THIRTIETH ANNIVERSARY LIMITED EDITION

A Million Wild Acres

200 Years of Man and an Australian Forest

ERIC ROLLS

Foreword by Les Murray

Includes Tom Griffiths' *The Writing of A Million Wild Acres*

HALE
& IREMONGER

First published by Thomas Nelson Australia
This edition published in 2011 by Hale & Iremonger
an imprint of The GHR Press
Level 8, 182–186 Blues Point Road
McMahons Point NSW 2060
www.ghrpress.com

National Library of Australia Cataloguing-in-Publication entry

Author: Rolls, Eric C. (Eric Charles), 1923–2007.
Title: A million wild acres : 200 years of man and an
Australian forest / by Eric Rolls ; forward by Les Murray ;
introductory essay by Tom Griffiths.
Edition: 30th. anniversary ed.
ISBN: 978 0 8680 6714 8 (hbk. : limited ed.)
Notes: Foreword from 'Eric Rolls and The Golden Disobedience'
by Les Murray ; introductory essay 'The Writing of A Million Wild Acres'
by Tom Griffiths.
Subjects: Forests and forestry – New South Wales – Pilliga
region – History. Frontier and pioneer life – New South Wales.
Australia – History. Pilliga region (N.S.W.) – History.
Other Contributors: Murray, Les. Griffiths, Tom, 1957–
Dewey Number: 634.9099444

Cover design by Xou Creative
Printed and bound in Australia by Griffin Press

FSC
www.fsc.org
MIX
Paper from
responsible sources
FSC® C009448

The paper this book is printed on is certified against
the Forest Stewardship Council® Standards.
Griffin Press holds FSC chain of custody certification
SGS-COC-005088. FSC promotes environmentally
responsible, socially beneficial and economically viable
management of the world's forests

10 9 8 7 6 5 4 3 2 1

Acknowledgements
to this 30th anniversary edition

I thank everyone associated with the Watermark Literary Society Inc. for sharing my dedication to the work of Eric Rolls, and especially Lyndal Coote for her untiring support and assistance. I warmly thank Les Murray for permission to use an excerpt from his 1982 essay 'Eric Rolls and the Golden Disobedience' as the Foreword to this edition. Les's generosity is indicative of their mutual esteem. I give warm thanks, also, to Tom Griffiths for permission to reproduce his insightful essay 'The Writing of *A Million Wild Acres*'. I thank photojournalist Peter Solness for the superb photograph of Eric with White Cypress Pines, the National Parks and Wildlife Service, Baradine, for the photograph *Pilliga bushfire aftermath* and designer Lucy Schuman of Xou Creative for the excellent cover.

My warm appreciation to Angelo Loukakis for initiating this publication, and to publisher Michael Rakusin and editor Glenda Downing for the great pleasure of our association.

Elaine van Kempen
The Camden Haven, March 2011

For Douglas Stewart
who encouraged my first writing

I have built a forest. It is the opportunity to
build what one loves into something permanent
that makes this very difficult game worthwhile.

Foreword

It delights me to learn that Eric Rolls' *A Million Wild Acres* is to be reissued.

...I grew up near and often in the great forests of the New South Wales lower north coast; our house was less than two miles from the edge of the Myall State Forest, and four more large State forests lay within the ambit of my childhood; my father had been a bullock driver and timber-getter in those forests before he married and started dairy farming—and yet even I was almost seduced by the myth of the alien bush, as I began learning to write poetry...

The part of the bush I grew up in is first mentioned in Eric Rolls' book on page 70, as he describes the surveys carried out by Henry Dangar to find suitable country for the newly formed Australian Agricultural Company:

> The one area left that seemed likely to contain the company's grant lay between Port Stephens and the Manning River. In February 1826 Henry Dangar made a thorough reconnaissance. And he found good land. There is beautiful cattle country around Stroud, Dungog, Gloucester and Taree. Further east, though it was obviously not the rich farm land that Dangar would choose for himself, there was fair open grass land. It was not the wooded tangle of today.

The poor grassland country down around the Myall Lakes, now all under eucalypts and red-barked angophoras and great tracts of paperbark forest standing in rushy grass on white clay soils...was deemed suitable for fine-wool sheep, and the world of the local Aborigines was destroyed to accommodate them. Within a few years, footrot and the soils' deficiencies in copper and cobalt, defects unknown to nineteenth-century science, had wiped the sheep out. And with the Aborigines no longer there to burn the country over continuously, the lonely Myall Lakes scrublands we know today, with their tremendous wealth of wildflowers, began to cover the grassland over. Back in the hills I come from, north-west of there, the rainforest which had always withstood the Aborigines' fires in moist gullies began to expand as the settlers and cedar-getters usurped the black people, then retreated again before the white man's axes and crosscut saws. The scattered clumps of sclerophyll forest, never large or dense in Aboriginal times, began to surge outward, spreading down off the ridges to cover the valley flats which had carried only a few trees to the hectare in pre-European days. When my father was a young man, he and his brothers could ride everywhere in 'the State', as they called the vast forest reserve near their home, seeking the giant timber trees that stood among the younger spindlier growth. As my father told me recently, 'You hardly had to make roads for the bullocks then. You could see through the bush for hundreds of yards.' Now, you could barely get a horse through most parts of the Myall State Forest, among the vines and wattle thickets and dense stands of young trees which flourish there after eighty or ninety years of mill logging and sleeper cutting...

It is Eric Rolls' controversial and perhaps revolutionary contention that the forests of Australia as we know them are no more than a hundred to a hundred and thirty years old. Apart from the tracts and patches of rainforest that follow the eastern face of the Dividing Range from far north Queensland down almost to Victoria, and a few large pockets of sclerophyll forest mainly in areas of high rainfall, he contends that Australia bore the appearance in pre-European times of a vast parkland kept open and well grassed by constant burning off. It was a *paysage humanisé* and *moralisé* which the Aborigines had maintained for untold centuries; the wilderness we now value and try to protect came with us, the invaders. It came in our heads, and it gradually rose out of the ground to meet us...

Rolls' general theory of the Australian forests is anchored in the particular story of one forest, the Pilliga (from Kamilaroi *peelaka*, a spearhead), which lies beyond the Dividing Range in New South Wales and extends from Narrabri in the north to Coonabarabran in the south. Its eastern extremity is close to the village of Baan Baa and in the west it peters out around the small town of Baradine. It is characterized by a mixture of eucalypts, acacias and callitris trees, usually known by the collective name cypress pine, and is enormously rich in birds, animals and flowering plants...

Slowly, with a leisurely accretion of detail from sources that range from printed books to previously unread family diaries and Lands Department archives, Rolls tells the story of how European animals, plants and humans spread northwards on each side of the Dividing Range and took over this belt of sandy country. It is not purely human history, but ecological history he gives us, showing how the real explorers were as likely to be escaped cattle and introduced grasses as men. By the time the hard men of the infant colony and their convict slaves arrived to take up new country, cattle had usually preceded them and begun compacting the ancient spongy soils with their hoofs, driving out the native ground-plants with the chemical and light-occluding properties of their huge droppings. He is unsparing of the rapacious human landtakers, but will not take the easy course of repudiating them. As he writes (pages 10–11):

> The tormented community generated its own men. Some hard gobbets indeed were thrown up. Those attracted later as settlers were the same type—capable, adventurous, and extraordinarily adaptable, difficult, crude, vigorous, dishonest, selfish, violent. They differed only in the extent to which each of these qualities was developed. Some were more violent than others, some less adaptable. They developed Australia.
>
> If these men had remained in Britain they would have had no influence on their times. Society would have restrained them. In Australia they moved outside the law. It is no use wishing they were different. To do so is to dispense with our culture. No other men could have done what they did. Australia might have been abandoned as a British settlement.

...The story of the Pilliga forest is one of advance, disappointment and retreat by pastoralists and then by small farmers. It is possible that we have never had so penetrating a study of the realities of settlement before; certainly I do not know of one which interrelates the human and non-human dimensions so intimately. Also, and it is a country man's point, Rolls realizes that more of Australia's history took place outside the law than within it, and more attempt was made to hide than to record it. He has a knack, born of sympathy and human knowledge, for detecting the outlines of concealed knavery even a century old. History is not just the propaganda of dominant groups, but also the public record of approved classes of human beings, and there is a way in which country people in Australia are apt to miss out on their due by being neither acceptably Upper nor recognizably proletarian, and their wary reticence compounds this still further. Given rapid changes of ownership of runs, by chicanery, bad luck, disease, opportunism or poor judgment of country, and changes in government policy such as John Robertson's Selection Acts of the 1860s, few were able to amass large stable fortunes. Dynasty and great wealth are features of many parts of the New World of European settlement, but are far less important in Australia, and the difference sets us off from many apparently comparable societies. The ecological result in the Pilliga was that neglected runs and failed selections went under surging masses of gum and cypress pine seedlings by the 1870s. Cypress pines came up ten thousand to the hectare, and soon there was no room for grass to grow. Foxes and competition for grass destroyed the rat-kangaroos which had previously kept the seedlings nibbled down, and the disappearance of the Aborigines meant that burning off was no longer regular and cyclic. Happening occasionally, sometimes as a result of lightning strike or accident, fires had the opposite of their historic effect: they now induced the appearance of millions of seedlings. The blue-green peelaka spearheads of cypress pine trees filled up the country. Rabbits, arriving soon after the first great spurts of growth, tended to keep the forest in check to some extent, until myxomatosis in the fifties of this century wiped the rabbits out, and bush fires in the same decade were followed by soaking rains. After the fifties, the Forestry Department, which had assumed that milling in the Pilliga would eventually cut the timber out, began to think in terms of sustained yield from the region. And unless the periodic threat of a new international airport in the Pilliga 'scrub' becomes a reality—let us hope Rolls' book makes that less likely—the area may at last have reached some sort of natural balance of human and non-human life. Not that such balances last forever...

...I think Australian readers have already come to see Rolls' book as genuinely representing a broad rather than a sectional sensibility, however, and existing on a plane we instantly recognize as common

Australian property rather than the atmosphere of an elite. I have heard conservationists growl at Rolls, and call him 'that old fraud', but I can't see how he damages their cause; he may, indeed, have burnt off a derivative form of ecological consciousness and let one more truly adapted to Australia spring up. He gives an originally imported notion the 'sound' of common acceptance, partly by freeing it from overtones of a mandarin desire to reform and civilize us. And so there is no strain of intimidation in our assent to his book.

The ruling literary culture of our time exhorts us to many disobediences. Very many of these are fraudulent or by now worn out, but there is a disobedience I value and call the golden one—and that is disobedience of the dominant literary sensibility itself. It is often wise, in the New World, to write literature as it were against the grain of Literature, because then you avoid the resistance which literary claims very often provoke, perhaps at a deep level, in the minds of readers whom Literature as usually understood in late colonial societies often seems to threaten with relegation if they resist its assumptions. We have grown used in recent years to highly mannered forms of prose fiction, many of them derived in this country from Patrick White's method of dabbling small exacerbated qualifications of extreme sensitivity over narrative and character alike in ways which constantly threaten to snub us if we do not render abashed assent. Few writers, perhaps, have followed White's other trick of inverting ordinary snobbery and transposing it into mystical election, but a myriad of other transformations and inversions of snobbery are around, to the point where the marks and shibboleths of enlightenment and competitive modernity have become a study as intricate as the quarterings of European heraldry encountered by Voltaire's Candide...But even playing tricks on a divisive and alienating mandarin tradition is not the same as discovering new styles and departures in art, and perhaps freeing it to reflect more of reality than a received sensibility allows. In its steady 'middle' voice, Rolls' narrative seems to be attempting nothing less than a complete account of its large subject. The whole truth, with no let-outs of polemic or withheld sympathy or portentousness or even of the chic brilliances which often disguise hollowness of vision. In its very different tone, and in a context of half-personal documentary rather than fiction, Rolls' enterprise may be seen as Proustian. But only tangentially, because in achieving his effect of completeness Rolls has done something which the aristocratic literary traditions of Europe make hard even to conceive: he has penetrated to the condition of the best 'primitive' art. In painting, the term primitive refers to art executed by people without formal training; in literature, where it is much rarer as a genuine and productive thing, we may take it as meaning unaware of the received sensibility...Rolls' own early 'Sheaf Tosser' poems had a comparable 'primitive' quality which impressed many good judges who could see beyond the roughnesses and repetitions. It now seems that this essence in his early poems has stayed alive in Rolls and kept him from conformities, so that he might consummate it three decades later in a prose masterpiece.

Claims have been made that Rolls' *Million Wild Acres* will be seen as one of the great books about Australia, rivalling *Voss*, *Such is Life* or *Capricornia* as the 'ultimate statement about national experience'. The book has a larger scope, perhaps, than any of those, but I am unsure of the precise meaning of that term 'ultimate statement'. Rolls' history probably contains as much poetry, in the wide sense, as any of them, without their dimensions of fiction, and none of its poetry consists in 'purple' writing...

...To cut through alienation by simply ignoring the received sensibilities which produce it is a form of what I call the Golden Disobedience, and that disobedience seems at the moment to be available to non-fiction writers in greater measure than to other writers of literary texts. Poets may come next as writers to whom the Golden Disobedience is available. Novelists and playwrights, with honourable exceptions, seem to come a poor third. Rolls sidesteps all the received literary manners, and tells 'people's' history in a way which belongs to them rather than to most these days who would speak of The People. And in doing so he creates a great work of art in which a central native tradition is renewed, altered and immeasurably deepened.

Les Murray

Excerpt from 'Eric Rolls and the Golden Disobedience', first published *Quadrant*, December 1982.
Reprinted in Les Murray, *A Working Forest: Selected Prose*, Duffy & Snellgrove, 1997

The Writing of
A Million Wild Acres
Tom Griffiths

Soon after *A Million Wild Acres* was published in 1981, I read the book and realised that I had encountered something momentous.[1] I felt as Les Murray did when he wrote of Rolls's book that he read and re-read it 'with all the delight of one who knows he has at last got hold of a book that is in no way alien to him'.[2] I was living in Melbourne and I was moved to write to the author, whom I had not met and could hardly dream of ever meeting, and who seemed to me to live in an extraordinary, magical and especially dynamic place. It was slightly mystifying because I recalled once as a child in the 1960s being driven through Coonabarabran, and I could remember the vast tracts of the Pilliga Scrub (as it was disdainfully called) rolling endlessly past the car window. It had not seemed extraordinary, magical and especially dynamic then. Had it changed? Had I changed? Had this man's book opened my eyes? All of the above. I had never before realised how strongly words on a page could animate actuality.

In my mid-twenties and freshly home from my first trip overseas,

---

1   This is an amended version of an essay first published in John Dargavel, Diane Hart and Brenda Libbis (ed.) *Perfumed Pineries: Environmental History of Australia's Callitris Forests*, Centre for Resource and Environmental Studies (CRES) and the Australian Forest History Society, Canberra, 2001, pp. 184-94.
2   Les Murray, 'Eric Rolls and the Golden Disobedience', in his *A Working Forest: Selected Prose*, Duffy and Snellgrove, Sydney, 1997, p. 158.

I wrote Eric Rolls a brief letter, telling him that *A Million Wild Acres* was one of a handful of books about Australia that I would like to put in the hands of any visitor to help them understand my country. Now I would make even greater claims for it. I think it is the best environmental history yet written about Australia, and I would especially hope it could be read not just by visitors but by all Australians. I wrote that letter to Eric not because I wanted or expected a reply, but because I had to write it. But he *did* reply! He told me of the work he was doing on his history of the Chinese in Australia, offering me a brief, vivid snippet of his life. I now know that Eric gets lots of letters like mine, and that he replies to more than I would have thought possible. I've been looking at some of them in the archives. Eric's papers, mountains of them, are in at least three libraries. And amongst them you can find testimonies from people moved by his books to write, even though writing does not always come easily to them. Some people normally unfamiliar with written words, are clearly living Eric's words. One wrote in stumbling script: 'This is the first book I have ever read. Thank you for writing it. I enjoyed it so much I am now going to try reading other books.'[3] Another wrote at more length, but also with spelling difficulties:

Dear Eric,
    Just a note or a few words, to say how much I liked your two books, A Million Wild Acres, 'They All Ran Wild'. The best I have seen. I will get your other books and read them soon.
    I would of liked to been with you, and read all the books and papers, and places you went to-get all the true information. A great bit of work. I do not no how many times I have read 'A Million Wild Acres'. I no I have read 'They All Ran Wild' twice last month.
    ... I lived all my early life at Pilliga. I will tell you more later. I like reading History of Australia. And you love the Bush, and no all about it.
    ... If you are ever over this way call in and have a yarn, and stay with your family. We have plenty of room. I will write again to you soon, hope you get some rain. 'And keep writing', all the best.
        Yours truly... [4]

---

3   Interview with Eric Rolls conducted by Tom Griffiths, Newcastle, 19 February, 2000.
4   K.C., Letter to Eric Rolls, 3 November, 1989, in Rolls Papers, Mitchell Library, Box 37D.

And here are the words of another reader, admitting (like me) that she did not often write fan letters, but in this case could not stop herself:

> I enjoyed your book more than I am capable of expressing. You made the Pilliga come alive on the page and I hope you make trillions.
> … On nearly every page I found something to exclaim over (mostly I exclaimed how on earth did this man have time to fit in the farming!)[5]

Well, I think Eric often wondered that himself. He has written of the constant battle between acres and words, the farm as both a source of his originality and a growing distraction. As the success of *A Million Wild Acres* both settled and unsettled his life, he did a stocktake:

> On my sixtieth birthday I happened to be working out how many years it would take me to write the next five books: say another three years on this one, eighteen months, two years on that, seven years' research and writing on the next big one. Then I realised with considerable shock how old I would be. I decided from then on to work words a day every day instead of acres.[6]

In his book *Doorways: A Year of the Cumberdeen Diaries* (1989), Eric told us of his workspace, his desk, as it was at his farm on Pretty Plains. He always wrote with his back to a broad window, the words in front of him, the acres behind. 'The imagination works better against a blank wall', he said. But the sun on his back warmed him, reminded him of the outside world he was trying to capture on paper. Of his Silky Oak desk, he wrote: 'everything on it knows its place. Words come to it that I am not expecting.' On his desk were a pile of handwritten notebooks, eleven dictionaries and books of words, a typed outline of the current book. He added five new pages of writing to the pile each day. Empty blocks of lined A4 paper sat beside him, and the two fountain pens that had written all his books. In front of him was a large, disconcerting pile of letters that needed

---

5   L.A. c. 1995. Letter to Eric Rolls. Rolls Papers, Mitchell Library, Box 37E (69).
6   Eric Rolls, *Doorways: A Year of the Cumberdeen Diaries*, Angus & Robertson, Sydney, 1989, p. 11.

answering, and that we now know he would probably eventually get to. There was a big splinter of fragrant sandalwood, a tail feather from a Swamp Pheasant, little soapstone turtles from China, a branding iron and two blocks of Mulga.

Now imagine him there and let's watch Eric wrestling with both the words and the acres in the late 1970s as the book he has always wanted to write materialises into chapters, but never fast enough. I am going to quote from his letters to Sue Ebury, the editor at Thomas Nelson Publishers with whom he worked on *A Million Wild Acres* and also to his agent, Tim Curnow.[7] And remember as you read them that Eric has firmly declared that 'Unless you feel so intensely about writing that you are prepared to murder anybody who stops you getting to your desk, it's no use thinking of being a writer.'[8]

When Eric offered the idea of the book to his publishers in October 1974 (and they accepted it immediately and enthusiastically), he hoped that it might be finished in seven months.[9] On the first of June 1976, with years of experience, observation and research behind him, he takes a deep breath: 'The frame of the book is already mostly planned – it is only wording to be considered.' And three months later: 'I've got within a fortnight of beginning to write and am getting excited.' A year later, in September 1977, Eric writes that he has not signed the Nelson contract yet because he is 'frightened harvest is going to fall on me like a guillotine when there are two chapters still to go. I don't want to let anyone down and enough money has come in to keep me writing until harvest – so I'll just do my damndest and see how far I get.' 'Most days [he says] I read about six hours and write for six – if it is not ready on time it won't be for lack of trying.'[10]

But the acres continually interrupt the words. Another year later, in September 1978, he explains:

> I lost three precious weeks writing when the lad who was working here burnt himself as he began crop spraying – he is still off work but I'm back to the writing. The tractor we use for odd jobs was burnt completely. I had to finish spraying then do

---

7   Eric Rolls, Letters to Sue Ebury and Tim Curnow, 1976-80. Rolls Papers, National Library of Australia, MS 7027, Box 1, Folder 2.

8   Interview with Rolls, 19 February, 2000.

9   Eric Rolls, Letter to Anne Godden, Publisher, Thomas Nelson (Australia) Ltd, 11 October, 1974. Rolls Papers, NLA, Box 10, Folder 67.

10   This and several quotes in the text that follow are from Rolls, Letters to Ebury and Curnow, 1976-80, Rolls Papers, NLA, MS 7027, Box 1, Folder 2.

the summer ploughing. It is cruel changing over from writing to farming unexpectedly. And I'd been concentrating so hard I was not even living in this century when it happened.

'[O]ne nearly gets torn in halves sometimes trying to lead two lives', he exclaims. But he acknowledges that 'Without the farm there would have been no book, even if it delayed publication.'

In his house, he virtually re-enacted the settlement process he was describing. Just getting the right pioneers into the right places at the right time was a demanding and arduous job. He recalled:

I lined all the men up against one wall – 37 men – each had a pile of papers, each named, all their years, and then I had the map at the other end of the room. I'd pick up a pile and march the man across the room to his place on the map. … You had to see him getting there.[11]

A reviewer of the book, the environmental historian and philosopher, George Seddon, later described these early chapters of the book as:

like the Book of Genesis, with its endless 'And Joktan begat Almodad, and Sheleph and Hazarmaveth, and Jerah'. There is a walk-on-walk-off cast of thousands, and the detail is numbing – but this *is* the Pilliga Book of Genesis, and I think the author was right to put it all in.[12]

In July 1979, Eric reflected on a job nearly complete:

The end of the Pilliga book is in sight, thank God. I'm appalled that it has run so long over time. Each estimate I made seemed certain – I know how much I can do a day. Then what seemed certain plans for the farm would come unstuck and I'd have to do a couple of months hard work. It is hard not to go on writing and leave it. But one has to be practical. If we went broke in the middle of the book it would cost more time than ever. And there is not much leeway on the land now. Fixed costs are enormous and increasing. As much as I love the farm, it will have to be

---

11   Interview with Rolls, 19 February, 2000.
12   George Seddon, 'Dynamics of Change', *Overland*, 87 (May 1982), pp. 55-60 at p. 59.

sold. It will not only cost me too much time but too many books. I'm also afraid it will cost me years of my life. It is excruciatingly difficult each time coming back to an unfinished chapter. So much reading has to be done again – days of it.[13]

And on 4 October that year, 1979, he records: 'I've just written the last word of the Pilliga book.'

Three years of intense writing, in the available spaces. But for years before there had been the source material of experience, of life on the soil, of walking and talking the forest, collecting scats to analyse animal hairs, learning the names of plants often for the first time, mastering in words the craft of the timbergetters. And all that correspondence! Eric's papers spill out with letters requesting and receiving information: To the Curator of Mammals at the Australian Museum, 'How rare is the rat kangaroo?' … and could they possibly as one old timer attested 'be seen hopping about in dozens on a moonlight night'? To the Patent Trade Marks and Design Office in Canberra, 'Can you tell me anything about early patents for barbed wire in Australia?' To the secretary of RAS Kennel Control, 'Can you tell me if there is still a breed of dog known as a staghound?' To the President of the Quirindi and District Historical Society, 'Do you know exactly how the old acetylene lights worked?' To Mrs King of the Tamworth Historical Society, 'Have you any local information about the construction of George Clarke's stock yards at Boggabri – near Barber's Lagoon?'[14]

It is the detail that matters, and it is getting it right that matters, too. 'Much of the game of writing history', he declares at the start of the book 'is keeping it true.'[15] And keeping it true, for Eric, means not just finding out what happened, but also finding a sense of wonder about it, and understanding it in such detail and with such precision that he can make the story live. Use of the active tense – and his books bristle with it – requires quite specific knowledge. The passive tense, by contrast, allows slippage and can mask ignorance. Rolls's prose is bracing and vivid. 'At times', he says, 'I can even smell what I'm writing about.'[16] His books won many awards, but he was particularly proud to win the Braille Book of the Year and the Talking Book of the Year, for he often said: 'I write to make people see.' There

---

13   Rolls to Ebury, 12 July 1979, NLA.
14   Rolls, Letters requesting information, 1973-80, Rolls Papers, Box 1 Folder 3, NLA.
15   Rolls, *A Million Wild Acres*, p. vii.
16   Interview with Rolls, 19 February, 2000.

is also a 'swagger' to his style – and he consciously cultivates it – because it enables him to tell a story with conviction. This careful accretion of authentic organic detail generates the power of *A Million Wild Acres*. Les Murray celebrated this in a wonderful essay called 'Eric Rolls and the Golden Disobedience'. Eric's disobedience, explained Murray, was his freedom to sidestep received literary sensibilities, his ability to transcend the conventional boundaries between fiction and non-fiction, and between humanity and nature. Murray considered the book to be like an extended, crafted campfire yarn in which everyone has the dignity of a name, and in which the animals and plants have equal status with humans in the making of history. He compared its discursive and laconic tone to the Icelandic Sagas.[17] Through his democratic recognition of all life, Rolls enchants the forest and presents us with a speaking land, a sentient country raucous with sound.

Years later, Eric reflected on the writing of this book:

> I began to think that the whole forest seemed to be an animate thing, with voices, and that perhaps I ought to give the trees themselves an identity, and then I thought that's absolute bloody nonsense, you've got a wonderful story to tell, just tell it in a straightforward manner in the best way it can be written. One of the reviews said that the whole book reads as though the trees themselves were telling the story, which delighted me. If I'd tried to do it that way, the book would have been hopeless.[18]

One of Eric's earliest public performances made nature animate. Every Friday afternoon at his kindergarten in Grenfell, his teacher Miss Postlethwaite used to tell the class stories. She would do this from her slightly elevated stage, with a mat at her feet. But she was rather dull. So one day, five-year-old Eric put up his hand and said 'Miss Postlethwaite I'd like to tell a story this afternoon'. She said 'Alright, come out here.' Eric was prepared and knew what he would do. It was sowing time on the farm, so he went up the front and pretended he was a grain of wheat. He jiggled down into the ground, buried himself in the earth, and pulled the mat over his body. Then the roots grew and the legs stuck out. Then leaves sprouted and the arms waved. The little boy wriggled and danced. As Eric recalled:

---

17   Murray, 'Eric Rolls and the Golden Disobedience'.
18   Interview with Rolls, 19 February, 2000.

So I grew up, and a header came along and stripped me, and then the sheep went into the paddock and I got eaten.

He started telling stories every Friday afternoon, and adults began to join the gathering, too, making quite an audience. 'I realised that telling stories was a good thing to do if you did it properly.'[19]

It was 1928 and soon Eric's father was driving his family north from Grenfell to Narrabri to take up his own farm. Well, it was not really his own farm; the rabbits owned it. The farm was too far from any school Eric could attend so he had to wait until he was seven to begin lessons with Blackfriars Correspondence School. Eric recalled how he 'spent two exciting years with a pack of dogs walking about hunting rabbits into burrows and hollow logs' so that his father could chop them or dig them out.[20] He slept on the verandah of the wooden homestead, waking at night to watch the play of moon shadows and in the early morning to see the light come onto the Nandewar Ranges. Eric later won selection to Fort Street Boys' High School in Sydney, where, as he recalled, he taught the other kids how animals reproduced and they taught him how humans did. He missed the chance to go to university because he got chicken pox just prior to his exams, and then the Second World War intervened. After serving in Papua New Guinea, he returned to Australia where he farmed his own land for forty years on the edges of the 'Pilliga Scrub'. Eric believed that contact with the soil preserves a writer's essential sense of the ridiculous. He wrote more than twenty books, as well as hundreds of articles and essays, mostly in the second half of his life.[21]

The central story of *A Million Wild Acres* is a simple and compelling one, told richly and persuasively. It is, in Eric's words, about the growing of a forest. His original achievement was to confront and provoke Australians with the idea that in many areas of the country, landscapes that had once been grassy and open are now densely vegetated, that there might be more trees in Australia now than at the time of European settlement, that forests – which we so readily and romantically see as primeval – could often be the creation of our own act of settlement. How many trees make a forest, he asked? 'It is not a paradox that the fires that once kept our forests open should

---

19   Interview with Rolls, 19 February, 2000.
20   Eric Rolls, 'Before the Bitumen', MS submitted to *The Sydney Review* on 21 July 1989, Rolls Papers, Mitchell Library, Box 37A.
21   Tom Griffiths, 'Eric Charles Rolls (1923-2007): He worked with words and the land', *Sydney Morning Herald*, 7 November, 2007.

now cause them to grow denser.'[22] Eric brought an observation that was commonplace in local lore forcefully into the scientific and historical literature. Many of today's forests, Rolls reminded us, are not remnants of a primeval jungle: 'they do not display the past as it was, they have concentrated it.'[23]

Ross Gibson, who (with John Cruthers) made the award-winning film *Wild* based on Eric's book, described his history of the Pilliga as an 'unruly tract of local history' and 'a deliberately feral book'.[24] *Feral* is a fitting adjective for the work of the author of that other landmark book, *They All Ran Wild: The Story of Pests on the Land in Australia* (1969). Eric was fascinated by the meaning of 'wild'. It is often used to describe nature that is seen to be untouched and pristine. But for Eric – a farmer – 'wild' nature was feral, mongrel, hybrid nature, nature stirred up, nature enlivened by human presence and intervention; it was dynamic, historical nature.[25] So the forest that he grew in the pages of his book was 'concentrated' and volatile.

A Million Wild Acres was Sue Ebury's title. Eric's own earlier suggestions had celebrated the novelty of the nature he described: 'Pilliga', 'An Exaggerated Country', 'Unexpected Forests', 'Phoenix Forest', or 'Ungentle Men Unsettled Land'. At first Eric had his doubts about Sue's suggested title: 'I'm a bit dubious about another title with wild in it', he replied, ' – I am partly civilised.'[26] He is fascinated by the invaders, the cattle, rabbits, foxes, their adaptability and sheer vigour even as they wreak damage. And he respects the 'wild men' too, the 'ungentle' white settlers of Australia. He is impatient with those who disown them. 'This book', he writes in *A Million Wild Acres*, 'is not written by a gentle man'.

The book challenges the traditional contrasts of European settler thinking about nature. It revolutionises those assumptions that disturbed nature is somehow always lesser nature. Such views brought Eric into conflict with aspects of the green movement. At the same time as recognising the fragility and integrity of native ecosystems he wanted to acknowledge the creative ecology of invasion. This relish for the fecundity of life and an irrepressible optimism also underpinned

---

22   Eric Rolls, *A Million Wild Acres*, Nelson, Melbourne, 1981, p. 248.

23   Rolls, *A Million Wild Acres*, p. 399.

24   Ross Gibson, 'Enchanted Country', *World Literature Today*, 67 (3), 1993, pp. 471-76.

25   R Gibson and J Cruthers, 'WILD – Outline for a Film', Rolls Papers, Mitchell Library, Box 37A (69).

26   Rolls, Letters to Ebury and Curnow, 1976-80, Rolls Papers, NLA, MS 7027, Box 1, Folder 2.

Eric's joint advocacy of the causes of nature conservation, on the one hand, and human immigration to Australia on the other. He was always determined to see the creativity of encounter.

When Rolls was writing *A Million Wild Acres*, the conservation battlegrounds in Australia were the rainforests, most notably at Terania Creek in 1979.[27] As Rolls acknowledges in his final chapter, woodchipping was also an issue and had become shorthand for indiscriminate forest clearing and exploitation. Rolls considered it a necessary industry committed to unnecessary destruction.[28] So his book was written in the midst of those campaigns, when forests were depicted as timeless and primeval, and human disturbance meant the destruction of trees. He wrote a detailed regional study showing that forests could also be the creation of settlement. He wasn't the first to notice this phenomenon: the anthropologist, naturalist and explorer Alfred Howitt, for example, presented his observations of the increasing density of forests in Gippsland to a scientific audience in 1890.[29] The power of *A Million Wild Acres* was that it gave voice to a myriad of these earlier observers. And Rolls told a multi-causal story of how it had happened in one region, a place he knew intimately. He saw system and pattern and creativity in it. His book attracted little scientific or green criticism for over a decade and a half, awaiting another political context. By the mid to late 1990s, the frontline of conservation battles had moved from the logging of old growth forests on public land to the clearing of native vegetation for farming on private or leasehold land. In this new context, Rolls's argument about the history of tree density was misinterpreted for political purposes by both farmers and scientists.[30]

---

27 John Dargavel, *Fashioning Australia's Forests*, Oxford University Press, Oxford, 1995, pp 184-85.

28 Rolls, *A Million Wild Acres*, p. 402.

29 Alfred Howitt, *The Eucalypts of Gippsland*, Royal Society of Victoria, Melbourne, 1890.

30 For example, in 1995, the NSW Farmers' Association sponsored a report by D G Ryan, J R Ryan and B J Starr called *The Australian Landscape –Observations of Explorers and Early Settlers*, Murrumbidgee Catchment Management Committee, Wagga Wagga, 1995, which linked *A Million Wild Acres* to modern debates about tree clearing and controlled burning, and was used by opponents of vegetation clearing control regulations (especially those introduced in NSW in August 1995). The report's perceived political influence earned it more attention than it deserved. An opposing study by J S Benson and P A Redpath ('The nature of pre-European native vegetation in south-eastern Australia: a critique of Ryan, D G., Ryan, J R. and Starr, B J', *Cunninghamia*, 5(2), 1997, pp. 283-328) criticised Ryan, Ryan and Starr and also sought to discount Rolls's book because of the legitimacy his Pilliga story could be seen to give to some clearing of native vegetation. For a local correction of Benson and Redpath, see J R Whitehead, 'A discussion paper on human impacts on the vegetation of the Coonabarabran Shire', in Coonabarabran Shire Council, *Vegetation Management Plan, Vol. 3: Appendices*, Shire Council, Coonabarabran, 2000.

There was also continuing scientific and cultural resistance to recognising the significance and sophistication of Aboriginal burning. As Judith Wright wrote in 1982 in reviewing *A Million Wild Acres*:

It is as strange to me as to Rolls that some scientists and others still dispute the effect of Aboriginal fire-management, or even that there was such management. Again and again in my own reading of stock-inspectors' reports in the Queensland of the sixties and seventies, there is reference to the change in pasture growth and shrub cover which followed the vanishing of the Aborigines and the fierce protectiveness of squatters for their timber fences, huts, yards and vulnerable slow-moving flocks of sheep. But no doubt such evidence is too much that of laymen to be trusted by academic ecologists.[31]

The politics of this issue are so embedded and have such a long history that they are often unconscious.[32] Scientific disdain for Aboriginal ecological knowledge was once racist; now it is sometimes simply anti-humanist. In other words, the same scientific suspicions can apply to settler knowledge – indeed to local knowledge of any kind – because it is human, anecdotal and apparently informal. So the debate about Rolls's work sometimes presents itself as a clash of disciplinary styles, a methodological tension between the sciences and the humanities. The very qualities for which literary scholars and cultural historians celebrate Rolls's book – its vernacular and organic dimensions, holism, and narrative power – can be seen by others to diminish its scientific credentials. But Eric himself continually paid tribute to scientists, and his book, *Australia: A Biography*, was dedicated to them.

Eric was never afraid of a dangerous idea. He liked to tell it as he saw it. It got him into trouble of course. When Pauline Hanson called Aborigines 'cannibals', he responded that she was more savage than any cannibal. When he wrote an article about the damage that cats do to the environment, the *Sun-Herald* reported that they had never had so many letters and phone calls about anything they had ever published, and Eric received violent threats, including one woman who threatened to burn his home, his car and to destroy everything

---

31   Judith Wright, 'A Chronicle of White Settlement', *Island Magazine*, 12, 1982, pp. 44-45.
32   Tom Griffiths, *Hunters and Collectors: The antiquarian imagination in Australia*, Cambridge University Press, Melbourne, 1996.

he owned. When researching an essay on the use and abuse of water resources for the *Independent Monthly* in 1992, he told the editor, Max Suich, of how his research had provoked a dark, watery threat:

> I had no idea that things are as serious as they are, or that it will take so long to rectify them, or that there are such murderous forces at work opposing change. It is quite startling to be told 'you better pull your punches or you'll end up with concrete shoes'. I haven't pulled any punches.[33]

And he is just as ready to run the gauntlet of the conservationists as he is the developers or the bureaucrats. He is especially critical of all of them if they are 'short on history'.[34] There is a fearlessness about Eric's work, as well as a swagger. And there is a complexity to *A Million Wild Acres* behind the compelling narrative power. It is a truly original work, yet it speaks directly to so many people; it is unique and pathbreaking, yet it also seems to represent an organic integrity and a common vernacular. That is Eric's extraordinary artistic achievement. That is why readers write to him, and why reviewers compare *A Million Wild Acres* to the Book of Genesis, or a campfire yarn, or an Icelandic Saga. That is why it is possible for this book to be the first book someone might ever read.

---

33   Rolls, Letter to Max Suich, 6 October, 1992, Rolls Papers, Mitchell Library, ML 1719/83, Box 26 (69).
34   Eric Rolls, 'Questioning a few fervent opinions', *Island*, 53, 1992, pp. 26-31.

Contents

Maps

Preface

An author seldom searches for the subject of a good book. It envelops him stealthily until he must write it. If he is overtaken by a big subject at the right time, he is a fortunate author.

At no other time could this book have been written. Thirty years ago it would have been gloomy indeed. The fragrant yellow pine, the red dense ironbark was milled with the prospect that its extermination was controlled. There were few wildflowers in southern Australia. Most of the bush was bared by rabbits. There were few enough native mammals, fewer birds than now. Thirty years ago I would have predicted the end of many species.

The fascinating details of our forefathers were locked in secret drawers. The previous generation still shrank tenderly from our history. When the Mutch indexes of births, marriages, deaths and convict records were first exposed in the Mitchell Library, descendants filched the unnerving cards that bore their names. Even yet family trees are compiled with main branches excised. Entries in the *Australian Dictionary of Biography* are wary.

I have shown no concern for those who are ashamed of their ancestors. It is a foolish shame. In the unscientific selection of human breeding, genes good and bad are quickly dispersed. One's great-grandfather has little enough opportunity to exert his influence. But what if a villainous great-grandfather was permitted a look at those descendants who wish to disown the truth of him? Would he not be bitterly ashamed of them – so afraid of life as to deny his genes?

William Cox was an important man. He was also a rogue. In the biography written by his great-granddaughters he was disembowelled and restuffed with all the qualities thought fitting in an ancestor. They erected him as a comic effigy of an important man.

Neither education nor social advantages decided the success of our first settlers. A remarkable contract of sale is extant dated 1836. It bears the flourishing signature of George Bowman and the cross of Samuel Clift. George Bowman was a wealthy, educated free settler. Samuel Clift was an ex-convict who could neither read nor write and who received his first land as one who answered the 'description of persons entitled to grants of land by virtue of their being married to respectable females'. Both men were successful in Australia during their own lifetimes. Both established families who have been persistently successful on the land in northern New South Wales.

The term 'squatter' needs explanation. I have used it only in its later meaning of a man who drove his stock beyond the law to pasture on the Waste Lands of the Crown. The first men known as squatters were the cattle thieves and sly-grog sellers who floated round the edges of all first settlements. A marvellous manuscript preserved among land records in the State Archives of New South Wales sums up the characters of twenty-three such squatters. It was scrawled in 1838 by a contemporary who kept a hard eye on his neighbours. He called his assessment 'A Mornerandum of the Squatters of Georgean a Part of Argyle & Rocks Borrough general caracter'.

'…N7 A Man Name Phillip Hickey living on Bowlon Hill Retailing Rum and Keep Two Generous Women and well known in Berima and at OConors plains as a Good Customer to the Contractors and has Mary Haycock living with him as a Vagobond &c &c'

'…N11 Michael Hogan on the Creek from Terromo to Bowlong who had only a few head of Cattle about two years ago now has a Large herd Keeps a Dairy and will Bring half as much Tallow to Sydney as he will Butter he had not the second Shurt when he Came up Now has Bales of Blue Cloth Retailing to Stockeepers he never grows any Grain I have seen his Family of ten head thirteen pigs twelve dogs to support without any Industry only the Hazurd, fresh saddle Bridle and a new Rideing Coat his wife Riged in the Greatest stile, it did not answer him to stay in Terromo Removed down the Creek more Lonesome place…'

In the spelling of place names I have used the first known version of a name for the first mention, then changed to the modern spelling. When it seemed essential I noted the change. Often I have not done so. If the reader finds Bugaldi Creek and the village of Bugaldie spelt differently on the same page, that is not carelessness. That is how The Boogaldi and Boogaldi Creek have come to be spelt.

Much of the game of writing history is keeping it true. But what is the truth? When the *Singleton Argus* records John Wilkinson as shooting Joe Governor at 300 yards, is it trebling the deed of its local hero? The coroner at the inquest in the Caledonian Hotel accepted the distance as 300 yards (274 metres). But such a shot with doubtful ammunition, a fast running target and an open-sighted rifle aimed by a fifty-six-year-old man who had run a kilometre in pursuit is unlikely. One must accept other newspaper versions and the police estimate of 300 to 350 feet, or about 110 metres.

All one can do is read everything there is to be read, add it to one's own experience, then pick the way through a maze of stories. But with the most contentious story, the growth of Australia's modern forests, there was no doubtful choosing of the way, no stories at variance. There was one clear documented path that only a forgotten few have taken before me.

Acknowledgements

These works sat on my desk through two years of writing: M.H. Ellis's *John Macarthur*, H.R. Carter's *The Upper Mooki*, W.A. Wood's *Dawn in the Valley*, J.F. Campbell's *'Squatting' on Crown Lands in New South Wales*, Brian Fletcher's *Landed Enterprise and Penal Society*, Errol Lea-Scarlett's long outline of the Eather family in *Descent*, and *Henry Dangar Surveyor and Explorer*, a monograph by John Atchison and Nancy Gray. Without the information in those, my job would have been extended by years.

Mrs Joanna Richards, an experienced and excellent genealogist and research assistant, saved me weeks of time and many trips to Sydney by answering for me 'Whom did he leave his money to?' or 'Did he go to gaol when he was arrested for getting so rowdy drunk at the funeral?' When I collected her stack of letters together I was startled to find she had written 70,000 words of answers.

Mr Hans Brunner spent many days assessing difficult hair samples from the Pilliga forests and gave me fascinating information for the chapter on mammals. I thank him also for correcting what I wrote about his extraordinary work.

I thank Dr John Atchison, Mrs Jillian Oppenheimer, Ms Beth Williams, Mr Geoff Douglas, Mrs Liz Dovey and Mr Alan Morris for their careful reading and correcting of the typescript. All removed errors and made a better book. Even the well-known Spotted Bower-bird that had lived with us for years irrationally became a Western Bower-bird during writing.

I am grateful to Dr L.A.S. Johnson and his staff at the National Herbarium for the many plant samples they identified and questions they answered. I knew nothing of the plants when I began looking at the Pilliga forests. Chapter eight should make it obvious how carefully the National Herbarium answered my questions.

Many people went to a great deal of trouble to find photographs and to give me information. I thank Mr Bruce Cameron of Boggabri for a tape of Mr Bob Trindall's ninety-odd years of memories, and Mr Harry Abbott for a tape on Harry Joy. His father had known Joy well. I thank Mr Bert Ruttley for the hours he spent bringing the forest alive for me. Bert said he was not going to die until he read the book but unfortunately he could not wait. I thank also Bert Ruttley's daughter, Mrs Mary Hitchen, the Caseys, Young Dan and Old Dan, Mr Jack Howlett of Baradine and Mrs Nancy Gray of Scone, the Reverend E. Noble of the Presbyterian Church, Bowenfels, and Mrs Hart of the Presbyterian Church Archives in Margaret Street, Sydney, Mr Frank Winchester of Lithgow, Mrs Rutherford of Bathurst, Mr and Mrs A. Kensit of Baan Baa, Messrs Bob Logan of Narrabri, John Grosser of Gunnedah, Les Clark of Boggabri, Mrs Ethel Purdy of Baradine, Mr Claude Carr and Miss Jane Carr of Yaminbah, Mr Phil Langdale of Crickenbah, and Mr Dick Law for a very good night around the bar of the Imperial Hotel in Wee Waa.

I thank Brigadier M. Austin of the Department of Defence for a legal opinion about Governor Brisbane's declaration of Martial Law but since the civil courts continued to operate his declaration is not accepted as true Martial Law.

I thank Mr Vic Mills of Bugaldie for information on Chalk Mountain, Mr J.R. Giles for letters about wild pigs, Mr Barry Fox and Dr David Briscoe for allowing us to join them on an enjoyable hunt for the Pilliga Mouse, the Messrs Noel Worland, Ernie Chiswell and Doug Mackaway of the Forestry Commission, Baradine.

I thank Messrs Guy Court and Charles Perfrement of the Tamworth Historical Society for their prompt copies of some superb photographs, Mr Claude Kassell of Coonamble Historical Society and Ms Maris Golding of the Forestry Commission of New South Wales for their help in finding old photographs.

I thank Mrs Laura Purdy for introducing me to Mrs Ethel Merckenschlager, her old aunt with such good memories, Mr Roy Edwards for notes of his experiences in the forest, and Messrs Ned

Edwards and Donald Magann for their stories of when they had worked together sixty years before.

I thank those friends who responded so enthusiastically to my last-minute long-distance telephone calls for photographs: Mrs Brian Ridley of Ridley and Hamilton Writers' Service, Canberra, Mrs C. Gray, Mrs John White and Mrs P. Knight; and I thank Mr R.W. Crane of Baradine who spent so many hours taking new photographs and copying old ones. That work could not have been done had not Joan, my wife, managed his pharmacy while he worked in his dark-room.

My whole family helped profoundly. Joan also ran the farm while I was away on research, Kim, Kerry and Mitchell trapped mammals during their holidays, searched for termites, took photographs, drove the tractor. Joan travelled hundreds of kilometres in search of photographs. They made the book with me and I thank them all for enjoying it.

I thank Mr Clive Willis of Sydney for the months I spent writing in his spare house at Narrabeen. The book was written during four years of support from the Literature Board of the Australia Council. I am deeply grateful for that help. With Australia's small population and consequent small market, books requiring massive research are intolerably difficult for an author to finance. Although an author is ruthless enough to produce his work despite all difficulties, these fellowships make things so much easier for his family, and they surely are worth considering.

I thank the staff of the Archives Office of New South Wales and of the Mitchell Library, State Library of New South Wales, for their considerable help over several years and for permission to quote from documents in their possession; and I thank Mr John Dunnet of Narrabri for access to early copies of his newspaper, the *Courier*.

I thank Mrs A. Rich for her many hours of scrupulous typing and Mrs D. Dangerfield for typing a batch at short notice in a last-minute rush.

The beautiful maps were prepared by Will Newton. The book was edited by Sue Ebury, one of those exceptional editors who can clear faults without meddling.

I

Explorers and Livestock

Setting up the Board

It is as long as the good road between Narrabri and Coonabarabran that runs down the middle of it; it is as wide as the narrow tracks dozed out for timber trucks between Baan Baa and Baradine. It is busy with trees, with animals and with men. It is lonely and beautiful. It is a million wild acres. And there is no other forest like it.

When John Oxley saw it in 1818 there was little forest there as the word is used now. The meaning of forest has grown with the forests. 'Brush' he called it in small areas, 'a very thick brush of cypress trees and small shrubs.' 'Scrub' he called the stunted growth on the dry ridges, 'mere scrub.' Most of it, about 800,000 hectares, was a 'forest' of huge ironbarks and big white-barked cypress pines, three or four of them only to the hectare. We would not now call it forest. 'But that is open grassland' we would say in bewilderment. 'One would scarcely have to clear it to cultivate it.' Australia's dense forests are not the remnants of two hundred years of energetic clearing, they are the product of one hundred years of energetic growth. This book is the story of how one forest grew.

What Oxley saw he did not like. 'Forbidding . . . miserable . . .' he said, 'a sandy desert . . .' Oxley was using the term 'desert' in the sense of deserted, not dry. It was a decidedly wet desert in August 1818.

Oxley, Surveyor-General for sixteen years, is not well regarded. He discovered the Liverpool Plains and good land along the Brisbane

River but, in deciding that the interior of Australia was an inland sea, he changed the wild rumours of convicts into a general misconception. He built up his own good farm but he failed in managing the business side of it. He was unsuccessful as a trader with America. Those around him who prospered had been blatant manipulators of the grain market or dealers in rum with no concern for consequences. Oxley was meanly petty and no match for the vigorous rogues. He would sell a couple of his crossbred sheep as pure merinos. He was disappointed when John Macarthur would not sanction a marriage to his daughter Elizabeth. Oxley already had three daughters by two different girls. He made the final miscalculation of dying young, at forty-two or three (it was not known exactly when he was born) before he could outlive his errors.

When Oxley passed through what is now the Pilliga forest he was travelling east. He had set out to go west towards the supposed inland sea. Now he was making for the Pacific Ocean. And some of the ways he was taking there were difficult. 'Have you been there?' a sleeper cutter asked me in a Wee Waa hotel. 'Have you seen where the bastard went once he got east of the Peel? No one'd foller him.'

But Oxley's route was mostly decided by the weather. His party had been following down the Macquarie from Bathurst. On the western plains the river disappeared into marshes. Even in dry times there is a confusion of channels and reeds. One follows by boat what seems to be the main channel and two metre high reeds close in ahead. One turns to go back and it seems they have closed in behind. But in dry times the marshes can be easily skirted. Then thousands of extra hectares are used as grazing leases. It is fine cattle fattening country.

It might have taken Oxley weeks to skirt them. The Macquarie was in flood, and Marthaguy and Merri Merri creeks had filled their lagoons and swamps. Between the Macquarie and the Castlereagh rivers there was a barrier of reed and water a hundred kilometres long and a hundred wide. Oxley climbed a little hill west of present Gulargambone and named it Welcome Rock, 'for anything like an eminence was grateful to our sight'. From Mount Harris, a higher hill five kilometres away, he looked back east over flat black plains towards the Warrumbungles, 'a most stupendous range of mountains'. They do look good from out there, too. Not even the distance of a hundred and twenty kilometres can smooth their outline. It is as jagged as a gapped saw.

Westward there was marsh. Then the Macquarie began to come down in a huge flood. It seemed the whole plain must go under water. Oxley headed for the mountains. 'A delay of a few days would have swept us from the face of the earth.' The mountains he thought 'distinguished by the name of Arbuthnot's Range'. Arbuthnot was a Treasury official. Luckily no one has remembered that name. Warrumbungle, the European version of the Kamilaroi name, has persisted.

There were fifteen men with Oxley, horses and dogs. It was a good party. George Evans who had been first to explore the country west of the Blue Mountains in 1815 was second-in-charge. Charles Frazer, Scottish superintendent of the developing Botanic Garden, was plant collector. Dr John Harris who had imported spotted deer from India to his Ultimo estate went as a volunteer although he was sixty-four years old. Five of the convicts had accompanied Oxley on a previous trip that ended in swamps on the Lachlan.

The Castlereagh was in flood so they camped for a week until the water dropped, then they crossed about twelve kilometres north of Gulargambone. Oxley marked that river on his map as a slanting squiggle leading nowhere but he correctly estimated its source in the Warrumbungles.

Two boats that had carried a lot of the stores were left behind on the Macquarie. Now the packhorses and saddle horses were loaded with 160 kilograms each, a massive burden through the bog. As they approached the mountains they came into open forest of ironbark and cypress pine. The ground looked sandy and dry and the horses were led in gratefully. They floundered to their girths, and for a kilometre or so 'the horses were not on their legs for twenty yards together'.

Oxley climbed Mount Bullaway on the western end of the range. From there he could see north-east over the present forest area to the Nandewar Ranges beyond the Namoi River. That range he 'honoured with the name of the Earl of Hardwick' but that name, too, has been mostly forgotten. Then the party travelled north along low ridges into the rich lovely Goorianawa Valley. Some of those ridges were forested then as we know forest now – sides and summit dense with cypress pine and shrub undergrowth. The valley was open and boggy. Oxley did not even like that country. He wrote of 'utter loneliness . . . in these desolate wilds'. The place had been made eerie by a thunderstorm. 'The reverberations of sound among the hills was astonishing.' Australian thunderstorms are a marvel few places in the world experience. The lightning does not flicker calmly in broad sheets. Jagged lines connect across the sky as though the side of a furnace is cracking apart.

Oxley skirted the present dense Yarrigan forest and crossed Bugaldi

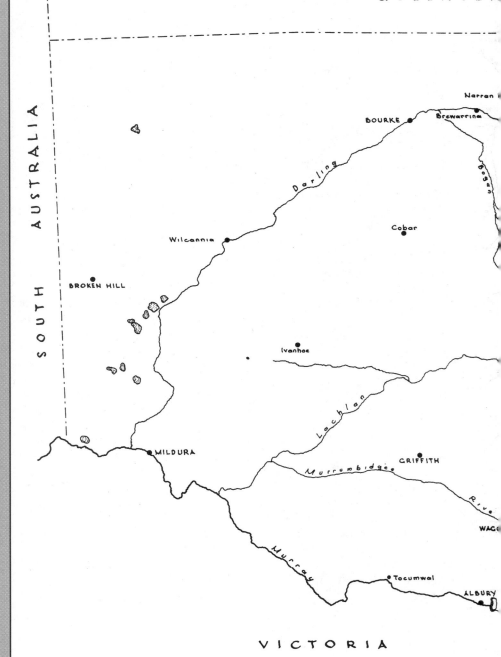

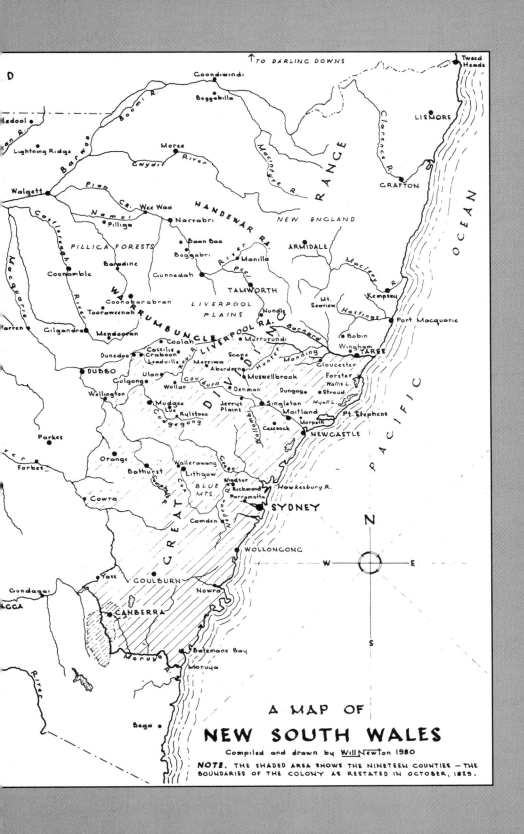

A MAP OF

NEW SOUTH WALES

Compiled and drawn by <u>Will Newton</u> 1980

NOTE. THE SHADED AREA SHOWS THE NINETEEN COUNTIES — THE BOUNDARIES OF THE COLONY AS RESTATED IN OCTOBER, 1829.

Creek into Yerrinan forest. The country was 'quite open, interspersed
with miserable rocky crags on which grew the cypress and eucalyptus'.
They found 'a new and large species of eucalyptus'. This was the
Yellow Box, still growing just north of the railway level crossing at
Bugaldie, where Oxley crossed the present Coonabarabran-Baradine
road. Yellow Box is a fine-leaved eucalypt good for shade and good for
bees to make honey. It is more gum-like than box-like, since the limbs
and upper trunks strip their bark. The lower bark does not strip. It
clings in red-brown tatters.

In the early 1970s the Warrumbungle Historical Society plotted Oxley's route from Mt Harris to the Liverpool Plains. There are local
criticisms that the committee spent too much time in aeroplanes and
not enough time on foot going thoroughly over the ground. This is fair.
But nevertheless they presented a convincing route along most of the
way, and they correlated Oxley's stated positions with the true positions thirteen kilometres farther east. Several of the peaks he mentioned are easily identified, and not where he said they were. Oxley
had two chronometers with him and both gave trouble. Chronometers
are notoriously troublesome instruments. Neither worked at all after he
crossed the Castlereagh.

So allowing for that error, Oxley's party came into the valley of Dandry Creek which he called 'Wiltden Valley'. This creek flows into
Baradine Creek, south-east of Baradine, and now divides the Wittenbra State Forest from Timmallallie. Here there was firm soil and good
grass but the water so tasted of iron it could scarcely be drunk. Several
species of acacia were in full flower and 'a vast variety of other flowering shrubs of the most beautiful and delicate description'. This area
was destroyed but grew back, more lovely now than when Oxley saw it.
There is little good timber so few men ever go there. In the spring it is a
wildflower garden. There is a patch of the tall columnar bright yellow
Acacia leucoclada (it has no common name) that grows nowhere else in
the forest. And there is a grove of Black Cypress Pine covered with
lichen so profusely, the trees look snow-covered. It might be lichen in a
Tasmanian rainforest, not the dry north-west of New South Wales.

Farther up the creek Oxley reported banksia. This still grows outside
the edge of settlement, well shaped trees of *Banksia marginata*, a cream-
flowered honeysuckle. Then Oxley came down off the higher country
and headed north-east towards the Nandewar Ranges. This country is
split chequerwise by low ridges into irregular sandy flats and valleys.
Creeks flow north-west into Baradine Creek and north-east into

Yaminba Creek. The formation cannot now be seen for growth, not even from the air. In 1818 the ridges were scrub-covered, and the flats were sparsely timbered with apple (*Angophora*), ironbark, and Blakely's Red Gum dwarfed to mallee size. The grass, mostly spinifex (*Triodia*), grew in separated spiky clumps. It was good cover for thousands of Rufous Rat-kangaroos. The dogs would not eat the rat-kangaroos; the horses would not eat the grass. The ground was boggy.

After two days hard going the explorers came into a dense brush of young ironbarks. It was late in the afternoon. They hoped soon to find water and a place to camp. Aborigines had recently burnt the area. Ground and tree-trunks were blackened. The sunlight came bluish through the canopy of stiff leaves. There was scarcely space to lead the horses through the gloom. Then they suddenly bogged to their bellies. For five kilometres the weakened horses ploughed furrows through the soupy mud till they came out on to firmer ground. When their drastic loads were taken off they lay down where they were, panting like dogs.

'Quicksands' Oxley called these bogs. They are not true quicksands. There is quicksand in some of the creeks, small round white grains of sand in water, that will drop a man or beast through almost as quickly as if he was falling in air. The bogs occur where the subsoil becomes oversaturated. It turns to slurry over a lower impervious layer. On top there is a sandy crust perhaps six millimetres thick, perhaps eighty or a hundred. An eighty millimetre crust will support an astonishingly heavy load. A twenty tonne trailer load of wheat might pass over a couple of times then drop through empty once the crust is cracked. A car can roll safely over a twelve millimetre crust, then vibrate through if it is left standing with the motor running. Our mailman stopped to open a gate on what seemed a hard patch of road. His car was settling on its chassis as he went back to drive it through.

The slurry is usually about thirty centimetres deep; it might be two metres. 'Spewy' is the farmers' term for such subsoil. Once vehicle or beast has broken through, it is difficult to haul it out. The top keeps breaking away as it does when a skater tries to pull himself from a hole in thin ice. Dead horses have been found in the forest cemented in up to their necks in a dried-out bog. A patch of bullock horns has been seen poking up like fungi out of the soil.

Oxley spent one more day trying to travel north-east but he could find no way through the bogs. His horses were hungry and weak, their backs galled from the pack saddles. He turned south towards the eastward spur of the Warrumbungles. Where he turned is in the

southern section of the Pilliga East State Forest, about fifty kilometres
south of Narrabri and about ten kilometres east of the Newell
Highway. He was east of Yaminba and Borah creeks.

These creeks flow parallel four to five kilometres apart. They join
and form the big Bohena Creek that flows north into the Namoi River
near Narrabri. Oxley followed them up to the hills. He was on solid red
ground and glad to be out of the sand. The forest 'must at all times be
impassable' he wrote. 'In wet seasons it is a bog; in dry ones there is no
water.'

Then he went over the range and came to the edge of the black-soil
Liverpool Plains. 'Horses as well as men had cause to rejoice . . . from
miserable harassing deserts' they had come to this 'beautiful and fertile
country.'

Nombi (pronounced more like Nummabee probably) the Aborigines
called it. Girrawillie Creek ran through it. William Cox took it up no
more than twelve years later, the first run formed on the fringe of the
present forest area.

Oxley continued east through the northern section of the Liverpool
Plains, some of the richest land in the world. He crossed the Peel River
near Tamworth and found a difficult way over the Great Dividing
Range. On the eastern slopes he climbed a mountain more than seventy kilometres from the coast and saw the sea. Mount Seaview still
testifies to his unimaginative naming. Then the party followed down
the Hastings River, named preposterously for the Governor of India,
to the lovely harbour called Port Macquarie for the Colonial Governor
who had sent the expedition out.

They turned south down the coast and struck rivers and long inlets,
lakes and more marshes. Their dogs died of tick bite or were paralysed
by the poison. The horses knocked up and one drowned. A man was
speared by Aborigines. Dr John Harris saved him and all the party
reached the penal settlement at Newcastle early in November 1818, a
little more than five months after setting out from Bathurst.

Nobody followed Oxley's tracks as they later followed Mitchell's.
Apart from being a roundabout route, it was too early. Of those who
were to settle the north, some had not yet arrived in the Colony; some
were building up their stock numbers; and an astonishing number,
born in the Colony, were growing up.

They were growing up with a purpose: to breed cattle and to grow
wool. The whole Colony was growing up. The amorphous squabbling
outcast community now had a function undirected by government and
mostly disapproved of. Unwelcome shapes were arising out of chaos.

Governor Phillip, the remarkable organiser who established the Colony on 26 January 1788, had little more idea than any of his contingent of a thousand why the Colony was there. Each saw himself in Australia for private reasons, the majority because as convicts they had no choice. But the British politicians who had sent them there, quietly and rather carelessly, had diffuse and private reasons for the sending. The Colony would grow hemp for rope and coarse sail making, with convicts as slaves; it would grow flax for linen and fine sails. It would cut timber for masts to supply Indian fitting yards. It was a sea base and refitting port, a whaling base, a gaol. It was a trading post that would function outside the monopoly of the East India Company, or oppositely a port to secure the China trade for the East India Company. The last probably was the main intention. Three of the first transports were East India Company vessels under orders to proceed to Canton as soon as their cargo was discharged in New South Wales. The First Fleet pioneered a new route to Canton. But the scheme was 'very undigested' said the Duke of Richmond, a junior minister, the only ministers in politics who dare make honest statements.

The site of the first Colony was a natural gaol, very difficult to get out of. There was ocean on the east, the wide deep moat of the Hawkesbury River on the north, and mountainous walls to west and south. Phillip did not choose it intentionally for that purpose. He did not realise he was fixing a great city on a bad site. He could not have done anything about it if he had. Already he had moved from Botany Bay where he had been sent because the swamps made him fear malaria. So it was important to get the men off the ships, to get houses and storerooms built, to get land ready for crops. Sydney had higher land and a beautiful harbour. It was too late for more exploration by sea. Who could have known that the ideal site of Port Stephens was not far to the north? And who then knew the significance of gaps in the ranges?

In the beginning there was no energy for questioning. The Colony had to concentrate on little more than keeping alive. For two and a half years there was no contact with Britain, then, a month after the arrival of the *Lady Juliana* with food, news and two hundred healthy London prostitutes, there was the appalling arrival of the Second Fleet with holds full of convicts put down in irons made for negro slaves and left to rot for eight months. Two hundred and eighty-one had died on the voyage and were thrown overboard. Of the seven hundred and forty-three that arrived alive in June 1790 few could walk. Most of them, sick and stinking, were off-loaded with hoists. Perhaps Australia gained some independence from that contact. Its parent, distant Britain, had become abominable.

But for four or five years many of the colonists were starved to the point of inertia. They had enough food to ward off scurvy and beri-beri but insufficient to work on. The first farmers on whom the Colony depended lacked knowledge but above all they lacked energy.

Phillip went, a sick man, in December 1792 and left the easy-going Major Grose, commandant of the New South Wales Corps, as Lieutenant-Governor. The New South Wales Corps replaced the marines, too dignified to work, that Phillip had found useless. The New South Wales Corps had been recruited by Grose in the British Isles from military prisons, from the disgruntled who had missed promotion, from the adventurous and the opportunists. Some, drunks and deserters, had been given the alternative of the lash or the Corps.

When Grose took over, the government farms that Phillip had fostered at Parramatta and Toongabbie were beginning to grow more grain, private gardens were flourishing, there were the beginnings of trade with India and the Cape of Good Hope. Grose relaxed Phillip's strong discipline and for a while there was a holiday spirit in the Colony. Then came rum – any strong drink that could be brought in by ship or distilled out of grain in the Colony. Nowhere else in the history of the world has alcohol been used as a coin. It was given absurd value. The holiday became a holiday of the morals and turned to long-lasting malignity. Wives were bought for rum, and judges. A parcel of ¼-hectare land grants was bought for a cask of rum placed in the centre of the land. Clerks in charge of the convict registers erased recorded terms of conviction and marked in shorter terms for $24 a head, or its equivalent in rum. Labourers were paid in rum or later in unmarketable grain that had to be discounted fifty and sixty per cent through dealers to pay for goods marked up five and six hundred per cent. The grain market was gerrymandered by all who could get control of it. Government stock were stolen and borrowed. The Reverend Samuel Marsden as magistrate hauled a miller before him one Sunday morning and fined him because his turning mill was desecrating the Sabbath. His own mill turned throughout the hearing. No man who could advance considered anything except that advancement.

The tormented community generated its own men. Some hard gobbets indeed were thrown up. Those attracted later as settlers were the same type – capable, adventurous, and extraordinarily adaptable, difficult, crude, vigorous, dishonest, selfish, violent. They differed only in the extent to which each of these qualities was developed. Some were more violent than others, some less adaptable. They developed Australia.

If these men had remained in Britain they would have had no influence on their times. Society would have restrained them. In Australia they moved outside the law. It is no use wishing they were different. To do so is to dispense with our culture. No other men could have done what they did. Australia might have been abandoned as a British settlement.

No gentleman ever succeeds in doing much. The greater the achievement the greater the violence directed towards that achievement. This book is not written by a gentle man.

James Ruse was thrown up early, a convict and our first good farmer. Vigour was most developed in him. He had the energy for thorough digging. There were neither ploughs nor draught animals available. So when the fallen timber was burnt he turned in the ashes with a spade. Then he hoed the ground 'never doing more than eight, or perhaps nine, rods in a day,' he told contemporaries, 'by which means, it was not like the government-farm, just scratched over, but properly done.'

And John Macarthur was thrown up early, an ensign of the New South Wales Corps, its leading opportunist. He came by the horrible second fleet in 1790 with his young wife Elizabeth, a maid, and a baby son. Francis Grose, his commanding officer, favoured Macarthur. He first made him paymaster of the Corps, then in 1793, as Lieutenant-Governor, granted him nearly one hundred hectares of land next to James Ruse at Parramatta with ten convicts to work it. Any officer who wanted land was given it but the others farmed with less ambition than Macarthur. He established himself as the most important man of the early years. More than any man he ensured the success of the Colony – his violence was the greatest. In directing it towards fine wool for his own benefit he established the Australian woolgrowing industry. For much of the next 150 years wool was Australia's major export. Woolgrowing is still an important industry.

But Macarthur was too violent. He dissipated its energy against a succession of men: Captains Gilbert and Traill, Judges Barron Field and Richard Atkins, Colonel Paterson, Governor Hunter, John Raine in an absurd squabble over a dam at Parramatta – almost everyone, eventually, he came in contact with – and Governor Bligh. That last magnificent row cost him years of exile in London.

Some of these men were abominable. Traill was responsible for the Second Fleet massacre. Atkins, the first remittance man in Australia, was drunken, cheating and ignorant of the law he administered viciously. Bligh was foul-mouthed and overbearing and a danger to Macarthur because he threatened to withdraw the Camden grants of land where the wool was grown. 'Are you to have such flocks of sheep and herds of cattle as no man ever heard of before? . . . You have got five thousand acres of land, sir, in the finest situation in the country but by God you shan't keep it!' But Macarthur did not pursue these quarrels with the idea of removing obstacles to wool-growing. They became for the time the main pursuit. They cost him half his life.

Without Elizabeth, Macarthur would have been nothing. She had the energy and the grand sense to carry out his ideas. For eleven of the years between 1802 and 1817, the most important years of their stock breeding, Elizabeth managed the farms while John Macarthur spent two long periods in England as a result of his quarrels. In the end his violence scattered in madness. It turned even against marvellous Elizabeth whom he cursed for being unfaithful. He threw his daughters out of the house and cursed his sons in a lucid fury that sounded distressingly sane. But by then his brilliant sons were managing.

Until men and stock broke over the western and northern mountains Macarthur had the most land in the Colony and the best. And his great estate at Camden known first as the Cowpastures was discovered not by men but by the Colony's first cattle. They wandered off when their convict attendant fell asleep. It was the most successful exploration in the first twenty-five years.

Exploration by land was not encouraged in the early years. The succession of governors and acting-governors up to 1810, Phillip, Grose, Paterson, Hunter, King, Bligh, Johnston, Foveaux and Paterson again, were trying to consolidate what there was, not extend their difficulties. New land meant new roads and more opportunity for convicts to abscond. Even the next governor, Macquarie, was wary.

Hunter encouraged exploration by sea and Bass and Flinders went out enthusiastically. But the first explorations by land were more private attempts to look over the beautiful barrier of the Blue Mountains than official expeditions.

Governor Phillip had named those mountains in two sections after a couple of marquesses: Carmarthen Hills and Lansdowne Hills. But they were always referred to as the blue mountains, and thus they became the Blue Mountains. All distance is blue because of Rayleigh scattering, a reflection in all directions of the low wave lengths of light from minute particles. The Blue Mountains are unusually and outstandingly blue. It is a trick of height and distance and temperature and the high oil content of shrubs and trees. A vapour of oil droplets scatters the light and a dense weave of blue rays covers the mountains.

Lieutenant Dawes, young officer of marines, went out first in the year after settlement. Sedate, scientific and religious, he tramped through the hills with little bags for soil samples and questioned the Aborigines about Noah and the Flood. Science had not advanced beyond religion in those days. The Aborigines had certainly heard of a flood. Dawes was delighted.

William Paterson tried next in 1793 as newly arrived commandant of the New South Wales Corps and as an explorer who had made a name for himself in Africa. He tried to follow westward up the Grose River that joins the Nepean to form the Hawkesbury but cliffs and gorges turned him back. Then Henry Hacking, the aging quarter-master of little *Sirius* of the First Fleet, went out and, after him, George Bass in 1797. Tall and good-looking, Bass could scale the mountainous waves of Bass Strait in tiny boats with Matthew Flinders but he had no hope in the Blue Mountains.

More and more convicts took to the bush and headed for the mountains. 'Over the hills and to the north lay China' they said. They were told the interior was desert or perhaps it was mangrove swamps. Then Irish convicts arrived, hustled out of their country so fast after religious squabbles it was forgotten to send their papers with them. No one knew why they had been sent or how long their sentences were. They arrived in a ferment that bubbled into the rest of the community. 'Over the hills and to the south' they said, 'there is a European settlement' – a fairy kingdom of great wealth where no one worked. Several set out to join it.

So Governor Hunter in 1798 sent men to find a strange outlaw, John Wilson, and ask him to take a party of Irish convicts over the mountains and prove there were no settlements. Wilson said he knew of the skeletons of fifty men who had tried to reach China but he would lead the party across.

Wilson was one of the first of the bush rangers, men who ranged free in the bush. It was years before the words were run together and bushranger came to mean an outback highwayman. He had come out as a convict and was only nineteen or twenty years old when he finished his sentence. Then he took to the bush and lived with the Aborigines. An escapee named Knight joined him. Occasionally they robbed settlers' houses. None of these men could keep away completely from settlement. Then they unaccountably tried to steal two white children, nine-year-old girls. They were caught and sentenced to hard labour but

escaped. Hunter must have considered Wilson tough enough to keep
Irish convicts in order.

The Irish convicts were soon convinced. They turned back. Wilson
and his companions travelled south-west for a few days till they, too,
had to turn back. Two months later Wilson took another party out.
Old Henry Hacking joined it and also David Collins, the marine officer
who had stayed to become Judge-advocate. They followed up the
Nepean River, then up the Warragamba to where it is joined by the
Wollondilly. They climbed a spur and followed the high country that
feeds the Wollondilly all the way through to its source east of
Goulburn. They climbed Mount Towrang but the western view from
there is hilly enough. They did not see the Goulburn plains.

No more interest would have been taken in the journey even if they
had. No new land was needed. Wilson returned to the Aborigines and
was murdered in a quarrel over a woman. So many of those who tried
to live with Aborigines were murdered because they ignored the marriage laws. The women were not available by selection. Marriage was a
rigid tribal arrangement.

In 1799 more Irish convicts arrived, members of the Society of
United Irishmen who had been trying to re-enact the French Revolu-
tion in Ireland with the aid of 1,500 French troops. They arrived with
ready-made fables about the new land. All the old stories were reinforced. They persisted through Hunter's term to King's. At last an exasperated Governor King decided he would have to scotch the
rumours. He would demonstrate the deserts or the swamps. He called
on Ensign Francis Barrallier to cross the mountains.

It was not easy to get Barrallier. William Paterson of the New South
Wales Corps, now Colonel after his spell as Acting-Governor, told
King coldly that it was beyond his instructions to release an officer for
exploring. King loved a joke. He detached Barrallier as his aide-de-
camp then 'sent him on an embassy to the King of the Mountains'.

Barrallier was unusually capable. He had four soldiers and five convicts with him. Aborigines known and unknown joined him on the
way. The log that Wilson had kept four and a half years earlier would
have been useful to them but no one thought of it. They spent the last
two months of 1802 trying to find a way out of the chasms of the Nattai-
Wollondilly river system westward across the north-south ridges.

Not many Aborigines knew a way over the mountains either. There
was little commerce between the tribes east and west of the mountains.
Barrallier met an Aboriginal who had come from the west but he was

with a party unfriendly to the Aborigines accompanying Barrallier. There was quarrelling and threats to kill, and no one told Barrallier where the man had come from until he had gone.

Barrallier presented a detailed account of his explorations to King. It was written in French in atrocious handwriting. King consigned it to Lord Hobart in the hope that he could get it translated. It was filed away and not translated until it was published in *Historical Records of New South Wales* ninety-five years later.

By 1805 there was a little more interest in new land. When a group of bush rangers who roamed west of the Hawkesbury declared that they had been over the mountains to plains on the other side, Governor King coaxed them to do it again with promise of reward. They reached the cairn of stones erected near present Linden by Lieutenant Dawes sixteen years before, but shortly after they lost their energies in rough country and returned.

The Blue Mountains are difficult. By world standards, the Great Dividing Range of which they are part is a range of low hills nine to twelve hundred metres high with a few higher peaks. They were pushed up about a million years ago as a long narrow plateau over three thousand kilometres long and two hundred and fifty to five hundred kilometres wide. Now it is in the middle period of erosion. Everything soft has gone. What is left are the bones, sandstone and basalt, rough as any skeleton. It does not matter to an explorer if a mountain is only a thousand metres high when he is confronted with a hundred and fifty metre wall half-way up. In a few million years most of that will wear away too. What will be left will be small conical hills like the spectacular volcanic residues on the north-western edge of the Liverpool Plains.

Now the mountains challenged George Caley, Sir Joseph Banks's energetic and cantankerous botanist. Soon after the return of the bush rangers he set out with 'four of the strongest men in the Colony who had been accustomed to live in the woods'. Caley had often been in the foothills collecting plants. He began from the same place as the bush rangers, at the junction of the Grose and the Hawkesbury. But he followed in the direction of what is now Bell's line of road and travelled farther than anyone had before, only to be turned back by a succession of valleys 'which may with more propriety be called chasms'. Caley wanted to seek a way round but his four strong men balked. On the way back they saw two ravens in a tree. 'They've lost their way,' said a member of the party.

King decided that there was no point in more attempts to make the crossing. Even if someone clambered over and farmers followed, 'What is their produce to be done with, except for feeding swine?' And who would clamber over? Few men had the persistence of Caley and he arrived back exhausted.

The crossing was eventually made by keeping to the ridges and thus avoiding the chasms. Those first cattle that strayed to the best piece of land found in the first twenty-five years had done what is seldom possible in Australia, followed up a coastal stream. Cattle keep watch on their masters and as soon as their convict herdsman lost attention they slipped off quietly and found the Nepean River. They fed up the river to the glory of the Camden Cowpastures and there they stayed.

No one remembered exactly how many cattle escaped. They had been brought from the Cape of Good Hope in the First Fleet. There was old Gorgon, the bull, four or five cows and a bull or heifer calf. Five hundred men searched for them but they were not found till 1795. A convict employed to catch and shoot game for an officer's household was told of them by an Aboriginal. He went to see for himself. A hunter was employed by every man who could afford one. Those with money did not go hungry for long in New South Wales. Sheep and cattle were too few to kill. Domestic pigs and poultry supplied some meat, game most of it. 'With the assistance of one man and half a dozen greyhounds which I keep, my table is constantly supplied with wild ducks or kangaroos. Averaging one week with another these dogs do not kill less than 300 lbs weight.' So John Macarthur wrote to his brother James in London. The most important social distinction in early New South Wales was not between free and convict, rich and poor: it was between the fed and the unfed.

Governor John Hunter rode out to see the cattle. They were fat and wild. One big bull charged so viciously he had to be shot. It took six balls from the muzzle loaders to bring him down. Perhaps it was old Gorgon himself run as wild as his progeny and showing off. Surely he was still head bull. A total of sixty-one adults and calves was counted, a remarkable number for such a small herd to reach in seven years. None of the later importations cared for at the settlement had done as well.

That journey of the first cattle to the Cowpastures is important, not only for the land found, but because many of their prolific descendants were taken into Government herds. Their blood was in the rough early cattle, colonial cattle. Australia was developing not only its own men but its own livestock. The cattle, the horses, the sheep were markedly different to those bred elsewhere. They too were vigorous and the right sort to people Australia.

What breed was Gorgon and his cows? There are good descriptions of the cattle found at the Cowpastures, the best by Governor King of a bull he got a very close look at. It came out from among cows the Governor's party was inspecting, pawed the ground and charged suddenly. King's retinue all galloped to the cover of a clump of trees. His horse was slower to move. When he reached the clump there was no room to fit in and no one offered him any. King turned to face the bull alone. As it raked at his horse he smashed it across the nose with the handle of his riding-whip and it turned away.

It had 'majestic horns' wrote King, and long legs, 'a most Noble animal . . . as large as the finest Ox I ever saw in England, his skin sleek and shiny'. Elsewhere he explained that 'The rising on the top of the shoulders is not that of the Buffalo Breed . . . they are formed like the Tame Bull, Gorgon . . . with a thick neck and broad high shoulders.'

But King nowhere mentioned their colour to aid identification nor, it seemed to me at first after a long search, had anyone else. The cattle were of Zebu extraction because of the humps. Without knowing the colour it was not possible to get closer than that. No one previously has identified these cattle.

Barrallier twice mentioned colour in that long unread journal. His route had led up through the Cowpastures and the wild cattle then numbered several hundred. He found a bull that had been gored in a fight lying dead in a gully. It was 'of a reddish colour with white spots'. Several weeks later he came across 'a superb black ox which looked at me without being frightened'.

At the end of the eighteenth century the breeds of cattle were not fixed as they are now. Old colours could still protrude in calves. The Africander breed which is now predominately deep red can still show white on the underline. At that time the red was paler and there was much more white in the breed. Spotted beasts were possible. Black Africanders are rare since the breed developed in a slow five hundred year trek through the deserts and semi-deserts of Africa. Sand imposes its colour on the animals that live on it. European rabbits selected for sandy as soon as they reached the South Australian deserts.

Because of the pronounced humps that he imposed on his descendants, because of that one red bull with white spots, one can be sure that old Gorgon was an Africander. And because of that black ox, a dominant colour in cattle, one can deduce that at least one of the first cows was either one of the new Africander crosses that South African farmers were then making with European breeds, or, more likely, a Vaderlander, an old breed always black with unobtrusive neck humps. Modern stock of that breed which was developed by a family named Uys are known as Drakensberger.

Africander cattle are of distant Zebu ancestry but the flaring shoulder humps have rounded and moved farther up the neck. They have lost the Zebu jog-trot and their calves bellow distress instead of wailing it on one long note. These cattle fixed the shape and the colour of a Zebu-Shorthorn cross to produce the deep red Santa Gertrudis.It was a brilliant breeding experiment and one that Robert Kleberg Junior never admitted. George Peppin in Australia made an even more successful experiment with the small early Australian merino. He crossed it with the Lincoln and produced the big, plain-bodied Australian merino that could walk dry miles to water. Peppin never admitted that outcross. Stock breeders have the same absurd idea about pure blood as Hitler.

For three years after the cattle strayed there were no known cattle in the Colony. Then in 1791 Captain Parker, master of the storeship *Gorgon*, bought cattle at the Cape and after a difficult trip landed eight cows and three bulls alive. They were described as Black Cattle so they must have been Vaderlanders. There were other black breeds in South Africa but they belonged to black tribes that would not sell them. Certainly other breeds had black individuals but it is inconceivable that Phillip so favoured black he instructed Parker to select black beasts from other breeds that were mainly red, yellow and white.

More cattle were brought in from wherever they could be got by Government and by individuals. A chartered ship sent to Bengal in 1795 brought back one hundred and thirty-two Zebu cattle. They were penned on the gun-deck with mats laid to stop them slipping and they were put in tight enough to support one another as the ship rolled. Wind-sails supplied fresh air. Twenty attendants cleaned the mats and fed and soothed the cattle. Each time the ship tacked they turned them all comfortably uphill. Only one cow died on the voyage.

The *Supply* and the *Reliance* came from the Cape in 1797 with another load of Vaderlanders. Hunter described the *Supply* as 'a complete mass of rotten timber' and he could not send it back for any more.

Cattle were brought from Madagascar, from Spain, from Britain, and some of the small breeds kept as milkers aboard ship were dropped off – short-legged English Polls from St Helena, one cow from St Catherine's, the lake port in Ontario, and an Andalusion cow left by

Commodore Malaspina in 1793 on a visit with two Spanish discovery vessels. Communication was slow but widespread at the end of the eighteenth century.

A Devon bull, an old breed, and a few cows of the developing Shorthorn were brought from England by Captain Kent, master of the leaking *Supply*, who farmed for a few years in New South Wales. In 1800 there were over a thousand head of cattle in the Colony, not counting the wild herd. Other stockbreeders brought in cattle of their choice. The Reverend Samuel Marsden, for some years eclipsing Macarthur as the leading farmer and stockbreeder, imported Lincoln Reds and the polled Suffolk Duns, an indefinite breed that disappeared into the Red Poll. Ayrshires, just beginning to develop their showy modern colouring, were brought in for milk, and another consignment of cattle came from the Cape by the *Perseus* in 1802. This time the Cape cattle were 'very nearly of the English breed . . . a superior kind to most that come from that place'.

One or two breeders favoured the ancient Longhorns with a preposterous two and a half metre sweep to their horns. And Sir John Jamison, one of the first squatters to move to the Namoi, had good Devons and, later, a few early Herefords on his Nepean estate. The lovely pattern of white on deep red was not fixed in these cattle until the 1850s. That pattern was found to be dominant, and the roans and irregular white streaks on the body, and the freckled faces (broken baldy) of the early breed disappeared.

The cattle were well looked after, as one would expect after the months of effort in getting them here. The only fences were paling or post-and-rail round gardens, orchards and crops, so the feeding cattle were tailed (followed) by stockmen and brought back to yards at night. As numbers increased (and they increased quickly to 11,000 by 1810) it became impractical to yard them each night and stockmen moved their herds to accustomed watering-places in the late afternoon and allowed them to bed down in the open.

The wild cattle continued to increase quickly. There were estimates of thousands by 1804. Each governor had dreams of quietening the cows and bringing them in to breed with the Government herd. But they persistently outran the horsemen and dodged the wings built to guide them into yards. Horsemen were sent out to shoot bulls and salt their meat but after a few were shot the others became unapproachable. Many of the bulls would charge on sight. Sometimes a whole herd would advance, seemingly more savage than curious.

The Zebu ancestors of Africander cattle were very wild. They were fed out for several months of the year by nomadic Indian tribesmen who used them as night guards. These cattle are intelligent and allow those they know to handle them. The wary cattle rested in a ring around the sleeping men and even the heifers would charge in a mob and kill if a strange man or dog approached.

We sometimes buy Brahman (improved Zebu) crosses for fattening. They are interesting cattle to handle, and will play with me in the paddock once they know me. They mill around holding out their noses to smell my hand, then snort and gallop away as though frightened, only to turn soon and gallop back to mill again. When I laugh and talk to them they settle down and can be moved easily from paddock to paddock on foot. But if a stranger comes near they are always uneasy and sometimes, when confined, they panic and will not even listen to me as I try to soothe them. Their wild ancestors are with them still. I would have been very frightened if the Cowpasture cattle had milled around me.

Governor King laid claim to 1,300 of those cattle. Governor Arthur Phillip had owned two of the five cows that escaped. When he heard of the discovery he wrote to King stating that a proportion of the descendants was undoubtedly his and he gave that share to King. That might have been reasonable. But, since the wild cattle were uncatchable, King took 200 of the tame Zebu and black cattle in their place. It was as shabby a deal as any rogue in the Colony made. Certainly he advised Lord Hobart after he had taken delivery: 'I beg to throw myself on your Lordship's candour.' But it was $14,000 worth of cattle no man would have judged him entitled to. King was sick and prematurely aged – he died four years later in 1808 – and nothing was said in his lifetime. After his death the arrangement was disallowed.

The Cowpastures were made the preserve of the wild cattle. A guard-house was built and a man stationed to prevent shooting. No land was to be made available where they roamed. Then, after his first long absence of three and a half years, Macarthur returned from England in 1805 with an order from Lord Camden for 2,000 hectares about Mount Taurus. The ineffective Camden did not know that that hill, named after the first big bull was shot there, was in the centre of the Cowpasture reserve. The grant galled every governor in Macarthur's lifetime. Few in Australia had faith in wool.

Apart from the quality of the land and his hopes for wool Macarthur was well aware of the advantages of living close to such a large herd of cattle. His men found a way of dealing with them. They shot the cows and roped the calves. The cattle had spread along seventy kilometres of the Nepean River. Strong young bulls selected cows, moved away and established a new territory. Sometimes two or three bulls with up to a hundred cows moved off together. Outcast bulls roamed the mountains in mobs of up to twenty. It was impossible to guard them all. Many Nepean settlers added wild calves to their herds.

When the Blue Mountains were finally crossed by Blaxland, Lawson and Wentworth in 1813, Governor Macquarie considered another attempt to muster the wild herd so that they could be driven over the range. He thought of making the whole interior their preserve and giving the Camden lands to settlers. Quiet cattle were used as coachers but no one was successful in mustering adult wild cows until young George Johnston, Superintendent of Government Stock and son of one of the main men involved in the deposing of Bligh, built winged yards in several places and turned out quiet cattle to mingle with the wild. Johnston was an outstanding horseman and he was well mounted. His father had been presented with the first good stallion in Australia. In two or three years he yarded and tamed almost 900 cows and shot 178 bulls for their hides, then, early in 1820, he was killed in a fall from his horse while running in another mob. But the best of the wild cattle had been taken and, finally, in the late 1820s, the degenerate remnants were run into a walled gorge in the rough Razorback Range north of Picton and shot.

The Government cows were given in ones and twos and threes to encourage settlers. They were given out on loan with payment expected in kind (another cow for a cow) in three years time. They were sold to any who could afford to pay for them. The breeds were separated in three mobs, those from England and Europe in one, the little Zebus from Bengal in another, and the Vaderlanders and the Africanders from the Cape in the third. All were branded with the broad arrow. Several thousand were maintained, divided into herds of about three hundred in the care of two stockmen. Each herd had its own yard at a watering place, and huts were built for the stockmen near the yards. One room at each hut was 'reserved for the exclusive Accomodation of the Superintendent of Government Stock to reside and sleep in' on his tours of inspection.

These were the cattle that settlers and squatters first moved over the Blue Mountains and up to the Hunter and eventually to the Liverpool Plains. In attacks by Aborigines, by the carelessness of stockmen, by the impossibility of holding them all on unfenced land, many escaped. There were wild cattle always in advance of settlement. The mixture of breeds degenerated into small hard Jersey-like beasts, black and white, rusty coloured or dun – the Colonial cattle, the Goulburn roans. The savage little bulls – 'all horns and balls' is the grazier's description of such beasts – would follow a man along the mountain tracks and attack at first opportunity. They were found in the Bulga Range when settlers moved on to the Hunter River. There they were accounted for as the descendants of Channel Island cattle that Cook left on the coast. Cook carried no cattle to leave there. The only mammals he carried on his first trip were pigs. He did not release pigs in Australia but he took a sow and her litter ashore when he anchored in the Endeavour River in north Queensland.

Oxley found tracks of wild cattle on the Macquarie in 1817, 150 kilometres from the nearest known cattle at Bathurst. They were early in the Snowy Mountains and down the Lachlan. Allan Cunningham mentioned in 1827 that it was well known that stragglers were in the foothills of the Warrumbungles. William Gardner, an amiable Scottish school-teacher in New England during the 1840s and 1850s, told a strange story of cattle found 200 kilometres up the Swan River in Western Australia by the first settlers who moved inland in 1829. Gardner who wrote huge manuscript volumes of early history, inaccurate and unpublishable, saw wild cattle spread from Sydney to the Swan: 'the greatest width of this island is 2,500 miles . . . herds of wild cattle must have gone over and may be at present grazing on the interveening country'.

There were still descendants of these cattle about in the 1920s. They moved into the prickly pear in Queensland after it had overrun the Brigalow country and driven out men and softer breeds of cattle. There was nothing to eat but pear and the cattle adapted. Their prickle-studded tongues atrophied to stumps and they lost all knowledge of water. If moved to grass away from the watery slabs of pear they would die of thirst beside a dam. Their gait changed. The calves born on that country moved more like antelopes as they leapt through the pear clumps. A few were captured and given a run in camp drafts at local rodeos but they could outrun the horses in the time allowed.

The first horses vital for the working of cattle were not attractive. They also came from India and the Cape. The Cape horses were nags – run-down crosses of the Arab and ancient Moorish Barb. 'Narrow and sharp-backed' James Atkinson described them in his *Account of the State of Agriculture and Grazing in New South Wales*, 'fall off much from the rump to the tail, low necked and large headed.' The light-boned, goose-rumped Arabs imported from India did not improve them. Major George Johnston's good stallion was given him by the Duke of

Northumberland who was probably doing something for a bastard son. It arrived in 1802. 'A noble animal nearly seventeen hands high' Governor King described it, but he thought the $20 service fee too much for government mares. The next year the merchant Robert Campbell imported Hector, a Persian·stallion. Persian horses were as fast as the Arab from which they derived but taller and heavier. There were some better mares to mate him to. Officers of the New South Wales Corps had brought in light, well-shaped horses from the Cape, the offspring of Spanish Jennet stallions. Hector nicked with these mares, and the Australian Blood Horse was established. From these were bred in thousands the heavy remounts for the Indian Army and the present great Australian stockhorse.

The early pigs were black and short, and they fattened to grossness. That was an advantage in the days of general hard physical labour. Fat supplied energy. Milch goats and poultry were prolific, but there is no record of breed. The first few sheep were shepherded without dogs. Hunting dogs, mostly heavy greyhounds, were brought in early. There were soon so many they were a nuisance in the streets. But even by 1803 when there were over 11,000 sheep in the Colony, Governor King reported 'We are very much in want of a breed of shepherd's dogs . . . If such a thing could be procured it would be of great utility'.

Meat was the only product considered of the first sheep brought to the Colony, the strange Afrikaner or Cape Fat-tails. Like Africander cattle these sheep evolved with the Hottentots. The same conditions developed men, their cattle and their sheep. In the eighteenth century, big flocks ran in the dry areas of Cape Colony. They were common shipboard livestock. When the trade route to India and China went by way of the Cape of Good Hope, vessels both outward and homeward bound called to take a supply of live mutton on board.

There are many species of fat-rumped and fat-tailed sheep. The remarkable Russian Karakul is an offshoot, selected for the patterned furry coats of the day-old lambs marketed as astrakhan.

In the fat-rumped species, as the sheep matures, the rump bulges with fat in two big cushions meeting in the centre. The tail, a ten centimetre naked vestige, is lost within the folds. In the fat-tailed species the rump does not swell. The tail itself develops according to breed either as a short bag thirty centimetres wide filled with four kilograms of fat, as a dumb-bell swinging level with the hocks from a few centimetres of ordinary tail, or as a grotesque, tapered tube beginning broadly and ending in a long narrow tip naked on the underside and trailing along the ground.

These sheep are sometimes specially fed before slaughter. Then the tail develops fantastically and can weigh fifteen kilograms or more. Such tails are strapped to skids or even little trolleys that are pulled about by the sheep.

The Cape Fat-tails were thought to have the blood of both fat-rumped and fat-tailed sheep. They had long flopping ears and frizzled hair in various shades of black, brown and bay, usually spotted with lighter colours. If not shorn the coat was cast each spring like the coats of horses and cattle as a new coat grew through it. The shorn hair was good for mattress-making. The tails of the majority were short, broad and flat, naked on the underside as are the tails of all sheep, and they ended in little kinked twists as though the tails of pigs had been pinned on. The tails weighed two or three kilograms. Some sheep exhibited their unselective breeding with long tapered tails. When the breed was popular in South Africa the fat was commonly used as butter, just as dripping, the rendered fat of cattle and sheep, was used in Australia.

The forty-four fat-tailed sheep loaded at the Cape when the First Fleet called there soon died in coastal Sydney. The Afrikaner Fat-tail evolved in deserts. Eight ewes and three rams landed with the black cattle on the *Gorgon* in 1791 fared better. They could be moved a little farther inland to Parramatta.

Sheep were brought from Bengal, too, walked there for shipping down mountain passes from Tibet. The chartered *Atlantic* brought two rams and eighteen ewes of that breed for the government flock in 1792. They were black or dark grey mostly, small but prolific, bearing two, three and four lambs at a time. They grew about two hundred grammes of wiry fleece called 'cat's hair' in the wool trade and they dressed about eleven kilograms. The fat-tailed, less the tail, were not much heavier.

Private individuals as well as the Government were building up flocks. More fat-tailed sheep came from the Cape, more hairy sheep from Bengal. John Macarthur imported sixty Bengal ewes in 1794, or perhaps it was thirty in 1793 – he changed his stories according to circumstance.

In 1797 eight, nine or ten fairly pure Spanish Merinos were brought from the Cape on that last trip of the old *Supply* with the *Reliance*. The commissary, John Palmer, himself a landowner, had been sent with Captains Kent and Waterhouse to buy livestock. Palmer bought the black cattle already mentioned and more fat-tailed sheep, then he was offered a small flock of merinos by Mrs Gordon, widow of a colonel recently killed in action. The sheep had been bred from a gift by the

King of Spain to the Dutch Government at the Cape. Colonel Gordon seems to have taken over the sheep simply because no one else was interested in them. Palmer was not interested in them either. He wanted meat not wool. The two captains bought the sheep privately, thirteen each. They knew nothing about wool and bought them perhaps as a speculation, perhaps out of curiosity to see how they fared in the Colony.

They did not fare well on the voyage home. Captain Waterhouse wrote: 'The passage to Port Jackson is generally made in 35 to 40 days, this one 78 . . . We met with one gale of wind the most terrible I ever saw or heard of, expecting to go to the bottom every moment . . .' The animals ran out of food, 'they lived on air most of the time'. The black cattle stood it well enough and the fat-tailed sheep. Kent lost all his merinos except one ram. Waterhouse lost four, five or six of his – he did not remember exactly.

There were three merino rams and five or six ewes left alive. The ewes were isolated and mated only to merino rams. Since a vigorous ram can serve a hundred ewes if he runs with them all year, the merino rams were available for cross-breeding with Bengal and fat-tailed ewes. Although they were not vigorous each might have impregnated forty or fifty of the prolific Bengal ewes as well as his share of the few merinos.

One wonders at the discomfort of a merino ram when he first mounted an Afrikaner Fat-tail. A wide three-kilogram bag of fat is a formidable chastity belt. A merino ram and a ram of any British breed mates by rearing and dropping his forelegs over the shoulders of the ewe. His thin-tailed mate, even if her long tail is not docked, twists it to one side and the ram's long thin penis meets no obstruction. Fat-tailed ewes cannot swing their tails out of the way. The rams, which are notably virile, use a different technique. A fat-tailed ram slides up a ewe's back. As he begins the slide he hooks one foreleg beneath her tail and moves it to one side. Then his brisket catches it and pushes it further out of the way. When his forelegs grip the ewe's shoulders he pulls his belly hard against her tail and clamps it clear of his penis.

Rams of other breeds never perfect the trick. But there has been much experimental crossing in South Africa. Persistent rams of both British meat breeds and merinos succeed in penetrating fat-tailed ewes often enough to impregnate them, especially when the ewes are not too fat.

Merinos improved the wool quality rapidly but, most strangely, that was attributed more to climate than to breeding. The merinos were not popular. They were delicate and there was insufficient meat on them.

Much more interest was taken in a consignment of nuggety South-
downs for crossbreeding. They improved meat quality but did nothing
for the wool.

Some robust sheep came in from Ireland, known always as the 'Irish
sheep'. They were English sheep put aboard ship in Ireland and no
guess can be made as to their breed. They grew fair wool and they were
not merinos since there were few merinos in England and export was
forbidden. They also were used in crossbreeding. Major Johnston had
one Spanish ram, like the stallion a gift from the Duke who might have
been his father. 'Badly chosen' Samuel Marsden wrote of it, 'little or
no value here.'

Captain Joseph Foveaux, administrator for several months in the
two-year upset after Bligh was deposed, was the biggest early sheep
owner; the Reverend Samuel Marsden grew the best wool. Macarthur
owned about a thousand mixed sheep by 1798 but he was not 'extravagant enough to kill mutton.'

By 1800 there were over 6,000 sheep in the Colony, mostly
crossbreds. Macarthur had kept a small flock of pure merinos separate
from his crossbreds but he had no great area of land then and no
definite plans for woolgrowing. He even offered his whole flock to the
Government at $5 a head. While King was making up his mind,
Macarthur had one of his most violent quarrels. He fought a duel with
Colonel Paterson and shot him in the shoulder. King had Macarthur
arrested.

His indignity was such only a court-martial would satisfy his
honour. Macarthur had such presence his absurd reaction was taken
seriously. King ordered him to England for court-martial. While he
was waiting for a ship to come in he bought all of Foveaux's sheep, one
thousand two hundred and fifty. Elizabeth took charge of them on her
farm at Seven Hills and began her long period of management. Now
they were the biggest sheep owners in the Colony. As an afterthought
Macarthur packed a few merino fleeces to take with him when he sailed
in November 1801.

There was no court-martial. There was nothing Macarthur could
be charged with. What was discussed was wool. British mills were in
trouble. Wars with France and threats of war with Spain had cut off
supplies. Macarthur's samples looked good. He tricked Lord Camden
into the Cowpasture grant. At public auction he bought merino sheep
forbidden to be exported and arranged a Treasury warrant to export
them. In 1804 he set sail for the Cowpastures in his own ship, the *Argo*,
bought for whaling. Aboard were sheep, ploughs, plants and seeds,

and four young men trained in wool-sorting. The figurehead was a golden fleece. Australia's wool industry had begun.

Animals wanted and unwanted prospered in Australia beyond all expectation. The finical first merinos were certainly well cared for. All Macarthur's sheep, even when they numbered thousands, were housed at night during rough weather. But their success depended not so much on the care and the climate and the grasses which at first were good, but the hybrid vigour introduced by the outlandish crosses with the hairy Bengal and the Afrikaner Fat-tail sheep.

The merinos John and Elizabeth Macarthur bred from their crossbred ewes look rough by today's standard – a flock of them could still be seen in the 1970s at Camden Park estate maintained much as they were 170 years ago. But sales of ewes from Macarthur's flock, from Marsden's, from smaller breeders, all of them graded-up from crossbred merinos, established the first big flocks. Since the sheep that later stocked South Australia, Victoria and Western Australia were the descendants of crossbred Bengal and Afrikaner Fat-tail sheep brought from Norfolk Island to Tasmania, probably every present-day merino has a trace of their blood.

The early sheep were quickly upgraded. The small importations of merinos could be held pure behind log or paling fences to breed a continuous supply of rams for mating to crossbred ewes bought in the Colony.

Cattle improved more slowly. Few cows were imported to mate to purebred bulls nor was it possible to fence off herds of breeding cattle on distant runs. As many good bulls were imported as stockbreeders could afford. These were mated to the rainbow-coloured Colonial cows. But since not enough bulls could be imported for mating to the rapidly increasing herds, the best of the young crossbred bulls had to be left unemasculated as sires.

There is extant the *Register of the Female Herds of Government Cattle* kept in the beautiful script of John Maxwell, Superintendent of Government Stock at Bathurst from 1823 to 1826. The cows were kept in herds of 400 and each cow was described under the headings Colour and Marks. They were brindle, red, black, yellow, white, brown, blue, all of various shades, with spots and marks carefully recorded: 'dark brown with a mealy nose'; or 'light brindled, some white on inside of joints'; 'white, red ears and sides mottled with light red'; 'light red, white on the chine, rump, belly, breast, on tail and a star on the forehead'; 'dark brown, snail horned'; 'black, some white on belly, polled'; or 'red and white, colour a muddled mixture'.

New men arrived as well as stock and a surprising number of new children were being born into Australia as the only land they knew. In 1807, out of a population of about 7,500 there were 395 married women, 807 legitimate children, and 1,025 natural children. Marriages were encouraged officially but living 'tally' was the preferred thing. That arrangement was not the common one of the master taking advantage of his maid, it was the tallying of tastes between a labourer and an emancipist servant girl or even two convicts holding working tickets of leave. The expression came from an old method of keeping account of money lent by individuals to the British Government. A stick with notches cut in it to signify the amount was dated then split down the centre. The lender took one half, the stock; the Government retained the other half, the counter-stock. When the lender needed his money he presented the stock. This was compared with the counter-stock, and if the number of notches tallied, payment was made. Women living tally were treated as partners rather than possessions.

Macquarie overcame social bigotry but he could not overcome sexual bigotry. It was built into nineteenth-century Englishmen. 'A scandalous and pernicious custom' he declared it, 'so shamelessly adopted throughout the Territory.' But it was an excellent arrangement.

The only things not thriving in the Colony were Australian grasses. Their roots had run in a spongy soil full of humus. They were accustomed to fire, to drought and flood, to deficiency of nitrogen and phosphorus, to the gentle feeding of sharp-toothed kangaroos at their clumped butts, and the picking of their seeds by parrots and pigeons and rats. They had never had their whole seed heads snatched in one mouthful; they had never been trampled by cloven hooves; their surface roots had never had to run in hard ground.

The methods of management hastened the destruction. The areas about yards and sheds where the sheep and cattle were folded at night were trampled hard and bare. These areas ringed outward with the constant droving backward and forward. There was barely time for the sheep to feed after being driven out in the morning before it was time to start them back.

Ground never stays bare for long. Before English grasses and medics accustomed to trampled ground were sown and found to thrive, hardy but inferior Australian cousins of the good grasses took over. The best grass, the tall sparse-seeded Oat Grass (*Themeda australis*), all but disappeared. So did *Poa caespitosa*, the Weeping Polly Grass of rich damp places. The excellent Forest Blue Grass (*Bothriochloa intermedia*) was replaced by the unpalatable Red Leg Grasses, and several species of soft *Danthonia*, Wallaby Grass, by a wiry relation. Mostly the tufted Spear Grasses (*Stipa*) and Wire Grasses (*Aristida*) found they liked the new conditions. High in fibre, low in protein and energy, they grew prolifically. Their cruel seeds twisted into wool and flesh. Sheep scratched and lost weight. Landholders burnt the grasses as they seeded. They grew even better.

Even at Camden the pastures quickly deteriorated. Gum saplings sprang up and Native Blackthorn. Then came drought, then rain, then in February 1812 caterpillars, millions of Army Worms that ate crops and the new-sprung grass. Stock starved and died. Some men moved illegally past the Cowpastures. Macquarie threatened them with arrest and impounding of stock. Gregory Blaxland looked again at the mountains from his Brush Farm.

2

The First Moves

A Difficult
Game

The Blaxland brothers, John and Gregory, had arrived as the Colony's prize settlers. They had money from the sale of estates, though not as much as the Government thought they had; they were conventionally respectable, properly married and with backgrounds of army, land and trade; they were good friends of Sir Joseph Banks, the botanist, who more than any man in England overlooked the affairs of the Colony. They came out tended like a pair of stud bulls. And they behaved with all the unpredictable bad temper of bulls.

Gregory arrived first, in April 1806, with his wife, three children, servants, a few head of sheep and cattle, a swarm of bees in his cabin, and crates of iron and tools for use and for sale. The British Government paid fares and freight. Governor Bligh took their goods into Government storage when they arrived in Sydney until Gregory selected a land grant. For the expenditure of $6,000 improving the land he was to receive one thousand six hundred hectares and forty convicts to work it, all of them fed and clothed at Government expense for eighteen months.

John arrived with his family and servants a year later. He came as part-owner of a ship, the *Brothers*, fitted up for sealing. John as elder brother had more money. For the expenditure of $12,000 on improvements he was to receive three thousand two hundred hectares and eighty convicts. Governor Bligh gave a dinner to introduce Mrs Blaxland to the Colonial ladies.

The rows began soon enough. Few could get along with Bligh. Little could please the Blaxlands. They displeased the succession of governors by showing no interest in grain-growing – their interests were trade and meat. They built a dairy and abattoirs in Cockle Bay, now known as Darling Harbour. In present Market Street they built stockyards and a butcher's shop. Their milk, butter and cheese was sold where Myer's great store is now at the corner of Market and George Streets.

John ran the business in Sydney, Gregory bought the livestock. Meat was scarce and dear when the Blaxlands began trading. They reduced the price, but they were given no credit for that. A firm friendship with Simeon Lord, ex-convict shipowner and merchant, made the Colony suspicious of them.

To supply salt for the preservation of meat and hides the Blaxlands built a salt works at Parramatta. A supply of salt was put aboard the *Brothers* and it was sent off sealing in southern waters under the command of Captain Russell. When he returned with an excellent haul of 38,000 good skins worth $60,000, there was a row between the captain and the Blaxlands of comic ferocity.

It happened after the deposing of Bligh while Major Johnston was administrator and began in March 1808 with a letter from John Blaxland to Johnston. He wanted Russell taken off the ship for reasons listed as both civil and criminal. The captain had brought a cask of rum ashore hidden in a barrel of bottled porter and sold it illegally – 'a kilderkin of the ship's spirits' a court was later told, 'wrapped around with two hammocks and stowed in a hogshead of the ship's porter'. He had delivered ship's stores to the house of Elizabeth Guest, his mistress: paint, cheese, sugar, butter, crockery. Someone else had been given half a bushel of split peas and another had been given meat. He had been heard to declare if the ship would not carry the sail set, she could drag it. And worst of all, and not stated very clearly, the captain had not used all the salt. If he had employed his men more wisely, he might have brought back an even bigger cargo of cured skins.

Johnston did not reply. John Macarthur replied as Secretary to the Colony. He had an interest in the *Brothers* through the English firm that had part share with John Blaxland and wanted the ship on its way as soon as possible. He demanded evidence of Blaxland's authority.

Blaxland refused to deal through Macarthur. He continued to write to Major Johnston and Macarthur continued to reply. Eventually the captain was brought before a bench of magistrates to answer the charges. It was found there was insufficient evidence to bring him to trial. The captain returned to his ship.

A few days later the Blaxland brothers and Simeon Lord went aboard. Soon all three were in court charged by Captain Russell with assault. There had been some side play in the interval with a fantastic story by Gregory Blaxland. About half past eight one night he rode to the home of an army officer, Captain Anthony Fenn Kemp, and said he had a story to tell so serious it could not be told within the house, someone might overhear. So in great agitation and apparently drunk he walked up and down outside while he told of a plot on the Hawkesbury to murder Macarthur.

At the trial of the Blaxlands and Simeon Lord, Captain Russell announced he was going 'to avoid prolixity and circumlocution' and describe 'the nature of this assault . . . in distinct words'. Thereafter he meandered for more than half an hour before he explained what happened. Simeon Lord came aboard waving a stick and calling Russell a thief, a rogue, and a damned cowardly scoundrel. Russell told the Blaxlands to go home and sell their milk and cabbages. Gregory Blaxland threatened to drive his teeth down his throat. Russell asked if they would like to hear 'some gun fart' and turned to run for his pistols. The Blaxlands grabbed him. Elizabeth Guest ran out of the cabin and screamed. Lord called her a 'damned bitch' and waved his stick about some more. The captain was 'violently pushed . . . from the mizzen mast to the taff rail'.

Simeon Lord and John Blaxland were found not guilty. Gregory Blaxland was fined ten dollars, 'five pounds lawful money of Great Britain'. Captain Russell was indicted for perjury. And at that trial he was sentenced to seven years transportation. The judgement was so blatantly unfair the judge and two magistrates were dismissed from office. No second trial was held. Too many in the Colony were thought capable of swearing to anything.

Captain Russell sailed with the skins. He was put under a $5,000 bond to surrender himself in England for perjury if such a charge should be brought. John Blaxland followed in another ship to ensure that it was. At Cape Town John Blaxland was seized on orders from Sydney and thrown into jail. He was kept there a month before he was allowed to sail on to England. In London it took him three years to sort out court cases. While there he had another little spell in gaol for debt. He had failed to meet a bill in the hands of John Macarthur.

Gregory developed his grant where a creek now known as Blaxland joins South Creek east of Mulgoa, and settled in to live at Dundas, north of the Parramatta River, on an attractive farm called Brush Farm first owned by John Macarthur. He also managed his brother's affairs but perhaps he managed his own rather better. John complained bitterly when he returned that he had not had his share of convict hours. The complaints were made to the Governor. The early governors had as intense an involvement with the people of the Colony as has a headmaster with the pupils of his school.

Gregory's herd was building up. He had bought eighty head, the pick of 1,700 of the mixed Government cows, and he had mated them to the four English bulls brought with him on the boat. He realised his land would soon be insufficient. The mountains confined him. He began exploring up the Warragamba River and at the back of the Cowpastures. He talked to those who had tried to cross the mountains. And he formed the theory that the only way across was by keeping to the highest ground. The streams led through chasms to sheer walls. The logical starting place was at a natural ford on the Nepean where a lagoon formed Emu Island in times of flood. The watershed of the Grose had to be kept on the right, that of the Warragamba or Western River on the left. By the time he suggested this theory to his friends, Lawson and Wentworth, the Army Worms had eaten him out again and his stock were starving. The crossing of the mountains had the most forceful of all motives: selfishness.

These three men are important to the story of the Pilliga forest, not only because the crossing of the mountains opened one of the ways to the north but because Lawson, Wentworth, and the Blaxland brothers' sons continued to explore. They squatted on big stations on the southern and eastern fringe of the present forest area.

Captain William Lawson had been trained as a surveyor but he bought a commission in the New South Wales Corps and came to Sydney in 1800. He spent six years at the garrison on Norfolk Island, then by purchase and grant he built up farms at Concord and Prospect until he needed more ground for his stock. Lawson was one of the very few early colonists that it might have been pleasant to know. He had enormous energy which he spent mostly on exploration and the building up of his flocks, and only occasionally on the destruction of his fellows.

At thirty-nine he was the oldest of the three. Gregory Blaxland was thirty-five. William Charles Wentworth was twenty-three, an unattractive tall youth, snobbish, unsettled, squint-eyed and frail. He was a

true Colonial, born in 1790 on the way to Norfolk Island, where his
father was appointed hospital assistant. His mother was a convict,
Catherine Crowley, whom his father, D'Arcy, had pulled out of the
hold to be his bedmate on the journey out. The girl was fortunate to
escape the hold. The transport was the *Neptune* under Captain Traill.

The women convicts were usually not as hardened criminals as the
men. It was policy to send out all women offenders in an attempt to
balance the sexes. Most of the convicts, men and women, were
thieves – times were hard in the British Isles. But the amounts stolen
were often made to seem more trivial than they were. Many British
courts made it practice to reduce the value of stolen goods to an amount
below that demanding capital punishment. Simeon Lord, for example,
who had made off with great bolts of Manchester cloth – one hundred
yards of calico, one hundred yards of muslin and twenty-one assorted
lengths – was charged with theft of cloth of the nominal value of
tenpence.

The amount that determined a capital offence varied from court to
court and varied greatly from ten cents to four dollars. But if the right
value was given to the stolen goods an offender could be sentenced
immediately to transportation without the bothersome first step of
transmuting a death sentence before transporting him.

D'Arcy Wentworth had been first an ensign in an Irish company
then an apprentice to an Irish surgeon. He had later experience in London hospitals. On Norfolk Island he became Superintendent of convicts. He continued to live with Catherine Crowley and two more
children were born. The father ate in the officers' mess, mother and
children drew rations as convicts.

The family came to Sydney when D'Arcy Wentworth secured a post
as assistant surgeon. He later became principal surgeon and a considerable landowner. Tall, good-looking, blue-eyed, the women loved
him. After Catherine Crowley died in 1800, D'Arcy Wentworth lived
with a married woman in his houses at Sydney and Parramatta while
another woman helped break the journey between the two houses.
Several more children were born. D'Arcy acknowledged them all and
provided for them. But only Catherine Crowley's made names for
themselves.

William was sent to England for schooling. There were plans to
make him a surgeon, too, but a family friend devastated that hope. 'A
very improper profession for Him as from the Cast in the Eye' she
wrote, 'it leads Him differently to the object he intends.'

So he returned to Australia in 1811 as Acting Provost Marshall, a post secured for him by a distant relative, Earl Fitzwilliam. William associated himself with the aristocracy through this relative. His mother was not considered. William's artificial world was shattered when he learnt his father had been tried three times in England for highway robbery, a capital offence. He had been attempting to replace gambling losses. He seems to have escaped punishment by announcing that he was transporting himself to Australia. He would accept the first vacancy as medical superintendent of convicts.

Despite his frailty young Wentworth was energetic. He was given a land grant of 700 hectares on the Nepean, and from there he, too, had been into the mountains looking for a way over. Only the Governor, Macquarie, was uninterested in a crossing. He did not forbid the expedition but he gave no encouragement. Gregory Blaxland dined with him a few days before the party set out and the attempt was not mentioned until he was taking his leave. Then Blaxland referred to it. Macquarie wished him success, 'but there was a reservedness in his manner I could not account for'.

Apart from Blaxland, Lawson and Wentworth, there were four servants in the party, five dogs and four pack-horses. One of the servants was James Burns, a member of Caley's expedition of strong men. There was no designated leader. It was Blaxland's idea. Lawson as a surveyor naturally kept account of the route.

He did so in great detail and with extraordinary accuracy. He was only three kilometres out in a reckoning of ninety-five. Sometimes he counted steps as the Roman soldiers counted them, 2,000 long paces or 2,200 short paces to the mile. Mostly he estimated distance by time, three and a half kilometres to the hour. Each change of direction was noted so accurately their route could still be retraced. In this extract the fractions refer to miles; the year was 1813:

> Monday morning 17th May at Nine o'clock struck our tents and loaded our Horses with our provisions and about two Hundredweight of grass for each Horse and proceeded by the path we had cut the two preceeding days our course WSW ½ W ¼ NW ¼ WNW ½ W ⅛ NNW ¼ W by N ¼ SW ½ W ¼ SW ¼ Groce Head bore N by E Mount Banks NW by W W ½ SE ¼ WSW ¼ SW ¼ SSW ¼ WSW ¼ SW ¼ S ¼ SW ¼ W ¼ SSW ¼ WSW ¼ – Encamped the Mountain very Scrubby and rocky obliged to go for water into a very Steep gully abt Six Hundred feet deep our Horses had no water this Night.

It was difficult going even on the main ridge. The nights were damp and they had to wait each morning until the dew was off else they would have been soaked and cold in the first few minutes of walking. Fogs hung in the valleys sometimes until two o'clock in the afternoon. The ridge in long stretches was less than twenty metres wide with a drop into the fog on either side. It was like walking on a plank above the clouds.

There were few big trees. The first eighty kilometres led mostly through brush and scrub. Already the colonists were adapting words to define exactly their own country. Brush was a dense growth of mixed shrubs. If there were timber trees scattered through it they were designated: pine brush, cedar brush. Scrub was usually found in drier country: a sparser growth of stunted eucalypts with scattered shrubs, or else a growth of one species of small tree with no undergrowth as in mallee scrub and Brigalow scrub. The word forest did not consider the timber trees scattered through it. 'Forest land is such as abounds with grass . . . the Grass is the discriminating Character and not the Trees.' So Governor King explained one of Caley's reports of his explorations.

The word creek changed its meaning early, too. In England a creek was a tidal inlet. It is notable but not strange that there was no word to describe the dense growths of big cypress pine or eucalypts that now cover big areas. Except for some localised growths that were not found until years later, there were no such growths to be named. When stands of big stringybarks were found near Nundle, for example, or the Karri and Jarrah forests in Western Australia, or the great rainforests in far northern Queensland and in parts of the North Coast of New South Wales, the words to describe them were quickly found: big scrub.

The explorers blazed a trail clearly through the stunted trees that formed the scrub by taking off strips of bark in line on each side of the track. Through the dense low shrubs of the brush they hacked their way. At midday each day they made camp, then blazed and cut a way along the ridge until late afternoon when they walked back to camp. The next morning they moved the pack-horses along the prepared way, made camp and prepared the next morning's route. If they found a patch of what they called forest they cut grass to carry on while their horses fed.

Because of the low growth the ridges could be traced from lookouts. When one ridge ran out the beginning of the next could be seen across the col. If the mountains had been covered in dense high eucalypts as they are now, the crossing might have had to await the invention of the aeroplane to show a way through the maze.

It is strange that no Aboriginal tracks were found. There was no regular traffic over the range but Aborigines went in there, probably from east and west, when the banksia, known as honeysuckle, was in flower. The big creamy bottlebrushes full of nectar were steeped in water and the sweet scented liquid drunk with delight. But the tracks would have been unclear with irregular use and few Aborigines would have been willing to point the way. It is thought young Archibald Bell followed an Aboriginal track when he marked out the Bell's line a modern road follows.

When the explorers broke out on to western grassland they were exhausted. Their food was nearly done; boots and clothes worn out; they all had diarrhoea. They went on for ten kilometres. There was grass enough 'to feed the stock of the colony . . . for the next thirty years'. They had what they wanted. They turned back.

'Admitting that we have not traversed the mountains', Wentworth wrote, 'we have at all events proved that they are traversable and that, too, by cattle – a circumstance which by those who were allowed to possess some local knowledge of the country, has been hitherto deemed impossible.'

Macquarie all but ignored them. He called George Evans before him, the assistant surveyor who had been out of favour for supporting the deposed Governor Bligh, and instructed him 'To endeavour to effect a Passage from a place called Emu Island in as nearly a due Western Direction as possible over the Blue Mountains'. It was as though the crossing had never been made.

Evans is little enough known. In Australia the most incompetent explorers are the ones best remembered. Robert O'Hara Burke is known to everyone. Alfred Howitt, a brilliant explorer who rescued King, the last survivor of Burke's party from Cooper's Creek, is known to few.

Evans, also, was outstandingly capable. James Burns was again one of the party, his third time in the mountains. And they revealed the interior of Australia. There were no swamps where Evans saw it, no deserts. He had cut into an unknown fruit and found flesh instead of stone. 'The soil is exceedingly rich and produces the finest grass intermixed with variety of herbs; the hills have the look of a park and Grounds laid out . . . I named this part "Macquarie Plains".' That area is north of present Bathurst.

Evans was capable of exact observation and sound conclusion: 'I have called the Main Stream "Macquarie River" . . . I think the lower parts of the Plains are overflowed at times, but do not see marks to any height; the small trees on the lower banks of the River stand straight, not laying down as you see them on the banks of the river and Creeks at Hawkesbury.'

Evans was the first white man to taste the marvellous Murray Cod. 'Nothing astonished me more than the amazing large Fish that are caught; one is now brought me that weighs at least 15 lb.'

On another expedition Evans found the Lachlan River, and land 'better than ever I expected to discover . . . if a further trace into the interior is required . . . I respectfully beg leave to offer myself for the Service. I see no end to travelling. I . . . describe it . . . by comparing the Country to an Ocean, as it is nearly level, with the Horizon from N.W. to S.W.; small hillocks are seen at great distances of a pale Blue, shewing as Land appears when first discovered at Sea; Spaces clear of trees may be imagined islands, and the Natives Smokes, rising in various points, vessels; it is a clear calm Evening, near Sunsetting, which shewed every part advantageously.'

Evans did not have the education to push himself. The Lett River in the Blue Mountains, no river at all, was hilariously misnamed because of his bad spelling. The party was moving along the bank of a little stream and Evans noted in his journal: 'The numerous Valleys carry off the Water in rainy seasons into the riverlett.'

Earl Bathurst, Secretary of State for War and the Colonies, when Macquarie sent him the journals, saw mostly the spelling and missed the fine accuracy of observation. 'He does not appear from the style of his Journal to be qualified by his education for the task of giving the information respecting this new country which it is desirable to obtain.' Bathurst wanted botanical and geological reports. On the next exploration to the west, Evans, undoubtedly the superior explorer, was under the command of Oxley.

Macquarie had sufficient interest in the new country to name it. It was a joke one would have expected of King. He punned on Westmorland in the north of England and called it *West-more-land.*

The only good land remaining east of the mountains was monopolised by the wild cattle. Macquarie admitted that settlers and emancipist farmers had nothing to choose from, so a road had to be built to the west. William Cox offered to build it. He, also, is important to the forest story. He was a man of prodigious energy who was involved in the earliest squatting in the north. There have been Coxes on the land and usually in Parliament ever since that road was built.

William Cox had come to Australia briefly in 1797, then returned early in 1800 with his wife and four small sons as the newly appointed paymaster of the New South Wales Corps. He came out in charge of a shipload of Irish rebels. 'General' Joseph Holt and his wife were aboard too. Holt was one of the rebel faction leaders who was allowed his freedom provided he kept out of Ireland. Cox and Holt became close associates.

The Irish rebels had a good trip. Cox took care of any men under his control. They were fed better than usual and in good weather all were exercised on deck. There were few deaths aboard the *Minerva*.

In Australia Cox took over from Macarthur as paymaster and bought his Brush Farm. He persuaded the haughty Holt to act as his manager and bought several more farms. Holt was an excellent manager and got good work out of convicts without cruelty. The usual punishment was a three kilogram hoe instead of the standard one and a half kilogram. In twelve months there were one hundred hectares under wheat and maize, one thousand sheep, two hundred pigs and twenty head of cattle bought in twos and threes from Government stock. Holt was also farming on his own account in a small way and sometimes doing a little smuggling and a good deal of illicit distilling.

Despite their capabilities and their undoubted good nature both these men were thorough rogues. Cox was a fine master to work for but no man to do business with. He built up his farms on Regimental funds.

This was not theft. One of the perks of a paymaster's position was the use of the funds under his management. It was a sort of overdraft on which no interest was paid. But any call on the money had to be met immediately. Macarthur (or Elizabeth) had prospered with careful use of the fund. Cox overspent. In 1803 he was caught almost $16,000 short. That was all Government money. But Cox had acted as banker to private individuals and spent their money, too. It is not possible to tell from the records whether they ever got it back.

The Government was repaid quickly. Cox assigned his estate to trustees, and farms and stock were put up for auction. It was the first big auction in the Colony – 450 hectares of land, over 1,800 sheep and almost 100 head of cattle. The cows made much the same money as they did in 1977, up to $160 for the best cows with calves. Spanish merino ewes made seven dollars; the little mixed breeds four. Two days of sale realised $16,000.

'General' Holt was soon in trouble, too. The sudden reduction in management duties gave him time to work up a little Irish rebellion in Sydney. This time he could not keep himself out of trouble. He was sent to Norfolk Island.

Cox was sent to London to face trial for malversation, not too serious

a fraud. But he seems to have escaped trial altogether. He returned to
Sydney in 1810. Macquarie made him magistrate at the Hawkesbury.
And 'General' Holt was soon back to take up the management of what
was left of Cox's farms.

One can gain the impression that if a man was not actually in irons
during Macquarie's term his character fitted him for any position.
Macquarie was a sound judge of men. He was not interested in what
they had done but in what he thought they could do. He was also well
aware that the only men he had to choose from were criminals or
opportunists.

Cox made an excellent magistrate. He did not like the general
restriction on movement thought necessary to keep convicts in their
allotted places. He issued his own travelling passes. 'Captain Cox's
Liberties' they were called. The people loved him.

He took contracts for public works, gaols, schools, anything the
Government needed building in Windsor. Even if he had had no training for the job some of the buildings are still standing to prove his com-
petence. The court-house at Windsor begun in 1820 is the best known.
It is still in use – such a lovely solid building one wishes its purpose was
more genial than the maintenance of law.

When he was asked to build the western road Cox first thought of
himself. He demanded a good grant of land. Then he considered his
men. He needed about thirty fit convicts and their reward was to be
freedom when the road was made.

A storeroom was built for tools and rations and a gipsy-like covered
cart with bed and cupboards for Cox. He wanted to be always on the
job. Road-making began at the Emu Island ford. Trees, shrubs and
scrub were cut down, hauled aside and roots grubbed out. Rocks were
levered off the line with pinch bars or blown up with gunpowder.
Sometimes a big rock was moved with block and tackle anchored to a
tree. The road was nowhere less than four metres wide. It was
stipulated that carts should be able to pass without danger.

All went well until they reached the western edge of the mountains.
There was a sudden two hundred metre slide. Cox sent three men
scouting for a better route with offers of a reward if they found one.
None could be found.

No satisfactory route has ever been found. Major Mitchell, the
Surveyor-General, eventually built a better road, and his route is still
in use. It was made to the same scale Napoleon used going over the
Pyrenees to Spain. It is steep, with elbows and many turns. Laden
semi-trailers in low gear now break axles, then if they are unlucky they

lose their airbrakes, then if they miss a safety ramp they crash. The first trains came off the mountains down a crazy zig-zag.

So Cox decided to make a road that a cart could travel down with a light load. There would be no possibility of travelling back with any sort of load whatever. It would however be a sound route for stock to travel. Fattened cattle could be driven up for slaughter. Sheep could walk their own wool into the mountains and there be washed and shorn. But Cox thought it would limit the produce of the new country. He called it 'a very great drawback'. He issued all hands a gill of spirits.

The whole road was completed in six months, an extraordinary achievement: 170 kilometres of good clear track and a dozen or more wooden bridges from Emu Island to the Macquarie River. Some of the working party were occasionally detached, too, for work at Cox's new Clarendon estate at Windsor. Hardworking men all fed at Government expense could not be resisted. And before the road was finished someone had taken time off to move several hundred of Cox's hungry cows over it to the good western grass.

The terrible descent down Mount York was in use for seventeen years. It did not limit traffic. The users solved their own problems. The descent with loaded carts was made with big logs attached lengthways behind to act as brakes. At the bottom of the hill the logs were un-hitched and the carts drove on. Few bothered to roll the logs out of the way. The passage of several carts blocked the road. Governor Macquarie complained of the continual expense of sending convicts to clear it.

William Lawson who was later Commandant at Bathurst made an attempt to ease the gradient. He said his new track 'would keep a gentleman to drive his chaise down it without getting out'.

But his improvements did not help much with the passage up of loaded carts. That was solved ingeniously. Big rings to act as pulleys were fixed to rock faces. Ropes were tied to the chains hitched to the leaders of a loaded team, run through a ring and back to the tail of a team of bullocks pulling downhill. Carts were hauled up in stages from ring to ring.

Governor Macquarie himself went to inspect the new road in May 1815 shortly after it was finished. Mrs Macquarie accompanied him, William Cox, Sir John Jamison, John Oxley – there were about forty in the party. They fixed on the site for a town and named it Bathurst after the Secretary of State for the Colonies with a military volley, the Union Jack flying from a flagstaff and three cheers.

The party spent seven days at the site of Bathurst, riding along the Macquarie, driving by carriage to Mount Pleasant – and surely drinking too much. A diary kept by Major Antill, one of the party, states that when it was time to leave 'They gave three cheers . . . away started all the carts, and some of the saddle horses, going off in different ways full gallop. In a moment all was confusion and dismay . . . Two caravans belonging to the Gentlemen were upset, and the shaft on one broken'.

The next day when well on the way home they sobered up enough to realise a man was missing. Someone remembered he had drunkenly insisted on walking down to an Aboriginal camp. He was never found.

One would have expected men and stock to pour over the new road. Macquarie was cautious. He wanted advice from London about use of the new country. He was fearful of mass escapes of convicts and of trouble with the Aborigines. He was uneasy about maintaining a settlement at the end of such a difficult road. If the wild cattle could be mustered and driven there it would make the rest of the Camden lands available to settlers and save many problems. He stationed military guards on the road and any man wishing to travel it had to make written application for a pass.

Government sheep and cattle were sent over with men to shepherd and tail them. Some of the cattle were left to form a station at the Vale of Clwydd, the old name for the valley leading down to Coxs River, not the valley marked on modern maps. The sheep and the rest of the cattle were driven on to the Bathurst Plains.

It was Evans who named these plains: O'Connell Plains, Bathurst Plains, Macquarie Plains. There are so-called plains all round the Bathurst district still marked on maps. They are rolling, grassy, treeless hills with little creek flats between them or longer and wider stretches of river flats. The colonists called any treeless areas plains provided they were not steeply hilly. Except where old names have been retained, the word plain now refers to such areas as the expanses of Coonamble or the Galathera plain north of Narrabri. As far as the horizon there is no rise, no dip. The plains are like flat, black ocean. In the marvellous mirages of hot summers, they often look like true ocean, a surging blue which indistinctly joins the sky. There is nothing else to be seen. Even the trees are drowned in blue light. At other times there are optical illusions. Cars approach like double-decker buses because each carries an image on top. An inverted windmill stands on top of an upright mill, both wheels clearly turning and glinting. Rarely, scenes are mirrored in the sky. A hundred metres in the air sheep and cattle walk about and graze.

William Lawson was the first private individual to get permission to move stock across the road. On 21 July 1815 William Cox saw him at the Emu Ford. Cox wrote in his diary 'Mr Lawson crossed the River with 100 Head of Horned cattle for the West country; his Horses appear so bad, I do not think he will get his cart there at all'.

A month later Rowland Hassall, Superintendent of Government Stock, was camped in a hut on the mountains on his way to inspect the stock stations. The night was cold, wet and windy. 'About 2 o'clock we were greatly alarmed by some person knocking and calling at the Door where we slept which proved to be Leiut. Lawson on his return from Bathurst after leaving his herd of Cattle in one corner of the Plains . . . we were nearly all affrighted at his appearance, what with his meager face, being wet, cold, starved, with a blanket over his shoulders in the dead time of night . . . but the most dismal of all was the Dreadful account he gave of the Season and the country . . . he pointed out that the Snow a few miles ahead was 2 Inches Deep, that the road to Bathurst was so boggy that no one could pass, that it had rained every day and that never in all his life had he gone thro' such labour, hardship and fatigue . . . After Mr Lawson had refreshed himself with such comforts as our little stock afforded, he left us about 3 in the morning for Emu ford.'

Lawson did not complain easily. 'Old Ironbark' he was nicknamed later. When horses were scarce he used to walk from his farm at Prospect to Sydney thirty-five kilometres one day and home the next.

Thomas Arkell, the Government Stockkeeper in the Vale of Clwydd who later squatted on the Lachlan, was having a miserable time of it, too. Hassall found him with one hundred of his cows and calves dead. They moved what were left farther west.

It would not have been cold that killed them. Probably they were wormy, and certainly the grass had insufficient nourishment. The dried-off summer grasses were too low in protein and in minerals. Australian soil had never been called on to support either plants or animals greedy for phosphorus.

At Bathurst things looked better. Cox's cattle 'about 400 in number are wonderfully recovered and look healthy and well'. Hassall had a sheep killed that dressed almost twenty-five kilograms and all had been very poor when they were sent over the mountains. By the end of October 1815 Government stockmen could be sent out to bring back a hundred fat Government bullocks for slaughter.

William Cox took up his grant in the new country, eight hundred hectares across the river from Bathurst that he called Hereford. He was appointed magistrate and Commandant of the military detachment and the Government stockkeepers and convict farmers. Cox was grateful for the position. Those without a Government job were having a hard time of it. Apart from droughts and caterpillars there was a trade depression in the Colony. Also Cox found himself in a good position to take advantage of the Government. He came to a happy arrangement with Richard Lewis, the storekeeper.

When beasts were killed, the smaller went to the Government men, the bigger to Cox's. The convict farmers worked as much on Cox's land as on the Government's. He borrowed three Government working bullocks for two years. As for the tallow from the killing shed, it was all Captain Cox's. What would Government do with a bit of fat?

There was an inquiry and William Lawson took over as Commandant in 1819. Cox was undaunted. The Government building contracts were coming up and his Clarendon estate at Windsor was thriving now that he had relief grass for his stock. There was no need for such petty dishonesty. Cox could boast: 'We manufacture cloth for Trowsers and frocks from our coarse wool, also Coarse Blankets, boots and shoes from hides tanned upon the estate, we make our own hemp, we keep a Taylor to make up the Cloathing a smith for a Blacksmiths forge a carpenter also a Wheelwright when we can get one.' Butter and cheese were made in the dairy. He grew grain: maize, wheat, barley and oats. He ran cattle, pigs, sheep, poultry. Clarendon was a self-contained community of about sixty people.

Blaxland, Lawson and Wentworth were each granted four hundred hectares of the new country for their share in findng it. Lawson was the only one in the position to take it up. He had his army pay to support him when the farms were not profitable. The job of Commandant at Bathurst suited him handsomely. He was on hand to develop his land on the Campbell River, to buy more at Macquarie Plains and to go exploring for grass he did not have to pay for. But Lawson did the job honestly.

William Wentworth was too sick for farming and grazing. The struggle over the mountains had affected his lungs. He went off on a sandalwood-getting venture to Raratonga in the hope that a sea trip would improve his health. They got no sandalwood. Four sailors and a white woman were clubbed to death by natives and Wentworth barely escaped trying to rescue one of the sailors. The deaths left the ship shorthanded so on the return journey Wentworth acted as navigator. He had practised on the voyage out from England.

He returned to England but the climate made him sicker than ever. He tried to get a job back in Australia as Collector of Customs or as Tender Master overseeing Government contracts on a commission basis. Not even his relative, Earl Fitzwilliam, thought him fit for the jobs. So William went to France for two years and wrote a book, *A Statistical, Historical, and Political Description of The Colony of New South Wales and its dependent Settlements In Van Diemen's Land, with a Particular Enumeration of the Advantages which these Colonies offer for Emigration and their Superiority in many Respects over those Possessed by The United States of America.* Although it encouraged settlement it criticised the power of the governor and the restraints on trade.

After that he felt well enough to return to England and take a law degree at Cambridge. He enlarged his book during those years and it ran through two more editions. He did not have as much luck with a proposal of marriage to Elizabeth Macarthur. She had already been refused to John Oxley because he did not have enough money. Wentworth as a bastard had no chance.

Gregory Blaxland was too broke to take up his 400 hectares. He had no Government position. His interests had been cattle and meat, not wool, and now there was too much meat and prices were low. Most of the seals had been slaughtered. No one wanted sandalwood. (Wentworth's venture would have been profitless even if it had been successful.) Three men, one of them old D'Arcy Wentworth, had been given monopoly of the rum trade for the building of a hospital. Simeon Lord's business had failed. Blaxland seemed to have no spirit left to take his stock over to the grass he had spent so much energy looking for. He sold his grant for $500.

But he presented to Governor Macquarie the idea of a joint stock company for the breeding of fine wool sheep. It was a brilliant scheme. Sheep were to be bought of the best breeding obtainable and in large numbers to give better scope for breed improvement. 'No grant of land to be taken, nor any permanent Establishment made, nor any Building erected, the property of the Company, except stores for the Wool if considered necessary. Native boys to be taken as shepherds in preference...'

The company was to continue for ten years, then the stock would be sold and the proceeds divided. Gregory wanted to manage the scheme and appoint one of his sons as an overseer who was to live with the sheep. Their pay was to be ten per cent of annual sales.

It was Macquarie's worst mistake during a long and good term in office that he refused this scheme. Blaxland made himself lovable to no one and Macquarie so disliked him he could see no good in any of his ideas. Others in England took up the plan and the ponderous Australian Agricultural Company was formed without Blaxland's economical ideas. Eager shareholders including twenty-seven members of Parliament poured in money, so the company spent it on buildings, overpriced cull stock and the hiring of too many men, some of them drunkards and tied to the company by long-term agreements.

Gregory Blaxland was a bitter man. 'Every hope I had of advantage . . . was blotted out and distroyed,' he wrote. 'Other men and other families were allowed to make their fortunes from our exertions.'

But the Australian Agricultural Company made nobody's fortune. It eventually had a substantial influence on Australian stockbreeding, though more on cattle than on sheep. But it averaged less than two per cent dividend a year until the company was reconstructed in 1852 and its first big profits were made in the 1960s, 140 years after formation.

Between 1817 and 1820 a very different group of men explored the rough little dry hills to the north of Windsor. They, too, were seeking grass but they also sought farmland safe from the tremendous Hawkesbury floods. These men were of more lowly origins but they had no intention of remaining so.

Benjamin Singleton made two attempts without much luck. He had come to Australia as a three-year-old in 1792, the son of an out-of-work English farmer who had taken a London job as warehouse porter and stolen a length of cloth.

William, the father, built up a good farm on the Hawkesbury when he was released. He was flooded out three times and had to sell. No one then knew the sources of the river. Floods came unexpectedly. In 1806 the water rose about fifteen metres in a few hours. Several hundred farmers, one tenth of the population of the Colony, lost all they had: houses, crops and livestock. Haystacks floated out to sea with pigs, dogs, fowls and goats crowded on top of them.

Benjamin and his brother James built watermills at Kurrajong and on the Hawkesbury, and took Government contracts for the grinding of grain. But Benjamin spent enough time away from the mills to make himself an expert bushman.

On his second trip north the Aborigines were unfriendly. He kept a log, unpunctuated and usually brief. On this difficult night, 5 May

1818, he had an exciting story to tell: 'Disturbed by the voice of Natives Cracking of Sticks an Rolling Big rocks Stones Down towards us every man of us rose and fled from the fire secreting ourselves behind trees with our guns an ammunition where we could have a View of the fire Doubting if we staid by the Fire every Man was lost spent the Whole of the Night in that Condition Raining Very Hard the Native whom we had with us was timid than any of us Saying he was sure he should be Killed.'

The next day they fell in with about two hundred Aborigines who had never seen a white man before, except one who spoke a little English. 'We told them that we wanted to go to Bathurst or to find good land They Pointed to the N Eastward saying we go there in Two Days where there was a Large river so Large they Could not Swim Over it saying they Could not Drink it which we suppose by that means it was Salt we told Our Native to Asked them which Way it run they said Both Ways by that means we suppose the tide must rise an flow.' But they feared the Aborigines so went no farther.

After Oxley's return a few months later Macquarie became interested in Singleton's story. The penal settlement at Newcastle could be serviced only by boat. The isolation was deliberate. Only resentenced convicts were sent there. But if good land was found on the Hunter, and if an overland route was found to it, the convicts could be transferred to newly discovered Port Macquarie and the Hunter lands opened to settlers. He sent John Howe to investigate.

This extraordinary man was Chief Constable of Windsor. He came to Sydney in 1802, a free immigrant, with a wife and two small daughters. He farmed a grant of forty hectares at Ebenezer, bought a store at Windsor, then in 1810 also set up in business as an auctioneer. He became a builder by chance. Tenders were called for a bridge over South Creek. None were received so Howe decided to build the bridge himself. It was about seventy metres long, the largest bridge then built in the Colony, and he finished it in seven months. The rows of fifteen metre piles were driven three metres into the bed of the creek.

Thereafter Howe, like William Cox, took all the building contracts he could get: streets and roads, wharves at Windsor, and a toll punt across the Hawkesbury with orders from the Governor that no other punt was to ply within three kilometres.

Howe reached the Hunter at his first attempt. He did not know that it was the Hunter and there was no chance to explore much of the river. Howe was sick, and the party short of food. He saw enough to declare 'It is the finest sheep land I have seen since I left England.'

The next year, 1820, Howe went back to the Hunter with a big party. Benjamin Singleton was in it, George Loder (born in the Colony, and Howe's son-in-law), Daniel Phillips, another man of no importance to this story, five convicts and two Aborigines. In addition, three men went as volunteers: Thomas Dargon (often spelt Dargin) who was another son-in-law of Howe's, Philip Thorley, born in the Colony, and Andrew Loder, also born in the Colony in 1799 and brother of George. The Loder brothers' father had been a private in the Indian Army who came to Australia and joined the New South Wales Corps as a private. When most of the Corps was sent home after Macquarie's arrival, he became gaoler at Windsor.

This time there was no question that the river was the Hunter. They came across convict cedar-getters and followed the river down to the penal settlement. And there was no question of the extent of good land. 'In our way down the river' Howe reported, 'we came thro as fine a country as imagination can form and on both sides of the river from upwards of 40 miles (I may say) will at least average two miles wide of fine land fit for cultivation and equally so for grazing.'

There was no easy track to the Hunter but it was easier to service than Bathurst. Farmers could get goods in and out by sea as well as over the rough track. The difficult convicts were moved to Port Macquarie. The Hunter was opened to settlers.

Most members of Howe's party received grants. John Howe, the Loder brothers, Benjamin Singleton and Thomas Dargon moved cattle to the Hunter in October 1821. They did not abandon one bewildered man with them as William Lawson did with his hundred cows at Bathurst. They feared trouble with Aborigines so they sent 'a sufficient number of men to be a protection'. St Patrick's Plains Howe named this area of river flats and undulating hills.

On 22 December 1821 Benjamin Singleton inserted an advertisement in the *Sydney Gazette*:

ST. PATRICK'S PLAINS   MR B. SINGLETON
begs leave to inform the Public, that he will take charge of any Person's Cattle at the above-mentioned Plains. Terms 10s a-head per annum; taken for no less period than three years. Apply at the Kurry Jung Mill.
N.B.   Responsible for any number which may be entrusted to his charge.

He was probably acting in conjunction with John Howe but it was Ben Singleton's job to take care of the cattle. He moved with his wife

Mary and five young children to the Hunter to await their coming. Philip Thorley and his wife, also Mary, accompanied them. The track down the Bulga was so steep it became the custom to unload pack-horses and manhandle the goods down.

Then, as now, permits were required to move livestock. During 1823 and 1824 permits like the following were issued for the movement of 433 head of cattle to the care of Singleton.

> Permit Joseph Onus and Robert Williams, Settlers at Richmond to pass from Windsor to the Station of Benjamin Singleton on Patrick's Plains with the undermentioned cattle and servants viz.
>
> 100 Head Cattle, Branded JO on near hip
> 40   do   branded R̲W on ditto
> Thomas Ward, Convict per Henry
> assigned servant to Jos. Onus
> This pass to be in force for Twenty One
> (21) days only from the present date.

Colonial Secretary's Office
Sydney 24th, October 1823   F. Goulburn

Many more had been taken to Singleton during 1822 but if permits for those movements are extant they have disappeared into the gigantic muddle of the State Archives. The Hunter developed quickly. Apart from cattle going to Benjamin Singleton, private individuals moved sheep and cattle to the vague area of grants and purchases of various sizes: forty hectares, five hundred hectares. Who could be clear where forty hectares lay on the Hunter when there was neither surveyor's peg nor fence on the whole length of the river?

Two hundred kilometres west on the other side of the mountains William Lawson was out again in search of grass. The year 1821 at Bathurst was droughty and William Lawson was principal stockowner. Already there were about 6,000 head of cattle and 28,000 sheep in the district. They had not come in a sudden influx over the mountains. They had been driven over in hundreds and bred to thousands in the area. The sheep were tended by careful shepherds who had to walk because horses were expensive and who were allowed no dogs lest they hurry the sheep. The crossbred hounds, the only dogs then available, certainly would have.

On William Lawson's first northward search in August 1821 he was out for only five days. He made too far east and found himself in the impossible country west of present Cessnock. There was no way

through on horseback. Even now most of that country can be seen only
from the air or on foot. Thousands of square kilometres of the wide top
of the Dividing Range have degenerated into a mass of mounded-up
hills seventy to one hundred metres high. It looks as though it has all
been turned up roughly by a giant shovel and left to weather in clods
for a few months till weeds in the shape of eucalypts have begun to
grow.

James Blackman, chief constable and Superintendent of Public
Works at Bathurst, then went out, probably under Lawson's orders.
He travelled due north over unattractive hills and came to the good
land along the Cudgegong River. Lawson went up to see for himself in
November 1821. He chose land just north of present Mudgee, called
Munna by the Aborigines, then continued north for a quick look for
more good land. He found it on the Talbragan and Carbon plains on
the Puterbatter River, now the rich wide flats of Craboon on the
Talbragar River. He hurried back to Bathurst to get in touch with his
friends George and Henry Cox, sons of William, who had been farming very successfully at Mulgoa.

George Cox rode out to inspect the country on 30 November 1821, a
few days after Lawson's return. William Lee, a Bathurst settler, accompanied him and Richard Lewis who had been so obliging to
William Cox as Government storekeeper. He was now in their employ.

Lawson had blazed the track clearly. George Cox kept a journal, a
log of distance, and drew a map of the route. Where the Cudgegong
swings west near present Gulgong, the party kept north on Lawson's
track to the Talbragar. Although a journal entry shows that he was
aware the river was the 'Talbroogah', both log and map strangely refer
to it as the same river as the Cudgegong. These men were instinctive
bushmen. The maps they made might be wild but they never lost
themselves.

George Cox, too, admired the Warrumbungles from a distance of
seventy miles. He saw their southern spread, Oxley had seen their
western. 'There is in view from the ridges we were on an uncommon
high mountain to the NW½W in a range with 5 or 6 high peaks on it,
which gives it a most remarkable appearance.' He was as impressed by
Munna on the Cudgegong as Lawson, 'a most beautiful and luxuriant
flatt of ground', and especially by the Talbragar River flats, as he
ought to have been: '. . . the grass on the clear land is short and very
sweet but by far the greatest proportion of the Food is herbs of the
greatest variety and richness . . .'

George and Henry Cox mustered 500 head of cattle belonging to

William Lawson and their father and set out from Bathurst for the nearer land at Munna. The Cox brothers took up the left bank of the river. Lawson as discoverer was given his choice of the right bank. He did not accompany the drovers. Early in January 1822 he went north again to find a way on to the Liverpool Plains. Already he was planning a succession of runs. But that third trip advanced him no farther. He found the Liverpool Range too rough to cross.

The Cox brothers built huts and yards at Munna then they moved some of the cattle twenty kilometres down the river to more good land at Guntawang and built another set of yards and huts. Theophilus Chamberlain, a ticket-of-leave man who had been overseer for William Cox at Clarendon, was left in charge. Somehow he immediately outraged the Aborigines. They attacked. There is no record of what he did. Most trouble was caused by seizure of women. It was common practice until well into the 1840s to chain Aboriginal women in the huts.

On 7 February 1822 William Cox wrote from Clarendon to Sir Thomas Brisbane who had taken over from Macquarie:

'My son Mr Henry Cox is this instant returned from Bathurst (and so ill from the heat that he cannot proceed further) with information that the Natives have driven away the persons who was in charge of the Stock at the River Cudgegong with the exception of one man who it is supposed is killed it also appears that the natives let the Horn Cattle out of the yards and got possession of the sheep that my sons kept there for Rations which they were killing when the men came away . . .'

Henry Cox had reason to be exhausted. Life did not move as leisurely in those days as is now supposed. George Cox first saw the country at Munna on 3 December 1821. William Cox's letter was written sixty-six days later. In that time George had inspected the country from Munna to the Talbragar and ridden back to Bathurst, a distance of 220 kilometres; Henry and he had established two cattle runs about 130 kilometres north of Bathurst (that involved not only the mustering and droving of the cattle and ration sheep and the building of huts and yards but the organising of provisions for several months for the several men who were left there); and Henry had ridden about 300 kilometres to Clarendon, near Windsor, to tell his father of the attack while George sought help at Bathurst.

William Lawson had returned from his third trip by then but he was away somewhere else out of Bathurst. The sergeant he had left in charge of the military detachment refused George Cox a posse of soldiers so George gathered up five or six willing men, armed them as best he could, and rode back. The truth of what happened has got mixed with later troubles and disappeared into a fable of seven white men killed and many Aborigines. Guntawang was abandoned so presumably they simply mustered what cattle could be found, shot what Aborigines could be found, and retired to Munna.

Within months Guntawang was reoccupied by two young brothers, John Richard and Edwin Rouse, twenty-one years old and sixteen, the elder born at sea, the younger in the Colony.

Richard Rouse, their father, belonged to an old English family but he came to Australia with little enough, a chest or two of tea that he sold at a good price. He lived in a tent with his wife and two young children on the site of the present Sydney Cricket Ground for several months of 1802 then took up a forty hectare grant at North Richmond. Margaret Catchpole, that well-known woman convict, had delivered John Richard on the ship *Nile* on the way out. When Edwin was born Margaret Catchpole was on hand to deliver him too. She wrote to an uncle and aunt in England:

'Sydney October th 8 1806

'. . . i went thear to nurs one Mrs Rouse a very respectfull person thay Com from englent free thay respect me as one of ther owen famely for Mrs Rouse with this Larst Child she had tould har husband that she must died Becurs i was not thear Mr Rouse did Liv up at Richmond at his farm But the Govner giv him a places to Be super and tender and marster Bilder at the Lumber yeard Parramitta then then i was Left over seear at his farm But it was so Lonsum for me so i left But i hav got fouer yowes and nin Breeding goates 3 wethers and sevenn yong ones that is all my stock at present Mr Rouse keep them and Charg me nothing for them . . .'

Independent but sociable, Margaret Catchpole preferred to be nurse and midwife to overseer. She was paid in livestock usually or grain. There was little money in circulation. And she should have had six pigs also but they were drowned in the 1806 flood. 'This places have Binn so flodded that i thought once must all Binn Lorst . . . as you well know i hav a good spirit i was tring to sav what i Could and then i and Mrs Dight and har 3 Children went upon the Lorft for safety wee had not Binn thear a Bov i owear Befor the first Chimdey went dowen and middell warl went then i expected the next Chimdey to goo and all the warles and then to Be Crushed to dead for the weater wase a Bout five feet deep in the howes . . .'

Margaret Catchpole had gone to Richmond to nurse Mrs Rouse and Mrs Dight at the insistence of Mrs Palmer, wife of the Commissary.

Her first job in the Colony had been as cook in the Commissary's household. Both Mrs Dight and Mrs Rouse had acted as wet nurse to one of Mrs Palmer's babies. That was usually a lowly occupation – by custom the lusty peasant girl feeding the young of the delicate aristocrat. Neither Mrs Dight nor Mrs Rouse were socially inferior to Mrs Palmer. Paid wet nurses were not available to insipid women in Australia. Women were too few. This was simply a case of two healthy women with milk to spare saving the child of a woman who had none.

Richard Rouse accepted Governor King's offer of Superintendent of Public Works at Parramatta. In that year, 1805, he owned one horse, two cows and ten ewes, plus goats, pigs and about eight hectares under crop. Apart from the forty-hectare grant that all settlers received, Richard Rouse received further grants for public service, one of them at Rouse Hill. He was thorough in his job as Superintendent. In addition he became an auctioneer at Parramatta. Richard and his wife, Elizabeth, had nine children and by the time their sons were old enough to go looking for more land, they owned enough cattle and horses to stock it for them.

Their sons had almost decided to settle at Lue, east of Mudgee, where James Walker, a man vital to this story, later formed a station. But they fell in with Mike Leahy, an Irish ticket-of-leave man employed by the Coxes, who was taking a dray up to Munna. Leahy told them of the good land abandoned at Guntawang.

The Rouse brothers bred cattle and horses there. It was ideal horse-breeding country with stone enough to keep hooves trim, grass enough to give vigour but not to fatten out of shape, hills enough to develop wind and surefootedness. Richard Rouse bought the best mares that could be bought, the blood of Robert Campbell's Hector and Major Johnston's big stallion. He later imported horses. His brand at Guntawang and Rouse Hill, ℞ , became famous throughout the Colony. Known as the crooked R it was looked for on a coach team like the insignia on a modern truck.

William Lawson failed in a fourth attempt in December 1822 to find a way to the Liverpool Plains. Allan Cunningham, the botanist, had also tried and failed. His horses strayed.

Sir Edward Parry, the Arctic explorer sent out to save the Australian Agricultural Company, described Cunningham as 'a clear-headed, clever and scientific man, an excellent surveyor as well as a first-rate botanist'. In 1823 he went north again, turned east and crossed over the col in the Dividing Range near present Cassilis (Lawson had been over before him), then for about one hundred kilometres he climbed up and

down the exhausting succession of rough north-south ridges that run
off the east-west Liverpool Range, and through the creeks that flow
between each ridge via the Goulburn or Krui rivers into the Hunter.
Somewhere near present Murrurundi (his estimate of longtitude was
rather worse than Oxley's) he gave up hope of finding a pass to the
north. He circled south into the Hunter Valley, north-west back over
the same col in the Dividing Range, and continued west in search of a
pass. At last when he climbed a high point as a lookout 'to my utmost
gratification . . . a very considerable depression in the back of the main
ridge, distant about three miles, afforded me a clear, although limited,
view of a part of the open plains'. Upon them stood the little conical
hills he had seen from another lookout. All the evil difficulties of the
trip were over and he had found 'a Hope at the bottom'. So he named
it Pandoras Pass. The party climbed up and over and there halted. The
horses were tired and provisions too short to go any farther. Considering Cunningham's hopes for that pass he might better have thought of
the Arabian Nights and called it Sesame Pass.

But it was never widely used. The track he took coming out of the
Hunter Valley is now the modern road that runs along the granite
ridges through Merriwa and Cassilis to Coolah and Coonabarabran. It
was more important in the days of bullock wagons when Maitland supplied the north than it is now. Pandoras Pass was later used for some
years by drovers and teamsters coming out of the Liverpool Plains. In
dry weather they could take that road to Sydney and dodge the difficult
Hawkesbury crossing on the road through the Hunter Valley. In
modern times the road over Pandoras Pass is not maintained.

For the original pouring out on to the plains other passes were found
east of the Dividing Range by those coming from the Hunter, and only
twenty kilometres westward of Pandoras Pass across the Coolaburragundy River, where the rough range smooths out, the way was easy
for those coming up from Bathurst.

Back on the Cudgegong, Cunningham came across Tom Frome,
Cox's head stockman, looking for stray cattle. He was probably still
looking for the rest of those driven from Guntawang. Frome was the
man reported as supposedly killed in William Cox's letter. Cunningham did not refer to him by name. He called him simply 'a stockman
of Mr Cox' in his journal. It is difficult to find names for any stockmen
or shepherds let alone records of their lives. They were considered of
no importance. Yet the success of any pastoral enterprise depended on
them. It was difficult to settle both cattle and sheep in strange country
especially if Aborigines were about. Straying stock had always to be

searched for so their lives depended on their bushmanship – they had no compasses. And if they were ticket-of-leave men, their continued liberty depended on the well-being of the stock in their charge. No one had mercy for a shepherd with missing sheep.

But in May 1824 shepherds and stockmen, more frightened of Aborigines than their masters, abandoned stock and came into the settlement at Bathurst. In a sudden violent flare-up the Aborigines had speared seven men in one day on three stations within forty kilometres to the north of Bathurst.

From the beginning of settlement there was an astonishingly close relationship with the Aborigines. It was rare for a white man to be killed by unknowns. When a shepherd in a lonely hut was speared, if he saw the man who threw it, he knew him by a name. And, when stockmen rode out to shoot Aborigines in retaliation, they counted the dead by name. But the names they called them were cursory and degrading: Bobby, Saturday, Sunday, King Billy. Most Europeans could not be bothered learning to pronounce Aboriginal words and in choosing names for Aboriginal acquaintances they took less trouble than teamsters in naming their working bullocks.

The whites were often more savage than the Aborigines who were sometimes simply outraged, sometimes bewildered into violence by persistent transgression against their moral codes.

There was early trouble on the Hawkesbury. The Aborigines found that maize was good to eat and assembled to strip the crops. To them, food in the field was common property. No man might usurp it. It was incomprehensible to them and considerably frightening that sixty-two soldiers of the New South Wales Corps should ride out in 1795 to drive them off the river on which they depended for so much of their food.

By the early 1800s many of the tribe had accepted the new ways and were living with the settlers at Richmond and Freemans Reach along the Hawkesbury. Numbers of Aboriginal children were brought up in settlers' homes. But there was a core of the tribe antagonistic to all whites. They raided huts and sometimes killed the occupants in a carefully reckoned payback system. Their Aboriginal names were listed.

In 1816 a group of the Hawkesbury Aborigines most strangely crossed to the west, presumably out of their territory, and attacked the Government Stock station on Coxs River. They dispersed the cattle and the stockmen fled. Seventeen soldiers were sent out to protect the restored station.

At Bathurst there was persistent discord. About twenty stockmen and shepherds including the final seven were murdered in the first ten years. Many Aborigines were murdered in retaliation. Most of the trouble was probably over women. The Aborigines were willing to lend women as a courtesy. It was unforgivable to keep them. It is doubtful if any amicable arrangement could have been made for permanent partners. Who could make an amicable arrangement, anyway, with a stockman capable of raping a woman bound so she could not move? And if a decent white man had arranged a tribal marriage, who could accept the responsibility of sharing his goods with his wife's relatives as he had to by all Aboriginal laws? Although tribes differed in language and in many of their customs, some laws were general.

William Lawson got along with the Aborigines better than most men. He was well aware that the whites were usually the first aggressors and as commandant the Bathurst tribe trusted him. When Lawson retired as commandant to settle his new discoveries the Aborigines still turned to him for advice. On 22 December 1823 Lawson wrote to Major Goulburn, the Colonial Secretary:

'A man by the name of Miller a settler . . . shot a native and it appears without any cause or provication. They came immediately to me at Campbells River for protection and demanding justice, saying if they did not get satisfaction they would kill him Miller or some of his children. I had told them some days previous if the white men ill treated them they were to go and complain to Major Morrisset who would punish the white men which they perfectly understood and they promised at the same time not to kill the white men or the stock. Miller is committed to take his trial.'

It is not known what caused the seven murders at Bathurst in May 1824. The general alarm of the whites can be well understood. It was caused as much by the manner of the deaths as the fact of them. One corpse especially was a truly spectacular horror.

Two of the seven bodies were burnt almost to ashes in a burnt hut. The others had been stripped naked and spears thrust through their hearts 'with anatomical precision'. So reported Stephen Wilks, one of the surgeons who carried out the post mortem. Their heads were smashed in by woomeras. But John Donnolly had suffered more than death. He had been killed at a distance from his hut and the dingoes, hawks, eagles and crows had found him: 'the eyes picked out from the orbits, and the soft parts from the face, the entrails, belly and all the flesh of the lower extremities devoured . . . the voraciousness of the birds, however, finding a readier access to that portion of their prey which lay within the chest than through the bony casement of the ribs, those remained entire covered by the skin . . .' The preserved flesh over the chest displayed four spear wounds all angled towards the heart.

Governor Brisbane declared martial law west of the mountains. For four months seventy-five soldiers rode about in small parties, each under the charge of a magistrate, and kept the Aborigines moving. Brisbane reported that none were killed, they were simply kept in a continual state of alarm until the elders came in and asked for peace.

There was no peace. As soon as the soldiers were withdrawn the Aborigines stole cattle, and stockmen rode after them with guns. Theophilus Chamberlain and two of Cox's stockmen tracked Aborigines with forty head of cattle for 150 kilometres north-west of Munna. When they caught up with them they must have been only twenty kilometres from the Castlereagh. In attack and counter-attack they shot nineteen Aborigines and burnt piles of weapons.

One hundred and twenty-two of Cox's cattle were still missing as well as some of William Lawson's. So four magistrates, six mounted settlers and about forty soldiers rode out from Bathurst. 'Shoot them all and manure the ground with them' advised George Cox. The magistrates had to go because it was not legal to shoot an Aboriginal unless a magistrate was present to certify that it was necessary. The *Sydney Gazette*, 30 September 1824, hoped 'This will put an end to this sanguinary and desultory warfare'. It also noted 'Some of these men know the country well'. More than William Lawson and the Cox brothers had been riding the country for grass.

During the 1820s each district developed a style that became fixed for many years. Parramatta and Windsor were thriving areas of small farmers – the dungaree settlers, emancipist families dressed in cheap blue Indian cloth – and all the businessmen associated with communities: innkeepers, punt owners, blacksmiths, millers, coach-builders. Along South Creek and the Nepean were wealthy estates like Regentville of Sir John Jamison who gave lavish dinner parties to his friends and who entertained strangers at riverside picnics to demonstrate the beauty of Australia. The county of Argyle beyond the Cowpastures, where Macquarie had directed most of the starving stock while he made up his mind about Westmoreland, developed into a varied collection of farmers and small cattle owners, men of all classes. About them in the rough hills lived the never-to-be-respectable, the men and their women who preferred to live 'by the hazard'. They were not cattle duffers – they worked on too small a scale. They were the moonlight gully-rakers getting off with a few unbranded calves to their own hidden yards or with a fat beast for the tallow-pot under which there was a good fire to burn any sections of branded hide.

Although cattle were used at first in all forward moves, Bathurst developed into a sheep walk. Lawson's report of his first experiences and the early disaster to the Government herd made the whole area suspect for cattle. Farming there was not attractive nor was it encouraged. The best land was reserved for the Crown. And, apart from the distance to markets, the first settlers could not get the site of their grants confirmed. They were shooed about like fowls in a garden.

In 1822 fourteen of the Bathurst settlers sent a petition to Governor Sir Thomas Brisbane: 'The greatest part of your Excellency's Memorialists Received the Indulgence of Grants of Ground March 1818 that your Excellencys Memorialists has used every laborious exertion to put the said ground in a good state of cultivation but from the alteration which occurred three times during the said Four Years has been attended with a considerable expense and your Memorialists are apprized from the Surveyor General of Lands that is again your Excellency's Intention to remove the Lines which will inevitably Ruin your Memorialists by the Exchange of their Cultivation Grounds and also their Dwelling Houses.'

The Hunter River, after the first scramble for grass, became the area where immigrants were sent to make their selections, two hundred hectares for each thousand dollars of capital. The new immigrants were encouraged by Wentworth's treatise of climate and prospects in his book and also by the lengthy report of John Bigge, British Government Commissioner who spent seventeen months investigating the Colony. The humane Macquarie was devastated by that report. Australia's future, it proclaimed, lay not in small farms where convicts rehabilitated themselves but in the big farms of men with the capital to develop them and in the wool from the big flocks of joint stock companies and wealthy individuals using convict labour. Bigge was right. Macquarie considered men; Bigge the future. There would have been no sale for the small farmers' produce. Macquarie's plans were too early.

Benjamin Singleton was disturbed by the immigrant land seekers soon after he settled on the Hunter. Already Australians had become possessive. Convicts considered that since England had cast them out Australia was now their land and, encouraged during Macquarie's term of office, they expected blocks of it to be available when their sentences were served. Those born in Australia, now a considerable

number, felt their own land was being snatched by interlopers.
Although not born in the Colony, Benjamin Singleton was so young
when he arrived that he knew no other land. By discovery and by his
years in Australia he felt entitled to his choice of land on the Hunter.
His grant of eighty hectares had not been surveyed nor John Howe's
320 hectares so Ben Singleton had made his selection and built a hut for
himself and stockyards for communal use.

Then 'Major' James Mudie arrived to set up his pretentious Castle
Forbes. Where Singleton had settled Mudie also felt a proprietary interest. He had come from England with money enough to work 800
hectares and he had an order from Governor Brisbane dated 3 August
1822 for the same land. Henry Dangar, a young Cornish surveyor, was
on his way to peg it out.

Because of the remoteness of the western country William Lawson
could make use of his public position to go in search of land on his own
account and take it up with impunity. Benjamin Singleton had sound
reason to feel disgruntled that he could not do the same. John Howe
protested to Oxley but to no avail. Their grants had to be taken
elsewhere. Singleton did not hurry to re-establish himself on his next
choice at the present town of Singleton. Mudie's first crops were
damaged by Singleton's straying stock.

James Mudie had been a sub-lieutenant of marines. He was
nicknamed 'Major Medallion' after the financially disastrous publication of a book dealing with war medals issued in the reign of George
III. A vile man, he demonstrated beyond doubt that the free could be
more savage than the convict. He dressed his men in numbered
uniforms of mustard yellow branded with Mudie's name as assignee
master. He considered them as sentenced to an everlasting expiation of
their crimes and refused tickets-of-leave on paltry excuses to men overdue for them. Five young convicts, flogged beyond all justice, escaped
and shot at the overseer in final protestation. All were hanged. In court
they asked to display their backs as evidence that hanging was
preferable to a return to Castle Forbes.

Benjamin Singleton began looking towards the next line of ranges as
an escape from the detested immigrants. Perhaps out on the Liverpool
Plains he could get first choice of land. He tried to arrange it legally but
a letter from the Colonial Secretary's office dated 12 May 1823 gave
him no encouragement:

'Your letter of the 27th ult. has been received offering to discover
a practicable Road from Patrick to Liverpool Plains on the Condition
of obtaining a Grant of Land:- but sufficiently fast for every purpose

of Settlement, without holding out any public inducement, will the enterprise of Englishmen, and the moveable riches of the Country composed of its flocks and Herds bring to light all the hidden features of the Colony.'

It is unlikely that that letter deterred Singleton from searching but it was the young newcomer, Henry Dangar, who found a way over. He had come out in 1821 as a free settler but since he was a trained surveyor John Oxley appointed him to his staff soon after his arrival. For six months he worked in the Camden and County of Argyle areas then he was sent to the Hunter River when settlement began. From the time of his arrival there in March 1822 to the middle of 1824 he had been hard at work surveying the river itself by boat, pegging the boundaries and assessing the values of the farms that were there, surveying the farms that were to be, surveying townships – the old name for parishes – and Government reserves. It was tedious work measuring and checking. He had several Aboriginal youths with him and six convict workers, sometimes an assistant surveyor. They used the old link chain – bars with circular conjoined links, one hundred links to the chain of sixty-six feet. That old measure, link, is as foreign to all except surveyors as the metric measures now so absurdly imposed on us are foreign to everyone.

A careless convict chain-man left his chain lying in grass one afternoon and could not find it. Another was borrowed. When the old chain was eventually found Dangar compared the two. His chain had stretched by two links. Weeks of work had to be done again.

Dangar had a superb eye for country. Few were good judges of strange land. His work was constantly interrupted by settlers seeking advice. 'I have to take my grant in this area. Which is the best land?' Henry Dangar had marked out his own 400 hectare grant near Singleton's at the present town of Singleton. He called it Neotsfield after St Neot, his birthplace.

Dangar was unsettled by the wild enthusiasm of some of the immigrants. He was pegging land for men who were multiplying the future by hundreds and thousands. He had no intention of being left out. In July 1824 when his team was measuring north of the Hunter near the present Liddell power station, he saw the distant Liverpool Range above the intervening hills. So he left his team at work and rode north along an easy route that is generally followed by the present highway through Muswellbrook, Aberdeen and Scone. North of Scone, within sight of a possible route over the ranges that Cunningham had not seen, he turned back. Four days was enough to be away from his job on an unofficial exploration. He found the land along the stream he called Kingdon Ponds as good as anything he had seen in the Colony. He had another grant to select, 520 hectares in return for service to the Government. His brother William was about to sail from England. By grant and by purchase Henry Dangar hoped to take up a substantial slice of the good valley.

But the finds were too important to be kept secret. He drew a map of his discoveries for John Oxley and arranged an official exploration. It had two purposes, the main one to find where a river William Lawson had called the Goulburn joined the Hunter. He had reported it flowing south-east on one of those northern journeys when he went too far east to get over to the Liverpool Plains from the westward side of the Dividing Range. The other object was vaguely stated, 'To explore to the north west'.

The party set out on 7 October 1824 from Philip Thorley's farm on the Wollombi Brook. Thorley and his wife were the couple who had come into the Hunter Valley with Benjamin Singleton. The Goulburn junction near present Denman was soon found. Dangar thought he was wasting time. There was nothing vague about his ambitions. He hurried his party north-east on to his two-month-old track.

H. R. Carter, a farmer and grazier on the Liverpool Plains, as was his father before him, followed Dangar's track to the plains in 1972. By aeroplane, by foot, by horseback, with a copy of Dangar's map in his hand, with modern maps and photographs and help from those who lived along the way, he retraced the journey exactly and recorded it in his book *The Upper Mooki*.

From the site of present Scone Dangar travelled north-west up the stream he had called Dart Brook on his previous trip. At its head he turned south then west for twenty kilometres up and down some of the same ridges jutting out of the rough walls of the range that Cunningham had walked over. Near a south-flowing creek called Coulson about 150 Aborigines attacked suddenly, one of the rare attacks by unknown blacks. One of the party was speared in the head, not deeply enough to kill him, and for three hours they halted and kept guard. Eventually they abandoned their pack-horse (dead or alive, it is uncertain which) with most of their provisions and all their cooking utensils, and rode on over the range by a very steep pass and down the northward flowing Macdonalds Creek.

Dangar found the plains as good as he hoped. He turned a half-circle to the right, crossed a creek to be known as Millers which was very soon to be squatted on, travelled up Little Jacks Creek and south over the range again to the point at the head of Dart Brook that he had left four days before. The pass back was little better than the pass up. It was a horse track, a cattle track, but no road.

There is a modern road from Merriwa to Willow Tree that goes over the range up the centre of the oval Dangár traced in the two crossings. But it is rough enough, little better than the neglected road over Pandoras Pass.

Those ways to the plains that Dangar found were used in the first crossings. But no one else crossed for another two years. The intervening country between settlement and the Liverpool Range had still to be fill in both east and west of the Dividing Range. Explorers moved out of curiosity. Stockowners moved only when they had to.

It was a busy two years. Immigrants and colonials filled in the area by purchase, by grant and by permissive occupancy, curious circular temporary areas that allowed a man to build up his stock and learn the country without committing his capital immediately in purchase of land, and that gave the Government time to get land surveyed before committing it by sale.

George Loder took up a circle in 1824 south of the Hunter near Cockfighters Creek, now called Wollombi Brook. Cockfighter was the name of one of John Howe's horses that bogged when crossing the creek. George Loder was married to Mary Howe. He and his brother, Andrew, had both received grants on the Hunter for their part in Howe's expedition. George also held land at Windsor. His lambings had been good and he had the sheep to stock more country.

These permits granted 'temporary occupation of two geographical miles in every direction around your stockyard to be erected at . . . until such time as Government may choose (six months notice being previously given) to revoke this indulgence and resume possession to itself '.

The Colonial Secretary was aware such a description made a circle. Some of the permits simply gave possession 'in a circle round your stockyard'. Such holdings were never intended to be fenced nor to cater for close neighbours. Few were issued for the Hunter district. That land was all taken up by more permanent title as quickly as it could be surveyed.

Early in 1824 two Scotsmen, James Walker, son of a wealthy Perth merchant, and Andrew Brown, his young overseer, went westward over the mountains. James Walker took up 800 hectares by grant called

Wallerawang by the Aborigines. This land on Coxs River is the site of the present big power station north-west of Lithgow. Andrew Brown took up forty hectares for himself on Farmers Creek which he called Cooerwull on the western outskirts of present Lithgow. Neither was a good choice of country. Andrew Brown who later selected huge areas of some of the best country in Australia for himself and for James Walker had not yet developed his eye. James Walker remained always the businessman dependent on his overseers to run his properties. He had gone into the British Navy instead of his father's business, but he was retired in 1822 on half pay at the age of thirty-seven when the long wars with France were over and Britain was reducing her forces. His choice of land was affected by the need to find a climate where he could live free of the distressing asthma that struck him on the voyage out.

He and Andrew Brown arrived in Sydney in September 1823 with a cargo that had become usual: ploughs, hoes and spades, blacksmith's, farrier's and carpenter's tools, and all the merino sheep there was room for on board. James Walker loaded twenty-seven sheep. Nine died on the voyage.

Those who knew country had all passed Wallerawang by. There was much movement from Bathurst in all directions during 1824 and 1825. The Lawsons and Coxes were in advance of those who went north. After being driven out of Guntawang, once the stock had settled down at Munna, the Cox brothers moved upstream instead of down and opened up more country on the Daby plain near present Rylstone. Then in May and June 1824 Coxes and Lawsons applied for circles of the land found by William Lawson on the Puterbatter or Talbragar River, then often called Lawsons River.

Almost certainly they had already occupied it. No one risked losing land to the less scrupulous by first seeking permission. John Lawson, erratic eldest son of William Lawson and Sarah Leadbeater, asked sanction for occupying his standard 3,200 hectare circle at Cawburn, the rich Craboon flats his father had first spelt Carbon. His cattle were branded WL on the near hip.

Sarah Leadbeater was the lively convict girl William Lawson had begun to live with on Norfolk Island. That family was victualled like the Wentworths. William Lawson married Sarah in 1812 when his third son, Nelson, was six.

William, the second son, occupied a circle across the river north of John's on the Coolaburragundy River. It is unlikely the two herds of cattle were run separately or that either son stayed with the stockmen.

These were simply outposts for breeding-up. In 1824 John was helping his father at Prospect, east of the mountains. William was in charge of the Bathurst farm lands.

Young William Cox, brother of George and Henry, sent his cattle higher up the Talbragar towards the Cassilis country to a 'plain called by the natives Nandowey laying about east north-east 45 miles from Mudgee at the junction of two creeks running westward into the Thulberago [Talbragar] river which is the third to the north of Bathurst'. His brand was WX. And the violent Theophilus Chamberlain was once again put in charge of a station.

So the pawns were moving up the board, long prongs of men and stock each side of the Dividing Range. And so far all were moving within the law.

3

The Squatters

The Rules are Ignored

When preparing to write the next chapters I made thirty-odd piles of mixed papers on one side of a room. Each pile dealt with one man. At the other side of the room I laid two maps on the floor, a modern map of the Pilliga forest prepared by the Forestry Commission and an Occupation of Lands Office map of the same area drawn in 1881. The last map was divided into named blocks of land: the stations that the men moved to. I seemed about to play a simple game of draughts. Who would I move where? How many would become Kings?

The game had been played. What I had to do was analyse it. It was not a simple game. Each man moved to rules more complicated than chess. And it was a rough game that extended outside the law of the land and often outside any moral laws. But few men stayed on the board for long. Flood, drought, depression, land laws kept bumping the board and many slid off. It was rare for numbers of men to succeed in any district in Australia. German Lutherans seeking religious freedom prospered in the Barossa Valley in South Australia. They lived in fervid austerity until the land yielded them more than they needed. In the Western District of Victoria, the supreme pastoral area of Australia, determined and businesslike Scotsmen managed their own stations and many succeeded. Italians grew sugar cane luxuriously and profitably on the steamy north coast of Queensland where others would not work. Those three districts only were generally successful. And even there little land has passed down through several generations.

Individuals prospered magnificently: Tyson who played the eastern cattle markets like a trader shuffling international currencies; Kidman who played with the entire river system of the centre. His cattle followed flood-irrigated feed to market. These men won exceptional fortunes. But usually any result was checkmate.

Before Henry Dangar could peg his grant on the land he had discovered near present Aberdeen, where the rich Kingdon Ponds valley runs down to the Hunter, a carnival of Scotsmen and English labourers, tradesmen and shepherds, arrived by the *Hugh Crawford* in 1825 to establish a farm for Thomas Potter Macqueen. The men brought their wives and children with them, tools, farm implements, livestock and '2 – 3 pair of the real breed of rough colley dog', the first sheep dogs known to be brought to Australia. They even brought a Scottish piper. The land order was for 8,000 hectares. It was a lavish venture. Macqueen did not accompany them. He was an English member of parliament who was something of a confidence man. He had borrowed $60,000, much of it from his mother-in-law, the Dowager Lady Astley, to equip the farm.

But his men were outstandingly capable. Peter McIntyre as agent and manager had engaged them. When Henry Dangar was instructed to peg out Macqueen's huge claim as well as another 800 hectares for McIntyre himself, he was distressed to find that a good Scottish farmer knew as much about land as a good Cornish farmer. McIntyre insisted on making his own choice. He spent weeks walking the Hunter Valley then settled inevitably on the land on Kingdon Ponds. McIntyre was unconcerned about its remoteness and also about the stories he had heard of savage Aborigines and bush rangers who had lately become bushrangers. On 3 September 1825 he wrote to Sir Thomas Brisbane, 'Tho they have Plundered and forcibly Robbed Several, Burned Houses and Corn Stacks, and even violated the Wife of a respectable Settler . . . I have no doubt of being able, with my Highland Lads, to defend myself and property, or to run down any of these desperadoes who come near my Residence at Segenhoe, which is the highest settlement upon the banks of Hunters River.' The residence was still to be built but half of Macqueen's grant had then been pegged.

Henry Dangar was as firmly of the opinion that findings was keepings as Benjamin Singleton. He had planned to take up much more than his grant on Kingdon Ponds. When his brother William arrived from England in May 1825, Henry arranged with him to take his 320 hectare grant alongside the 520 hectares Henry wanted for himself. In addition they decided to pay a deposit on another 800 hectares. To make certain of getting it, they bought orders for grants from two settlers. That was illegal but it was common practice. He protested his prior claim to John Oxley, his superior, and Governor Brisbane who had made the grant.

Brisbane had been recalled and was too discomfited to do anything but await Ralph Darling, his successor. John Oxley was adamant that new settlers had first claim. Since Macquarie's departure it was policy to encourage them. Henry Dangar pegged four thousand hectares for Macqueen, and wrangled with Peter McIntyre for twelve months over the rest. During that time Henry Dangar made two journeys of exploration for the newly formed Australian Agricultural Company.

The purpose of that company was: 'the cultivation and improvement of Waste Lands in the Colony of New South Wales'. It was inaugurated by an act of the British Parliament on 21 June 1824. There were 10,000 shares of $200 each, not fully paid. The accent was to be on wool. The company was granted 400,000 hectares to produce it on.

A slab of country eighty kilometres long by fifty wide was difficult to fit into the map of known Australia. Oxley thought the Liverpool Plains too wet for sheep – he had seen them in an extraordinary year. Allan Cunningham went out to the plains in April-May 1825 and found them even wetter. He travelled north-west out of the Hunter on another of what he called 'botanical tours', over Pandoras Pass again, and down Coxs Creek. It was in high flood. South of present Boggabri, within twelve kilometres of the Namoi which he did not see, Cunningham decided the flood water was permanent swamp and turned back over the pass to Bathurst. He made an entry in his journal to remind himself how bad the plains were: 'A brief statement of L.P . . . inundated – useless – height of floods – woods irrigated – ironbarks boggy – unsafe situation of stockkeepers.'

The Australian Agricultural Company's advisory committee – all connected with John Macarthur – thought the Liverpool Plains too remote anyway. So Oxley instructed Dangar to set out from the area of the Muscle Brook (Muswellbrook) – named because of the mounds of mussel shells left by feasting Aborigines – and travel in a north-east by east course through country no one had seen to Port Macquarie, then travel south down the coast, keeping inland about thirty kilometres to examine rivers Oxley had crossed at the mouth in 1818.

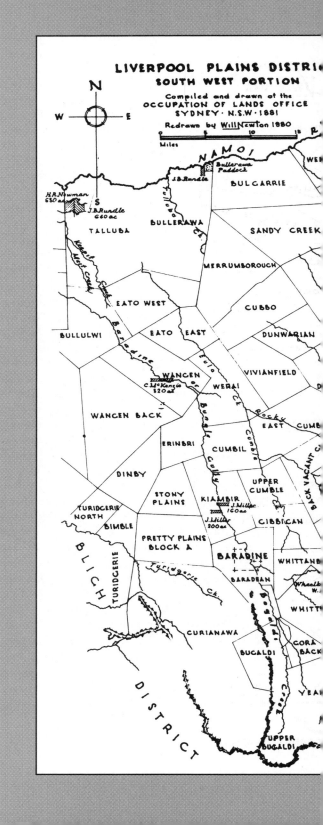

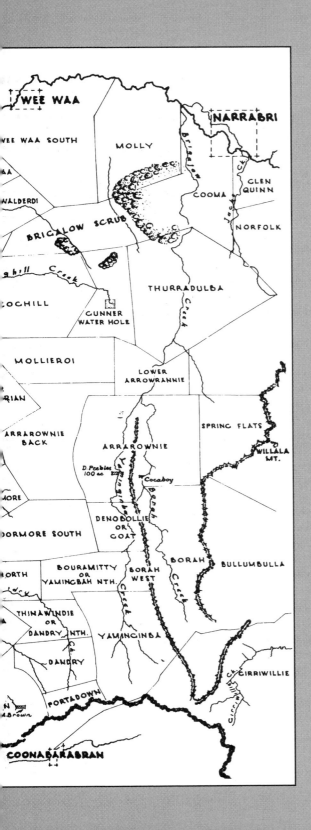

In August 1825 Henry Dangar walked up his beloved Kingdon Ponds. They led him naturally to Pages River, and there the wild country to the north-east turned him naturally over the gradual pass in the Liverpool Ranges through present Murrurundi. Cunningham had turned back a few kilometres too soon in 1823. The rest of the trip was a failure. He travelled north along the high country east of the Liverpool Plains and found no access to the east over the Dividing Range till he reached the Peel near present Nundle. Then he travelled south-east down the wild Barnard River into the country he was supposed to traverse, east along the middle Manning, and north-east to Port Macquarie. The going was so hard the horses died of exhaustion, and the party arrived at the penal settlement at Port Macquarie on foot. The coastal exploration had to be abandoned. No suitable tract of country was found.

So when Robert Dawson as managing agent of the company arrived in Sydney in December 1825, with livestock and men, there was no land available. Two chartered ships brought them out, the *York* and the *Brothers* that John Blaxland had a share in. There were two thoroughbred stallions and five mares, twelve head of cattle, and 708 merino sheep, 179 of them Spanish Merinos bred in England, the others the big French Rambouillet strain bred originally from a few hundred ewes and rams besought by Louis XVI from the King of Spain, then augmented by thousands driven out of Spain by greedy Napoleon.

The livestock were paddocked in the Government Domain until they could be driven to a farm at Bringelly, near one of the Blaxland properties, rented to hold them temporarily. The people were taken out directly to the farm. After months aboard ship they arrived there at night in pouring rain – twenty-five men, fourteen women and forty children – to find the buildings could not contain them.

The one area left that seemed likely to contain the company's grant lay between Port Stephens and the Manning River. In February 1826 Henry Dangar made a thorough reconnaissance. And he found good land. There is beautiful cattle country round Stroud, Dungog, Gloucester and Taree. Further east, though it was obviously not the rich farm land Dangar would choose for himself, there was fair open grass land. It was not the wooded tangle of today. It all looked fit to produce the fine soft-handling Australian wool the company was formed to produce. There was insufficient experience of sheep-breeding in the Colony to know that there were diseases in sheep in that country that could not be coped with then: worms, liver-fluke and the footrot the French sheep had come with. And trace elements were unheard of. Thousands of hectares about the Myall and Wallis Lakes are copper deficient. Some of it is also deficient in cobalt.

Footrot is as it sounds – a bacterial infection that attacks the soft layers of hooves. The horn lifts away from the rotten tissue that usually becomes flyblown. There is still no easy cure.

Worms and liver fluke are parasitic diseases that are still with us but for which there are now good drugs. Sheep breeders drench strategically so that the parasites never overwhelm their flocks.

Cobalt deficiency causes a change in the wool. The delicate crimped elastic fibres straighten out into glossy bristles. The sheep die slowly. Copper deficiency is insidious. It shows up sometimes as bighead or water in the head (the old English 'sturdy' disease) for which there are also other causes. But it usually shows up as a general unthriftiness difficult to diagnose.

The Australian Agricultural Company settled in on Port Stephens. Another shipment of merinos was due, expensive fine-woolled Saxons selectively bred in Germany. Like Governor Phillip at Port Jackson, Dawson was committed by expediency. The land looked good enough. There seemed to be no other choice.

By 1825 the Hunter River was overstocked, a startling increase. Flocks had been well tended and calving and lambing percentages high. Men rode in search of grass and in search of a better pass over the Liverpool Range than the Dart Brook pass Dangar had used in his circling return in 1824.

By 1826 the Hunter was eaten out. Stock were taken up the farthest branches of the river in search of grass. Ben Singleton rode to see his friend, Henry Baldwin, a thriving ex-convict farmer at Wilberforce across the river from Windsor. Henry's rascally second son, Edwin, was about to marry Ben's fifteen-year-old niece, Alice Clark. The Baldwins mustered their cattle, probably running on the Hunter; Ben Singleton mustered his two hundred head. They boxed them together and Benjamin Singleton and seventeen-year-old Otto Baldwin drove them over the Dart Brook pass. The climb was so steep the stockmen clung to trees as they gasped for breath. No one yet knew of the better pass Henry Dangar had discovered a few months previously.

Out on the good grass of the plains they moved west about twenty-five kilometres to a creek in an area the Aborigines called Yarraman-bah. Perhaps it had been recently named. Yarraman became a universal name for horse among the Aborigines and it was only thirty kilometres to the south that Dangar had abandoned the pack-horse. They settled their cattle on water. The year was 1826. If one discounts the unknown cattle thieves always in advance of settlement, they were Australia's first squatters. A government order was shortly to put them out of bounds.

It was probably from Yarramanbah that George Clarke, one of Singleton's assigned convicts, bolted north and joined the Kamilaroi tribe of Aborigines on the Namoi. He lived with them for years, and it is only from Supreme Court records of his trials for theft in 1832 that the presence and the position of several squatters on the plains are known. Where else are criminal records the only record of land settlement?

Next over the range came cattle belonging to Joseph Onus and Robert Williams, very successful settlers at Richmond and on Cockfighters Creek (Wollombi Brook). They had been one of the first to send agistment cattle to Benjamin Singleton. It was a family partnership. Joseph Onus was married to Ann Eather, a girl born in the Colony. Robert Williams lived with Ann's younger sister, Charlotte.

Robert Williams was born in the Colony in 1794, the only son of a First Fleet convict and a convict mother who arrived three years later. His parents did not live tally, they married in 1791 two months after her arrival. Robert Williams was given no grant of land. His father was a small farmer but by 1826 Robert had bought 400 hectares on a creek flowing into Wollombi Brook, he had built a house, put up nine kilometres of good fencing and he had stock enough to breed from: 280 cattle, 100 sheep and fifteen horses and mares.

Joseph Onus, sometimes spelt Oness, was himself a convict who came out in 1803. He had married Ann Eather before he was pardoned in 1812. He was astoundingly successful as a farmer. Beginning on ten hectares at Richmond he built a two-storey house about 1820 that was still standing in the 1980s and referred to as the Farmhouse in Richmond tourist brochures. By 1826 when he sent his cattle over the range he owned 640 hectares of land at Richmond and on the Wollombi Brook, 100 sheep, 20 horses and 300 cattle. It was twenty-one years since he was sentenced to life imprisonment.

It is unlikely that Joseph Onus rode over the range with the cattle. He was now the farmer businessman employing much labour. He maintained eighty convicts with no help from the Government. Robert Williams probably went to select the site but he too would soon have left the stockmen in charge and returned to his farm. These runs were established as outposts for breeding up, and at first mostly cattlemen were interested. But whoever went with the cattle found permanent water on a creek now known as Millers, and Boorambil was established for Onus and Williams a few kilometres east of Yarramanbah.

On 5 September 1826 Governor Darling, stern and cold, directed John Oxley to draw a line on the map that ruled them out of bounds. It would have caused some marvellous argument if anyone had taken it too literally – there was no map accurate enough to draw it on. The northern boundary extended westward from Cape Hawke, near present Forster, to the Wellington Valley. The western boundary followed the Macquarie River south and extended to the Lachlan. The southern boundary ran east to Campbells River, then south-east along that river and extended to meet Batemans Bay. No land could be selected under any tenure outside that boundary. No more of the circular tickets of occupation, an excellent idea of the usually ineffective Brisbane, were to be issued. Soldiers were not stationed to prevent men going over the Blue Mountains or into the Cowpastures. And the squatters did not move secretly. The line was intended to show where the law of the Colony ended. Even if Governor Darling preferred it as a prison wall he knew it could not be maintained.

Early in 1827, or perhaps 1826, William Nowland mustered his hundred head of cattle, drove them over the invisible barrier, over the considerable barrier of the Dart Brook pass and east on to Warrah Creek. William Nowland himself went with them. He told about it years later in a letter to the *Sydney Morning Herald* of 23 January 1861. He probably also took with him cattle belonging to Philip Thorley, the young farmer who was first to the Hunter with Ben Singleton, and Tommy Parnell, jovial innkeeper at the Richmond ferry. Certainly the cattle on Warrah later ran in those three names.

The creeks that then had cattle on them, Warrah, Millers and Yarramanbah, flow north. They conjoin in a flood plain that overflows in wet years into the Mooki River. The three runs were on the slopes where springs fed permanent waterholes in the creeks. Lack of water on the plains was a drawback for many years. The first wells put down struck brackish water. It was not until modern times that the sea of good irrigation water was found below the salty shallower water. The plains are now farm land and still beautiful. When they were first seen they were covered with high grasses, mostly panics. The lightly timbered tongues of land between the creeks ran down to the rich spongy plains like green headlands into a brown sea of grass. Low grey islands of Myall were the only trees. Sudden ridges and isolated conical hills broke the flatness.

William Nowland was the son of a superintendent of convicts at Norfolk Island and later at Castle Hill. He and his three brothers were all born in the Colony. In 1827 William was twenty-three and apprenticed to his older brother, Henry, as a wheelwright. Another brother, Michael, was a blacksmith. Later as squatters, as innkeepers, as mail contractors and coach owners, the Nowland brothers and their sons were known throughout the north.

As soon as the cattle had settled down to a regular pattern of feeding and watering and the stockmen could keep check on them, William Nowland loaded a pack-horse and set out with one man to find a better pass over the range. They rode for three months, harassed by Aborigines, until finally they found the way south over the good Murrurundi pass Dangar had found in 1825. For some reason Henry Dangar did not advertise that pass, the third he found in twelve months. When William Nowland wrote his letter to the *Sydney Morning Herald* thirty-four years later, he was still unaware anyone had used the pass before him. Indeed no one knew Henry Dangar had discovered it until 1969 when Dr John Atchison who was studying records of the Australian Agricultural Company found an undated map. There was no complementary journal but John Atchison proved the map from the company records.

Nowland blazed the trail, rode to the Hunter, loaded a dray with supplies and drove it to Warrah on a gradient 'a team could take two tons over'. It was wet, the wheels cut in and left a clear track behind. Ten thousand hungry cattle followed it out to the plains. If Oxley's invisible boundary had been the Great Wall of China, it would not have deterred the squatters.

There is a discrepancy in Nowland's dates. The *Australian* 9 May 1827 reported the numbers of cattle on the plains. In his letter Nowland says he established Warrah in April 1827, then spent three months looking for the pass. Yet he is clear that most of those who went on to the plains followed his track. I feel sure that he was right about that. Dates are easier to forget than facts. So after thirty-odd years he put down either the wrong month or the wrong year. Probably Warrah was formed in April 1826. That gives time for the cattle to move.

There was also much activity on the western side of the Dividing Range. In December 1826 the Lawsons and Coxes made their last attempt for ten years to keep within the law. On Christmas Day 1826, William Lawson wrote to John Oxley from his estate on Prospect Hill: 'I have selected my Land which I purchased from his Late Excellency, Sir Thomas Brisbane, on the North Side of the Puterbatta Rivulet, laying about N.E. from Mugee, distant about fifty miles from Mugee, that I wish to be put in possession of the land as soon as possible, so that I can proceed to Cultivate for the Ensuing wheat season.'

The land he wanted to confirm as his was the permissive occupancy above the junction of the Coolaburragundy and Talbragar rivers that his son William had sent cattle to in 1824. Oxley made a memo that the land was outside the limits and Sir Ralph Darling ordered. 'He cannot be allowed to have this Land – Refer him to the regulations.'

Lawson did not care where the land was marked on the map provided he established it was on the Puterbatter (Talbragar) River for later surveying and provided he kept it. So he corrected the direction and shifted both land and river nearer Mudgee. That expert surveyor and explorer who could find his way anywhere wrote, 'On the subject of the Land which I purchased from the Late Governor, I must have made a Mistake as to its Situation, it lays about NNW from Mugee and about Thirty-two Miles at the Puterbatter River, on the north side or on a Small Creek which runs into it.'

For the first fifty years in Australia those who obeyed the law were left sadly behind. Land laws especially usually served to confirm what had been done illegally. But before that purchase and before he stepped over the line as a squatter, William Lawson had done well by legal grants and purchases. At Prospect and at Bathurst the family held over 4,000 hectares.

The Cox brothers or their stockmen had been exploring again, unofficially and with no records kept. William Cox, their father, bought the best of his permissive occupancies but usually he let others take them up while his stock moved forward to other good land. They had civilisation behind as a buffer and unlimited land in front.

In December 1826 Cox's cattle were north of Lawson's, if one supposes, as was usually the case, that land applied for was already occupied. At those distances cattle on the site were the surest claim. Many were riding then in search of land, in pairs usually, a man and his stockman, with a pack-horse. They carried corned pork or beef, flour, sugar, tea and a bottle of water. Water for the horses had to be found each day. Towards sundown they would pretend to make camp on the water. They hobbled the horses and turned them loose, boiled the billy, had a meal. After dark, to fool any watching Aborigines, they quietly packed up, re-saddled the horses and rode on for an hour or so before sleeping. It was never a relaxed life. They had to be as wary as any animals at water.

On 9 December 1826 William Cox made application for the advance of his cattle. Both William Lawson and the Coxes wrote educated hands. 'The Whole of the Tickets of Occupation Occupied by myself and sons in the District of Mudgee, Daby and to the N.East of Bathurst having been taken up by Grants and Purchases by different individuals, I find it necessary to send my young cattle still further in the same direction. I shall in consequence feel obliged by His Excellency allowing me to send a Herd of Cattle to a place called by the natives Binnea, it lays about N.N.East from Mudgee and is supposed to be distant from thence about 50 or 60 miles . . .'

William Cox had obviously not been there. He was then sixty-two, married again after his first wife's death in 1819 and beginning a new family. He managed Clarendon and left exploring to his grown-up sons, George, Henry and Edward. The fourth son, William, was managing a farm in the Hunter.

John Oxley noted that 'if the distance from Mudgee be accurately stated the situation requested by Mr Cox is on the S.W. side of Liverpool Plains'. So it is, on Binnia Creek on the far western edge of the Liverpool Range on the easy gradient to the plains that Cunningham missed by twenty kilometres when he went over Pandoras Pass. Two properties still retain the name Binnia. The present road from Coolah to Mullaley runs between them. The Coolaburragundy River, if one does not follow it too far into the mountains, leads to that way round the ranges. Cox's and Lawson's stockmen had been two years in the area. They probably found the way. Binnia Creek is only fifty kilometres – no more than a good day's ride – north-east of the Craboon-Dunedoo plains near the junction of the Coolaburragundy and the Talbragar where the Lawson brothers took up their permissive occupancies in mid-1824. But via Pandoras Pass, Binnia Creek is over 100 kilometres away, and one has to circle south round the western edge of the range to get there.

So the cattle of William Cox, the first squatter on the Liverpool Plains by a route west of the Dividing Range, did not go over Pandoras Pass as has always been supposed. They walked easily round the end of the Liverpool Range that William Lawson and Allan Cunningham spent so much energy trying to cross. Although the route is easy to negotiate it is hard to find. High rough hills unobtrusively become smoother and a little lower.

William Cox's application is important not only because it establishes the route but because it mentions the rapid filling-in of the country between Bathurst and the Talbragar River. Nobody apparently has found that letter before me and the early general settlement of that big slab of country was overlooked. There is no other direct evidence for it. The duplicates of stock permits and of permissive occupancies were sketchily enough kept in some years and survey dates give the impression that the land was bought many years later than it was. Surveyors had no hope of keeping up. The Land Board told Governor Darling in 1826 'Unless the arrears of survey are brought up, it will be almost impossible for Your Excellency to prevent the greatest irregularity and confusion.'

Without that one application of William Cox's, without that one letter of William Nowland's, the story of land settlement in the north would be sketchy indeed. So much of Australia's history took place outside the law there was more attempt to hide it than to record it.

Between 1826 when they were first ruled out of bounds and 1836 when their transgressions were legalised, some who rode north are not known, some who are known cannot be located, and few left record of when they went. Some, and regrettably I do not know who, went out with stolen cattle, bred them up on distant waterholes and reappeared as respectable squatters.

The Hawkesbury Benevolent Society was a respectable enough body but it considered free grass before the law. Thomas Dargon, John Howe's son-in-law and fellow explorer, who had charge of its herd of cattle, could not find enough grass on the Hunter so in 1827 John Gaggin, a stockman, drove the cattle up William Nowland's fresh dray track to the plains and settled them on Phillips Creek, one of the heads of the Mooki River. That creek west of Yarramanbah was named for its discoverer, Daniel Phillips, a small farmer and energetic wanderer, who also had taken part in John Howe's 1820 expedition. Earlier two governors, Hunter and King, had employed him to 'explore . . . the Colony in search of Curiosities'. He left no record of a life that may have been fascinating.

Formed early in 1819, the Hawkesbury Benevolent Society gave relief to the district's paupers. William Cox, Lieutenant Archibald Bell and Henry Baldwin were among the initiators. Income came from the sales of cattle bred from a donated herd. Since the donors were careful to cull their own herds when making donations, the Society owned the roughest mob of Colonial cattle. On the plains its stray mongrel bulls,

branded 4D, were a nuisance to those trying to upgrade herds. William
Nowland and his younger brother Edward took charge in 1831 and introduced better bulls. 'I put at least one pound per Head on their Herd
of 2000' wrote William Nowland in 1856.

George and Andrew Loder sent up cattle and sheep, the first sheep
on the plains, to a creek they spelt Kuwherindi. The year was not
recorded but it was probably 1827. In 1832 Ned Dwyer, the Loder
brothers' superintendent, told Sir Edward Parry of the Australian
Agricultural Company who admired his garden that he 'grew some
wheat once' as though he had been there for years. Longanay the
Aborigines called him, Long Ned. He lived with his wife in a slab
house by the pleasant Quirindi creek that the Aborigines pronounced
something like Gooarinda. He had been an Irish convict sent out in
1816 as a 'seditious and disorderly person'. Nothing is known of the
woman who lived with him. She was probably the first white woman on
the Liverpool Plains. The couple kept domestic poultry and milking
cows and grew good vegetables, necessities few bothered with. Ned,
with several shepherds and stockmen under him, had charge of 1,700
sheep and 1,100 cattle. An intractable Irishman to the last, he always
walked even when mustering cattle.

Thomas Eather sent stock early to the plains, 150 head of cattle and
two brood mares. Probably his stock ran on Boorambil with those of
Onus and Williams. Thomas was the brother of Ann Onus and also of
Charlotte Eather, the girl Robert Williams lived with. They had ten
children but never bothered to marry. Friends and relations frequently
pooled their stock and employed stockmen between them. Until herds
and flocks increased to thousands and there was competition for land,
the main consideration was keeping down expense while the stock bred
up. The cost of sending supplies to distant stations was high.

Since Thomas Eather had been overseer to Joseph Onus on his big
Hunter River farm, many of his herd of 150 would have been Onus's
cattle given to him as payment. Few stockmen were paid wages until
the 1850s. Rations and cattle was the usual pay.

An energetic man, Thomas Eather was born in the Colony in 1800.
He learnt the trade of shoemaker and by the age of twenty he employed
several convicts in his own business at Windsor. Then he branched into
land and took up a small lease on the wide shallow Wollombi Brook in
the Hunter Valley. He acted as overseer for Joseph Onus whose farms
were on the nearby flats while he cleared his land.

Thomas Eather's father, also Thomas, arrived as a nineteen-year-
old convict by the Second Fleet. He had been sentenced to death as a

seventeen-year-old in 1788 and spent over a year in the grim Hulks, those tied-up derelict ships that housed the prisoners sent to perform the rough dockyard jobs no paid labourer would take on: shovelling ballast, unloading colliers, quarrying stone for breakwaters, scraping and painting guns.

Those who survived the Second Fleet massacre were of superior strength. Some of them had used it savagely. There was a vicious practice known as 'feeding pigs'. Children as young as ten-year-olds were prisoners in the Hulks. The older boys stole their food, ate the best of it and threw the young ones the scraps. But even some of those young ones survived to reach Australia.

In Australia the first Thomas Eather lived with Elizabeth Lee, a convict girl who arrived in 1791. There is no record of their marriage but perhaps they did marry: their first three children were baptised as the children of Thomas Eather and Elizabeth Lee, the last five as the children of Thomas and Elizabeth Eather. It was a vigorous and successful family. In days when life was short, the youngest of the Eather family at death was sixty-five, the eldest ninety-one. Seven of them married and had big families. There are now thousands of Eather descendants in New South Wales and Queensland. Some of the Eathers' first land is in the hands of fifth generation descendants, a rare progression in Australia.

In 1828 a stockman named Alexander Bloomfield drove cattle belonging to John Burns, a Richmond settler, and James Robertson, a Sydney watchmaker and jeweller, beyond all others on the plains to one of the permanent waterholes then in the Mooki River that flows north into the Namoi at Gunnedah. James Robertson was born in Scotland but worked for years as a watchmaker in London. A friend of Sir Thomas Brisbane, he was assured of a good welcome when he came to Sydney with his family in 1822. Apart from his business he took up valuable land grants, two hundred hectares at Seven Hills north-west of Parramatta and thirty-four hectares of North Shore waterfront that is now Cremorne. He had spread to the Hunter before the move to the plains, where his eldest son, James, managed for him.

John Burns has no part in this story. His partner, James Robertson, is important because of his third son, John, who became Sir John, five times premier of New South Wales and propounder of land laws that redirected settlement. But he began as overseer to his father on a run on the Namoi, then took up a run in his own name that is now in the heart of the Pilliga forest.

Peter McIntyre rode up from Kingdon Ponds for a look at the plains as soon as he heard of the Dart Brook pass in 1825. About 1828 he sent his cattle up and they began a northward drift that ended six years later in the New England. They were then a herd of several thousand.

The determined Peter McIntyre cost Henry Dangar his job in 1827. After his strenuous exploration for the Australian Agricultural Company, Henry Dangar returned to routine survey work and to the interrupted argument with Peter McIntyre who accused him of altering survey pegs, of refusing to mark land, and of offering bribes. The row grew so heated Governor Darling instituted an inquiry. It was found that Henry Dangar had certainly tried to use his public office to his own advantage so Governor Darling dismissed him.

He sailed for London with petitions and protests. All were futile. But the trip itself was not futile. As on Macarthur's trip for court martial there were unexpected results. Aboard ship he began work on 'a complete emigrant's guide', *Index and Directory to Map of Country bordering upon the River Hunter*. The book was published in London in 1828 and sustained the growing interest in the Colony. It was a different book, not an explorer's probe into new country that settlers then felt hesitant about going into or a general discussion of politics and prospects like Wentworth's book, but a detailed description of one area where many immigrants had already settled and where land could be bought and sold. He discussed values and profits and made detailed suggestions about the best use of capital.

The map itself was beautifully drawn but grotesquely out of shape. Apparently Dangar, who seemed capable of finding his way anywhere, carried no instruments for determining longitude. It was not till 1834 when Mitchell produced an accurate map of the Colony based on a trigonometrical survey, much of which he had carried out himself, that a traveller could use a compass with a map to find the way.

Shortly after Henry Dangar's book was published and while he was still in London, there came an upheaval in the Australian Agricultural Company. It changed his future.

Over two thousand good merinos had been shipped to Australia for the company in the first two years. They were exceedingly well-cared for on board. Losses were only five per cent, a remarkable figure considering some of the ewes were in lamb – lambs were born during the journey. But the sheep were not thriving on the Port Stephens country.

Suddenly the fears that the company would become a monster like the East India Company powerful enough to control Colonial woolgrowing turned into charges against Robert Dawson of bad management. The sound neat buildings he had been praised for were found to be built on a swamp; the hard-working employees became overseers with high-sounding titles who did no work; his good relations with the Aborigines and the laughing girls who worked as maids changed to insinuations of a harem forty strong; he was found to have taken up land of his own and to have spent more time on it than the company's. Probably there was some truth in all the charges. He was not a strong manager, though his position was impossible, anyway: the self-interested local committee had authority over him. The solution was ludicrous. The local committee stepped in to save the company.

It consisted of James Macarthur, son of John, John's nephew, Hannibal Hawkins Macarthur, and his son-in-law, Dr James Bowman. There was another member of the committee, Hannibal Hawkins Macarthur's brother-in-law, Captain Phillip Parker King, but he was on service with the Royal Navy and never an active member. The local committee had been no help whatever to Dawson. They declared the Liverpool Plains too distant for settlement (John Macarthur was uninterested in squatting) and they had taken dishonest advantage of Dawson's inexperience in Colonial stock buying. They had treated the company as a great opportunity to sell the culls from their herds and flocks at high prices. Dr Bowman even sold 300 sheep in the wool then shore them before delivery.

Now Dr Bowman sacked Dawson and put John Macarthur, at that time barely sane, in charge. Macarthur sacked many of the other employees too, some of them unsackable because of contracts. He closed down the Sydney office which cut off communication with London; he put the Aborigines in clothes, which destroyed their grace, and he ordered them to go to church on Sunday or lose their rations.

Sir Edward Parry, Arctic explorer, handsome, religious, was sent out to restore order. Henry Dangar was offered the job of surveyor to reassess the company's lands and to seek suitable new country. He married Grace Sibly in England and set sail again for Australia.

On the Kingdon Ponds William Dangar, by grant and by purchase, had collected together much of the land that Henry had gone to London to fight for. In order to keep Henry from pursuing his own ends, one of the clauses in his contract stipulated that he was to have no interest in land or livestock. Henry had been permitted to keep the order for the 520 hectares promised by Governor Brisbane. So he gave his brother William power of attorney and went ahead as he pleased.

During 1828 a census was taken. The several hundred living outside the boundaries were ignored. Those born in the Colony added up to a substantial number, 8,727, more than those free by servitude, twice as many as those who had come free. In 1836 girls counted as children in that census were the 'very nice-looking young ladies' who startled Charles Darwin at a Macarthur dinner party by exclaiming proudly, 'Oh, we are Australians and know nothing of England.' More than Benjamin Singleton looked sourly at the immigrants.

John Lawson, eldest son of William, vented his discontent in a longwinded, garbled, unjust, foolish memorial to Governor Darling in 1829. He was then 26 and about to take up a 420 hectare grant on the Cudgegong River. He thought he was entitled to a larger area because of the number of his stock.

'. . . Your Petitioner therefore most respectfully takes this medium of bringing under your Excellency's consideration the reasonable claims which Petitioner presumes, he as a free born subject in possession of considerable means, is entitled to at least in common with Emigrants arriving in this Colony with not one third the capital, and who are in the habit of deriving from the Government in preference to the Native born youth.

'That in thus expressing to your Excellency the foundation for soliciting a grant in extension, Petitioner trusts that your Excellency will not conceive him dictatorial, as Petitioner answers your Excellency that nothing would induce him to deviate from that distinguished deference due to your Excellency as the representation of the Sovereign . . . the system hitherto observed by Government in reference to the native born youth of the Colony, has been remarkable for the partiality exhibited towards the Emigrants, and which System your Excellency's Petitioner humbly submits as tending to blast every prospect that the Colonial Youth have a right to look forward to, towards increasing affluence and independence . . .'

A Land Board report attached to that memorial explained that John Lawson assisted his father at Veteran Hall, the Prospect farm, his father's 'more extensive concern beyond the mountains being entrusted to the management of his younger sons, Messrs William and Nelson Lawson'.

James Chisholm, once a sergeant in the New South Wales Corps, now a family friend and wealthy banker, sounds rather uneasy in his support of the application.

'Old Mr Lawson has cash to a considerable amount in my hands . . . this applicant is not considered to be so steady as his brothers who have previously been before the Land Board and his father does not entrust him with the management of his affairs to the same extent as them . . . I think it is likely that he will shortly settle upon his own land as I know his father is very anxious to have him settled.'

While he was trying to get John settled, William Lawson took over Binnia, and William Cox's cattle moved on to Nombi, the lovely country Oxley described when he came out of the sandy forest. It was 1829 or 1830, no later. John Brown, the stockman who brought up a lot of their cattle, was an ex-seaman born the year the Colony was founded. He lived through the entire nineteenth century and died in 1907, one hundred and nineteen years old.

Others joined William Cox and William Lawson. Young Charles Purcell, a Nepean settler, or his stockmen, moved cattle west of Nombi to Girriwillie, on the head of the creek now known as Girrawillie that flows through Nombi into Coxs Creek near Mullaley. Charles Purcell, born in Gibraltar, came out as an infant in 1810 with his father who was a lieutenant in the 73rd Foot, the regiment that relieved the New South Wales Corps. By 1830, Andrew Brown, first squatter on the Castlereagh, had chosen his first run and was planning to move James Walker's cattle and some of his own. The Rouse brothers were about to extend from Guntawang. James Brindley Bettington, married to Rebecca, William Lawson's eldest living daughter, sent his cattle out to the western part of the Liverpool Plains somewhere, probably with Nelson Lawson's cattle, though he soon formed his own stations on the Castlereagh. Nelson Simmons Lawson was William's youngest living son. He formed Bone and Premer, east of Nombi, and probably took his cattle over Pandoras Pass. The pass lay on his southern boundary.

William Lawson has little further part in this story. The Lawsons did not advance north beyond Binnia into the Liverpool Plains or down Bone Creek, now known as Coxs, to the Namoi River. They consolidated in the country they knew. Buying and leasing they took up huge areas on the Macquarie, Castlereagh, Talbragar and Coolaburragundy rivers. In the late 1830s when the first grand rush of squatters was over, William and Nelson in partnership mustered a herd of surplus cattle and sent them with stockmen leapfrogging over the runs along the Namoi to the Barwon. It is doubtful William Lawson ever saw the Barwon country. Sarah died in 1830 and he lived on at the Prospect farm, Veteran Hall, named for the company formed by those of the New South Wales Corps who remained in Australia. He became a member of the Legislative Council but he never found politics as interesting as new grass. He died in 1850. Nelson had died the year before, John died a few months later so William inherited most of the estates. The Prospect farm was eventually taken over by the

Metropolitan Water Sewerage and Drainage Board and drowned by the Prospect reservoir. Sarah's coffin was dug up in 1935 by workmen laying pipes.

The good grass on the plains was revealed just in time. A three year drought followed the marking in of boundaries. It affected all the settled areas, Bathurst, Mudgee, Goulburn (Argyle) and Camden. It instigated the moves west of the Dividing Range but most of all it affected the overstocked Hunter. What grass there was powdered to nothing, the river all but dried up. The settlers had overestimated the country.

The new settlers were not Londoners with a city man's ignorance of the land. Most of them had centuries of farming and grazing behind them. They were aware of varying stocking capacities. The English lowlands will carry twenty to twenty-five ewes to the hectare with their forty lambs for three months of the summer. The hills of Scotland and Wales will run one sheep to twenty-five to fifty hectares. How did the Hunter settlers make such a mistake?

They had come to a new land. The damage could not have been foreseen. So different was the Australian soil before cloven-footed mammals pounded it that a modern sheep-breeder sent to a similar area would overestimate almost as seriously.

In England droughts were of short duration, a couple of months at most. If a field was overstocked for a time there was no disastrous damage done. A season would restore it. In Australia thousands of years of grass and soil changed for ever in a few years. The spongy soil grew hard, run-off accelerated and different grasses dominated. Even on the black soil plains where the self-mulching soils cannot be damaged permanently by hooves or by the plough, the plants have changed. A modern grazier will look at his cattle fattened excellently on barley grass and burr medic and say 'You can't beat natural pasture'. Those two plants are probably the principal stock fodder in Australia. Both came from Europe.

Benjamin Singleton summed up the effects of the drought in a memorial to Governor Darling in 1829. He was seeking a swamp at Wallis Plains (Maitland) that he wanted to drain for maize growing, an impractical solution to a drought. Someone else had already applied for it anyway.

'Your memorialist has been an inhabitant of the colony for the last thirty-eight years . . . and during the whole never experienced such unfavourable seasons as those of the last three years during which your memorialist has been at a very heavy expence in agriculture on an extensive scale at St Patrick Plains when every prospect failed the Produce of the different crops of wheat and maize being little more than the seed expended on the ground . . .

'That your memorialist having a family of ten children cannot but feel the greatest anxiety from the unfavourable appearance of the weather . . .'

Governor Darling noted on one corner, 'Ascertain from the magistrate at St Patrick's Plains what this man's general character is. There appears some doubt as to his being quite correct but this is not enough.'

So James Glennie J. P. gave him a reference: '. . . He has a large family and has been unfortunate in a watermill which he erected on St Patrick Plains owing to the long continued drought. He is a very honest sober man and I consider him worthy of the indulgence asked . . .'

What was incorrect about Benjamin Singleton except that his enthusiasms did not inspirit him, they overcame him? The idle mill was genuine misfortune. No one could have foreseen that the Hunter would dry up to a trickle and the four hundred dollars spent on the mill would lie unproductive almost until the time it was destroyed by flood. But what of the *Experiment*, built for the Parramatta River trade to carry thirty tonnes of cargo and a hundred passengers? It was powered by four horses in a treadmill and the jeering passengers left it on its only trip.

He was miller, innkeeper, punt owner, ship-builder for the Hunter River trade in conjunction with his son-in-law, George Yeomans. He was district constable for a year, a prejudiced constable who subjected the free immigrants to harsher laws than the colonials. He was butcher, brewer, squatter, and more constantly farmer at Singletown, now Singleton.

In October 1829 a new government order restated the boundaries of the Colony. The former lines bulged as though the hooves of cattle being driven to grass had snagged them and pulled them forward. The northern line now extended west along the Manning River and the Liverpool Range till it met a northern extension of the Wellington Valley. The new western line extended down that valley as before, it passed west of Bathurst then continued south through present Yass and beyond it to the latitude of the Moruya River. The southern boundary was the short easterly line from that point across the Dividing Range to the mouth of the Moruya. Nineteen counties were enclosed.

For those thinking of squatting, it restated where land was free. More and more went out – down the south coast, beyond Goulburn, west of Bathurst, north-west, south-east down the Lachlan and the Murrumbidgee. This book deals only with those who went north.

Joseph Brown, twenty-one-year-old son of David, an ex-convict Hawkesbury settler who had recently died, drove hundreds of cattle past William Nowland's station on Warrah Creek, past Ned Dwyer at Kuwherindi, past other unknown nomads to the Peel River, and took up Wollomal on both sides of the river, a few kilometres downstream from present Tamworth. Unlike most squatters he lived there with his stockmen.

Major George Druitt who gave his name to Mount Druitt west of Sydney where he took up a grant of land sent several hundred head of cattle west of Yarramanbah to adjoin the Hawkesbury Benevolent Society's rough herd on Phillips Creek. It was then about four years since Ben Singleton and Otto Baldwin had established Yarramanbah and the place had grown. George Yeomans who was married to Ben Singleton's daughter, Elizabeth, had sent stock there, too, as had George's younger brother, Richard, and a couple of other men. William Osborn had charge of nearly two thousand cattle and a thousand sheep for six or seven owners.

Major George Druitt was almost as great a rogue as William Cox and had the same wayward charm as Thomas Potter Macqueen. He came to Australia in 1817 with the 48th Regiment sent out for a spell of duty in New South Wales. A girl, Margaret Lynch, stowed aboard their ship, the *Matilda*. During the voyage the captain married her to an army private, but Margaret did not take the marriage seriously. It might not have been legal anyway. In Australia she lived with Druitt. He married her in 1825 after their third child was born.

George Druitt became civil engineer and like William Cox supervised the building of roads, bridges and public buildings, some of them designed by the convict architect Francis Greenway. His work was good, but he was eventually accused of embezzlement, so he sold his commission, in those days a valuable negotiable asset, and pleaded his case in London. No charge was laid. Thereafter he concentrated on land and was one of the first to move into an area that later became Pilliga forest. His sons Joseph and Edward managed for him as soon as they were old enough. As his flocks built up George Druitt became conventionally respectable: a justice of the peace, foundation member of the Australian Racing Club, member of the Agricultural Society and shareholder in the Bank of New South Wales.

John Marquett Blaxland, son of John who came to Australia as such a favoured immigrant, rode up from his Hunter River farms in 1830 and formed a run north of Druitt's where Phillips Creek joins another creek and broadens into the Mooki River. It eventually became two runs, Phillips Creek and Gilcoobil which was anglicised into Kickerbell, a name still retained for the remnants of the huge run. Only forty kilometres west Nelson Simmons Lawson's cattle were on Coxs Creek. Those who came to the plains east and west of the Dividing Range had almost met.

In 1824 John Marquett Blaxland had tried to emulate his uncle Gregory. He blazed what he declared to be a better track from the Hawkesbury to the Hunter and was given a 250 hectare land grant for it, but it was a clumsy roundabout way that no one ever used. He did not marry and died young in 1840, five years before his father who had become a substantial landholder by grant and by purchase. He took no further part in squatting.

Kickerbell was eventually bought by Gregory Blaxland's eldest son, also named John. That family took no part in unlicensed squatting. Under later land laws a younger son, Gregory, drove sheep out of their climate to Nymbwoidia (Nymboida) on the North Coast of New South Wales, and later to the Burnett River in Queensland, where he was killed by Aborigines. Gregory senior spent his life devising schemes that came to nothing: the Joint Stock Company for growing wool, a sixteen thousand hectare tobacco farm on timbered land near Camden to be leased to tenant farmers, or the growing of oil seed crops on sufficient scale to light all the lamps of Britain. The new cheap gas lights made the venture unprofitable before he began. His frustrations overcame him when he was seventy-five and he hanged himself at his lovely Brush Farm.

Also in 1830 Cyrus Matthew Doyle sent cattle somewhere out on to the plains in the care of another good Irishman, William Fitzpatrick. Edmund, his brother, sent eighty-five head with them. Cyrus came to Australia in 1803 as a ten-year-old. His mother, Sophia Isabella, had paid her own fare and the fares of her three children to accompany Andrew, her husband who was technically a convict. He and his brother, James, had been army clothiers in Dublin. In November 1801 they were both sentenced to transportation for life, the crime not stated in the *Rolla* indentures. But the brothers had money, a fair education and highly placed friends. So James was permitted by Governor King 'to dispence with his attendance to any duty' and he prospered as a Windsor publican. Andrew was assigned to his wife in Australia and led a

normal life. He was not even subjected to the indignity ordered years
later for such assignees: a Sunday morning muster with other prisoners
then a compulsory church service. But he almost went to gaol eighteen
years after his arrival in the Colony when he got rowdy drunk at a
funeral. The *Sydney Gazette* of 19 May 1821 reported the incident:

'On Monday, the 7th instant, a special Bench of Magistrates was
convened at Windsor, at which William Cox, Esq. presided, to investigate the curious conduct of an individual, which for turpitude and
atrocity, we believe, is unparelled in our colonial records. The circumstances are simply these: – The funeral service of the late
THOMAS ARNDELL, Esq. was being performed in the Church at
Windsor on Sunday the 6th inst. by the Rev. Mr MARSDEN; in the
act of which solemn duty the Reverend was openly and publicly interrupted by a settler of Portland Head, whose name is Doyle. He had
been disturbing the whole of the persons with whom he was associated
in the pew, for a length of time before, by his unbecoming conversa-
tion; and giving way to his impassioned imagination, he suddenly
started up, and gave the Minister, and the word of God, the direct lie!
Of course, such a character was immediately seized; and the following
Monday taken before the Bench, the Members of which were pleased
to order him, <u>the said Mr Doyle</u>, to be imprisoned in His Majesty's
county gaol at Sydney, for the space of three calendar months – to be
solitary confined – and to be fed on bread and water . . .'

Since there are no gaol records for him, apparently he repented and
was reconciled, as the law allowed the disturber of a preacher. Certainly he continued to prosper as a Hawkesbury farmer. He bought
land for each of his seven children. Cyrus married Frances Bigger,
daughter of a local farmer, and lived in a two-storey house on the east
bank of the Hawkesbury on the farm his father had bought him called
Ulinbawn. Like the Eathers, Doyle descendants are widespread. In
1831 Andrew Doyle boasted, 'We are now the Happy parents of 53
children and Grandchildren – And I beg to state Mrs D. was the first
Gentlewoman ever arrived in the Colony from Ireland.'

William Dangar (and Henry unofficially) sent cattle to form a second station on the Peel upriver from Joseph Brown. Young William
Cox sent up sheep and cattle somewhere, probably a share of increase
as pay, from the big farm Negoa (between present Muswellbrook and
Aberdeen) that he managed for his father, the road builder.

And John Town, newly married to Elizabeth Onus, Joseph's
daughter, sent his cattle out. His father had sent 100 head to the care of
Ben Singleton in 1824. Young John tried to run his cattle at Richmond

and by 1830 he was squeezed for room. Like Robert Williams he could get no grants of land. Some seemed to get all they asked for, others had not the knack of pleasing governors.

John Town tried hard with his first application for a grant. He wrote it himself:

North Richmond May 2^d 1828

I John Town Jnr
   Humbly Addres your Excellencey the Governer of New South Wales and its Territores in the fowlling manner as I am now become owner of two hundred and fifty head of hornd cattle and also twelve horses And am in possion of no land I humbly make application to Your Excellency for the purchase of land for my cattle to graze upon as the holders of land in this quarter has Debarrd my cattle from either grazing or Running upon there lands
PS As I am newly commencing busness for my self and it the first application that I have made to your Excellency the Governer: or any of the former Gentleman that held like situations I hope that your Excellency will be so kind as to look into my situation
   I again Address your Excellency if it would please your honour to give me the purchase of six hundred and forty acres of land. I also Pettion Your Excellency in the fowlling Manner: as my stock is increasing daily if it would please Your Excellency to favour me with the Grant of land also
   I Remain Sir your Humble and Obident Servant.

The scrawl and the misspellings caused this memo on the back: 'Request Mr Bell to give infm respecting this man's character and condition in life.'

Lieutenant Archibald Bell, J. P., Superintendent of Police, Windsor, and father of young Archibald who marked Bell's line of road over the Blue Mountains, reported '. . . John Town, Junior, is the Son of the Proprietor of the Mill at the Curryjong and Keeper of a Licensed House at Richmond. Mr John Town Senior is a man generally supposed to be very independent in circumstances . . .'

Another application made three years later, beautifully written by somebody else, had no more luck than that one. John Town, the miller and innkeeper, was a Lincolnshire tailor sent out for life in 1800. His son John was born in 1802, mother unknown. John Senior later married Mary Pickett, a convict girl who arrived in 1809.

John Eales sent sheep over the Currabubula gap in the hills that separate the Liverpool Plains and the Peel valley and established Duri

in 1831, a run he held for years. He came to the Hunter in 1823, a
ruthlessly ambitious free settler. He began farming with one convict
only and was nicknamed One Man Settler. But he soon demanded his
entitlement of twenty convicts, employed free men besides, and farmed
his 800 hectares with great success. In 1829 he grew 10,000 bushells of
maize as well as wheat and barley on the Hunter banks between present Maitland and Raymond Terrace where he later built a mansion,
Duckenfield.

Edwin Baldwin, brother of Otto, had made a move with his cattle in
March 1830. He mustered all he had, branded the calves, and headed
them for the plains in charge of two stockmen, David Hudson, and
William Osborn who had ridden down from Yarramanbah. But they
had mustered too many of their neighbour's cattle with them and the
district constable rode after them. Edwin was too barefaced a cattle
thief to be tolerated. He had drafted off big calves belonging to his
neighbour, Alex McLeod, branded them with his father's brand, HB,
and mixed them with his own cattle. Their mothers were left bellowing
against the boundary fence. He had also taken a cow or two belonging
to John Earl, another neighbour, and even more stupidly, a three-year-
old strawberry roan bull that had grown up in a paddock next to him
and that John Earl had praised to Edwin only a week or two before he
stole it.

Edwin was brought to trial and charged as Edwin Baldwin alias Edwin Rayner. That makes him sound more sinister than he was. All it
means was that Edwin's father, Henry, did not marry Elizabeth
Rayner, his mother. Henry arrived in 1791, sentenced to seven years.
Elizabeth was not a convict. She arrived free in 1801 with Israel
Rayner, probably her brother, a shoemaker who came as a free settler
and lived at Parramatta. Henry and Elizabeth had twelve children,
some of them named by devious association: Wellow, Edwin, Eva,
Otto, Wynn, Arlette, Harvest (born late November as the crops
ripened), Tulip, Virgo (and she died poor girl, virgin enough at twelve
weeks), Be Marr (Elizabeth Marr was a baptismal sponsor), Dio (a
son) and William.

James Glennie, J. P., magistrate at Hunter River, asked at the trial
for his opinion of Edwin's character, remarked sourly 'I never heard a
good character of Baldwin'. So inevitably the Chief Justice, Francis
Forbes, sentenced Edwin to death. That usually had no more meaning
than the Queen in *Alice's Adventures in Wonderland* shouting 'Off with his
head'. All capital offences carried the death penalty. In the same bundle of Supreme Court papers judgment of death was recorded against

the stealer of a coat worth $15 and against a drunk who made 'burglarious entry into a dwelling house . . . with intent to commit a larceny'. A shepherd was sentenced to death who had been found one night with crossed sticks erected beside a tied-up ewe from his master's flock, and hot water and knife ready to butcher it. And an unfortunate at Maitland was sentenced to death 'for feloniously having a Venereal Affair with a bitch dog . . . he was . . . found lying on his side with his Trowsers down and one of his arms under the body of the bitch and his penis in her private parts'.

In none of these cases was the sentence intended to be carried out. But in Edwin's case the judge added 'I ordered execution to take place at such time and place as the Governor should appoint'. The noose was very near.

All settlers wanted to preserve their cattle but none wanted to go as far as hanging the son of one of their fellows. Old Henry was then a substantial landholder and squatter with over 1,500 cattle, 2,000 sheep, a big brick house at Wilberforce and good outbuildings, another good house and sheds on the Hunter farm, and most valuable of all, hundreds of pounds of ready cash. So Edwin was saved by a petition of 'highly respectable settlers'.

He celebrated his continued existence by producing a double family: one by his young wife Alice, Ben Singleton's niece, the other by Christian Nowland, widow of Edward who had had charge of the cattle belonging to the Hawkesbury Benevolent Society. Edward Nowland died young in 1842 after a sudden illness.

The Kamilaroi Aborigines who had harassed Henry Dangar and William Nowland on the plains were mostly disposed of in one determined engagement. Two men left accounts of it: William Gardner in one of his great handwritten volumes and Martin Cash, convict and later bushranger in Tasmania, who wrote a book published in 1870, *The Life and Adventures of Martin Cash*. Neither man was accurate but the accounts agree well enough.

It happened about 1827 or 1828 near Onus's newly formed Boorambil. The Aborigines might have issued a challenge to the white stockmen as they sometimes did to settle their own differences, with day and hour formally stipulated. The whites had no intention of exposing themselves. When they saw the long line of painted warriors approaching, all the stockmen who had gathered (Cash said seven, Gardner sixteen) took cover in a well-built hut with slots in the walls to poke rifles through. When spears and boomerangs thrown against the

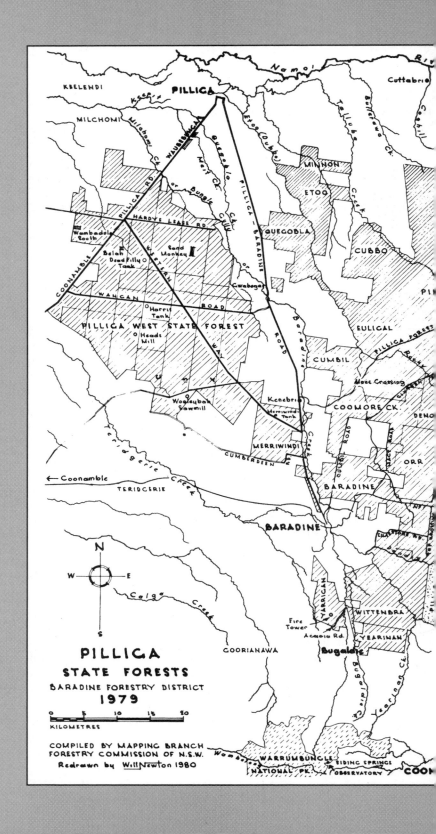

PILLIGA
STATE FORESTS
BARADINE FORESTRY DISTRICT
1979

0   5   10   15   20
KILOMETRES

COMPILED BY MAPPING BRANCH
FORESTRY COMMISSION OF N.S.W.
Redrawn by Will Newton 1980

Few roads are marked.It is impossible to show several thousand
kilometres of forest roads on a map of this size.

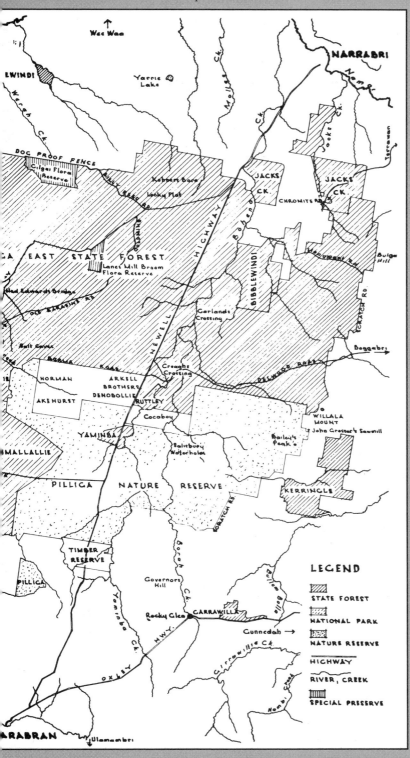

walls in derision failed to bring the whites out, the Aborigines stormed the hut and tried to unroof it. They persisted for hours. Perhaps two hundred were shot, most of the young men of the tribe.

Another tribe of Kamilaroi to the north became expert cattle thieves under the tuition of George Clarke, Ben Singleton's runaway convict. He was known usually as George the Barber since he had been a hairdresser in England. The Aborigines accepted him as the ghost of a warrior come back to them from another world. Clarke was educated and intelligent and learnt their language quickly. He probably organised the cattle raids to make up for his deficiency as a hunter.

East of Boggabri on the Namoi River there is an anabranch with a half-moon lagoon still known as Barbers. There he built stockyards, the first on the Namoi, out of rails and the hides of cattle stolen from Joseph Brown's Wollomal, ninety kilometres upstream on the Peel, a tributary of the Namoi. Green hides were tied together and warped from tree to tree with soaked strips of hide. As the ties dried, the hides were stretched tight and hard. Some panels were made of rails also lashed to trees with pliable strips of wet hide. The yards were strong.

About the end of 1830 George Clarke crossed the range with a small party of Aborigines and went back to Ben Singleton's farm. Singleton had never reported him missing. 'Major' Mudie criticised him constantly for his lenient treatment of convicts. Clarke's skin was blackened and he was patterned with the tribal cicatrices that made him a full warrior. He had at least two wives, one of whom was to prove notably faithful to him.

Singleton put Clarke to work again for a few weeks and as he worked he told marvellous stories of a great river flowing north-west to the Gulf of Van Diemen. He said he had followed it to its mouth where he saw Aborigines with bows and arrows who told him of men who came in boats to cut scented wood and others who came for a sort of sea slug. He described mammals like hippopotamuses and monkeys as big as orang-utangs. A rocky island stood in the river's mouth and on it a burning mountain. He offered to lead Benjamin Singleton to the river.

There is a burning mountain in Australia near Wingen, north of Scone. A coal seam has been alight for thousands of years. Blue smoke comes up through deep cracks and hot rocks are coated with yellow sulphur. During the 150 years since it was first seen the fire has crept about a hundred metres up the slope.

With George Clarke as guide, Benjamin Singleton and Richard Yeomans set out for the great Kindur River. They would have passed the burning mountain on their way north. But they did not get far.

One night on the Peel Aboriginal tribesmen came to Clarke. He slipped away with them silently and when Singleton and Yeomans woke in the morning they were abandoned.

It was too dangerous to travel on alone. They returned to the Hunter. And that time Benjamin Singleton reported Clarke as a runaway. From then on his name appeared in the lists that were regularly published showing age, height, colouring, marks, from whose employ – curiously like the lists to be published later of impounded stock. But Benjamin Singleton's description was even shorter than his exploring log: 'Clarke George, from Mr B. Singleton.'

The dream of the Kindur did not die. Ben Singleton and Richard Yeomans planned an expedition to explore it. They intended to leave in October 1831 and offered through the *Sydney Herald* to outfit up to twelve men to accompany them along the Kindur to the Gulf of Carpentaria. The mouth of the river had unaccountably shifted.

But on 22 August 1831 the *Sydney Herald* published a comment which was startlingly sensible. It came from John Thompson, assistant surveyor to Major Mitchell who had succeeded the dying Oxley as Surveyor-General:

'It is much more probable that Peel's river falls into the Darling river ... the Peel has been traced to its junction with another river ... should the travellers succeed in tracing beyond this confluence, to the confluence with the Darling ... and return by the way of the Talbraga country, they will effect one of the most important discoveries that has yet been made.' Major Mitchell himself grew enthusiastic about the exploration.

Clarke quite stupidly began robbing the new huts on the plains as soon as he returned to the Namoi. Now he was the Flying Barber with a young convict associate, Peter Kenny. They made such nuisances of themselves a mounted sergeant, Sandy Wilcox, with a black tracker set out to capture them. He took them in six days in a camp on the black plains north-west of present Baradine and brought them down to the Bathurst lock-up. There Clarke wrote out the story of the Kindur which Mitchell read. He decided immediately to go in search of it himself, and set out the next month in November 1831. Clarke expected to go as guide and interpreter but was told he had to face trial.

No sooner had Mitchell left than one of Clarke's gins came down and set him free. She passed him a file at night. But they lost hours on their way north getting rid of the heavy leg irons. He was soon retaken and charged with thefts from all corners of the plains. The Supreme Court informations were ponderous documents. This is the charge against him that shows Nombi first occupied by William Cox's cattle:

'In the Second Year of the Reign of Our Sovereign Lord William the Fourth, by the Grace of God, of the United Kingdom of Great Britain and Ireland, King, Defender of the Faith.

'NEW SOUTH WALES (TO WIT.) – BE IT REMEMBERED, that John Kinchela, Esquire, Doctor of Laws, His Majesty's Attorney General for the Colony of New South Wales, who prosecutes for His Majesty in this Behalf, being present in the Supreme Court of New South Wales, now here, on the First Day of February in the Year of our Lord One Thousand Eight Hundred and Thirty-two at Sydney, in the Colony aforesaid, informs the said Court, that George Clarke otherwise called George the Barber late of Numbi in the Colony aforesaid Labourer and Peter Kenny late of the same place Labourer on the Twenty-eighth Day of September in the Year of Our Lord One Thousand Eight Hundred and Thirty-one with force and arms at Numbi aforesaid in the Colony aforesaid, Three Muskets of the value of Six pounds, two Bayonets of the value of Ten shillings, Two Blankets of the value of One pound, Three Rugs of the value of One pound, One Axe of the value of Five shillings, One Frying Pan of the value of Five shillings, One Kettle of the value of Five shillings, Five Tin Pots of the value of Five shillings, Five pounds of Flour of the value of One shillings, Five pounds of Bread of the value of One shilling, Five pounds of Beef of the value of One shilling, One pound of Gunpowder of the value of Two shillings and Six leaden Bullets of the value of Six pence of the Goods and Chattels of one William Cox in the dwelling house of the said William Cox there situate then and there being found then and there in the said dwelling house feloniously did Steal take and carry away against the form of the Statute in such case made and provided and against the peace of our said Lord the King his Crown and Dignity

John Kinchela
Atty General.'

Peter Kenny was sentenced to work on the roads in irons for three years. George Clarke was sentenced to death, commuted to transportation to Norfolk Island for three years. His faithful gin never saw him again. He was eventually hanged for theft in Tasmania.

It is strange that there are no stories of half-caste children by Clarke. He lived with several wives for almost five years. Since he was accepted as a tribesman his children would have been allowed to live. John King, the survivor of the Burke and Wills expedition, left a daughter on the Cooper. Until the tribal life of the Aborigines broke down, all half-caste babies born from casual or forcible encounters were killed as unfit to live, just as deformed babies were always killed.

Benjamin Singleton has no further part in this story. His man was the first white to live on the Namoi, his cattle led the eastern prong that soon moved to the forest. He moved farther out on the plains to one of the ridges and formed a station he called Pine Ridge but his stay there was brief. In 1842 he went bankrupt along with hundreds of others in the Colony. Even Singletown had to be sold. But again, for a time, a new Kindur sustained him: money in Chancery supposed to be left for him. He and his wife, Mary, set sail for England. The family stories had no more substance than Clarke's. Benjamin Singleton returned to Australia to die.

Major Thomas Livingstone Mitchell, brilliant, painstaking and irascible, came to Australia in 1827 at the age of thirty-five. He joined the army as a nineteen-year-old, and was with Wellington in Spain, mapping and reconnoitring often under fire during the Peninsular wars. After the French troops were driven out of Spain and defeated finally at Waterloo, the Chief of Staff, Major General Sir George Murray, sent Mitchell back to make a historical record of the war. For several years he wandered through Spain and Portugal measuring, mapping and sketching the major battlefields.

Mitchell came to Australia as Deputy Surveyor-General but with clear understanding that he would succeed Oxley when he retired. 'You must not expect to find Captain Mitchell a great scholar' wrote Sir George Murray who recommended him to the Colonial Office, 'but a skilful, accurate and a practised surveyor, and a very good draftsman. His plans are indeed beautifully executed.'

So many Australian explorers went, or were sent, chasing rainbows: inland seas or good stock routes where there was only desert. On his way to seek the great Kindur River in November 1831, Mitchell rode up from Parramatta, crossed the Hawkesbury by ferry where one still crosses by ferry, then travelled a good new road built on a line he had surveyed to the upper Wollombi. He called on several Hunter River settlers on the way north, crossed the Liverpool Range by the well-used Murrurundi Pass and hired an Aboriginal guide at Quirindi whom Long Ned Dwyer recommended. On a near summer's day Mrs Dwyer 'enveloped in numerous flannel petticoats' moved among 'undraped slender native females . . . who appeared to be treated by her with great kindness'. The guide showed them the best track for their 'wheelbarrows' (carts) to Joseph Brown's Wollomal on the Peel. The overseer found them another Aboriginal guide, 'Mr Brown', and the party travelled west down the Peel, past where it was joined by the Muluerindie (the head of the Namoi) to its junction with the Mooki near present Gunnedah. There the Namoi flows north as Clarke said it did and Mitchell explored its fertile banks.

Mitchell had a good team. It was not the string of almost anonymous men that went with most explorers. Principals only were usually thought worthy of mention. Mitchell named each man and his reason for choosing him. Equipment was chosen with the same care. Two of the carts were specially made light enough to be manhandled if necessary. The salt pork was boned to cut down bulk and weight. Fold up canvas boats were carried.

Certainly Mitchell's perfectionism was carried too far. He moved with an exploring army not a troop of forward scouts, and the military discipline that sometimes shows through his excellent narrative was galling to tired men. 'I had the satisfaction to see my party move forward in exploring order' he wrote, and later 'It was a standing order . . . that no man should quit the line of route to drink, without my permission.' As his men pitched his tent each night they had to align it on the meridian by compass so that he always knew he faced south when he looked out the flap.

Mitchell found George Clarke's abandoned yards and near them many old native gunyas with cattle bones strewn outside them. There he left the Namoi and headed north-east where the Kindur River was supposed to begin. He crossed a big creek which he named Maule's River after an English friend. 'Mr Brown' had returned to Wollamol, afraid of the local Aborigines, and Mitchell could find no Aboriginal to tell him the name of the creek. He had a rule he too often broke that places should retain their original names. 'New names are of no use', he wrote, 'especially when given to rivers or water-courses by travellers who have merely crossed them . . . we derive from such maps little more information than we had before . . . So long as any of the aborigines can be found in the neighbourhood . . . future travellers may verify my map.'

The Nandewar foothills were too rough for the carts so Mitchell returned to the Namoi and followed it north as the easiest way of skirting the mountains. He liked the country where Maules Creek joined the Namoi: 'The river widened into smooth deep reaches . . . the richest part of the adjacent country . . . covered with a fragrant white amaryllis in full bloom.' This was the lovely *Calostemma* or garland lily found there now as isolated specimens. Mitchell launched the boats: 'I feel sanguine about our progress.' But they tore on snags so often they had to be abandoned.

At Narrabri the Namoi River swings to the west and flows to the Barwon. Mitchell liked the look of the flat black plains to the north. 'Beautiful open country' he called it. He headed across it to try to cut the Kindur as it came out of the mountains but what he found was 'not the great river . . . but only the Gwydir of Cunningham'.

Since his venture on to the plains in 1825, Allan Cunningham had made a long northern trip in 1827 out of the Hunter, up along the mountains west of the area now called New England to the Darling Downs, then back along the western edge of the Nandewar Range. Mitchell unaccountably ignored the result of that exploration. If there had been a great river flowing west Cunningham must have crossed it. Cunningham found the Darling Downs superb, but like Oxley he was too early. He pointed to country that the squatters could move to later. Their immediate concern was unstocked country nearer. Mitchell had the knack of going out at exactly the right time. On one of his later journeys he met squatters following up his tracks as he returned.

I own a copy of Mitchell's *Three Expeditions into the Interior of Eastern Australia* bought in 1841 by a landseeker. All the way through the second volume he made marginal marks and underlined mention of the best country in the extraordinarily good Victorian country Mitchell called Australia Felix. Here and there he wrote directions to himself all round the margins. On two blank pages at the back in tiny writing he expounded to himself 'Method for fully examining the country about Portland Bay – if Arriving by water'. The country he fixed on as best became the marvellous Mount Sturgeon of the Armytages employing up to 400 men in a great rich valley on the upper Wannon in Victoria. But he was much too late to get any of the good land he so enthusiastically considered. It was taken up immediately not by men who waited to read about the discoveries but by men who formed big overlanding parties to follow up Mitchell's tracks.

Despite his disillusion with the Gwydir, Mitchell followed it to a river he decided was the Darling that Sturt had discovered flowing into the Murray. He made an accurate estimate of the flow of the western rivers and returned at the end of February 1832. Sir John Jamison, a close friend of Mitchell's, immediately sent up two drafts of cattle from farms he had bought on the Hunter. One mob crossed the Namoi and settled down on the rich country round the ready-made yards of George the Barber. The other mob was driven up Bone Creek (Coxs) that flows into the Namoi opposite Barbers Lagoon. They established another station seventy-five kilometres upstream on the eastern bank, south of the hilly remnants still known as Tommy and Billy Ridge. Nelson Simmons Lawson had cattle immediately west and south. Now the eastern prong and the western prong of stock had closed on the plains like a pair of pincers.

Bone Creek was named Bowen Creek by Oxley. 'Bone' might have been mere misspelling since it was also spelt 'Boan' but it might have been a cynical misinterpretation of the name after a bad year. Mitchell in his *Three Expeditions*... told of Snodgrass Valley in the Hunter quickly becoming Nograss Valley as the 1826–9 drought set in.

It is not known who took Sir John Jamison's stock to the two stations. The Aborigines killed five stockmen in their hut near Barbers Lagoon a few months after they arrived. The *Australian* reported the deaths on 3 May 1833 but mentioned no names and attributed the station to 'Mr Renkin' instead of Jamison. George Ranken or Rankin was a well-known Bathurst settler who squatted to the south-west across the Lachlan. The station was not abandoned. Sir John Jamison sent up more stockmen to muster the cattle and take charge, surely an unnerving experience.

Along with Sir John Jamison, Cyrus Doyle advanced his cattle a few squares from wherever they were on the Liverpool Plains. He sent out his tall son, Andrew, just turned sixteen, to join his stockmen and they drove about two hundred head of cattle down the Namoi to the good plains Mitchell had described near present Narrabri. The name was first written Nunebey. Several Aborigines went with them. John Purcell, probably an ex-convict and no relation to Charles on Girriewillie, was in charge.

Donald McLauchlin, one of Peter McIntyre's original Highland lads, drove up a big mob of Macqueen's bullocks to fatten on the Mooki. McLauchlin had ridden the river several times in search of country. The land he took the bullocks to was near the present village of Breeza, pronounced something like Pirryja by the Aborigines. In defending his territory he once leapt on a bareback horse and chased a trespassing squatter with drawn sword. The chase lasted twenty kilometres but the squatter's horse was too fast.

Robert Fitzgerald, the very successful son of successful ex-convict parents, in a strange partnership with William Lawson, sent cattle to join Nelson Simmons Lawson east of Bone and Premer. Their cattle fed as far as Yarraman Creek, several creeks west of the similarly named Yarramanbah Creek.

During 1833 several other squatters moved forward. Some of them anticipated being driven out by the Australian Agricultural Company. In February 1833 six thousand young sheep spread among William Nowland's cattle on Warrah Creek. William Telfer had charge of them, an extraordinarily capable shepherd indentured to the Australian Agricultural Company. He brought the sheep over the Barrington Tops from Stroud along a rough track that no longer exists and lost only six on the way. The Australian Agricultural Company had sought better land.

Sir Edward Parry had arrived in Australia in December 1829, Henry Dangar a few months later. Their movements were restricted for a few months since both wives were heavily pregnant and their husbands wished to be near them. Lady Parry shortly gave birth to twins, Grace Dangar to another son to join the baby son she already had.

Parry was anxious to make a good impression in Australia. 'Waited on the Governor immediately' he wrote in his diary, 'most kindly received.' And a few days later he spent a day returning calls, 'being anxious not to give the slightest offence to anybody'. Calling and returning of calls had not then developed into the silly card game of the 1870s but reputations in 1830 were vulnerable and sensibilities raw.

On his first tour of inspection Parry was startled at the way the Hunter River settlers lived. Accustomed to servants in England, many of them, and lacking the skills of tradesmen, they were not making a neat job of adapting. He stayed a night with one settler, George Graham, and his cousin named Oliver. 'Mr Graham's father kept his hunters in England. They now live in a miserable slab-hut of their own building, open to admit wind and rain in most parts, badly thatched with reeds of which the colour is not to be seen within for the smoke and dirt with which it is covered – no floor – the fire place a recess made of slabs – their beds a sort of cot slung with bullock's hide to the rough rafters, and everything giving the idea of filth and wretchedness. They wait entirely on themselves, chop their own wood, boil their kettle, wash their cups and pannikins, plough, reap and everything else themselves. They slept under their cart for three weeks keeping watch with a loaded gun alternately.' Nearby the Maclean's hut was worse, and Mrs Maclean was 'Colonel Snodgrass's sister – a woman accustomed in Scotland I understand to all the elegancies and comforts of life!!'

Life was growing harder for the later settlers. By 1830 their numbers had outstripped the convicts available as labourers. But despite Parry's assessment of wretchedness one must believe that the majority were enjoying themselves. I began farming in 1948 living in a tent, boiling the billy on an open fire, washing in the Namoi River. It was the lovely country where Maules Creek runs into the river. Life then, as it is now, was decidedly enjoyable.

Henry Dangar began exploring again and assessing land for the company. It was now obvious that much of the Australian Agricultural Company's Port Stephens grant would have to be surrendered. Sir Edward Parry agreed. It was also obvious that the company's holding would have to be fragmented. Not even the Liverpool Plains could encompass the two hundred thousand hectares surrendered without including too much unwatered country. So it was decided to retain the good Stroud-Gloucester strip, to work coal pits at Newcastle as a separate venture, and to apply for approximately one hundred thousand hectare blocks both on the Peel River and on the northern slopes of the Liverpool Range where those first over the range had bred up their stock.

The company's plans had been set back before Henry Dangar had made his final investigation because Governor Darling was recalled. He joined the lengthening list of unhappy Governors the seething Colony had broken. Parry received from Darling 'the most affectionate attentions'. Most others found him ungracious to the point of repulsiveness.

William Charles Wentworth, back in the Colony, had been agitating the discontent through his new paper, the *Australian*. He returned in 1824, not the young aristocrat who went to London, but a vigorous plebeian. He had fallen bitterly to earth while he swallowed the nasty fact of his father's trial, then he set out to climb a different ladder. Trial by jury, he advocated through the newspaper he published in defiance of Darling's censorship, government by elected representatives. The emancipists flocked to him as leader of the Radical Party. Here was another Macquarie. He lived with Sarah Cox, the daughter of Frances Morton and Francis Cox, an emancipist blacksmith. After two children were born he married her but he was as inconstant as his father, D'Arcy, and had several children by other women. 'A vulgar ill-bred fellow' Darling declared him.

Not all the wealthy, or all those clear of any convict background, reviled Wentworth. While Parry was preparing a laudatory farewell address to Darling, Sir John Jamison walked in. Parry was startled to find that Sir John was anxious not to offend the Governor but he was even more 'anxious to become popular with the Radical Party ! ! !' Yet Governor Macquarie with the same ideas had written off Jamison as 'intriguing and discontented'.

The night Darling sailed out of Sydney Harbour in October 1831, William Wentworth gave a celebration barbecue at the lovely Vaucluse house that still stands. There were piles of 4,000 loaves and casks of Cooper's gin and Wright's strong beer. A whole bullock roasted over slow coals. It had been turned slowly on a huge spit since the previous day. Twelve sheep turned on lesser spits. The guests feasted by the light of two bonfires, 'upwards of 4,000 persons' declared the *Australian*, surely an enthusiastic exaggeration. 'A mob regaled upon Cooper's gin and a roasted bullock' wrote Parry. He had no pleasure in Darling's going. The new Governor, Sir Richard Bourke, was not so enthusiastic about the company.

Major Mitchell objected to the boundaries Dangar and Parry proposed. He wanted natural features as simple boundary lines not the zigzags Dangar drew to cut out useless country. Mitchell had sympathy for the squatters who would be displaced. Parry insisted they were nomads who were willing to move again. Bourke supported Mitchell.

Parry went over their heads through the Court of Directors in London to the Secretary of State for the Colonies. Bourke tried to compromise by giving the company temporary occupation of sixteen thousand hectares on Warrah Creek where William Nowland and his partners, Philip Thorley and Thomas Parnell, had their cattle. But in August 1833 he was directed to yield all the land required: 125,000 hectares on the Peel and 100,000 hectares of the Liverpool Plains stretching from Phillips Creek to Warrah. Some of that land is still held by the company which in 1978 owned 94,000 hectares of rich farming and grazing country. Farming, one of its principles that was neglected for 130 years, made the company prosperous in modern times. In 1976, by Royal assent, it transferred domicile from Britain to Australia. Head office is now at Tamworth on the Peel.

So between 1832 when Sir John Jamison and Cyrus Doyle sent cattle to the Namoi, and 1836, when all laws came over the Range and the Impounding Act and the Scab in Sheep Act drove the last resisting squatters off the Australian Agricultural Company's grants, there was a slow drift of men with cattle and sheep to the Namoi and to the southern edge of the open sandy plains that are now the dense Pilliga forest. Their employers sent them now in the hope that the land laws would catch up with them and they would be given title.

Sir John Jamison's stockmen moved down-river about thirty kilometres from George the Barber's stockyards and laid claim to forty thousand hectares of good land north of Maules Creek stretching on both sides of the Namoi. On the east bank it ran between Maules Creek and Bibbla Creek as far as the Nandewar Range. On the west bank it spread across the creek then known as Banbar, now called Tulla Mullen, the Aboriginal name for the main waterhole on the creek. Banbar became Baan Baa, the name of the present village. Two more stockmen were killed there by Aborigines towards the end of 1833, and one man, Farley, who escaped, was drowned in the Namoi the next year swimming away from bushrangers. The bushrangers returned a few weeks later and the two surviving stockmen shot them.

One of the bushrangers was Macdonald, a brilliant bushman and aloof Scot, who would be known by no other name. For years he led raids on Hunter River farms and Liverpool Plains squatters. Sometimes he retired to Courada, a lonely settlement of bushrangers on the head of Terry Hie Hie Creek beyond Mount Courada, north-east of Narrabri. It was formed probably about 1826 or early 1827. Cunningham on the way to the Darling Downs in 1827 found cattle dung on Bingara Creek only fifty kilometres to the east and on the way back he found an open shed about eight metres long and two wide built recently by white men. The uprights were sunk deeply into the ground and the tops squared with a broad axe to take the roofing timbers. The flat roof was wattled and thatched with eucalypt branches. It seemed to be built as a temporary shelter.

George Clarke told of the settlement at Courada and Aborigines confirmed it. Twenty men lived in three huts, one of them shingled. They had horses and two ploughs and grew their own wheat. Night and day a sentry guarded the difficult approach. Two expeditions of mounted police sent to find them travelled too far north. Troughs that these men built were in existence until modern times. If no fires have been through the area they could be still there. They were installed on a slope above a black soil flat within sight of the spectacular rock faces of Mount Waa. Mount Courada itself, widely known as Castle Top, is an extraordinary landmark: a massive cube of rock on top of a dome.

The highest trough was set in under the outlet of a little spring. It was a long, hollowed-out log. Each end was grooved and fitted exactly with a solid half-moon of timber to hold the water. The end board opposite the spring had a depression cut in it so that the trough overflowed into another trough set in beneath it and so on in series down the slope. They were designed to water a lot of cattle. But something must have gone wrong with the duffing plans. The Aborigines reported that they had a few cattle only. Macdonald found the settlement abandoned shortly before he was shot at Baan Baa.

When Sir Edward Parry in 1832 inspected the land Henry Dangar chose for the company he wrote down a list of twenty-three squatters who would be affected by the move. Various writers have distorted this into a list of men ousted by the company in 1832. That is not so. Possibly none of them moved as early as 1832. Some were scarcely affected. Long Ned Dwyer at Quirindi had to do no more than restrain the movement of George and Andrew Loder's stock to the south. To William Lawson and Robert Fitzgerald it meant little more than the loss of an impermanent watering-point. Joseph Brown simply moved all his cattle to the northern side of the Peel. And John Blaxland's stockmen at Kickerbell, like Ned Dwyer, had to watch the southern boundary.

Joseph Onus and Robert Williams were displaced from Boorambil and since they found choice land on the Namoi, they probably moved about the middle of 1833, when Sir John Jamison's stockmen moved downstream to Bann Baa. Robert Williams did not accompany them. Even three years later he did not know where his cattle were or how many he had: 'A considerable number' he stated in a memorial with lordly unconcern, '. . . supposed to be now depasturing on the Unlocated Lands on the Banks of the Namoi River.'

It is even more unlikely that Joseph Onus rode up on that trip than on the move over the range in 1826. Almost certainly Thomas Eather went up with John Bazely, Onus's head stockman, and formed three stations, one for himself and his two brothers, Robert and Charles, one each for his brothers-in-law. Joseph Onus's cattle fed where I began farming on the east bank of the Namoi south of Maules Creek that was designated the southern boundary of Sir John Jamison's station. The Aborigines called that creek Kaihai, and the area about the junction Benial. The station was called Theribry. Robert Williams's cattle fed on the Boggibrie run south of Onus's.

The Eather's station was on the west bank of the river, south of Banbar Creek that ran through Jamison's. Thomas Eather held it for years and finally gave it to his son Charles in 1861. He serviced it by dray from his farm on Wollombi Brook, a month to go up, a month to come back. It is impossible to believe that he was not personally involved in its selection. It was the land Mitchell referred to where garland lilies grew. Thomas Eather named it after a little hill across the river that Mitchell referred to as Einerguendie. Thomas Eather spelt

it Inderiniandie which was finally anglicised through many variations
to Henriendi.

James Robertson had to move. Alexander Bloomfield, his superintendent, leapfrogged down the Mooki to the Namoi in 1833 and
formed Cowmore just north of present Gunnedah. Robertson would
not pay the licence fees that were later introduced so there is scant mention of that station in the records of the Occupation of Lands Office.
According to his son, John, who became Sir John, he also occupied
land round Boggabri in 1835. It must have been a brief occupation
since there was soon no room for him to fit there. However a hill to the
north of the town is still known as Robertsons Mount, usually ab-
breviated to The Mount.

Warrah had to be yielded to the Australian Agricultural Company.
The stockmen must have regretted leaving it more than the absent
owners: they had good tobacco growing and a vegetable garden. The
three owners drafted off their cattle. Thomas Parnell sent up his son,
Thomas, to take charge of them and he drove them down the east bank
of the Namoi to a run he named Bull (probably pronounced Pool) next
to Robert Williams's Boggibrie. Philip Thorley went to the west bank
of the Namoi downstream from Robertson's Cowmore. William
Nowland tried to hold ground on the plains. He ran his cattle with
those of the Hawkesbury Benevolent Society but boundary disputes
and law cases kept him restless for years.

William Dangar and Henry who had just completed his job with the
Australian Agricultural Company moved their cattle about fifteen kilometres off the Peel up the Cockburn River to good country at Moonbi
that Henry found when he examined the Cockburn for the company.

The several owners at Yarramanbah moved and scattered. William
Osborn, so useful for mustering the neighbours' unbranded calves,
took charge of cattle somewhere on the plains for Charles Ezzy, a Richmond innkeeper. Otto Baldwin sent sheep and cattle north of the Peel
and across the Namoi to its junction with the Manilla River. There he
formed a station he called Diniwarindi where the town of Manilla is
now. The Baldwins held it for years. Richard Yeomans, since 1830 an
innkeeper near Maitland, died suddenly. George Yeomans probably
sent their cattle somewhere northward, possibly to Diniwarindi, but he
was more interested in boat-building and innkeeping than squatting,
though in the 1840s, in partnership with Otto Baldwin, he established
Bugobilla (Boggabilla) on the Macintyre River, named by Cunningham for his friend Peter McIntyre.

George Druitt had to move his stock off Phillips Creek. His men drove sheep and cattle around Cox's stock on Nombi, and north-west of Charles Purcell's on Girriwillie. They came off the black soil to the heavy red loam and sand along Yaminba and Borah Creeks. Druitt called the station Yamingabee. Part of it is now farmland, most of it is in the Pilliga Nature Reserve.

Some squatters were forced to move in 1834 by shortage of water. They advanced a few squares, and others who had not joined in the first move to the plains now came forward from the Hunter. George Bowman, not related to Dr James Bowman, brought up a mob of two-year-old mixed sexes. He rode up himself from his prosperous farm on the Hunter. George Bowman was the son of one of the earliest free settlers. John Bowman, his father, was encouraged to come out in 1798 by the offer of a free passage. With George Bowman rode Martin Cash, the convict and bushranger, John Johnston, an assigned convict who was hanged in 1838 for murdering Aborigines on Henry Dangar's Myall Creek run, and a stockman, hutkeeper and bullock-driver with a drayload of stores. Bowman found the land next to Robertson's unoccupied. So he left the three unnamed men to build a rough hut and temporary stockyards near present Gunnedah where the Mooki joins the Namoi. There they fattened the steers and grew the heifers into breeders but Bowman did not hold that good country. Two years later he moved north-east of Doyle's Narrabri station to Terry Hie Hie. And whoever had charge of his cattle then thought themselves the first white men on the upper creek till they found the bushrangers' good troughs.

William Sims Bell, eldest son of Lieutenant Archibald Bell, fitted in on the Namoi south of Otto Baldwin, where the big Keepit Dam is now. His father and young brother sent thousands of sheep and cattle somewhere into the north. John Howe made a move into squatting and sent his son, James, downriver from William Sims Bell to the site of Carroll. Robert Pringle fitted in on the Peel downstream from the Australian Agricultural Company's boundary. He came to Australia as a free settler in 1824 and felt his way as manager of a Hunter farm for six years, then bought the farm from the absent owner. John Town senior sent his cattle past Phillip Thorley's to the rich flat black plain he called Milkengourie. Young John Town was busy with the Woolpack Inn at North Richmond and had no part in the move. And Edward Cox, living at Mulgoa and wealthier now than his brothers since a friend of his father had left him property, moved both sheep and cattle that had bred up on the Talbragar north to the Castlereagh. He formed adjacent sheep stations, Urabribble and Ulamanbri (now Ulamambri), just east of present Coonabarabran. The cattle were driven on east past Girriwillie, past Nombi to Coxs Creek and down it to its junction with the Namoi at Boggabri. It was 1835, the year John Robertson said he went there. Perhaps their stockmen fought it out. It was Edward Cox who stayed. He called the station Namoi Hut. William Cox's stockmen on Nombi probably knew it well and had surely been there before Mitchell. Nombi was only sixty kilometres away, one good day's ride down a big creek, and they had been there for six years.

On 22 October 1836 Sir John Jamison wrote to the Colonial Secretary:

Sir

I have the honor to request that you will be pleased to lay before His Excellency the Governor the following application

Sir John Jamison Knt residing at Regentville applies to his Excellency the Governor for a Licence for one year from the 1st of January next to depasture sheep, cattle and other stock upon the Crown Lands situated beyond the limits of the Colony which he has been in the occupation of four years past about 250 miles from Capertee in a northern direction His stock yards fronting each other on the right and left bank of the river Namoi about fifteen miles below Barbers stock yard and known by the name of Baanba bounded by Mrs Onus's station on the right bank and on the left by Mr Cox's station and extending down the river about fifteen miles. Sir John Jamison declares that he is free and single and that he intends to depasture his said stock under the charge of Mr Thomas McKenny free that he possesses considerable estates in the County of Cumberland, Capertee etc.

Sir Richard Bourke scrawled on the back of the letter, 'Send Sir J. J. the printed form'. The law had caught up. Squatting had become respectable.

4

Licences to Depasture Beyond the Limits

A New Game to New Rules

The area of one and a half million hectares that now contains the Pilliga forest, the Pilliga Nature Reserve, and the encircling and encroaching farmland is bordered on the east by the Namoi River flowing north past the towns and villages of Gunnedah, Boggabri, Baan Baa and Turrawan to Narrabri, and on the north also by the Namoi River that turns west at Narrabri and flows past Wee Waa and Pilliga, then out of the area through black plains into the Barwon at Walgett. In some places, the river divides yellow sandy soil from rich black. The southern boundary is the Gunnedah-Coonabarabran road that leads out of the northern end of the Liverpool Plains a few kilometres west of Mullaley into low hills running off the Warrumbungle Mountains. As one travels towards Coonabarabran the road exactly divides the red downs that George Druitt took up as Yamingabee from the black downs of William Cox's Nombi and Charles Purcell's Girriwillie (now Garrawilla). The town of Coonabarabran and the Warrumbungle Mountains define the south-west corner. The broken western boundary is partly the often dry Teridgerie Creek that runs north-west out of the Warrumbungles then west through the very flat black plains into the Castlereagh north of Coonamble, and partly the bigger and more permanent Baradine Creek that runs near Teridgerie Creek for about ninety kilometres of its length then turns direct north and loses its main channel in impermanent swamps and lagoons and gullies meandering into the Namoi in the north-west corner between Pilliga and Walgett.

The first holders of licences 'to depasture Crown Lands beyond the Limits of Location' took up what they called stations. They followed the water and soon circled the area though they came to it from several directions. Governor Bourke offered them an indefinite future: whatever land they could hold against their neighbours, to run whatever stock they owned for one year for a fee of twenty dollars. It was less a condonement of squatting than a statement of the authority of the Crown, as in Brisbane's occupational permits, to 'revoke this indulgence and resume possession'. The threat hampered nobody. Occupation increased.

John Johnston, a Hunter River settler, sent John Farrell with sheep and cattle to occupy the land round present Gunnedah that George Bowman had recently vacated. John Johnston who also spelt his name Johnstone and Johnson was no relation to Bowman's stockman of the same name.

James Robertson sent up his nineteen-year-old son, John, recently returned from working his way round the world, to take charge of his cattle on Cowmore, next to Johnston. John Robertson rode down the Namoi to Boggabri and west to the Castlereagh, looking out for a sheep station for himself. He admired the tall straight ironbarks thick enough in parts to be a forest 'such as we hear of as existing in other lands'.

William Charles Wentworth who had taken no part in the first squatting rush now sent up James Watson, a convict with a ticket-of-leave, in charge of a thousand head of cattle. It is unlikely Wentworth rode up with him. He had just bought the fine house and grounds, Windermere, on the Hunter. His interests were now politics and money-making. He had done with exploring. James Watson soon established three stations: Burburgate on both sides of the Namoi downstream from John Johnston and Robertson, Tiberenah (later Tibbereena) on both sides of the river downstream from Sir John Jamison's Baan Baa, and Galathra on a big black plain north-west of Doyle's station, then spelt Nunabry. It is impossible to tell whether Nunabey as it was first written was more as the Aborigines pronounced it, or whether the e was a misreading of somebody's r. Later the name changed nearer its modern spelling and became Nurrabry. Perhaps the original n was a misreading of rr. Perhaps rr was a misreading of n. In the handwriting of one of the clerks who kept these records the letters e, rr, and n all look much the same. Cyrus Doyle, Andrew's younger brother, could have resolved it. He spoke Kamilaroi fluently and was later initiated into a tribe.

The cattle feed on the black plains was excellent fattening. Indeed, neither the rate of gain nor the quality of finish can be bettered in a modern feedlot. The pasture has changed since sheep and cattle fed on it though not as much as red soil pastures. All the original grasses still grow, though in different dominance, and grasses now grow more thickly since imported medics keep the phosphate-rich soil rich also in nitrogen.

The best of the first grasses were Flinders (*Iseilema*), Kangaroo or Oat Grass (*Themeda*), Early Spring Grass (*Eriochloa*), Umbrella Grass (*Digitaria*), Native Millet or Panic (*Panicum*), Sago Grass or Slender Panic (*Paspalidium*) and Mitchell Grass (*Astrebla*). Perennials most of them, they were heavy-seeded and grew rather sparsely in big clumps. The top growth died in drought time and the plants looked dead, then after a good fall of rain they shot green from the butts. The clumped growth allowed them to keep some of their roots intact when the puffy soil yielded up too much of its moisture and tore the clumps apart as it split open in zig-zag gashes up to six metres deep and fifteen centimetres wide.

Between the clumps in good seasons grew a mixture of palatable herbs named sometimes for their resemblance to English plants: native carrot, crowsfoot, lamb's tongue and yellow vine, tar vine, Boggabri. Nitrogen was supplied by low growing Lotus species often called Barwon River Trefoil, or the delicate Glycines that twined up the grass stems, or occasional plants of vigorous *Swainsona*, the purple-flowered Darling Pea. These few leguminous plants were so precious to the pasture most of them protected themselves against grazing kangaroos and emus with poison.

But there was less water on the north-west plains than on the Liverpool Plains. Galathera Creek had a few impermanent holes but it was mostly no more than a dry gully. Robert Pringle had taken up Gurley on a similar creek north-east of Galathra in 1836. He held it for two or three years only. 'The usual condition of that country is drought' he declared and sold his licence, yards and huts for two horses and saddles.

It was not till the 1880s when bores tapped the marvellous underground water that much use could be made of the feed on the plains. Then overgrazing by sheep gave too much room for Darling Pea to grow. For twenty or thirty years it took over and grew in masses. It is not only poisonous but addictive and does not provide enough nourishment to support life. Pea-struck animals eat nothing else. They lose condition rapidly. Their gait changes to a high-stepping stagger and

Details of the country north of the Liverpool Plains.

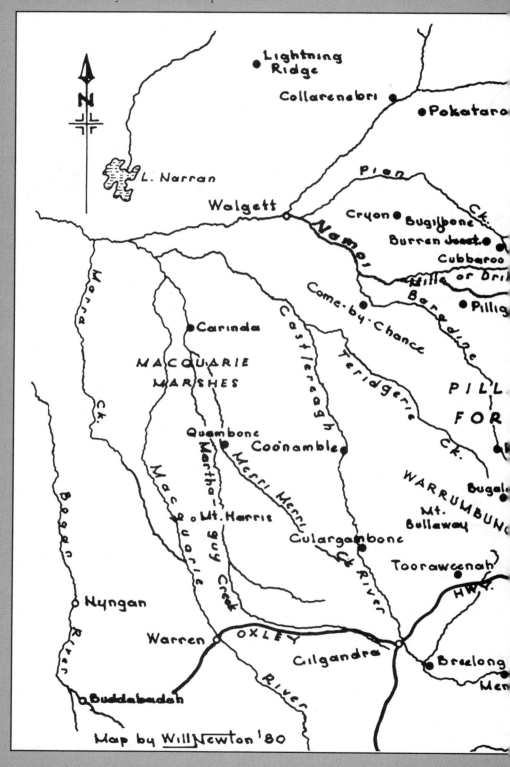

Map by Will Newton '80

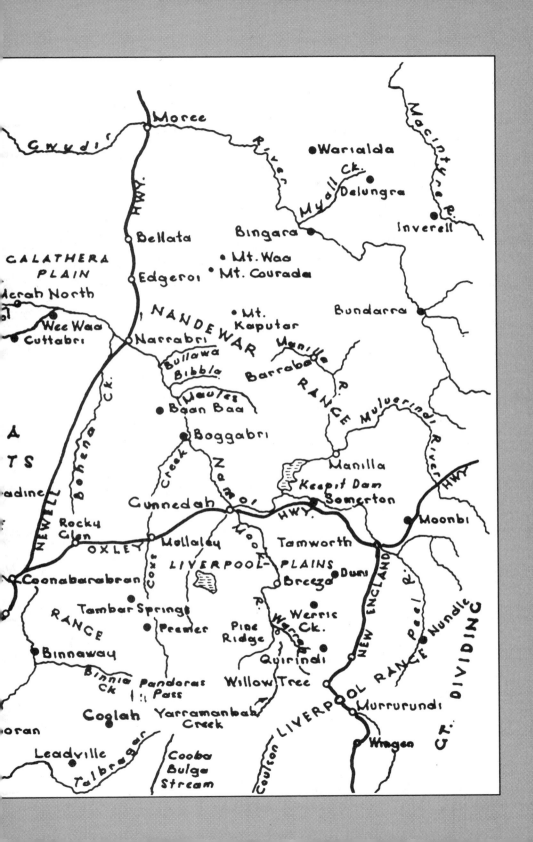

their expressions to a fixed stare. In the last few days before death some are compelled to walk in a straight line. I have seen a sheep, in a later wild growth of pea occasioned by rabbits in the 1930s, tramping endlessly with its head pressed against a fence post. Sometimes when an affected sheep walks into a tree the front hooves catch on the bark and the sheep lifts itself as high as it can reach with its front legs. It supports itself on its hind feet and beats against the trunk with its front hooves for hours.

The excess nitrogen provided by the Darling Pea changed the grasses. Fast-growing annual windmill grasses (*Chloris*) and umbrella grasses (*Digitaria*) soon predominated and crowded out the Darling Pea which likes bare spaces to grow in. Then the burry pods of imported medics that had spread through the Hunter and the central west of New South Wales were carried up in the wool of sheep. The seeds grew to provide nitrogen in place of the Darling Pea and, since medics grow well among grass, the new status of grasses has remained. The inferior imported Barley Grass (*Hordeum leporinum*) has spread over big areas, especially country that has been farmed. But the plains provide more stock feed now than they did one hundred and forty years ago and the fattening capacity has not deteriorated much.

William Wentworth also sent stock higher up the Namoi to a station called strangely The Monilla and Glen Riddle. Monilla was Manilla. The station spread on both sides of the Namoi and up the Manilla River on the north side. So Otto Baldwin on Diniwarindi must have been sharply squeezed to let him in. Indeed, eleven or twelve years later in the description each gave of his run in the 1848 *Government Gazette*, the boundaries along the Manilla River overlapped about three kilometres.

All stockmen, almost everybody travelling in the country, carried shotgun, rifle or pistol to shoot Aborigines, to shoot game, as a protection against the plentiful bushrangers. But nobody asserted his pride with his pistol like the gun-toting cowboys of American legend. Australian boundaries were settled by discussion, by fists, by swung whips and stirrup irons – nasty enough weapons – by Donald Mc-Lauchlin with his sword. Later they were settled by deceit, by bribery, by appeals to the Commissioner, by court cases pompous as jousts.

In 1836 or early 1837, possibly before Wentworth, possibly after, John Button, a storekeeper related distantly to Henry Dangar's wife Grace, sent a stockman named Prise (possibly a misspelling of Price) with a mob of cattle to form a station on the Namoi. He settled at Turrawan on the west bank of the river, the forest side, between the western portions of Baan Baa and Tiberenah. With Prise – nothing is known of him, not even his initials – came his wife, Mary. In the ten years since Ned Dwyer took his wife or companion over the Liverpool Range no other white woman is known to have crossed it. Surely she was the first non-Aboriginal woman on the Namoi.

While her husband tailed the beef cattle, Mary Prise managed the dairy. Cheese provided a quick income for many of the early stations. It was a return load for drays bringing up stores.

John Button was one of a dozen or more Dangar relatives near and distant who came to Australia. His brother Charles came out with him. By 1836 all five Dangar brothers were in Australia. The gregarious and ineffective Thomas came with William in 1825. Then followed John Hooper Dangar and lastly the youngest, Richard Cary Dangar. In addition, Henry Dangar's brother-in-law, James Sibly, came out with his wife, and Jeremiah Brice Rundle, a cousin. Samuel Wellington Cook and his wife, Elizabeth, sister of the Dangar brothers, came from Canada in 1837. For an uneasy year or two their business interests – mail runs, stores, inns, cattle and sheep stations, farms and surveying – all entwined.

William Nowland, tired of his cattle being disturbed at water on the Mooki by trespassing sheep, sent one herd in March 1837 beyond all others on the Namoi to the western end of a chain of lagoons, swamps and channels known as Drildool. In flood time this complex acts as an anabranch of the Namoi. East of Wee Waa brown water sweeps out in a northern curve through Merah and Cubbaroo and back into the Namoi west of Pilliga. In the 1970s it acted also as a drain for excess water from irrigated cotton fields.

The Aborigines resented William Nowland's intrusion and gave him a more difficult time than white neighbours on the plains. One of the stockmen was pinned to his saddle by a spear through his trousers.

Thomas Arndell, a Hunter River settler, sent some of George Loder's 1,500 head of cattle round to Merah to join William Nowland. He was the son of surgeon Thomas Arndell at whose funeral Andrew Doyle made such a fool of himself, and he was acting as executor for George Loder, his brother-in-law. Both the Loder brothers died in their late thirties when they were well on the way to becoming wealthy. George died first in 1834 and did not see the completion of the lovely two-storey house he was building. His widow, Mary, managed the inn they had bought from squatting profits and finished building the house which still stood in the main street of Windsor in 1979. She married Thomas Dargon after her sister, Eliza Dargon, died. He had been an innkeeper before he began farming. Andrew Loder was killed in a fall from his horse in 1836 when riding home to the Hunter from Kuwherindi. When their executors, John Wiseman, married to George Loder's daugther, Mary, and Thomas Arndell, drafted up the sheep, they counted out ten thousand each. Andrew had four thousand head of cattle in his own name, George fifteen hundred.

Joseph Onus also did not live long to enjoy his wealth. He died suddenly in 1835 at the age of fifty-four. So Ann Onus in 1836 made application as administratrix for a licence for Theribry. She knew it as Benial. She then owned, or held in trust for her young sons, two thousand hectares of farmland at Richmond and on the Wollombi Brook, five thousand ewes and two thousand cattle. William Sharp (he first spelt his name Shairp) who married her in February 1837 married a comfortable fortune. Since none of the Married Woman's Property Acts had then been passed, a woman's possessions became legally her husband's. He came to Australia as a free settler in 1826 with two thousand dollars, sufficient to establish him on a five hundred hectare farm on Wollombi Brook. As usual the land was not surveyed for years. When finally the surveyor pegged it, one boundary line cut off most of his newly cleared cultivation, another ran through the middle of a new house he was building. Ann Onus's brother, Thomas Eather, had been involved in a wrangle for seven years over blocks on the Wollombi Brook. Five men had to place themselves on a line of pegged farms. They mistook a waste piece of land as the first farm so each man worked the farm next to the one he had title for. They had crops growing and buildings up before a surveyor found the error.

During 1836 and 1837 there was also activity on the southern and western boundaries of the forest area. When the Coxes applied for their depasturing licences, William had turned Nombi over to George and Henry in partnership. They were running hundreds of cattle and thousands of sheep in the care of Antonio Roderick. They also listed fourteen children between them. George was married to Sophia Bell, sister of William Sims Bell, Henry to the daughter of a Bathurst settler. Now they sent a couple of flocks of sheep to join Edward's on the Castlereagh and formed a station first spelt Cooleburebarun. It changed by degrees to Coonabarabran.

Job Webster Cheeseborough, acting for J. B. Bettington who was prospering as a Sydney merchant and already had three stations on the Castlereagh or near it, sent cattle north round the eastern slopes of the Warrumbungles down Teridgerie Creek. On the plains where red soil changes to black, where Sandy Wilcox had caught George the Barber, he established Teredgere. Job Cheeseborough, an excellent manager, later took up a run in his own name and made a widespread reputation as a classer of merino sheep.

About the same time, late 1836 or early 1837, Andrew Brown, James Walker's outstanding manager, rode round the north-west end of the Warrumbungles with a mob of Walker's steers to grow and fatten into bullocks. He came the way of Oxley in 1818 and he came in person to select the station. Brown, a careful Scotsman, had a share of the steers and he kept close watch on his every asset. On Baradine Creek he found a long waterhole near where the town is now so he built a hut and settled the cattle down. He spelt the station Barradean. But the best fattening country was behind him, so he also claimed the rich black Goorianawa valley he had followed down from the slopes. Soon Barradean was regarded as an outstation of Curianawa.

The steers came from a string of well-established cattle and sheep stations Andrew Brown had chosen for himself and James Walker along the Castlereagh and southern and western slopes of the Warrumbungles. After the bad choice of Wallerawang and Cooerwull, Andrew Brown soon developed his eye. He put together some of the richest grassland in the world, a rare black soil found only on those slopes and about Coolah where the subsoil has some stone in it and the ground holds together in drought time instead of crazing like the mud in a dried dam. It grows Kurrajong instead of Myall.

The Rouse brothers who also built a private empire were not far behind Andrew Brown on the move to the Castlereagh. But of all the squatters who advanced to their squares on the map, Brown became the one undoubted king. He found little enough joy in it – he was too conventionally religious. He lived until he was 97 and was active until he died. For most of his years in Australia he kept a diary, a dreary enough record though a valuable one. Coupled with dozens of extant letters of James Walker's and letters and reminiscences of the Archer brothers who later worked for Walker before earning their own fame, Brown's diary shows in detail how these big stations strung out over three or four hundred kilometres were managed. But few of the manuscripts date before 1837 when most of the stations were functioning and nobody thought to tell when they began. That has to be searched for elsewhere, sometimes deduced.

In the winter of 1826 on the poor dry grass at Wallerawang James Walker had lost more than 400 of his crossbred sheep as well as 9 of his precious merinos. Nevertheless, in an application to buy more land in 1827, he stated he had 1,800 crossbred sheep, 64 merinos, 312 head of cattle and 15 horses. He certainly was not running all those on the eight hundred hectares of Wallerawang. Undoubtedly young Andrew Brown had already been scouting northward and he had sent shepherds and stockmen to feed the stock on unoccupied pockets of grass and water. William Walker, James's younger brother, held land to the north, four hundred hectares granted in 1825, at Lue, east of Mudgee, where the Rouse brothers were about to settle before they were told of Guntawang.

William Walker had prospered as a merchant and shipowner. He came to Sydney from Calcutta in 1813 as agent for a British shipping firm with a branch in India. His job in Australia was to establish another branch of the firm and to collect debts from Robert Campbell, a well-established shipping merchant who had been shaken in the depression that eventually broke Simeon Lord and almost broke the Blaxlands and many others. Robert Campbell's difficulties were caused by unpaid debts to him but he soon settled his own and remained a good friend of William Walker's even when William set up business in opposition.

When Andrew Brown explored to the Castlereagh in 1830 he was looking out for land for himself as well as James Walker. Convicts farmed ten hectares of his eighty hectare grant at Cooerwull but it was chosen mostly as a site for a water-driven flour mill. The remaining seventy hectares would not carry many of the 200 head of cattle and 300 sheep he had already earned as overseer.

James Walker bought and leased more land at Lue but Andrew Brown established the properties. James Walker also bought an interest in William's business and in 1831 the brothers went to London to form a branch. James intended to stay a short time only but he married his cousin, Robina Ramsay Walker, granddaughter of a Scottish laird, and the couple settled so comfortably in London James became unwilling to return. For seven busy years Andrew Brown had full charge of the farms and stock in Australia.

By 1833 he had moved his own stock and some of James Walker's to the Castlereagh and established Biambil (now Biamble) north-east of present Mendooran for James Walker, and Cuigan (now Caigan) immediately north for himself. Two good properties still retain those names. Then Andrew Brown went in search of a kingdom to stock as soon as he had the numbers.

Andrew Brown got on well with the Aborigines and they directed him to good country but in almost sixty years of diary entries he never mentioned them. Nor did he ever exult in his own strength, yet he was so well built, when he stripped to wash in the Castlereagh, the well-muscled Aborigines felt his arms and legs in wonder. Instead, especially as his wealth grew, he made fatuous January references to the Grace of the Good Lord Who had carried him successfully through yet another year.

Early in 1834 eighteen-year-old David Archer, James Walker's nephew, arrived at Wallerawang to learn Australian ways under Andrew Brown. He was the first of nine Archer brothers who eventually came to Australia, sons of William Archer, an unsuccessful Scottish timber merchant who settled in Norway.

David Archer helped Andrew Brown in the establishment of the Castlereagh stations. Those who now live on that river love to tell visitors it is the only river in the world that flows to all points of the compass. Certainly it does flow to all points. It comes out of the Warrumbungles flowing east past Coonabarabran, turns south past Binnaway, south-east past Mendooran, then, in big undecided sweeps, it heads in a general westerly direction to Gilgandra. In its wanderings between those towns a series of big and little creeks come into it on both banks. At Gilgandra it straightens out and changes course again. It flows north-west through Gulargambone to Coonamble, north for a stretch, then west into the Macquarie and with it into the Barwon.

Andrew Brown and David Archer began exploring up into creeks running south and west out of the Warrumbungles into the Castlereagh: Yarragrin, Gundy, Bidden, Mogie Melon, Wallumburrawang, Tooraweenah, Nullen, all anglicised Aboriginal names. They established stations on each of them and named them after their watering-points. Wallerawang remained headquarters for James Walker. Andrew Brown lived there though he was developing Cooerwull as his own headquarters. The new stations spreading north from them consisted at first of the usual slab hut with a stockman or two in charge of a hundred head of cattle, or one or two shepherds with three or four hundred sheep each, a hutkeeper, and portable wooden hurdles to secure the sheep from Dingoes at night. For several years the shepherds drove the sheep back to Lue or Wallerawang for shearing. It was much easier to move the wool on their backs than carry bales in drays where there were no roads.

Young Charles Darwin called in at Wallerawang in January 1836 towards the end of his five years of wandering and observing as naturalist aboard H.M.S. *Beagle*. The shearing of 15,000 sheep cut out the day he got there and more men than usual were about. Darwin found the all male atmosphere unsettling. 'Although the farm was well stocked with every requisite, there was an apparent absence of comfort: and not even a single woman resided here. The sunset of a fine day will generally cast an air of happy contentment on any scene: but here, at this retired farm-house, the brightest tints on the surrounding woods could not make me forget that forty hardened, profligate men were ceasing from their daily labours, like the slaves from Africa, yet without their just claim for compassion.'

The next morning to cheer him up David Archer took him on a kangaroo hunt but not one could be found. 'It may be long before these animals are altogether exterminated', wrote Darwin, 'but their doom is fixed.' It was bad prophecy. Most of the bigger kangaroos after an initial set-back thrived on settlement. After 'bad sport' but 'a pleasant ride' Andrew Brown took Charles Darwin along pools in Coxs River that runs through Wallerawang and showed him Platypuses swimming. He shot one for Darwin who marvelled at its head and beak. The stuffed specimens he had seen were shrivelled and out of shape.

The copy of Darwin's book I read was published by Henry Colburn in London in 1839. It was the first edition of the first of many publishers to publish Darwin's first work. I always ask for the oldest edition of a work in a library. The excitement of handling rare books sharpens the imagination. This book was particularly rare. It had been David Scott Mitchell's own – his signature was in it. It was one of the books that founded the great Mitchell Library. Yet nobody had ever read it. The pages were uncut.

Darwin correctly sensed the atmosphere where numbers of convicts worked. They were intractable employees, most of them, and their employers and overseers intractable masters. There was a too widespread belief that a monthly flogging was encouraging. In four months of 1836 at Bathurst about two hundred local employees averaged over fifty lashes each. These were given for trivial offences. Several of James Walker's employees were brought in on more serious charges. 'The two flocks of ewes got mixed up', stated one hutkeeper in evidence, 'and after two days attempting to separate them the shepherds agreed to take them into Loowee to be drafted. The following morning they were late and I called them twice to get up. The second time I called them, both the prisoners rushed out. The prisoners Rogers said that he would get me . . . He laid hold of an axe and made two or three strokes at me with it. He then flung the axe at me. After that he struck me with a shovel . . .' David Archer testified that the hutkeeper was covered in blood.

Andrew Brown took four violent employees of James Walker's

before the magistrates during 1836. All were sentenced 'to be worked in irons for 12 calendar months and returned to his assignee at the expiration of his sentence'. Did they come back to Wallerawang smiling and eager to work?

James Walker in London was encouraging free emigrants into his employ. He wrote to William Archer, now in Norway, of sending out four Highland shepherds, three of them married, and farm workers from Ayrshire with others anxious to go.

William Brown, Andrew's brother, a millwright, came out to build the watermill at Cooerwull. James Walker chose the millstones and shipped them out, a pair of French burrs. Andrew Brown decided to concentrate on his own affairs. He wrote to James Walker that he wished to go home for a year or two and that David Archer would soon be capable of taking over from him as manager.

James Walker arranged for David to be joined by two of his brothers, William and fifteen-year-old Thomas. 'We have so many people coming home here', James Walker wrote to their father in 1837, 'that the idea of the remoteness of Australia is quite changed'. He began to think of going back himself. 'Since we have heard of A.B. wishing to come home, my wife is really anxious to go out and see the place.' But James Walker's asthma was troubling him and he could not stir himself. 'He vacillates incessantly and is unstable as water,' his nephew, Edward, wrote of him, 'I doubt whether he would be able to do much even if he went out.'

It was his asthma that finally drove him to action. In the summer of 1838 he decided he could not survive another winter in England and he arrived in Sydney with his wife in April 1839, a few months before Andrew Brown sailed home to marry his cousin, Christina Henderson. It was common policy among the wealthy to marry relations to keep the wealth within the family. A year or two before he left, probably by the end of 1837, Andrew Brown had the big network of Walker and Brown stations functioning efficiently as two units.

Four of Walker's best stations were well north of Brown's complex: Yoolandry on the Castlereagh south of present Coonamble, Coonamble itself, first spelt Conambril, Magometon to the east named after a little hill some old men still pronounce in the Aboriginal fashion, Makomadine, and Goorianawa farther east running down to Baradine. The first track from Coonamble to Baradine passed only over Walker property. Between Magometon and Goorianawa there were waterless black plains. Mule trains carried supplies in before dray tracks were cut.

The Australian Agricultural Company used mules down the rough Peel Line William Telfer cut to Gloucester and the company brought in South American muleteers to handle them. Cobb and Co. later used mules to haul coaches on dry Queensland runs. They are hardier than horses under extreme conditions. But mules soon lost favour when wire fences were built. A fence was no barrier to a mule and too often they were not to be found in their paddocks when needed.

Biamble became Walker's main sheep station employing over sixty men (no women) by 1839. Yoolandry was the main cattle-breeding station. Coonamble began as an out-station to it: a hut and one stockman with a mob of heifer weaners to be kept away from the bulls till they were old enough to mate. The steers, the castrated male weaners, were driven sixty kilometres to the bullock station, Goorianawa, to fatten. Two men only ran Goorianawa and Baradine for years. When a draft of bullocks was fat, a stockman, usually George Gibson, rode up with an Aboriginal boy from Wallerawang, cut them out and drove them back the same way over the mountains to market in Sydney.

An astonishingly close check was kept on these distant stations. Every two or three months someone in authority rode round them, counting the cattle and sheep, listing the supplies needed, loading the cheeses cured at the well-manned sheep stations, and the occasional keg of salt-preserved butter for sale. Andrew Brown usually inspected his own stations, a round trip of about eight hundred kilometres. Illumurgulia (a name retained only in the parish of Allamurgoola) stretching on both sides of the Castlereagh near present Gulargambone, was his chief cattle station in 1838. It was well managed by John Hall. Andrew Brown found him in June 1838 'at plough putting in wheat' and received a present from him that was rare where there were no women: three chickens. On the way home at Caigan he loaded the drays with 500 cheeses for sale in Sydney. They weighed probably eight to ten kilograms each. Pressed with stone-weighted wooden levers, then wrapped in brine-soaked woollen cloths and cured in bark-covered dug-outs in the dairy houses, the usual station cheese was too salty, too hard, yellow and greasy, but it sold readily enough and paid well enough to make. Brown depended on it to cover much of the running expenses of the stations. Illumurgulia alone was soon producing two tonnes of butter and cheese a year.

By August Andrew Brown was back at Cooerwull seeing to ploughing for wheat, a very late sowing. He drafted off fourteen head of poor cattle and sent them to fatten at one of the out-stations in the care of two Aboriginal boys. Small numbers of stock were frequently moved from station to station. As few as three head of fat bullocks for rations were sometimes driven two or three hundred kilometres. The fat mobs sent to Sydney usually numbered a hundred to a hundred and fifty. He drafted off 652 'wedders' for market in Sydney with nine to be delivered on the road, ration sheep that someone had bought. Both the educated and the uneducated frequently used dd for th. I found a delightful character outside the scope of this book nicknamed Boddered Joe.

As soon as his ploughing was finished, Andrew Brown rode three hundred and fifty kilometres to Baradine to see to the drafting of Walker's bullocks. George Gibson started for Sydney with 150 head, 120 of them Walker's and thirty as Brown's share. On the way back Andrew Brown called into Tooraweenah, one of his sheep stations, to make a count. 'Found three flocks of sheep there' he noted in his diary 1 October 1838, 'tho not feed or water sufficient for one. Marked lambs in Conley and James's flocks and counted them

James's flock	ewes	384	
	wethers	4	
male lambs		184	
females lambs		193	
wethers killed		1	
died ewes		5	since last muster
Conley's flock	ewes	385	ought to be 397
ewe lambs		170	
male lambs		125	
Counted Duttons flock			
	rams	30	
	wethers	376'	

He told James and Conley to take their flocks about twelve kilometres north to better feed in the open forest along Tunderbrine Creek, hold them there till the 27 or 28 October, then bring them back sixty kilometres south-east to Caigan for shearing. Since they had to camp out he allowed them to draw an extra ration between them for four weeks. They would not have had saddle horses – shepherds were not thought to be worth them – but a couple of pack-horses or mules to carry their flour, sugar, tea and salt meat and a couple of sheepskin rugs wrapped, perhaps, in a sheet of canvas as their only protection from the weather. They would have had dogs of some kind, though

good sheepdogs were still very rare in 1838. Once on Tunderbrine
Creek they would have cut branches or hauled logs to build a temporary yard for the sheep at night. While travelling they would have
had to camp the sheep in the open. And Conley could afford to lose no
more. The twelve sheep he had already lost would have cost him six
months wages. Yet a shepherd's life was thought to be so easy his pay
was lowest of all.

In between inspections in the last months of 1838 Andrew Brown was
seeing to the building of a woolshed and yards for Walker on Biamble,
to his own sheep-washing and shearing and wool-scouring at Caigan,
and to the building of a house at Cooerwull for the bride he was to
bring there.

The building of a good house was a complicated sequence of jobs
that had to be done on the site. Before the carpenters could hammer a
nail, the blacksmith had to make it. Before the bricklayers could lay a
brick, the brickmaker had to find suitable clay to make the bricks and
build a kiln to bake them. But before the kiln could be built masons had
to find suitable stone and cut it. Then there was limestone to be carted
and fired in another kiln for mortar, and a pit to be dug for the sawyers
since their long saw was drawn vertically through the logs. Axemen
had to cut the logs and bullock-drivers haul them to the sawyers and
the shingle splitter. Dray loads of dry wood had to be carted to the
kilns. Sandstone had to be cut for flagging. The glazier mixed his put-
ty, made his frames and cut his glass. The painter stirred his heavy
pigments into oil. And all did their jobs well. Most of the house was still
in use after 140 years.

By September 1839 Andrew Brown was aboard ship on his way
home and a rare personal picture he gave of himself in his diary is not a
pleasant one: 'I fired at several albatross without effect the shot having
no impression. At last one rising so high over as to permit the shot to
strike under the wing it fell immediately.'

The Rouse brothers, John Richard and Edwin who took up Guntawang, George, their younger brother, and Richard, their father,
built a wider network than Walker and Brown, though none of them
held as much as individuals, nor did they live so long. In their various names they fitted between the Lawsons and the Coxs on the
Cudgegong and the Talbragar, they travelled down the Macquarie as
far as a waterhole named Warren (now a pleasant town), and they were
later among the first on the Barwon. On the Castlereagh they took up
Mundoran (now the town of Mendooran), Breelong where Jimmy and
Joe Governor began their long wild run, and a couple of other stations

adjoining it, then they drove a big mob of sheep up the Wallum-burrawang Creek past several Walker and Brown stations to the headwaters and formed Woronbongles. It lay between the present Warrumbungle National Park and the Coonabarabran – Gilgandra road. Edwin Rouse took charge of it himself with sixteen free men and eleven convicts under him. When he went there, probably in 1836, the nearest stock to the east were George and Henry Cox's sheep at Coonabarabran. From Woronbongles (later called Terraconang-adgere) they spread south-east down other creeks. They later vacated the highest country and moved out of this story. The great crooked R brand passed down and in the 1970s was in use by Richard's great-great-grandson. Other versions of crooked Rs are used by other members of the family. Richard Rouse's lovely home still stands in fine order at Rouse Hill, and up to 1978 it had been continuously occupied by six generations of the family, till the Hamiltons and the Terrys, both descendants, one family upstairs, the other downstairs, rocked the old house's future with bitter quarrelling.

North of the Namoi there was a temporary halt to settlement during 1837. The stockmen Thomas Arndell sent to Merah were so frightened of the Aborigines, they abandoned the Loder's cattle and returned to safety. Alexander Paterson, the first Commissioner of Crown Lands for the Liverpool district, rode up from his headquarters at Jerrys Plains north-west of Singleton to inspect the stations in October 1837. Merah is almost four hundred kilometres from Jerrys Plains which is south of the Liverpool Range, but no nearer accommodation was provided. At most stations Paterson was told that though the feed was good the cattle were poor because the Aborigines frightened them and kept them unsettled. While on the Namoi he was told that two of George Bowman's stockmen had been killed on Terry Hie Hie when they tried to seize two Aboriginal women, so he rode across to confirm it, admiring the feed on the way but regretting the lack of water. Then he rode north to the Big River, as the Gwydir was called when it reached the plains, where two more men had been killed. An intelligent Aboriginal boy who spoke fair English said three white men lived with the Aborigines and incited the raids.

No search was made for the white men. Major Nunn rode up from the Hunter with a squad of mounted police and shot enough Aborigines to keep them quiet for a while. Merah was settled again. Loders held it for years.

Alex Paterson had to resign a few months later: '. . . riding has again

brought back my complaint with a severity that renders it torture to sit
on horseback.' And David Thomson, Royal Naval surgeon at Inver-
mein, now Scone, certified that he was 'labouring under a fistula in
ano at present in a state of great irritation'.

Perhaps Nunn's expedition gave confidence of police protection,
perhaps men were simply ready to move, but much land north and
south of the Namoi was filled in during 1838. John Button, the Cornish
postmaster and keeper of Thomas Dangar's inn and store on Pages
River, near present Murrurundi, extended from Turrawan, and sent
cattle round to fit in at Cubbaroo between William Nowland's Drildool
and Loder's Merah. Overreaching himself, he formed another run on
a little creek in the plains to the north and another opposite Cubbaroo
on the south side of the Namoi on Bullerawa Creek, a short creek that
now begins in the Pilliga forest and flows north through grazing and
farm land into the Namoi.

William Nowland was not for long the man farthest down the
Namoi. Charles Purcell sent surplus cattle from Girriwillie to
Tureeweewah only fifty kilometres from the Barwon at Walgett and
George Druitt sent cattle off the Yaminba and Borah Creeks to Mille
joining William Nowland on the west. By the next year more of
Druitt's cattle were way up on the Boomi anabranch of the Barwon,
and at Brewana (now Brewarrina) where the Barwon washes over a
long sandstone shelf and becomes the Darling. It was on this shelf that
the Aborigines had built the intricate Brewarrina fisheries, four hundred metres of stone-walled paddocks as wide as the river with entrances to trap fish swimming upstream or downstream. The paddocks
led to a maze of smaller yards and ended finally in cul-de-sacs with big
stones at the narrow entrances to be rolled across after the laughing
splashing crowd drove the fish in. It was a ceremonial ground and a
feasting ground whenever muddy freshes set big numbers of fish moving. The yards were damaged when the first paddle-wheel steamers
scraped over them in the 1860s. As the river trade increased the
Aborigines decreased and there were soon insufficient to maintain the
walls. A weir was built at the site and now white and black assemble
when the fish are moving to snatch them as they jump up the fish
ladders.

Other men joined George Druitt on the creeks flowing through the
red and yellow sandy soils. George Druitt had moved east off the
Yaminba Creek. He held the better land on nearby Borah Creek and
extended east to the black downs watered by a little creek called

Bullumbulla that flows via other creeks into Coxs. So the name Yamingabee was lost. When Charles Fitzsimmons brought cattle to the same creek he heard the name as Yaminginba. He drove sheep west to the Bugaldi Creek that joined Baradine Creek on the west bank near James Walker's Barradean hut. The land he occupied on both stations now juts into the Pilliga forest as good farm land. Charles Fitzsimmons might have lived on one of them – when he bought two blocks in Brisbane in 1842 he gave his address as Liverpool Plains – but although he held them for seventeen years he left nothing to identify him. He is a name with no flesh.

James Evans, a Gloucestershire 'farmer's man' sentenced to seven years in 1820 who prospered as a settler and innkeeper, sent sheep and cattle to Dandry Creek (Oxley's Wiltden Valley) that follows much the same path east of Baradine Creek as Bugaldi Creek follows on the west. Some of his stockmen continued on down the creek with cattle, past Walker's Baradine, to where the creek breaks up into gullies running into the Namoi. There they formed Bungulgully, a station that added to Evans's prosperity and that his family held for a hundred years or so.

Young John Robertson formed his station in the forest he liked so well, Garrowramere, spreading across Borah and Yaminba creeks downstream from Druitt and Fitzsimmons, but he stocked it with cattle instead of the sheep he first favoured. He made no money on it, nobody made any money on it – it was a disaster as a station. But it is fascinating because of the men involved with it. None of them were fools. It looked to be good grazing land. What grew in the forest before sheep and cattle changed it?

Garrowramere and the land to the north-east of Bohena Creek was ironbark forest as the colonists understood forest. Botanists who like the sound of foreign terms would call it savannah woodland. It was grassland with scattered big straight Narrow-leaf Ironbarks (*Eucalyptus crebra*) spaced about fifty metres apart. There were few young trees. The frequent fires of the Aborigines and the plentiful rat-kangaroos that eat young trees stopped almost all regrowth. Here and there patches of young trees that missed being eaten shot up till they were safe from fire and grew into the sort of ironbark scrub Oxley reported. When Garrowramere had neighbours and boundaries more or less defined, it was known as Arrarownie. It then contained the dense scrub of ironbarks Oxley had passed through in the sapling stage in 1818.

South-west of Narrabri swinging in a wide arc between Bohena

Creek and Coghill Creek at Cuttabri was a Brigalow forest so thick the roots laced together on the surface, and five metres off the ground the long shiny leaves crowded in a canopy grey as galvanised iron. Wherever there was a clearing big clumps of Brigalow Grass (a *Paspalidium*) thrived on the nitrogen produced by the Brigalow.

All the rest of the area, perhaps 600,000 hectares, was a pine forest (*Callitris columellaris*), broken in places by Bimble Box flats or Yellow Box slopes or stretches of Belar or oak, even belts of stringybark on the southern hills. The pines also were big and straight and they were in the last hundred years of their lives. Over much of the area they were spaced even wider apart than the ironbarks.

Among both pine and ironbark grew a scattering of other species of eucalypts, of casuarina, of acacia, cassia, hopbush, and so many others – a small showing of the modern profusion. But the ridges that form a grid through all the south and the east carried heavy growth then as now. It was scrub. No tree dominated in height or in numbers. It was the seedbank of shrubs and flowers and the nursery of insect-eating birds.

The plants that interested the squatters as feed for cattle and sheep were dominantly summer grasses. One species of Early Spring Grass (*Eriochloa*) grew as well on the sandy plains as the other grew on the black plains. The excellent Blue Grass (*Dichanthium*) grew on box flats and Darby's Oats (*Arundinella*) along creeks. The tall Oat Grass and Kangaroo Grass (two species of *Themeda*) grew on sandhills. Any sand-hill near a hut was always fenced in as a choice horse paddock. There was Silky Browntop (*Eulalia*) and several species of umbrella grass (*Digitaria*) and the bulky but less valuable panics. Where rat-kangaroos were plentiful not much grew except the inedible *Triodia*, usually called Spinifex because of its resemblance to that coastal grass. The little mar-supials made nests within its spiky clumps and kept everything else around them well eaten down. So they made room for the Spinifex to spread.

Among the grasses grew yellow vine (a smaller leaved species to the one that favoured black soil), crowsfoot, docks, the little rhagodia (saltbush) and pigweed that is good feed if eaten with other plants but poisonous with oxalic acid if hungry stock eat too much. Aborigines harvested the pink-fleshed pigweed (*Portulaca*) when it was seeding and piled it into mounds. After a few days they turned it and shook it and the tiny black seeds fell thickly on the ground like a pile of gunpowder.

Then they ground it with round stones as pestles and flat stones as mortars, mixed it into a paste with water and ate it, sometimes raw, sometimes baked in ashes, and fattened on it amazingly during its brief season.

Nitrogen was supplied by trees and shrubs of acacia and cassia and up to twenty species of showy peaflowers.

The effect of European stock on the sandy soil grasses was more immediate than on the blacksoil grasses. It was worst on the worst country – the acid country, the country very low in phosphorous like Arrarownie. As on the Hunter and the Nepean the spongy soil grew hard, especially where sheep were shepherded. The same inferior grasses took over as on the Nepean: Red Leg Grass, Spear Grass, Wire Grass.

There was much activity in the Dangar family during 1838, all of it unpleasant. James Sibly, put in charge of the Pages River Inn, had set out to drink his way through the cellar. In less than twelve months his wife left him and the inn failed. And since Thomas Dangar was no businessman and John Button little better, the store and mail run John Button was managing failed together with the Bird in Hand at Scone that Thomas Dangar was managing. The sheriff took over and advertised sales of property unless the debts of 'Dangars and others' were paid forthwith. Henry Dangar, lost for a while in the confusion and the resulting family squabbles, advertised all his property for sale, even the farms on Kingdon Ponds he had fought so hard for. But his brother, William, helped him save his empire (there were then 22,000 sheep and 3,000 cattle on it) and so did the Sydney money-lender, Thomas Burdekin, at enormous interest. His forty per cent was the final destroyer of Benjamin Singleton, but the Dangars extricated themselves. Jeremiah Brice Rundle took over the management of post office and store from John Button whose name continued to show as licensee of the Namoi River stations. He was probably nominal holder only – Rundle and William Dangar owned them.

In the midst of the money troubles another calamity that eventually rocked the whole Colony overtook Henry Dangar: the vile massacre in June 1838 of the forty or fifty remnants of a tribe of Aborigines on Henry Dangar's Myall Creek station north-east of Bingara on the edge of the New England.

The mountain Aborigines were originally helpful to the stockmen. They directed them to good land and water. Relations soured when stockmen and shepherds stole women or wantonly destroyed the remarkable wallaby nets knotted out of Kurrajong fibre. The Aborigines speared sheep and cattle for no more than their kidney fat. Fat was such a treat to them it was given a mystic quality and was always torn out of slain enemies. So there was shooting and spearing, turn for turn.

Under Old Daddy, an unusually tall, amiable Aborigine, a tribe had settled down in Myall Creek and neighbouring stations. Some of the women slept willingly with the stockmen. The stockmen laughed and played with the Aboriginal children. In June when Hobbs, Dangar's superintendent, left for a few days, a party of stockmen picked up pistols, guns and swords and rode to where the Aborigines were making camp near one of the huts. Those of the tribe in the camp made no protest. The women slung their babies on their backs and stood quietly while the stockmen tied men, women and children together by the necks on a throwing rope. Then they led them away. Old Daddy who was not tied walked beside them crying with a couple of untied children who said they would follow their mothers. Where there was plenty of dead timber to burn them, the stockmen slashed their heads off with their swords. John Johnston who rode to Gunnedah with George Bowman was among them. Next day they rode the mountains in search of the rest of the tribe that had been away. They gave no sound reason for the massacre. It was suggested they might have been ordered to clear the run of Aborigines.

Governor Gipps, appalled, brought the stockmen to trial and in doing so appalled the squatters. Few of those associated with squatting had not killed Aborigines. Henry Dangar engaged three counsel to defend them and opened a subscription list to pay the fees. Money poured in. Nevertheless seven of the stockmen were hanged. Nobody, black or white, had thought it possible.

And it had the opposite effect to that desired. Aborigines from Port Phillip to the Moonie River in Queensland, all well aware of the incident, developed a 'Ha, ha! You can't touch me' attitude. They speared sheep and taunted their shepherds or cut steak from living bullocks. When found cutting up a speared beast one Aborigine told a stockman, 'You're ogle-eyed. It's a kangaroo.' On both sides the need for revenge deepened.

But settlement never slackened. The Barwon filled in during 1839. That was the year William Lawson sent cattle there. Young Thomas Parnell married to Isabella Doyle, big Andrew's sister, sent round surplus cattle from Bull. Many others moved out. Thomas Eather from

Henriendi went beyond them all, an extraordinary move to Muggarie on the Narran River near present Angledool, over a hundred kilometres north-west of the junction of the Namoi and Barwon. Thomas Eather and the men he left there must have been able to get along with Aborigines. The station was so remote that even when it was described nine years later for the 1848 *Government Gazette* there were no neighbours. In 1847 three of Thomas Eather's young nephews, Abraham, Thomas and James, were working at the station. Abraham, one of his brothers and two other young men left to bring up more cattle. By the time they got back with the mob, probably a couple of months later, the waterholes had dried up. John Griffiths, an orphan reared with the family, died of thirst. The others abandoned the cattle and barely got through. Aborigines found them and helped them in.

At the Coonabarabran station in 1839 relations with the Aborigines were not pleasant. Graham Hunter, the Commissioner of Crown Lands for the Bligh district wrote to the Colonial Secretary from his headquarters at Coolah (spelt usually Cooler, or sometimes Cooler Creek, and once, Coolerbarrendine), 2 September 1839: '. . . I found the Superintendent (R. Heening) living with an aboriginal black woman I immediately warned him of the consequences and took the woman, gave her to the black whom she belonged On my return to this place I found from the black whom the woman belonged that R. Heening and a ticket of leave man of the name of Hugh Griffis had come after the black with a pistol and taken the woman from him . . .'

So George and Henry Cox's superintendent, Roger Heenan, lost his depasturing licence and Hugh Griffiths lost his ticket and became a convict again.

Edward Mayne, the new Commissioner for Liverpool Plains, was critical of the squatters. '. . . In no country . . . could they have ventured to do with impunity what they have tried to do here The universal practice has been to proceed with a large herd of cattle and sheep and sit down in any part that may best suit them and then leave that property often to the value of thousands of pounds in the care of a couple of men . . . neither of them of responsible character . . .'

Tamworth was developing as a village when Mayne became Commissioner. James Charles White, a clerk with the Australian Agricultural Company, had set up as a storekeeper there in November 1835. It was an ideal site: both the busy head station of the company's Peel River sheep stations and the camping ground for teamsters taking supplies from Maitland north to the New England or west down the Namoi. The Reverend William Cowper, the company's chaplain,

rode up from Port Stephens, a month-long trip, for annual church
services.

But an autocratic man, brother of the London Police Commissioner,
Edward Mayne moved down the Peel about thirty kilometres from
Tamworth, where he was expected to set up his headquarters, and
built a house and office he called Summer Hill on 130 hectares sliced off
the western boundary of Robert Pringle's Bubbogullian. The modern
village on the red hill is now called Somerton. Then he began
speculating in cattle that another brother, Captain William Mayne,
ran on the shares for him on Warialda station on the edge of the New
England. He borrowed the money and he paid twenty to eighty dollars
a head for cows at the top of the boom in prices caused by the scramble
to stock new land.

In 1841 Edward Mayne took up a station in his own name, Pian
Creek, an anabranch shooting off the Merah-Drildool anabranch.
That was not illegal, indeed the Legislative Council in 1839 had
specially made it legal for Commissioners to hold land, but although all
his Commissioners dabbled Governor Gipps was strongly against it.
Edward Mayne bought Pian (it would have been worth little more than
the cattle on it) from Mary Prise. She put her lopsided cross on the
document of sale.

Her husband, John Button's stockman, died in 1838. Mary Prise
managed the station as well as the dairy until 1840 when John Button
scraped up enough money to return to England, and his brother,
Charles, took over as nominal licensee. By then Mary Prise had one
hundred and fifty head of cattle as her own and her husband's share as
pay, so she sent a stockman downriver to find her a station. She held it
for a few months only before selling to Mayne. Although she could
neither read nor write she was wise enough to sell out as soon as the
price of cattle began to slip. Mayne held the run for another twelve
months until the water dried up, then he moved those cattle also to
Warialda. He delayed paying his licence fee for several months then
assessed himself a low fine. Governor Gipps was furious.

During the three years from 1839 to 1841 William Osborn, still
managing for Charles Ezzy, moved seven or eight hundred head of cattle off the Liverpool Plains round to the good station, Molly, between
the Brigalow scrub and the Namoi River with Bohena Creek as the
eastern boundary. Gilchrist and Alexander, names only, came to Wee
Waa on the north side of the Namoi and in doing so squeezed the
Loder's cattle on Merah farther up the anabranch. It must have been

an amicable arrangement – one of the Loders managed for them. Wrongly spelt with a wrong initial, it is impossible to tell which.

Mayne and Boydell, probably the Commissioner's brother and Charles Boydell from the Hunter, briefly took up Gunadaddy, a big stretch of country between Druitt's Bullumbulla and Edward Cox's Namoi Hut. The first simple spelling of that station changed first to Gullandaddah, then to Ghoolendaadi, names that look more Aboriginal but are probably much farther away from the pronunciation. Sometimes it was known as Melville Plains, a jarring name among the Aboriginal names, however distorted they were. After the squatters left Bathurst and the Hunter behind them, where all farms were named reminiscently, they asked the Aborigines where they were and so named their stations, but the British are wretched linguists and the words were heard so badly it is profitless to give meanings to them. All names had meanings in Aboriginal languages. Not even names of persons existed simply as sounds.

Even those with knowledge of the language made absurd mistakes. 'What does *guida* mean?' asked Reverend W. Ridley who published *The Kamilaroi Language* in 1866. He was seeking a meaning for the Gwydir River. 'A red place' the Aborigines told him. So he translated Gwydir as 'river of red banks'. 'This river . . . was named in honour of Rt. Honourable Lord Gwydir' Allan Cunningham wrote when he crossed it in 1827.

The Kamilaroi language was spoken between the Liverpool Range and the Moonie River in the north, from New England west to the Barwon. And except in onomatopoeic words like *Kukuraka*, the Laughing Kookaburra, each syllable had a meaning but, as in Chinese, two or three syllables together usually added to a new meaning. Kamilaroi was an intricate and gutturally musical language. Each syllable of a word carried equal strength. Nouns, pronouns, participles and verbs were declined by suffixes and there were more cases and more tenses than in English. There was an emphatic imperative as well as a normal imperative and also a taunting imperative. Irony was part of the Kamilaroi character.

Consonants were spaced by vowels. If an Aborigine tried to pronounce doctor he said *dokeda*, pumpkin became *pumuken*. When two vowels came together they were separated by a gasped aspirate, sometimes sucked in, sometimes blown out. George Bowman's station, Terry Hie Hie, was pronounced *Turry aih hai* and used both aspirates. I have heard old white men with little education say it that way. They had seen no anglicised version of the name to confuse their memories of how it was pronounced.

There were no separate sounds for *b* and *p*. There was a sound made with the lips halfway between the English positions for those letters. The sounds *d* and *t*, *g* and *k* were distinguished but there was much less distinction than in English. If a Kamilaroi Aborigine had tried to repeat *big bucket*, *pick pocket*, *be buggered*, what he said would sound the same for each, though his ear was so excellent he would recognise a difference. European pronunciation of Aboriginal words was worse.

Five different meanings have been given for Narrabri by Europeans who knew Kamilaroi all based on *ra* as the second syllable. Since the first spelling was Nunebey it might have been *na* which would alter the meaning. Any meanings for Coonabarabran are based on *coona* as the first two syllables. They were probably *coola*. Not even the two or three speakers of Kamilaroi still alive in the 1970s could tell what the names of towns and stations meant. Nobody knows what the names were.

Robert Williams whose cattle went to Boggibrie station died at the end of 1839. He left the station to Charlotte Eather, the mother of his children. John Panton, a busy Sydney merchant and eldest son of the postmaster-general, administered the station for her as executor for twenty-two years. Even after he bought land on the Darling Downs, John Panton kept close watch on Boggibrie from his home at Ipswich.

Andrew Doyle's two young brothers, Cyrus and Bartholomew, joined him during 1839. Young Francis might have come up then, too, although he was only fourteen. They brought up several hundred sheep which they took south across the Namoi to Cooma and Thurradulba. They moved a couple of drafts of cattle off Nurrabry down, too. Bohena Creek separated them from Molly on their west. Thurradulba joined John Robertson's Garrowramere. They sent one flock of sheep belonging to their father, Cyrus, farther east and formed Willylaw between a range of low hills, now known as the Willala hills, and the north-west corner of Edward Cox's Namoi Hut.

In 1840, Patrick Quinn, with permission from the Maitland bench of magistrates, came up to work for Andrew Doyle on a ticket-of-leave. These combined passports and work permits were granted to well-behaved convicts after they had served about half their terms. Those sentenced to life had to wait eight to ten years. Since a man with a ticket was free to work for anybody and was paid wages like any workman, some vicious masters sought excuse to delay the issue. The tickets were not free. An annual fee of one dollar had to be paid for renewal until a pardon was granted. That was no trivial sum – as a percentage of average wages it amounted to about one hundred dollars in 1979. Some men found themselves too sick to work. There are pathetic references in contemporary newspapers to 'wretched-looking' men surrendering tickets because they could not support themselves.

Patrick Quinn arrived in Australia in 1831 on the eighth trip of the *Asia* from Ireland. 'Nil reads/writes' his shipping indent stated, '. . . Native place – Clare laborer offence – unlawful oaths tried Clare 2.6.1831 Life no former convictions 5' 5¾ ", ruddy freckled complexion, sandy hair, light brown eyes. Remarks – right middle finger turned backwards.'

He was convicted for swearing oaths to a secret society. Probably he had been one of the Whiteboys, Roman Catholics acting against the Protestants who were seizing their land by English law. There are no men more violent than those who think they have the backing of God. The Andrew Doyles had sought to save their possessions, their right to work, even their right to vote, by turning Protestant. Thousands of the Irish upper class changed religion.

But Patrick Quinn got on well with the Doyles. He soon had his conditional pardon which gave him full freedom in Australia but barred his return to Ireland. By 1843 he was overseer at Nurrabry. By 1845 he managed it while Andrew Doyle managed Killarney, an extension immediately to the north.

Some of the men who took up stations about 1840 are unidentifiable. Arthur Selwyn and his partner Brown who lacks even an initial took up Bugilbone and Berryabar joining the western boundary of Druitt's Mille. Berryabar stretched both sides of the river. The southern section joined the eastern boundary of Evans's Bungulgully.

J. B. Reid drove sheep to Cumbil Creek which runs into Baradine Creek near Wangen and he managed the station himself. Later he sent shepherds down to the edge of the Brigalow scrub and established Moralgarry or Sandy Creek, watered by Coghill Creek. Whoever gave his name to that creek has never been heard of since. Ezekiel Wright brought cattle to a long stretch of the creek east of Reid's sheep and formed Coghill south of the Brigalow. He lived there, too, one of the few resident owners.

On 1 May 1840 a twenty-four-year-old immigrant named Henry Parkes wrote home to his sister, Sarah, in Birmingham. In Sydney, with a young wife, a baby born as the ship sailed up the New South Wales coast, and threepence in his pocket, he had gone to work for Sir

John Jamison at Regentville as a prelude to his long, famous, bankrupt career as a politician. 'Sir John agreed to give me £25 for the year' Parkes wrote, 'with a ration and a half of food. This amounted to weekly:

　10½ lbs Beef – sometimes unfit to eat
　10½ lbs Rice – of the worst imaginable quality
　6¾ lbs Flour – half made up of ground rice
　2 lbs Sugar – good tasted brown
　¼ lb Tea – inferior
　¼ lb Soap – not enough to wash our hands
　2 figs Tobacco – useless to me.

'This was what we had to live upon and not a leaf of vegetable or a drop of milk beyond this. For the first four months we had no bed other than a sheet of bark off a Box-tree, and an old door laid on two cross pieces of wood, covered with a few articles of clothing . . . the morning sunshine, the noon-tide shower, and the white moon-light of midnight gushed in upon us alike. You will perhaps think . . . you would have had a few vegetables at any rate, for you would have made a bit of a garden . . . the slave-masters of New South Wales require their servants to work for them from sunrise to sunset, and will not allow them to have gardens lest they should steal a half hour's time to work them.'

'My dear Mother' wrote another immigrant, 'the living is not very choice here being Beef and Bread one day and Bread and Beef the following.' Neither James Walker nor Andrew Brown supplied tea and sugar in the rations to any station where dairy cows were run – they thought milk a sufficient drink.

Life looked different to the employers. 'Wallerawang is such a nice place' James Walker wrote to his niece in Scotland, 'so rural, so romantic – so unlike what you all live in.' By 1841 he had settled back comfortably in Australia. 'He had a wonderful liking for . . . camping-out, and "roughing it" as he called it' Thomas Archer wrote of him, 'and his geniality was never so marked as when jogging along with his whole commissariat packed in a pair of saddle-bags across his horse and his spare wardrobe strapped to the pommel of his saddle.'

But he could not find his way anywhere unless he had a broad road to guide him and he was equally as diffident in business. Edward Walker, his nephew, was critical: 'A most tiresome person to have any dealings with and his worrying timid habits seem to increase with his age.' Yet he planned an attack on Lambert and his gang who were robbing his drays on the Wallerawang–Lue road. With an Aboriginal to guide him he led a party over foggy hills before daylight and grabbed the bushrangers as they led their heavily-loaded pack-horses along a narrow track.

About July 1841 James Walker rode to Baradine. He had just returned from the Governor's ball in a Sydney bright with new gaslights. Now he was at Baradine with William Archer to farewell three Archer brothers, David, Thomas, and John who had come out first to master a little coastal trading vessel. They were off to Queensland with eight thousand sheep to form stations for David Archer and Co. Edward Walker, back in England studying for the ministry after a spell at Lue, was a non-working partner. William Archer had taken over from David as James Walker's superintendent.

They had planned to leave twelve months before, in the first rush to the Darling Downs after that energetic Scotsman, Patrick Leslie, had confirmed Allan Cunningham's opinion they were good. David Archer bought a light dray and a bullock waggon in Maitland, loaded them with supplies and travelled up the road through present Cassilis that Cunningham first used. Before he could lift his sheep that were running on Biamble, scab broke out among them. So he searched till he found unoccupied feed and water on a creek running south-west from Tooraweenah. Written now as Terrabile Creek, pronounced perhaps Turrabilly by the Aborigines, it was usually called then, as it is now, Terrible Billy. Thomas Archer with a party of the helpful Castlereagh Aborigines was sent up to strip bark to roof huts and a temporary woolshed. The Castlereagh tribes offered little resistance but they died as quickly as any of the tribes. Smallpox, influenza and syphilis were as deadly as bullets, arsenic or swords.

So David Archer moved his sheep to isolation, shore them, then doctored them for twelve months – hard and nasty work. Three diseases were common among the early flocks: scab, catarrh and footrot. Crawlers, sheep so lamed by footrot they could not stand, were an allowable reject in any sale. It is still illegal to sell sheep with footrot. The other two diseases are no longer with us. They were eradicated eventually by an extravagant and compulsory slaughter. Catarrh was a contagious infection of the nose and throat. Three-quarters of some flocks died twenty-four hours after the first running noses were seen. Scab was caused by a mange mite. Itching sheep chewed at their wool and rubbed against logs and trees until they rubbed their wool off in patches and their skin raw.

One of the early treatments, and the one Colin Archer used, was to pick up each shorn sheep and dip it into a barrel of arsenic solution.

The men's fingers swelled and the nails went black. It was difficult to keep the frightened men at work. A better and less dangerous treatment was to dip the sheep in tobacco water. But tobacco was expensive and hard to get. Sir Edward Parry had economised for the Australian Agricultural Company by buying tobacco stalks instead of leaf. William Gardner on one of his huge handwritten papers proposed 'galvanism' as a cure. Chains were to be draped across the backs of tightly penned sheep, looped round a body here and there, then connected to a battery. Wool on the sheep's back is a good conductor, he explained, 'the tube of the wool being then filled with yoke and oil from the animals body'.

When the three Archer brothers set out with a party of convicts, Aborigines, free men and a cranky Irish bullock-driver, the Darling Downs were all taken up. With many other latecomers, they went exploring with their sheep. And they were eventually successful. They opened up the Eidsvold country on the Burnett River north of Brisbane which they named for Eidsvoll, the town in southern Norway where the Norwegians in 1814 drew up a constitution asserting their independence from Sweden.

Other brothers joined them. They discovered the Fitzroy River in 1853 and established a chain of stations including Gracemere that the town of Rockhampton spread to. They planted a garden jutting into a lagoon as their father had done in Norway. Gracemere became a showplace. Colin Archer who fitted out a ketch to bring their supplies in and take their wool out returned to Norway in 1861 and made his name as a shipbuilder. He built the *Fram* that Nansen used in the North Sea and Amundsen used in the Antarctic. His rescue boats, fast and safe in the wild winter storms of the northern seas, were stationed among all the fishing fleets. An edition of Norse stamps in 1941 commemorated him.

Major George Druitt died in 1842. 'Mr Laban White', auctioneer, put out a catalogue of furniture for auction at the Mount Druitt home. Beautifully printed on solid paper, folded and bound, it listed the contents of 'Drawing Room, First Parlour, Hall, Second Parlour, Dining Room, First Bedroom, Second Bedroom, Third Bedroom, Fourth Bedroom, Spare Room, Yard, In the Paddock'. Henry Cox bought 'one large handsome wardrobe' out of the second bedroom for 'eleven pounds sterling'. There were only pigs and a few head of cattle in the paddock. Over 2,000 head of cattle and about the same number of sheep passed to George Junior and Edward with Bullumbulla (sometimes spelt Burrumbulla) and Mille.

Pay chits are extant, drawn by George and Edward on their father before his death, for the running of those stations. Some pay chits were written on printed forms. Most of them were scrawled on torn-off pieces of paper, and by the time they had passed through several hands and travelled hundreds of kilometres in pockets or saddle bags, they were usually presented for claim in tatters. They all had this form:

£7.15.6   Burrumbulla Jany 13th 1842
    At ten days sight please pay Alexander Taylor or order seven pounds fifteen shillings and six pence on a/- wages
To George Druitt J. P.   Edward Druitt
    St Marys

They were roughly torn off to the approximate size of a modern cheque. The figures in the top left hand corner were boxed in with straight horizontal and wriggling vertical lines.

Dr James Smith Adams settled at Coocoobiandi in 1842, the first doctor on the Namoi. Dr Rogers had come out from England to practise for the Australian Agricultural Company in a slab and bark hospital at Tamworth on the Peel in 1838. Rogers was better qualified than Adams who might have completed his apprenticeship or might not. The only information about him concerns his squatting. He took up Yarraldool between Brown and Selwyn's Bugilbone and Charles Purcell's Tureeweewah. Coocoobiandi was no more than a one hundred and fifty hectare house and cow paddock cut off the corner of Edward Cox's Namoi Hut with the permission of Commissioner Mayne. The Aborigines gave the name to a hill with a high smooth rock face known now as Gins Leap, six kilometres north of Boggabri. There are local stories that an Aboriginal woman was chased over it in a tribal row. Dr Adams – he is remembered as Baldy – built his house and surgery at the northern end of the rock.

After Adams left for Port Phillip in 1852, Dave Grover (whose descendants still live nearby) built an inn there. The Rock Inn thrived as a coaching inn until the railway came through in 1882.

Alfred Denison, later private secretary to Sir William Denison, his half-brother who was to become the first Governor-General in Australia, bought Gullandaddah from Mayne and Boydell in 1842. John Lloyd, twenty-six years old and member of an Irish family with aristocratic friends, took over as superintendent. Although he had only been in Australia twelve months, he was soon managing over 13,000 sheep and had the reputation of one of the best superintendents in the Colony.

The Doyles took part in the move to Queensland but they went up the Barwon on to the Moonie River three hundred kilometres west of the Darling Downs. Young Bartholomew, writing to his father, Cyrus, from Narrabri on 19 January 1843 carefully gave the good news first:

'Our cattle and sheep are doing very well indeed, having abundance of grass and water; you may consequently expect a goodly number of fat cattle shortly; indeed I wish much that we had not removed any part of our stock, and particularly not to the Mooney, which you are aware is at least 240 miles beyond this. I regret to say that Bolin, your principal stockman at the Mooney, arrived here yesterday with the unwelcome news that the blacks on the 2nd instant had taken 3 horses from the hut where they were fastened, killed them and let our cattle on the station (amounting to 500 head) out of the yards and driven them away. Bolin says he has not a beast left. You have consequently four men at present up there at heavy wages for no purpose . . .' Towards the end of the letter he mentioned, as though it was of least consequence, that another man had been killed. Joseph Onus junior and his brother-in-law John Eaton, had lost 1,100 head of cattle off the same river. Patrick Quinn rode to Maitland, where Cyrus was then living, for more horses so that they could ride to the Moonie and muster the cattle.

The Aborigines on the lower Gwydir and Macintyre and on the Moonie made more resistance than any others. But if they had made a systematic attack on the scattered stations they could easily have wiped out all the whites in the area. They were certainly capable of planning such an attack. They seem simply to have been reluctant to do it. Attacks were retaliatory and thus sporadic. Once a wrong was paid back the account was settled. They made more systematic attacks against cattle. They trained their dogs to round them up as shepherds' dogs rounded up sheep. Some tribes were said to have hundreds of dogs, a mixture of Dingoes and pups of several breeds begged from stations, and their progeny. Then with the dogs holding the mob together they ran them till they were exhausted and speared them at will. The meat would have been full of adrenalin, cherry red and tough, but they did not eat much of it. They ate the fat, and ripped open the bellies of the pregnant cows for unborn calves.

Each commissioner had a squad of Border Police to help him keep order. The proud Mounted Police, by tradition trotting – never cantering – at a steady ten kilometres an hour, would have nothing to do with the Border Police, recruited from ex-convicts. Edward Mayne did not like the look of one lot of reinforcements. He wrote to the Colonial

Secretary '. . . some of them do not appear calculated to form an efficient police – they are mostly what is termed "old hands" . . . one of them in particular arrived in 1833 has been assigned out three times and has had four punishments one of which was twelve months to an iron gang . . . when arrived at Muswellbrook he got drunk, caused much disturbance . . .'

A troop of good light horsemen could not have kept order from the Liverpool Range to the Moonie River. The Border Police made rounds of the stations, painstakingly detailing distances travelled, numbers of stock, amounts of cheese made, arresting Aboriginal murderers now and again or bushrangers, looking for cattle thieves, perhaps sometimes even robbing a dray themselves. By 1846 most of the Border Police had been disbanded. One or two picked men were kept on at each headquarters.

Edward Mayne was dismissed in 1843. One hundred and five pounds sterling paid into his bank account by the government to buy horses for his Border Police was seized by the Sheriff. Governor Gipps was more furious. Mayne was broke. His expensive cows were now worth a dollar a head.

The Colony had overproduced wool and meat and underproduced grain. It could not sell its own produce yet it had to pay for expensive wheat from India and South America and rice from China. In modern times Australian graingrowers as well as woolgrowers and meat producers depend on overseas markets. We use a little only of what we grow.

It was the third depression for the Colony. Merchants as well as squatters were shattered in 1842–3. Edward Walker wrote from Cambridge on 6 December 1843 of 'the wide dispersion into all the numerous ramifications of the Colony of my Father's enormous Capital'. William Walker who had been managing his London office closed it down and sailed out to salvage his Australian affairs.

Edward Mayne had $800 in salary owing him so the seized money was quickly repaid. But he had been slow in paying in fines and rentals collected from others as well as his own licence fee for Pian Creek. And he fed his horses corn. Governor Gipps thought they ought to eat grass. Mayne was emphatic he had done nothing dishonest and fought his dismissal. He appealed to Lord Stanley for a full investigation but was never given one.

After his dismissal he tried to keep the good six-roomed house he had built of timber and stone. Robert Pringle joined in hounding him. He told his shepherds to feed their flocks to Mayne's door and starve him out. Mayne was not treated justly. Finally in 1846 he was declared unfit to hold a pastoral licence so he lost his house with no compensation. By then Governor Gipps himself had resigned, a crushed man. But the Colony had begun to recover.

Boiling-down saved it – the steaming of carcasses in huge pots for their tallow. Sheep worth five cents or nothing at all had sixty cents worth of fat in them. Tallow was valuable on the London market. 'Who cares for fleece, we'll get their grease,' wrote Edward Walker.

James Ebsworth of the Australian Agricultural Company first experimented in 1838 and was astonished at the amount of tallow a sheep produced. But he did nothing more about it. Stock were then valuable. Henry O'Brien, first squatter on the Murrumbidgee, boiled more sheep in the middle of the depression and on 22 May 1843 published a long letter in the *Sydney Morning Herald*. He quoted the price of tallow in London and the cost of getting it there. He proved the minimum value of a sheep in fair condition was sixty cents and thus multiplied the value of Australian sheep and cattle by ten.

It seemed the letter was no sooner written than the fires were under the boilers and the flesh in the vats. Two hundred thousand sheep went through works in Sydney, Maitland, Muswellbrook, Melbourne, Geelong, Portland, Adelaide in less than twelve months. And they were not simple establishments to erect. The first vats were wooden. Oak staves seventy-five millimetres thick were bound with iron hoops to take steam under pressure. When the quartered flesh of thirty or forty sheep was packed in, a heavy well-fitted lid was screwed on top. Huge boilers supplied steam under pressure through pipes seventy-five millimetres in diameter for ten hours. Then the tallow, eight to ten kilograms from each fat sheep, up to one hundred kilograms from each fat bullock, was run off through pipes in the side of the vats. It was tried in separate pots and sealed in casks. Some works combined a soap factory.

Within six years over two million sheep a year were boiled down and over two hundred thousand head of cattle. Giant iron vats held three hundred sheep and nearly three tonnes of tallow poured from them at a time. Warlike Britain bought it all for making the glycerine used in explosives.

5

Runholders and Selectors

The Rules are Modified

The recovering Colony was no longer a penal colony: transportation ceased in 1840. So the newly respectable Colony was given representative government, a partly elected council that assumed much of the power of the Governor but left him chief authority. It first met in 1843. It did not lessen the difficulties of governing.

Sir George Gipps tried to put a stronger hobble on the squatters while they were still financially weakened. 'We see here a British population spread over an immense territory', he reported to the British Government, 'beyond the influence of civilization, and almost beyond the restraints of law . . . women are beginning to follow into "the bush" and a race of Englishmen must speedily be springing up in a state approaching to untutored barbarism . . . the squatters in general live in huts, made of the bark of trees; and a garden, at least any thing worthy of the name, is a mark of civilization rarely to be seen.'

For the first time 'runs of land' began to be talked of, one of those marvellous expressions that come from nowhere into immediate use. What Gipps wanted to do was limit the size of the runs, increase the period of tenure, and encourage the building of houses by offering eight-year extensions if a house was built on freehold purchased from the run within five years. He suggested further extensions if more freehold blocks of 128 hectares (that made sense when it was half a square mile) were bought. He fixed an annual license fee of eighty dollars. 'The lands are the unquestionable property of the Crown,' he explained, 'and they are held in trust by the Government for the benefit of the people of the whole British Empire.'

The squatters, probably correctly, saw the purchase conditions as a disguised tax. There was uproar. In the new Legislative Council, twenty-four elected by the people, twelve appointed by the Governor himself, the aging William Lawson was almost a lone voice in support. Even Robert Lowe, the brilliant barrister saved by Gipps from starvation when he was unknown and had no briefs, would not support him. An outlandish albino, nearly blind, with a heavy shield across his pink eyes, carrying a stockwhip and wearing a Panama hat, loyal to nothing but ambition, Robert Lowe reviled Gipps in his climb to fame in British politics and a peerage.

And William Wentworth, since Gipps seemed about to cost him money, changed sides for the time. He was always the champion of what served him best. He had also 'vowed eternal vengeance' against Gipps for cancelling the sale of the eight million hectares of New Zealand he had bought from seven Maori chieftains for $400 a year each for the rest of their lives. So he spoke against the proposed bill in Council. He spoke against it before the 350 gentlemen assembled in the saloon of the Royal Hotel in Sydney. The *Sydney Morning Herald* reported his very long speech on 10 April 1844: '. . . In the district of Bathurst he had 10,000 or 11,000 sheep, and 2,500 cattle – at present he pays one license for them; but when this new regulation comes into operation in 1845, he will have to pay eight squatting licenses; and instead of paying 10 l. as formerly, he will have to pay 80 l. Again, at the Liverpool Plains, instead of one license he will have to take out seven; so that instead of the sum of 20 l. now paid by him, he would have to pay to the amount of 150 l. . . . to say that it was rent was a misnomer. Was it a debt? No, because the representative of the people had nothing to do with it. What was it then? He would tell them what it was – it was a tribute – it was an imposition such as a lord put upon his serf – fit for Tunis and Tripoli – worthy of the Dey of Algiers – it was intolerable – it was a nuisance which should not be endured – which the representatives of the people would not endure. (Tremendous cheering.) . . . all the value of this country, whether of this city or of its remotest acres, has been imparted to it by its population; and consequently the country itself is our rightful and first inheritance . . . these wilds belong to us, and not to the British Government.'

What would Australian politicians of 1981, formal and obscure in their deviousness, make of him?

George Gipps began to shamble. He was too tired to meet such power. He held up James Walker as his example of the misuse of land. A 'magnificent squatter' he called him, which made him a different man to the dithering asthmatic Edward Walker and the Archers saw. Gipps did little sums. He added up every hut that Walker's shepherds were stationed at, he added up all the vacant land between his runs, and credited him with twenty-seven runs covering one and a half million hectares for which he paid ten pounds sterling.

Gipps was partly right. Andrew Brown had occupied more country for James Walker than he would need in the next ten years. And Gipps's suggested bill was mostly sound. But he had run against the rum trade in a different form. He had no chance. He resigned and went home to die. Sir Charles FitzRoy came out to take his place, content to do nothing but enjoy himself while the Legislative Council ran the country. Even his easy philosophy was shattered in December 1847 when he lost control of his coach horses in the domain, ran into a tree, and killed his wife and aide-de-camp.

In the end the new Land Act of 1846 defined by an Order-in-Council of 9 March 1847 was a fair enough compromise. A runholder was given a term of fourteen years to graze stock, and farm only that ground he needed to grow food. He was to pay $20 a year for a run that would carry 4,000 sheep or 640 cattle and pay $5 extra for each additional thousand sheep that he ran or the equivalent in cattle. For the first time runholders defined their boundaries.

Sir John Jamison did not live to define the boundaries of Baan Baa or to see his fortunes revive. He lost heavily when the Bank of Australia failed. A few months before he died in June 1844 he married Mary Griffiths, the daughter of his dairyman, who had been his housekeeper. During the years of entertaining she would have been the servant in the background. When the indignity of a lowly marriage no longer mattered, he married her as a financial arrangement. He had seven children by her as well as a few by other women.

So Baan Baa passed to Lady Jamison. Sir John Jamison's knighthood was well earnt. It acknowledged his brilliant work as a young physician in the British Navy in curing an outbreak of scurvy in the Swedish Navy. He was sent to Sweden at the urgent request of the King of Sweden. But T. D. Mutch, a New South Wales politician in the 1920s, who in his later life compiled a huge and valuable card index of births, marriages and deaths, was unkind enough to refer to his widow as '"Lady" Jamison'.

William Wentworth managed Baan Baa for her for a short time from

a distance which probably accounts for the detailed description of the
boundaries in the 1848 *Government Gazette*:

'Estimated area –107,520 acres

'Estimated Grazing Capabilities – 2,000 cattle.

'Baan Baa on the Namoi River, extending 8 miles on the west side of
the river, and going into Button's paddock by a line west from the
marked tree on the edge of the plain to a mountain known as Ballal,
and from thence to Tarremullen waterhole; on the west by a line running north to a bald spur in the Brigalow range, and from thence on the
north to a waterhole in the Namoi River, known as Bundur Wallur in
Button's paddock, to a bald spur in the Brigalow range, on the eastern
side of the Namoi River, from the confluence of Onus' or Ghooi Creek
to Bundur Wallur, at the junction of Bibelah Creek with the Namoi,
being 8 miles; bounded on the south by Onus' Creek up to Onus' hut,
and from thence to the southern point of a brush mountain about three
miles east from Onus' hut; on the east by the Pundawai range; on the
north by a line east from Bundur Wallur to bald spur in the range opposite a mountain called Deeriah.'

The holder of every run from Port Phillip to the Darling Downs tried
to describe it. Aboriginal place names were naturally spelt differently
by every man who mentioned them. Some of them as printed were
also misinterpretations of somebody's handwriting and are almost
unrecognisable. Some mistakes are funny. When James Weston who
had taken over the Coonabarabran run from the Cox brothers told a
clerk his southern boundary was Jack Hall's Creek, it was written
down Jackall Creek.

Usually descriptions were brief and vague, as Hyam Joseph described Cumbil (or Cumble) that he had bought from J. B. Reid:

'Estimated area – 12,800 acres

'Estimated Grazing Capabilities – 2,000 sheep

'Sandy forest, bounded on the north by George Pounder's marked
tree; on the south unbounded; on the east unbounded; on the west
Wangan Creek.'

George Pounder is an unknown. He was probably somebody's
stockman setting up on his own. He came to Werrai on Etoo or Cumble Creek (now Dubbo Creek) in 1847 with 300 head of cattle and 5
horses. And when he died in 1871 all he had worth mentioning in the
will he signed with a cross was his horse Jonathon, a saddle and bridle.

His Jewish neighbours, the Josephs, who did not live on their sandy
runs, grew wealthy indeed. Hyam Joseph, an auctioneer and shipping
agent, lived in Auckland, New Zealand. He bought Sandy Creek from

Reid as well as Cumbil. Moses Joseph, probably his brother, had taken up Merrumborough and Bulgarrie, adjacent vacant land in 1845. It extended east of Button's Bullerawa to the Namoi. They ran about 6,500 sheep in partnership, and both employed the same overseer.

It is difficult to trace relationships in Jewish families. There is a shortage of surnames, and surnames are used as given names much more frequently than in English. Solomon Moses and Moses Solomon both lived in Sydney at the same time as the Josephs. Moses Joseph's father who also came to Australia was Joseph Joseph. Sons name their sons after grandfathers and brothers, and their sons repeat the names. Soon there is confusion.

Moses Joseph had hawked his cheap handmade jewellery around English country towns. When he was caught stealing the stock of a fellow pedlar in 1826, he was sent to the Colony for life. He worked out his sentence with a firm of Jewish merchants in Sydney then opened a tobacconist's shop. It thrived. He married his cousin, Rosetta Nathan, 'a respectable and virtuous woman', in the Colony's first marriage ceremony performed according to Jewish rites. Governor FitzRoy granted him a rare absolute pardon in 1848. In partnership with his father he dealt in town blocks in Sydney and the developing towns of Brisbane, Maitland, Tamworth and Armidale. He bought thousands of acres of grazing land in the New England. His sheep must have done well enough on the forest runs because in 1857 he extended to Dunwarian, probably the last bit of unclaimed land in the area. His fortune grew so great that even when he backed the wrong side in the American Civil War and invested 250,000 pounds sterling in the Confederate States the chief effect of the loss was merely to prevent him becoming a millionaire.

A Jewish contemporary, Lewis Wolfe Levy, did almost as well. With David and Samuel Cohen he established the Maitland firm of grocers and suppliers, David Cohen and Co. When the firm foreclosed on a Tamworth grocer, Lewis Wolfe Levy went up to take over the shop. Levy and Cohen later held runs in the forest area but as holders of mortgages not as graziers.

L. W. Levy established an inn in Tamworth, too, and advertised his wine with innocent honesty in the *Maitland Mercury* of 15 September 1847:

' "Tamworth" Inn
   Peel's River

' . . . L. W. L. having purchased directly of the importers, largely of both Foreign Wines and Spirits – which he reduces with very little and clean water only – he is assured by connoiseurs that these, as well as his Ales and Porter, are the "real thing" and not the colonial rubbish.'

By 1854 his customers' palates had apparently improved. The firm then advertised 'The Grog of D. Cohen and Co. Stands pre-eminent over that of other Spirit Merchants; and it may be fairly stated, and without fear of contradiction, that it is 15 per cent cheaper to the purchaser, merely from the non-introduction of water, and absence of adulteration . . .'

Shepherds and stockmen drank from the 'water-carts' of the sly-grog sellers. They dodged the mounted police, the runholders and their managers, and drove round the out-stations with casks of their own distilled brews. It was raw and poisonous, most of it, and they were not fussy who owned the wool, hides, sheepskins or tallow they traded for it. If one of their customers died, they burnt cask and liquor and moved on. One of the first white women over the Liverpool Range was the companion of George Burnett, a sly-grog seller. When mounted police disturbed them in 1838 on the Hunter side of one of the rough passes drovers still often used as short cuts, they loaded their casks hurriedly and followed their customers to the plains.

Captain C. F. H. Smith of the Mounted Police caught up with a grog-cart doing a Christmas run down the Namoi in December 1847. At Baan Baa he found all hands drunk so he rode in pursuit to Turrawan and captured it.

Robert Hallilay Milner who had bought Turrawan (or The Broadwater) from the Buttons in November 1845 was himself a good drinker and might not have welcomed the police. He came to Australia early in 1842 as surgeon superintendent of the emigrant ship *The Duke of Roxburgh* from Ireland. He was gazetted a competent medical man in the Colony which entitled him to practice. So he settled on the Namoi with his wife, Caroline, not many kilometres downstream from Baldy Adams at Gins Leap. He built a little hospital, ran a few hundred head of cattle, drank too much and treated the patients brought to him, some of them the wrecks of too many grog carts and shanties.

John Allman, the Commissioner who took over from the unfortunate Edward Mayne, was an enthusiastic drinker. The son of Captain Francis Allman who established the penal colony at Port Macquarie, he had been a clerk and postmaster as a young man, then Commissioner at Wellington. After his move to Tamworth he was seldom enough on duty. Roderick Mitchell, his young assistant and the brilliant son of Sir

Thomas, finally reported in April 1846 that his superior had been absent 238 days in the previous twelve months. 'He is, I believe at the present moment involved with nearly every innkeeper from New England to Maitland and the sum due to each of them is more than gentlemen usually incur at such places.'

Worse, he had drunk the ticket-of-leave money, the fines, some of the rent, and the proceeds of the sale of four cast police horses which might well have been the horses Mayne had trouble paying for when the Sheriff seized his money. So Allman, too, was dismissed and Roderick Mitchell at 24 became Commissioner. Richard Bligh, grandson of the deposed governor, was his deputy.

Sir Thomas Mitchell was out exploring again during his son's term, seeking a route overland to the Gulf of Carpentaria and still hoping, somewhere, to fall in with the Kindur. Roderick sent the Border Police to follow his tracks into Queensland with the news that Leichhardt had forestalled him. When the erratic Leichhardt lost himself and his party in 1848, Roderick Mitchell was asked to lead a party in search of him. He had then been transferred to the Darling Downs. In a hurry to reach Sydney, instead of waiting for a steamer at Brisbane, he boarded a light sailing boat, was washed overboard in a storm, and drowned.

Leichhardt, a friend of the Archer brothers, who more than any explorer went out in search of himself, disappeared with his party somewhere in the central Australian desert as totally as if they had evaporated. After the publication of Patrick White's *Voss* he lost even his identity until E. M. Webster restored it in 1980 with *Whirlwinds in the Plain.*

Caroline Milner was one of about 300 women who came north in the 1840s. Before that influx the only white women known to have been in the north were Ned Dwyer's companion, Mary Prise, George Burnett's keg mate, two women at Tamworth and Mary Facer who came up in 1839 with her husband, James, a carpenter, to put up buildings for Andrew Doyle at Narrabri.

By 1845 five women lived at William Sharp's Therribri. With twelve men employed to look after 2,000 sheep and 700 cattle, it was one of the best-manned runs in the north. A few convicts were still serving out their time on other runs including one convict woman at John Johnston's Gunnedah. She had two free companions.

There was a woman on Druitt's Burrumbulla, on Thomas Eather's

Henriendi and Fitzsimmons's Yaminginba, at Pilliga and Coghill and two at Purcell's Garrawilla. Big Andrew Doyle's wife, Catherine, another daughter of John Howe, lived with him at Killarney.

Now gardens were being dug and more acres put in to grow wheat for flour. Calico was stretched across walls to make ceilings beneath bark roofs, and the wide cracks that had opened between wall slabs were papered over from inside. There was still a trade in Aboriginal women on the distant runs. Roderick Mitchell told of one gin being sold for a mare and foal. But the newspapers were now growing calmer about the imbalance of the sexes and lonely men 'exposed to the severest temptations . . . and grossest excesses of immorality'. For many convicts, as for prisoners today, homosexuality was an only resort.

Samuel Marsden's daughter, Elizabeth, held a run in the forest, though it is unlikely she ever saw it. In 1843 a J. Marsden on Yarragin at the head of Baradine Creek was included in Graham Hunter's itinerary. There were two men including Marsden on the station and 250 head of cattle. There is no known J. Marsden who might have lived there connected with the Rev. Samuel Marsden, nor any Marsden of any initial. Yet when James Evans described the boundary of Dandry, he put the Rev. H. H. Bobart on his west. Henry Bobart married Elizabeth Marsden before her father's death in 1838. He succeeded Marsden as incumbent of St John's, Parramatta.

The run was never in his name. After the mysterious J. Marsden it was licensed to Mrs Bobart as Yearunan (Yearinan). She sold it to Andrew Brown in 1848.

Even by 1845 there was little land to be taken up anywhere within 800 kilometres of Sydney. Late comers either had to buy or go far out. Although the last few vacant squares on the forest map were still being filled during the 1850s these were either moves to country obviously inferior from the beginning or else a squeezing in between runs on to land that had not been regularly stocked. The law did not allow the holding of vacant land, or even allow for the spelling of land. Graham Hunter, Commissioner for the district of Bligh, a high-handed and vindictive man, not only watched the stocking of his licencees but their morals. His treatment of Roger Heenan at Coonabarabran was fair enough but a man named Pearce on the Castlereagh lost his licence because he was living in adultery with a white woman. He gave the middle of one of James Walker's lightly-stocked runs to somebody else because he found no stock there.

A few of those who came to their squares on the map while Gipps's new laws were being argued have still to be mentioned. Brutal as most of them were, they were brave. And the first to the forest area have an importance beyond those who went first to most places because what they set growing is a miracle. If scientists with modern knowledge, if agricultural scientists and foresters, bacteriologists, chemists, meteorologists, botanists, agronomists, ecologists, were shown the area as it was in 1840 and told, 'Here is a good place to grow a self-regenerating commercial pine forest', they would laugh and say 'It is impossible. The soil is too poor, the rainfall insufficient, the summer too hot, and no commercial forest tree regenerates well enough to make timber anyway'.

So Henry Cavan, probably a stockman, came to Wittenbra down the creek from Mrs Bobart's run with two or three hundred head of cattle, stayed five years, then left with his licence fees unpaid. And John Miller (or Millar) came to Kiambirie north of Baradine with 190 head, and his descendants held it as Kiambir or Kienbri or Kenebri for over one hundred years. He was probably related to Lockhart and William Millar, early residents with their sheep on the Liverpool Plains.

Lieutenant Thomas Lodge Patch, retired sick from the Indian Army on half pay in December 1843, sent stockmen with about 1,500 head of cattle to Pilliga on the south side of the Namoi immediately east of Brown and Selwyn's Berryabar. That land had probably been previously occupied by an unknown. It is good land and unlikely to have stayed vacant for so long. There is a cursory reference in Roderick Mitchell's manuscript records to a station there called The Clubs or Ace of Clubs.

Patch first called his run Pealica and if that is how it was pronounced, *Peelaka*, then it meant spear-head, and thus by association with shape, the lovely casuarina, the River Oak. *Pela*, a spear, has become our Belar, another casuarina.

Soon after, in partnership with one of the four Glennie brothers (probably James, the Hunter River magistrate and farmer), he sent cattle up the Baradine Creek to Wangen, the site of the present village of Gwabegar. The Glennies were sons of Dr William Glennie, principal of a private school in Dulwich, Surrey.

Thomas Capp was given a licence for a run down the creek from Wangen. He called it pretentiously Capp Stations. It was one run only on a section of the creek known as Milchomi. The water dried up so he moved his 500 head of cattle to the Namoi. Arthur Selwyn on

Berryabar and Thomas Lodge Patch at Pilliga protested to Roderick Mitchell that Capp had taken ten miles of their river frontage. Capp defied them and said he intended to stay.

He and his brother, Charles Solomon Capp, were half brothers of Andrew Loder's children. Their parents, Joseph and Charlotte Capp, had both been convicts. Joseph was a carpenter who made coffins for the Hawkesbury Benevolent Society after he was free. For a time he plied a punt that he rented from John Howe across the Hawkesbury at Windsor and was once brought before the magistrates for refusing to ferry one man over. He said it was not worth his while for a penny. Although he was merely warned, the *Sydney Gazette* of 23 October 1823 published the hearing 'as a hint to all toll men . . . the public are not to be annoyed by their caprices'. And the fact was, the paper pointed out, it was not a man only, it was a man and his dog. Capp was entitled to charge threepence.

After Thomas and Charles Solomon were born, Charlotte Capp went to live with Andrew Loder as housekeeper. She had five sons by him, the last one, James, born in 1836, the year his father was killed.

Thomas Capp's neighbours, supported by Roderick Mitchell, forced him off the river so he bought Coghill with permanent water from Walter Bagot who had held it for only a year after buying it from Ezekiel Wright in 1848. Bagot was already out on the Barwon. He was related to the famous Bagots of South Australia and later invested with his brothers in New England. In 1846 he took a mob of cattle down the Barwon and Darling and marketed them in Adelaide. Only B. Raye, superintendent of a Barwon run, had been ahead of him with seven hundred head. Once the unknown Darling stretch was behind, the overland route along the Murray was well marked. It had been in use since 1838. It was Roderick Mitchell who suggested the Adelaide market. He wrote to his father that he had lifted the value of the Darling runs twenty-five per cent.

Walter Bagot was not concerned by long distances to market. In 1854 he advertised in the *Maitland Mercury* for stockmen to 'Drove cattle to the neighbourhood of the Melbourne diggings'. Gold had been discovered by Edward Hargraves on 12 February 1851.

More accurately, Hargraves, a showman rather than a digger, so engineered the announcement of the known fact there was gold in Australia, digging had begun before the Government had a chance to stop it. All the Government could do, as in the case of the squatters, was license what had been done. There had been odd finds of gold since 1823. A shepherd named McGregor had been quietly smashing it out of a quartz reef east of Wellington for years. The news passed from shepherd to shepherd. But gold and a colony of ex-thieves were thought not to go together. Hush! Cover it up.

'I cannot describe the state of the township. They are all mad . . .' the correspondent of *Bell's Life* reported from Bathurst on 13 May 1851. 'Business at a stand still and every body off to the diggings.' A nugget weighing over one and a half kilograms was turned up 'like a root of potatoes'. By June, one of the coldest Junes known, a line of drays drawn by bullocks and horses was bogged in the snow-soaked road over the Blue Mountains. Joseph Druitt from Mille (now Millie) stopping to fossick on a trip down to Maitland found a piece of gold-bearing quartz in the Warrumbungles. He reported his find to the *Maitland Mercury*.

'I have seen some notes of my uncle James about the Gold discovery at Bathurst', Edward Walker wrote to David Archer, 'and the poor old gentleman seems on the brink of despair.'

William Wentworth decided there was no future in cattle or wool with shepherds and stockmen running off to the diggings and no convicts coming in to replace them. Even overseers and a few squatters were packing drays with picks, shovels, tents and panning dishes, and joining in the latest rush. Wentworth had a third share in fifty-one Indian coolies brought to the Colony in April 1846. They were given a free passage over with their wives and children, free passage home in five years, and provided on board with 'a brass pot, a brass plate, blanket, cap and dhooty and jacket'. Clothing allowance was scant, pay low and food half a ration. The Indians, not the meek slaves they were expected to be, went begging through the streets of Sydney. Wentworth was forced to increase the pay and double the clothing allowance and food ration.

In the last months of 1846 Wentworth headed the committee of the Legislative Council appointed 'To enquire into, and report upon, the Despatch of the Right Honorable the Secretary of State for the Colonies, to Governor Sir Charles Augustus FitzRoy, dated 30th April, 1846, respecting the renewal of transportation to this Colony'.

The committee, carefully considering their own interests, recommended 'that no fewer than five thousand male convicts be annually deported to this colony'. They wanted 5,000 women, convict or free, to come with them. Immediately meetings were called all over the Colony 'to protest against it being made a land of slaves'.

When a ship load of Chinese labourers arrived in Sydney in October 1848 there was criticism because no women came with them. It seemed no labour could be got happily from anywhere. William Wentworth had lately erected a boiling-down works at Windemere. The smell of money cloaked the smell of the slaughter-yards in his lovely grounds. How could he run that works without men as well as care for thousands of sheep and cattle? In 1852 he offered all his runs for sale: Tibbereena, Burburgate, Manilla and Glen Riddle, Cowmore that he had taken over from the Robertsons with its licence fees unpaid, Bull he had bought from Thomas Parnell, and Galathera on the black plains. John Lloyd who had left Alfred Denison to take charge of all Wentworth's runs formed a company to buy them. There was still little money for investment and less faith. Wentworth was anxious to sail for London. Thomas Sutcliffe Mort arranged the sale. He was a young Lancashire salesman who came to Sydney, concentrated on the auction of wool, and formed the woolbroking firm of Goldsbrough Mort & Co. He later sent the first shipment of frozen meat to London from another of his companies, the NSW Fresh Food and Ice Company.

Mort found two men named Croft and Tooth willing to buy a share of the runs. Since no other buyer could be found, Mort himself, although it was questionably legal for an agent to buy a share, put up the rest of the money. He wisely got Wentworth to sign a document that he was aware Mort was a partner. Twelve months later John Lloyd, tall, handsome, with a mass of dark wavy hair, too quick-tempered to work with partners, bought the syndicate out for $16,000 more than they paid for it. He had faith in the pastoral industry.

Andrew Brown had faith in God Who had already done him a service in saving Mrs Brown from an illness so severe his diary entry reads as though he had composed her epitaph: '30 September 1853 . . . on the 24th July a Man in the prime of life was struck down whilst preparing dinner and died in a few Minutes illness on the same night Mrs Brown was taken so alarmingly ill that we had great fears that the time of Her departure was come thanks many thanks to an All Merciful God who in his goodness has averted so great a calamity and lengthened the days of one so valuable and valued by a fond husband and affectionate children domestics and neighbours . . .'

The entry is cryptic. Did the man die in Brown's house? Were they poisoned? For the next thirty years the diary catalogued his wife's headaches.

As for the labour outlook, he noted on 31 December 1853: '. . . the want of labour will be so great as to imped every attempt to carry on work . . . my only sure hope is in the mercy of an all wise Providence who can bring light out of darkness and show the way of escape from difficulties and dangers when man cannot of himself let me then rest on Him for help and be not dismayed.'

So acting on good advice he took out warrants for the arrest of two indentured Chinese shepherds and a servant who had bolted for the diggings. And he brought out more Chinese: '24 April 1854 Three horse teams accompanied by four China Men as Shepherds and hutkeepers started for Caigan today.' It must have been a thoroughly bewildering experience for gregarious townsmen and methodical farmers of small plots to be set down in a waste of grass with a flock of sheep. And the few Chinese who had seen sheep had seen flocks of five not five hundred.

For over thirty years the forest area was busy growing wool, fattening wethers, breeding cattle. Some runs changed hands often, both the good and the bad; some runs stayed in the same hands for two or three generations. A few owners lived on their runs. Most of them did not.

Some runs had a roundabout connection with one family. Coghill was transferred from Thomas Capp to William Loder, his half-brother. Then it went out of the family for ten years. Patrick Quinn bought Coghill and Tibbereena south which he named Glen Quinn in 1855. He had left Andrew Doyle and set out on his own. Then Thomas Gordon Gibbons Dangar bought it, stepson of the bankrupt Thomas who designated himself genteely as retired. Although T. G. G. Dangar had a long connection with other runs in the district, Coghill passed probably by mortgage to J. B. Rundle, a relation of his stepfather's, in a few months. Then Charles Solomon Capp, brother of Thomas who was then dead, bought it in 1865 and held it till he died in 1884. He left it to his widow, Mary.

Charles Capp's son-in-law, Woodley Cole Slyman, managed Coghill for a couple of years. There is a local story that during a violent thunderstorm his shearers refused to go on shearing with their steel handpieces in the open bark shed. He shouted Scottish oaths and snatched up two pairs of the discarded shears. 'A wee bit of lightning canna hurt a man!' He ran out into the open thrusting the blades at the sky. And down came a bolt of lightning and killed him.

He came from Cornwall so perhaps they were Cornish oaths. Anyway, there are still men who can find his grave. It is marked by heavy ironbark posts in dense forest near the site of the old homestead on the creek bank. He was killed in 1867.

Cyrus Doyle found the sheep his sons sent to Willylaw did not thrive so he left the run. It lay vacant for years at a time but was taken up spasmodically. When there was no one on it, stockmen and shepherds on adjacent runs would have used any feed that grew there. Good stockmen and shepherds were always on the lookout for a bite of extra grass.

John Eales, ex One Man Settler, who established Duri had spread back over the Currabubula Gap to the plains. His shepherds, as ruthless as their master, had care of 30,000 sheep by the late 1840s, and they used them to worry neighbours' cattle at water, and deliberately misjudged boundaries so that their sheep bulged into the next runs. Eales spent months of his life in court, disputing boundaries, suing and being sued for wages, for trespass, for wrongful impounding. He won some cases, lost some. Since he was a good businessman he must have found the stolen feed more than worth the court costs. As well as his grazing runs, he owned a prosperous coal mine and he was also principal shareholder of the Hunter River Steam Navigation Company that he founded in 1839.

Right through the 1850s there was endless litigation. Lawyers thrived. Eales was viciously aggregating money. Most of the litigants, more human, more absurd, were protecting their dignity rather than their property. They rode into Maitland or Bathurst at the head of their troop of witnesses. Each side took over a hotel at the opposite end of town. For a week or more stockmen and shepherds ate and drank at the disputing squatters' expense and outlied one another in court. John Allman, in one of his sober moments as Commissioner, said he usually avoided putting stockmen on oath. It was the only way of avoiding perjury.

The attitude of the squatters had changed. Now each run was a private business in competition with neighbours, not dependent on them for protection against loneliness and Aborigines. Under growing civilisation they developed a more cultured savagery. Australia now had an extra colony with customs houses on its borders. Victoria separated in 1850.

Even by 1848 Wee Waa was developing into a village, the first on the Namoi. There were four slab huts and a clerk of petty sessions. W. J. Slack had run a public house there for a year or two and taken subscriptions for the *Maitland Mercury*. It was no longer necessary to ride to Tamworth for mail. In February 1848 Joseph Griffiths began a subscription delivery from Tamworth to Wee Waa and it ran every alternate Monday if the sub-contracted mailman was sober. Lanky William Blakely carried it on from Wee Waa to the Barwon till he drank too much at Mogil Mogil one day – where there was probably a shanty – tried to cross the river by canoe, capsized and drowned.

More shanties had sprung up along the Namoi by 1850. The mailman rode leisurely from one to the other. It usually took him six days to ride 220 kilometres. Once he got so drunk he lost the mail. Parties rode out in search but it was never found.

The man bringing the pack-horse mail from Pages River over the Range to Tamworth was a good drinker, too. In June 1850 he lost the pack-horse with the mailbags. A bullock-driver found it four days later. That mailman had a roundabout route to develop a thirst on. He had to skirt the Australian Agricultural Company's boundary of its Peel lands. The company allowed no through roads for fear of travelling sheep with scab – a genuine fear.

Even the mail service between Australia and England became erratic between 1848 and 1852. The Lords of the Admiralty decided to transfer the contract to steam vessels and cancelled the old contracts as they began their deliberations. After almost two years the Secretary of the Association for the Promotion of Steam Communication with Australia wrote to the Chancellor of the Exchequer on 13 November 1850 to remind him the mails had been forgotten.

The northern mails in New South Wales improved when Henry 'Boshy' Nowland secured the contracts for his coach runs. By 1854, when there was a good steam service to Britain, his hard-driven Royal Mail coaches were racing the mail north in strict short time. Like long wagonettes swung between cart-wheels, two shaft horses abreast and one in front, they pitched so roughly passengers who could afford it travelled privately or rode. Light two-wheeled dog-carts driven tandem were a favourite for those with new money. The older squatters drove down in sulkies or spring carts, their splintered shafts laced with greenhide. But they drove good horses. That was a matter of pride.

Abraham Johnston built a post office and store at Gulligal on Burburgate in 1854 and Gulligal became the northern mail centre for six or seven years.

The Reverend Edward Williams, his parish the vast Liverpool Plains, held service now and again in the little Wee Waa court house. There was a yearly race meeting after 1850. James Glennie brought horses, so did the Doyles, George Pounder from Werrai, young Andrew Loder (George Loder's son) from Merah, and others outside the scope of this book. Up to six horses took the field together and the meetings lasted two days.

A cricket club was formed in 1851. Edwin Evans, son of James who formed Dandry and Bungull Gully, was too young to be interested. He became famous in the 1870s, 'the best all-round player in Australia'.

The nearest doctor remained Doctor Milner at Turrawan till he died in 1858. But Holloways Pills or Ointments were a very broad cure-all for diarrhoea and constipation, ague, asthma, bad legs, bad breasts, headache, jaundice, piles, sore throats, tumours, venereal affections, worms of all kinds – the full list ran down half a column of the *Maitland Mercury*. David Cohen & Co. were apparently prepared to market them by the wagon load from their 'large consignments' at West Maitland. 'It is apparent that the sale is immense in the Northern Districts of New South Wales.'

Any friendliness that might have appeared at race meetings, or church services, or games of cricket disappeared when there were stock on the move. Thousands of stock were being driven to market. Andrew Brown mustered 10,000 sheep in 1856 and sent them for sale to Victorian miners clamouring for meat. Yet no one had thought of providing for stock routes. Shepherds and stockmen guarded their masters' grass with malignant intensity. Joseph Druitt advertised that if any stock were driven through Millie he would prosecute the owner and impound the stock. 'A Liverpool Plains Squatter' wrote to the *Maitland Mercury* 1 February 1854 to ask how Druitt was going to move stock from Millie to market without crossing somebody else's run. If such runholders 'intend acting up to the notice . . . they must be prepared to receive payment in kind'.

John Robertson forfeited Arrarownie in 1847 with the rent unpaid. Then he went to Sydney to prepare for a parliamentary career formulating land laws. Even before he left others had been applying for the run under different names. Jockeying for a bit of somebody else's land or even all of it under a different name was part of the game. Arrarownie was abandoned again in the 1851 drought. All the water dried up.

Colin MacKenzie who gained experience with Edward Cox at Ulamambri applied for a licence for Yokeyberly in 1847. Roderick Mitchell granted it 'provided it did not constitute a trespass'. Elizabeth Bobart protested it was the name of a waterhole on her run, Yearinan, so MacKenzie had to wait for his land till he bought Wangen from Patch and Glennie in 1850. In November 1854 he had a crop of wheat 'now ripening for the sickle'.

Since at first the law allowed only enough ground to be cultivated to satisfy the needs of the licence holder, and under later land laws because of distance to market, farming methods remained primitive in northern New South Wales for almost fifty years after South Australian farmers growing wheat as a business began to develop their own machinery.

By 1856 when runs were limited in size to 4,000 hectares for one licence fee, the Commissioners of Crown Lands were confronted with multiple applications for pieces of oversized runs under different names, their boundaries vaguely described often with the deliberate idea of confusing the Commissioner. Ceelnooy Lagoon, north-west of Baradine, used by Wangen till 1856, was applied for as Ceelnooy Lagoon, Ceernooy Lagoon, Kilnary, Kilmery. It is now the site of the Wooleybah sawmill, by 1980 one of the last two mills working inside the forest area.

William Carlow bought Dandry from James Evans in 1855. He came an unusual way, across from Port Macquarie in 1846, and he came with his wife Catherin, his sons and at least three daughters, an advent to a land short of women. He was 58 years old when he came and it is not known what he did in the nine years before he bought Dandry. Probably he worked for James Evans.

Jane Carr, their granddaughter, ninety-two years old when I saw her in February 1978, told me her grandmother's father, John Salisbury, was sold as a slave off a ship – a twisted but fair memory of the arrival of the convict ships when masters waited on the wharves for their assignees to be drafted to them.

David Matthews who married one of the Carlow daughters was a stone mason. He bought sixteen hectares of freehold on Yaminba Creek that extended into the farm known now as Sandbank. From sandstone on the creek bank he carved the early gravestones in the Coonabarabran cemetery. The Carlow graves on a hillside up from Dandry Creek are marked by his carving – heavy slabs with fluted tops as headstones, small oval-topped slabs as footstones. He, too, was said to have been sold as a slave off a ship but that was probably a memory of the savage Master and Servants Act when bonded tradesmen were given free passages in return for twelve months work on rations and a low wage. Rewards were offered for the return of any who absconded and their descriptions were published as though they were criminals.

A bonded German immigrant named Conrad Moss took Cyrus Doyle to court in 1854. He thought he had come out as a vine dresser but Cyrus Doyle did not persist with his vineyard. Moss worked at fencing, ploughing, feeding pigs. Once he had to skin a dead cow, an unpleasant experience when the newspapers so often reported the death of men who had skinned sheep and cattle that had died of the mysterious Cumberland disease. Stock and men continued to die of it until 1888 when scientists from Louis Pasteur's Institute in Paris identified it as anthrax and inoculated 300,000 sheep with Pasteur's new vaccine.

Moss finally went to court when he was ordered to go with a stockman taking cattle to Narrabri. His wife was pregnant. He would have been away four to five weeks. During that time she would have drawn no rations, she would have had nowhere to live. The bench, showing unusual sympathy, cancelled the agreement. Until shrewd employers began to welcome women as cheap labour, a wife was regarded as an extravagance in a working man, and neither rations nor wages allowed for her.

John Boyle married another of William and Catherin Carlow's daughters, Hanora. He applied for a licence for Weerabarwa in 1856, a big waterhole on Baradine Creek that was sometimes referred to strangely as Wheelbarrowa. Both James Walker and James Cooper who had taken up the discarded Wittenbra protested that he was applying for part of their runs so he applied for Gebian, vacant land to the east, but James Weston of the Coonabarabran run got it as Gibbican. By then Weston had put up a roughly-built hotel in Coonabarabran, the first building in the town, and a water mill on the river to grind wheat.

The protest was one of James Walker's last acts. He died suddenly of a stroke in November 1856.

Boyle stayed in the district – doing a bit of cattle rustling, I was told – and eventually his sons bought Gibbican.

In 1847 Robert Campbell Tertius – distinguishing himself neatly from the two other Robert Campbells of the merchant house – had put money into the district. He staked David Ryan in that part of the Wee Waa run north of the river – Ryan soon paid it off – and he bought Bora and Burrumbulla with 9,500 sheep from Joseph Druitt in partnership with his brother-in-law, James Orr. Orr's father had been an army officer serving in Ireland, and after land he had bought there was seized in an insurrection he brought his family to Australia. James managed the runs until 1852, when he bought them in partnership with his older brother, Ebenezer, who had been postmaster at the mushrooming Boyd Town on the south coast of New South Wales.

Robert Campbell concentrated on the wharves his father and uncle had established, on dealing in town blocks, and on the gold buying that made his fortune. As soon as he heard of the gold discoveries, he tendered to buy all that the government received in two months.

James Orr tried Indian coolies as shepherds but they could not manage sheep under Australian conditions. When most of his men ran off to the diggings he brought up Chinese coolies and they managed very well as shepherds and as shearers. Using wheelbarrows they built an earth dam across Borah Creek to make a deep pool for sheep washing. The Orr brothers also trained Aboriginal men and women as shepherds.

The newcomers in the late 1840s and the 1850s were the first who did not shoot Aborigines to maintain their position. Those Aborigines left lived on the runs, taking employment spasmodically, hunting spasmodically where game were left, mostly living on beef, flour and sugar. Their lithe bodies, the women's especially, bloated into grossness. The Aboriginal diet was well balanced over twelve months. Their need to move, the walkabout compulsion, was almost certainly a dietary need. They walked to different food. When tribal life broke down the wandering became restlessness without purpose, their diet a disaster. The good thick drink they made by steeping the nectar-rich cones of banksia flowers in water was replaced by empty sugar bags cut in squares and soaked in tins of water. In search of the nourishment it did not contain, they drank the sweet water till their bellies distended.

So much had attitudes to Aborigines changed where they were no longer a threat, James and Ebenezer Orr offered a reward in the *Maitland Mercury* 20 October 1855 for the capture of the murderer of an Aboriginal.

'Fifty Pounds Reward

'Whereas a Native Black, named Charley, employed by us as a shepherd at a station called Sam's Well, near Borah, in the District of Liverpool Plains, was barbarously MURDERED on Friday evening, the 28th of September, while tending his flock in the bush; and strong suspicion resting upon William Wright (also then in our service, and who has since absconded) as the perpetrator of the above deed, for whom a warrant has been granted, we hereby offer a reward of Twenty Pounds to any person who will lodge the said William Wright in any of her Majesty's gaols, and Fifty Pounds on conviction of the murderer of the said aboriginal Charley. Description of the above named William Wright:-

Height, about 5 feet 7 inches
Age, about 30 years
Hair, light brown
Complexion, sallow
Sharp featured, and inclined to stoop in his walk
Country. State of Massachusetts, United States of
America.'

Unlucky diggers from other countries who had not made their fares home were seeking jobs, as well as the unwanted thieves and bad men run off the fields.

Ebenezer Orr took over the management of Borah and Burrumbulla. Summer and winter, he dressed his fattening shepherdesses in long red flannel. The head station where he lived was Burrumbulla. When working sheep on Borah he camped with his shepherdesses in a big fortified cave in a little hill near the creek. The cave has now fallen in but it existed until the 1920s with the remains of the barricade of upright poles – no one knows why it was needed. An Aboriginal bora ground was nearby where the sacred initiation ceremonies were held. Big Yellow Boxes with carved trunks marked the site until well into this century, when sharefarmers, greedy for another hectare or so to put under crop, burnt them.

At shearing time the woolly sheep were driven up the west bank of the creek to the shed. The shorn sheep were driven back down the east bank. The red girls behind their flocks showed up for miles.

Thomas Gordon Gibbons Dangar came to Cubbaroo in 1851 as the young manager for William Dangar of his interest in the Button runs. Thomas Cook, William's nephew, managed the runs William owned outright. One of the most successful of all named Dangar, Thomas Gordon Gibbons Dangar was the son of Matthew and Charlotte Selina Gibbons. Matthew Gibbons died when Thomas was an infant and his widow married Thomas Dangar a year or so later. She died when her son was only nine years old, and the kindly Thomas reared him and gave him his name. He had nothing else to give him. T. G. G. Dangar had to make his own way.

After a few years as manager he moved south across the river and made his home at Bullerawa where he lived for over twenty years, for much of that time the 'roads and bridges' member of Parliament for Gwydir. William Dangar retired and went to London in 1857. Thomas Cook and Thomas G. G. Dangar then leased the runs. Thomas Cook eventually inherited his share. Thomas Dangar might have had some help from his foster uncle but mostly he borrowed from J. B. Rundle – the runs periodically appear in Rundle's name. Off and on he owned a broad strip of connecting runs extending south from Bullerawa about forty kilometres into the present forest area: Bullerawa, Talluba, Keppit, Grugi, Eato (or Etoo) West, Eato East, Werai, Vivianfield, Cumbil, Upper Cumble, Back Vacant Cumble, Coormore, Coghill, Upper Dunwarian, North Wangen, Milchomi Back No. 1, Milchomi Back No. 3.

In manuscript description of the boundaries of Eato made in 1851 – inferior country that had been used off and on for its water – an old hut named Tubba, or Dubbo is mentioned. One wonders how old the hut was. Was it older than the thirteen or fourteen years since known men might have built it as an outstation?

By 1856 Henry Dangar was a sick and aging man living in Sydney. He had been parliamentary member for his home district Northumberland during the passage of the 1847 land laws. His slow Cornish wit could not match Wentworth's and Lowe's and he found it a confusing experience. In partnership with his youngest brother, Richard Cary, he built meat canning works near Newcastle. It opened for business at the end of 1847 and the British Admiralty ordered large quantities. Just as the works promised to be successful, the huge sales of meat to the gold diggers forced the price so high the Dangar brothers could not compete and they closed down. Henry and Grace went to London for a holiday. He had a slight stroke aboard ship and decided to sell all his land. William, seemingly always there to lean on, organised the sales. When Henry and Grace returned to Australia in 1855 after a second trip abroad, Henry was given a welcome dinner at the Caledonian Hotel at Singleton, an evening surely of stupefying dullness. Sixteen men were present, 'the table groaned with a profusion of good things; the wines were of the first class'. Until four in the morning they ate and drank formal toasts to the Queen, to Prince Albert, to their son the Prince of Wales, to all the other Royal children – they then numbered about six more – separately, to the guest of the evening, the pastoral and agricultural interests, the town and trade of Singleton, the clergy, the ladies, Mr Gaggin and the magistracy of Singleton, the surveyor of the northern roads, the chairman, vice-chairman, Mrs Dangar, Mr William Dangar. There might have been more. The correspondent who reported it to the *Maitland Mercury* of 17 November 1855 added '&c'. 'Most of these toasts were ably responded to.'

With the breakdown in the tribal lives of the Aborigines had come the third major change influencing the land. By the 1850s, in many places by the 1840s, grasses were changing and the ground was growing harder. Then everywhere in settled districts regular burning of grasses by Aborigines stopped. Australia had been cultivated by fire. Even tribes living in the central deserts burnt as rain approached to attract game to new sprung grass. The coming rain controlled the area burnt. The country was vast. The Aborigines were few. Perhaps the desert country was burnt every four or five years.

In the more highly populated, better rainfall districts the Aborigines burnt progressive patches along stream banks. Sometimes they put the fires out when they had burnt enough by beating them with broken-off leafy branches of eucalypts, excellent beaters I have often used. Kangaroos and Emus were supplied with a succession of the sweet new shoots of grass that attract them. So the Aborigines kept their game in good condition and they always knew where to find it. Much of Australia had been burnt once or twice a year for thousands of years.

The cattle had changed too. Some breeders had almost bred out the mixed early blood. By the 1850s there was frequent reference in advertisements of cattle for sale to herds 'improved by A. A. Co's bulls'. Herefords were still few. Most of the better cattle were Durhams, the big roan cattle the too-small modern shorthorns were bred from. Even then the giants of the breed were disappearing, the fat bullocks that dressed 600 to 700 kilograms and weighed about 1.3 tonnes liveweight.

But they were still big cattle. When Patch and Glennie split their partnership and offered their Pilliga and Milchomi runs for sale at the beginning of 1854, Mort & Co. advertised the cattle as a special feature, and also – how much conditions had changed – they emphasised the nearness to market.

'. . . the quality of these cattle are unexceptionable. Eight thorough-bred Durham bulls bred by G. Fenwick, Esq., late of the Paterson, got by his celebrated bulls, Thrifty and Harlequin, out of the Australian Agricultural Company's thorough-bred heifers, have been running with the herd the last six years . . . as a specimen of the quality of these cattle, it may be remarked that the last draft boiled down by Mr Bourn Russell of Stony creek, 10 January 1853, consisting of 100 bullocks and 30 cows, produced 250 lbs of tallow per head. The cattle are quiet and well broken to the runs . . .

'Pilliga, well-known to be one of the most fattening, best watered and extensive runs in the Lower Namoi . . . is distant 290 miles from Maitland, and 300 from Sydney, being an easy drive of three weeks for fat cattle to either market . . . the improvements comprise a comfortable Slab Cottage, containing sitting-room and two bedrooms, floored and comfortably furnished with Store behind Kitchen, a stockman's Hut, detached with four compartments, a three-stall Stable, with box for breaking-in colts or for an entire horse.

'A most commodious and substantial Stock-yard in which 3,000 head of cattle can be worked, being subdivided into nine parts, amongst which are branding and milking yards, and lanes and gates for drafting . . .

'One stockman and two natives can manage the whole affair . . .'

H. R. Newman who bought it failed within ten years. J. B. Rundle who made much money lending on mortgage then foreclosing took over. Rundle was an astute businessman. In partnership with Richard Cary Dangar he formed the firm of hardware merchants that became Dangar, Gedye and Malloch. He associated with two of Henry Dangar's successful sons in other thriving businesses.

Sheep had changed as well as men and cattle. No throwbacks to fat tails or brown hair had been seen for over twenty years. Edward Cox from his main stud at Dabee advertised 450 two-year-old merino rams for sale with a testimonial from Marcus F. Brownrigg of the A. A. Company saying he had bought ten, and 'I am almost disposed to prefer them to the imported rams we have received into our flocks'.

But there was still a lot of work to be done with Australian merinos. They cut only a kilogram of wool. Most breeders except the Macarthurs concentrated on Saxon rams, descendants of sheep housed, rugged, fed and pampered on little German farms as though they were spinning gold. They had lost their constitution and in Australia the ultra fine wool deteriorated to dusty cobweb. The bigger French Rambouillet and secretly the English Lincoln had to be used to restore vigour.

Different breeders had different ideas and bred distinctive merinos. It was not until the late 1960s that anyone realised how very different they were. The progeny of crosses made in Victoria and Condobolin, NSW, between different strains showed hybrid vigour.

After selling all his runs – he had land on the Lachlan, Macquarie and Murrumbidgee as well as the Namoi runs John Lloyd bought – William Wentworth retired with his family to London in 1854. That year John Lloyd, too, went to London, a sick man. Ten years living on corned beef, damper and black tea had ruined his health. Europeans had little more idea of good diet than the Aborigines after they stopped seeking their own foods. And the weak English beer, that like the Aborigine's nectar was rich in nutrients, was as unpopular in Australia as it had become in England. Distilled spirits (rum) was the favoured drink. It made men drunk and supplied no food.

Edward Lloyd, John's brother, took over as manager and another brother, Charles, came from England to help. He had been managing a woollen mill for a wealthy cousin. John Lloyd sent fencing wire from London soon after he arrived, sufficient for seventy kilometres of five wire fence. He thought sheep would do better running free in paddocks instead of being shepherded, an idea generally scorned for another ten years. The wire arrived at the end of 1854 but the track across the Breeza plain was boggy. It lay waiting for months on the wagons till the track dried. It was the middle of 1856 before the first fence was run fifteen kilometres round a lambing paddock near the house on Burburgate. Someone had put up short lengths of wire fencing in Victoria in 1854. The paddocks on Burburgate were the first big wire fenced paddocks in Australia.

Paddock changed its meaning in Australia as much as creek or forest. An English paddock was a small enclosure in a field. Many hedged English fields would have fitted in the Burburgate paddocks.

Edward Lloyd bought connecting runs in his own name. The Orr brothers sold him Borah and Burrumbulla. James left the partnership and Ebenezer bought Yaminba and Garrawilla. Edward Lloyd also bought Ghoolendaadi from Alfred and Henry Denison then in partnership (Henry was Sir William's full brother) and Arrarownie that had had several owners since John Robertson. Charles took over as manager of the Namoi River runs but Edward kept an interest. The three brothers functioned as Lloyd Brothers, bought other runs, and built up Burburgate as the notable head station of an astonishing string of runs down the Namoi from Manilla to Wee Waa, 180 kilometres of seldom-broken line sometimes both sides of the river, sometimes one side only, then from Wee Waa north in a broad strip for another eighty kilometres almost to the Gwydir at Moree. They held, as Charles Lloyd spelt them, Manilla, Glenriddle, Cowmore, Collygrah, Bundabolla, Gulligal, Burburgate Proper, Bull, Dripping Rock, Boggabri, Baan Baa North and South, Wallah (Bundur Wallur of Mary Jamison's description), Tibbereena, Wee Waa North, Gundermain, Gallathera, Edgeroi, Gurley, Bimble, an aggregate of over 500,000 hectares of rich country.

Before Burburgate was completely fenced, seventeen shepherds had charge of the sheep in flocks of a thousand to fifteen hundred. The names of the shepherds are a mixture of given names only, surnames only, full names and foreign names: Tommy, Rooney, Cocking, Sim Ki, J. Griffiths, Ah Li, Simon, Carney, Wm Landers, Thos Landers, Jourdan, G. Griffiths, Haw, Le Goui, Alec Hill, Charley, J. Dick. Sometimes men asked for work who claimed no name at all.

By 1859 the Lloyds were running over 100,000 sheep. They killed a thousand or more a year for rations on all the runs. A hectare or two of garden on Burburgate supplied vegetables. They established an orchard and a vineyard. The woolshed complex was 300 metres long.

William Wentworth, hearing of the success in London, grew rancorously jealous. In 1859 he began a suit in Chancery to have the sale of his share of the runs put aside. The time in which such a suit could be brought had almost expired; no lesser court would have accepted it. Wentworth argued that the value of the runs had been misrepresented at the time of the sale and that Mort's taking of a share made the sale illegal. He demanded half the value of the properties in 1859 plus a half share of the profits for the six years since he sold them.

For five years the highest legal brains of Great Britain argued the case at their leisure. If it had not been for that acknowledgment Mort got Wentworth to sign he might have won. Wentworth lost. It cost him twenty-five thousand pounds sterling. He got justice.

When Wentworth began his suit in London in 1859, John Robertson and Henry Parkes were campaigning for election to the four-year-old responsible Parliament. Both of them were to become knights, both premiers several times. Although it was early in their careers, both had been already seasoned in government. Henry Parkes declared he was a free trader and opposed to state aid for religion. He pointed to one of his successes as chairman of the committee which inquired into the electric telegraph: 'The gentlemen who were the foremost in opposing it were the first to celebrate its opening in champagne.'

Henry Parkes's position in life had lifted considerably since the letter to his sister nineteen years before. Financially he was rather worse off. He no longer had threepence in his pocket. Before his election was announced he appeared before the Chief Commissioner of Insolvency with a deficiency of almost 11,000 pounds sterling.

John Robertson, handsome, bigoted, anti-Victorian, was also a free-trader. 'Why should we bloody well close our gates to all the world in order to trade with those bloody fellows across the Murray, who produce just the same as we do, and all they can send us is bloody cabbages?'

But his main concern was a land law. He took up the cry of the rapidly increased population, 'Unlock the land'. He argued that the

squatters' leases had to be broken as they expired, and in his passion
his language was austere. 'The land is either their freehold, or it is not'
he told a meeting at Murrurundi. 'If it is, let us admit it; if not, surely
the land should now be open to the people.' He proposed 'free selection
before survey.' He was elected.

In 1860 as Premier and Minister for Lands he introduced bills which
enabled a selector (any man, woman or child) to go on to a run and peg
out an area of 16 to 128 hectares which he could buy on terms at five
dollars a hectare. He had to live on his selection and make improvements to the value of five dollars a hectare. Robertson, like Macquarie, wanted a nation of farmers.

The bills caused an astonishing disruption of parliament. The lower
house dissolved twice within months and new elections had to be held
each time. When a strong majority for the bills were elected and they
were passed as Robertson wanted them in the Assembly, the Council
blocked them. Since parliamentary government was introduced the
Council was again wholly appointed. There was a fixed minimum
number of councillors but no maximum, so the lower house arranged
for the appointment of sufficient new agreeable members to get the
bills through. When the new members walked into the House, all the
old members walked out. Nobody was left to swear them in. A whole
new Council had to be appointed.

Once the bills were passed, runholders and selectors continued the
farce. Some genuine farmers got good land and worked it – sufficient
to increase production significantly. But alas, the bills were 'framed for
honest men'. Too many swindlers selected deliberately to make
management of the rest of the run difficult, then sold at a profit to the
runholder anxious to gain back access to water or buildings. The
runholders peacocked their land by buying sixteen hectare blocks
spaced strategically to make selections unattractive. Some borrowed,
bought too many patches, and ruined themselves. They sought mineral
reserves where there were no minerals. They paid men fees for the use
of their names as dummies.

Andrew Brown thanked God for His hand in the expert protection
given his runs: '31 December 1865 . . . water reserves made preventing
free selection wherever these are relieves me of much anxiety and af-
fords better prospects for future returns for these and every other bless-
ing I offer sincere thanksgiving to the Giver of all blessings.'

For fourteen years men enjoyed themselves outwitting the law until
in 1875 John Robertson, too pig-headed to admit its imperfections, was
forced to block up the biggest of the loopholes.

But land use is dominated by weather and the chance of profit, not by land laws. The north was still too remote for grain growing as a business. Selection mostly waited the coming of the railway. Scab in sheep and the 1864 flood that followed two years drought had more effect along the Namoi than land laws.

In 1863 Charles Lloyd noted in his diary: 'January . . . Heard of miserable lot of sheep suspicious passing down river belonging to Vivers . . . in February (early) heard rumours of scab appearing amongst sheep on several stations through which Vivers' sheep had passed . . . most awful news – as it meant ruin to several sheep owners . . .'

Forty to fifty thousand of Lloyd brothers' sheep became infected. Charles Lloyd experimented with dipping mixtures. He mixed together the main components of old remedies that were partially effective: lime, sulphur and tobacco water. A thorough dipping of the sheep in swim-through baths killed the mites. Scab could be eradicated. Charles Lloyd later went to the Cape Colony at the request of the government to advise on treatment of scab. His mixture, dangerous to the men using it if it gets into the lungs, was still in use in modern times.

Twelve months after the scabby sheep moved upriver, in February 1864, the Namoi came down in the highest flood yet known. 'The flood came so fast in the night', wrote Charles Baldwin who was managing Diniwarindi for his uncle, Otto, 'and it being dark and pouring down rain, that we were obliged to put the children and three women in the boat and tie it to the porch of the back door. We waited till daylight when twelve of us started in the boat. We had to pull quite half a mile. We only saved one bag of flour (for nineteen of us), no salt, one bag of sugar, and some tea that was in the water all night.'

Charles Baldwin had just built a new home, he had imported all the furniture, he had an expensive new carriage. The house collapsed and everything went soon after they rowed away.

At Manila a man named Fitzgerald who worked for the Lloyds, lived in a slab hut by the river with his wife and stepdaughter. All drowned. Burburgate head station went half a metre under water. Four to five thousand sheep drowned. Sixty to seventy men, women and children – Chinese, Aboriginal and European – spent three days in a loft above the huge woolshed. George Bowman, caught at Baan Baa south – the Lloyd brothers had recently sold it – on his way to Terry Hie Hie, spent the night on the roof of the house with water almost to the top of the walls. Harper, the new owner, told the story.

'About dusk we saw the woolshed torn up and carried past us with two men on the top – an old man named George, and one of the shearers; it was most melancholy to hear them bid us "good bye"; just then the roof parted between them, and carried them each different ways, fortunately they struck against the tree and we saw the men saved by climbing into them.' When the water went down two of his shepherds walked in after two days and nights in a tree to report all the sheep gone.

The Milner's house at Broadwater had been built three metres vertically above the height of the 1840 flood. The Aborigines told them there would never be higher water. Mrs Milner still lived there among a good vineyard and orchard. The water went thirty centimetres into the house. She continued to manage the run. Broadwater has had a strange connection with women. After Mary Prise and Mrs Milner, Gael Penrose farmed what was left of the run in the 1970s.

'Our hitherto promising little village of Narribri presents a fearful wreck of desolation,' somebody reported to the *Sydney Morning Herald* after the flood. Narrabri was growing on both sides of the river: round a slab cottage and a stockman's hut beside the Greyhound Inn that the Lloyd brothers had built on Tibbereena north soon after they bought it, and round Peers's private hospital built on a corner of Glen Quinn in 1859.

Patrick Quinn saved his food – he got it into a loft just in time – but he lost his 'office equipment'. Since he could not read or write he might not have regretted it much. He had only recently been held up by bushrangers on his way back from Maitland, a regular hazard on the northern road. Coming down the range from Murrurundi towards the Willow Tree Inn in December 1863, his buggy was stopped by two men, one with a double-barrelled shotgun, the other with a pistol in each hand. They made him drive into the bush, unharness and hobble his horses. They emptied his pockets, returned a cheque, his watch and chain, and enough silver to get him home, then one of the bushrangers watched him at gunpoint while the other held up each traveller that came along. After five hours they had sixteen captives. Then came Nowland's coach. They ran it off the road, robbed the passengers and slashed open the mailbags. They overlooked a bag of gold in the boot. One man tried to get away and the man with the pistols shot his horse. Then they loaded their booty on their pack-horse and made off into the mountains. As they were going one man told Patrick Quinn he knew him well. He would come and have Christmas dinner with him.

Quinn was then thriving as a land owner. He had bought out the Josephs, held their runs briefly, then resold at a profit. As well as Glen

Quinn, in 1864 he owned Wee Waa south and other runs north of the Namoi.

Andrew Doyle who had moved with his family across the river to Cooma had no heavy losses but water entered the house. His half-brother, Alfred John Doyle, had taken over the Narrabri run.

The runholders on every river in the north had the same stories to tell. Losses were enormous. After some of the flood water had dried up, Charles Lloyd set out in March to visit Callandoon, a run his brother Edward had bought on the Macintyre near Goondiwindi. He had to travel via New England to get there. It was a hard journey through water and mud all the way. At Callandoon he found the manager drunk on his bed. He had begun to drink as the rains began. Twenty thousand sheep had drowned and expensive imported rams. The Lloyd empire never recovered.

Although big Andrew Doyle was not ruined by the flood, at 49 he was about to make a ruinous move to the Barwon. His first wife, Catherine, had died after their tenth child was born. He married again and was beginning a new family. He was a huge, restless man, two metres tall and so strong be could take a four-bushell bag of wheat weighing 110 kilograms in each arm off a wagon and carry them up steps into a shed.

To finance his new runs he borrowed from the relentless John Eales. So Cooma and Thurradulba show in Eales's name as mortgagee. Andrew Doyle bought a run on the Barwon near Brewarrina, and Bundabulla to the north on the Bokhara River. Before the mortgage fell due he had sufficient wool on wagons on the way to market to meet it. It rained, the wagons bogged, the time expired and Eales foreclosed. Andrew Doyle did not live many years after that. He died prematurely aged at 65.

In a day when all houses were low and dark, Ebenezer Orr built a house so low and dark on the bank of Yaminba Creek that people did not like going into it. The roof was flat and the walls barely 1.8 metres high. The height of Australians has increased markedly over the last 150 years. Some of the convicts were less than one metre tall, many were less than one and a half metres. Not a nail was used in the house. All joints were morticed and pegged with wooden pegs.

Ebenezer Orr made a good garden near the house and grew lucerne on a black flat near the creek. The stockyards covered almost half a hectare.

At least two of his Aboriginal shepherdesses lived in the house with him. By one of them he had a daughter, Mary. While she was still young, the grass on Yaminba began to fail. Orr had also owned Arrarownie briefly. That run persistently looked better than it was. He sold Arrarownie, abandoned most of Yaminba and moved his head station to the good land of Garrawilla. When Mary was eight or nine years old he married a Sydney woman and made another home in Sydney. He wanted Mary reared as a white child so he took her from her mother and paid the Carlows to rear her. She went to school in Sydney – Orr paid for it – and grew into a good-looking young woman, but she could not fit happily into the white world and cried often because she was black. She married a man named Cain but died an alcoholic in early middle age.

After Yaminba was abandoned, Joe Launt, a poddy-dodger (stealer of unbranded calves) who had been knocking about the creeks for a year or two, decided to extend his activities. He had come up with his sons about 1857 from a run north of Coolah called the Black Swamp and camped on a waterhole on Borah Creek called Cocaboy. He never paid the licence fees on the Black Swamp and under later holders the name passed into Australian tradition as the Black Stump. Joe Launt might have bought a block of freehold at Cocaboy – old maps show a narrow rectangle jutting out from the creek – but more likely he leased a few hundred hectares from the successive owners of Arrarownie.

Cocaboy to this day has a reputation as a place of mysterious noises. The Launts soon moved downstream to live and on a lonely spot between the two creeks built a house and a set of cattle yards capable of holding 2,000 head. They became the spelling yards for well-organised cattle rustlers operating between Victoria and the new colony, Queensland, that separated in 1859. It is unlikely that Joe Launt was a principal in the cattle rustling. He was too foolishly talkative. Probably he tailed the quiet Victorian and Queensland cattle the rustlers used as coachers. They drove stolen Queensland cattle down for sale in Victoria with a lead of Victorian cattle and brought Victorian cattle back with a Queensland lead.

Some posts of the yards are still standing. The solid ironbark has withstood 120 years of termites and bushfires. The rails are all gone – the police cut them down in 1864 – but from the mortice holes and the shaped tops of the posts one can see there were four rails and a cap rail. When I walked in to find them in 1974 two posts in one of the gateways were still in good order. Shaped slip rails were slid into holes cut with a mortising axe in one of the posts, dropped into L-shaped slots mortised in the other post and held in place with stout wooden pegs.

Perhaps the rains of early 1864 disrupted the rustling. Joe Launt and his sons, George and Joseph, began picking up a few too many from their neighbours. Fred Lowry, a relation of the Launts, rode with them sometimes and a half-caste well known in the district named Billy Purcell, surely a son of Charles Purcell who took up Garrawilla. A man named Allan McPhee or Wilson, usually known as Billy Bullfrog, rode down from Warialda to join them. McPhee's brother was wanted for murder. Fred Lowry's brother had been shot by the police a few months before.

Ebenezer Orr missed cattle off Garrawilla. Worse, he missed Betsy, a twenty-year-old Aboriginal shepherdess, his favourite at that time. She had run off with Joe Launt, or more likely, one of his sons. Orr tracked her to Launt's house and brought her back. He kept a closer watch on his cattle.

In February 1864 he rode to Coonabarabran for constables Ward and Gill. That town was growing, too. James Weston's son had gone blind so he sold the run and his hotel to Alfred Croxon about 1858 and retired to Maitland. Alfred Croxon rebuilt the hotel as the Travellers' Inn and applied to buy land for splitting into town lots.

Ebenezer Orr and the two constables, with Tommy, an Aboriginal employed by Orr, as tracker, rode towards Garrawilla. They found calves bellowing for their mothers, and tracks in deserted sheepyards where cattle had been recently drafted. Tommy tracked calves and horsemen on a roundabout route over stony ridges where it was hoped no tracks would show. From one of the ridges they saw four horsemen driving 140 head of cattle slowly while the cattle fed. They followed them at a distance to Orr's old house on Yaminba Creek and watched the cattle turned into a log-fenced paddock. The men went into the house.

They waited till after dark and rushed the house during a sudden shower of rain. They grabbed George Launt and Billy Purcell. There were three other men in it. Billy Bullfrog made a dive for one of the doors. A constable grabbed him by the belt. The belt broke and Billy escaped. Young Joe Launt and Fred Lowry dashed out another door. Constable Ward shot Lowry and Joe Launt surrendered.

They buried Lowry where he fell, sandwiched between two sheets of bark. The Dingoes dug him up so someone buried him again a bit deeper. It was usual to dig graves near homesteads as a protection from Dingoes.

Patrick Quinn saw Billy Bullfrog rowing across the Namoi near Glen
Quinn and rode for the police. They tracked him to Warialda and
caught him on Gragin station where he worked. But his three names
confused his identity too thoroughly even though his horse was
branded OR for Orr. The Launt brothers and Billy Purcell were tried
at Mudgee. They were found not guilty too. It was difficult to get convictions for cattle stealing. Too many jurymen had themselves stolen
too many cattle.

But old Joe Launt, not directly involved with the cattle stealing, got
two years hard labour in Bathurst gaol. Furious at the arrest of his
sons, he rode the district declaring he would make old Orr bloody glad
to leave the district; he would leave him as poor as a shag on a rock; he
would scab his bloody sheep. When he told Orr's shepherds the same
thing and when they found him riding round Garrawilla with cut
squares of fresh scabby sheepskin in his saddlebags, they reported him.
He was brought to trial at Mudgee in July, the first man tried under
the new Scab Act of 1864.

Distraught by their losses the Lloyd brothers broke their partnership
after long loud quarrels. Charles Lloyd married a wealthy Sydney girl
in 1865 and sailed for England on his honeymoon, a crazy voyage with
a drunken captain who lost his reckoning going round Cape Horn and
brought the ship too far south among icebergs, then, free of them after
a worrying few days, he could not find the Falkland Islands where he
intended to get supplies. Within sight of the coast of Ireland, the seas
rough and the captain helpless, the passengers hailed a passing pilot-
boat and transferred to it for the run into harbour.

Among Charles Lloyd's diary notes of balls and dinners with titled
families in England and Ireland, the Moseleys of Leaton Hall are mentioned often. The honeymooners attended a lavish ball given in honour
of James Moseley on his twenty-first birthday. James was to come to
Australia within a few years and buy Glen Quinn and Turrawan.

Back in Sydney early in 1867, a week or two after landing, the Lloyds
lost their baby daughter born in England. Families of ten to fifteen
were common in the nineteenth century – birth was often a yearly
event, and deaths came often enough to disrupt lives every several
years. Children died with startling suddenness.

Charles Lloyd bought back into Wallah that his brother, Richard,
an engineer in Paris, had taken over in an unpleasant family adjustment of debt. Charles and his wife went up to manage it and after the

halls and castles they had stayed in on their honeymoon and the comfort of rented Sydney homes, they lived for several months in an old bark hut on Wallah.

Edward Lloyd lost all his runs and took a job with the Bank of New South Wales. John Lloyd retained Burburgate, heavily mortgaged to Ebenezer Vickery, a hard-fisted Methodist boot-manufacturer and colliery owner.

By 1869 Burburgate had been fully restored after the flood and much more fencing done. It was reputedly the best-improved run in Australia. Fenced lambing paddocks of about 2,000 hectares faced the river on both sides. Beyond them were paddocks averaging about 12,000 hectares, each equipped with huts and yards, and beyond them again on the north well-watered unfenced stations on which the sheep were still shepherded: Dripping Rock, Mihi, Mulligaloon and Wee-yan, where the good Wean Picnic races are now held each year. Burburgate had its own boiling-down works capable of handling 1,000 sheep or 100 head of cattle a day. A cooper made the tallow casks on site. More than 20,000 fat wethers were turned off a year and 100 head of cattle a month. The wool clip was a thousand bales or more of scoured wool.

Ever since the wool industry began sheep had been washed before shearing to avoid the slow difficult haul to market of unneccessary weight. Dust, grass seed and natural greases amounted to half the weight of a fleece. The sheep wash was usually a crude affair built in the bed of a creek dammed with an earth bank to give sufficient depth of water. The woolly sheep swam through the soaking pen to men who soaped them, then let them swim on beneath staging where men with long T-shaped poles scrubbed them and ducked them right under water. The washed sheep climbed up the bank on a wooden ramp and walked along a corduroyed race to the covered shed, where they were penned on an elevated grated floor that let their round balls of dung drop through. It took them a week or more to dry. The water dripped from them like sweat. The receival pens in a shearing shed are still known as sweating pens.

On Burburgate the water for washing was pumped out of the Namoi river into tanks by a centrifugal pump driven by a steam engine. The water in the tanks was heated by steam and directed by spouts on to individually penned sheep. A splash barrier protected the men from constant wetting.

But even with such expensive machinery, river water and creek water stained the wool permanently and the starved sheep lost condition. As roads improved and railways extended, washing went out of fashion. Wool was sold in the grease and scoured at the mills. Garrawilla piped the wash water from a clear spring and persisted with washing up to the 1880s, years after other runs had stopped.

Charles Lloyd in 1861 installed scouring machinery and by 1869 much of the Burburgate wool was shorn in the grease. The wool, classed into matching lengths and fibre diameter, was pushed in wheeled bins along a tram track and over a weighbridge to heated soaking vats in the centre of the long shed. Then it was rolled through tanks of alkaline solution and out through an immense mangle to steam-heated drying racks. Another tramway carried it to the pressing room. The big bales were stored in a high open-ended wool room at the far end of the shed, built so that the wagons could pull alongside it to load.

The haul for the teams was already getting less. The railway had reached Muswellbrook in the Hunter. It was almost to Wallerawang westward. Gunnedah was a town. The old name The Woolshed, attributed to the village from John Johnston's bark shed, was no longer heard. A village had begun to grow round the Gulligal post office on Burburgate to the consternation of the Commissioner of Crown Lands who regarded the innkeepers and storekeepers as illegal occupants. He had moved some of them in 1866.

Ebenezer Vickery, with 129,000 pounds sterling invested in Burburgate on mortgage, certainly owned more than half of it. He thought it a 'fine property to hold' and in 1869 put in his own manager under an agreement to pay John Lloyd a thousand pounds sterling a year out of profits. He agreed to advance John Lloyd who had no money at all 250 pounds to go to London to raise sufficient money to buy out Vickery's interest. Vickery was to furnish him with a copy of the accounts and plans of the run.

In January 1870, in the office of a Sydney solicitor, Vickery presented a deed for John Lloyd's signature with the threat that if he did not sign it immediately he would be arrested under orders of Vickery's bankers and prevented from going to London. Too beaten to refuse, and trusting Vickery's word instead of the print, John Lloyd signed away Burburgate for 250 pounds sterling, and Vickery hurried him aboard ship a fortnight sooner than he intended to sail.

He arrived in London with no documents, querulous, vague and unintelligible. Perhaps he had had a stroke, perhaps he had become an alcoholic. He complained so incessantly to his solicitors of everybody he had been in contact with they could not single out the complaints against Vickery as of any more consequence than the rest. The trip to London was a waste of time. He returned to Australia.

And immediately made himself obnoxious by threatening to select on Charles Lloyd's Baan Baa. 'Which he eventually did to me great injury' wrote Charles Lloyd. So John was one of the first selectors in the north. At that time he had not a friend left.

He finally made a solicitor understand what had happened to him. The matter came to court in 1873. In argument and appeals it was not settled until 1878. It was proved John Lloyd's interest amounted to about 100,000 pounds sterling and Vickery seized it for 250 pounds. It 'shocks the conscience of a Court of Equity', said the judge of the Supreme Court in summing up.

Vickery was charged with all costs. He kept Burburgate – his heirs still own part of it – but he had to pay a fair price for Lloyd's share. It was too late for John Lloyd. He died three years later.

About 1867 Frederick York Wolseley bought Arrarownie. He had come to Australia in 1854 at the age of seventeen and got the necessary colonial experience on his brother-in-law's run in the Riverina. Meanwhile his elder brother, 1st Viscount Wolseley, Colonel of the Royal Irish Regiment, had taken part in the Burmese War, the Crimean War, the Indian Mutiny, the Chinese War, with several more engagements to come. As listed in Burke's *Peerage, Baronetage & Knightage* these awful wars have the significance of cricket matches.

Frederick Wolseley enclosed about 4,000 hectares with a twelve wire fence 28 kilometres long to protect his sheep from Dingoes. He thought barbed wire would be more effective and manufactured barb was not then available. The usual barbs were sharp flat strips of metal indented in the middle so that they could be sprung over plain wire. Wolseley's fencers used a hand tool – it might have been his own invention – that twisted short lengths of wire tightly on to the strained wire in the fence and left the ends poking out sharply. Every fifteen centimetres along the 336 kilometres of tarred black wire the fencers wound a barb. Yet the fence was not high enough to keep Dingoes out. They climbed over. But Wolseley was wholly engrossed in plans he had for a shearing machine.

For two or three weeks of the year, seldom more than a month, the silent woolsheds wake up and sing. The high-frequency metallic buzz of the handpieces, the slow knock of the diesel engine, the slap of the long belt and the harsh whispering of the overhead gear driving the friction cones all combine in an unmistakable drone that can be heard hundreds of metres away.

I walked into a shed using blade shears in 1950. Jim Dyer of Buangor in the Western District of Victoria used the blades until 1956. He specialised in superfine wool, especially lambswool, and he wanted none of the short second cuts or skin pieces always associated with machine shearing. Shearers and shedhands talked in normal voices. One could hear the click of each pair of shears as they closed after the long slow blows. The loudest noise was the scrape of the blades against the pedal-driven grindstone now and again as a shearer gave his blades a touch-up. A shedhand stood by each shearer brushing away fribs (the shorter pieces of wool on the legs before it runs into true hair near the hooves) so that they did not tangle in the fleece. Two men at the sorting table searched for occasional grass seeds. The wool was exquisite, stretchy and soft as down. The lambswool made 572 pence a pound in 1953, 1,050 cents a kilogram, a price not exceeded until 1980.

Such attention to quality can no longer be made to pay. Jim Dyer's wool is still as good. But in the 1970s the average price was a fifth of what it was in the 1950s and costs ten times higher. In its brief season his shed now sings as loudly as everybody else's.

Frederick York Wolseley soon found that Arrarownie would be no help in financing the manufacture of a shearing handpiece. He went home to England for more money, worked on the design for a year or two in Melbourne, then in 1876 bought Euroka, a run near Walgett. With the help of a remarkable blacksmith named George Gray he developed the first commercial handpiece, usually known as the Wolseley hotbox. It was said that learners who had not the knack of setting the irregular rocker screw developed hands as red as boiled lobster claws.

After Wolseley bought Euroka, Tom Williams, a tall half-caste stockman still remembered for his ability as a roughrider, moved most of the stock from Arrarownie to Euroka. Wolseley's nephew, Erle Wolseley Creagh, took over management of Arrarownie. There was little enough to manage. Out of favour with his family, he was cast out of England in 1876 at the age of seventeen and abandoned as a remittance man in the homestead by Borah Creek.

Cuthbert Fetherstonhaugh came to Goorianawa in 1869 to manage the run for the Walker estate. James Walker's widow, Robina, had died in 1867. A hard riding Irishman who spoke German like a native (his bankrupt father had taken the family to Germany where living was cheap), he had run wild horses on the Goulburn River; he had been a preacher for a time, too unorthodox for his dean; he had managed a run in the Riverina where he was chased by three bushrangers firing shots at him. He outgalloped the range of their pistols and led them across a difficult river crossing where one of them drowned. Barcroft Boake wrote a ballad about him but unfortunately none of it is worth quoting. He came to Goorianawa with his gay, pretty wife, 'one of the belles of Melbourne' her very old daughter told me. She drove her own lively chestnuts four-in-hand and she matched her husband with the reins.

Edward King Cox, son of Edward, bought Baradine, probably as drought relief country, from the Walker estate in 1867 but did not keep it long. A village was then developing on a surveyed reserve. Two or three selectors came on to the creek. The rest of the Baradine run was absorbed again by Goorianawa, owned mainly by James Walker's daughters and Thomas Gabriel Walker, a distant cousin. His only son had died as a youth two years after his father.

Robina Walker had sold Coonamble and Magometon in 1863 together with 7,000 cattle all bearing the Walker brand, WR conjoined. But she held Wallerawang and some of the other runs. After her death her daughter, Georgina Lyon Wolgan Walker, married Edwin Barton, the engineer who constructed the crazy Zigzag Railway down the western side of the Blue Mountains.

They lived at Wallerawang, and their son after them. In 1948 their unmarried grandson and granddaughter, James Lyon Walker Barton and Loveday Barton, lived there. A youth employed by them, William Benjamin Harvey-Bugg, shot them both one Sunday morning as they returned to the house from church. The Bartons were 'too kind to me' he illogically explained to the Court.

The Walker and Barton families, some of their employees, and Bobby, an Aboriginal of the Wallerawang tribe, are all buried in the private walled cemetery on Wallerawang. My wife, Joan, and I went there to see it in 1975. Coxs River where Charles Darwin examined the dead Platypus was in flood and we could not drive across the ford to the house. We had to circle the property and come in by another road. Notices at all the gates warned that trespassers would be prosecuted.

There was no one home. It was spitting rain. Smoke from the great stack on the powerhouse at Wallerawang poured down over the property. A great web of wires enmeshed it. The cattle in the paddocks looked good. There was an astonishing collection of machinery in the big sheds. But the old house was neglected. There was cow dung on the path and rough long-tailed sheep in the garden. We tramped about the wet paddocks trying to find the cemetery. The place seemed eerie. We knew Harvey-Bugg was out of prison, an ideal man to keep the property clear of trespassers. We found ourselves absurdly watching the windows for movement or a rifle barrel poking out.

The cemetery was on the side of one hill hidden by another. A stepped-down brick wall one and a half metres high enclosed it, eighty metres long by twenty-six wide. At one end a few ewes and their lambs were camped – shut in there to keep down the grass. They were too long unshorn, uncrutched and daggy. At the other end was the skeleton of a cow.

James Walker's grave is covered by a sandstone slab supporting on six pillars another massive horizontal slab. Lesser members of the family are remembered by lesser slabs, some horizontal, some standing, some levered out of place by vandals.

There is a plan to dam Coxs River to form a lake to supply the powerhouse with water. If this is done most of the property, like Lawson's at Prospect, will go under water.

Andrew Brown still prospered during the 1860s and 1870s and he still held Yearinan, near Baradine. The water mill on the uncertain little creek at Cooerwull was too often idle so he had long ago converted it to steam. Then, looking for more profit, he converted the flour mill into a tweed factory in 1857, and opened his own coal mine to fuel his engines. There is a blank space in the town of Lithgow above the tunnels of his mine.

He complained to his diary in February 1868 that 'all locks and a great many bales of this year's wool is seriously injured with clover burr'. R. Meston, investigating Cumberland disease (anthrax) for the Government in 1859, had reported on the spread of medic. 'Bur medick occupies nearly all the alluvial soils of the Macquarie, Lachlan and Castlereagh, and is fast spreading towards the Hunter as well as Liverpool Plains . . . It is the black clover of the British farmers who hold this species of lucerne in detestation.' Although it certainly lowers wool values and causes bloat in cattle in lush springs, it has increased the carrying capacity of Australia's pastures.

From 1865 until well into the 1870s a boiling-down works operated at Euligal on Dubbo Creek, a part of the old run, Werai. Cheese was made there, too. During the summer cheese and tallow were stored in big cellars. It was carted to the rail head in winter, at first via the western end of the Liverpool Range through Cassilis to Morpeth, later to Muswellbrook, and later still down the western road through Mudgee to the Wang as Wallerawang was called. Dan Jones had two wagons on the run. He brought stores as back load: tea, sugar, big sacks of flour, currants in casks.

I spoke to a number of men who had seen the ruins of the busy factory before they were burnt and before the big holding paddocks were enveloped in dense scrub. But there are no records of who owned it. J. J. Eason is said to have owned Euligal about that time but no memories connected him with the boiling-down works. He even left no record of his association with the land. Perhaps he bought a piece of freehold that sometimes traded freely then without reference to the Department of Lands.

Some runholders were buying extra freehold from the Crown to protect yards and outstation sheds from selectors. Although there were few selectors in the north in the 1860s all runholders were edgy. Many water reserves were determined on northern runs during 1866 and 1867.

One of the earliest selectors in the forest area was Charles Colwell who selected sixty-four hectares of creek frontage on Baradine run in 1872. He called the selection Ulee Wallen. Although the area is still farmed it would now be a bad choice of country. He could have taken first pick of the rich Goorianawa valley. But the first selectors of farming country were limited to well-cleared sandy loam, the only soil their light mouldboards could plough. The stump jump mouldboard was not developed till late in 1876. Few disc ploughs were used till the Sunshine Harvester Works made the Stump Jump Disc Cultivating Plough in 1906.

And the early wheats were not suited to the Australian climate. The white-grained Golden Drop and Spalding, and the red Pedigree were English and European wheats that ripened in the autumn as the days shortened. The Australian summer was too hot so they had to be sown in the winter to ripen in the lengthening days of spring. Tall growing and heavily flagged (leafy), if rain gave out in the spring they burnt off and set no grain at all.

Charles Colwell knew the district. Born at sea in 1837 he had come to Wambolong on the western end of the Warrumbungles with his parents about 1850. He soon spread west from Ulee Wallen across good open plains he called Pretty Plains (we now own part of them) to Teridgerie Creek where he bought more land called Bimble. Eventually nine of his twelve children selected land along that creek.

Thomas G. G. Dangar married Catherine MacKenzie, daughter of the man who grew wheat so early at Wangen. He built a good home on

Bullerawa. No one in the north built mansions costing a hundred thousand pounds sterling like Thomas Chirnside or Sir William Clarke and several others in the Western District of Victoria. But whereas homes on most northern runs were valued at about two hundred pounds, the home on Bullerawa was valued at two thousand.

By the river he built huts to house twenty-five ex-convict workmen who had grown too old to work. He supplied a cook who called them to meals by ringing a big brass bell. Thomas Dangar later donated the old bell to the Pilliga school.

W. C. Cormie, son of David Cormie who was manager for Thomas Dangar, used to watch the old men bathing naked in the Namoi when he was a child. The cat o' nine tails had so scarred their backs they seemed to be covered in scales not skin.

James Moseley, the Irish friend of Charles Lloyd, took over Glen Quinn and Tibbereena from Patrick Quinn about 1871. At the age of sixty-eight the scab had ruined him. He had so little equity left in his runs, Namoi runholders took up a subscription to support him.

In 1873 James Moseley contracted to shear sheep from neighbouring runs in his big shed. Showing the astonishing adaptability of so many early landholders, he built a swing bridge across the Namoi so that he could handle sheep from both sides of the river. It was a crude enough bridge, sides of packing cases nailed to barrels to make a narrow walk. The two halves were towed together in mid-stream by boat and lashed with ropes. But it was many times better than ferrying sheep across by boat, the only alternative.

By the early 1870s there had been no regular burning of the forest area for about twenty-five years. Cattle and sheep had displaced many of the rat-kangaroos. With nothing to destroy seedlings, acacia scrub and white Cypress Pine here and there extended off the ridges to flat land. Seedy grasses had all but taken over and the corkscrew seeds of wire and spear grasses worried sheep. Runholders began to burn again. In the winter they hoped to destroy grass seed, in the summer to drive back the scrub.

But over the next ten years the weather pattern became as important in triggering the growth of forest as the marvellous parade of men. The year 1875 was droughty. So many stock moved in search of grass or water or to forced market, sufficient provision was at last made for them. The Lands Office defined strips about 400 to 800 metres (a quarter to half a mile) wide as travelling stock routes along most northern roads and tracks. Some routes had been gazetted in 1874.

The width had become customary much earlier on the routes to the Victorian goldfields. They were unfenced and usually unmarked so runholders and their employees estimated them as ribbons, drovers estimated them as continuous expanses. Rows over moving stock continued.

During the drought a new industry started in Narrabri, by then the main town on the Namoi. J. Morath and L. Mountford set up steam sawmills employing thirty-four men. In January 1876 a timber reserve was declared immediately south of Wee Waa to ensure a supply for the town. When Arthur Dewhurst, district surveyor, tried to define another reserve for Narrabri, two hundred and ten of the inhabitants protested. They wanted an unrestricted market for the magnificent timber to the south of the town. Most of the logs had been drawn from the north because of the difficult river crossing. But T. G. G. Dangar had promised a bridge. The Government reduced the size of the suggested timber reserve.

In March 1877 James Ward was appointed the first forest ranger in the area to regulate the taking of timber. All timbergetters had to be licensed. They could cut no pine less then thirty centimetres in diameter. In August 1877 the first forest reserve was declared in the area. It consisted of the northern section of Coghill below the Brigalow and the southern section of Molly. It was named Robertson in honour of John Robertson who first referred to the excellence of the timber.

The year 1877 was another drought year. Waterholes in creeks dried up, the lower Namoi became a series of muddy waterholes. Cattle had to walk up to thirty kilometres to water. Thousands of cattle and sheep died. The sandy forest soil stirred into dust.

During 1877 and 1878 the Government declared more forest reserves. The whole of Ceelnoy run was declared, extensions were made to Robertson, and another small area was declared on the western boundary of Molly called Gurleigh, probably from the same Aboriginal word as the run Gurley north of Narrabri. James Ward estimated there were four mature pines to the hectare in the reserves and twenty-five young pines. In places he counted a hundred or more young pines to the hectare. Even that is not dense growth. It gives a spacing between trees of ten metres.

The drought broke partially in 1878; 1879 was wet with extraordinary storms in places. Between daylight and midday on 4 March over 300 millimetres of rain poured on Cumble and neighbouring runs. The year continued wet. Coarse grasses sprang thickly from their butts and seeded heavily before winter. The cattle market was low. There were too many cattle even after the drought losses. When their cattle fattened runholders sent them to the boiling-down works and brought 200,000 extra sheep into the area. They burnt the dry grass to clear the seed and give the sheep a green pick.

And where the fires ran years of pine seed came to life.

6

The Forest Takes Over

The Game Ends

The pines came up ten thousand to the hectare. 'One year the stockmen saw the little pines just up to the top of the horses' hooves,' one man told me. 'The next year the pine tops brushed their boots as they rode. And a year or two after that – those old stockmen used to ride at ten past ten, knees cocked out from the saddle like wings – well, they had to jam their knees in hard behind the pads or the pines would have pushed them backwards out of the saddle. Soon they just mustered their stock and got out. There was no room for grass to grow.'

But it was mostly a less sudden growth than that, and a slower withdrawal. And the growth was not confined to the Pilliga forest area. Everywhere that sheep and cattle had changed the grasses and burning began again after a long break, everywhere the number of rat kangaroos were reduced, trees leapt away. In New South Wales pine scrub came up down the Lachlan and gum scrub on the flood plains of the Murray and Murrumbidgee. On the North Coast the lovely dense rainforest broke its narrow confines along the stream banks and began to climb the sides of the hills. Years earlier mixed eucalypts had started in the Blue Mountains. Andrew Brown commented on the area near present Kurrajong on his way to Sydney to catch the boat in 1839: 'The first part of our route today led through a very rich soil heavily covered with timber there had been some grants given to Pensioners there some

years ago who were allowed rations by Government for some time during the recpt of which they cleared and enclosed small parts of their
locations but when the rations ceased to be issued they all left their
properties which are now covered with young trees much closer than
the original forest . . .'

Most of the growth was commercially useless. Thousands of hectares
of pine on the Lachlan had to be tediously cleared with the axe. But the
growth was valuable because it suddenly threw a protective net over
plants and animals that might otherwise have disappeared. In the
Pilliga the pine eventually also made good timber.

Despite the growth of patches of pine, energetic human life continued in the Pilliga forest. Dave Peebles bought eighteen hectares of freehold by a big waterhole on Yaminba Creek not far from Erle Wolseley
Creagh and built a hotel and blacksmith's shop called Ayrlands. It
catered mainly for teamsters coming out of the Hunter through Cassilis
or up from Mudgee to Narrabri and beyond. But at a shilling a meal
and a shilling a bed, locals rode there, too, for a night out.

Mrs Peebles was a huge woman. She had to turn sideways to walk
through the bar door. Her daughter, Ellen, married Bob Miller,
brother of Jack on Kiambir. When Bob Miller took his bullock wagon
to Mudgee for stores (the rail reached there in 1884) Ellen Miller lifted
her younger baby daughter on the side-saddle in front of her, put her
older daughter up behind, and rode fifty kilometres back to Ayrlands.
Bob Miller died early of typhoid fever. When old Dan Casey, son of
Ellen Miller by a later marriage, told me that story in 1975, his half-
sister who rode in front was still alive.

One night after Ellen Miller had ridden to Ayrlands for company, a
man walked to the door of the room where she was talking to her sister.
'Walk out!' he said. 'I beg your pardon?' 'Never mind about begging
my pardon. Walk out!' And he pointed a revolver at the two women.

He forced them into the bar where his accomplice held a revolver on
the rest of the staff and the guests. 'Don't move from here till ten
o'clock.' The men with the revolvers left.

'Me old grandmother – she soon got a bit fidgety,' Dan Casey told
me. 'She began to move around a bit.' She had a look where she kept
her cash and found a thousand dollars missing. Two men were later
charged with the theft, one of them a man called Cain, either the man
who married Mary Orr or a near relation. Both were found not guilty.

Joe Launt, settling down to a more conventional life, took up a selection on Yaminba Creek not far from where his sons were surprised in
Ebenezer Orr's old house. Although the house had been abandoned for

years, Joe Launt thought it wiser to go by night to steal the bits he needed from it to add to the comfort of his own house. Coming back one dark night with a window he tripped and fell. He jinked his neck but saved the window. It was still in good order in 1978. Jane and Claude Carr showed it to me in one of several rooms of Launt's house that still stood at the back of their own. Jim Carr, their father, married Mamie, one of the Carlow girls, and bought the Yaminba selection from Joe Launt.

In 1882 the rail came through to Narrabri. When considering an extension to Moree in 1887, T. G. G. Dangar made some comments on the railway system in the House which are still applicable and which governments in modern times have foolishly disregarded: ' . . . The only objection to it can be on the score of its not paying; but I ask, do our roads pay? From a railway you will get a little return but from a road you will get nothing. In 1873 the Commissioner for Roads reported that it was an utter impossibility to make any roads on this black soil country . . . it is only throwing money away . . . we actually got a bit of road made up at Walgett which has cost . . . almost £3,000 a mile. The railway from Narrabri to Gunnedah cost the country £2,900 a mile. The proposed line from Narrabri to Moree can be made for far less than that sum . . .'

Ahead of the railway and behind, selectors picked over the land and made their claims each Thursday, selection day. Many of them worked on the railway to earn money for machinery and improvements. A few took the job of railway gatekeeper. Everywhere the line crossed a road big white wooden-framed gates with iron bars were installed and beside them a cottage for the gatekeeper. There were almost as many gatekeepers along the railway lines as innkeepers along the roads.

Later selectors worked as shearers, teamsters, fencers. 'None of us had any money,' Donald Magann told me. He drew a block of Crown Land north of Baradine in 1908 on what had been part of the Baradine run. By then it was heavy forest and he had to clear it. 'All we had was our hands. We had to have credit at the stores and we had to have work.'

The influx of settlers to the railway in the 1880s triggered off much buying of waterfront freehold by runholders. J. B. Rundle bought over 1,300 hectares to maintain his water on Pilliga, most of it along Baradine Creek, some on mere depressions where perhaps his manager intended to put in ground tanks if he had to. By then Rundle was a member of the Legislative Council and the holder of several hundred thousand hectares of land. James Fletcher, on Wee Waa south, bought three long thin 18-hectare blocks on the Namoi, little more than lanes to water.

It was a law common to most countries that no man could usurp big areas of land by buying only waterfront. The British Government instructed all colonial governors that no more than one-third of the length of a block of land could front water. Thomas Mitchell in dry Australia reduced this proportion to one part frontage to a length of four or four and a half parts back. And seemingly without anybody giving instruction, it became Australian law that ownership ended at a stream bank, not in midstream as in England. It was a sound law that in modern times has been abused. In maintaining public access to river, lake and sea, governments and councils have destroyed thousands of kilometres of beautiful waterfront with noisy highways.

By 1884 Sir John Robertson had lost his grip on the land laws. His laws had divided New South Wales nastily into two opposed classes, squatter and selector, and had not increased production enough to compensate for the bitterness. Worse, in a reversal of all Robertson had planned for, run had joined to run and, despite the selectors, had aggregated into giant 'pastoral holdings'. J. S. Farnell who had worked for years in the Lands Office before becoming a member of parliament introduced a bill that was carried enthusiastically, restricting selection to half a pastoral holding, the 'resumed area'. On the other half, the 'leasehold area', the runholder had authority for at least ten years.

As a result of that law there is a mass of detail about the runs of New South Wales in the records of the Lands Office for 1885, 1886 and 1887, some of it printed, most of it in manuscript: maps, letters and surveyors' reports.

The Pilliga forest area was encircled and engulfed by eight big holdings. Ghoolendaadi on the east had swallowed up Namoi Hut and Henriendi, temporarily out of the Eather's hands. It stretched down Coxs Creek from the present village of Mullaley to the Namoi, took in the town of Boggabri, and joined Baan Baa south opposite the junction of Maules Creek and the Namoi. On the old scale of forty chains to the inch it took a sheet of parchment 180 centimetres by 95 to encompass its 72,000 hectares and even then an extra piece had to be pinned on for a protruding corner. It was well improved, with 500 kilometres of fencing. John Kerr Clark, the owner, thoroughly peacocked the whole area as well as buying much land within the Boggabri population reserve.

On the south Girriwillie and Nombi had run together as Garrawilla, a rich property. Selectors had begun to come on to Goorianawa which had not extended though it was still one of the biggest holdings. On the west of Goorianawa, old Teridgerie had combined with several other runs and become the lovely Calga of the Ryder brothers. The rich black plains Andrew Brown had walked past because there was no water were now watered with seventy-two tanks and dams. South of the travelling stock route between Coonamble and Baradine three runs only extended the seventy kilometres between the Castlereagh River and Baradine Creek, Warrena, Calga and Goorianawa, and north of the stock route three other runs extended the distance, Nebea, Urawilkie and Charles Colwell's Bimble.

On the central part of Baradine Creek, Mrs Catherine MacKenzie's Wangen sprawled over fifty thousand hectares of Wangen, Wangen Back, Bullulwi and Erinbri. Her husband had died and she was then a wealthy widow living on Sydney's North Shore. She owned fifteen runs in the Warrego district of Queensland as well as Wangen managed by her son, Murdoch. But Catherine MacKenzie herself argued the division of the run with the Lands Office. Much of Wangen had been overgrown by the new pine, oak and acacia scrub so at first she tried to retain a broad strip along the creek as her leasehold. Since the new law stipulated that the runs should be divided equally in quality as well as in area, that division was not allowed. But in a series of letters she argued her case shrewdly and forcibly, and retained the best of the run anyhow.

On the north three big aggregations of runs joined one another, stretching about seventy kilometres down from the Namoi into the present forest area, Pilliga, Bullerawa and Merah Pastoral Holdings. J. B. Rundle protested the suggested division of Pilliga – he claimed out of twenty-seven kilometres of river frontage he had been left only two kilometres – but his authority as Legislative Councillor was of no value to him: the Lands Office questioned his figures. And indeed he had measured the frontage left him by selectors along all the turns of the river and the suggested leasehold frontage in a straight line. Moreover he complained of the crookedness of the boundary lines, a just complaint – they zig-zagged in all directions. He was told the boundary followed valuable fencing and was composed of 'straight lines directed to the cardinal points'.

Most of the Pilliga run is still farmland and good grazing land. Among the selectors who took up long thin blocks fronting the Namoi in the 1880s were R. Holcombe, W. Phelps, G. Phelps, and J. N. Phelps. They were particularly successful settlers and their descendants now take up substantial space in northern telephone books.

The east-west road crossing the Coonamble-Pilliga road shown on modern maps as Hardys Lease Road or sometimes by the more descriptive name, Two Rail Fence Road, marks the southern boundary of Milchomi, the southernmost part of Pilliga Pastoral Holding. No part of the old fence remains, though it stood for over a hundred years. As in all post and rail fences, the ends of the rails were shaped with adzes to fit neat rectangular holes chipped into the split posts with the long thin blades of mortising axes.

Channels from Pilliga bore and Milchomi bore now water about fifteen properties on the dry sections of the old pastoral holding. The first bore in Australia was sunk on Llanilo, a dry run west of Walgett, in 1872. It struck subartesian water at about fifty metres. Then in 1879, David Brown, the manager of Kallara on the Darling, grew curious to learn if bubbling mud springs meant water under pressure below. He was satisfied by another bore to fifty metres that poured water out of piping carried eight metres above the surface. Contractors built drilling rigs to a French pattern – the word artesian comes from the French province of Artois – and their hardened chisel bits punched round holes towards water 200 metres down, 2,000 metres down, over much of Australia. Hot sulphurous artesian water streamed through hundreds of kilometres of ploughed drains.

By 1884 the New South Wales Government, acting with astonishing speed and interest, had its own boring plants in the field testing for water, and had begun a series of deep bores twenty-five kilometres apart to furnish dry stock routes west of the Darling. Some bores that have flowed for almost a hundred years were giving out by the 1970s. When the flow finally stops in some remote dry areas, windmills and pumps will give a few more years grace, then the country will be abandoned. The stocking capacity is not high enough to sustain the huge cost of seeking more water at 2,000 metres.

T. G. G. Dangar, suffering from diabetes, had sold Bullerawa by 1885 to Duncan MacRae who combined nine of the former runs as Bullerawa pastoral holding. The southern portions, now Quegobla, Etoo, Euligal and Coomore Creek State Forests, were already overgrown. 'I never go near this area as I am afraid of getting lost', Mac-Rae's manager told a Land Board meeting, '. . . there has been no stock on it in my time.' But it was this southern part that was cut off for selectors. It was thought the scrub could be cleared for farming.

Merah was still in the hands of the Loder family. The pastoral holding stretched over nine of their former runs thirty-five kilometres north of the Namoi and thirty-five kilometres south. George Loder owned it, the son of Andrew Loder and Charlotte Capp. He lived at Abbey Green out of Scone, where he spelled and topped off the cattle his son, William Mark, sent down from Merah to market.

George Loder tried to keep the rich country north of the river as his leasehold but the holding was split north-south. However, he did not abandon the sandy country where the scrub was coming away. Throughout the late 1880s and 1890s he employed shepherds, especially in the summer, to follow the patches of grass on his own land and the land his neighbours had abandoned. When the summer grasses died in the winter, the sheep were moved back across the river to the herbage on the black country.

His shepherds drew the ration that the first shepherds had drawn nearly one hundred years before: eight, ten, two and a quarter – eight pounds of flour, ten pounds of meat, two pounds of sugar, and a quarter of a pound of tea. The tea was more stem than leaf. 'Fencers' tea' it was called, 'Mostly posts and rails.' The sugar was treacly Javanese sugar in coarse hemp bags. It made the tea black and bitter.

Bob Trindall whose father built a hotel at Cuttabri on Coghill Creek on the resumed portion of Merah remembered some of George Loder's shepherds, especially John Gilbert, an American. He lived with an Aboriginal woman, Sammy. 'I come straight from the city of New York' he told everyone he met. 'I'm a true born American.' Bob Trindall was born in 1878 and died in Boggabri in 1978, a few months past his century.

Those who tried to hold on to single runs where the scrub was taking over found life hard. Henry Gardner wrote to the Minister for Lands from Upper Cumble on 10 February 1885:

Sir
. . . with referance to the Dividing
the run Upper Cumble
Leased by me
I beg to Say that I have
not got the Means to Imploy
a Draftsman in consequence
of Drought and Poor country
my returns is not Suffecient
to keep my Family in
Provisions . . .

His four-roomed cottage with a shingled roof had a floor in it (there were many dirt floors) but cottage, separate kitchen, school room and sheep yards were worth only $200. He had two miles of dog leg fence.

These popular fences were based on short posts sunk about fifteen centimetres into the ground. Each panel was formed by butting a long rail against one of the upright posts and leaning its top on the next, then butting another long rail against the bottom of that post and leaning it on top of the first. They naturally crossed in the middle of the panel. When similar rails were put in the adjacent panels, their ends crossed over the tops of the upright posts. Each upright post thus had rails butted against it on each side and rails leant on its top from each side. Other shorter rails were driven into the ground each side of the upright posts and leant towards the line of fence so that they crossed in the cross on top of each upright. More long rails were then lifted into the forks. These fences were as insubstantial as a tower of cards. Each rail supported and was supported. A rogue horse or cow could demolish panels a day.

Charles Herbert Battye, inspector of runs, reported on Upper Cumble in 1887: 'The whole area is all inferior scrub country. The scrubs are young ironbark, pine, oak, wattle and other scrubs, with a thick undergrowth . . . a flock of 600 or 700 sheep . . . all the stock he had except a horse or two . . . looked very poor indeed . . . even in this good season.'

But Henry Gardner and his brother Pross held on for years. They cleared a bit and farmed a bit. Probably their sons went shearing or timbercutting. They put a bank across one end of a lagoon that filled from the creek in flood time and made a half-moon lake where the children rowed homemade boats. People came out from Baradine for the sport. They extended the house and some of the big box trees that died when their bark was stripped for the roof stood until recent times. But finally Upper Cumble was abandoned. The Gardners selected out Magometon way.

Alexander Cormie on Cumbil (or Cumble) explained he had 'No permant warter . . . 3,000 acre ucless country north and south divisions . . . 2 miles of dog leg fencing'. His brother, David, setting out on his own, had bought the run but died a year or two later. Alexander held it for seven years then opened a butcher's shop in Pilliga. 'Leaving out the carrickabar scrub the area would carry a sheep to 20 acres', he explained to a Land Board hearing about the resumed part of his abandoned run, 'and then the grass seed would kill the sheep.' The red-twigged acacia known as Curracabah that came up in thousand hectare masses has strangely been replaced by other acacias growing in the same profusion. I have not found a single specimen in hundreds of miles of driving and walking where it grew so thickly, though it can still be found scattered along rocky ridges.

Healthy old aloes still mark the site of the Cormie homestead where the Pilliga Forest Way now crosses Dubbo Creek. No trees have yet grown where the sheepyards were, and there are graves on the creek bank, those of an old convict shepherd and young Samuel Cormie who died of whooping cough.

From Portadown, an unmarked run sliced off Dandry, William Hodges wrote a bewildered letter to the Minister for Lands on 13 July 1885:

'Sir,

'In Referring to the lines Referring to the Boundrys of the Portadown Run, I cant accept as shown in the Tracing as it cuts off all my Homested and Improvements and by acceptin the same I should not have 10,000 ten thousand acres of Land and to comply with Request Referring of sending the Papers Back in the time Requested I Beg to state there is no Mail Runing by my Place so that my letters oftimes lye for sometime before I Can get them unless I send into Coonabarrabran Every Week and I Beg to State that I have Been away from home fer some time. I have made a Light Pencil Marke on the traceing as Showing the Lines I Beleve to Be my Boundary of the Run so the Sketch cant be Right . . . '

He had eight hectares of cultivation fenced in, the only fence on the run.

Dave Grover who built the Rock Inn north of Boggabri had taken up Norfolk on Jacks Creek south of Narrabri. He built a house on it and six miles of fencing but soon abandoned it.

Even James Seivl (he had quarrelled with the rest of the Sevils or Sevilles and thereafter spelt his name strangely) with some good country on Borah had difficulty. In December 1885 he told a Land Board hearing at Coonabarabran 'Last March I put 4,500 sheep in the paddock below the homestead . . . I mustered them about the middle of last month and I got about 2,400, and they were in very poor condition.'

Ebenezer Orr had also found that area useless. It is bloodwood and gum country and grows neither useful grass nor useful timber if the profit content of 'useful' is considered. Now as part of the Pilliga Nature Reserve it is a delight of birds and rare fish in the creek.

James Seivl in 1885 had already ringbarked over two thousand hectares of new growth and old growth on the good Bimble Box country

that is still farmed. Ringbarking is the circular frilling of the bark of
a tree with overlapping axe cuts into the sap wood. The crown dies
slowly over a couple of years but since eucalypts have astonishing
defences against accident, many ringbarked trees sucker from the base.
So the ringbarkers have to be followed up two or three times while the
tops are dying by sucker bashers swinging their axes upside down to
knock off new shoots.

Since timber on leased land remained the property of the Crown, all
ringbarking was done under licence. Ringbarking was encouraged.
Permission was rarely refused.

When James Seivl's son, William, took over management he continued with the ringbarking. 'Going in big licks for improvements' the
Narrabri Herald reported in 1887, 'building, fencing, scrub clearing.'

John Fletcher on Andrew Doyle's old Cooma was devastated by the
splitting of his holding. His big house and woolshed were built on
freehold land near the railway terminus at Narrabri West. Various
reserves alienated all the northern section of his run: a big population
area, a public water reserve in such a position that the public made
good use of it, travelling stock routes to the south and west, and four
long awkward strips that were trial survey lines for railways from Mendooran to Narrabri and from Narrabri to Walgett. Fletcher was left
with only his freehold, not particularly valuable because the town of
Narrabri developed first to the north of the river, and the newly
overgrown and never fertile southern section joining Brigalow scrub
and the abandoned Norfolk.

When he protested about the isolation of his homestead, the Land
Board provided 'a driftway for access . . . leading as far as possible
towards the Namoi River'. So his stock, after walking down a lane,
could get within smell of water, and he could ride within sight of his
homestead. What did he have to complain of?

Jack Miller selected the best of Kiambir and let the rest go. William
Head took it up. His descendants still owned sawmills at Baradine in
the 1970s. He did not prosper on Kiambir. When he received his stock
assessment in 1895, he pointed out that he had lost sixty of his hundred
head of cattle in the drought. 'I am not in a position to pay', he wrote,
'i have to go carrying in woolseason time to pay the rent and i am quite
willing to give the place up.'

His brother George held Thinawindie (probably pronounced
Tahoonawondai in Kamilaroi) on Dandry Creek. Perhaps he had an
eye on the patches of good timber because he could do little more with
the run than grow four hectares of wheat on creek flats.

Another brother, Robert, had taken over Gibbican (pronounced always Gibbean) that was little better than Thinawindie. The Boyles had forsaken it for Bohena (old Thurradulba) joining Erle Wolseley Creagh's Arrarownie on the north. The Boyles had plans of a hotel to rival Ayrlands but their reputations were not substantial enough to earn them a licence. The ironbark bed logs of the long building they put up were still there in the 1970s with a few dead White Cedars nearby and a dead fig, a live climbing rose and several huge nasty oleanders, five metres high with a six metre spread. The Boyles drew their water from a barrel with the bottom knocked out sunk into the sand in the creek. Hard riding men, scrub dashers, they were always on the lookout for cleanskins. Their house site is marked on modern forestry maps as 'Garlands', one of the hopeful later owners of the poor land.

The McGhees, aristocratic Irish relations of Erle Wolseley Creagh, bought Bohena from the Boyles. In the drought of 1902 they bought chaff from the Argentine with the harmless-looking little grey seeds of Spiny Bùrr Grass in it. It thrived on the sandy soil and is still spreading through the north-west, known widely as Bohena Beauty. The smooth seeds are borne in clusters of viciously spiked burrs. The exquisitely sharp points bear double rows of barbs so small they can be seen only under a microscope. When a spike is pulled out of flesh the barbs are left behind, invisible and irritating.

During the 1918 drought a cattleman named Cruickshank from Wee Waa bought Bohena as drought relief. There was then a big waterhole in the creek and, as always, even in drought time, there were pockets of green grass in the poor sand, and shrubs that cattle would eat if hungry enough. The new scrub came to be regarded as drought relief country, sustaining cattle for several months if nothing better was available.

Charles Colwell on Bimble was upset by a map showing an alteration to his northern boundary. 'I am quite against the alteration', he wrote to the Under Secretary for Lands in 1891, 'I having Sank a Tank about 200 yds from the Boundry Fence . . . the tank is 3,600 cubic yds extrecation ivery gallon of water used for sinking of this tank had to be carted from Dinby house tank a distance of 3 miles for 10 Men and 10 Horses with the Kind concent of Mr C. E. Taylor . . . there can be No Dispute arise as I Purchased the Turidgerie North Run . . . from the Government by auction . . . Kindly forward any correspondance you wish to Send Me direct to Me the Agents charge two high.'

But the alteration was a correction to the map only. An error had been found when marking in new selections.

Charles Taylor who got his colonial experience with Edward King Cox bought Dinby in 1885. It was a subdivision of Pretty Plains Block A which Charles Colwell probably named. By 1885 they were no longer pretty plains, they were overgrown. Nelson Proctor who sold Dinby was glad to get out: 'The whole of the run is scrub country except a few scalded plains. I have had no stock on it for the last 18 months it is overrun with wattle, pine, and budtha and belar scrubs I have to water stock all summer months.'

But Belar means good country. Charles Taylor employed a gang of Chinese to provide permanent water. Using picks, shovels, and wheelbarrows they dug four deep holes across the shallow Dinby Creek and piled the soil – two or three thousand cubic metres of it – in a wall across the creek downstream of the holes. When the dam was built he employed the Chinese ringbarking and in the 1970s his grandsons still owned much of the land.

By 1884 Alfred Croxon had held the Coonabarabran run for twenty-seven years. Then his new neighbours on Belar, looking over old maps, thought they found a fault in the boundary lines and claimed a big slice on the south. Croxon pointed out that neither he nor James Weston had had any protest about the boundary in thirty-seven years. But the file of correspondence grew startlingly thick when all the neighbours joined in with boundary suggestions. It seemed the matter would go to court till land agents settled it by declaring 'It is still open to the lessees of adjoining runs to set forth their claims, if they have any, by an action against him for trespass, a course which they do not appear to be more likely to undertake during the next 25 years than their predecessors have ventured to do during the last quarter of a century'.

So someone in the Lands Office made a note in pencil, 'Mr H. thinks these papers may now be put away'. And J. G. pencilled, 'Yes Papers may now be put away'. They were tied with pink ribbon and filed. And judging by the dust which dropped in my lap as I untied the ribbon, no one had looked at them since.

M. Wright, manager of Yearinan in 1888, was one of several who commented on the new growth, 'The scrub is increasing very fast, principally pine and wattle. The scrub has increased very much during the last 18 months, since the heavy rains.' He also commented on the new selectors, 'All the land available for agriculture has been taken'.

Until the frightening bank crash of 1893 when thirteen of Australia's banks closed their doors (they had overinvested in land like the finance companies in the 1970s) eager selectors paced out and pegged their

favourite blocks. James Nash took a big slice of Yearinan. His descendants are nearby. Fred Border and Eric Matthews and six or seven
others pegged sixteen hectare farms on Bugaldi Creek and grew fruit,
potatoes, pumpkins, and a little wheat. They carted their produce in
drays to Walgett, Coonamble, Coonabarabran, wherever they thought
they could sell it. It was a hard life, but Border's and Matthew's
descendants are still in the district.

There are still beautiful orchards in the area. In 1979 one could drive
into Curnuck's orchard on Yearinan Creek or towards the Warrumbungles to Morrissey's La Perouse and find hundreds of peach trees,
slipstone and clingstone, laden to the ground, pears, apples, plums,
walnuts, nectarines, or a delicious crossbred called Nectared that Ted
Morrissey was one of the first to grow. He once marketed vegetable
seed all over the world.

The descendants of other selectors who came into the forest area in
those years have stayed: Keeping, Ditchfield, Beck, Deans, Redden,
Meyer, Sherwood. Alfred Croxon's descendants stayed as selectors
and settlers. There are undoubtedly more who established present-day
families. I made no special search for them.

The Browns had sold Yearinan by 1885 and were no longer
associated with the forest area. In 1878 Andrew Brown had turned over
all his freehold, his runs and his stock to his two sons, John and
William. John lived at Caigan. William died young in 1882. Their
sister, Grace, was always sickly. Andrew Brown's diary records 'Dear
Grace's pains in the side' almost as frequently as Mrs Brown's
headaches. Several of John Brown's children and grandchildren died in
their youth. 'Drink and T.B. did for the Browns' one is told in
Lithgow. There are few kindly memories of longlived Andrew Brown.

He always took an intense interest in the Bowenfels South public·
school. He inspected it regularly even when well into his nineties and
gave an annual prize to the child who topped the class. In 1870 a
Roman Catholic boy came top. Brown, just elected an elder of the
Bowenfels Presbyterian Church, gave him a cruel present, a book
deriding the boy's religion. Robert Foster, the local member of Parliament, mentioned the book in the House. The Director of Education
wrote to Andrew Brown for an explanation. He replied abruptly, 'I
have no desire to make observation on the subject of these communi-
cations'.

In his very wealthy old age he assumed regal authority. He attended
church as though attending his own glory. Somehow he has been

credited with building the lovely old church at Bowenfels, out of Lithgow, in 1842. It was built by public subscription – Andrew Brown was merely a subscriber – and finished in 1850. The roof was originally shingled. This has been replaced but the wide sandstone slabs in the walls are sound. So is the cedar, pit sawn and adzed, that lines the lower inside walls.

To the original building Andrew Brown later added a wing. In 1885 the Presbyterian Assembly granted exclusive use of this wing to Andrew Brown and the boys of the Cooerwull Academy, a school Brown built. Every Sunday morning the boys of the Academy marched to the church and took their allotted pews. No other member of the congregation was allowed to enter until Andrew Brown and his family arrived in an open carriage with two liveried footmen standing behind the coachman. Ushers met them and conducted them to their pews. Then the humbled congregation entered.

In May 1892 when he was 95 he sat with the Rev. W. A. Smith and another elder of the church 'to consider certain rumours affecting the moral character of William Pitt, a member of the Church'. Poor Pitt and three witnesses he had offended were called before them. They struck his name off the roll and declared him no longer a member of the church. Then they prayed.

The Presbyterian Church was even more successful than the Catholic Church in maintaining order among the working class. Priests demanded that those who broke their laws knelt before God in the confessional, a more nebulous judge than the panel of grim seated elders a deviant Presbyterian stood before.

Some Presbyterian ministers kept a prurient reckoning of the months between marriage and the birth of a first child. The Anglican church had been as savage earlier in the century. In May 1850 Edward Walker wrote to David Archer from his first incumbency in England 'We have been Called to a very painful trial in the little Church here . . . viz to separate from us a very old member of the body who turns out to be a downright Infidel and Arian – he openly denied that Christ had existed from all Eternity! In other words robbed Him of His Godhead! I had often suspected him for his language was very strange but he never let the cat out of the bag until Sunday 28 April last! when to our surprise and horror, he contradicted me in my exhortation and when I said Christ had existed from all Eternity he said "Nay. You're wrong there- you're wrong there" . . . the brethren . . . urged upon us to put him away at once, as a heretic and infidel.'

There is a happier religious scene in the children of Baradine carrying chairs from houses and the hotel to the hall where the minister from Coonabarabran rode for service every second month. Or in the Rev. William Ridley's trip down the Namoi in 1871 and finding the big Evans family of Bungul Gully at their regular hymn singing, or the 'fine hopeful circle' of Scots in the even bigger family of Benjamin Bruce Campbell of Bulgarrie. At their irregular visits to distant places ministers often married couples and christened the first two or three children. Couples sensibly lived together until a parson turned up.

In 1976 Joan and I drove down to go through the session books of the Bowenfels church for references to Andrew Brown. The council had given me permission to go through the books but when we arrived they were not to be found. For several hours a tall, handsome, crafty Scotsman, one of the elders of the church, ran us round in circles. We opened empty cupboards and searched trunks of rubbish. At last the exasperated minister, just out of hospital, got out of bed and rang his elder. He spoke for ten minutes before the elder would admit that instead of putting the books where he was asked to put them he had given them to a member of the local historical society to read. That gave a better insight into the character of Andrew Brown than the session books when they were finally brought to me.

Two of Andrew Brown's stockmen formed their own runs with their share of the cattle as pay, and their descendants are still in the central west. George Gibson who used to draft the fat cattle at Baradine married Edith Aldridge, Mrs Brown's young Scottish 'lady's companion', and established a run north of Coonamble and several more on the lower Macquarie. Sandy Ferguson who managed Tonderburine in the 1850s took up land near Gulargambone and his four sons extended it.

The famous Brown horse brand, ⏋B , was resurrected in the 1970s by Harold Poole, the owner of Caigan.

Cuthbert Fetherstonhaugh, manager of Goorianawa that Andrew Brown established, bought an interest in it from the Walker estate in 1877. Mrs Dorothy MacMillan, his daughter, remembered the place with delight when I spoke to her in 1974. There was no proper home when her mother went there as a bride. On wet mornings she took macintosh and umbrella to breakfast in the detached kitchen. But her father soon built a fine new house on sloping ground. It had big verandahs all round, and wide hollow wooden walls filled with sawdust as insulation. There was a central room they called the lobby that the other rooms opened into, a cool place in the summer.

Mrs MacMillan remembered a canvas boat her mother made for keeping food. It hung in the breeze on the verandah. A wooden tray beneath it filled with water kept the canvas damp by capillary attraction. Compartments held butter, milk, cream, cooked meat.

Water was piped as far as the garden from two big willow-fringed dams higher up the slope but it was not reticulated within the garden. Each evening a Chinese gardener took buckets on a pole balanced across his neck and trotted water to the vegetables and flowers. Visitors came from all round the district to see the roses. They grew over a huge trellis that sheltered beehives. Mrs Fetherstonhaugh had grafted three roses together on a briar stock: little yellow banksias, vigorous climbing Cloth of Gold and yellow Maréchal Niel. They bloomed at different times and for months there was a succession of yellows.

Cuthbert Fetherstonhaugh's wild driving is still remembered. He reckoned he could take a team of four up Mount Bullaway that showed clearly from the homestead. It was a steep five hundred metre climb on foot. He hitched four lively horses to a drag, a heavy coach-like vehicle that could be extended to take an extra seat. He extended it for stability and set off. And he got a good three-quarters of the way up before the drag capsized and rolled with the horses into a gully. Fetherstonhaugh climbed down and cut the unharmed horses loose. The drag had to stay there. Billy Armstrong who bought The Summit forty years later found it there. Only the iron frame was left.

The sheepyards were built above the house across a gully that had washed out a metre or so wide and more than a metre deep. The track from the house to the yards ran up the slope for a few kilometres round the head of the gully and back down to the yards. One morning Fetherstonhaugh was driving a couple of buyers to inspect yarded sheep. 'Why are we going right up here, Mr Fetherstonhaugh?' asked one. 'Couldn't we drive straight across there?' 'Yes, of course we could' he replied. He turned his team, cracked the whip. And it is said that Fetherstonhaugh and the horses got across with the shafts but the buggy and the buyers stayed in the gully.

In the difficult 1890s Cuthbert Fetherstonhaugh grew restless, or short of money, or both, and sold out. John Campbell bought it. He had built up a string of good holdings, Goolhi that was old Burrumbulla, Urawilkie joining Bimble, and several others.

The land will sustain hard work but no riotous living. His sons and daughters dispersed most of the land. One wild night in a Coonamble hotel at a party to celebrate renovations, the Campbell sisters heated a poker in the open fire and burnt 'Charge it to Dad' in big letters in the proud new carpet in the lounge.

Huge flocks of sheep continued to use the stock routes through the abandoned scrub lands. In 1887 the Fletcher brothers of Boolcarrol north of Wee Waa brought 20,000 from Brookong in the Riverina (where Cuthbert Fetherstonhaugh chased the bushrangers), a distance of about 800 kilometres, in thirteen weeks. Creeks and rivers were all flowing in a good season. They built seven bridges on the way. The last one over the Namoi at Wee Waa was nearly thirty metres long. They lost only sixty-three sheep on the way.

They must have carried barrels to float spans across the Namoi. Sir Thomas Mitchell explained how smaller streams could be bridged. If a tall tree was fallen from bank to bank, shorter timbers could be laid on it crosswise from either bank. They in turn supported more timber laid crosswise. Eventually when all the rails were lashed in place and all the gaps filled in such a bridge was strong enough to take laden carts.

Drovers usually swam cattle across streams. If a mob is big and a bridge narrow, those behind get impatient and take to the water. Those that go in downstream are safe enough, those that go in upstream can be swept under low bridges and drowned. The tail of 500 cows crossing Narrabri Creek bridge in 1887 took to the water and climbed up the bank into Chinese market gardens. The shouting Chinese chased them with sticks and the shouting drovers, concerned only with getting their cattle together, chased the Chinese with stockwhips. Although Chinese market gardeners were invariably scorned, they undoubtedly saved thousands of Europeans from scurvy in the goldrush days. No one except the Chinese would have bothered growing vegetables. They knew more about diet.

Roads were being widened, bridges being built all through the north-west during the late 1880s. T. G. G. Dangar, although sick and living in Sydney, was still the very active member of parliament. Bridges he had promised over Bugaldi creek were nearly built by October 1887 when the *Narrabri Herald* was advertising, 'Carriers, look out for business! Urawilkie, Goorianawa and other sheds are stacked with wool.' Tracks the wagons made getting wool out of Goorianawa can still be seen after ninety years.

A network of coach runs using the improving roads supplemented the railways. Where there were no bridges over streams they bumped over the system of transverse logs known as corduroy or simply floundered through the mud and sand. The big Cobb and Co. had competition from local coach lines, Thomas Lovelee and the Charters brothers in Narrabri, the Nowlands, descendants of the pioneers, in

Coonabarabran. They used the excellent thoroughbrace coaches made in Australia to an American pattern. The body of the coach floated on tensioned laminated leather straps and rocked gently to and fro instead of jolting up and down like the first coaches on steel springs.

Mail contracts called for an average speed of ten kilometres an hour. Where roads were wide enough, five horses were harnessed, two wheelers on the pole and three leaders. On narrow roads they drove four-in-hand. The coachman held four or five reins in his left hand, his long whip in his right. He sat on a high open box seat and even on the frostiest mornings he did not wear gloves lest the reins slip through his fingers.

The coachmen were changed about every ten hours, the horses every two hours after travelling about twenty kilometres. Changes of horses were made at inns and shanties. There were six wine shanties between Coonabarabran and Gunnedah. In 1979 the old stables still stood at Milchomi homestead west of Pilliga where Cobb and Co. made a change at Dowden's Inn on the Narrabri-Walgett run. That was over 220 kilometres of hard going and five horses always went to a team. Night and day grooms had the change horses ready and the trip was made in under twenty-four hours.

In the Namoi flood of 1886 when coaches were days late and teamsters could not move for weeks, the steamer *Bunyip* set out to make a quick trip with stores from Walgett to Narrabri. She lost the main channel in a sea of water at Bugilbone and her skipper made back to Walgett lest he get stranded off the river. That is the only attempt known to reach Narrabri. The Namoi was regarded as too shallow and too snaggy for paddle-wheel steamers. Yet there is an inexplicable entry in the *Narrabri Herald* of 12 November 1884: 'District News Wee Waa No steamers have come up the lagoon for some time. The price of potatoes and onions are very high, the Chinese having all the trade to themselves. Anxious enquiries are made daily as to what has happened to Charley Morgan's steamer "Who'd a Thought It". Report says she got foundered going over the Molly bar.' There is no other mention. All early copies of the *Narrabri Herald*, the only ones in existence, were mutilated for a special Narrabri Jubilee issue in 1933. The compiler, a member of the family owning the paper, used some of the cuttings and lost the rest.

W. B. Trindall opened a wineshop and coachstop at Cuttabri on the edge of the Brigalow about 1880. He had been a teamster on the Walgett-Morpeth run and found it profitable to carry a couple of casks of rum which he sold by the nip off the wagon. When the wineshop prospered he applied for a hotel licence, dug a pit and began sawing pine for a twenty-two room hotel. He and an English immigrant, Tom Hawke, also cut the shingles for the roof and the hardwood pegs that nailed them in place. It took them two years to build it, working most days from daylight to dark. They opened for business in January 1884.

Beneath the sign The Beehive Hotel, there hung a board with a verse on it:

> 'We are all alive within this hive,
> Good liquor makes us funny,
> So if you're dry, step in and try
> The flavour of our honey.'

A traveller going by one day with no money called in and said if he was given a rum he could better that verse. So he had a drink and recited,

> 'I am a fly and I'm very dry
> And I'd like to taste your honey
> But if I step in your bees might sting,
> Because I've got no money.'

William Trindall, the young married son of the owner of the hotel, was killed on Millie, then owned by one of the Capp sons, Joseph, in 1888. He had been loading wool on one of his father's wagons at Bugilbone. One morning he could not find his horses. He was told they had strayed on to Millie and Dick Weldon (Burren Dick), a stockman, had impounded them. 'I'll go and pull the bastard's nose' said Billy Trindall and galloped off.

At the Millie yards he found Burren Dick with the horses. 'You bloody bastard, what did you yard my horses for?' Burren Dick picked up a stick and cracked Trindall on the head as he leapt off his horse. Then they fought. Billy Trindall found himself short of energy. 'I give you best' he said. He took his horses and rode for the Halfway Hotel at Bugilbone. There he died a few hours later.

Dr Charles de Lepervanche of Narrabri, the first doctor in the north-west trained at university instead of as an apprentice, carried out the post-mortem. The *Narrabri Herald* reported his findings in detail: the external wound on the head, the length and shape of the cracks in the skull, the great clot of blood on the brain 'eight inches round and weighing six ounces'. Dick Weldon was charged with murder. He got two years hard labour in Maitland jail for manslaughter.

Two northern doctors are well remembered, Dr de Lepervanche and

Dr A. J. Park, both of Narrabri. Dr de Lepervanche came up in 1870 on a shooting expedition as a young graduate of the University of Paris and he decided to stay. A simple man – his brother Gabriel who came with him set up as a baker – he is remembered with affection. He was prepared to ride 180 kilometres to the country beyond the Barwon if a patient was too sick to be brought in. He grew some of his own drugs in a garden by the river bank and in a big cellar beneath his house he bottled wine consigned in barrels from France. He died at the age of 91 in 1933.

Dr A. J. Park who came in 1898 and practised for fifty years is remembered with respect. He made a name for himself as a surgeon and diagnostician throughout the north. Patients came from Queensland to see him. Although he lived until modern times – he died in 1948 – he knew the difficulty of emergency operations at night in the early 1900s when the only light was a kerosene lamp held by a nurse.

Although both doctors did well enough financially they retained their humanity and with it their respect. Modern doctors obsessed with their profession as a business earn no more respect than successful grocers.

Edmund Fuss, the pharmacist in Narrabri in 1884, advertised *'No More Doctor's Bills'*. But what he promised as a 'great blood purifier' and 'general stimulant and tonic' was the 'Aerated Sarsaparilla' he made in his second occupation of 'Lemonade and Cordial Manufacturer'.

John Reah Dick who came as pharmacist to Boggabri in 1898 displaced John Humphries, the storekeeper, as part-time dentist. He had kept a hard-backed chair and a pair of forceps and treated his brave customers for nothing.

In the end the land act of 1884 had no more effect on land use than Robertson's acts. The bank crash, drought, the rabbits, nullified everybody's hopes. Rabbits came late to the central north of New South Wales. In 1887 when rabbiters in Victoria and South Australia had been earning good livings for years and wealthy rabbiters in the Riverina were driving their buggies four-in-hand, an inspector came up to have a look at a pocket of rabbits on Cooma. He found them confined to about three thousand hectares. Someone had released a few there about 1872 and they were spreading gradually. Some months later a forest ranger, T. H. B. McGee, saw two rabbits on Yearinan. Others came up from the south, others were brought up by hopeful rabbiters. By 1910 they could be driven into winged yards 7,000 at a time.

The four or five good years between 1879 and 1887 were the only years in which it was possible for the new forest to come away. By the next good rains in the 1890s there were sufficient rabbits, as enthusiastic eaters of seedlings as the disappearing rat-kangaroos, to stop most new tree growth. The extent of country to be abandoned was determined by the 1890s. Except for a thickening of the undergrowth in places in the several wet years following the breaking of the 1902 drought, there was little more growth of pine or scrub until 1951, when a huge fire germinated seedlings on land soaked by heavy rain in 1950. At the same time myxomatosis destroyed the rabbits. And the lovely tangle which is the modern forest came to life.

Governments do not like to see men or land out of their control. As men rode out leaving the overgrown land behind them, the Government was considering how the land could be cleared to entice them back. A new lawmaker, Joseph Carruthers, (he later became Sir Joseph) began speaking of 'a million farms for a million farmers'. Closer settlement became the new slogan. It aroused more general interest than the federation of colonies into the Commonwealth. That seemed to be a game for the politicians.

After federation in 1900, a succession of land acts defined new tenures to cover every type of country: scrub lease, snow lease, inferior lands lease, improvement lease, settlement lease, and homestead selection, the most important of all. It provided a 'living area', a farm where a hardworking farmer might live with his family in reasonable comfort, which meant frugally. Governments are afraid of wealthy landowners. They have too much power.

These laws applied to New South Wales only but there was the attitude that the new farmers would be farming for the nation. Exports of wheat would build the Commonwealth. Between 1901 and mid-1903 there was drought. Droughts are inevitable and necessary. They rest and rebuild the soil. But they are usually rather local and have no general effect. The 1902 drought was the longest, the driest, the most widespread yet known. In 1903 Australia imported 300,000 tonnes of wheat, almost half of what it exported in 1901.

Hope sprang again with the rain. By 1905 the New South Wales government had decided its forestry reserves were too big. The whole Pilliga area was assessed for wheat farming and an enthusiastic report made on the land round Baradine (though it was unsuitable for

immediate settlement because there was no rail) and between Narrabri and Pilliga along the new Narrabri-Walgett railway.

In 1905 a Tamworth syndicate of businessmen bought what remained of old Burburgate, divided it into fifty-eight farms and put it
up for auction. They hired a special train to bring in the buyers and
sold at an enormous profit.

Frank Campbell, one of the several sons of Benjamin Bruce Campbell, selected Lucky Flat on the eastern boundary of old Coghill. By the
early 1900s it was still an open, attractive piece of country. It was called
Lucky Flat both for its bowling-green appearance and its good water.
Bert Anderson and Charlie Lucas, teamsters, had put a well down
there in the 1902 drought to water their horses. They expected to go to
forty metres for a rather salty supply. Instead they struck good water at
eight and a half metres.

The Campbells knew the area well. They had been associated with
Bulgarrie, Cubbo and Dunwarian for over forty years. Frank Campbell was engaged to one of the McGhee girls. He erected three or four
posts of the house he intended to build for her, then rode out with the
two men who worked for him to bring in a beast to kill. Their rough
gallows was ready for it, a long pole with a rope tied to one end,
hinged in a fork of a strong sapling. As they raced after the cattle,
Frank's horse tripped on a root exposed in a washout. The horse fell
and Frank was killed.

No one else took up Lucky Flat. It became a teamster's camp and
the forest gradually took it over. The gallows pole wedged in the fork as
the sapling grew. It lifted off the ground and fifty years later dangled
high in a big tree.

The Trindalls selected a block on Brigalow Creek east of their
Beehive Hotel. They were not farmers. The selection served as a base
for their thousand-odd head of cattle they moved about wherever they
could find feed. Mrs Trindall ran 300 Angora goats at Cuttabri. Bob
Trindall remembered their long waved hair and the distinct crease
down the middle of their backs. Doctor Failes of Coonabarabran who
bought a block of Goorianawa also ran Angora goats. Seventy years
later when mohair was again valuable, another Coonabarabran doctor,
G. R. Varley, had a fine flock on a farm in the Warrumbungle
foothills out of Coonabarabran.

At Merebene on Baradine Creek, a part of old Wangen that is still
farmed, two English brothers named Hogg established a big vegetable
garden in the 1880s. They fenced in forty hectares with palings and put
in a steam pumping plant on the creek to flood irrigate it. Inevitably

they went broke. Where was their market? The modest growers on Bugaldi Creek could supply all the local towns.

Mamie Carr shepherded their sheep on Yaminba. A tall, lean woman, she dressed always in a long black frock. As she walked swiftly behind her sheep the skirt billowed out behind her. She looked from a distance like a great black bird harrying the flock. She is remembered as clearly as Ebenezer Orr's more colourful shepherdesses fifty years before her. The sheep were yarded where George Druitt first yarded them. Manure built up so deeply yard was built on yard. The third fence, high on the outside, was low on the inside by the time the Carrs fenced Yaminba. A big grey mound still marks the site.

Jim Carr extended Launt's old house and built a notable fireplace. The sandstone hearth, cut from the same quarry as David Matthews cut his headstones, measured about three and a half metres by three. Each side of the chimney was a low door. A horse snigged a heavy log about three metres long up to one door. Both doors were then opened and a long chain run across the hearth to the log. The horse was taken round to the other side of the chimney, hooked to the chain, and the log was pulled into place. When smaller logs were laid alongside, the fire burnt for days.

Paths on the clay soil sank into furrows. A photograph taken in 1920 of the Yaminba homestead shows the huge chimney and a triangular ditch from garden gate to house, house to separate kitchen, and kitchen to gate.

Jim Carr's cattle ran unattended in the scrub, a general practice. During an unprofitable few years around 1910, he neglected his cattle and they developed into a formidable herd, still remembered with awe.

George Ruttley selected a block of Arrarownie in 1897 down the creeks from Launt's first house and duffing yards. He did as many did who were giving it a go with little money: selected the minimum 80 acres (about 33 hectares), then used abandoned country around him. He had been battling on Rocky Creek for three years, tailing a few cattle and shooting wallabies for the scalp money. Scalp money was paid on many Australian animals thought to be pests as well as the imported rabbit. He grew good vegetables on Rocky Creek. A sandstone shelf led down to the water, the only sandstone for many kilometres. He cut a few steps to make it easier to carry water up in buckets to the vegetables growing in the rich soil of an old sheep fold on Cumble. On Arrarownie he shepherded a few hundred sheep and made a bare living. After ten years he took the iron roof off the house, loaded his possessions on his big five-horse dray and moved his family to another selection on old Coghill called Nelcroi, a farm known now as Far Park. Jonquils and irises, a dead pepper tree, some sawn pine, mark where the abandoned house was among the apple (*Angophora*) forest that has grown there.

The soil on Nelcroi looked rich. It was still spongy and full of humus, a piece of Australian soil still in its original condition. The top five centimetres could be raked through the fingers. The sheep left distinct tracks until they hardened the soil in a few years. George Ruttley died young of Bright's disease. The family left the selection and an oak forest took over.

George Ruttley's son, Bert, and Jim Carr's son, Claude, both still alive in the 1970s, remembered Erle Wolseley Creagh who worked out his penance on Arrarownie until his uncle, Viscount Wolseley, died in 1913 when he was permitted to return to England.

After an unprofitable attempt to breed horses for the Indian market when he first came as a youth, he did little at all. He had a good orchard with beautiful figs and a few hectares of cultivation to grow feed for his horses. He kept the big paling sheepyards in repair and the three-rail fence round the house paddock that restrained his horses and the goats he milked and ate. Sometimes he employed young Bert Ruttley to repair that fence. Bert said there never seemed much that needed doing. He was employed more as someone to talk to. At the end of the day when Bert left to walk home, the lonely man followed him talking. He would say goodbye, walk a few steps towards his own house, then turn to talk again. Some days he turned three or four times before he could face walking back to the empty house. There he washed his hands in the tin dish on a stand outside the door and went in to play his grand piano. Before the last Aborigines left the creeks, a group of them came each evening to hear him play. They walked quietly into the house and sat on the floor in a half circle around the piano.

He read late into the night – his shelves were covered with books – and slept late. His relations did not stint him for money. The house was comfortable. When the old shingles began to leak he covered them with corrugated iron. The mailman always had a big bag of mail for him. He got newspapers from overseas and from Sydney and he never threw one out. After reading it, he folded it and placed it on a pile. In the end his front door led in through a corridor of newspapers, a collection of thirty-six years. Even the reading of a newspaper necessitated washing his hands. Perhaps he was trying to absolve a memory like Lady Macbeth.

In his youth he would make quick trips to Coonabarabran riding or driving seventy kilometres there and seventy back in a day. A day or so before the trip he sent a black boy ahead to leave changes of horses at the several inns. In his fifties he sometimes walked the fifty kilometres to Narrabri and lead a pack-horse. He made frequent trips to Sydney.

When word came of his uncle's death, he sold the two horses he had left and his goats, abandoned books and piano and sailed for home. But he did not stay long in England. After his mother's death the next year he returned to Australia and lived at Cunnamulla in Queensland.

Timbergetters and swagmen, stockmen and cattle thieves camped in the house. They lit their fires with the newspapers and jumped on the keys of the piano. Someone burnt the house down about 1920. The site is still marked as Creaghs Crossing on Royal Australian Survey Corps maps. By 1979 the forest had not yet taken over the house paddock. A few posts still stood, a few Pepper Trees and White Cedars. The figs that bore until recent years had finally died.

In 1907 Harry E. Joy from South Australia won a contract to clear two thousand hectares of what had been the resumed area of old Cooma. It was an experiment in land settlement. The country was surveyed into twenty blocks of about four hundred hectares each. One hundred hectares of each farm was to be cleared ready for a stumpjump plough so that a settler could support himself while he cleared the rest. The price Harry Joy submitted was the lowest by far. For years he had been sweeping down the Tintinara scrub in south-east South Australia by the astonishingly modern method of towing a heavy cable between two steam traction engines.

Joy came to Narrabri with two 8 HP tractors and two women companions who scandalised the local wives. Some of them might have been envious. Joy was easy-going and good company. But despite his unconventional and advanced ideas he was never particularly successful. The first tractors were not heavy enough for the Pilliga timbers and he was soon running months late with his contract. He bought two 16 HP Fowler tractors and lengths of heavy discarded anchor chain to make a cable. The work speeded up.

One afternoon as he jolted over the railway line, the big hook attached to the end of his cable fell off the tractor and snagged a rail. He pulled an ugly bow in it before the slow-revving steam engine let him know it had a load. The train was due. Joy unhooked, turned round and pulled the rail the other way. He had it reasonably straight again when the train came but he watched fearfully till the last carriage rolled by safely.

The big steel driving wheels of the tractors were fitted with bolt-on angle iron grips. Joy cut his firewood easily by laying dead pine logs lengthways in front of the wheels and driving along them. The grips dented the logs into easily broken off thirty centimetre lengths.

Bert Ruttley worked for Harry Joy as an eleven-year-old. Children worked then as a matter of course. Five and six-year-olds were often experienced shepherds. Many children on the land are still given responsible jobs when they are very young. From the time they were six our own children could help a ewe in a difficult lambing, or cut the fat steers out of a mob of a hundred with their lively ponies. They loved such work after school or in the weekends.

Bert had been shepherding 500 sheep for Trindalls. When William Trindall added another 600 to the mob and refused to pay any more money, Bert left the flock to the Dingoes and sought other work. The care of sheep involved less work in those days than it does now, since there was little trouble with flystrike. The imported green blowfly which lays its eggs on urine-stained wool did not build up to serious numbers until the 1920s. But 1,100 was a considerable number to shepherd in timbered country.

Even so, the work with Joy was harder than shepherding. Bert's job was to follow the chain through the tangle of fallen timber and with a forked stick poke the chain as high as he could reach up the trunks of the standing saplings to give it better leverage. Big trees had to be pulled individually. Bert uncoupled the chain, then recoupled it the other side of the trunk so the sweep could continue. Men following with mattocks, shovels and axes trenched round the big trees and chopped through the roots. Then the tractors hauled them down with chains fixed high up the trunks.

Several White Russians, refugees from riots in their own country, were later employed in the clearing gang. Big men with big black beards, at first the locals feared them, then they grew to like them. Many hands were needed in a clearing operation. The pulling down of the trees was the quickest and easiest part of the work. Then the fallen trunks had to be snigged and rolled together for burning and the broken branches piled lengthways on top. New chums stacked them crisscross and were left with a multitude of ends to throw in. Logs too big to handle were cross burnt into lengths. A straight dry branch was propped across the log from each side and a shovelful of coals placed where they met. Even big green logs could be burnt through if the cross-burning poles were pushed up regularly as they burnt. Fires had to be tended night and day. Burning-off fires smell good. All Australians know the piquant smell of eucalypt leaves burning. But many timbers – oak, belar, budda, myall for example – burn like incense.

The Government soon found it was not necessary to clear any of the blocks to attract settlers. More than twenty eager farmers ballotted for each block of timbered land thrown open at Wee Waa. Victorian and South Australian farmers sold their farms at good prices and came to the cheap land with capital to clear it. Joy cleared a lot of land privately by contract. He brought in two massive ploughs to rid the cleared land of roots, a mouldboard and a seven-disc. Neither had stumpjump action. Heavy cast iron wheels held them to their work. Stick pickers followed, stacking and burning.

The Wee Waa Voluntary Workers Association was formed during the 1914-18 war to clear the scrub blocks belonging to men who had enlisted. Newfangled cars drove out with the old sulkies and drays. Women brought picnic lunches. But the enthusiasm ran out after two or three hectares were cleared. The backbreaking work seemed rather worse than going to war.

It was only within reasonable cartage distance of the railway line – about fifty kilometres – that wheatgrowing developed quickly as a business. And even there the northern settlers were slow to use the latest machinery. They were not businessmen seeking to employ surplus capital. They were farmers seeking to make the best use of what money they had, and at that time labour was cheap.

Settlers came to Baradine but their farming methods were crude enough until after World War I. The year's harvest, ten to twenty bags, was carted in a drayload or two to Neilson's or McIntyre's flour mills in Coonabarabran. Enough bags were sold to pay expenses. The year's supply of flour, bran and pollard for the fowls, bran to mix with oats for the working horses, was carted home again.

At least the horses were run in paddocks with reasonably substantial fences and were available when needed. Andrew Brown's early ploughing on his usually well-managed Cooerwull depended on how far the bullocks wandered during the night. His diary for 1842 records early starts and late starts and two or three day searches for missing bullocks.

But until several years into the twentieth century most northern farmers persisted with two-furrow fixed mouldboard ploughs made to a Scottish pattern of 150 years before. The ploughman walked behind them, directing his horses by voice and rein, guiding and levelling the plough by the handles. If a share ran under a missed root, the horses had to be uncoupled and brought round to drag it backwards. Sometimes the plough kicked when it hit a root and a handle cracked the ploughman in the ribs. If it hit something as solid as a stump, the unyielding plough often somersaulted. The surprised ploughman had no time to let go. The handles flung him forward at the heels of his horses. If he did not keep calm and call 'Woo!' in a normal voice, the horses were likely to take fright and haul the plough over him.

The English and European weeds that troubled the Hunter farmers had still not reached the north. The main purpose of the several cultivations necessary in modern times is to kill imported weeds accustomed to hundreds of years of cultivation. So the little mouldboard ploughs could be followed by a harrow to break up the clods and the seed sown immediately on the next fall of rain. The harrow was often no more than a log with iron spikes driven into it, perhaps a system of heavy chains attached to a pole.

The seed was broadcast on top of the ground and covered lightly with another run of the harrows. The old method of pickling for bunt, a fungus disease that replaces the grains in the head with stinking black balls of smut, aided germination. All seed wheat was first soaked in a solution of bluestone, and thus it was ready to germinate when the harrows covered it. The broadcaster was a spinning flanged plate driven by a chain from a cog fitted to the axle of a dray. It flung the seed out in a twenty-metre wide strip.

But many first crops were sown by hand. Bill Grosser whose sons and grandsons now farm thousands of hectares of old Ghoolendaadi sowed eight hectares by hand when he came to the north from Victoria in 1909. He set out butts of pickled seed at measured intervals through the paddock to replenish the casting bag hung from his neck. He threw the grain in alternate sweeps of his hands as he walked.

Since the 1840s South Australian farmers had been harvesting up to four hectares a day with strippers made to the patterns of John Ridley and John Wrathall Bull, and cleaning the harvested grain with John Stokes Bagshaw's Champion winnower. Settlers in northern New South Wales used reaping hooks to harvest their small areas until the century was nearly over. Catherin Carlow on Yaminba Creek reaped with the best. 'Not many of the men could keep up with old Gran,' Jane Carr, her granddaughter, told me, 'Gran could do her acre a day.' The crops were reaped before they were dead ripe to avoid shattering, tied in sheaves and stooked. When the grain was ripe the sheaves were carted into a shed and the grain thrashed by men beating with greenhide flails alternately up and down.

Those with bigger areas cut their crops with the extraordinary reaper and binder that mowed the standing crop, rolled it into sheaves, knotted a length of twine round each sheaf, and dropped it on the ground. It was invented in America by Cyrus McCormick, one of the few non-Australians to lead in the development of harvesting machinery. The lines of sheaves were carted in and stacked in sheds, or built sheaf by sheaf into big firm stacks in the paddocks and thatched to protect them from rain. Then the farmers waited for the thrashing machine to arrive. A contractor at Binnaway, south of Coonabarabran, owned two of them. For months a team of men travelled through the north from stack to stack, threshing the grain, bagging it in big four-bushell bags that weighed about 110 kilograms, and restacking the straw for stock feed as it was ejected from the machine. Farmers worked together and supplied much of the labour to cut down expense. Horses drove these machines through a system of pulleys and belts by tramping in a treadmill or more usually by circling in pairs at the end of a pole that turned a wheel.

Some time in the 1890s Jack Miller of Kiambir bought a stripper and winnower. He harvested his own crop then took the machines contracting. Farmers heard the whining buzz of the beaters from miles away and rode over to see the machine working. Jack Miller sat on the stripper and lifted the comb up and down as the crop varied in height. A lad on a pony, the whipper-up, rode alongside the horses and kept them to a steady three miles (almost five kilometres) an hour.

The spinning beaters on the stripper knocked the heads off and in the same action thrashed them on a curved serrated steel platform. Grain, chaff and short straws were flung together into a box at the back. When the box was full, the stripper was driven to the stationary winnower. The men working the winnower spread a tarpaulin on the ground behind the stripper, opened the lid of the box, seized the ropes attached to a board, and slid the dusty boxful on to the tarpaulin. The stripper went back to the crop and the two men at the winnower worked hard to clear the tarpaulin before the box filled again. One man tin-dished the chaff into the hopper (fed the winnower), the other wound the handle that spun the fan, shook the sieves, and elevated the clean grain into a bag. Dust stung their eyes. Fine wheat hairs spiked their necks, the folds of their arms, their waists. They sweated and itched.

Some farmers were over conscious of the price of the Indian jute bags. They soaked them overnight in a farm ground tank to make them more yielding and hung them on fences to dry. The bag sewer dumped each bag and topped it up before he began to sew, then, before he made the last four or five stitches, he rammed the corner of the bag with a pick handle to make room for a little more wheat. Some rammed the corners with a device known as a bag-filler, a hopper soldered to a length of downpipe – an awkward top-heavy tool. Even then the most stringent farmers were unsatisfied. They instructed their unfortunate bag sewers to turn the bags over, slit a bottom corner, and ram in another kilogram or so of wheat.

Much of the hesitancy about spending money on wheat-growing machinery was due to the uncertainty of the yield. If a year was dry, the unsuitable European wheats set no seed. If a year was wet the fungus disease, rust, turned crops into a red mush as they headed. In 1889 most farmers in all colonies lost all their crop.

But when the rain came after the great drought of 1902 they could plant Federation with confidence. William Farrer, a plant-breeding genius, worked for twelve years without pay and without recognition to produce wheats suitable for Australia. He believed that our wheats needed to be early maturing, short-stemmed and scanty-leaved. A rainfall of 500 to 600 millimetres allowed no extravagance with soil moisture. While chemists maintained that the only answer to rust was to develop a poisonous spray, Farrer persisted in crossing wheats that showed some resistance to rust. He believed correctly that resistance would be intensified in the crosses. In 1898 he was invited to continue his work with the Department of Agriculture. F. B. Guthrie, a brilliant cereal chemist with the Department, had devised a method of milling small quantities of wheat and testing the flour for baking quality. He helped Farrer select his crossbred wheats. Federation was their great success. It established the modern Australian wheat industry.

Farmers bought stumpjump disc ploughs equipped with seats, a marvellous comfort even though the seats were hard. The best de-signed ploughs were mounted from behind. A farmer climbing up the front of his plough had to leap nimbly if too fresh horses took off with-out orders.

Donald Magann of Baradine rode in to see a trial of H. V. McKay's harvester in Coonabarabran about 1908 or 1909. This astonishing machine had been in use in Victoria and South Australia for over twenty years but few northern farmers had seen one. They ran behind it holding out their hats to catch the tailings then shook them and blew on them, checking for wasted grain. The paddock where the trial was held is now part of the town of Coonabarabran.

Built by Hugh Victor McKay when he was only eighteen the stripper harvester reaped, winnowed, and filled bags with clean grain as it moved. The first models were framed with Tasmanian Blackwood (*Acacia melanoxylon*), hard, knot-free and strong yet light in weight, a great timber. This Australian machine changed the method of harvesting throughout all that part of the world anxious to use machinery instead of men. Even in the 1970s a huge amount of the world's grain was grown by methods that had not changed in a thousand years.

It was at H. V. McKay's Sunshine Works out of Melbourne in 1907 that unions demanded a wage that acknowledged a workman's family. McKay did not grant the wage willingly. Although a brilliant self-trained engineer he was an unyielding businessman. His workers got their rise after long strikes and a court case. The judge, Mr Justice Higgins, spoke of a 'basic wage' and allowed a worker sufficient to live with a wife and three children 'in frugal comfort in a civilised community'.

Tined seed drills came on the market, then combination implements with multiple tynes that cultivated the ground as well as sowed the seed. They became the modern Australian combine that has been sowing crops with notorious inaccuracy for seventy-odd years.

In November, December and January of each year stacks of bagged wheat grew in railway yards in towns and villages. Horse teams and bullock teams carted in the bags about one hundred to a load. Lumpers took the bags on their shoulders off the wagons and walked up leaning planks to stack them. Few in the north grew more than forty hectares yielding four or five hundred four-bushel bags.

Some farmers in the south put in bigger areas. Mack and Austin at Narromine had seven four-furrow disc ploughs working one behind the other, each plough pulled by a five-horse team. An overseer rode the paddock keeping check on the work. George Henry Greene at Iandra, Grenfell, had sixty-one share farmers growing over eight thousand hectares by 1909–10. It was the last season there for my grandfather, Thomas Rolls, who had made what he needed to develop his own land. About 700 men took off that massive harvest. Modern farmers efficiently replaced men with machinery and are no longer big employers of labour. So they lost their influence with politicians and their importance.

The three-bushell chapman sack came into use. Weighing eighty-two kilograms instead of one hundred and ten when full of wheat, it was a less killing load for the lumpers. Headlie Shipard Taylor, another young Australian engineering genius, built the first header in 1913. He used a sliding knife to cut the heads off instead of beaters to knock them off and he built long wooden fingers to lift storm-flattened crops up to the comb. Elevators carried the mass of heads on their short straws to the drum where spinning grooved bars crushed them against a grooved concave sheet of steel and threw husks, straw and threshed grain on to riddles shaking in a blast of air. The tailings blew out the back, the grain was elevated into a five-bag box. H. V. McKay bought the patent and Taylor went to work for him to oversee construction of his Sunshine H. S. T. ground-drive header. Sunshine was written across the front elevator casing in big fancy writing and red embossed lines signified rays. Eight horses pulled them in two rows of four by a system of pivoting bars known as whiffle-tree swingle bars that the trace chains attached to. The toothed segment on the big steel driving wheel growled on the little pinion and the high-pitched moan of the open cogs driving the drum could be heard kilometres away.

The new machinery gave farmers confidence. Even if rust-resistant Federation was battered to the ground in summer storms, headers could recover most of the grain. The Government had already become over-confident. Wheatgrowers along the railway line were all doing well enough, even those who paid twenty-five dollars a hectare for Burburgate blocks. The newly cleared land west of Boggabri and south of Narrabri, Wee Waa and Pilliga was mostly growing payable crops. The farmers around Baradine cleared more land to grow wheat. The Coonabarabran flour mills, even though one hundred kilometres from rail, bought their grain. Ignoring the species of trees that signposted good country from bad, the Government pegged blocks deeper among the new-grown saplings.

If one drives north towards Cuttabri through the present forest one travels through a dry flat oak scrub with patches of good pine. Suddenly one runs into good cleared farmland. The soil looks the same. At first glance even the trees growing along the roadside look the same. Then one realises that Bull Oak, *Casuarina luehmannii*, has changed to Belar, *Casuarina cristata*. Modern farmers have cleared to the last Belar and run their fences where the oak begins. But many early would-be wheatgrowers ringbarked oak and grew little in its place. Bob Beavis on Rosewood (part of old Coghill), a believer in deep ploughing, broke up his oak country thirty centimetres deep and did not grow enough to feed his bullocks.

In 1912 five blocks of Upper Cumble growing pine, Western Black Wattle (*Acacia hakeoides*), Narrow-leaf Ironbark and gum, the last three certain indicators of country unsuited to European plants, were allotted to settlers. A Dutch family, the Lubbs, came on to one of those blocks in 1915 via South America where they ploughed their land with a wooden pole fitted with an iron share at one end and handles and two sliding props to keep it at the right angle at the other. Cheap Mexican labour sowed and reaped the crop by hand. All five settlers built houses, ringbarked their country and watched suckers and new scrub come up behind them. So they applied for timber licences, cut and sold the millable pine and eventually abandoned the blocks. The houses fell down or were burnt. The chimneys still remain. Harry Collins, one of the settlers, built them solidly of big sun-dried bricks. He followed the runholders' old road through Upper Cumble, and, where box trees showed the clay was non-crumbling, he dug his bricks out of the hardened wheel tracks.

Prickly Pear, that vigorous exotic cactus, joined in the wild growth of Australian plants. It took over much of old Wangen and spread east of present Gwabegar. It filled in the open spaces in the Brigalow country. And it ensured that some of the settlers on the doubtful country failed even sooner. They tried to plough the pear out and multiplied it a hundred times. Every piece of sliced-up stem grew. Of eighty excited settlers, many of them ex-servicemen, who took up leases near the new rail terminus at Gwabegar in 1924, almost half abandoned them to the forest again.

Kerosene tractors, Hart-Parrs and Fordsons, came into the north in the 1920s. Southern farmers had tried steam traction engines but they were too cumbersome for farm work and it was a formidable job to keep them supplied with wood and water.

Bill Grosser bought one of the first tractors in the north, a 1923 Hart-Parr. In the 1970s his grandson, Ron Grosser, restored it and demonstrated it at the yearly agricultural equipment field days held at Gunnedah. The engine turns slowly, only 750 revolutions a minute, with an occasional cough. That cough was a characteristic noise of farming districts. It carried through the higher-pitched, faster note of the early Fordsons.

The power take-off on the Hart-Parr is driven by a heavy rhinoceros-hide belt. This outlandish piece of equipment was fitted in 1929 because the original cowhide belt stretched too much on the short drive. It was still tight and supple fifty years later.

It was little fun starting the Hart-Parrs. The crank handle fitted on the near side and the designer had allowed insufficient room between the starting dog and the driving wheel. When the wheels were studded with the necessary steel grips, the crank handle could be swung a three-quarter turn only. As a bright afterthought the designer fitted a wooden shear pin so that nothing important broke if the handle swung too far. But the wooden pins broke too often at the wrong time and a hurrying farmer often left the crank handle lying on a bag in the shed when he drove out to the paddocks. Then, if he needed to start the engine again, he pulled on the flywheel and risked mangling his hands in the friction clutch.

The next model Hart-Parr dispensed with the troublesome shear pin but that made it impossibly dangerous to start with the crank. If the engine fired a little late the crank handle could not be withdrawn in time. The farmer smashed his knuckles on a steel spud, or smashed the crank handle, or the starting dog – possibly all three. But the clutch had been moved off the flywheel leaving it clear. It became universal practice to start the tractors by swinging the flywheel.

Most farmers continued with horses until well into the 1930s. Then they bought a Case Model L, or a McCormick-Deering W30, or a Minneapolis-Moline, usually known as a Twin-City – reliable tractors without quirks. The operator sat exposed on an iron seat with only a stiff steel spring to cushion him from the jarring of the steel-spudded wheels. Each time a spud came up – they were spaced about fifteen centimetres apart on both wheels – it threw dust against one of his cheeks. At the end of the day he wore a dust mask. He breathed through channels in the dust. He spoke through grotesquely enlarged lips.

At harvest time, to save paying an extra man's wages, farmers extended the tractor controls to the header seat. The header driver sat on the unyielding perch on his Sunshine H. S. T., drove the tractor moving three or four metres in front of him with his left hand, worked clutch or brake with his feet, while his right hand adjusted the throttle, lifted the comb up and down, set the crop lifters and now and again wound the little handle that turned the levelling auger in the grain box behind him. When the box was full, he stopped the machine, leapt off and emptied it into bags at the bagging outlets. The full bags were stood in line across the paddock to wait the itinerant bag sewers.

Policemen, school teachers, shop assistants joined the regular sewers at weekends. All were paid by the hundred and there was good money to be made. Some developed remarkable skill. They put twenty-two stitches in well-filled bags at the rate of thirty to forty bags an hour.

Motor trucks took over the carrying from horse and bullock teams. Motor driven elevators made lumping easier so fewer lumpers handled many more bags. Without the gruelling necessity of walking up sloping catwalks, the lumpers built their stacks twenty-one tiers high. The lumper's badge of office was a hood made out of a flour bag to protect the back of his neck from the rough jute. Towns grew proud of their lumpers and boasted of their tallies. But Dick Tumbers of Boggabri was acknowledged over a wider area than any other. He stacked up to 4,500 bags a day.

Inevitably Federation took rust – changes in rust species keep pace with plant breeders – but not before it was known as Old Federation to distinguish it from a later cross, Hard Federation. Farmers possibly aided the rust because they were reluctant to dispense with the pretty stemmed high yielding Purple Straw, one of the less rust-resistant ancestors of Federation.

Tall, slow-growing Ford took over as a main variety, and high-yielding Nabawa, bred at Wagga as early as 1912 and strangely unrecognised until the Western Australians found out how good it was. The north ignored the popular, soft-grained Bencubbin that the southerners grew and planted Fedweb and Hofed, the rust-resistant wheats of another plant-breeding genius, Dr W. L. Waterhouse of Sydney University.

In 1946 he released Gabo, a wheat bred for blacksoil plains where the fertility is extreme and the rainfall low. Its every characteristic was tailored to fit it for where it had to grow as though it was built not bred. It is the greatest success any plant breeder has ever had and it changed Australia's farming. It was rust-resistant, the most rust-resistant then developed. It was high yielding, the highest yielding then developed. It was quick-growing so that it could be sown any time during winter or early spring when there was enough moisture. The grain was easily threshed yet it did not shatter. It was high in protein, yet good to mill. It was short stemmed so that summer storms did not tangle it as much as the tall-growing species.

Jim O'Reilly, the agronomist at Gunnedah, oversaw wheat-growing on blacksoil. He had come to the district as a graduate in 1928 so was well ready for the new wheat. He drove to farmers' meetings with one piece of string in a bottle of sand and another piece in a bottle of marbles. He explained that no matter how much nourishment the marbles contained, if the string was a root it made insufficient contact to draw nourishment from them. He told the blacksoil farmers that the soil beneath them was structured like a bottle of marbles. Conventional methods of cultivation were useless. They had to work shallow with tyned implements to consolidate the soil for the roots to run in, the opposite to red soil farming.

So the settlers on Gurley that Robert Pringle was glad to sell for two horses and saddles put their black plains under wheat and found it the richest of land. So did the settlers on the Galathera plain, and Ghoolendaadi, and Onus's old Therrebri and Cox's old Nombi. The Liverpool Plains went under wheat, and the plains between Coonamble and Baradine, and Doyle's old Killarney and the plains to the west beyond Wee Waa. Farmers fitted their old tractors with rubber tyres or bought new tractors already equipped with rubbers. They fitted old generators, batteries and lights and drove night and day. The cold at seven or eight kilometres an hour on an open tractor on a frosty night is unbelievable. I've taken off two pairs of gloves and slapped my hands together till my fingers had enough feeling to open my penknife to cut the twine on the bags of seed. My toes pained through two pairs of socks and boots thrust inside a cocoon of wheatbags seven thick. I've thought of knocking off but the lights of other tractors whose drivers were braving it have kept me there. Stupefied by noise and cold we sat and spiralled round our paddocks sowing wheat.

Soon the wheat was held in bulk silos instead of stacks, and carted to shipping ports in bulk railway trucks. Until the 1960s most farmers still bagged the wheat on their farms. Carriers loaded the bags on their trucks and took them to the silos where contract tippers emptied them down the elevator chutes. The itinerant bag sewers adjusted their methods. They skewered the top of a loosely-filled bag with a needle thirty-five centimetres long, threaded it with a length of binder twine, drew the needle back, then tied the ends of the twine across the top of the bag. They devised quick methods of cutting the twine. Most rolled it round twenty-litre oil drums, slashed it down one side, and tied the lengths together in bundles. They came into the paddocks about daylight, the twine dangling from keepers on their hips. They left at dark. Some sewed up to 1,200 bags a day. Bag sewing and tipping employed a lot of men in country towns. Then farmers equipped their header boxes with augers, carriers fitted bins to their trucks, and the grain was carried in bulk from paddock to ship.

Modern scientists work constantly to produce wheats ahead of the races of rust changing to catch up with them. As one wheat succumbs another is released. Nicholas Derera, a brilliant Hungarian, is director of wheat breeding at the University of Sydney Plant Breeding Institute north of Narrabri. He has produced some blacksoil wheats capable of huge yields but his major quest is not yet solved: to breed a white-grained wheat that will not germinate for about three weeks after it is ripe. Sprouting of grain in the head during wet summers ruins the milling quality of too much hard northern wheat. Although Australia has always marketed only white wheats we might yet have to grow red wheats that have a natural period of dormancy. Nicholas Derera has red wheat crosses ready for that day.

In the late 1940s an honours graduate named Markias from the Philippines worked on some of the Pilliga forest soils that were obviously deficient in phosphorous yet gave no response to applications of superphosphate. He found the soils too acid to support European grasses or legumes. In wet 1950 he achieved spectacular results by inoculating lucerne and barrel medic with nitrogen-producing bacteria, coating them with lime, and sowing them with a mixture of half lime and half superphosphate. A jubilant Government saw a million hectares of intractable forest brought to order. They threw open nine big blocks in the heart of it.

Five of the blocks averaging about 2,800 hectares each were along that part of Borah and Yaminba Creeks that Ebenezer Orr was glad to abandon. Four of the blocks were on the old run west of Ayrlands known as Denobollie or Goat. Various men had leased it but none of them apparently ever stocked it. It was always scrubby forest with the scaly bloodwood as a dominant tree, useless for any moneymaking pursuit.

The conditions of the leases demanded extensive pasture improvement. But most of the half dozen men who went on to them advanced cautiously. Allan Simson built a home for his family near the long-abandoned Ayrlands hotel. But he was rather bewildered by his acquisition. His son Mac told me he seemed to think the land generated money of itself. Neville Salisbury and his partner, Lane, who also owned a stock and station agency in Walgett, built a house near the lovely pool in Borah Creek known now as the Salisbury Waterholes but in a year or two they took the iron off the roof and left the rest of the house to disintegrate. The Arkell brothers, wealthy businessmen from Wollongong, took up two blocks of Denobollie. They cleared it all and built houses and sheds on it. They found, as the others did, that only exceptional years supported Markias's theories. Normal years, as

usual, produced nothing profitable. But, most strangely, they still own
it. Now and again they send a man up with a mob of cattle to stock it,
perhaps even to plough a few hundred hectares, though it has never
become less obstinate about yielding profit.

One man, Norman Akehurst, had a spectacular smash. He sold a
coffee plantation at Rabaul at the height of a boom in coffee, came to
the forest with a marvellous sum to invest and took up two blocks,
about 5,500 hectares altogether, next to Arkell's. He called it Mala-
goona after the good plantation he seized from the jungle. 'It is rich
land' he said, looking at the bloodwood and ironbark scrub, 'see the
trees it can grow.'

So he cleared it with bulldozers, the whole huge area. He fenced it
and ploughed it and sowed pasture and crops. He graded roads. He
built two good houses and big fowl yards, electric light rooms, sheds,
stables, an underground cement tank to store 140,000 litres of run-off
water from the biggest shed, a brick barbecue in his front garden. He
sank bores and equipped them with pumpheads, diesel engines, tanks
on steel stands and troughs. He bought sheep.

The pasture died, the crops died, the sheep died, Akehurst died. His
family drove out and abandoned the lot.

I drove in to see it in the remarkable spring of 1974. There was a five
hundred hectare mass of four species of acacia in full bloom in the front
paddock. About the first deserted house grew forty hectares of low
mauve boronia. In the background among regrown bloodwood and
ironbark as far as one could see were the nodding blue heads of lilies,
lilac-margined white westringia and deep purple False Sarsaparilla
climbing among the creamy balls of Mountain Hickory.

The forest had had a final say. It converted a fortune into something
completely beautiful and completely worthless.

Sixty-odd years before, at the turn of the century, Jimmy Governor
had tried to make a final statement for the Aborigines.

7

The Breelong
Blacks
A Sinister Comedy

A hare chased by a slow dog obviously enjoys the chase. It skips along looking back over a shoulder. It spurts safely ahead, doubles back on its tracks, then springs a metre or more to one side to leave a big gap in the trail. It runs into a patch of high grass and threads a maze of tracks through it, then sits up on a nearby vantage point and listens while the panting dog thrashes about trying to unravel the scent.

Jimmy Governor, a part Aboriginal, chased for months through the central north of New South Wales by more than two hundred mounted police, and, off and on, by about two thousand civilians, enjoyed the chase more than anything he had ever been allowed to enjoy. He was a good bushman and an expert tracker. He had been employed as a police tracker at Cassilis. He might have gone up into Queensland and hidden himself for years. Instead, he fooled with his pursuers. He left signs of his passing so obvious that the most inept civilian must find them. When he wanted to he could disappear by driving sheep back over his tracks, or by walking along railway lines that left no marks. Then he would announce his presence again by spilling flour all over somebody's floor, or by burning a house. Once, he and his brother Joe hid in a culvert and let a party of mounted police ride over the top of them. But Jimmy and Joe Governor were no harmless game. Jimmy had finally been offended out of all dignity, and he was trying to win back his self-esteem by eliminating all those who had offended it. Nine people had been viciously murdered, and there were known to be more on the list. The Governors frightened people over a huge area 400 kilometres long and 300 wide.

The Governor's mother, Annie, was born on Caigan, Andrew Brown's first station on the Castlereagh. Her mother was Polly, an Aboriginal servant at the homestead, and her father a red-headed Irishman named Jack Fitzgerald. He died before Annie was born, so she was brought up as an Aboriginal. She married Sam Governor who later changed his first name to Thomas. He was a bullock driver on the Mudgee-Muswellbrook run. Although he earned his living as a white man he was Aboriginal enough to carry a nulla nulla. A panel in the bar-room door of the Royal Hotel at Leadville bore its imprint for years. He had three other sons besides Jimmy and Joe, all of them darker than half-castes. One of them, Roy, was safely in the Brewarrina lock-up during the hunt, doing five years for larceny. Another, Jacky, was charged with vagrancy a month or so after the first murders and thrown into Mudgee jail as a precaution. All his black friends at Wollar were locked up with him. It was the memory of this high-handed treatment that Jimmy was trying to expunge.

Joe was brought up by little Andrew Doyle (son of big Andrew who established the Narrabri run) in hilly country on the Goulburn River west of Muswellbrook. In those days the children of poor parents were often left with whoever would feed them. Little Andrew once belted Joe for kicking a milking cow. This was not forgotten. Little Andrew was on the assassination list.

Jimmy went to school at an Aboriginal mission on the Talbragar River and at Gulgong Primary. For a year or two Miss Porteous taught him in a little shingle-roofed school a few miles out of Coonabarabran. He learned to read and write fairly fluently and did not leave school until he was fifteen. Many contemporary white children spent only two or three years at school and left at twelve. Jimmy had his grandfather's red hair, a striking feature with his very dark complexion. He was a handsome youth. Jobs were not hard to get as fencer or stockman. At the weekends he came into Gulgong and played cricket with the local youths.

Joe had the Aboriginal outlook. He did not like constant and monotonous work for money. He preferred to live with the blacks and work for a few days when he got hungry. Mostly he made all he needed possum-shooting for skins.

Jimmy had dreams of living like a white man, but however hard he worked he could not make a white man's money. Aborigines had no rights by law and they were usually fobbed off with rations and pocket-money. Jimmy thought he might do better as an Aboriginal. He took the job of black-tracker with the Cassilis police. Trackers were despised by the whites and hated by the blacks. After seventeen months he tried to go white again. He left and went horse-breaking. As a horse-breaker he could not be so readily taken down. Horses were broken by contract at a price per head. Jimmy was good. He began to make money.

On 10 December 1898 when he was twenty-three, he made a decided jump into the white world. He married sixteen-year-old Ethel Mary Jane Page, the white daughter of a Gulgong miner. He had got her pregnant to ensure the contract.

It was a sad mistake. The girl was a whiner and a tale-bearer. Her family would have nothing to do with Jimmy. He could not cast off his black relations. Now that he was making money they began to come around him. They built humpies near his hut and demanded food. By tribal law Jimmy had to support them. He did not enter the white world: his wife ended up living in a black's camp out of Gulgong. The local white women ostracised her cruelly.

After his son was born, Jimmy tried to move into a happier atmosphere. He took a job fencing and splitting posts for John Mawbey of Breelong, a fair-sized property on the Wallumburrawang Creek that runs into the Castlereagh east of Gilgandra. It was part of the big Breelong run that was first taken up by the Rouse brothers. Mawbey was one of those who liked to employ Aborigines because he could treat them harder. Jimmy was supposed to be working contract but he was still paid partly in rations – "Tucker and ten bob a hundred' for post splitting. A good man could cut seventy to eighty ironbark posts a day if the trees were big enough and split easily.

Things went well enough for a month or so. Jimmy was working hard and getting enough to eat. Ethel complained a bit. She was working one or two days a week at the homestead about two kilometres from their hut on the creek. She did the washing and filled in the rest of the day with odd jobs. Mrs Mawbey told Ethel often that a white woman had no business marrying a black. It wasn't right. She ought to leave Jimmy. Helen Kerz told her the same things more forcibly. She was a twenty-year-old trainee teacher at the Breelong West school, and boarded with the Mawbeys. Five or six of the nine Mawbey children went to school there.

Joe Governor and his friend, Jacky Underwood, came to see how Jimmy was getting on. They had been shooting and trapping possums around Dubbo. They put up a rough gunyah on the creek and claimed rations. Ethel and Jimmy had to eat a little less. Jacky Underwood was about thirty-nine years old, one-eyed, and slow-witted. He had an alias, Charlie Brown. On some police documents it was written the other way about: 'Charlie Brown (alias Jacky Underwood)'. Neither was his real name. 'Jacky Underwood' was borrowed from a drover who had once employed him at Mudgee. 'Charlie Brown' was a convenient tag. He probably knew his Aboriginal name. Both his parents were full-bloods but both are unknown. He was born in Queensland somewhere.

Jimmy got what work he could out of Jacky and Joe for their food. Ethel had to put up with jeers from the women at the homestead about the place turning into a black's camp. She told all this to Jimmy tearfully but in great detail. Another full-blood arrived, Jacky Porter, and Jimmy's young nephew, Peter Governor, who had been lamed in a fall from a horse. They put up another gunyah. They claimed rations.

Now it was difficult to feed them all. Mawbey did not like the encampment on his property and he grew harder. He condemned one hundred of the split posts. Eight inches by five inches free of sap at the small end was the usual specification. (That is now expressed grotesquely as 200 mm by 125 mm.) If too big a margin was allowed for error the posts were awkwardly big and heavy, slow to stand in the ground, and slow to bore for the wires. In trying to split to the right size a post might easily run out ten millimetres small at the top.

Probably these hundred posts were light. Jimmy did not seem outraged at having them condemned. Then Mawbey and his two elder sons began to cart away the condemned posts. That was not to be tolerated. If the posts were not fit to be paid for they were fit only to rot in the bush. There was a quarrel. Mawbey agreed to pay for the posts.

Then there was trouble with Mrs Mawbey. She was short-weighing the flour and sugar for Ethel, or Jimmy thought she was. After that Ethel had fancier stories to tell about what was said at the homestead.

On 20 July 1900 the Governors were almost out of food. Ethel walked up to the homestead to ask Mrs Mawbey for flour and sugar. She did not get any. She was told again a white woman had no business living in a black's camp. 'Black trash', said Helen Kerz, 'You ought to be shot for marrying a black.'

Ethel went back to the camp in tears. When Jimmy came home from work she asked him to take her away. She did not want to hear herself talked about any more. Jimmy could not see how it would be different anywhere else. He said he would go and get the rations from Mawbey. He would complain, too.

Jimmy had been talking a bit about going bushranging. Ned Kelly had been dead only twenty years. He was still a living hero. Jimmy had been thinking a bit about murdering Mawbey, or better, of taking Mrs Mawbey to court. 'I'll make her mind her own business' said Jimmy. It was a satisfying fantasy, Mrs Mawbey going to jail for libelling Jimmy Governor.

It was not a brave setting out to see Mawbey. Jimmy took slow Jacky Underwood with him. They had a boondi or nulla nulla (a club the shape of a baseball bat carved usually from heavy Myall or Yarran) and an old shotgun without any cartridges. They drifted about in the bush for about two or three hours possum-catching. Since they had no cartridges to shoot the marsupials, they took them Aboriginal-fashion. They looked through the top of each eucalypt towards the moon. If there was a possum it showed up dark silver against the disc of the moon. Then one climbed up quietly, clubbed it if he could, or shook it down to the man on the ground if it was on branchlets out of reach.

The Mawbey men were bagging wheat. The winnower was in a shed at the former homestead, one and a half kilometres from the new one. Mrs Mawbey's uncle, Reg. Clark, usually slept there, and two of her sons, Reg. and Sydney. Now they were working long hours, so John Mawbey slept there too. He often slept there when he was farming.

Jimmy and Jacky Underwood did not get there until ten o'clock. By that time they were cold and had lost their courage. The presence of so many in the house was daunting. Jimmy did not say much at all; he simply asked for flour and sugar. John Mawbey promised to send them down in the morning. He asked them to come in and warm their hands at the fire. They said 'No thanks'. Mawbey went to bed. Jimmy and Jacky went back to their camp.

Perhaps Ethel then egged Jimmy on. His account of the night must have sounded lame. Flour and sugar was not much assuagement. Jimmy said he would go and see Mrs Mawbey. He would tackle her about what she had been saying. Jacky Underwood again went with him. They still had the boondi. Somewhere they picked up a tomahawk or two. Almost certainly Ethel followed them, and probably also Joe and Peter Governor and Jacky Porter. How could they have kept away? It promised to be too good a row to miss. That whitey missus bastard was going to hear a few things from a black bastard for a change.

Jimmy knocked on the dining-room door. 'Are you in, Mrs Mawbey?' She was about to go to bed and answered from somewhere inside. Jimmy shouted at her. 'Did you tell my wife she ought to be

shot for marrying me? Did you ask my wife about her personal
business?' Jimmy was trying to be dignified. The words were stiltedly
formal. Mrs Mawbey opened the dining-room door. Helen Kerz, in a
long nightgown, inevitably stood beside her. Mrs Mawbey said
something about going home to bed. Helen Kerz decided it was Jimmy
who ought to be shot. 'A black fellow like you has got no business marrying a white woman.' Jimmy was sensitive about his colour. He
smashed Mrs Mawbey across the mouth with his boondi and knocked
Helen Kerz to the floor with a fist. He wanted personal contact with
her. 'Then I got out of temper' said Jimmy later in a statement.

The result was hideous. There were ten people in the house. Three
girls and Helen Kerz slept in a bedroom; Mrs Mawbey slept with three
boys on a closed-in verandah. The two youngest sons, Cecil and
Garnet, six years old and three, slept in a cot in the separate kitchen.

Jimmy leapt into the dining-room. Helen Kerz was screaming. She
got to her feet and ran into the bedroom, slamming the door. The
screaming woke fourteen-year-old Percy Mawbey and his sickly
cousin, George, who was sleeping with him. They dived under the bed.

Mrs Mawbey was getting to her feet. Jimmy clubbed at her again.
She called for help. Percy recognised his mother's voice and came out
from under the bed. He ran towards her. George heard him threaten to
shoot someone then moan and fall as Jimmy almost beheaded him with
a tomahawk. Mrs Mawbey was on her feet again and Jimmy clubbed
her down on top of her son. This time her skull was smashed in.

Jacky Underwood was chopping down the bedroom door. George
Mawbey under the bed heard Jimmy urging him on: 'Go on, Jacky.
Dash out their brains!' Elsie Clarke, Mrs Mawbey's eighteen-year-old
sister, cringed in her bed. Jacky Underwood took a few chops at her
while eleven-year-old Hilda Mawbey jumped out the bedroom window. Her older sister, Grace, took Helen Kerz by the hand and pulled
her out the window after Hilda. All three ran down the path towards
the creek.

Jacky Underwood did not do much after his few slashes at Elsie
Clarke. He did not even kill her. She remained conscious enough to
hear and survived her drastic wounds. After a long spell in hospital she
was able to testify. She asserted that as the three girls escaped Ethel
Governor called from outside 'Look Jimmy, there goes the girls'.

Anyway, Jimmy Governor raced after them. Grace threw the garden
gate shut behind her and Jimmy ran into it, barking a hand. But she
was hampered by her long night gown. Jimmy soon overtook her and
killed her. Young Hilda was a fast runner and seemed to be getting

away. Jimmy left Helen Kerz while he went after Hilda. She headed for the creek but tripped over a log in the bed. Jimmy killed her, too, then went looking for Helen Kerz who had tried to hide. Her white nightgown gave her away. 'You can't plant on me' said Jimmy, 'I'll have you'. He clubbed her ferociously, then threw the boondi beside her. Threads of flannelette were snagged on it, flesh, blood and hair.

When he came back he prowled through the house looking for the other boys. Jacky Underwood told police after his capture that he knew George Mawbey was under his bed but he said nothing to Jimmy. He told him they were all gone. He also said that he shoved one of the girls under a bed and put a blanket over her. There were no girls left. It must have been nine-year-old Bertie who was saved. Jimmy overlooked the cot in the kitchen. Cecil and Garnet slept unharmed throughout the uproar.

Then it was time to reckon up. 'How many did you kill?' asked Jimmy. 'I kill one' said Jacky. 'I did all the murders' said Jimmy. 'I think you do most of 'em' said Jacky. They left.

Now it was quiet in the house. Bertie jumped out a window and raced to tell his father. The screams had carried the kilometre and a half between the houses. The men were already on their way. George went out to meet them.

Mrs Mawbey was still alive as well as Elsie Clarke. She lived long enough to make dying depositions. 'My name is Sarah Mawbey. I believe I am dying. I know I am badly hurt.' The statement of a dying person carried more weight in a law court than the unsworn statement of the living. So the unfortunate woman had to admit her fears to the policeman with his notebook before she came to the statement the police wanted. 'Jimmy Governor hit me with a tomahawk. I only saw two men. I could hear more outside. I could hear all of them.'

None of the Mawbeys could set out immediately after the murderers. Hilda Mawbey could not be found in the dark. There was the doctor to be summoned from Dubbo, the police from Gilgandra, and the frightened children to be cared for. Sydney who had been sleeping with the men was only twelve. Jack, the eldest son, was away. There was Reg. aged eighteen, John Mawbey and Fred Clarke to act. The Governors got several hours start.

Jimmy ran back to his camp to pack up. Jacky Underwood behaved in entirely Aboriginal fashion. He needed comfort. So he moved a couple of kilometres from the house and made a fire. 'After a bit I go on to the camp and find Jimmy there. They was all leaving the camp and crossing the creek. Jimmy say he going to capsize the train going to

Muswellbrook.' Jimmy was seeing himself as a real bushranger. Jacky was thinking only of the hills. He wanted to follow them through to Townsville. 'We go into the big mountains we be all right. Jimmy say "We are going to kill a man and a boy near Mendooran".'

Ethel Governor, Jacky Porter and Peter were all taken the next day. They had only moved twenty kilometres. Ethel blamed Jimmy and Jacky for all the murders and said they were on the way to Wollar to murder Jimmy Coombes. She denied being anywhere near the house the previous night and also exonerated Jacky Porter and Peter. She tried to save Joe, too. Ethel was keen on Joe. She had begun to sleep with him sometimes. He was not as moody as Jimmy.

Ethel turned Queen's evidence at Jimmy's trial and testified against him. She got herself out of trouble and later remarried. She had nine more children.

Jimmy, Joe and Jacky Underwood travelled fast. They went east past Mendooran, past Merrygoen and camped in the hills fifty kilometres from Breelong. They did not murder the man and the boy. Jacky talked Jimmy out of it. He had seen enough murder. They did rob a bark hut for food: sugar, tea and tinned fish, plus tobacco, a shirt and a cap. Then they moved on to a creek and sat down beside some rocky waterholes to boil their billy. A party of civilians rode on to them and fired shots. All three escaped into the bush.

Jacky Underwood lost his spirit. It was no fun being shot at. Jimmy and Joe ran south. Jacky saw them no more. He dawdled after them. It was too difficult trying to get to Townsville on his own.

Jimmy and Joe travelled another fifty or sixty kilometres. They robbed two houses near Gulgong and threatened to come back and murder the owners if they told the police. They boasted of the others they were going to kill. Escape was no part of their plan. They set out to frighten as many as they could.

Then they went north-east towards Ulan. Jimmy had once asked Sandy McKay for some tucker. Sandy had replied 'Go and earn your tucker, you black bastard, the same as I have to do.' They found him at work in his vineyard. Joe split his head open with a tomahawk. That was Joe's first murder. He ran into the house and chopped at Mrs McKay. She was badly wounded but did not die. They threatened her adopted daughter but let her run off in panic while they stole some money, a horse and saddle and bridle. They double-banked along the Cassilis road until they found another horse, then they circled south again and had some fun with an Indian hawker on the road to Wollar.

They bailed him up in his covered waggon but did no more than announce their assassination list. Jimmy Coombes was still on it and a
man named Neville. The O'Brien family was not mentioned.

The Governors came on them at a place called Poggie, midway between Wollar and Merriwa. O'Brien was away. He was a former em-
ployer. It is not known how he had offended. Mrs O'Brien was at home
and her eighteen-month-old son. A midwife was staying there too,
Mrs Theophilus Bennett. Elizabeth O'Brien was heavily pregnant.

They shot Mrs Bennett three times and left her for dead. She did not
move when they kicked her. Then they chopped down Mrs O'Brien
and split open the skull of her son with the tomahawk. They took some
money and a pair of boots. As he was leaving Jimmy took out his big
knife and slashed Mrs O'Brien's womb open to reveal the unborn
child. Mrs Bennett recovered.

The horses were found abandoned in nearby scrub. Jimmy and Joe
walked for a while. They called on the threatened Neville but he was
away from his hut, so they sat on a log near it and rolled cigarettes from
tobacco and newspaper. The butts and matches were left lying about.
It was an ostentatious visiting-card. They then showed their bushcraft.
They walked into rough country till they came to a fence then they
walked along the wires. It was a wallaby fence, ten barbs laced together
every sixty centimetres. Where it led into hard granite country they
jumped off and left no tracks.

There was a state of terror over a wide area. The *Mudgee Guardian*
kept it simmering on a notice board posted outside the office. Five hundred police and civilians searched the country bordered by Mudgee,
Gulgong, Cassilis, Merriwa. All farming had stopped, farmhouses and
timber-getters' camps were deserted. A reporter called on thirty-five
homesteads and found only four occupied. In one of those, forty-three
women and children were under the guard of four men. Forty-odd
people camped in the Ulan church.

Jacky Underwood was taken on the fourth day after the murders. He
calmly walked into a selector's house near Leadville and asked for
food. Shaw, the selector, recognised him. He kept him eating and talking, offered him a job, while Mrs Shaw ran two kilometres across the
hills to a neighbour to ask him to ride for the police. There were no
police to be ridden for. They were all out riding the bush somewhere. A
party of civilians rode with Jacky Underwood into Leadville and locked
him up. John Seabrooke, a labourer, and a mining overseer named
Scoble, in charge of the Mt Stewart mine, sat outside the cell until 11

o'clock the next day when a constable arrived from Mudgee to take over. Jimmy Governor's father had found that lead and silver mine. He did nothing with the find, probably because a part-Aboriginal had no rights of property. He was graciously given a horse, cart and harness by those who developed it.

Jacky Underwood was convicted of the murder of Percy Mawbey, almost certainly murdered by Jimmy Governor. He was hanged in the old Dubbo gaol. 'I'll be in heaven for dinner' he said, as he stepped on to the platform. Certainly he would have imagined a fire to eat it beside. In 1974 the local historical society re-erected the gallows he was hanged on. The gaol is a gruesome tourist attraction.

Jimmy and Joe circled around the Wollar area. They stole another horse, shotguns, rifles, cartridges here and there. Little Andrew Doyle's relatives came and took him to their home out of Scone for safe-keeping. Little Andrew was very deaf and had a displaced hip. He carried a big ear-trumpet and used a walking stick. It was probably that stick that Joe had been belted with. The Governors came to his house a few nights after Little Andrew had been persuaded to leave.

Jimmy Coombes was not killed either although he was first on the list. There was only one more murder. Jimmy Governor had once poisoned Dingoes for old Kieran Fitzpatrick out of Wollar. Somehow all Jimmy's dogs had got poisoned too. Jimmy blamed Fitzpatrick. He was almost eighty. They shot him first then finished him off with the tomahawk.

Bloodhounds were brought up from Sydney, and six black trackers from Fraser Island, Queensland, expert beyond comprehension of white eyes and proud of their skill. Local Aborigines laughed at the idea of black trackers being used. They said none of them would dare lead police to the murderers. They would go always in fear of their lives if they did. Jimmy and Joe were acting out all blacks' fantasies. It was less than twenty years since the last black ears had been nailed to Queensland huts as trophies. A lot of them were women's ears, too. 'Go for the breeders' was the common cry.

Jimmy and Joe moved west past Gulgong. They shot a sheep on Rouse's old Guntawang and were surprised roasting a leg a few miles north-west on Spicers Creek. They had to run off from the half-cooked meat and leave their tea and sugar behind. They covered their tracks for a few days after that. No one knew where they were. Newspapers ridiculed the police and criticised the civilian parties. 'A great many gallop all over the place in large bodies' wrote the *Sydney Morning*

Herald. 'Many never leave the roads where they are of no possible use, and they stampede for the nearest hotel or wineshop before dark.' So did the police. The Queensland black trackers complained about it. They wanted to camp when it got too dark to see the tracks and move on at daylight.

Superintendent Thomas Garvin, in charge, was not happy with his police either. 'Two sub-inspectors should not be in one party,' he directed his officer in Mudgee. 'Neither should a number of senior sergeants be in the one party. Valuable time is being lost through police following each other in such large numbers leading to portion of districts being unsearched and unprotected.'

This unprotection worried many. Everyone would have liked a policeman sitting on his doorstep. W. F. E. Cole, J. P., wired the Inspector-General of Police from Coolah on 30 July 'Town without police protection for ten days. Black murderers reported twenty miles from here. Many men away. Panic in town. Meeting of whole population unanimously request me to ask that at least one policeman be sent here immediately.'

Jimmy and Joe were unaware of this farce. They were finding hiding out rather dull. They moved north-east up Coolah Creek towards Cunningham's Pandoras Pass and began to expose their movements again. They stole a rifle, boots, cartridges and reloading tools from a German settler named Schiemmer, then went on over the pass to the edge of the Liverpool Plains. No one was following them and they grew very cocky. They stole more clothes and boots (perhaps Schiemmer's did not fit) from a kangaroo-shooter, Andrew Byrne, and left two notes for the police at his camp. Then they stole two grey horses and held up a boundary rider. 'We are doing a bit of bushranging,' they told him. Jimmy exchanged him hats.

They rode out on to the plains towards Tambar Springs, fired a few shots at a teamster named Squires and made off with one of his horses. The third horse was a nuisance so they took it back again and gave Squires a taunting letter to give to the police. It detailed all the movements of the searchers in the few days that Jimmy and Joe were hiding.

After that they moved fast and carelessly, westward on to Nombi, the run taken up so early by William Cox, then north-east through Ghoolendaadi towards Boggabri. Sometimes they rode, sometimes they walked. When riding they cut fences to get through. It was a broad trail they left.

People at Coonabarabran and Baradine, not knowing which way the
Governors were heading, began polishing up their marksmanship.
Bruce Pincham, a Baradine sawmiller for sixty-five years, remembers
his uncle out practising with a pistol. 'He wouldn't have worried the
Governors much. He couldn't hit a fruit-case at ten yards.' When Phil
Langdale bought Crickenbah on the Borah Creek in 1919 there was an
old dead gum in the creek at the back of the house well studded with
shot. John Sevil (unlike his brother, William, he spelt his name conventionally), the owner in 1900, used to walk to his back door and practise quick firing with his shotgun. He had cowbells hung as alarms to
all the fences near the homestead.

The police did not know which way the Governors were heading
either. There were twenty-seven of them in Baradine one day, not at all
anxious to move out into the forest.

The Governors walked through the cemetery at Boggabri and made
down-river through what used to be the old Baan Baa run. At dusk
they were seen sneaking through the long shadows of the paling fence
round the Turrawan railway station. A mounted constable galloped
over and called to them to stop. As they raced for the thick pine forest,
the constable leapt off his horse and took aim with his rifle. His horse
pulled back as he squeezed the trigger, the shot went wide, and the
frustrated constable had to walk after his runaway horse. B. Lye, a
civilian with him, grabbed for his old Martini-Henry but in his excitement fumbled a .303 into its enormous breech. The rifle did not fire.
The Governors moved into the safety of thick scrub and came out on to
Bohena Creek.

They stuck up Bateman's selection demanding food and went north
to Mrs Burns in a railway ganger's house. 'Give us all you got.' They
ran by night along the railway lines so the police could not tell which
way they had gone.

But as bushrangers they had to keep on playing the part. They announced their whereabouts again next morning at the Round Swamp
seventeen kilometres out of Wee Waa by sticking up Dave Jones and
Walter Self, teamsters. They took two good ponies, saddles and
bridles, and left at the gallop. Where to?

'You all better get home quick, the Governors are about.' Jack
Miller had walked up to the little school near old Kiambir out of
Kenebri to warn the children. Old Dan Casey told me he still remembers it clearly. He was twelve. He ran most of the eight kilometres
home. Each bend in the road was a terror. He feared to go round it to
see what was in front; he feared to look behind.

George Ruttley on his selection of old Arrarownie fortressed the doors and windows of his house with gum logs. His son, Bert, remembered him sawing them all lest the Governors hear him chopping.

Miss Porteous who had once taught Jimmy Governor at Coonabarabran was then living at Bugaldie, south of Baradine. The Porteous family had owned the Bugaldi run. She must have been kind to her pupils because she had no fears at all. 'Jimmy would never hurt me.' The Kenebri children also need not have been afraid. The Governors went past seventy kilometres away. They rode the teamsters' brown ponies up Middle Creek on the western boundary of old Molly, then cut fast south-east through the Brigalow to the big Bohena Creek again. Jimmy could not resist the wide deep clean white sand that had filled the creek bed. He smoothed out a patch with a stick and laid the imprint of his big knife in it. Then he broke off a gum branch and stood it upright beside his sign so that the dullest searchers must find it.

They robbed Harry Kuhner's tent on Bohena Creek. He was camped about seven kilometres north of the junction of Borah and Yaminba Creeks. Harry was sleeper cutting in the area that Oxley had turned back from. The forest of young ironbarks mentioned by Oxley had now grown. They smashed Harry's shotgun and stole his rifle. There were rumours that they had twenty-seven rifles, surely a too heavy load.

Although one would have expected police to be always impeccable with names, Superintendent Garvin in his official report misread somebody's handwriting and Kuhner was spelt Keeliner – a good German name turned into an absurdity.

The Governors passed within two kilometres of the Ruttleys' fortified house and up Borah Creek past lonely Erle Wolseley Creagh. There were only two shivering boys at Ayrland's hotel. George Ruttley as a fourteen-year-old and a younger brother had charge of it while Dave Peebles was in hospital. He had lost a thumb in tangled reins when his pack-horses fought.

John Sevil got no opportunity to use his shotgun. His alarm bells never sounded. Jimmy and Joe spent the night quietly in his woolshed reloading cartridge cases with their stolen equipment. There is a woody hill on the other side of the creek from the Crickenbah homestead still known as Governors Scrub. Orr's old house where the Launts were surprised in 1864 was only ten kilometres to the west.

People who stayed in their houses were now leaving food in the kitchens at night in the hope that the Governors would simply take it and go. There is a lovely local story that as Mrs Lou Worrell was going to bed at Melrose she looked at her batch of freshly-made cakes on the kitchen table and said 'I'm not leaving these here for Jimmy. I'll put them to cool on the dining-room table. Jimmy can have this stale bread and cold meat.' In the morning the cakes were gone, a pile of freshly ironed clothes was ruffled as a sign of his coming, and outside, between two brick chimneys, were the prints of Jimmy's bare feet where he had stood and listened through the cracks of the unlined walls.

But alas, somebody else ate those cakes. The only night the Governors could have come to Melrose, near Kenebri, was the night they spent in the Crickenbah woolshed. There was no time to have ridden to Kenebri and back. Anyway the tracks followed unbroken up the creek. The police were on to them like bloodhounds the next morning. The actual Bloodhounds had been sent home. The Governors were too fast for them. They were averaging about forty kilometres a day.

I once took part in a search where Bloodhounds were used. A man was lost in the Nandewar Ranges. The hounds took us out of the hills down on to the flat country. It was easier going but it was the wrong direction. A Bloodhound gives the impression of having no sense other than smell, and that not reliable.

Jimmy and Joe travelled fast up Borah Creek by a circuitous route that knocked the ponies up. They abandoned them sore-legged and winded near Rocky Glen. Saddles and bridles were left on. It was there the Governors rested in the culvert while the search parties rode overhead. It was a wooden slab-covered culvert across a gully. Now it is seen as a dip in the main road near the Oxley resting place between Coonabarabran and Gunnedah.

On foot again, the Governors went south on to old Garrawilla and robbed a Chinese hawker. They moved back east towards the Tambar Springs country again, robbing huts as they went. They were seen coming out of one with two bags full of supplies. With plenty of food they then holed up again for three days. Search parties crisscrossed the ranges but not even the Fraser Island trackers could find a sign. Where the ground was not too hard to show anything there was a confusion of sheep tracks.

Jimmy Governor explained after his capture that sheep were used deliberately to obliterate tracks. Sometimes they even carried dirt with them. If they had to step across ground where prints would be left they dusted them over by throwing small handfuls of soil into each mark. Stones were also used. A stone thrown slantwise and hard into a footprint bounced off out of sight and left a mark more like an animal scratch than a human print.

The police began to get letters suggesting ways of taking the Governors: leave poisoned food about; dress policemen as women and station them in lonely huts pretending to sweep floors and cook meals, not smoking or lazing about outside; lace a bottle of rum with morphia and leave it in a pantry; engage six Chinese vegetable hawkers to drive their carts about the roads with two policemen hidden under the vegetables in each cart.

Some of the letters were weird. This was scrawled on a roughly torn-off piece of paper, unsigned. The envelope was franked '2d. to pay' in blue crayon. 'A man has killed Jimmy Governor tell the Sydney police, they do not know, tell them at once. This message came through at a spiritualist meeting 10.30 p.m.'

And there was this, signed H. Casson. 'I am a gifted second-sight Sear and have been many times rewarded with unprecedented success in completely clearing up the mysterious and intricate . . . I beg to place my services at your disposal in effecting the capture of the Breelong blacks . . . Should my services be required I shall want a piece of cloth about two inches wide stained with the blood of the last murder committed . . . at present I am so situated that I am unable to go at my own expense. Also whilst I am at search . . . I take no food except fruit . . .'

The Inspector-General made a note on the back 'Liverpool police may ascertain who the writer of this letter is – probably a lunatic.' The Liverpool sergeant who went to interview the man wrote that he was an inmate of the Liverpool Benevolent Asylum. He added laboriously 'He is not quite sane in his mind.'

It was worse not knowing where the Governors were than when they were marking their line by robbed houses. Angus Campbell and Harry Baker, an excitable American negro, boundary riders on Garrawilla, heard a knocking on the door of their hut one night. They dived out the back window and ran seven kilometres to the homestead in bare feet. Next morning their billy-goat was lying against a wall of the hut chewing his cud. His tracks were all round the door that had a few fresh scratches where he had been trying his horns.

Three days was long enough for the Governors to lie low. They came out of hiding and robbed a succession of huts, taking rifles, blankets and food. Most of it was thrown away, the rifles usually smashed. In one hut they left three notes for the police, two of them said to be obscenely derisive. In the third Jimmy blamed Ethel for all that he had done. Unfortunately none of these letters were kept with the police records of the hunt. Probably they were kept by individuals as souvenirs, perhaps destroyed.

Then followed several days of great activity. Jimmy and Joe moved on to creeks in the Bundella-Blackville area on the northern edge of the Liverpool Range where Nelson Simmons Lawson and Major George Druitt first took up runs. The police were camping in houses by night and hiding in them in wait during the day. So Jimmy and Joe began moving down on to the houses after dark and firing shots through them. Near Blackville they found an unoccupied house and burnt it during the night. Then they walked barefooted over the Yarraman Gap, so rough it has never been used as a track, to the headwaters of the strangely named Cooba Bulga Stream that flows via other creeks into the Goulburn. A police party was waiting in Ambrose Rawlinson's house. Jimmy and Joe watched until the police and Rawlinsons left, then they came down and burnt that one, too.

Police were camped on the creek but Jimmy and Joe did not even bother moving out of the area. By midday next day they were only seven kilometres away on Cattle Creek. They called on Mrs Baylis who was alone, and left a supply of cartridges with her. She was asked to give them to the police with their compliments. Jimmy said the police might find them handy to shoot him with.

The Governors had now been outlawed and could be shot by anybody with impunity. Under the warrants that had been originally issued for their arrest, police were ordered 'You and every of you, without delay, do apprehend and bring before me, the said Coroner, or one of Her Majesty's Justices of the Peace in and for the said Colony, the bodies of the said Joe Governor and Jimmy Governor . . .' There was a reward of $400 each.

But what was required under those warrants was live bodies. Anybody, especially a civilian, killing either of them except in self defence might have been charged with murder. Outlawing made it safe for anybody to shoot them. But it was a complicated and strange procedure. A notice had to be inserted in the *Government Gazette* advertising a time and place at which those to be outlawed had to surrender themselves to prevent the outlawry. This notice had to be advertised in newspapers and on posters that were likely to be seen by the runaways. One gathers that to be absolutely legal it ought to have been delivered like a summons. The rewards were increased to $2,000 each.

Now the Governors made certain those rewards would be hard earned. They went east along the rough Liverpool Ranges. A party of police who camped in a deserted hut were mistaken by civilians for the outlaws. They were surrounded during the night and in the morning the first policeman stepped out into a ring of cocked and aimed rifles. 'A serious tragedy was narrowly averted,' reported Garvin.

By the time they were tracked to Murrurundi, the Governors had covered about seventeen hundred kilometres in exactly six weeks. Two men who had followed them all the way were Herb Byers and his mate, Bob Woods. Local stories have persisted that Herb Byers had been engaged to Helen Kerz and was out to avenge her death. It seemed a logical story until I found that Byers was not the only local supposed to have been engaged to her. All contemporary newspapers published many pages about the murders, the chase and the people involved. Since none of them mentioned a lover for Helen Kerz, it is unlikely she had one. Bob Woods's father had once arrested a bushranger. Perhaps his son was trying to emulate him. Herb Byers was a crack shot and a kangaroo shooter, a professional hunter. Jimmy Governor was new and interesting game, and, now that the reward had been increased, profitable game. Byers could not have made that sort of money kangaroo shooting.

South of Nundle, on top of the main Dividing Range, Jimmy Governor fired two shots at James Heyman, the leader of a civilian search party. He was lucky it was Jimmy who fired them. Joe was the better shot. They were both seen running away downhill. The six Fraser Island trackers were brought on to the trail less than twenty minutes old. As they followed the tracks downhill, Jimmy and Joe doubled back under cover and walked right past the tracking party to the main range again.

Sub-inspector Galbraith in charge of the trackers was incompetent. Garvin was critical of him in his report 'His party upon this occassion was in my opinion unnecessarily large, namely, four Civilians, a Constable, Himself and 6 Trackers. A similar blunder was I regret to say, made by him at Chilcott's Creek and that mistake should have been a warning to him to have acted differently upon this occassion.'

The proud trackers were now more unhappy. They resented being made fools of. They tried to point out that good tracking is more than simply following where the quarry has been, it is anticipating where it will go. They wanted to station men ahead – they had learnt a great deal about how the Governors behaved. They wanted other searchers spread out widely to cut off such doubling moves as the Governors had just made. They also explained that only one tracker should keep to the trail. The others should circle widely on each side. That way they could cut corners if the Governors ran off at right angles and perhaps save hours. These Queensland Aborigines seemed unconcerned about the reaction of New South Wales Aborigines if the Governors were caught. But all six were held doggedly on the tracks.

It was inordinately difficult country that Jimmy and Joe had taken to now, the wild Tops country between Nundle and Gloucester at the headwaters of the Manning and Hastings rivers. It was wet. There were scrubs and vine-tangled mountains, precipices, gorges, rivers and creeks. The searchers often went hungry. It was hard to bring in food.

Much of that country is still uninhabited, though thoroughly explored. The map shows unfamiliar names. Every little creek has been named by someone. But because almost nothing is known of the language of the Aborigines of the area, many of the names sound harsh and strange. One at least is musically beautiful, Cooplacurripa, but there is also Tugrabakh and Konunk Kosh Kosh, Cockerawombeeba Creek, Tuckybunyubah, or Cobakh Creek.

At the last place, on 22 September, Jimmy Governor came down into open country and met fifteen-year-old Isabella Burley, the daughter of a local farmer, on a track through the bush. He threatened to shoot her, then raped her. 'Did you do that awful thing to that girl, Jimmy?' 'Yeah! But it wasn't the first time she'd been tampered with.'

The illogical justification of the rapist that acceptance of one man opens the way to any has barely yet (in the 1980s) lost force in courts of law.

Despite the roughness of the mountains, there were a few big cattle runs on the slopes. On flats along rivers and creeks small farmers had settled. Higher up there were timbergetters' huts. Jimmy and Joe kept themselves in food. They robbed house after house. Always flour bags were opened the same way – split down the side. Flour was tossed about the floors, sometimes oatmeal and pepper were mixed with it. Notes were still being left. Jimmy unkindly pointed out that they were lying in hiding and watching search parties go past within fifteen metres of them.

Jimmy and Joe made no attempt to live off the land. It was beneath the dignity of good bushrangers to eat wallaby. Once they overcame their scruples. They went to the hut of a man named Smith on the Barnard River. He had no food but he did have a fat pet wallaby in the yard. They shot it and cooked it on the spot.

At Cooplacurripa they set fire to blankets in a bark hut and hung a chaff bag to carry the flames to the roof. Peter Regan, the owner, returned while his bed was still smouldering.

On 12 October they were west of Port Macquarie at the junction of

Yarras Creek and the Hastings River. At four o'clock in the afternoon they sneaked up on a hut where Constable Richard Harris and Jimmy Landsborough, a New South Wales black tracker, were hiding. One of them shot Harris in the hip through a crack in the wall. Harris was not badly wounded. He and the tracker ran outside and fired at the Governors as they ran away. They dodged and returned fire. No one else was hit.

Jimmy was having trouble with Joe. Joe was getting careless. Jimmy liked to circle a hut for an hour or so reading tracks before he went near it. Joe was always in a hurry and impatient of careful checking. Next day at the same time in the afternoon they came towards a hut twenty-six kilometres north on the Forbes River. They dodged from log to log and from tree to tree but they came without checking. Sixty metres away Jimmy got suspicious. They both turned and ran. Byers and Woods were in the hut. At 120 metres Jimmy stopped and looked back, foolish as a fox in a spotlight. Byers fired and Jimmy dropped. He called out 'Joe' and rolled on the ground. Byers and Woods came out of the hut and fired at Joe. He took cover and fired back. Then Jimmy got to his feet and began to run. He staggered and fell a couple of times but then ran more strongly. Byers and Woods followed but it began to grow dark. Jimmy and Joe escaped.

There was a blood spoor to follow after that, big clots in places, and a bloodied mountain pool where he had washed. But they still could not be found.

Four days later they were fired on again on the Hastings River. They split up after that. 'Only one track here, boss,' said a Fraser Island tracker. 'One fella walk same place as the other,' said a New South Wales tracker. 'No.' The tracks were not deep enough for the weight of two.

Wounded Jimmy was left on his own. He had been hit in the mouth. The bullet knocked out four teeth and went out his cheek. He found it hard to eat. He hung about the orchards and apiaries on Bobin Creek north of Wingham, living on orange juice and honey.

On 26 October 1900, ninety-eight days after the Breelong murders, John Wallace, a beekeeper at Bobin, missed his afternoon tea. He was burning off in what he called his 'bush paddock' and when he went to boil his billy about three o'clock in the afternoon, billy, mug and tucker-bag were missing. He kept alert after that and just on dusk he saw a man walk up to one of his fires. Wallace watched him for a quarter of an hour or more, decided that it must be Jimmy Governor preparing to camp, so he went away quietly and collected seven neighbours, four members of the Moore family, Tom Green, Alex Cameron and John McPherson. They surrounded Jimmy in a wide circle during the night and at about 2 o'clock in the morning crept into a tighter circle. Each man was stationed about fifty metres from Jimmy. It was barely light when he woke and ran. Five shots were fired from shotguns. All missed. It is difficult to understand how so many shots could miss at such close quarters. Probably when shooting at a man there is an unconscious desire to miss. Jimmy was about one hundred and eighty metres away when a shot from Tom Green hit him. He fell. Even then he was hard to find. The men tramped about in the wet knee-high bracken.

He was found when it grew lighter, still alive. There were forty shotgun pellets in his back and thighs, none of them deep. He rode into Wingham on a mattress in a spring cart.

Four nights later Joe Governor made a careless fire on John Wilkinson's property on the Gooroongoola Creek north of Singleton. Wilkinson was returning home from Muswellbrook and saw it. He went for his brother George and they, too, checked first that there was a man asleep there. Then they sat at a distance and waited all night. At daybreak they walked up to Joe and called out 'Surrender!' He leapt in the air, grabbed for his rifle, missed it, and ran for the creek. John Wilkinson pulled the trigger and the cartridge misfired. He chased Joe, shot twice more, and missed each time. Then he went down on one knee, took more careful aim, and shot Joe through the head at 110 metres. He somersaulted over the bank of the creek and died in the water.

He was laid out on a stretcher in the Caledonian hotel at Singleton, more or less on show. Someone ghoulishly noted 'You could strike a wax match on the soles of his feet'. Presumably he had demonstrated it.

The University of Sydney asked for his brain and skull. Professor Wilson of the Medical school told a reporter that it was not true that Joe Governor's whole head had been sent. Their interest was scientific only. The brain would tend to show 'aboriginal character', the skull with the bullet wound in it 'would be useful to illustrate bullet wounds'. But it was a headless body that was buried outside the walls of the Singleton cemetery.

The Governors were too Aboriginal to sleep without a fire and Jimmy was proud of the fact that they had had one every night even when searchers were very close. There were scorch marks on his clothes, and little round holes burnt by sparks. They had made frequent use of burning-off fires. If they had to light their own it was made in the cover of rocks or gullies. Little sticks were used that flared quickly without much smoke. At first light they 'slithered'. Jimmy was fond of that word.

He was taken to Sydney by steamer from Taree shackled by a leg-iron to a ringbolt on deck to leave his hands free for smoking and playing euchre. His attendants played with him most of the voyage. Jimmy usually won. He made no attempt to justify himself. 'A man gets run into these things,' he said.

The police spent days justifying themselves. Newspapers had ridiculed the police because all three murderers had been taken by civilians. It was demanded that Herb Byers be paid a substantial reward for wounding Jimmy. There are pages of answers to these criticisms in the Governor files, all of them obviously first thoroughly discussed by those who were to make them. Similar phrases were used in every report.

Byers put in a detailed account for his expenses in the chase: for corn for his horse, for payments to storekeepers, innkeepers, to a farrier who shod his horse. It came to £79 19s 9d. None of it had been actually paid out; it was all owing. Perhaps he intended to pay it.

Inspector Sykes, at West Maitland, wrote 'I am at a loss to understand how he could have compiled such an account; he was a careless, improvident, impecunious fellow'. Byers had already been paid $130 reward. Inspector Garvin was sour about this additional demand. 'He should be paid only for the time he was attached to police parties . . . £9.18.3. This with the £65 paid him already will make £74.18.3, very handsome payment . . . for three months work he appointed himself to carry out.'

Apart from the mishandling of the Fraser Island trackers the police could probably have done no better. In each district local bushmen were engaged as guides. Their suggestions were followed. In the Tops country especially guides were essential, else numbers of searchers might have been hopelessly lost.

Jimmy and Joe Governor hoped to be black Ned Kellys and as such they failed. Jimmy knew it. There was a flare of pride when he was introduced to one of the Fraser Island trackers. 'Who's he?' he had asked. 'Willie Watts, the head of the Queensland trackers.' Jimmy looked at the red braid down the legs of the tracker's uniform. 'I thought he was a Salvation Army boy,' he said. But he was subdued before the steamer reached Sydney. 'Bushranging's not the fuckin' game it's cracked up to be.'

He would never be anybody's hero. Tomahawks and knives are not heroes' weapons. Jimmy had frightened far too many people. He was hanged at Darlinghurst gaol.

8

Timber and Scrub

If the forest had been as dense in 1900 as it is in the 1980s, Jimmy Governor might have had an even better game with his pursuers. He could have boxed them up in huge impenetrable thickets of Spurwing Acacia or lost them on hands and knees in tangles of fallen dead Spearwood and varying live scrub. He could have hidden there for years and, if he had deigned to live off the country, it would have supported him.

It would be sensible to sum up the scattered references I have made to the marvellous growth of the forest. When the first squatters sent their stock in, the ridgy country on the east and south carried the same heavy growth as it does now, a remarkably coastal scrub which I shall specify later. Not all the growth extended to the flats, not all the ridges were covered. The rest, apart from the great arc of Brigalow in the north, was grassland dominated in the east by three to four big ironbarks (*Eucalyptus crebra*) to the hectare, and in the centre and west – about half a million hectares – by three to four big pines to the hectare. The White Cypress Pine is known in 1980 as *Callitris columellaris*. It has persisted unchanged through numerous Latin tags. A few pines that were seedlings in the 1830s were still alive in the 1970s to show how big the pines grew before profuse growth crowded them. John Grosser who owned a one-man sawmill and 400 hectares of timber on the eastern edge of the Pilliga Nature Reserve had three or four old pines he kept as seed trees. In the 1970s they were nearing the end of their lives of about 200 years. North-west of Kenebri off Dry Sand Road grew two big pines. These trees were twenty to twenty-five metres high and up to ninety centimetres in diameter at breast height. That is not big by coastal standards where Blackbutt logs two metres in diameter come in on the trailers as single riders. But the biggest pine milled in modern times is less than half the size of those old pines.

The old ironbarks were even bigger. Some would have fitted two only to a modern trailer. There are giants that died in the 1902 drought still standing as witness. Among the ironbarks and the pines grew their scattered seedlings. In places there were small belts of dense saplings. And there were belts of Bull Oak and Belar (*Casuarina luehmannii* and *C. cristata*), of Western Black Wattle (*Acacia hakeoides*), and especially of Curracabah, once known as *Acacia cunninghamii*, a name recently found to cover three species. The early reports of dense patches of it were not misidentification. Bert Ruttley who knew individual trees among myriads of the same kind told me that a wattle with long flowers and red stems, common when he was a boy, no longer grew. He knew it by no name, but he gave a good description of Curracabah. Other trees and shrubs – several hundred species – grew singly or in sparse clumps.

The first change noticed throughout Australia, and the principal change, was in the texture of the soil. Cloven hooves destroyed the mulch of thousands of years in five to ten years. So the grasses changed. As the Aborigines were displaced they ceased their husbandry of the land by fire. For varying periods over Australia there was no more regular burning. In the Pilliga forest the period was about twenty-five years from the late 1840s to the early 1870s. Then the seeds of spear or corkscrew grasses (*Stipa* spp.) and of wire grasses (*Aristida* spp.) began to worry sheep. The profuse long-tailed seeds depreciated the wool. But worse, they bored into flesh. These seeds move when dampened: the long straight tails twist into spirals on the first few drops of rain and turn the long pointed seeds into the ground like augers or down through wool into skin. It was common to find spear grass seed in mutton chops just as the broken-off heads of Aboriginal spears were sometimes found in the carcasses of cattle cut up for boiling-down.

So sheep owners shore in the autumn before the seed ripened, then burnt the dried off grass in the winter. In the spring it grew from the butts and gave a month or two of clean grazing before beginning to set its vicious seeds. Some men burnt again in late spring.

After the hard drought of 1877 the soil was bare and powdered. Extreme rains in 1879 brought away a dense growth of grass from butts and from seed. These herbaceous perennial grasses can appear quite dead after months of drought, then shoot green in three or four days after ten millimetres of rain. The old pines seeded well in the lush spring. When the stockowners burnt, pine seedlings came up thickly in the ash. Rat-kangaroos, eaters of seedlings, were in low numbers after the drought. Sheep had destroyed their cover as well as their feed. The pine grew unchecked.

In one of the periodic depressions in cattle prices that still trouble Australian graziers, thousands of extra sheep were brought into the forest area. The burning increased. More pockets of pine came away in good years in the early 1880s. Many runs were abandoned. When the 1902 drought ended there were more bursts of pine growth here and there. Scrub extended off the ridges and belts of oak came away.

Then the rabbits built up. Management of the area changed. Burning was irregular. The wandering shepherds burnt pockets here and there. Those cattlemen who used the abandoned forest as a giant common rode out and lit big fires ahead of rain. What seedlings these fires started were eaten by rabbits.

In 1917 the Pilliga West and Pilliga East State forests were dedicated and the New South Wales Forestry Commission took control. Although fire germinates pine seeds, it kills growing pines of all ages, so the Forestry Commission stopped the burning where it had authority. For forty-five years there was little fresh growth.

The thick pine grew in belts. Much of the forest area was still fairly open. 'Look at that!' an old man will say. 'Sixty, seventy years ago I shepherded a thousand sheep out there. I could let 'em all feed out and I could stand in one place and watch the whole flock. Only twenty year ago I could walk out there and shoot a kangaroo a hundred yards off easy. Now if I walked in there twenty yards and didn't watch where I was going I'd bloody get lost.'

By the long wet of 1950 years of litter had accumulated: natural fall, natural deaths, and the tops, branches and stripped bark that log-fallers and sleeper cutters leave behind them. Grass grew up among it and hayed off in the hot November of 1951.

Fire started near the Rocky Creek sawmill north-east of Kenebri on 16 November. It swept in double tongues south and south-east. The two tongues attracted one another. Fire is always sucked towards fire because of the displaced hot air. When they met, 'they went up like a masonic bomb', said one old resident of Baradine. The fire continued

on a wider front. It is the worst yet known in the area. I lived then east
of the Namoi about ninety kilometres from the fire. At midday the sun
was a dull orange circle in a green sky. Our eyes watered from the
smoke.

The rabbits' eyes were watering, too, blinded by the pustules of
myxomatosis. They died in thousands. So the growth that soon started
in the path of the fire had nothing to check it. It took control. Since the
1950s big areas of the forest where there is no millable pine have formed
a dense closed community. Plants are astoundingly successful where
there seems neither enough moisture nor enough nutrients to support
them. They are so interdependent their roots function as common
roots.

It is not a paradox that the fires that once kept our forests open
should now cause them to grow denser. The frequent fires the
Aborigines lit were mild grass fires and perhaps burnt no more than
twenty thousand hectares at a time. Seedlings came up in the path of
their fires but the plentiful rat-kangaroos easily ate them all.

Some modern scientists unaccountably discountenance the amount
of burning by Aborigines. It has to be estimated instead of measured
and that makes them uncomfortable. 'We are unable to assess quan-
titatively the impact of Aboriginal mans' use of fire on the vegetation,
and cannot extrapolate to pre-Aboriginal times.' Anyone who writes as
atrociously as that jeopardises my faith in all his thinking. It seems impossible to exaggerate the amount of burning in Aboriginal Australia.

Abel Tasman in 1642 was astonished by the fire-scarred trunks of
Tasmanian trees. Cook on his first sighting of Australia in 1770 noted,
'In the afternoon we saw smoke in several places by which we knew the
country to be inhabited'. He named a headland 'Smokey Cape'.
Governor Phillip complained the local timber was poor because it was
all damaged by fire. He told Lord Sydney in a letter written in 1788,
'The natives always make their fire, if not before their own huts, at the
root of a gum-tree, which burns very freely and they never put a fire
out when they leave the place'. George Bouchier Worgan, First Fleet
surgeon, recorded in his minute handwriting, 'It is something singular,
that all of this kind of Trees, and many others appear to have been
partly burnt, the Bark of them being like charcoal'.

William Lawson, approaching the Turon River on his way back to
Bathurst after his second trip north in January 1822 found 'the grass all
burnt for upwards of twenty miles'. Cunningham on his trip to
Moreton Bay in 1827 made many references to fires. When camped on

the Gwydir 'Large bodies of smoke rose from grass which had been fired on the river bank opposite the encampment'. Mitchell in his *Journal of an Expedition into the Interior of Tropical Australia* published in 1848 included a chapter on the Aborigines at the back. He declared, 'Fire, grass, kangaroos, and human inhabitants, seem all dependent on each other for existence in Australia, for any one of these being wanting, the others could no longer continue . . . But for this simple process, the Australian woods had probably contained as thick a jungle as those of New Zealand or America, instead of the open forests in which the white men now find grass for their cattle . . . The omission of the annual periodical burning by natives, of the grass and young saplings, has already produced in the open forest lands nearest to Sydney, thick forests of young trees, where, formerly, a man might gallop without impediment . . .'

Every explorer, almost every early writer, commented on fire. Later explorers commented when they found unburnt areas. Ernest Giles in the Gibson Desert in 1874, far into the sandhills and out of sight of the Rawlinson Range, found that 'No sign of the recent presence of natives was anywhere visible, nor had the Triodia been burnt for probably many years'. Elsewhere he said that 'The few native inhabitants of these regions occasionally burn every portion of their territories, and on a favourably windy day a spinifex fire might run on for scores of miles. We occasionally cross such desolated spaces, where every species of vegetation has been by flames devoured. Devoured they are, but not demolished, as out of the roots and ashes of their former natures, phoenix-like, they rise again.' I feel certain it was because Aborigines went into mission stations and stopped burning that the Desert Bandicoot and the Hare-wallaby disappeared from the central deserts. There were too few new shoots to sustain them.

Sylvia J. Hallam in her *Fire and Hearth* published in Canberra in 1975 included as an appendix thirteen pages of references to fire in Western Australia. She made no special search for the references. They all came from easily available published sources and ranged in time from Willem de Vlamingh off the coast in 1697 to the 1890s. The tribes of Aborigines in the south-west corner made a yearly ceremony of burning. It began with a corroboree and the fires were controlled by men with bough beaters. Since the chief aim of the burning was to concentrate kangaroos and emus on the new-sprung grass it was not desirable to burn too big an area at a time.

The tribes in that area of Western Australia repeatedly burnt the fringes of the Karri and Jarrah forests and kept them in check. These forests were the only big areas of thick eucalyptus in Australia at the time of settlement. And those forests, too, extended when burning stopped. Since the effect of fire in keeping country open was obvious, it seems safe to surmise that the Aborigines burnt also for that reason. They were intelligent, observant people and they did not like forest. It was hard to walk through, hard to find game in, and provided less grass.

Apart from their deliberate husbandry by fire, the Aborigines started many grass fires as an incidental result of doing something else. No tribes anywhere put their cooking fires out. A whirlwind can carry live coals a hundred metres and more to dry grass. They smoked bandicoots out of hollow logs by burning wet leaves and set fire to hollow trees if they were too solid to chop possums out of. If they had to travel by night, they lit fires to ward off evil spirits and they lit fires as a protective screen, as Sturt found west of the Darling, and Cook found when at anchor in the Endeavour River in north Queensland. The women lit fires when lizards hid in grass and the men joined in big hunts to trap kangaroos in circles of fire. Men and women carried firesticks from camp to camp both to preserve their fire and to keep themselves warm, and they lit fires now and again to revive the firesticks. They signalled by fire and smoke.

Lightning strikes supplemented Aboriginal fires. Some hot summers produce the extraordinary dry Australian thunderstorm. I have stood in the Narrabri saleyards and watched a single big purple cloud moving quickly over the Galathera plain forty kilometres to the north-west. A fork of lightning snapped to the ground and smoke soon rose. A kilometre farther on another flash struck the ground. More smoke rose. Property owners from the plains ran from the yards to drive home to their firefighting plants. The cloud started two more fires at similar intervals then dissipated.

Rough-barked Apples, *Angophora intermedia*, flare like torches when struck by lightning. Their rough flaky bark will smoulder through twenty millimetres of rain, then flare again a few days later and start a fire. Geoffrey Blainey in his excellent *Triumph of the Nomads* entitled Chapter Five 'A Burning Continent'.

Lightning starts fires mostly in summer and some years it starts many. The Aborigines started fires all through the year, but much of their deliberate burning was of herbaceous perennial grasses in winter. Yet opponents of prescribed winter burning to protect parks, forests and towns from devastating summer fires protest that it is 'unnatural', a foolish word since the condition Australia was in when the white man came was an artificial condition imposed by thousands of years of the fires and the Dingoes the Aborigines brought with them.

Peter Prineas, executive secretary of the National Parks Association of New South Wales, wrote to the *Sydney Morning Herald* on 29 May 1975 to berate another letter-writer about his remarks on a burn-off in the Blue Mountains: 'Is he trying to tell us that the native bush around Sydney evolved under a regime of regular and frequent winter fires: that low intensity burning carried out in grid pattern over vast areas is part of the natural scheme of things?'

People who ask rhetorical questions can hear energetic cries of 'No' as they write them. But all one can say to Peter Prineas is, 'Yes, that's just how it did evolve.'

Australian plants are marvellously adapted to fire. Nowhere else have plants developed this characteristic. Nowhere else have they had such practice.

Most eucalypts built complicated defences against fire. If the oily leaves burn in a quick top fire and the branches and twigs are not damaged, as often happens when a fire jumps a valley, new leaves grow from naked buds at the base of the leaf stalks. The naked buds are backed up by microscopic accessory buds which grow if a new shoot is eaten. If the whole crown of a eucalypt is destroyed, epicormic buds shoot from the trunk and the main limbs. The apparently dead trees grow fuzzy with new leaves that hide the blackened bark. Then two or three of the new shoots leap upward and develop into branches, and the rest drop off unwanted. If the trunk is destroyed by fire the eucalypt grows again from a big lignotuber under the ground.

Some eucalypts in cold, wet areas were exposed only to chance fires in drought time. The huge beautiful Victorian Mountain Ash, *Eucalyptus regnans*, has no resistance to fire. It withers like a tender annual and dies. But it experienced enough fire to become dependent on it to germinate its seeds. A Mountain Ash sapling takes about twenty years to mature, it lives for about four hundred years. So too frequent fires, too infrequent fires, kill out a Mountain Ash forest. The dense ash forests that have taken back some foolishly cleared land in the Victorian highlands need a fire about every three hundred years to produce their best, an impossible postulation.

Banksias, the stiff-leaved shrubs with bottlebrush flowers that interested Sir Joseph Banks in 1770, mature their seed slowly over about twelve months. Then the woody follicles enclosing them remain shut until the heat of fire or extreme drought dehydrates them and twists them open. Even then the winged seeds do not fall. A woody spring-like mechanism holds them in place until rain soaks it and makes it limp. The cream-flowered *Banksia marginata* that grows along Dandry Creek, where Oxley found it, lacks this trait but it does possess a lignotuber so that it can resurrect itself after apparent destruction by fire.

The seemingly robust coastal Waratah that produces heavy, deep red, many-bracted heads of flowers is regularly overcome by its competitors. It needs fire every six or seven years to give it room and allow it to send up new canes from its lignotuber. An extraordinary newly-discovered genus of plants in Western Australia, *Alexgorgea*, flowers ten to fifteen centimetres under the sand to protect its seed from fire.

The seeds of many of the plants that thrive in the new Pilliga forest germinate profusely after fire: *Boronia* spp. *Eriostemon* (wax flower), *Persoonia* (geebung), *Ricinocarpus* (wedding bush), *Actinotus* (flannel flower), *Acacia* (forty-three species), and the showy family of leguminous peaflowers, *Papilionaceae*, also with more than forty species. Ground orchids, especially the double-tails (*Diuris*), flower in clumps after fire, and grass trees send up spectacular spikes. The slow-growing grass trees (*Xanthorrhoea*) live for up to five hundred years. Undisturbed by fire they have been known to flower only once in fifty years.

On Christmas day 1974 someone boiled his billy on the Newell Highway north of Coonabarabran and did not put his fire out. There had not been a fire since 1951 and the growth was magnificent. Sixty thousand hectares burnt over the next three days, ground fire and top fire. Although the oil content of eucalyptus leaves is much lower here than in Victoria or Tasmania, the tops exploded a hundred metres ahead of the fire. It made a clean sweep of most of the Pilliga Nature Reserve. Even the soil beneath the ash looked dead. It had the texture of brick.

By June the eucalypts had all sprouted green. They were odd-looking trees with growth starting out horizontally from their wounded trunks. By September bloodwood, gum, box, mallee and ironbark were all beginning to look like Australian trees again. Some shoots on each had taken over and were lifting up as fair sized branches at an angle to the trunk. Much of the excess growth had already pruned. Eucalypts and most other Australian trees do not spread to catch the sun or droop to shed snow. They hang their waxy leaves edge-on to the sun to cut down transpiration, and their branches grow up at an angle so that they catch showers of rain like a funnel and channel it down the trunk to fine roots near the surface.

Our eucalypts look odd to foreign eyes. Scottish Mary Rose Liverani in her delightful *The Winter Sparrows* saw 'contorted trees whose skinny wizened branches, starved for water, swayed like tentacles over the sharp yellow grasses'. Francis Ratcliffe, the English scientist who established wildlife research in Australia, was confounded as a young man by the light the scant foliage does not break. 'The fierce Australian light pours through it', he wrote in *Flying Fox and Drifting Sand*, 'and floods the grass, the earth, and the trunks and limbs of the trees themselves, washing away the colour and leaving a monotone of bright yellowish grey'.

We drove through the recovering nature reserve in September 1975 along Kerringle Road leading to the Willala hills. Most of that track runs through old Arrarownie. On the flats round Baileys Peak, an isolated steep little sandstone outcrop with a trig. station on top, young plants of *Xanthorrhoea australis* were in magnificent bloom. There were thousands of thick creamy spikes, many of them over a metre long, glistening with nectar. The pungent scent was everywhere, a warm smell strangely like that of semen. Native bees and honey bees, wasps, butterflies and moths swarmed about them. The plants, although young, might have been up to thirty years old but the caudex or trunk of the tallest was no more than half a metre high and the dangling skirt of leaves obscured it. Old branched grass trees on the top of Mount Wambelong in the Warrumbungles are nearly four metres high and the bunches of leaves at the top are well out of reach. There are three species in the forest: *Xanthorrhoea australis, Xanthorrhoea australis* ssp. *acaulis* which never develops a caudex and remains a grassy clump, and *Xanthorrhoea johnsonii* with a slender flower spike that gives it the name of Kangaroo Tail. There are also natural hybrids. All grow only on the poorest country. Stems and leaf bases exude a resin that the Aborigines used to fix spear tips to shafts. Settlers used it as a varnish.

Iron grasses (*Lomandra*) which some botanists class as a relation of the grass trees grow over a wide area. There are three species. I have found only *Lomandra leucocephala* ssp. *leucocephala*. It flowers all winter. Exquisitely sweet-scented but too pervasive, one smells it often before one sees it. The flower heads are white cylinders two to three centimetres in diameter. Sometimes there are two or three heads on the short stem and they look as though they have been threaded on to it. The edges of the leaves fray at the base and ragged white membranes hang out. From a distance the leaves seem to be caught in a web.

All round the base of Baileys Peak we stepped carefully to avoid clumps of Pink Fingers and Blue Fingers (*Caladenia carnea* and

C. caerulea), another genus of orchids that likes fire. They are delicate plants and easily overlooked even in masses. *Caladenia caerulea* is no more than one small leaf almost flat on the ground and one blue flower on a ten centimetre stem. *Caladenia carnea* has a pink flower and a larger leaf like a single blade of grass.

One of the double-tails, *Diuris sulphurea*, grows in the same area. It sends up a much larger flowering stem from a much more substantial plant than the little caladenias. The flower is brilliant yellow striped with brown which gives it the name of Tiger Orchid. *Diuris abbreviata*, the Donkey Orchid, grows in spectacular clumps in the Warrumbungle foothills. The crossed tails that distinguish the genus are shorter in this species, and two yellow petals stand up like big ears. Both are out of their usual range. They are coastal and tableland plants.

Many, perhaps all, species of terrestrial orchids depend on insects to pollinate them. The proceeding has been studied only in the *Cryptostylis* genus. Edith Coleman first reported it in the *Victorian Naturalist* in 1927. No one believed her for years. Male ichneumon wasps, *Lissopimpla excelsa*, are attracted to the flowers. They hatch about six weeks ahead of the females and have energy to spare. The orchids smell like a female ichneumon wasp when she wants to mate. The centre of the flower looks roughly like her. So the male caresses the flower with his antennae until he thinks it is receptive, he curls his abdomen, grasps with his claspers, exerts his penis and quivers in orgasm. As he pulls away the pollinia catch on his claspers and are withdrawn. He transfers them to the next flower that attracts him.

The only epiphytic orchid that grows in the forest is a western species only, *Cymbidium canaliculatum*, a vigorous plant with dozens of racemes up to forty centimetres long of yellow-brown flowers splotched with red. It grows especially well in that part of the forest known as Cubbo on Budda (*Eremophila mitchellii*) and Fuzzy Box (*Eucalyptus conica*). Birds that eat the big brown fruit excrete the dust-fine seeds on the White Cedars near our house and occasionally one grows. Any epiphytic orchid that begins to grow on a gum is discarded with the bark. The Fuzzy Box strips its main limbs like a gum but not its trunk so an orchid in the first fork is safe. These orchids reach massive size in hollow trees and stumps. Their fleshy roots up to fifteen millimetres thick twist into a many-stranded cord up to seventy centimetres in diameter and several metres long. The mass weighs hundreds of kilograms.

Aborigines and settlers used the roots and the pseudobulbs as a cure for diarrhoea. They cut them or grated them and drank very small quantities of the liquid that oozed out. If one bites into the starchy roots they gum up the mouth uncomfortably. But the Aborigines ate them after prolonged washing and cooking.

Before the fire of 1974, if one looked south-west from Baileys Peak, the emerald cones of Black Cypress Pine (*Callitris endlicheri*) stood out from the undefined blue-grey mass of stunted White Cypress Pine and eucalypt. Pine seedlings are coming away there again. Pockets of the older pine were left. Fire always misses some areas, usually through sudden changes of wind at night.

Black pine is called 'sugar pine' by sawmillers because of the glistening white resin that coats the wood in granules as soon as it is barked or sawn. An experienced storeman is never fooled though occasionally a log-faller tries to ring one in. The timber is inferior and rots quickly, especially on exterior walls.

In places, especially near Creaghs Crossing, White Cypress Pine grows with three or four trunks and is a different shade of green. Locals know it as Mallee Pine but botanists cannot distinguish it. However there is a strange pine growing on deep sand commonly known as Poky-eye Pine because it does not shed its lower branches. It is a variable crossbred with thick-stalked warty cones. Botanists call it a 'phantom' because it seems to be a cross between White Cypress Pine and a species no longer found in the Pilliga, *Callitris preissii* ssp. *verrucosa*.

Each spring the forest and the Warrumbungles come into good bloom with individual plants and small groups of plants in full flower. Every several years when frosts are few and early, and winter rains extend into a mild spring, there is a general astounding display. Five hundred hectare masses of one plant sag beneath their load of blossom. In dry years the same plants grows almost unnoticed. They drop so many leaves they have to be searched for. The spring of 1974 was the best known. The sloped walls of Baileys Peak were yellow with Spearwood and Motherumbah (*Acacia doratoxylon* var. *doratoxylon* and *A. cheelii*). Both flower in long spikes and both are species of the western plains and slopes.

As soon as one stepped on to the big flat top, one seemed to leave the inland and step on to the Hawkesbury sandstone. A white-flowered form of *Philotheca salsolifolia*, one of those unfortunate plants that have attracted no common name, grew in every pocket of soil among the rocks. Members of the Society for Growing Australian Plants find the species difficult to grow, yet on Baileys Peak they flourished one and a half metres high where there was little more than a dusting of soil over sandstone. The five-petalled flowers covered the bushes and an aromatic smell came from the leaves as we pushed past them.

To the north-east about the base of the higher Willala Mountain, Red Ash (*Alphitonia excelsa*) grows almost as well as in coastal rain-forests. They are spreading trees to ten metres high and that September were hung with green fruit. Lichen roughened the smooth bark on the southern side. They looked out of place among the stunted bloodwood and angophora with long waxed leaves drooping to avoid the sun. The Red Ash holds its olive green leaves stiffly flat. There is so much saponin in the leaves they can be used as soap.

Motherumbah flowers on the top of Willala Mountain and so does a glorious shrub with no common name that grows in masses and masses itself in yellow flowers, *Phebalium squamulosum* ssp. *gracile*. That species is divided into the extraordinary number of ten subspecies. Most have an interesting oil content and scientists working on the oils of plants at the great New South Wales Museum of Applied Arts and Sciences would divide it into quite different categories to botanists.

In the spring of 1974 we drove north from the Willala hills along Scratch Road that is the eastern firebreak between properties and the Pilliga Nature Reserve in the south and the Pilliga East State Forest in the north. The beautiful Bush Iris, *Patersonia sericea*, was in bloom here and there, big three-petalled blue flowers on forty-centimetre stems. And there were bushes of *Gompholobium virgatum* with their little three-pronged leaves hidden by big yellow pea-flowers. A pinnate-leaved coastal hopbush, *Dodonaea tenuifolia*, grew in big clumps. It was hung so profusely with russet-edged fruit we saw it from a distance as a red mass.

There are nine species of hopbush in the forest. The commonest species, *Dodonaea viscosa*, forms its simple elliptic leaves with extraordinary precision, then leaf-eating insects and caterpillars distort the leaves into odd shapes, often merely a network of veins. Apart from the fact that the fruit hanging like papery lanterns from all species resembles true hops, the settlers made good beer and good yeast from the fruit. The resemblance is more than superficial.

We pushed the Land-Rover west along Monument Road, then only a grader track that no one else had used for two or three years. The forest was fast taking it back. No one knows how the road got its name. For twenty kilometres it led us through colonnades of Narrow-leaf Ironbark sixty to seventy years old, tall, straight-grained, and as beautiful timber as John Robertson admired in 1835 but growing much more thickly. Although the main growth did not change and we could see no difference in the soil, the understorey of dense acacia in full bloom changed three times. At first there was Motherumbah smothered in bright yellow spikes seven centimetres long, then a broad belt of the narrow-leaved Spearwood, *Acacia caroleae*, with golden spikes. That gave way suddenly to tangles of *Acacia triptera*, now known as Spurwing Wattle. The squatters called it Hookbill, a better name. The short phyllodes curve out stiffly from their firm attachment to the stem and end in cruel thorns. It would be a nasty job to bring the iron-bark out of those thickets.

The narrow track that is Scratch Road is kept open to four-wheel drive vehicles by an occasional scratch with a Forestry Commission grader. If one continues to travel north along it towards the Jacks Creeks State Forest one leaves the fence running beside cleared land and drives beside the unfenced and unused scrubby back paddocks of several properties. The scrub is so thick it is difficult to find anywhere to camp. On one trip we had to chop a clearing for the Land-Rover so we could park it off the road. We boiled our billy – it was winter and safe to light a fire – in the middle of the track.

What grows so densely? The trees are not thick. There is an occasional stunted white pine, much stunted Narrow-leaf Ironbark with an odd big tree among it, some Blakely's Red Gum, some Rough-barked Apple, and much stunted White Bloodwood (*Eucalyptus trachyphloia*). This tree is named for the crimson kino that leaks from it. It ooozes down the branches, down the trunk. Sometimes it drips straight to the ground and stains a square metre or so. It looks as though a beast has been slaughtered there. The cinnamon-coloured bark is appliqued to the trunk in little rectangular scales.

The understorey, a tangle of the living and the dead, changes according to its position on the series of flat-topped east-west ridges. The low ground and the flat ground is covered with a form of *Astrotricha longifolia*, or Star Hair, three metres high. Many-stemmed and dense, its smooth leaves are olive-green on top and grey beneath, its twigs are covered with cream hairs. Sunlight mixes cream, grey and olive-green together and long wide strips glisten silver as one looks down from the low hills.

The rest in winter looks anonymously grey, even the *Acacia implexa* that dominates big patches on the hill tops. In late summer it masses with white ball flowers, more delicately scented than those of the yellow-flowered acacias. In the Warrumbungle foothills it grows alongside Mountain Hickory, *Acacia penninervis*, with similar flowering.

For three weeks in rich summers the Coonabarabran-Baradine road winds through fifteen kilometres of dense white blossom.

When *Acacia implexa* discarded pinnate leaves for its long, curved, moisture-saving phyllodes, it retained some of the original genes. Young plants display both, sometimes in outlandish combinations. It grows well on our own property and occasionally I fence off a group of healthy seedlings. But they are short-lived. A fungus disease causes galls that can kill a tree ten metres high in a couple of years. Stems and leaves distort into bulbous fleshy masses. Wood grubs and caterpillars tunnel through them. The galls dry out as they feed. Other creatures inhabit the dry tunnels and crevices. I broke open a collection of galls on about fifteen centimetres of stem and found seventeen different creatures at home: spiders, ants, beetles, bugs, flies, wasps and larvae.

Acacia implexa breaks in places on Scratch Road and a tall rough grass, *Dimorphochloa rigida*, thrives on the nitrogen it produces. Five shrubs cover the slopes in an amorphous mass: a hopbush with threadlike leaves (*Dodonaea filifolia*), *Phebalium squamulosum* ssp. *gracile* (already mentioned on the top of Willala Mountain), *Bertya gummifera*, *Baeckea densifolia* (a heath myrtle that some desperate colonists used as a tea substitute), and *Casuarina diminuta* whose name had not been published when the National Herbarium identified it for me at the end of 1975. A few kilometres farther north it grows taller and dominates some areas, a favourite feeding-ground of black cockatoos.

Some specimens of *Casuarina diminuta* seem to be hung with unusual fruit: perfect, cone-shaped, scale-covered achenes on short stems. They are produced by a gall-insect, *Cylindrococcus spiniferus*, that injects a hormone into the stems.

In the central parts of the forest north-east of Baradine, known as Coomore Creek and Denobollie State forests, plants the beekeepers love for their pollen grow in magnificent abundance. Along Sunday Road and County Line Road, Common Fringe Myrtle (*Calytrix tetragona*) spreads as far as one can see. It droops so much under the weight of blossom the beekeepers call it Hangdown. In places it gives way to *Pultenaea foliosa* or *Pultenaea boormanii* up to one and a half metres high covered with the yellow and red pea-flowers known among a dozen others as Eggs-and-bacon. *Grevillea floribunda* grows in the same area. It can be found as rather insignificant plants through much of the forest. On the sides of some of the little hills on County Line Road it shows how well it can grow.

At intervals in the central part of the forest one comes upon broom plains, sudden patches of pure *Melaleuca uncinata* from fifty to five hundred hectares in extent. Early settlers and scrub dwellers tied bunches of it to handles and used it to sweep their sand floors. The needle leaves are high in oil and it is a terrifying experience to watch fire run into a broom patch. The whole area explodes at once.

A mallee here and there, *Eucalyptus viridis*, breaks some of the patches. Parasitic Dodder festoons some of the broom. The plants are flattened as though a heavy yellow net has been thrown over them.

In wet years bare patches among the broom stay damp for months and insect-eating sundews, *Drosera burmanii*, cluster there so thickly they redden the ground. They grow in the watertable along some of the roads, too. The pink rosettes, two to five centimetres in diameter, grow flat on the ground. Each leaf ends in a shallow cup attended by tactile hairs with a globule of clear sticky fluid on the tip of each. Flying insects, ants and spiders come to feed on the apparent nectar. If a fly sticks to a globule the hair bends inward under its weight. Other hairs slowly reach towards the struggling insect, dab their blobs on it and push it down into the cup. Enzymes in the sticky fluid digest the animal protein and over a week or so the hairs suck it down into the leaves. Bees get trapped and butterflies as big as the Lesser Wanderer. If one throws a pebble into a cup the plant rejects it. Imperceptibly during a fortnight or more the hairs lever it out.

We first found these plants growing on the wet bank of sanded-up Coghill Creek. *Drosera burmanii* grew in two colours, the common red-leaved form with little five-petalled pink flowers, and a green-leaved form with white flowers. Another sundew, *Drosera indica*, grew there plentifully, too, a rare find in New South Wales. These little green plants grow five to ten centimetres high and bear their hundreds of glistening blobs on short tentacle-like branches. They trap extraordinary numbers of insects, surely more than they need. Some plants only six centimetres high had over a hundred freshly-caught insects on them. The insects supply nitrogen. Sundews grow where the soil is so constantly damp nitrogen is either leached away or never fixed.

On Pine Road in Pilliga East State Forest what begins as a broom patch changes suddenly to a twenty hectare mass of Fringed Heath Myrtle, *Micromyrtus ciliata*. An odd scrubby ironbark grows among it, a few tall bushes of broom and some *Acacia conferta* with small phyllodes crowded along the stems. In spring the Fringed Health Myrtle is crowded with tiny white flowers. It is an isolated display. Elsewhere the plant grows as single specimens. There is no fringe apparent to the naked eye, but the leaves, themselves only three millimetres long, are bordered with minute stiff hairs. They can be seen if magnified about ten times.

In the flat Pilliga West Forest where the rainfall is lower than in the eastern sections the pine is at its best. The under shrubs vary with the soil. White sandy soil, red sandy loam and red loam run in wide successive bands to the north-west. These bands are no longer easily determined. The thick understorey hides them. W. A. W. de Beuzeville, the first forest assessor to work in the Pilliga, noted the soil changes in a paper written in 1915. He ascribed them to changes in the flow of Baradine Creek. The belts of white sand where the best pine grew were raised about half a metre above the rest of the country and were known as sand monkeys. All the creeks in the forest have raised banks. It is certainly possible that Baradine Creek silted up several times to the level of its bank then changed course.

Sanded up creeks were a natural feature of inland Australia even before sheep and cattle disturbed the soil. Both Aborigines and animals dug for water the sand protected from evaporation. But after the last big influx of sheep the creeks in the forest began to sand up unusually quickly. By the early 1900s all but the biggest waterholes had gone from the wide bed of Bohena Creek. It became a stretch of shimmering deep white sand. Now the last waterhole has been filled in for almost fifty years and the forest is taking the creek over. Perhaps in a flood early next century Bohena Creek will cut a new path and leave a sand monkey to mark its former bed.

De Beuzeville, a man who loved trees, reported a 'very old over wood with a very young under wood' in the western part of the forest. The Forestry Commission thinned that young pine underwood and it is now maturing into good timber. Spectacular belts of acacia run through it. Mudgee Wattle, *Acacia spectabilis*, covers itself with racemes of big yellow balls up to twenty centimetres long. The branches sag to the ground under the weight of blossom. This gives way to Western Black Wattle, *Acacia hakeoides*, or the low-growing *Acacia ixiophylla* with sticky dark green leaves and bright yellow flowers.

Where the acacias thin out and intermingle, vigorous *Cassia nemophila* (Desert Cassia) presents its butter-smooth peaflowers. Even from a distance its yellow shows clearly against the fuzzy yellow of the acacias. An Emu Bush grows there too, *Eremophila longifolia*. Emus relish its currant-like fruit. Indeed the shrub is so accustomed to producing its fruit for Emus none of its seeds germinate under natural conditions unless they have first passed through an Emu.

Across the Pilliga-Coonamble road on the western border of
the forest an acacia has grown into a tree thirteen metres high. The
bunched tops mass with yellow-brown flowers in spring. There are no
low branches. Phyllodes and flowers are high out of reach. A property
is named Yarran after this acacia, but it is not *Acacia homalophylla*, the
species usually known as Yarran. It is a very variable unnamed species
with some of the characteristics of Yarran. Near Gunnedah on the
Gunnedah-Connabarabran road it grows as a lovely bushy shrub.
Near our house there is a gaunt specimen, an old leaning tree twenty-
three metres high. The first phyllodes and flowers begin seventeen
metres above the ground. The scrappy samples I sent to the National
Herbarium were shot down with a .410 gauge shotgun. A group of its
seedlings came up near it so I fenced them off from the cattle.

One of the bands of red loam in Pilliga West grows Whitewood
(*Atalaya hemiglauca*) as an understorey. It stretches northward two
kilometres wide and ten long. Other trees and shrubs grow individually
or in clumps: Wilga (*Geijera parviflora*) whose little white flowers are
pollinated by blowflies, the beautiful Kurrajong, Bimble Box (*Eucalyptus populnea*), Boobialla and Dogwood (*Myoporum montanum* and *M.
deserti*), Bull Oak, Budda (*Eremophila mitchellii*) with delicately fragrant
wood, and so many others.

One tall, leafless shrub that grows on the Newell Highway north of
Coonabarabran is known disparagingly as Stinkwood. It is *Jacksonia
scoparia*. It also is sometimes known as Dogwood. It is beautiful when
weighted down with orange and yellow peaflowers, 'But don't put a
dead log of it on your fire' a sleeper cutter told me, 'It'd spoil anyone's
dinner – smells like a hundred farts'.

Forestry Commission workers cut out the oak where it threatens to
overwhelm their thinned pine. No one thins acacia but the log-haulers
and sleeper cutters curse it as an impediment and even many foresters
regard it as waste growth. But if one digs around the roots of acacia or
cassia one finds healthy kidney-pink nodules formed by nitrogen-
producing bacteria. The enormous growth of pine depends on them.

In the spring of 1974 I drove along Acacia Road, in the Yarrigan
State Forest south of Baradine, through yellow walls of Motherumbah
fourteen metres high. For a kilometre or so the flowering branches met
across the top and formed a yellow tunnel. Fallen blossom lay two
centimetres deep on the road. It seemed the road mirrored what was
above it.

On Duggans Road that runs along the north bank of Dandry Creek
opposite the amazing lichen growth mentioned in Chapter One and the

isolated patch of *Acacia leucoclada* ssp. *leucoclada* at Top Crossing, there is the dense low growth that harbours wallabies. Drooping Cassinia (*Cassinia arcuata*) is the main plant. Hundreds of hectares are bronze with it throughout the summer. It is known in Victoria as Chinese Bush since it overran the worked-out goldfields.

The country is sandy and ridgy and split by gullies. No good timber grows there. The black pine and angophora are stunted and misshapen. The Blakely's Red Gum is little bigger than mallee. A true many-stemmed mallee grows there, Dwyer's Mallee Gum (*Eucalyptus dwyeri*). The rather similar, single-trunked Hill Red Gum (*Eucalyptus dealbata*) grows beside it. Four low-growing acacias, the ubiquitous *A. deanii*, *A. conferta* with crowded leaves, *A. gladiiformis* and *A. buxifolia*, grow singly among the Drooping Cassinia or in places take over either one at a time or all together. A casuarina without a name covers big patches.

And among them, these too make wallaby country: *Hovea lanceolata* with masses of purple peaflowers, yellow Variable Groundsel, rust-coloured *Grevillea floribunda*, mauve *Boronia glabra*, *Persoonia sericea* and another geebung without a name, *Dianella revoluta* (the delicate Tinsel Lily with blue-berried fruit), *Melichrus urceolatus* (Urn Heath) with stiff prickly leaves and greenish flowers, Daphne Heath (*Brachyloma daphnoides*) in a tiny-leaved New England Tableland form, and one of the many eggs-and-bacon flowers, *Bossiaea rhombifolia* ssp. *concolor*.

Only thirty kilometres to the west there is good farmland and a different world. The area that was known as Pretty Plains has been cleared of its sudden excess growth and it is pretty plains again. The list of shrubs and trees scattered over the paddocks reads like an incantation:

> Kurrajong, Wilga, Budda, Boonery,
> Whitewood, Quinine Bush, Hickory, gum,
> Ironbark, Supple Jack, Needlewood, angophora,
> Pilliga Box and Bimble, cypress pine, Belar,
> Wild Lemon, Wild Orange, Currant Bush, Beefwood,
> Deane's Wattle, Bull Oak, Boobialla, Motherumbah.

They grow on a stretch of special soil. There is only about twelve thousand hectares of it altogether in a fifteen kilometre strip west of Baradine Creek. A good deep red and grey sandy loam covers a subsoil with free lime in it. Kurrajongs grow on it magnificently. So do cattle.

The Kurrajong was once known as *Brachychiton diversifolia* because of the extraordinary diversity of the leaves. When it was found that the Kurrajong in the far north of Australia was a different species, *diversifolia* was reserved for it and the southern species was named *Brachychiton populneum*. At a distance the shapely trees resemble poplars. Individuals grow to a noble size. One in a timber belt on our own property, forced up by tall trees alongside it, is ninety centimetres in diameter and approaching thirty metres high. An avenue of big Kurrajongs leads to the casino at Monte Carlo. Australian trees are grown widely overseas. Many Californians regard the Tasmanian Blue Gum as their finest native tree.

Aborigines made good use of the Kurrajong. In wet seasons they pulled up the yam-like taproots of seedlings and ate them, a pleasant enough and a substantial enough vegetable. I pulled up one seedling no more than fifty centimetres high that had a taproot one metre long tapering from seventy-five centimetres in diameter to ten centimetres. Some have bulbous roots up to twenty centimetres in diameter just below ground level with long thin taproots descending from them. The inner bark yielded strong fibre for netmaking. The shaped timber made good canoes and hard shields. The roasted seeds were a substantial food.

Kurrajongs belong to the same family as the Cacao tree that produces cocoa beans. The seeds are higher in caffeine than coffee beans and settlers frequently used them to make a drink. Leichhardt on his journey to Port Essington drank Kurrajong coffee for several months.

The Native Apricot, *Pittosporum phillyreoides*, is scattered through the western section of the forest. The Aborigines pounded its seeds into flour. There is one on our own property. As I write this chapter it is a lovely thing with its pendulous branches hung all over with apricot-coloured fruit. But if one merely brushes one's teeth with the hard flesh, a bitter taste lasts for hours. Leichhardt complained he could not eat the Emus that fed on its fruit.

The acid red fruit of the Emu-apple (*Owenia acidula*) was chewed by stockmen mustering far from water. It grows in the Warrumbungles and on the plains where sandy red soil shades into black. The Aborigines who also used it as a thirst-quencher knew it in various languages as Eurungie, Gruie, or Colane.

The Wild Lemon or Desert Lime (*Eremocitrus glauca*) grows sparsely near Coonamble and Coonabarabran and in clumps of several hectares each near the boundary of Taylor's old Dinbi. The small lemon-coloured fruit was eaten by the Aborigines. Settlers made jam of it and squeezed its juice for drinks. It has a mild clean acid flavour that is marred by its strange persistence. The wild lemon is a true citrus fruit and horticulturists have been interested in it for cross-breeding and as a grafting stock since it was first recorded in 1848. CSIRO scientists were experimenting with it in the 1970s. In 1976, Dr D. J. Hutchison, a research geneticist from America, inspected many of the known trees in South Australia and New South Wales, including those in this area, and collected seed and cuttings.

During the 1970s Dr Mark Buttrose of CSIRO's Division of Horticultural Research in Adelaide was working on Australia's principal inland edible wild fruit, the Quandong (*Santalum acuminatum*). Its flesh is acidic and astringent, though pleasantly so, and twice as rich in vitamin C as oranges. Since most domestic fruit was developed from thin-fleshed wild forms, Dr Buttrose believes that by crossbreeding different strains of quandong he can produce a valuable marketable fruit. A good clump of quandongs grows in the Merriwindi State Forest on our northern boundary. In summer the golf-ball-sized crimson fruit shows up for a hundred metres through the thinned pine. A species with yellow fruit is bigger and better eating. Settlers made a good quandong jam sweetened with honey. Children strung the oily kernels as beads or played with them as marbles. The hard close-grained wood was favoured by the Aborigines for making fire by friction.

One species of quandong with an edible purple fruit, *Santalum lanceolatum*, is better known as Sandalwood because of its fragrant timber. It was also known as 'the blacks' medicine tree'. They successfully used an infusion of its leaves to treat boils and festered sores and unsuccessfully the gonorrhoea the white man brought to them. It grows in the Willala hills.

The quandong is parasitic. When young the seed germinates in the ground normally, then the roots travel through the soil till one of them strikes the root of another plant. The meeting might be accidental, it might be the result of a deliberate search. The quandong root then grows a pad that clutches the other root and invades it with root tissue. No one knows what the quandong seeks from its host that can be tree, grass or small annual plant. Once mature it can grow alone.

The graceful Native Cherry (*Exocarpus cupressiformis*) that grows sparsely in the Willala hills is a more definite root parasite. It maintains its hold and in drought time looks green and healthy while the plants around it are withering. The strange fruit was cited by Englishmen as clinching evidence of the bizarre nature of Australia: the cherry with the stone outside. The little hard inedible nut which is the fruit is borne on the end of a thick red succulent edible stalk.

The contorted Supplejack that grows as a small tree on the western edge of the forest is not a parasite but it likes another tree to support its tendril-like branches until they age and harden. Sometimes one Supplejack supports another and they entwine together as one strange tree. If a Supplejack grows unaided the mature trunk records the writhings of the young shoot in search of support. Branches often twist together. Among educated and uneducated the tree is almost always mispronounced as Sooplejack. The tasteless new shoots were eaten by settlers and Aborigines. The early stockmen and shepherds burnt logs of it and leavened their Johnny cakes with its light white ash.

The big bulb of the lily, *Crinum flaccidum*, makes a good arrowroot-like flour. In a hard drought last century when neither teams nor steamers could reach Wilcannia on the Darling, one resident made good money digging lily bulbs and grinding them into flour. The plant grows best on sandy soil. It has contractile roots. The bulb develops on the surface, then the roots alternately grow and contract and pull the bulb up to a metre deep into the damp subsoil. It is such a beautiful plant with its big scented white flowers that each district where it grows claims it. So it is called the Darling Lily, the Murray Lily, the Macquarie Crinum, the Desert Lily, the Sandover Lily. We call it the Pilliga Lily. It grows well on several of our own paddocks. Sometimes we plough over the lilies when working the summer fallows and cut them off twelve centimetres below ground level. Straightway they send up long fleshy leaves and within a fortnight break into flower on stems almost a metre high.

Five Corners, *Styphelia laeta*, is a shrub with greenish flowers and small sweet, green, good-eating fruit. It came away in masses with the first scrub growth but has since thinned out. The unripe fruit leaves a floury astringent taste in the mouth. The soft dropped fruit tastes best but one must beat the Emus to it. Their little striped chickens cluster under the fruiting bushes. The droppings of the grown birds are studded with the five-cornered seeds.

Children at the old Rocky Creek sawmill also ate the little bright red fruit of the Western Nectar Heath (*Melichrus erubescens*). Mrs Laura Purdy of Baradine knew this stiff low-growing plant as Fiery Jack, a name worth preserving.

Aborigines ate the big seeds of the palmate cycads or burrawangs. Two species grow in the forest. *Macrozamia heteromera* is the most widespread. *Macrozamia diplomera* grows in the Warrumbungle foothills. There are hybrid plants where the two species meet. The oily nut-like seeds are contained in big pineapple-shaped cones. Untreated, they are deadly if eaten, causing violent vomiting and diarrhoea. It is thought to have been cycad poison that killed Dr Bogle and Mrs Chandler in those long-unsolved deaths in New South Wales. Aborigines ate them after washing them for days, wrapping them in the papery bark of Mela-leuca to ferment, then roasting them. No one now knows enough of the sequence of preparation to risk tasting them.

Not much more is known of Australian fungi. We are confident we can always recognise the Field Mushroom (*Agaricus campestris*) and pick them by the bucketful in good seasons. They grow best in unploughed paddocks that have been heavily stocked with cattle. Cultivation destroys the masses of perennial underground fungal threads that pro-duce the edible fruit. The edible Horse Mushroom (*Agaricus arvensis*) so common in Victoria, probably grows here. Very big mushrooms sometimes come up in the litter beneath angophora trees but we are not confident enough of our identification to eat them. White mushrooms of the *Amanita* genus are common, two or three species. Some species are deadly, some might be edible. Few know which is which.

Big firm white puffballs up to twenty centimetres in diameter grow among the forest litter. They smell delicious and are said to taste delicious but we have not risked eating them. Most of the other local fungi look too bizarre to be palatable anyway: the strange little cream-coloured Earth Stars with a dome in the centre of a fleshy rosette, the red Bracket Fungi growing on trees or the White Punk Fungi whose filaments invade timber and cause dry rot, the delicate long stemmed toadstools or the astonishing Basket Fungus. The last is a brown slimy oval growth about six centimetres long. If one breaks it open a lace of fleshy threads springs out from the centre and unfolds into a separate network ball about fifteen centimetres in diameter. It is sometimes called Crinoline Fungus.

Occasionally in the forest one comes across the sinister mushrooms of the *Boletus* genus. They are a bright cinnamon on top and a brighter yellow beneath with thousands of tiny pores instead of gills. If the thick flesh above the honeycomb of pores is broken open, it looks cheesy yellow with green patches here and there as though it is beginning to go mouldy.

It is only in recent years that Australians have reconsidered their grasses as something worth considering. When the best of them failed so quickly under the hooves of the first stock, all of them except those growing on black soil came to be regarded as worthless. The term 'pasture improvement' meant the ploughing out of indigenous grasses, spreading superphosphate and sowing with exotic plants. Increasing costs of such work have caused a reassessment of the hardy indigenous grasses. The time and money spent on exotics might better have been spent inducing our own species to produce more leaf and less seed.

But it is not only as fodder that our grasses are being considered. Members of the Society for Growing Australian Plants, especially in Canberra, are sowing them in expanses in their gardens to break the repetition of the shaved green mats of imported grasses in suburban lawns. Kangaroo Grass or Oat Grass (*Themeda australis*), the favourite of the early colonists, is the modern favourite. It does not produce the vicious seeds of so many others. It grows in masses on the forest fringes wherever it is not too much disturbed by stock. We cut big bunches of its light brown heads on purple stalks to decorate the little Baradine church at our daughter's wedding which excitingly disrupted the finishing of this book. Several city guests stopped to pick bunches along the Coonabarabran road on their way home the next day.

Two species of *Cymbopogon* are more decorative though rarer. *Cymbopogon obtectus*, Silky Heads, grows in thick patches at Creaghs Crossing. The long tufted leaves are purplish and strangely aromatic when crushed. The creamy woolly seed heads stand a metre high. *Cymbopogon refractus* grows in a few little clumps in a timber belt on our property. It produces less spectacular heads but always looks jaggedly interesting. The seeds poke out at angles on the end of short stalks produced regularly along the tall stems. It is known as Barbed-wire Grass. Blady-grass (*Imperata cylindrica*) has spread into the sanded-up creeks. Children living in the forest knew it as Sweet Roots Grass. They pulled up the fleshy rhizomes and sucked them like sugar cane. This grass is native but it is not restricted to Australia. The wild-growing Kunai of New Guinea is the same species.

The loveliest grass of the forest area is the annual *Perotis rara*, Comet Grass. It grows on such poor soils it is sometimes the only plant growing and is so short and sparse-leaved it looks insignificant for most of the day. The open cylindrical heads bear seeds with purple awns on purple stalks. Adjacent heads lace together. But they are so open the colour does not show up against the background of red sand. It is in the early morning when the dew is on it that this grass is beautiful. For an hour or so the purple awns and stems are reflected and refracted in the dewdrops. Then the grass loses all form and blurs into a purple mist.

Immediately north of Coonabarabran there are clumps of White Gums, *Eucalyptus rossii*. Coonabarabran features poplars in its streets but, even though they have made outstanding growth, they are

commonplace exotics. The White Gums which could distinguish
Coonabarabran are ignored and even bulldozed out of the way for
houses.

White Gums grow best on low slopes. They reach twenty-four
metres high with smooth straight white trunks. Often it is thirteen
metres to the first limb. The limbs are smooth and white, too, though
here and there oozing kino stains one pink. Some trunks are marked by
the black scribbles of the wood-eating larvae of a small moth, *Ogmograp-
tis scribula.* The grub eats its way through the narrow band of soft tissue
beneath the thin bark. It circles and zigzags aimlessly. Before it is fully
grown it turns around in a loop and begins to eat its way back along its
path. Hormones that it has previously excreted help complete its
development. It usually gets less than half way to where it began
feeding before it surfaces, hatches and flies away as a moth. The scribbles record its path exactly: a lightly etched single line from where it
began to feed, then a broader line terminating in a narrow loop.

There are unexpected plants in the Pilliga forest and in the Warrumbungles. Several species of common rainforest ferns grow in mountain
gullies, and the delicate coastal Necklace Fern (*Asplenium flabellifolium*),
encircles rocks and tree trunks. Flannel Flowers (*Actinotus helianthi*)
mass on the slopes after fire. They grow more than a metre high and at
first sight look as unreal as plastic palms. The ten green-veined, green
pointed creamy bracts that surround the insignificant hairy ball of
flowers seem indeed to be cut out of flannel. Among thousands of the
common Deane's Wattle that abounds on the flats, I found one
specimen whose leaves were sensitive to touch.

Some plants are confined to small areas. Some plants are rare.
Laird Welchman of Narrabri who induced Namoi Shire Council to
make some fine plantings of native trees found a white bottlebrush
(*Callistemon* spp.) in the overgrown bed of Bohena Creek. George
Althofer of Wellington who wrote well of mint bushes (*Prostanthera*
genus) in his *Cradle of Incense* found one new species of mint bush and
several not yet named among at least eleven different species in the
area. These showy aromatic shrubs have to be searched for. They
seldom grow in masses. A rare species with delicate blue and white
flowers in the shape of a six-pointed star (*Prostanthera cruciflora*) grows
beneath Gins Leap north of Boggabri near where Dr Adams had his
early surgery.

That austere tree, the Belar, whose leaves have been reduced to scales,
excites the ear not the eye. Wind rattles through a forest of eucalypts.

In a big clump of Belars it makes a humming noise that varies in pitch with the force of the wind. On gusty days Belars sing. An imaginative tribe of natives who tend huge flower gardens on the shores of Lake Kutubu in the Southern Highlands of Papua-New Guinea have also planted thousands of casuarinas (the genus that Belars belong to) in formation to catch wind from all directions. They have varied the density and the shape of the plantations to produce different notes. And on windy days they dance to the singing of the trees.

Sometimes plants can astonish one as much as if they had intelligence. I drove back one afternoon through the Merriwindi forest into the setting sun. It is an exploited thinned forest of pine with several species of box, ironbark and gum scattered through it. The eucalypts stand above the pines. There was a broken bank of clouds in the west. Some of them had risen above the forest. They shone with the reds and purples of a good Australian sunset. But there was nothing unusual about it. Then the highest eucalypts blazed orange. It was as though they had been switched on. Treetops lost their identity and became one glowing light. I pulled up to watch but even before the Land-Rover stopped some of them were going out. Leaves and branches showed again. But odd leaves continued to glow as though their filaments were slower in cooling. Then big sections of the forest, pines as well as eucalypts, lit up successively in orange masses and quickly faded. It was an intense light that seemed to come from within the trees. The whole spectacle lasted no more than a minute.

A yearly marvel is the pollination of the pines. The trees bud in early August. By mid-September they are brown and weighted down with pollen. Then the pines begin to release it. The pollen cones burst open in groups and spurt streams of pollen a metre into the air. The grains drift as a little brown cloud.

The spring of 1973 amazed men who had seen eighty years of pine flowering. In the early morning thousands of trees exploded together. Dense clouds rolled up from the forest. So much pollen drifted into a shearing-shed on the edge of the forest the shearers found it almost too dark to shear by early afternoon.

If one is near a pine when all the cones burst together, one hears a crack like a pistol-shot. The branches recoil and the tree shivers. One does not expect a tree to move in passion.

9

Timbergetters and Scrub Dwellers
A Different Game

The pines in the old open forest seldom branched below nine metres. Their thin light-grey bark was patterned with embossed triangles. The outermost flakes whitened with age. From a distance the whole trunk looked white. 'Old Greys' the millers called them.

The first timbergetters cutting for Mountford and Morath in Narrabri soon found they had to travel too far for trees sixty centimetres in diameter. By 1878 the legal size was reduced to thirty centimetres. The axemen chopped the biggest logs off at the first limb and rejected the tops, so much of the timber was knot-free. The high resin content made it termite-proof. When sawn it was honey-coloured with beautiful amber figures in it. From the 1860s to the 1880s Australia sent slabs to exhibitions in England and on the Continent for the world to admire.

The tongued-and-grooved lining boards in the old wine shanty at Cuttabri were twenty centimetres wide and showed no shrinkage. New licensees in the 1970s covered some of this timber with modern sheeting. The floor of St Cyprian's Church in Narrabri, laid in 1892, oiled and polished in recent times, is cypress pine at its best. This exceptional building was designed by John Horbury Hunt and has been maintained as he built it, even to the slate roof and the ironbark shingles on some of the walls.

The pines approaching one hundred years old that were milled in the 1970s had dark grey bark. Dozens of little branches radiated from the trunks. Only the bottom two or three metres were free. 'It's bloody hairy,' says a log-faller disgustedly as he takes his axe to trim the branches off a cut log. The old men who cut big pine in their youth declare it a different tree. 'This is a crossbred', they say, 'full of knots'. They call it 'black butt' pine.

The species has not changed, only the conditions it grows under. The modern timber is still superb. The knots add to its character and it is seldom that a knot loosens and mars a sawn board. As flooring, sanded and polished, it gives off a yellow glow with the dark brown whorls of the knots studded through it irregularly.

Pine was generally known as yellow wood. Licences issued for the Liverpool Plains in the 1840s recommended the holders as 'fit and proper persons to cut and saw yellow woods'. It was Governor Hunter who first claimed timber for the Crown. In 1795 he sent men along the Hawkesbury and its tributaries to blaze all trees suitable for building, and indent them with the broad arrow. Most subsequent titles to land except freehold reserved timber to the Crown.

Sir Henry Parkes made another definite move to preserve timber in 1871 when he established the Forestry Branch within the Department of Lands. It was under the authority of that branch that the first forest rangers were appointed. In 1881 the musical but erratic poet, Henry Kendall, was appointed Inspector of Forests, a job intended as a sinecure. But he set out to prove his worth and alcohol and the strenuous travelling overcame him. He died the next year.

Louis Schwager set up a steam sawmill in Gunnedah about the same time as Mountford and Morath set up in Narrabri. He selected a sixteen-hectare block near Gunnedah with an unusually heavy stand of big pine on it. The spiteful lease-holder – it is not known who he was – sent in his men to cut down and split up every tree. In 1883 Schwager moved to the Round Swamp between Narrabri and Wee Waa where Jimmy and Joe Governor stole the teamsters' ponies. Later he moved to old Coghill. In the 1970s his descendants were graziers and sawyers.

J. W. R. Horne established a coachbuilding works combined with a big sawmill in Boggabri and advertised his timber enthusiastically in the *Narrabri Herald*. This advertisement appeared on 22 July 1887:

HORNE! HORNE! HORNE!

J. W. R. Horne, of Boggabri, is always Blowing his horn about selling his Timber so cheap, yet he has not gone bung. He has only 60,000 feet of Seasoned timber in stock.

Please take notice that his Boards are FULL THICKNESS after
being plained.

Boards Plained 14 in. wide and 3 in. thick. Wall plates Groved if
required, at his noted

   Cheap Saw Mill, Boggabri

Horne prospered and in 1914 hired a chauffeur and bought a
Cadillac. It was the finest of the early cars in the north. However one
day Horne drove it himself. His sleeve caught in the hand throttle and
the car raced off the road. He drove home, put it away in his garage
and bought another make. After the old car had passed through several
uncaring hands, Ron Palmer, a Boggabri solicitor, bought it and
restored it. It still goes well, a fine old machine that has taken many
Boggabri brides to the church.

Some sawmills persisted with steam engines until halfway through
this century. In the 1970s there were still parts of old Robey, Clayton-
Shuttleworth or Marshall engines about most of the active mills. The
flywheel on some of them weighed three tonnes. At Wooleybah in
Pilliga West State Forest lay most of a fine engine made by Davey,
Paxman and Co., Colchester, England. Although it had stood in the
open for over twenty years since it was last used, the exposed rotary
governor slid on its 25-millimetre shaft at the touch of a finger. The
heavy weights that swung out in a circle of 45-centimetre diameter were
free on their pivots and so delicately balanced they moved at once when
I flicked the unit round.

Despite the steam sawmills, much of the timber used locally was
sawn by hand in pits until late in the 1890s. If house, church or
school was to be built, a deep trench was dug alongside the site and the
logs to be sawn hauled to it. Then a frame to support the logs was built
above the trench. The sawyer and his offsider levered a barked log on
to it and chocked it in place. They stretched a string soaked in blue or
dusted with whiting tightly along the length of the log and flicked it to
mark the first cut. The sawyer stood on top, his offsider jumped into
the pit. Their saw was about 1.8 metres long and tapering. The sawyer
worked the wide end and guided the cut along the line. The man in the
pit walked slowly backwards pushing and pulling steadily and blindly.
The saw cut on the downstroke and he worked in streams of sawdust.
He kept his eyes cast down to protect them and usually wore a long
veil. Every few days they shovelled the sawdust out of the pit.

There is a depression on our own property that marks an old sawpit.
One sometimes finds the mark of a pitsaw on unplaned cedar boards.
The teeth were never perfectly set and the deeper-cutting teeth left a

regular pattern of straight score marks. Each downstroke advanced the cut five to ten millimetres according to the hardness of the wood.

Good sawyers were proud of their craft. Jack Carlow from Dandry Creek is still spoken of, and his mate, George Forrest. They cut pine weatherboards thirty centimetres wide and twenty-five millimetres thick. It required exceptional skill to cut such wide boards evenly. George Hodge had a pit ten kilometres out on the Baradine-Coonamble road where he sawed timber for sale, surely an awful task when the amount to be sawn had no limit.

In 1909 the three Pincham brothers bought Hodge's timber supply and set up a steam mill. Bruce Pincham, the younger of the brothers, had been milling for sixty-five years when I spoke to him. His father and elder brother had had a pit saw at Ulamambri but young Bruce had been working in a post office before he joined them in 1909. He knew nothing of milling. As a check on costs he walked into a sawmill, looked at the pile of white, barked logs waiting to be sawn, and asked the owner what he paid for 'skinned' logs.

Because of the increasing interest in milling Pilliga forest timber, W. A. A. de Beuzeville was sent up in 1915 to survey the area. He was newly appointed to the new position of Forest Assessor.

J. Ednie Brown who was Director-General of Forests in New South Wales in the 1890s had stressed that our forests were insufficiently known. He had come from treeless South Australia where for years he had been planting the imported Radiata Pine as well as Australian trees. Some of the River Red Gum forests he established there in the 1870s are now magnificent stands. He admired the New South Wales timber: 'For durability, beauty of grain and variety, our timbers are second to none in the world.' He advocated an orderly system of milling so 'cutting and re-cropping will be going on continually'. But it takes governments a long time to absorb sensible advice.

When Wilfred de Beuzeville began his assessment, E. H. F. Swain was District Forester with headquarters at Pilliga. An energetic man, Swain maintained that timber was valuable and would become more valuable, and that the land that grew it should be preserved to grow it, not cleared for the plough. For almost thirty years he was Commissioner of Forests, first in Queensland, then in New South Wales, but the governments that appointed him continued the clearing. Swain compensated by setting up the valuable Division of Wood Technology which in 1973, as the Wood Technology and Forest Research Division, moved its headquarters to beautiful timber buildings in West Pennant Hills.

De Beuzeville spent twelve months in the Pilliga forest. He mapped
the whole area in a system of traverses by compass at intervals of half
a mile (.8 of a kilometre). He measured, then counted, the paces of
his horse and stopped about every ten chains (about 200 metres) to note
the topography and the timber. With one assistant, Ivan Krippner,
he averaged about thirty-three kilometres a day. His Cocker Spaniel,
a companion for years, trotted behind. His horses became so used to
the work they stopped of their own accord about every three hundred steps.

Later as Forest Ecologist he planned a grid of timbered highways for
New South Wales with the showpiece one and a half kilometres wide
stretching one thousand kilometres from Tocumwal to Goondiwindi. It
was to be planted for timber, for honey, for fodder, for beauty. A subsidiary belt of Kurrajong farther west was to run for 750 kilometres.
The project was to employ a thousand men for fifteen years.

It was an ecologist's dream and perhaps not even desirable when the
restricted amount of good land in Australia is considered. But the
scheme was imaginative and certainly applicable to some areas. De
Beuzeville's book, *Australian Trees for Australian Planting*, published in
1947 is still worth reading.

The Forestry Commission as it is today was set up in 1916. Ivan
Krippner, de Beuzeville's assistant, became District Forester at Narrabri. Red-bearded and long-faced, he was known as Jesus Christ. But
it was the middle of World War I and the commission made a slow
beginning. Krippner went to the war and returned to Narrabri briefly
when it was over. He was replaced by Gordon Burrows who introduced
the most vital concept of the new Commission: sustained yield, which
was a restatement of Ednie Brown's theories. No more timber was to
be cut than would be replaced by planting or by regeneration. The
Pilliga forest depends on regeneration, but during the 1930s and 1940s
when rabbits were thick foresters began to fear there would be no more
regeneration in the Pilliga. No plantings of *Callitris* have been successful in Australia though they have grown exceptionally well in South
Africa.

Gordon Burrows so loved timber and the forest he directed in his
will that his ashes be spread in it. When he died in 1958 Arthur Ruttley, another dedicated forester, spread the ashes in a ceremony at
Lucky Flat.

So that timbergetters could be directed to particular areas, reference
points were needed in the forest, and roads. A surveyor named Pen-
nyfather pegged the Pilliga West Forest, where the best pine was, into a

grid of squares with sides of about four kilometres. Each long line was blazed and designated by a letter of the alphabet. Every two to four hundred metres according to the density of the forest he put up a numbered shield, A1, A2 . . . B1, B2 . . . to the end of the lines.

Over the years the grid was extended wherever there was worthwhile timber. Bulldozers moved up the blazed trails followed by graders to make roads and firebreaks. By the 1970s there was a network of over five thousand kilometres of roads, most of them well maintained.

The depression of the early 1930s gave the Forestry Commission a supply of labourers willing to do hard repetitive work. They were sent with axes into the Pilliga West Forest to thin the overgrown stands of pine then about fifty years old. Some of them had shot to the lead but their growth was still restricted by the lesser trees around them. Those that had lost the race were chopped down leaving the successful spaced about seven metres apart.

Ben Harris, Big Ben, directed much of the thinning and the road-making. He came to Baradine as forest guard in a buggy and pair in 1917 and drove out by car twenty-nine years later after a long spell as District Forester. His send-off lasted a week and ended with a mock wake.

He also directed the construction of most of the ground tanks now in the forest to water working horses and bullocks and as a supply for fire control. He erected lookout towers with huts beside them that were manned throughout the summer. One wooden tower about twenty-five metres high was built at Lucky Flat in the Pilliga East State Forest north-east of Baradine, another on a little hill in the Yarrigan Forest south of Baradine and another in the Denobollie Forest halfway towards Lucky Flat on the strange formation known as Salt Caves (described in the next chapter). The first lookout at Salt Caves was kept by Pommie Timms before the tower was built. He had a range-finder set up on a sawn-off Black Pine stump.

When the local headquarters of the Forestry Commission was moved to Baradine in 1937, another high tower was built in the yard. In modern times the wooden towers were replaced by steel towers fitted with radio. In the late 1970s the regular manning of the towers was discontinued. Planes are used for spotting when conditions are dangerous.

The local headquarters of the Forestry Commission remained at Baradine in a pleasant building that featured the local pine. Narrabri tried energetically to get the offices moved back. There were moves, open and surreptitious, during the 1970s to transfer the offices to

Coonabarabran. Modern foresters are mostly city men and uneasy in
towns as small as Baradine. Some even give the impression they are
uneasy in forests.

The Forestry Commission stopped the wastage of the pine tops. Logs
had to run out past the limbs until they were less than 130 millimetres
in diameter free of bark. The barking of the logs continued into the
1930s. Then when some of the new-grown pine was cut the many limbs
made barking difficult. The knots held it on like pegs. So logs were
carted to the mills with the bark on. And it was found the better way.
The bark protected the timber from too rapid drying, and big stockpiles
could be made to tide the mills over a wet spell. Barked logs had to be
sawn within a couple of days in hot weather. If they were held longer,
the sawyer heard a series of creaks as the day warmed up and too many
of his logs split from end to end.

The first sawmills were established near the towns and teamsters
hauled the logs to them. The cut logs, up to twenty metres long, were
snigged by bullocks or horses along the ground to a convenient loading
point where they were barked. A wagon drew alongside and poles to
act as skids were leant against one side. The wagons had the table tops
removed. The loaded logs rode on the bolsters. Two men with cant
hooks and bars rolled the first white slippery log against the skids. They
passed ropes tied to the opposite side of the wagon top under each end
of the log then drew them back over the top of the wagon and attached
them to the base of an A-frame. Four bullocks pulled at the apex. They
walked steadily out in a straight line until the log rolled across the
bolsters against removable uprights that acted as stops. They halted,
turned, walked back and turned again ready for the next log which was
pulled against the first. Bullocks and horses grew so used to the work
they scarcely needed orders.

The full load was secured by chains tightened with twitch sticks.
They poked up from the load like fishing rods. Bullocks were mostly
used in log-hauling because they were steadier in sandy and boggy
country. Horses are nervous when ground gives way beneath them.
The wagons turned easily. The winding tracks they followed had to be
straightened when motor lorries took over. Ten to fifteen logs usually
made a wagon load. Paddy Keogh once put on thirty pine logs
weighing sixteen tonnes and carted them to a mill in Narrabri West.

When the haulage distances became too great, the sawmills moved
out among the timber, and the logs were snigged in by bullocks or
partly carried by horse-drawn jinkers. The teamsters were not put out

of business. They put the table tops back on their wagons and carted the sawn timber to rail.

A timber jinker was an inverted U-shaped rod running on two wheels with a pole about three and a half metres long attached to the top of it. Two or three horses pulled it over the top of the log to be drawn so that a wheel ran along each side. They pulled the jinker to within two or three metres of the butt, then they were stopped and backed. The pole lifted up in the air and the apex of the inverted U fell on the log. A chain was run under the log and hooked to the jinker. When the horses pulled forward the pole came down and lifted the butt of the log off the ground. The top trailed. Big logs measuring a thousand feet could be pulled in with three horses. The word 'super' was seldom used in that strange old measurement of timber. A thousand super feet is equal to 2.3 cubic metres, the awkward modern measurement. Royalty due to the Forestry Commission was calculated on super feet Hoppus until the changeover to metrics. Hoppus was an eighteenth-century English surveyor who calculated an allowance for the usual pipe in big timber. One super foot Hoppus equalled 1.27 super feet.

Although one might think it was a leisurely life making one trip a week to the railhead with a load of timber behind a team of bullocks, the teamsters were often pressed for time. Many of the millers supplied orders under contracts that stipulated delivery dates. A late delivery was often rejected. A teamster who lost a miller a contract soon found himself out of a job.

In the floods of 1921 wagon loads of timber bogged all through the forest, especially on sandhills where there was no clay subsoil. One teamster hitched a triple-pulleyed block and tackle between the tongue of his bogged wagon and the butt of a big box tree. He hitched his bullocks to the rope and gave the order to pull. The tree lifted out of the ground but the wagon did not move. A teamster on the haul from Schwager's mill on Little Rocky Creek to Wee Waa sank into spewy subsoil until the top of his load was below the level of the ground. He began to unload, the mud slid in and buried the lot. He dug it all out when the weather fined up.

Apart from the difference in temperament, bullocks pulled differently to horses. They were slower, averaging about three kilometres an hour to a horse team's five. They were not as strong. Eighteen bullocks drew the same load as twelve horses. Bullocks seldom needed extra feeding. They worked off grass provided they had plenty of water. Sometimes the forage was scant enough especially in forests. A bullock's breakfast was cynically defined as a 'good drink and a good shit'. Teamsters with horses usually carried chaff and oats. A roll of hessian with one end tied beneath the back of the wagon was unrolled and stretched to a convenient tree to make a trough.

Bullocks apply their strength differently. A draught horse pushes with his shoulders against a stuffed leather collar fitted around his neck. He lifts his head as he pushes. The high-stepping feathery-legged Scottish Clydesdales were the favourite breed in Australia. A bullock lowered his head and pushed the base of his neck against a wooden yoke held in place by an iron bow fitted round his neck and shaped so that it did not clamp his windpipe. The harder he pushed the more he lowered his head like a footballer in a scrum. The bullocks were yoked in pairs so that it was essential to match them in height and weight. Jersey crossbreds were favoured. They were livelier than pure beef breeds and did not overfatten when turned out for a spell.

The wood used to make the yokes had to be light and strong. River Oak was good. Phil Schneider, a teamster carting to Narrabri in the 1880s, was famed for the yokes he carved from White Tea-tree (*Melaleuca glomerata*) that grows in patches on the banks of the Barwon.

Mares worked with geldings in a horse team. Clydesdale stallions are tractable and can be worked alone. In a team mares on heat would distract them, and geldings might anger them as rivals. Cows never worked with bullocks. Castration of any male animal delays the ossification of the epiphyses, the cartilage at the end of bones that allows for growth. So castrates grow taller. This growth is especially accentuated in barrows and bullocks. A bullock is not usually heavier than a bull but it is always much taller than a bull or a cow.

It is much quicker to yoke up a team of bullocks than harness a team of horses even though more animals have to be handled. Bullocks are guided by voice not by reins. Each bullock learns his name and the orders to stop, go, turn right, turn left, back. A teamster who yoked up fourteen hides put his heaviest and strongest pair at the tongue of the wagon. They were known as the 'polers'. They turned the wagon and absorbed any side to side swinging of the tongue as the big wooden iron-shod wheels lurched over bumps. The 'pinners' or 'clampers' worked in front of them, named from the pin in the tongue to which the chains were hooked. Then came the pair known as 'the head of the pin', then the 'body bullocks', two pairs of them if fourteen were yoked. The front pairs were known as 'behind the leaders' and the 'leaders', the most experienced and most intelligent of the team.

When the teamster was ready to move, he brought his bullocks to attention, 'stood them up', with a crack of his long whip. The whip was his conductor's baton. It emphasised every order. He cracked it, he waved it with right hand or left hand, he reversed it and prodded a bullock into line with the butt. Sometimes he lost his temper and belted a lazy bullock with the handle or cut strips out of his hide with the lash. Most teamsters were gentle men and their teams worked willingly. But the long whip was their badge. Any old teamster tells one how long he 'drug the whip'. In the late 1970s at least ten teams still worked in New South Wales snigging coastal logs to sawmills, four of them in the Wollombi-Brunkerville area just west of Newcastle.

The teamster gave his orders in an easy singing voice. It was tiring to shout. So his bullocks had to have names that would carry down the line: Spanker, Cherry, Plum, Bonny, Nob, Darky, Boxer, Star, Trimmer, Dart, Bright, Rattler, Smoky, Saint – names were repeated over and over among the teams. The order to move forward was 'Gee!' and the nearside leader was always spoken to first. So after the first whip crack when the bullocks were listening the teamster would call 'Gee-e-e Spanker!' The team would then move but they all liked to be talked to so he would run all the way down the pairs: 'Cherry! Gee Plum! Gee Bonny! Gee Nob! Darky!' And when Smoky and Saint, the polers, were called, if the team was not moving briskly, he might add with a couple of whip cracks, 'Gee! You lazy buggers! Gee!'

'Stop!' could be simply 'Woo!' but more often it was extended into a musical call: 'Hey whop, hey erhey!' The order to back was 'Woo back!' and since bullocks do not like stepping backwards it was said assertively. Sometimes an unwilling bullock was tapped on the nose with the butt of the whip. Since the teamster always directed from the near side, the order to turn left was 'Come here!' usually slurred into 'Wee!' or 'Year!' and the order was directed to the leader on the opposite side, then repeated down the line. The order to turn right was 'Gee back!' directed to the nearside leader. 'Wooback!' was usually thrown in somewhere to show a backward movement. The language was a pidgin English which the bullocks thoroughly understood. And, as in New Guinea pidgin, degrees were defined by repetition. If the teamster called to his nearside leader, 'Geeback Spanker! Wooback! Geeback! Geeback! Geeback!' Spanker and Cherry would turn a little farther right at each 'Geeback!' until they headed back down the line. If Cherry looked sulky through inattention, the teamster would name him at the end of the call. Then the next pair were directed, and the next. Like a good conjuror the teamster kept up his patter. If, as

Spanker and Cherry were walking back down the line, he called 'Wee Cherry! Wooback! Year!' they would turn left and head away at right angles. An inexperienced teamster with an inexperienced team could get into a frightening tangle on a difficult turn.

The teamster usually had an offsider who walked or rode on the off-side. It was his job to speak to a bullock who was flagging or out of line, and to apply the crude brakes when going downhill. A team overrun by a loaded wagon was a hideous sight. On trips through sticky wet black soil it was also the offsider's job to poke the mud from the wheels. Scrapers kept the tyres free but a tonne or more of mud could soon collect between the spokes.

At river crossings, on boggy stretches, the teamsters helped each other through. A wing of horses (the offside or nearside line) could be quickly unclipped and hitched to another team to make a line three abreast. The bullock-drivers usually double-banked with two teams to a wagon. Narrabri Creek, an anabranch of the river, troubled a dozen teamsters carting out of the forest for years. Only the river was bridged. Wagons often capsized at a twisting difficult crossing at Wee Waa.

Teamsters congregated like modern truck drivers at regular camping grounds on good water. At Lucky Flat the teams watered from the unexpected shallow well. Four bullocks hauled a big canvas bucket by a rope running over a single pulley. An attendant tipped the water into long wooden troughs. At Pine Ridge on the Liverpool Plains, where Ben Singleton moved briefly, up to a dozen teamsters at a time sat out wet spells till the plains dried. They drank, they sang, they danced, they told tall stories, they matched their horses four or five at a time in 'scratch pulling' matches. Good horses had muscles torn or legs broken when they lost the tug-of-war and were dragged backwards.

They camped at waterholes in the forest where there is now no sign of water, or road, or clearing. The litter of broken yokes burnt in bush fires. They camped on the Castlereagh where William Field had a hotel and store on the Nandi flats out of Coonabarabran. They bought rum in nine-litre flagons and drank it out of tin mugs. They watered it down with cool water from porous canvas bags swung under the wagons.

The Australian waterbag was shaped like a small Gladstone bag with a screw-topped china pourer stitched into one end. They cooled by evaporation and cooled excellently but were dangerous if relied on as water carriers. Mitchell experimented with canvas waterbags when looking for a route from Sydney to the Gulf of Carpentaria in 1846. He sealed empty flour bags with mutton fat but did not persist with them.

Harry Hall whose father built a wineshop at Cuttabri after the Trindall's Beehive Hotel was burnt down in 1900 himself later held the
licence till he sold it in 1974. When the teams camped at Cuttabri he
remembered the Brigalow ringing with up to three hundred bullock
bells.

The best bells did not jangle unmelodiously. They rang with a clear
tone that carried a long way. Most of them were made by blacksmiths
from the good steel in wornout pit saw blades or crosscut saw blades.
Good bells were made at Condamine in Queensland by Samuel Jones,
an English-born blacksmith. He impressed his name on the tongues.
The best of all the bells were later made in the 1880s and 1890s at North
Wagga in New South Wales by August Menneke. When the steel was
shaped and glowing dull red, he wiped it over with a wool pad coated
with sieved sand and brass filings. The patchy orange glaze not only
made the bells look good, it gave them a sweet high-pitched tone.

When the teamster rode out to muster his team in the morning he
whistled up his Australian Cattle Dog, a breed usually known as
Queensland Blue Heeler. Too often he named his dog Zam-Buk, a
contemporary ointment famed as a good healer. At least one teamster
called his dog Time, as the best of all healers. They are good-looking
dogs and intelligent with black pricked ears, a few patches of tan about
the head and legs, and a washy blue speckled coat. They work
silently – barking dogs aggravate cattle – and can both muster and
hold. They enforce their authority by a quick hard bite on the heel. A
naughty horse who broke from the mob of free horses while the
teamster was catching another seldom risked breaking away again. A
cunning bullock who hid behind a big tree and turned like a clock hand
to keep out of sight of the searching teamster was glad to gallop into the
open when the dog found him.

The progenitors of the Australian Cattle Dog were bred at
Muswellbrook in the Hunter Valley by Thomas Hall in 1840 to replace
the ungainly, black, bob-tailed Smithfield dogs that made wild cattle
wilder. They barked, they were too slow, and when they got the opportunity they leapt for the nose to bite like a Welsh Corgi. Hall imported
a pair of short-coated, blue-speckled Highland Collies from Scotland.
The flecked coat was repeated in their eyes where white streaks in the
pupils designated them wall-eyed. They were fast intelligent dogs but
barked and headed so Hall crossed their progeny with selected Dingoes
that whine and howl but seldom bark and that bite instinctively at the
heel after centuries of grabbing kangaroos by the butt of the tail.

Hall bred good Dingo-Collie crosses for thirty years. After he died two Sydney brothers, Jack and Harry Bagust, fixed the modern breed. They crossed the best of Hall's dogs with Dalmations – bred as car-riage guard dogs – to introduce their guarding qualities. The crosses were not good musterers so another cross was made with a black-and-tan Kelpie, a sheep dog. The brothers 'bred a lot and drowned a lot' and by 1890 the type bred true. Queensland cattlemen bred so many they claimed the breed as their own. Despite their qualities they are not pleasant dogs to keep at a homestead. They guard too fiercely. No guest is welcome.

Some teamsters proudly matched their teams. Jack Cutler who carted wool through Baradine had twenty-four black bullocks. One man had a Red Wing brand wagon, a ginger horse, a ginger dog and twenty-four red Devon bullocks. Ray Hellyer, carting sawn timber to Coonabarabran after the rail came through, drove a team of Suffolk Punches, smaller and stockier than Clydesdales and not often worked in Australia. Henry Dangar was first to import them.

Throughout the country towns coachbuilders and wheelwrights, black-smiths, farriers, painters, saddlers shod and harnessed the horses and kept the vehicles repaired. Sometimes all these craftsmen worked together in one business. Thos Rampling in Narrabri in 1884 was 'prepared to turn out
    Coaches
        Buggies
            Waggonettes
                Spring Carts   on the
    shortest possible notice and upon the
        MOST REASONABLE TERMS'.
Later Lock and Ritter set up as coachbuilders and extended into modern times making good truck bodies. There were Sheridan, and later Perrin and Firth, in Coonamble, Fagan in Walgett and Gardiners in Coonabarabran. Jack Howlett, a fine modern saddler in Baradine, owned a beautiful sulky made by Gardiners that was about eighty-five years old in 1979. At that time there were still a few men at work who had trained as coach painters. They could trace the traditional white lines on the wheels of sulkies.

Some unusual timbers were sought for special jobs: Native Willow (*Acacia salicina*) for shafts, Rough-barked Apple for framework (though the magnificent Tasmanian Blackwood was acknowledged superior), and the coastal Spotted Gum (*Eucalyptus maculata*) for spokes, though local coachbuilders used ironbark which was as strong but very heavy.

The Gruie Tree (*Owenia acidula*) made long-lasting naves, the wooden hubs the spokes fitted into.

Wheels were set true or retyred on tyring plates, circular dished plates of cast iron about 1.8 metres in diameter and thirty-eight millimetres thick. Few are still in existence. They were always expensive and only the bigger coachbuilders used them. The iron tyres were fitted to the wooden felloes while nearly white hot and as they cooled they shrank on firmly. The wheels were dished out slightly to give them clearance and like car wheels were not reversible.

The blacksmith used an astonishing number of tongs – up to thirty that he made himself – to hold metals of different shapes and sizes. His bellows-boy pumped the three-metre handle on the double-acting bellows on the furnace with a fast upstroke and a slow downstroke. The blacksmith used a swage block for bending metal, a heavy cast block with varying grooves on the outside and holes of all shapes and sizes moulded through it. He rolled it about the floor until he found a hole that fitted what he wanted to bend. He used a hammer and a blade called a hardy for cutting rod. It had a square shank that fitted a square hole in his anvil.

His anvil might have had

PETER WRIGHT

PATENT

ENGLAND

on it, the best of all anvils. Even if he used it for forty years the hard skin on top would take no mark. Besides, he never risked scoring it by working cold metal. The anvils were forged of low carbon steel, packed in insulating boxes, covered with granulated carbon and heated to 900 degrees Centigrade in a furnace. The carbon melted into the molten tops of the anvils. Then they were slid from the furnace through a quenching spray of water.

A surprising number of anvils are still made for sale to Asian countries. Modern anvils are cast of higher carbon steel then flame hardened. Metallurgists think that method as good as the old. The few blacksmiths still at work in Australia do not agree. 'They're as soft as butter. Go to shape a bit of metal on one, all you'll shape is your bloody anvil.'

Charlie Fester, a blacksmith and farrier well-remembered at Baradine, had lost his left arm at the elbow but with a hook to replace it he shod the massive hooves of Clydesdales. Ned Edwards of Baradine went to Coonabarabran as a youth to learn the trade from Jack Mc-Carty, an inventive blacksmith but a heavy drinker. Many nights he began to rave. Then Mrs McCarty ran to a neighbour for help and young Ned, the neighbour and Mrs McCarty held the maddened man in bed. Old Dave Peebles continued to run the blacksmith's and farrier's shop at Ayrlands while his son Dave ran the hotel. Mark Byatt of Narrabri extended his smithy into a modern engineering works and because he knew metals and was proud of his work he continued to be successful. Jack Boyle, a descendant of the hard riding men on Bohena, was the last farrier in Narrabri. I have ridden a horse thirty-five kilometres in a morning to his wooden shed at the end of the town and home again in the afternoon.

The forest gave opportunity to men with no capital for an independent life as timbergetters and sleeper cutters. The rabbit industry offered life without a boss to thousands, the forest to a few hundred. As the extending railways needed more and more sleepers, axemen set up camp by a creek in the ironbark forest. Some built houses for a wife and family and lived in the one place for fifteen years. When the near timber cut out, they rode bicycles to work.

A few worked with mates to 'give them a back down on the saw'. Most of them were so independent they worked alone and rigged a 'chinaman' or 'dummy' at the other end of the two-man crosscut saw. A flexible stick was driven into the ground and one end of the saw tied to it. In later years bands were cut from discarded rubber tyre tubes as straps to improve the action of the dummy.

The first sleeper cutters chopped the big ironbarks down with axes. So did the first fellers of pine. And, since it was hard work and bending made it harder, they chopped the trees off at a convenient height. The wastage in the stumps was huge and unthought of. Then the untidy butt was sawn off and the log was measured into eight foot lengths. The length of sleepers in New South Wales was always eight feet. The width and thickness varied but was usually nine inches by five inches. Metric sleepers are measured in millimetres, 2,440 x 230 x 130. Two classes of sleepers were bought: square backs and round backs. A square back had to be all solid heart wood. A round back could have 'a bit of wane on it' – one end might run out into sapwood or even lack a few centimetres on each corner.

The sleeper cutter sawed the trunk into lengths until it was no longer big enough for sleepers. There was still much good timber left but he had no sale for it. He cut it off to rot.

He barked each length by bruising a line along one side with the back of his axe, rolling the log with a cant hook and bruising another

line. He swung the axe heavily and if the season was good and the
timber was sappy, the black heavy bark lifted off even a big log after he
bruised four or five lines. The timber beneath is pinkish white, damp
and pimply. A newly barked log looks like a woman stepping out of a
hot bath into cold air, exposed, goosefleshed and a little surprised. In a
dry time, when the trees are not growing, barking is a hard job. It
seems to be glued on. There is little sapwood on good ironbark,
perhaps twenty millimetres on a log ninety centimetres in diameter.
Some of the old ironbarks yielded sleepers from the limbs. Tom
Keegan of Baradine cut fifty-two sleepers from one tree, about 6.6
cubic metres of sleepers, and at least half of it would have been wasted
in the slabs too small for sleepers. There is no such wastage in modern
times. Trimmed sleeper offcuts are eagerly bought by graziers for yard
building. The sleeper cutter sells them under a fictitious name and gets
a good tax-free addition to his income.

The sleeper cutter often lit a kerosene lantern and sawed into the
night. He liked to have a few lengths barked and ready for boarding-
out and billeting in the morning. A billet is a piece with a sleeper in it
split off the main log. The board is his marker. It is a thin slab the size
of a sleeper section. He studied the grain in the small end of a log, applied his board so the longer sides ran with the grain and pencilled
round it. Then he took his chalked line, usually kept in a tobacco
tin full of whiting, stretched it along the log and with one smart flick
marked the line of his first cut. If he decided the log was a splitter, and
many of the big ironbarks split well, he drove steel wedges into the
bottom corners of his pencilled shape and, as the billet began to lift, he
rolled the log with a cant hook and drove in wedges progressively
along the chalked line. He always worked towards the big end to give
room for error. He used wedges of various sizes, sometimes two together for greater leverage. One man who drove a thick wedge into a
tight log reached down inside the crack to retrieve a small wedge. The
big wedge popped, the split closed and trapped his hand. No one came.
When his body was found weeks later the deep marks were still in the
sand where he had scrabbled with his feet to try to drag in his axe. The
blade lay no more than seven centimetres from the farthest stretch of
his toes.

There were no sledgehammers for the early sleeper cutters to drive
wedges. They made their own malls of Gunnedah Ironbark, an occasional cross between Narrow-leaf Ironbark and a box, probably Yellow
Box. The timber has the hardness and weight of ironbark and the
round grain of box. It will not split. Few are found. Logs of it were

used sparingly and treasured for years. When fitted with a steel rim the mall face bulged over it and held it tight. As the mall wore the rim slipped down. They were superior to modern sledgehammers. The tops of the wedges did not mushroom under their impact.

If the grain was not true enough for wedge splitting, the sleeper cutter 'grooved in' and 'blocked out'. If he made a mistake and felled a tree with an exaggerated circular twist in the grain he abandoned it. Such trees could not be handled till the modern power saw was invented. Both grooving in and blocking out were done with a squaring axe, a long-bladed implement with an offset homemade handle and untidy wedges driven into the eye at different angles. It looked an awkward tool. But each sleeper cutter spent hours testing and setting it. If he was expert in its use, 'you could slide your bare bum down one of his sleepers and never get a splinter'. The inexpert often had to tidy up with the adze, a mattock-shaped axe that he swung between his straddled legs.

One side of the squaring axe was flat to cut a true face, the other bevelled to push the sliced-off chips away. The handle was offset so the sleeper cutter did not bark his knuckles on the billet. Left-handed axemen and right-handed axemen set it to opposite sides. Hard close-grained Motherumbah (*Acacia cheelii*) or Needle Bush (*A. rigens*) made favourite handles. The carved handle was boiled then bent to the desired set and pegged till it cooled. Alf Waterfield of Baradine, usually known as Whiskers, is remembered for the long-lasting handles he made. He told no one what timber he made them of.

Once the handle had the correct sideways set, it had to be adjusted with several wedges to suit the sleeper cutter's height so that the axe hit the billet squarely on the full edge. He tested the point of balance on a forefinger. He lifted the axe and let it fall under its own weight and tapped the wedges till the cut was perfect.

A sleeper cutter kept two squaring axes: a special one for the finishing work and another for grooving out. But although any sleeper cutter would say he used his second axe for cutting a groove, he never called it a grooving axe. Applied to the tool the word lost its meaning. He called it a 'groving axe' or a 'gruvving axe'. With it, in a log that would not split naturally, he cut a groove fifteen centimetres deep along the chalk line. When he first came into the district, Alf Waterfield astonished the local cutters by lifting his squaring axe above his head and cutting with full force. It was usual to make a less confident half swing along the chalked line. Then the sleeper cutter finished splitting off the billet with mall and wedges, chocked it off the ground and squared the other side of the sleeper by blocking-in. He stood on top of the billet and used his felling axe to chop V-shaped notches into a second chalk line. He called the notches 'windows' and according to the toughness of the log he made them forty to eighty centimetres apart. Then he split off each block with his squaring axe. The squaring axe alone was usually sufficient to shape the other two sides.

Sleeper cutters soon found they could fell trees with the crosscut saw and thus save the time taken to square off the V-shaped end on a chopped butt. They made a first cut into the centre of the tree called a 'belly scarf' from the side they judged the tree would fall. They re-adjusted their dummies on the other side of the tree and sawed straight through in a horizontal plane about seventeen centimetres above the belly scarf which helped direct the fall and cushion it so the log did not split. The belly scarf also helped prevent a frightening 'whip back' when a tall evenly balanced tree jumped backwards off its stump and fell anywhere.

Some men cut extraordinary numbers of sleepers with a squaring axe. Oddle Edwards cut twenty-seven in one day on Wangen. His younger brother, Jim, averaged one hundred and fifteen a week for three weeks running. But they were the numbers boasted of, not the numbers averaged, and it was only possible when the sleeper cutter found a good big stand of free splitting timber. Usually he spent as long a time looking for timber as he did cutting. Bert Ruttley who classed himself as a good average cutter filled two drays a week for several years. A dray held sixteen. Loaded drays on the weekly trip to the railway depots could be heard coming ten kilometres away as they jolted in and out of the potholed tracks. The jarring shafts galled the horses. One man could bring in up to four drays at a time. He would drive two horses in the leading dray and hitch another on behind so he had spare horses to pull a bogged dray out of a sand monkey. The horses in the other drays, with promise of a good feed of chaff and oats at the end of the trip, willingly followed the first.

Sleeper cutters insist that sleepers cut with the squaring axe were superior because the axe closed the pores in the timber and protected it. The bruising shut of cut pores could have had only a temporary effect. Anyway the cells of timber run longitudinally. The early sleepers were superior because they were cut from selected trees. Nowadays any tree big enough is cut.

The food these men worked so hard on was rough enough. Jack Thompson and Jim Pullen who cut together often argued their preferences. Jim was a Salvation Army man and a slow talker. 'A ma-a-n when he's wo-o-rkin' needs plen-n-ty of sweet things such as bre-a-a-ad and ja-a-m and bre-a-a-ad and ho-n-n-ey.' His old mate, Jack, who had heard it often would stamp his feet till the dust flew. 'A man do not! A man when he's workin' needs somethin' substantial such as bread and fat.'

'I've eaten a lot of bread and dripping in my day,' old Ned Edwards of Baradine told me. 'There was never much meat about. The squatters would not sell it. We didn't like kangaroo and wild goat was awful. They ate too many gum leaves, and all you could taste was eucalyptus.' Ned was in his late eighties when I spoke to him in 1974. He boasted he had won sixty-four trophies at bowls, he had thirty-three grandchildren, and forty-four great-grandchildren, 'and a lot more to come yet, by Jesus!' School had always been too far away and he never learnt to write much but he taught himself to read just as his father had done. He had that brief spell of blacksmithing with Jack McCarty, he cut sleepers and bridge timber, he was a rouseabout in woolsheds and carried his swag between sheds, he was a shire maintenance man pugging the road between Baradine and Coonabarabran with a horse and tip dray. For many years he was head of the road gang in the Forestry Commission and with twenty-two men under him cleared and graded the first roads through the forest. They all pedalled out on bicycles early on Monday mornings with a week's supply of food in haversacks on their backs. He built Ned Edwards Bridge of round ironbark in the 1940s. The bridge is marked on Forestry Commission maps on Sixteen Foot Road in Pilliga East State Forest. The workmanship is outstanding. So is the quality of the timber. Almost forty years later the bridge was still as sound as when it was built.

Ned Edwards worked for several months on a fencing contract with Donald Magann, his cousin, who was trying to earn some money to improve the block of Baradine he had taken up. Donald's mother had been a housemaid for Mrs Fetherstonhaugh. He went to school till he was eleven, a common leaving age. Their boss on the fencing job was an uncle, Jack Munns, who had bought out several selectors on Goorianawa. They worked from daylight to dark then returned to their camp to cook the evening meal and enough food for the next day.

'He was a hard man' said Ned. Donald Magann was present that morning. He also was nearing eighty-seven years old. 'The only way we could get a bit of a rest was by suggesting a game of mumble peg,' said Donald. 'He loved that game and would play for hours.' Both old men got out their pocket-knives and knelt on the verandah to show me how the game was played.

Mumble peg was played on sand or loose soil with two-bladed pocket knives. The longer pointed blade was opened fully, the shorter round-ended blade, usually known as the castrating blade, was opened at right angles. The first player pushed the short blade into the soil so that the knife stood up with the handle and long blade in a horizontal line. Then he flicked the handle and spun the knife into the air. He scored points according to how the knife landed: one hundred if the long blade speared into the ground, fifty if the short blade speared in and the knife returned to the starting position. He scored twenty if the knife stood upright on its handle, fifteen if it stood on both blades, ten if it fell on its back with the short blade poking in the air, five if supported by the handle and short blade. If it fell flat he scored nothing. The players flicked in turn and kept score.

They had meat on that job. Each night Donald cooked the damper in one camp oven, Ned cooked the rest of the meal in another. 'We had meat, potato, pumpkin and jam' said Ned. 'No jam,' said Donald, 'No bloody fear! Jam was too dear.' 'Honey!' said Ned remembering, 'a sixty pound tin of honey. Or Cockies' Joy, we used to go for that'. Golden syrup, the cockies' joy, was packed in the same bronze tin until the 1970s. It was the one treat the battling selector permitted himself.

The early camp ovens, the universal cooking utensil for both hearth and camp fire, show brilliant technique in casting and the making of metals. The walls are only three millimetres thick. It is difficult to get iron to fill such narrow moulds even when the freezing point is lowered by the addition of phosphorous. Metallurgy is now a science not a craft and some of the old arts have been lost. Modern metallurgists do not know how the old camp ovens were poured. Like anvils, they are still made but the walls are now six millimetres thick. The modern ovens burn everything the unfortunate cook puts in them.

The old camp ovens cooked deliciously but the bush worker's meals were monotonous. The evening meal usually cooked while he was at work. In the early morning he put potatoes, pumpkin, salt meat and a little water in his camp oven, covered it with the well-fitting lid, then dug a hole and threw in about four centimetres of hot coals. He settled the camp oven on to them and shovelled in more coals till they covered the lid. When he returned at night it was ready. All he had to do was make his damper. On a sheet of bark or the blade of a shovel he kneaded flour, salt, water and a pinch each of cream of tartar and baking soda. He dusted another camp oven with flour, put it on a low fire till the flour began to brown, then added his damper. It cooked in half an hour. The early loaves of ground wheat the convict stockmen cooked in ashes were known as Johnny cakes. Sometimes a few currants were added as a treat. They were a superior food to the dampers made of white flour.

Diet had not improved in a hundred years. Like the squatters and ticket-of-leave stockmen, unmarried bush workers up to the 1930s were always on the edge of scurvy. They ate quandongs and Five Corners and geebungs when they came across them. When they broke out in sores they cooked and ate the ascorbic pigweed or the imported annual stinging nettles that grew near old rabbit burrows. Rarely they shot wild ducks and trapped rat kangaroos to eat. Most bush food was scornfully rejected as 'blackfellows' tucker'.

Billy Reed lived off the land and lived well. He was black.

> 'When passing through the farms
> He always dodged the houses
> For he never wore any boots
> And very seldom trousers'

wrote Syd Ruttley who knew him. Billy Reed cut sleepers in the nude. Everyone who knew him liked him and he is still spoken of with respect. A forest road through old Coghill is named after him.

Sleeper cutting was not his chief occupation. He began his working life 'nippering' for his father who was fencing on Coghill in its last days. Nippering was the usual introduction to work. Children about seven years old lit the fire, boiled the billy for the men, and carted water from the creeks. Billy Reed worked for Trindalls for forty years, mostly tailing the thousand head of cattle that roamed the forest. He cut sleepers when the cattle were settled or he shot Dingoes for the scalp money. Bert Ruttley sometimes camped out with him when Bert was a child. Billy would lie down overlooking a waterhole with his rifle beside him. Bert was told to be still and quiet. Billy seemed to go to sleep. But he was listening to the birds. He said the Noisy Miners told him what was coming to water. Sometimes when the birds called out and Billy made no move Bert feared he had gone to sleep. 'Hey, Billy!' he would whisper, 'Dingo?' 'Goanna' Billy would reply. And shortly a goanna slithered half his length into the water. 'Billy! Billy?' he would whisper again. 'Kangaroo!' And minutes later a big kangaroo hopped down warily. But sometimes Billy reached for his rifle as soon as the birds called, and it was cocked ready when the Dingo came to drink.

One day Trindall's horses that Billy rode turned up at the homestead on Brigalow Creek. One of them had a saddle on, always an ominous sign. A search party rode out but did not find him so Billy's brother was brought from Wee Waa to back track the horses. They found him dead in his camp, probably from pneumonia. His dogs, half-bred Dingoes, had eaten most of him. They buried what was left near Coghill Creek and squared a huge ironbark post to mark the grave.

Mag Morrissey, the last owner of Gibbican, used to cut a few sleepers. She is remembered by Mags Road in Baradine State Forest. She trapped Dingoes and ran a few cattle, too, but the scrub had mostly overcome all of Gibbican by the 1940s and 1950s when she was there. Most of her income came from her fowls. Each week she drove a sulky into Baradine with boxes of eggs and crates of cockerels to sell. Off and on, Joe Curran, a sleeper cutter, lived with her. In the absurd moral state of the community, he met disapproval with bravado. 'Meet the missis,' he'd say, 'Miss Morrissey!'

She met convention in the show ring by riding sidesaddle and regularly won the Ladies' High Jump at local shows. Women jumping sidesaddle at the Sydney Royal in the early 1900s cleared up to 1.8 metres despite their dangerous and unbalanced position on the horse.

She lived in a small rough house with a short wide iron chimney at one end of the main room. The chimney was backed on the outside by stones cemented together. Keith Pickette who owned a couple of thousand hectares of old Upper Cumble in the 1970s remembered having a meal with her. She cooked him a big steak. At the end of the meal she washed up in a tin dish on the end of the table, then turned and with a neat twist of her wrists flung the water up and out the top of the chimney.

Bert Ruttley cut a lot of wooden stock troughs in the years after World War I. The various species of box with tough circular grain made the best troughs but it was difficult to find trees tall enough and straight enough. He cut troughs eleven metres long out of ironbark. Trees were selected with a pipe to provide a beginning for the work of hollowing. He split off about one third of the log with squaring axe and wedges then hollowed out the big section with a reversed squaring axe. The bevelled edge made scooping cuts with no risk of splitting. A ridge was always left in the bottom of the trough. He took it out with an adze. Boards were tacked on both open ends with bagging as a gasket and sealed with clay or tar. Water kept cool in wooden troughs.

Bert lived in the forest for much of his life. In 1914 when he was sixteen he roofed his hut with one of the last bark roofs. The several species of stringybark yielded the best bark but in the forest it was available only as Red Stringybark (*Eucalyptus macrorhyncha*) on the slopes of the Warrumbungles. Box bark was next choice. All species provide thin hard bark. A frill was cut round the base of the tree, then with a long-handled adze another frill was cut about 2.4 metres higher. A longitudinal split was made in the bark and it was prised off with the sharpened handle of the adze.

When the sheet of bark was lifted off it immediately rolled up. Two men straightened it and held it to soften over a low fire. Then they spread it flat and weighted it to dry. The overlapped sheets were held on the roof by crossed saplings known as 'outriggers' or 'over purlins' lashed to the purlins. Bert lashed his with wire. On earlier roofs they were lashed with greenhide. Sometimes they were pegged down with wooden pegs. Ironbark pegs, round or square, dried slowly over a fire were almost as long lasting as nails.

The taking of bark was wasteful. A huge tree was destroyed for a couple of metres of bark. Aborigines used bark extensively for canoes, shields and dishes but they left wide strips between each cut. River Red Gums that yielded two canoes over a hundred years ago are still alive on the banks of the Barwon.

The more substantial early houses were covered with shingles, wooden tiles split from hard straight-grained timbers such as ironbark, Brigalow or oak. A tool called a froe was used in shingle splitting. It was a blade about twenty centimetres long with a handle inserted at right angles. The rather blunt blade was driven into the block of wood with a mallet. A quick twist of the handle extended the split and levered the shingle off. They were placed on like overlapping scales and gave a cover of three shingles at every point.

Many a shingled roof was eventually covered with galvanised corrugated iron, that marvellous 1847 patent of Morewood and Rogers at their Gospel Oak factory near Birmingham in England. 'G anchor O' each sheet was branded. Australian newspapers advertised it in the 1850s. By 1855 the factory was curving the ends of sheets and advertising it to cover verandahs, 'no rafters or under ceiling required'. The lovely Australian verandah was an adaptation of architecture in India where the inhabitants had had long experience of a hot climate.

In 1857 John Lysaght in Bristol somehow got round the patent laws and also began turning out galvanised corrugated iron. His brand was the Orb, 'a symbol of the industrial expansion of the Mid-Victorian Empire'. Australia became his biggest customer.

It is an excellent roof covering especially in the dry inland of Australia where it never rusts. It weathers to an unobtrusive grey and fits the landscape. But too many landowners in order to make it look a more expensive covering, paint it red or blue or silver, and the house stands out conspicuously like something foreign dropped there.

As well as Dingo scalps and wallaby scalps for the bounty, scrub dwellers marketed kangaroo skins for extra income. They stretched them on the ground to dry with little hard pegs of Yarran. Men and women tanned fresh kangaroo skins and stitched them together as blankets and rugs. A kangaroo skin rug was a good thing to have across one's knees coming back late by sulky from a dance on a winter's night.

Gordon Turner, a retired English industrial chemist who established Centralcure at Gunnedah in 1972 to process cattle hides from the local abattoirs, considered kangaroo skins one of the best of all leathers. His interest in tanning was so intense I felt he estimated the worth of my hide as he shook my hand. There is much wastage in kangaroo skins – both bucks and does get severely scratched when fighting – but the leather is light and strong and makes ideal uppers for shoes. However, prejudice and the law prevented the handling of kangaroo skins.

Ned Edwards in his youth chased Brush-tailed Rock Wallabies round Chalk Mountain out of Bugaldie to catch enough for a rug. Their tails made good covers for whip handles. The silver-grey fur of Brush-tailed Possums made more luxurious rugs. Platypus rugs were rarer. The few left in good order were valuable indeed by the 1970s. The soft dense-furred skins of Water Rats made the best rugs of all. If there are other pelts equal to Water Rat, none are superior.

Mrs Bert Buttley made slippers for her children out of rabbit skins. She tapped Rough-barked Apples and drew off kino for her tanning mixture. Her family did not remember any more of her method but her daughter, Mary Hitchen, remembered how exceptionally soft and warm the slippers were.

Tanning is a strange craft. It is a complex process by which fragile and perishable collagen is transformed by the absorption of tannin into tough permanent leather. The home tanners understood none of the chemistry yet they varied their formulas for different skins as though they understood it all. Old Whiskers Waterfield who cut smooth sleepers and made secret axe handles also had a secret tanning mixture. He, too, used the kino of Rough-barked Apples. Men riding in the forest found jam tins tied as collecting cups at the base of V-shaped cuts made through the bark into the cambium layer. A tobacco pouch he made out of the skin of an old man goanna in the 1920s was still in use in the 1970s. Reptile skins are difficult to tan yet after nearly fifty years the skin was as supple as basil and had not dropped a scale.

The thorough breaking of a hide while it is still wet from the tan-liquor has much to do with its softness. The long fibres have to be shortened. Eskimo and Indian women chewed skins for days. Australians worked the hides vigorously over a sharp-edged board or old file with the edge ground half round.

In forest and in town outside work at night was done by the light of the kerosene hurricane lantern until well into the twentieth century and many are still used. These portable lights with adjustable wicks were misnamed. A strong gust of wind usually left one disconcertingly in the dark. The kerosene to burn in them became available in Australia in 1858 and it quickly became a universal fluid. Four drops on a teaspoonful of sugar were given for a cold. It was a cheap and ineffective cure. The many cough mixtures available from a modern pharmacist are expensive and ineffective. It was mixed with mutton fat or glycerine and rubbed on chapped hands and was smelly and effective. It was poured into the sore red eyes of cattle and sheep with contagious pink-eye and was a considerable irritant. It was mixed with Stockholm tar and painted on cracks in horses' hooves which can no more be mended by external applications than a cracked boot. It was emulsified with soap to kill aphides in the garden. It was rubbed into children's hair to kill lice. It polished furniture. In substantial homes it filled some beautiful glass-chimneyed lamps.

Before kerosene the rough slush lamps lit camps and country houses and many used them for inside lighting until the 1890s. Old Mrs Merckenschlager of Baradine, born in 1882, clearly remembered her mother reading in bed by the smoky light. She dipped a rag in melted mutton fat as a wick, twisted it tightly and left it to set. Then she half-filled a jam tin with dirt – the wick would not burn any lower – inserted the wick and filled the tin with melted fat. In summer the fat went rancid and the smell of the burning lamp was powerful. Whale oil burnt more cleanly but it was expensive.

Those who could afford them used moulded candles, and later those who could not afford kerosene lamps continued to use candles. They were made six to twelve at a time in metal moulds. Candlewick was threaded through the mould and tied firmly in the centre then melted mutton fat was poured in, or the softer beef tallow with beeswax to harden it.

Acetylene generated by water dripped on carbide was used in bicycle lamps, buggy lights, car lights and houses. The stinking smell of phosphine in the wet grey residue of carbide pervaded everything near it. Some houses were lit by the dangerous Quirk system. A refined petrol called Shellite was forced under pressure from room to room through little copper pipes and burnt through mantled jets. This lighting was in several rooms of a house on a farm in the eastern section of old Baan Baa that my father bought in 1930. The jets were covered by too-ornate glass shades which I wish we had kept. We never dared use it. It seemed a certain way to burn the house down. We used Aladdin lamps that confined the flame from a wick behind an asbestos mantle. They burnt with a bright incandescent light till a careless adjustment of the wick or a breeze through a window caused the light to flare unnoticed. Then the mantle covered quickly with black carbon and one had to turn the wick low and wait ten minutes for it to burn clear.

By the 1940s most landholders generated their own electric power and they continued to do so until the extending electricity grid reached them in the 1950s and 1960s. Some big properties in far western New South Wales, some properties enclosed by the Pilliga forest, still generated their own electricity in 1979. It is unlikely the power lines will ever reach them.

Indian hawkers travelled the towns, the farms and the forest camps with rolls of cloth, made-up clothing and boots. Often they began their rounds on foot as 'bundle-basket' men with a wicker basket full of razors, knives, combs, needles and reels of cotton in one hand and a bundle of clothes tied in a white cloth on the head. After several years on foot Crean Box opened a store in Baradine. Most of them preferred the wandering life but progressed firstly to horse and cart then to covered wagonettes fitted with shelves and drawers. One day in 1908 as Gunga Sing travelled one of the tracks on Garrawilla his horses took fright as the first bot flies ever seen there buzzed about them. They bolted under an overhanging limb and swept the top off the wagonette.

Up to eight Indian hawkers camped regularly on the creek at Bugaldie. They bought fowls for a communal meal and knelt in prayer presenting the live fowls towards Mecca before they killed them. They cooked chapatis over the open fire in folding gridirons of fine wire mesh. Then all dipped into the same big pot of curried chicken.

An old woman named Humphries patrolled the district in horse and cart shooting wild horses for their fat and hair. Not as sinister but more mysterious, fortune-tellers set up dark tents hung with red and black curtains and read palms or stared at crystal balls. A procession of circuses came through on great loops out of one State into the next and came back several years later: Wirth's, Ashton's and Ridge's United States with Madam Ridge as ringmaster. She showed one night in the early 1900s at Underwood's mill on Rocky Creek in the heart of the forest. A hundred people turned up. Children who saw their first monkey that night remembered it all their lives.

Most entertainment involved participation. Sunday was not a restful day. Men rode thirty kilometres to a cricket match, played for six hours, drank for another two hours then rode home. Jack Underwood allowed none of his hands to play sport. He wanted full production at the mill on Monday. He also tacked up a notice 'All cigarettes must be rolled overnight'. Not all employers were as hard. Bugaldie, a village of several houses then as now, supported two hotels about two kilometres apart, The Cedars and The Duke of Wellington, and two cricket teams, Rosebuds and Bugaldie.

Tennis and football replaced much of the cricket in the 1920s. Each Sunday morning for years there was cockfighting on a vacant corner block in Baradine. The cocks fought with natural spurs. It was not as bloody a sport as modern cockfighting in Asian countries where lancets five centimetres long are strapped to each spur and sometimes another to the top of the head. Thus equipped the savage birds are as dangerous to handle as Taipans.

Dancing was the chief recreation. Jim Carr came from Yaminbah with his violin and his son Claude with his concertina or Alex Deans and George Harper from Coonabarabran. They rode for miles with their instruments slung round their necks. Each town had its favourite musicians. Sometimes there was a cornet player.

They played the old English square dances – the Albert, quadrille and the lancers – and round dances – waltzes and schottische – or the mazurka or Pride of Erin. The men wore dark trousers and stiff-fronted white shirts. The women wore long frocks and long sleeves. Short sleeves were never worn even by day. It was daring to show an ankle before the 1920s.

They danced in a little old barn at Bugaldie, or at the Ayrlands hotel. They danced at Yarrie Lake. Every Saturday after cricket they danced in a hall with a good pine floor the hopeful new settlers built on Upper Cumble. They danced on a sandstone floor at Rocky Glen and those who could not fit on the sandstone danced on couch grass. Wilf Watkins, fit from ringbarking on Garrawilla, danced all one night at

Rocky Glen and was still dancing at ten o'clock next morning. He wore out a new pair of shoes on the sandstone. He followed up the ringbarking with a team of fifteen men sucker bashing for three years. Where there were no floors they danced on the ground in the open air. They spent weeks preparing the site. Grass was chipped off and the ground was swept, watered and tramped until it was smooth and hard. The water was carted in square 450-litre black iron tanks on drays or sleds made out of forked branches. These common tanks doubled as shipping containers on the trip from England.

Dances usually followed race meetings. Two-day meetings were often held at Trindall's Beehive Hotel at Cuttabri and the Halls continued the meetings at their wineshop. It sometimes took the runners a week to get there led behind a sulky for two or three hundred kilometres. The prize money more than covered expenses. In 1884 the Beehive Handicap over one and a half miles was worth ten sovereigns. When the prickly pear came it grew thicker than the Brigalow and almost overcame the race track.

All the towns had regular horse races, most of them run formally to Australian Jockey Club rules. Fanny's Hotel on the Cooma Road out of Narrabri had footraces by night under gaslight. Around 1900 there were several hotels on that road and thirteen in the main street of Narrabri. Even little Wee Waa had five two-storied hotels. All of them offered accommodation and meals. When transport was slow landowners came to town infrequently and shopped for two or three days.

Many girls took their only chance of employment as hotel maids. They were not paid. They worked for food and clothes. Mrs Ethel Merckenschlager at the age of ninety-two told me she boarded at the hotel in Baradine while she went to school. Her father earned two and a half dollars a week as a bullock-driver for the Ryder brothers on Calga. Her board cost one dollar. So after nine months when she had learnt to read and write she took a job at the hotel.

When she married Max Merckenschlager they took up a block of heavy Belar scrub on Mosquito Creek south of Wee Waa. It was good country but they underestimated the difficulty of clearing Belar by hand. For years Ethel Merckenschlager bagged and watered her sand floors to keep them hard. They used home-made furniture and ate from tin plates. They saved newspapers for papering walls. Newspapers were pasted up with flour paste and painted over with stiff whitewash. Some women added blue for a change. Max Merckenschlager abandoned the farm after several years and went to work in a sawmill.

Mrs Ethel Purdy had more schooling than most of her age. Her father, Jack Treasure, was a sawmiller at Bugaldie and she went to school in Coonabarabran in a dowdy uniform of black shoes, black stockings, and dark long-sleeved calf-length dress. She proudly showed me her certificate from the University of Sydney for the Junior Public Examination held in Coonabarabran in June 1901 when she was fourteen. Five pupils sat. She was offered a job as governess, one of the few paying jobs open to girls. Her father would not hear of it. There was as much misguided pride in supporting daughters as in supporting wives.

Ethel Purdy had nine babies. 'We had no pills in those days' she told me with her old eyes twinkling, 'the women had to take pot luck and they always got potted'.

The elderly Cooper spinsters of Wittenbra in its last days supported themselves selling butter. All three brought it to Baradine in a horse and cart and sold it door to door.

Chinese market gardeners at Narrabri and Coonabarabran eventually replaced the travelling vegetable growers at Bugaldie. At Coonabarabran in the 1890s, the Chinese used a horse-driven device of their own making to lift water out of the Castlereagh. A wide endless belt of greased canvas with wooden slats nailed on at intervals ran under the water and up through a wooden channel. It looked crude but it worked.

Apart from the simple bucket, pulley, and horse-drawn rope for lifting water out of wells, horse works known as whims, whips or gins were widely used for drawing water. Originally the names might have specified different types of machinery but they were soon used indiscriminately. All the devices involved one or two horses circling at the end of a long pole. The action wound a rope on a wooden drum about three metres in diameter or simply lengthened and shortened a rope running over a swivelling pulley. In more elaborate set-ups the pole turned a big toothed cog that spun a smaller cog and turned a shaft running in a trench covered so the horse could walk over it. Other shafts and pulleys transferred the power where it was wanted. A whim on the government well on the stock route near Baradine was fitted with two 180-litre buckets, one coming up and one going down. They tipped automatically. A good whim on a good well could pump ten thousand litres an hour.

Mick O'Keefe, unusually tall for an Irishman, made storage tanks round Baradine to his own design. He erected a circle of pit-sawn ironbark slabs cross-braced together at the top and lined them with sheets of heavy gauge flat galvanised iron rivetted at the joins with big copper rivets, then soldered.

By 1910 windmills replaced the whims. Narrabri, as well as several other towns, became known as the Town of Windmills pumping from backyard wells. Each mill squeaked in a different key. Wells were forbidden when deep sewerage pipes were installed.

But for years in dry times battling settlers depended on hand bucketing of water from temporary shallow wells in the sanded creeks. Marcus Lubb, one of the sons of the Dutch family on Upper Cumble, watered a third of a hectare of garden through a hundred metres of wooden flumes sloping down from a scaffolding seven and a half metres high. He dropped a thirteen-litre bucket on a rope into the well, hauled it up, tipped it and dropped it again for hours. He tried using bigger buckets but the heavier lift slowed him down and he drew less water. During a drought on the plains in the 1920s he watered 300 head of Coonamble cattle sent on agistment. When the mob came in each evening he had two thousand litres of water ready in twenty-five metres of trough. The first fifty sucked it dry then the others pushed and bellowed while he hauled ten thousand litres more.

Between 1910 and 1925 thousands of cattle branded and unbranded, watched and unwatched, roamed the forest. They were not worth much but they were attractive to duffers operating between Narrabri, Coonabarabran and Coonamble. They would steal a small mob of quiet cattle in one area, drive them through the forest as coachers, pick up and brand cleanskins or change the brand on branded cattle, then sell them in another town. There they would lie quiet for a while then steal a few more and head back. They tied branches to their horses' tails to brush out their tracks until they were safely away. If police or stockowners were troublesome they might hide the cattle away on a quiet water for months. Then stories would be told of 'a creek in there with cattle on it got all the brands of the alphabet on them'. Stockowners were generally philosophical about stolen cattle or sheep until their own were stolen. Settlers said cynically 'You never tasted your own mutton till you had dinner at your neighbours'. For many it was a genuine belief that it was extravagance to kill one's own.

The belief was also genuine that unbranded cattle belonged to the finder. Stockowners as well as duffers rode the forest with branding irons and ropes in their saddle bags. When they saw a cleanskin they raced alongside it, galloped it till they 'took the gas out of it', reached down, caught it by the tail, and when its hind legs came off the ground they yanked suddenly and threw it on its back. The experienced horse stopped dead, the rider leapt off with his rope, dropped a noose over the horns or neck of the winded and confused beast, put quick half hitches round front legs and back legs and tied them back tightly to the head. Then he lit a fire to heat the branding-iron, adjusted the rope more securely, got out his knife and castrated the beast if it was a bull, branded it and untied it. At the next muster it was his.

Finally someone called a meeting of stockowners where it was decided to hold periodic general musters, count branded cows and allot cleanskins according to the number of cows of each brand. 'But old Tom, the greedy old bastard, he'd always get out there a few days too early and brand a few too many.'

The sport of camp drafting at modern rodeos is a standardisation of the work of drafting cattle in the open. Horses loved the work. So did the proud stockmen who polished their saddles and boots and wore clean clothes. P. P. Wright in an unpublished manuscript told of a muster of 20,000 head of cattle in the 1860s on Pian Creek where Mary Prise briefly took up her run. One hundred stockmen drafted them into about twenty lots. The number of cattle sounds exaggerated but Wright confirms it by defining the area they occupied as a circle of 'perhaps ¾ mile in circumference'. Twenty thousand loosely held for drafting would occupy that area.

Most of the stockmen held the main mob together. The men with the best horses drafted. If the mob was big several drafted on different faces at the one time. Each rode among the cattle quietly until he saw a brand he was looking for. Then he moved up behind the beast, perhaps flicked it lightly with his whip as a more definite indication to his horse. The horse needed few further orders. Its ears went forward in concentration and it did not take its eyes off the beast. It worked it slowly to the outside of the mob, moving from side to side as the beast turned and usually anticipating its movements. Then the stockman shouted and leant forward and they raced the beast clear towards the stockmen holding those of similar brand. If the beast swerved the horse leapt forward, met it shoulder to shoulder at an acute angle and pushed it round. The movement looks easy but it has to be judged exactly. If the horse hits at the wrong angle, if it hits too far back, legs tangle, and beast, horse and rider somersault at over fifty kilometres an hour.

Sometimes, to show how good their horses were, stockmen removed saddle and bridle to draft a beast. By dressage standards their riding style was bad. They sat slovenly, they held their reins too high, their leg aids were coarse. But their balance was perfect. No matter how the horse turned they did not shift. Thus the horses could move naturally without having to accommodate to a changing centre of gravity.

The felling of pine for the mills produced a roll of good axemen: Jim Grindley, Ivan Harris, Jim Kennedy, fast and untiring. All could cut their 10,000 super feet a day. Walter Arnold of Kenebri cut 8,600 feet of barked logs. He cut 13,000 feet in the bark, one hundred logs all squared, topped and trimmed. He marked on a Wednesday, cut on Thursday, and rode his bicycle home on Friday from the Wombo mill fifty kilometres out on the Coonamble-Pilliga road.

The daily average of the best axemen was a low percentage of their big tally. As in sleeper cutting the finding and testing of the trees to be cut took almost as long as the cutting. When there was plenty of superb pine only the best was taken. The axemen chopped a hand hold in the bark and tore upward. If the strip ran round the trunk it indicated twisted grain and he left the tree standing.

Bert Ruttley who worked for Jack Underwood at the Rocky Creek mill for thirty years did a lot of assessing of timber on private property, an exacting job. Although a mill owner never offered a landowner more than half of what his timber was worth, he needed an accurate figure to base any offer on. Bert walked in straight lines across the paddocks, measuring diameters, estimating height, tapping the trunks with the back of his axe. If an old tree was full of star cracks and useless, it sounded hollow; so did patches of dry rot. A hollow line indicated one crack only that could be cut out with the saw. He tested knots by chopping into the bark above them. If the chip flew out leaving the knot exposed the knot was dry. Too many dry knots made a tree useless. They fell out of the sawn boards and left holes. After he had tested a hundred trees he stopped to work out the average yield.

Each weekend for years he wore out four files gulleting the circular saws. That tedious job of lengthening the worn teeth is now done quickly with an electric grinder. Each morning he had two saws sharpened ready for a seven o'clock start. Bert mostly worked as benchman, the main man in the mill. He fed the logs to the big circular saw that stripped off one side. His tailer-out received the split log, discarded the bark and scantling, and returned the log over rollers for the next run through. The squared log passed down to men on smaller saws who cut it to size. The docker trimmed the ends off each sawn length. The planer on the noisy planing machine smoothed floor boards and weatherboards.

Elevators carried the sawdust to a burning heap at one end of the

mill, bark and scantlings burnt at the other end. All during World War
II Bert slept in the mill with buckets of water beside him. On windy
nights he was up most of the night putting out fires as they started. It
earned him no rest the next day. He started at the usual time. And no
matter how tired he was he had to keep alert. There is constant danger.

I carted the timber for our first small house from Bradley and
Wightman's mill in Narrabri in 1952. While I waited for the last of my
order to be cut I counted the fingers and thumbs on the five men working. They had thirty-seven between them. A relieving benchman at
Rocky Creek slipped as he fed the last few centimetres of a big log into
the saw. His foot flew up and was severed. At Wangmann's mill out of
Kenebri a saw flung out a wedge-shaped piece of wood. It gashed a
man's throat open and he died in minutes.

There was little compensation for accidents until modern times.
When attractive compensation was fixed for losses, some men considered it worth sacrificing a finger or two. One man running towards a
saw with outstretched finger began screaming metres before he reached
it. He knew how much it had hurt losing the first two.

During the 1920s interest in the Pilliga pine increased. Mills big and
small operated in the forest and in towns. The logs came in assessed for
royalty with the broad arrow hammered into their butts by the log
marker. Although Australian timber was admired and wondered at
overseas there was still a silly prejudice in Australia for imported
timber. Schwager's mill on Little Rocky Creek offered to cut joists
thirty centimetres by thirty centimetres and sixteen metres long for
A. E. Collins's new store in Wee Waa. The Sydney architect had
specified oregon so that inferior timber loved by termites was used
instead.

In 1922 Marshall Lord came with his big family to Gwabegar. A
huge man who eventually weighed 171 kilograms (twenty-seven stone)
he developed his business on the same scale: two sawmills, the general
store, the picture show, butcher's shop, baker's shop and hotel. He
lacked only the post office and police station. In addition he had faith in
the Cactoblastis and took up thousands of hectares of dense pear that
no one wanted. He soon ran 16,000 merino sheep where none could
have fed a year or two before.

Arthur Ruttley, a good forester and a brother of Bert, distributed the
first Cactoblastis caterpillars in the Pilliga forest. Ropes of eggs on slips
of paper were sent to him for pinning to slabs of pear. They were
delayed in transit and all hatched as he drove his car – it was about
1927 – towards Gwabegar and old Wangen where the pear was

thickest. So he scooped up the little caterpillars in handfuls and distributed them.

Arthur Ruttley had fought in World War I. Wounded in the face with shrapnel he was sent to hospital in England where he married the girl who nursed him. He had had no more than a year or two of school like his contemporaries but with his wife's help he attended the Forestry School in Canberra in the 1930s and in competition with university graduates topped the school.

Bob Beavis who ploughed so deeply established a mill at the Mollieroi crossing on old Coghill. He never swore and he found most disasters funny. His bullocks bolted one day with a load of logs on and jumped over the steep bank into the creek. The wagon capsized and the tangled bullocks writhed on top of one another. While the teamster tried to cut the yokes off with an axe, Beavis stood on the top of the bank and laughed, 'Crickies! Oh, by Crickies! Did you see the old turtle jump?'

He had borrowed from Bradley and Wightman to set up his mill and they soon took it over and extended it. A part-Aboriginal couple ran a boarding-house for the millworkers. They had several good-looking daughters who attracted old Dan Casey. He always kept an eye open for a good-looking woman or a stray beast. The family moved after a quarrel. The husband dug a grave for his wife beneath one of the beds in the boarding-house but she wisely left before he shot her.

Dan Casey considered Ruby Ruttley 'the prettiest thing in the scrub' but she kept aloof. Her sister Maud lived with George Johnson, a renowned bushman who had worked for Harry Joy. Johnson bought Thurradulba and set up a small sawmill there. He also kept an eye open for stray cattle. Constable Small from Wee Waa rode out one day checking on cattle brands. Maud was there alone. The constable tried to intimidate her by boasting what a good shot he was. He took a pack of cards out of his pocket, chose the ace of hearts and spiked it to a shrub. Then he stood off fifteen paces and put a hole through one corner with his pistol.

Maud was unimpressed. 'If that is the best you can do, copper, you don't scare me.' She reached inside her long wrap-around black frock, drew out an old revolver and put a shot through the little red ace. Revolvers and pistols were commonly carried until the 1930s.

The mills tried early trucks and traction engines to carry their timber but they were not an impressive improvement. Jack Underwood bought an International truck in 1925 to cart his sawn timber. With hard springs and solid rubber tyres it jolted the driver cruelly. After a shower of rain it sat and spun its wheels and the mill hands had to turn out to push it. Even with pneumatic tyres the trucks could not pull empty into some of the sandy country. Special low gears were fitted and three snig horses pulled them to the log dumps.

Steam traction engines bogged even more readily in the wet or in the dry. But provided the ground was solid underneath they could winch themselves out of a bog with the drum and cable attached to one of the wheels.

The Pincham brothers, after they moved their sawmill into Baradine, used two Maclaren traction engines and a Guy lorry with solid rubber tyres to cart sawn timber to Coonabarabran. The lorry was little more than a chassis and an engine. The driver sat on a box in the open. Sometimes Mrs Pincham rode in beside him for a day's shopping. She sat stiff and straight. Her long skirt flowed over the box.

The traction engines required a 'wood and water joey' in a spring cart to feed them. He cut dry wood and stacked it in heaps by the road. The engines carried a 900-litre tank to supply the boilers but that only drove them fifteen kilometres. The cart had to meet them several times with a 450-litre tank full. The engines sucked up the water quickly with a steam venturi. They ran quietly and slowly at about one hundred and seventy revolutions a minute. One heard them taking in and letting out regularly with a sighing sound as though they were breathing.

Max Merckenschlager worked as book-keeper at Pincham's mill for twenty-seven years. He spoke with a heavy German accent that never improved. His wife, Ethel, he called 'My Etel'. He dressed in a white shirt always. The Pincham brothers worked in grey flannel singlets. Anyone asking to see the boss was always sent to Max.

Eventually the Forestry Commission grew possessive and frowned on the stray cattle on its lands. And after the cattle were tidied up it was decided to tidy up the stray men. No one was thrown out but forest dwelling was insistently discouraged. However the 1951 fire moved many. Their camps burnt so they lived in town and drove to work.

The Commission had no equipment at Baradine to meet a fire on the scale of the 1951 fire. There was a small bulldozer, two light tractor-drawn graders and a La France fire engine that had been used by the American Army in New Guinea for spraying mosquitoes. It was an oddity that could not pump while it was moving, a dangerous thing to operate in a forest fire. Eventually top fire overwhelmed it while it stood spraying a grass fire and the operators barely escaped.

The District Forester, Sydney Starkey, had a bad heart and was uncomfortable outside his office. He understood so little of firefighting he made no arrangements for the men to be fed. 'Why can't they take cut lunches?' he asked.

Initially some of the firefighters were not worth feeding. With so little equipment they saw no point in risking their lives in a bit of scrub. They played cards and let it burn. A young sleeper cutter, not mentally normal, could not resist lighting a few extra fires. Others risked their lives trying to cut breaks for burning back with the little graders. Noel Worland worked the first sixty-three hours without sleep. Ned Edwards spent thirteen days and nights at the fire, his brother, Roy, eighteen.

Arthur Ruttley was sent up to take charge. He organised big bulldozers from coastal forests, five new graders from Sydney, water tankers from the RAAF. He flew in a plane load of forestry students to get experience. He recruited local volunteers and enough cooks to feed several hundred men. He kept everybody working. They put the fire out in three weeks.

Noel Worland watched the forest for further outbreaks from a De Souter aeroplane flown by Dick Burt of Baradine. The high wings were made of plywood and they drummed as the plane came in to land. The noise got louder and louder till at touchdown it seemed the plane must disintegrate. Dick Burt's cattle dog rode with Noel on the back seat and licked his face while he was spotting. Each time he pushed it away it growled venomously.

As transport improved most of the forest mills moved back to the towns and the new growth has almost eradicated their presence. A Kurrajong beside the road is all that marks the site of the busy Rocky Creek mill. Bert Ruttley planted it beside his house in 1925 as a seedling five centimetres long. A horse ate the top several months later but it grew from the butt into a big tree.

Log-fallers continued to use draught horses both for snigging and for loading until the 1970s. When driving round the forest roads at night one came on temporary yards of two or three strands of barbed wire strung between trees, and two or three big horses lifted their heads out of their feed bins to see what was going by. In 1974 we watched Fred Keegan putting on one of his last loads with a horse in the Yarrigan Forest south of Baradine. Spin, the load horse, was a black twelve-year-old with a white blaze on his forehead and four hairy white legs. He was mostly Clydesdale, the rest was Blood. He knew exactly what to do but he did not anticipate orders. That can be dangerous. The logs were small so one horse could handle them with a single rope. Fred kept each log straight as it went up the skids by pulling on a long broken V-belt slung over the small end. He called it his lariat.

Each completed tier had cross sticks laid on top of it for the logs in the next layer to roll on. Unloading at the mill was slow. The logs had to be levered off one by one with a pinch bar.

The modern method of loading is with a four-pronged fork on the end of a pair of arms three to four metres long operated hydraulically by a tractor. A three-tonne weight at the rear of the tractor keeps it balanced. The fork picks up logs four or five at a time, lifts them over the uprights fitted to the side of the truck as keepers and lowers them carefully on to the bolsters. Once the bottom layer is balanced evenly on the truck the rest of the load is dumped on quickly.

The unloading is spectacular. The driver stops a few yards short of the dump, undoes the chains, and removes the uprights on the driver's side of the trailer. Then he positions two ramps about thirty centimetres high in front of the trailer wheels on the other side. Some ramps are made carefully of welded steel, others are roughly sawn blocks of wood. But however crude the ramps every driver positions them exactly about two metres in front of the tyres so that front and back wheels reach them together. Then he gets into his truck, revs up, accelerates forward and jams his brakes on as one side of his trailer tilts in the air. The whole load flies off at once and the empty trailer bounces off the ramps.

Horses continued to be used for snigging. Some loggers used small crawler tractors but they are expensive to buy and expensive to maintain. Rubber tyres punctured on pine stumps and Budda stumps. But snigging is not easy work for man or horse especially in a thinned forest with sharp little stumps three-quarters of a metre high and a metre or so apart that can snag the log or stake the horse. On a dead pull draught horses like to hit the traces hard to get the load moving, then pull steadily. When snigging among stumps they often have to be stopped every metre or so and re-directed. It is like trying to inch a loaded truck forward when the clutch is grabbing.

Sleeper cutters changed to modern machines. Chain saws replaced the two-kilogram felling axes and crosscut saws; power saws replaced the squaring axes. They speeded up the work but increased the danger. The first chain saws vibrated intensely. After several years some men – usually the hardest workers – found their hands trembling uncontrollably, or worse, found that their fingers had gone white and lost much of their feeling, a discomforting and unforeseen disease known as Raynaud's Phenomenon. Not even the latest saws, advertised as 'vibration free', give immunity.

Fred Keegan slipped when trimming a fallen ironbark and his chain-saw ripped into the calf of one leg. He drove himself to hospital. Several days later his brother went out to pick up his tools. 'I thought I might as well finish off the log he was working on. I started up his saw, revved it up, not thinking, and, oh Gawd! There was meat and maggots flying everywhere! I never enjoyed my lunch that day.'

Australian use of the chainsaw is casual. A Swedish lumberjack by law wears hard hat, steel-capped boots, ear guards and face shield, steel-meshed gloves and padded protectors on knees and shins that will resist a saw for seven seconds. At a chainsaw competition at a local show the eventual winner finished his can of beer, took off his shirt as the bell went, and in thongs and shorts picked up his saw, started it, then gave an extraordinary display of sawing slots and square holes through big logs, of angle cutting, of felling, of speed sawing through hardwood and softwood and of accurate sawing when he sliced a cross section two centimetres wide off the end of a log about thirty centimetres in diameter. But he had no more than his skill to protect him from all dangers.

Marcus Lubb changed over to a power saw for sleeper cutting in 1955 before chain saws were used for felling. The circular blade of the power saw was turned horizontally to cut the tree down, vertically to cut it into lengths and rip it into sleepers. Two types of power saw were made, one with the saw spinning clockwise, the other anti-clockwise. The one that spun anti-clockwise threw chips and sawdust away from the sleeper cutter but there was always the risk when beginning a cut or if it struck a hard knot that it would rear out of the man's hands, swing over and saw him in half. The other machine, the one generally used, was safer provided the sleeper cutter cleared the ground of everything that might be thrown back before he began to rip a log.

One morning as Marcus Lubb finished the last cut on a sleeper his saw picked up the slab and speared it back into his left leg. It almost knocked him down but he regained his balance and took a step towards his saw. Something caught his left leg. He looked down and found he was standing on bone. His left foot, dangling by a broad band of flesh, trailed behind him. The road was three-quarters of a kilometre away. He crawled towards it. The dragging foot was so much handicap that if he had had a knife he would have cut it off. He was afraid he would bleed to death so he strapped his belt round his thigh. It made little difference. He reached the road and a car came by in time. After four months in hospital and another eleven months on crutches he went back to sleeper cutting. He was then approaching seventy.

Technically sleeper cutters work for the railway. Although each is paid at a rate per sleeper and he cuts under a licensed quota system he is covered by insurance under the Workers' Compensation Act. The Public Transport Commission replaced about 750,000 sleepers a year in New South Wales during the 1970s. Most of them came from the North Coast and the Riverina. The Pilliga supplied about 8,000 a month. Both concrete and steel sleepers have been tried – many thousands have been laid in South Australia – but they lack the cushioning effect of timber and are not as good.

However the number of trains on country tracks was so reduced by the late 1970s fewer sleepers were required. As sleeper cutters retired from the Pilliga forest their quotas were not reissued. And big ironbark was getting scarce. 'It's all cut out now' a Wee Waa sleeper cutter told me in 1975. 'Oh! I suppose that is a silly statement. There are still sixty or seventy men out there making a living out of sleepers but, by Jesus, you do a lot of walking looking for a tree! Forestry don't help you either. They give you a block, tell you that's where to cut them. One time they used to mark all the trees for you. Now they can't bloody find them. And when you've cut the block, they go through and ring all that's left. They only want pine now.'

Fortunately the obsession for monoculture lasted only a few years and big areas were not treated. Pine does not grow well in competition with eucalypts but the young ironbark that was killed might have been more valuable than the pine. In 1979 a subsidiary of the New Zealand company making Gallagher electric fence equipment set up a sawmill in Baradine to cut ironbark for electric fence posts. When this timber is impregnated with creosote under pressure it becomes non-conductive. So treated posts do not have to be fitted with insulators. The company had a world market for its posts and demand was increasing.

One still came on temporary camps of log-fallers and sleeper cutters in the 1970s. The last of the long term scrub dwellers, Penny and Reuben Harris, still lived on Harris Tank in the Pilliga West State Forest. By 1979 they had lived there thirty-five years in a few hessian and slab rooms. A bough shelter nearby housed bunks for hot days. They cut sleepers with squaring axes until 1975. Penny was left-handed, Rueben right-handed, so they worked one each side of a log. 'We gruvved 'em together' said Penny. The second-hand power saw they bought in 1975 did not increase their production much. Perhaps it got less afterwards. There were more things to go wrong and more to forget: files, cans of petrol, oil, tyre pump, spare belt. Sleeper cutting was never a business for them. It kept them in drinking money. They pedalled their bicycles to the hotel in Gwabegar. They lived largely off the land.

Near the kitchen there was a wire mesh stretcher with a deep layer of black hair beneath it. That was where the wild pigs were scalded. They cooked in a camp oven on an open hearth. Bronzewing pigeons made a good meal. 'Not supposed shoot them' said Penny. 'We do. Good to eat. Put a couple of birds in oven and onions, salt, pepper and water, all that, potatoes, peas and things. Good!'

The brothers regularly lost pig dogs in the big tank near their humpy. The dogs roamed freely and chased kangaroos that came to water. Sometimes a big kangaroo, harassed and frightened, grabbed a dog in its forepaws, hopped into deep water and held it under till it drowned – a favourite trick of kangaroos.

There have been some unusual methods of trying to earn a living from the forest. Hans Soltermann set up a mill north-east of Gwabegar to make parquet flooring from Brigalow. The hard dark-brown figured wood made superb flooring and Soltermann kept up an uncertain production for a couple of years in the mid-1970s. But there was an insufficient supply and Brigalow is a misshapen wasteful timber to mill.

During World War II men and women burnt charcoal for themselves and for sale to power vehicles equipped with the notorious producer-gas units, the messiest form of power there ever was. In the early 1970s the Ayoub family dug pits thirty metres long and one and a half metres deep on an old football ground at the Wooleybah sawmill to burn charcoal for use in backyard barbecues. They set up a semipermanent camp on Margos Road in the Pilliga West State Forest. Mrs Ayoub and her son, Phillip, saw to the charcoal burning. Her husband, Roy, carted the charcoal to market in Sydney and cut firewood for sale.

They filled the trenches with hundreds of sleeper offcuts, poured petrol round all four sides, then threw a match in. After the initial flare it took an hour or so for the wood to get well alight. 'Fire's picking up' said Mrs Ayoub as the flames leapt out of the trench. After several hours the mass glowed red but was still solid. Then they towed galvanised covers over the trenches, sealed them with dirt, and let the fires smoulder out. In four or five days the charcoal cooled and was ready for shovelling into bags.

The Ayoubs ate wild pig, too. They kept several in a pen and fed

them on second grade wheat and dead kangaroos. They briefly
employed an extra hand. He had nine children which Mrs Ayoub considered an extravagance, especially since he did not like getting up
early. She had to 'dog him' to get him up. One morning she dogged
him too hard, and when she was down in the trench adjusting an offcut
that had fallen crossways, he dropped the heaviest one he could find on
her foot and broke it. Soon after the supply of firewood and offcuts gave
out and the Ayoubs moved.

Driving back from Narrabri late one afternoon in 1974, I saw a truck
parked off the Newell Highway loaded with bundles of brush stacked
high in a netted frame. I followed its tracks inquisitively and came on a
camp of bearded, dirty, half-naked men drinking beer and whisky and
about to cook their evening meal on a plough disc hung by a wire
tripod over an open fire. A well-spoken man came out of the group. His
name was Levido, a member of a family of builders and architects from
Sydney. He had seen the lovely brush fences in Adelaide and thought it
would be good business to duplicate them on Sydney's North Shore.
He had a team of twelve men at work in a broom patch with scrub
knives, slashing *Melaleuca uncinata* into 1.8 metre lengths, tying it in
bundles and carting it out with a tractor and trailer. A truck load of six
and a half tonnes made one hundred and fifty metres of fence round
garden or swimming pool.

The business thrived for a few years. But it seemed a shame that
such a delightful distinguishing feature of Adelaide should be copied by
Sydney.

During the 1960s and 1970s some of the early names associated with
sawmilling went out of the business. The Lords sold at Gwabegar after
the death of Marshall Lord. The Maloufs left Coonabarabran for bigger business in Sydney. Greedy, energetic men, they had a marvellous
row with the Watkins brothers of Sandbank in the last years of the mill.
The title of Sandbank reserved timber rights to the Crown. The
Maloufs bought the Sandbank timber and moved on to the land to cut
and cart. No farmer, whatever his title, can bear the sight of another on
his land plundering the trees he has known all his life. Dave and Lyle
Watkins protested and were ignored. Then a ripping saw shattered.
The frightened mill hands crouched behind cover until the murderous
whizzing slivers clattered to the floor, then they searched for the
suspected bridge spike driven into the log. They milled no more Sandbank pine.

Three men who had been associated with timber all their lives sold out in the 1970s: Wilbur Wangmann and Jack Underwood of Kenebri, Lindsay Eather of Gunnedah. It made no difference to production. Logan's Timber Industries at Narrabri and George Paul, a newcomer to milling at Gunnedah, bought their licences and grew bigger. The Pilliga forest yields thirty-five thousand cubic metres of pine from up to a hundred thousand logs a year. Eight smaller mills had their share of this production in 1979. Only two of them still operated in the forest, the Wooleybah Mill and Head's Mill in Pilliga West State Forest. In addition John Grosser at his one-man mill within the eastern fringe of the Pilliga Nature Reserve cut pine from private property and from his own leasehold and freehold forest.

Young Dan Casey was foreman at Wooleybah during the 1970s. He had a private interest in a good herd of cattle he ran in the surrounding forest where there were grassy box flats. The Forestry Commission decided to bring cattle back into the forest to control the increasing undergrowth that was making logging tedious and dangerous. In the 1970s it offered big areas on 25-year leases. New barbed-wire fences gashed through the forest.

Most of the workers at Wooleybah were Aboriginal. Sawmill houses are never painted. They are designed to last only until the timber cuts out. Unpainted and unoiled cypress pine does not weather well. It splits and crazes. The rows of little houses exposed in a clearing among stacks of sawn timber look neglected rather than unobtrusive.

The Aboriginal millhands are good workers and dependable. They start on time each Monday morning though Dan Casey does not know how some of them drag themselves out. 'They don't eat all weekend,' he told me, 'they drink. After Friday knock-off they go to town. They buy a dozen bottles of beer to keep the kids quiet and as many flagons of sweet sherry as they've got money to buy. Their mates come down from Wee Waa and Walgett and they sit round the table drinking. At night they all crowd into one room to sleep. You see a couple of pairs of legs, three pairs sometimes, poking out the bedroom door and bodies asleep all over the floor. All they've got room to move is their eyes.'

In 1954 repairs were made to the Wooleybah school. In one of those outlandish blunders that public servants so expertly hide, whichever Government department was responsible for the building sent up a semi-trailer from Sydney with a load of cypress pine.

John Grosser, brother of Ron who demonstrated the old Hart-Parr, had lived for over forty years on his twenty-four hectares of freehold and three hundred and sixty hectares of forest lease. Driving along Scratch Road one came unexpectedly on a notice:

CAUTION
NO GRADING BETWEN
HERE AND SAWMILL PLANT

The track into the mill had little contour banks every fifty metres or so to stop water rushing down the track and cutting it out. Ron Grosser shovelled these banks on many kilometres of his roads. He laid bark wherever the tracks got boggy in the wet.

The mill was amazingly neat and organised for convenience. Little carts ran on rail tracks wherever anything heavy had to be moved. He thought the Japanese steel in the tracks was of poor quality so he painted it with rustproof paint. Sawdust was elevated into a huge mound well clear of the working. He strapped scantling in neat bundles and stacked it. He covered all sawn timber. When he had a few weeks' supply of logs in the bark on hand, he painted their ends to stop them cracking.

When we first came upon him he was milling pine from private property that had blown down in a violent windstorm three years before. It was so dry and hard he kept jets of water spraying each side of the ripping saw. Much of the pine was affected by dry rot. Some boards 100 millimetres by 50 in cross section had no more than five millimetres of sound timber. That did not matter to the company buying it, a firm marketing ready-built homes. It was junk timber for walls, floor joists and roofing. The unfortunate buyer saw only the sheeting that covered it.

'I don't like cutting such bad timber', said John Grosser, 'but the company pays promptly. It's a certain market.' John Grosser paid no royalty on it. The company bought it for half the cost of good timber. It seems a ready-built house might readily collapse.

John Grosser talked compulsively. When one pulled up he turned off the tractor driving his system of belts and began to talk. He seemed anxious to tell all he had learnt in years of isolation in one meeting. He kept recorded every day's events in detail in his diary. He kept outstanding pines as seed trees and experimented with the sowing of seed. It took up to 110 days to germinate. Sometimes he spoke of his trees as if they were aware of life. 'No pine seed struck here' he wrote to me in the planting season after the 1974 fire, 'to the memory of the thousands of pine trees burnt to death.'

He wasted nothing and regularly went back to the stumps of the pines he had cut to collect the resin which is extruded slowly over several months. He washed it, dried it and graded it for size with gold panning dishes fitted with mesh bottoms. The resin is sought after for use in incense-making, for artists' varnishes, and for the enteric coating of pills in pharmacy. It takes many stumps to yield a significant amount. Most loggers collect what they see but few market more than thirty kilograms at a time.

During the mid-1970s he considered selling out. Life had finally grown lonely. National Parks and Wildlife was willing to take over his lease country. After one officer had visited him to discuss selling, he watched him drive away in the late afternoon. He 'went south towards Bailey Lookout' John Grosser wrote to me, 'the weather was fine and the sun was down on the tree tops'. He had checked that the evening was normal. It is a momentous thing to discuss selling one's land.

In 1978 David Hynd, the new District Forester at Baradine, made a change to the ponderous method of marketing pine logs. By the old system a carrier with a contract to supply logs to a mill employed log-fallers. The Forestry Commission allotted him blocks in succession and sent men in to blaze each tree to be cut. When the logs were on the ground, the log marker measured the length of every log, then cut a chip out of the bark each side of the centre and measured the diameter with calipers. He stripped a piece of bark off the butt and wrote his figures on it: 25 8, or 30 10, or 14 5. The last was a thinning figure, profitable to millers, unprofitable to cutters and carriers since they had to handle so many more for the same money. The first figure was the length of the log in feet, the next was the diameter at the centre in inches. He put a crayon stroke on the butt to show the log was measured.

After the change to metrics he wrote longer figures in millimetres on the logs and the book-keeper at the mill calculated the load in cubic metres instead of super feet. Arnold Kuusik, a hardworking Estonian who was still book-keeper for the big Cliffdale mill at Gwabegar in 1979, astounded the local carriers when he first began to calculate their loads with an abacus. He flicked the beads quicker than a modern book-keeper with an electric calculator pushed the buttons. The log carrier paid royalty to the Forestry Commission. The miller paid the carrier on a contracted price. Few carriers ever believed they got paid for what they had on. There were always whispers of: 'The old bastard has been diddling them for years. He's got two sets of books, one for the mill and one for the carriers.' No one ever questioned the abacus.

In David Hynd's new system the Forestry Commission felled and delivered the logs to the mills. It cut out so many hours of tree marking and log marking. Millers were enthusiastic. By 1979 he was hoping to simplify the system even more and market the logs by weight.

The small town of Baradine, the neat villages of Kenebri and Gwabegar, exist only for the sleeper cutting and the sawmills. At night fires glow in the round rough high-walled corrugated-iron sawdust pits. Day and night the aromatic smell of burning resin drifts about.

10

Mud Springs and Soda Plains

Three marvels of the forest no longer exist: the mud springs, the soda plains and the salt caves.

One could walk fifteen metres into the old caves. The salt hung in columns like stalactites from the roof. Wild horses, wild cattle, and kangaroos went there to lick it. Women from the Rocky Creek sawmill pulled off columns and took them away in bags for curing meat. Picnic parties began driving in by car in 1926. There was no road. They picked their way through the open forest. The caves collapsed during the 1930s and left no sign of salt.

Their ruins are in a rocky outcrop in the Denobollie State Forest. A forestry hut for temporary quarters is at the top. Halfway up the slope a very deep well that yielded no water is covered up. It was sunk in such an odd place one can only suppose the wellsinker was fooled by his divining rod.

Salt comes to the surface in a depression near John Grosser's sawmill and lies as a white crust on top of the ground. Kangaroo tracks radiate out from it.

The soda plains were formed by sodium carbonate not sodium chloride. Women collected it, too, for scrubbing floors and some still had bags of it in the 1960s. Mrs Cormie's floors at Cumble were so white visitors hesitated before walking on them. There were a number of soda plains. The biggest lay on old Coghill about thirty-five kilometres south of Wee Waa. A dazzling white layer two to five centimetres thick covered about eighty hectares. Dogs hated the plains and ran away yelping with their tails between their legs.

The plains were fed by springs and seeping water. The edges were always damp and the soda spread slowly as the water evaporated. All water in the area tasted of soda. Those who drank it grew to like it and found other water tasteless. The main plain was still white in 1939 but patches of sandy soil were beginning to show through it and clumps of grass grew here and there. A few years later oak scrub took over. The soda plains probably disappeared because the increasing number of shallow bores sunk by settlers a few kilometres to the north lowered the water table.

The mud springs disappeared in the 1918 drought. They were a few kilometres to the north of the soda plains outside the present State forest on the edge of the gilgai and Brigalow country. Arthur Dewhurst, the surveyor, was so interested in them he sent reports to London and Philadelphia in 1878.

Bert Ruttley knew them well. There were a number on Nelcroi, the block his father took up. They were erupting pools of cold mud ranging from a metre across to several metres. The big ones were a nuisance to stock and had to be fenced off. Sometimes they stayed quiescent for days and the mud dried and crusted on top. If an unwary beast tried to walk across, it dropped as suddenly as in quicksand. Days or weeks later when an eruption began the remains were cast out.

Youths played with the springs. Most of them spurted and bubbled at intervals out of a central hole then subsided. Several boys would cut a pole about six metres long and twelve centimetres in diameter. When a spring stopped bubbling they put the butt of the pole into the hole and quickly upended it with long forked poles that allowed them to stand clear of the pool. As the pole dropped out of sight the boys ran and watched from a distance. Soon it speared into the air among a shower of mud.

The quicksand in the creeks never rejects its offerings. One morning in the 1920s Marcus Lubb watched a man driving a mob of horses along the banks of Cumble Forest Creek. Four of them broke away and jumped over the bank on to what looked like a patch of dry white sand. They disappeared. Marcus ran across – he was no more than twenty metres away. There was not even a bubble to be seen. The surface of the sand looked as though it had never been disturbed.

The sand in most of the creeks has now stabilised and will support weight at any time. Parts of Bohena Creek when there is the right mixture of sand and water are very dangerous. Even those living along it who know where to walk have found themselves suddenly up to their waists and glad to get out.

An Emu has been watched crossing as the sand was drying on top after a flood. The bird was aware that the crossing was precarious and tested every step. It stood on its right leg on the edge of the sand and prodded with its left leg. It put the left leg down then swung the right leg in an arc, stamping every few centimetres till it found a spot that seemed firm. Then it slowly applied its weight on its right leg and swung the left. It zigzagged for sixty metres across the sand and took a good half hour to reach the opposite bank.

Those creeks marked on the maps with several names, such as Milchomi or Bungle Gully or Baradine Creek, were originally named in sections, according to the runs they passed through. Many of the names were probably the Aboriginal names of the main waterholes. The creeks always flowed periodically then dried up into a series of widely-spaced pools. Now that the pools, too, have sanded up most of the creeks come down in flood after extreme rains, then dry up rapidly. Wild horses, pigs and kangaroos dig for water in the sand. At times when Baradine Creek is dry, springs break out through the sand. A good stream flows for several hundred metres then disappears again into sand.

In many places the water beneath the sand seems to be divided into pools. Wells go dry suddenly yet another well sunk only twenty metres away might yield a good supply.

Borah Creek in 1979 was still beautiful along its twenty kilometre stretch through the Pilliga Nature Reserve. It had flowed continuously since 1948. It trickled over pebbles and sandstone shelves and at intervals opened up into pools two hundred metres long and three metres deep. High sandstone walls faced some of them. Shelves and little caves and deep recesses at water level sheltered fish and shrimps on hot days.

The water was clear. Unfortunately in the Australian inland clear water means salt water. Borah Creek water is high in magnesium salts. Native animals thrive on it. But the farmers that border the creek south of the Nature Reserve cannot use the water on their gardens. Cattle drink it. The salt is at the limit of their tolerance.

Yaminba Creek running parallel to Borah Creek is a big, dry, winding creek. On some of the turns it carves out the black soil banks six metres deep.

Yarrie Lake west of Narrabri is not fed by any of the forest creeks. It is a strange shallow depression on a flat black plain. Before the country was farmed the plain was surrounded by open gilgai country that extended into Brigalow on all sides.

Most of the gilgai country in that area has now levelled out. No one knows why nor does anyone know how gilgai country is formed. It is an Australian oddity. Big areas of flat black country are broken by regular saucer-shaped depressions, perhaps thirty centimetres deep and one to three metres across, sometimes two metres deep and ten to thirty metres across. Gilgais in the one area are usually of the same size. They hold water for several weeks after heavy rains.

Yarrie Lake was not a big gilgai. In the 1880s it was fed by a small gully that ran into it from the south. It looked a perfect circle about 450 metres in diameter. The water was nowhere more than 1.8 metres deep. Most remarkably it was bordered by a circular sand dune 1.8 metres high. Observers likened it to the dunes surrounding some of the coastal lakes. James Moseley took parties to it from Tibbereena for picnics on the banks. It was never a good swimming hole. One had to wade through a hundred metres of shallow water and slippery black mud to deeper water.

A teamsters' track crossed the gully that ran into the lake. As the number of teamsters increased, their deepening tracks turned the water. It takes no more than a plough furrow or vehicle track to alter the flow of water on any of the black plains. Yarrie Lake dried up. The area had been made a Crown reserve. For forty or fifty years the lake bed was used as a cricket and hockey field.

Soil conservation work in the 1960s turned overflow from Middle Creek into the old bed. The water level drops low in dry seasons but after good rains the modern lake is much bigger than the old. The water is no deeper. The mud is as deep. But the sandhill has gone and the diameter of the circle has increased. Parties of water skiers go out regularly from neighbouring towns. There is room for seven boats at once.

Little enough remains of the long Aboriginal occupation though those who know what to look for quickly turn up relics. Peter Bindon of the Department of Prehistory, Australian National University, on a short visit to Baradine in 1975 found many stone tools around Mag Morrissey's old house. He said the site had obviously been an Aboriginal gathering ground. There was a big waterhole in the creek nearby to entice them there. It persisted well into this century. Three children named Clark drowned in it while their mother, in the care of a black woman, was giving birth to a fourth. Their father who owned Gibbican briefly was away.

There were no known signs of Aborigines about the Sandstone Caves, a series of chambers and vaults off the Newell Highway north of Coonabarabran. In a few hours by turning over and cleaning slabs that had fallen off the exterior face, Peter Bindon found sharpening grooves on one slab, and on another, red and hard with iron, a couple of sinuous lines, engravings of kangaroo and Emu feet, and a stylised nest of Emu eggs.

A cave in the Warrumbungle National Park behind the ranger's cottage has axe grooves near the entrance and a build-up of charcoal and litter on the floor that might yield something interesting when the cave is dug. Visitors are not allowed. Until someone in National Parks and Wildlife inadvertently published a photograph of it, the local rangers denied the cave existed.

There is an extensive sharpening area on a sandstone shelf in Kurrajong Creek on private property west of Baan Baa. One rock alone has twenty-three grooves in it. Already they are smoothing out as the shelf weathers. Such sites could only be preserved if modern Aborigines worked them as a demonstration of old crafts.

Old box trees on private property out of Baradine have oval scars where coolamons (trays) were taken. Carved burial trees and bora trees were cut down and sent to the museum early this century, or were burnt down accidentally in bushfires or purposely in clearing fires. There were carved burial trees along Teridgerie Creek still in fair condition in 1979.

The most interesting carved trees were on the Watkins brothers' Sandbank. Shield-shaped pieces of bark 180 centimetres long and 90 wide were cut out of the sheltered underside of four big leaning Yellow Boxes growing on the creek bank. The exposed wood was carved all over with stars and suns, boomerangs, goannas and smaller lizards and other signs Dave and Lyle Watkins could not recognise. One of the trees burnt down in the 1951 fire. The other three lived but deep charring destroyed the designs.

In a cave in the Willala hills – difficult to get to and, if one judges by the fallen rocks, dangerous to get to – there are three parallel grooves high on a wall and higher still, white and perfect, a human hand. It looks too recent to be genuine but any prankster would have had to go to inordinate trouble to put it there.

A prankster has been at work where Scratch Road crosses the Willala hills. There are small caves, a sandstone archway, and two high walls on which men have scratched their names for over a hundred years. At the back of one little cave, chiselled deeply in modern print, is 'RH 1825'. But high on an outside wall – he must have used a ladder – in rough and uncertain carving is 'J G LAUNT'. The date has weathered off. It was probably old Joe himself who put it there. On a more sheltered exterior face, in still perfect old-fashioned lettering, there is the earliest genuine date: 'J AVERY L SETON 1871'.

One comes across fence posts, some more than a hundred years old, in what now looks to be virgin bush. Some lines of posts put up by settlers never had wire in them. The splitting and erection of the posts satisfied fencing conditions of the lease and cost only the settler's labour. Wire cost money.

Old house sites are marked by graves and hardy garden plants, especially South American aloes with long grey leaves that flower on eight-metre poles every several years, or weeping Pepper Trees, often more drab than no growth at all, with stinking leaves. There are figs and oleanders a hundred years old and big White Cedars, those beautiful Australian trees that look as foreign as the others because they are deciduous.

Near Gwabegar on the bank of Baradine Creek a date palm still flourished in 1979 that Colin MacKenzie planted in the Wangen garden almost 130 years before. His grave stood a hundred metres away in a sandy wheat paddock among three huge Kurrajongs that must have been there when he was buried. The wrought iron fence around it allowed room for his wife who outlived the property and was buried in Sydney. The anguish she tried to express in the verse on his headstone has as much warmth as the marble it is engraved on.

Near Wooleybah mill there is the grave of a teamster's wife, Elizabeth Baccon. A forest ranger, David Cormie, and the Baccon family lived there beside a good waterhole in Six Mile Creek. One morning Mrs Bacon collapsed while pegging clothes on the line. Only four young children were with her. Her ten-year-old son, William, put the two youngest in a handdrawn cart, and he and his eight-year-old brother pulled it ten kilometres to Tom Ditchfield's selection in search of help. Their mother was already dead. The story, with an obnoxiously sentimental picture and verse, was featured on the Salvation Army calendar of 1915. The ironbark headstone her husband carved washed away in a high flood in the creek.

There was a fallen-in cellar in the ruins of Buggery, a selection off Dandry Creek. A succession of small farmers made no money there but the grapes that continued to flourish in the garden attracted pickers in January for many years. The Dandry Creek district has the same climate as the Bordeaux district of France. The cost of establishing a vineyard there would be huge but it would probably make the finest wines in Australia.

One occasionally comes across obvious ruins of houses in the forest, some of them fairly substantial. These were abandoned after the growth of the 1950s by log-fallers or sleeper cutters who had tried to combine farming and grazing a bit of leasehold with timbergetting.

A. A. Taylor, a sawmiller from Biniguy, took up a block of the present Jacks Creek State Forest in the 1930s. He intended to move his sawmill to the better timber of the Pilliga and graze sheep as an extra interest. He built a home for his family on Chrome Hill and dammed a gully for water. World War II intervened. The Government stopped private building and restricted the production of mills. The move could no longer pay. Alfred Taylor worked in Biniguy, his family lived on Chrome Hill. The children pedalled bicycles along Chromite Road to school in Turrawan ten kilometres away. The family were always short of money. Mrs R. Gunter, a daughter, told me she remembered her mother making out shopping lists of essentials only, then going through it and crossing out the least essential. In 1945 they left.

The forest has almost eradicated their presence. Even Chromite Road has almost disappeared. We tried to push our Land-Rover along it in 1974 to find evidence of the chromite mining. Acacias were three metres high between the wheel tracks. Then we came to an area where a windstorm had swept big trees across it so we walked the rest of the way.

We found a few mullock heaps along the ridge, a few shallow trenches. Two prospected for chromite there and took out experimental loads: Ellen Johnson, probably George Johnson's sister, in 1915, and Arthur Ruttley in 1929 before he decided to go to the forestry school. Chromite is a difficult mineral to mine. It occurs in pockets and one pocket gives no indication of where the next might be. The pockets were small on Chrome Hill and the ore low grade.

Several times during the 1960s individuals and companies tested the sanded creeks for rutile and zircon. They found tantalising amounts of both but insufficient to make mining pay.

And there were tantalising traces of gold in the ridges at the head of the creeks running into Coghill Creek. H. I. Jensen who reported on *The Agricultural Prospects and Soils of the Pilliga Scrub* in 1912 considered the area had 'a chance of becoming of importance as a mineral field'. A road known as Gold Mine Road runs south from Lucky Flat to the heads of Black Creek and Mollieroi Creek and there are stories of a profitable amount of gold taken out. But the man said to have taken it out did not take it and the Department of Mines has no record of mining there. Shafts were sunk on traces in the Warrumbungles in 1898 but nothing more was found.

However a secretive Swedish workman on Goorianawa spent every weekend for many years tunnelling into a hill on the property. No one even knows if it was gold he found. But when he died early this century he left more money to his relations in Sweden than he could have saved from his wages.

East of Baradine in the Timmallallie State Forest there is a road known as Limestone Road. An area of sixteen hectares was gazetted 'Reserve from sale for limestone' in 1884. Little was quarried.

Fullers earth, that green greasy adsorbent clay used in cloth making as a cleaning agent, was mined between Boggabri and Baan Baa in the early 1900s. A railway line was built to the site.

Companies in the 1960s bored for oil till they struck volcanic rock at nearly 2,500 metres to no avail, and the Geological Survey crew recorded deep narrow coal seams in the 1970s.

Shale oil seeps out of a rock off the Newell Highway twenty-seven kilometres north of Coonabarabran. Teamsters camped there and broke off pieces of rock to make their fires. After many years road workers camped there for months when they were putting the Newell Highway through the forest. They cut grooves in the rock to channel the seepage and collected the dripping oil for their lanterns. It was light and clear and burnt as well as kerosene.

In 1920 Davis Gelatine (Aust.) Pty Ltd began to mine diatomaceous earth on Chalk Mountain five miles west of Bugaldie. Rabbit burrows had exposed the light white spongy deposit, the biggest in Australia. A seam three and a half metres thick spread over sixty hectares beneath thirty metres of basalt. It is used for filtration and for making firebricks. Need is limited. Five or six hundred tonnes is extracted a year. In almost sixty years of quarrying no more than fifteen per cent of the deposit has been taken.

Up to 1950 six or seven men tunnelled through the seams towards the centre of the mountain. About thirty metres in, the white diatomite changed to black which was thought to be useless. So another tunnel was begun from the outside. Then they removed the two or three metres of diatomite between the tunnels. All the produce was bagged.

Since 1966 Vic Mills of Bugaldie has worked the mine alone with bulldozer and front-end loader. His father worked in the mine before him. He took out a year's supply in about three months. The harder black diatomite was found superior for firebricks. It has the consistency of coal so Vic Mills blasted it out. The teeth on the front-end loader merely scratched it.

The white face of the open cut shows three seams of volcanic ash. The face is exposed in several places round the mountain and the ash seams are regular. The first occurs at about ninety centimetres from the bottom and is twelve millimetres thick, the next at two hundred and seventy centimetres is five centimetres thick. The third near the top of the seam is about ten centimetres thick. The volcano must have died in one great burst.

Extraordinary fossils show up on the face though it is rare to get an unbroken one. The unstable diatomaceous earth split into vertical slabs and fish a metre long are broken in three pieces. But Vic Mills found many whole leaves and shells and sometimes a perfect fish up to twenty-five centimetres long.

A remarkable fossilised substance oozes out of cracks in sandstone on some of the rocky outcrops in the forest, especially on the Bulga, a hill north of Willala Mountain. It is dung-bitumen, usually seen as a thick, black dried spill on a sandstone shelf, but where a block of sandstone has fallen recently it has the consistency of heavy tar. It contains animal phosphorous and nitrogen and is probably the rather liquid excreta of dinosaurs which suggests that these huge reptiles made common heaps like alpacas.

The Warrumbungles have weathered too much to preserve anything. Close up they give the impression they will soon crumble right away. The trachyte remains of the cores of extinct volcanoes are spectacularly broken. Rock balances against rock and big slabs are ready to slide. Stunted Port Jackson Figs cling to rocks, their roots bulging cracks a little wider. Atop the Breadknife, like a sprig of parsley, an old White Cypress Pine has grown no more than two metres high. Its roots are well-anchored in cracks and illegal rope climbers tie their ropes to it for the long drop down the western side.

The Breadknife is well-named. It is a jagged-topped wall of green trachyte two to three hundred metres long, one to two metres wide, and up to a hundred metres high. It was formed when viscous lava poured into a long deep crack in the core of a volcano like metal into a mould. The lava set. Then the softer casting material weathered away over thousands of years and exposed the perfect cast.

It has cracked into blocks and some have fallen so climbing is forbidden. Expert schoolboy climbers begin their climb when there is just enough light in the eastern wall to show them where to drive their pitons. They wait at the top till the western side lights up, then climb down quickly and are back innocently on the walking trail before the park rangers wake up.

Some of the features of the Warrumbungle National Park have odd names. Myles Dunphy who had been secretary of the National Park and Primitive Areas Council made two energetic walks into the Warrumbungles in 1953. Only rough tracks and horse trails led into the area. None but local graziers knew it well. Myles Dunphy was so overcome by the extraordinary formations he turned to Gaelic mythology to find words wild enough to name them, and he littered the good map he drew with foreign heroes. It is disconcerting when sliding down a slope covered with stones formed somewhere in the depths of Australia to find that one is on Danu Scree or that after climbing through eucalypts and wonga vines one is on top of Macha Tor.

A rock especially favoured by rock climbers is Belougery Spire, notable for its lizards. At the point where climbers must get out their ropes to proceed further, the Warrumbungle Brown Rock Skink begins its existence. From there to the top of the spire it suns itself on ledges or hides in horizontal crevices. A sub-species of the common Black Rock Skink it is known only in the Warrumbungles and might be confined to that one peak.

North of the Warrumbungle National Park on Siding Springs Mountain is the Anglo-Australian Observatory, the finest in the world. Since 1977 unobtrusive and brilliant scientists have photographed deep space through the Schmidt Telescope with a 1.2 metre lens, a camera that looks close to the beginning of the universe, or watched bodies of almost infinite size through a computer-controlled mirror 3.9 metres in diameter. The glass was poured in Toledo, Ohio, ground and polished at the Grubb Parsons works in Newcastle, England, then shipped to Australia. It travelled by semi-trailer from Sydney to Coonabarabran under police guard, then bumped over forty kilometres of gravelled, rough, uncared-for road up the mountain to the machinery prepared for it. It weighed over fifteen tonnes. Through it astronomers have watched the pulsing lights from a neutron star 'as faint as a flickering candle on the moon' or watched a black hole, inconceivably gigantic, devouring stars. Ten billion light years distant, its awful mouth was one hundred million light years across.

And all that they watch, as immediate events, happened so long ago the ancient mountain the observatory is on did not exist.

Roads, still insufficient in 1979, lead into the Warrumbungle National Park from east and west. The park itself is not disfigured by roads. Good walking trails wind through it. The Forestry Commission has signposted the whole grid of roads in the exploited western and central sections of the forest and the roads are kept in good condition. In the Pilliga Nature Reserve, and in the eastern and southern sections of the forest where there is little good timber, some of the roads have been forgotten. All are maintained irregularly.

We use three maps when driving through the forest: the excellent Pilliga State Forests Map of the Forestry Commission, the Narrabri sheet of the 1:250,000 series of the Royal Australian Survey Corps, and the several sheets covering the area in the Central Mapping Authority's 1:50,000 series. All three are good. None is completely accurate. Wherever one drives, especially at night, it is necessary to count the roads one crosses and to remember all turns so that one can always go back to a known starting point. Drivers without maps have circled the forest all night winding themselves deeper into a maze.

Although one gets lost only if careless, it is sometimes difficult to get to where one wants to go, especially where tracks cross farmland between two sections of forest. One cannot distinguish dead-end farm tracks from the through road. In places it is hard to tell which is forest and which is private land. Some back paddocks were unfenced. Some leaseholds were unfenced. Driving up Borah Creek one came across a notice painted on a length of rusty iron nailed to a red gum:

NO SHOOTING
ON THIS
PROPERTY
CAUTION
PERSONS
SHOOTING
PIGS
GOATS
OR OTHER
STOCK
WILL BE
SHOT ON
SIGHT

Stan Rodgers put it up, a sleeper cutter who did not fence the boundary of his leasehold. He bred pigs behind fences and ran cattle on free range. A big dammed gully supplied his water.

The forest ground tanks like most excavated Australian tanks are not attractive. One expects a waterhole in a dry land to be an oasis. Bare yellow banks enclose yellow water puddled by wild pigs, wild horses and domestic cattle. About some of them rough new yards have been built to hold cattle running on forest leases. Round oak rails are twitched to trees.

Most tanks are fitted with windmills and corrugated iron tanks on wooden stands for quick filling of firefighting trucks. Little 1.8-metre wheels on 15-metre towers catch the wind above the trees. Some of the tankstands have makeshift showers beneath them. Teddy Williams, a retired sleeper cutter, lived at Dinner Time Tank near Harris Tank for years. He had a garden well fenced in and an intricate homemade self-watering system. His open shower, still in place in 1979, had sleeper offcuts laid on the floor. There was no tap to control the flow. He pulled out a .32 bullet that acted as a stopper in the end of a hose and sprayed himself.

Aboriginal families from Wooleybah drove west to Milchomi bore on Yetta for occasional evening baths in the hot water. Although one must travel across private property to reach most bores, those that supply more than one property have a two-hectare Crown reserve about them. The Bungle Gully bore a little farther west pours into a concreted trough. Bags as bath mats are permanently in place and forgotten cakes of soap. At wheat harvest time and cotton-picking time the big hot baths at Burren Junction north of the Namoi are a communal washing place. One never enters by the outflow end. Frothy blobs of toothpaste, clots of shaving cream float in the current.

Ghost stories abound in the forest. Lights flitted across swamps and disappeared into graves. A woman in a nightdress open at the top stood in the moonlight 'with her breasts shining' and a frightened horse bolted. At Cocaboy where Joe Launt had a camp men ran from the sound of cattle galloping at night and no horse stayed tied up. In the 1970s Yowies three metres tall or taller tore tarpaulins on parked semi-trailers or peered at motorists from the forest edge. A carrier with a load of pigs for Brisbane smelt a Yowie above his pigs. None left footprints at the only watering-places.

If one looks along the straight tracks in the thinned forest, pine shadows lie across them regularly like the rungs of ladders. The ladders seem to lead into infinity. And one can climb them to natural marvels.

II

Animal Life
Insects, Reptiles and
Others

In this exaggerated community of plants, the insects that feed on plants are in exaggerated numbers, as are the animals that feed on insects. So animals that feed on insect-eaters have also increased. It is a profuse and accelerated world that did not exist in such intensity until modern times.

Where there is much life there is much death. The fungi, the bacteria, the insects that return the dead to the soil are vital to the forest else it would smother in its own litter. The breakdown of dead leaves and wood in the dry Pilliga is astonishingly rapid.

Almost half the forest litter is recycled by termites. Their action is more complex than simple eating and excreting or ferrying plant remains about. In studies during the 1970s, CSIRO scientists found nitrogen-producing bacteria in the hind-gut of termites. Perhaps they aid the nodule-forming bacteria on the roots of acacias and leguminous herbs to supply nitrogen to the forest.

Termites have profited enormously by the growth of the forest. And they still profit by man's work in it. Timbergetters make an unnatural amount of forest litter. Even big logs of resistant cypress pine abandoned because of dry rot or transverse cracks, after years of weathering and threading with fungi, are finally destroyed by termites. Each post in the hundreds of kilometres of abandoned fencing marks a termite colony. And each side of the thousands of kilometres of formed roads and graded tracks there are termites in the grass and sticks covered by the soil banked up by the graders. Each species lives in the timber that pleases it and extends its colonies when conditions are right. Insects subsist like the plants. They thrive in the wet; stagnate in the dry.

We went out collecting termites for Dr Judith Reynolds of the Forestry Commission of New South Wales who was making a survey of the termite species found in that state. There were no flags on her map in any part of the Pilliga forest when we first saw it. Whoever of the family was home, whoever was visiting, drove many hundreds of kilometres over several months collecting termites from different soils and timbers. With little bottles of preserving fluid beside us, and dampened paint brushes to pick the termites up, we knelt for hours looking through watchmaker's goggles and scratching with knives along little tunnels through soil or wood. Not many species of termites swarm in obvious nests.

A colony can consist of one to two million workers and soldiers. Some species number one or two thousand at the most. There are always three main castes, the royal breeding pair, and the blind and sterile workers and soldiers. In most species there is a privileged fourth caste of male and female supplementary breeders. Some of these are chosen to become for a time new beings. They grow wings and compound eyes, then, when rain is approaching, they pour out through ways opened for them into the sunlight that would soon kill the normal termites, and they fly off to found new colonies. When they alight in some place that promises food they cast off their wings by propping them against the ground and arching their backs violently. Then they run off in pairs to seek a fault in a living tree or a crack in the damp underside of a log. There they eat their way together back into darkness, mate and begin to breed.

The queen in an established colony is maintained in a special compartment where she bloats into an immovable grub with a tiny head, perhaps thirty millimetres long and five millimetres wide, a little wider than her workers are long. The workers of all species are much alike in appearance – some are indistinguishable – and in behaviour. Like all creatures obsessed only with work they are dull. It is the soldiers that make the character of the colony. They are sterile and blind like the workers but active and markedly different among species in habit and appearance. About twelve soldiers of each species were needed to make identification certain and in the hours of searching for those numbers we learnt their characters. We found fifteen species.

The soldiers of *Amitermes lativentris*, a grass-eating species, are small and active with short, curved, notched jaws. These termites are scavengers as well as grass-eaters and their tube-like tunnels running a few inches underground come to the surface beneath pads of old cow manure and long-dead sheep. The walls of the tunnels are plastered with liquid excreta which sets smooth and hard. Every several metres they make low flat chambers a centimetre or two wide where perhaps twenty workers congregate.

The soldiers are in small numbers, about one per cent of the population only, and they function as scouts and explorers rather than defenders. If a soldier is exposed among the workers in a chamber he runs away and leaves the slow workers behind. Since several tunnels usually lead off a few centimetres after one of these chambers and the soldier might have escaped down any of them, it takes hours to collect twelve of this species.

The soldiers of the two species of *Coptotermes* found here investigate any disturbance to their galleries. As well as the long jaws they are eager to use, they are equipped with frontal glands that exude a sticky white fluid. Many species of soldiers squirt or ooze small amounts of a colourless repellent from head glands. The white fluid of *Coptotermes* identifies the genus. Since the gland extends beyond the head into the transparent abdomen these soldiers look white with hard amber heads. Although blind, they are well aware of the direction of danger. If a finger is held behind them they turn and run at it with jaws snapping and white blobs ready to smear. I watched a little black ant approach an exposed soldier of *Coptotermes frenchi*. When the ant was ten centimetres away the termite faced it, reared, and began to bob its head threateningly. The ant turned and picked up a defenceless worker instead. A soldier of *Coptotermes acinaciformis* placed in the palm of the hand sweeps white fluid with deliberate head movements then runs with jaws snapping. Now and again it stops, raises its hindquarters, lowers its head and hammers it quickly. This action is used in the nest as a warning signal. Some bite into flesh immediately and will not let go. If one tries to pull them off with tweezers heads pull from bodies but the jaws do not slacken.

Coptotermes attack living trees and in doing so they destroy much good timber. But many animals depend on these termites to provide hollow trees for nesting and shelter. As a big eucalypt ages, there are degenerative changes in the heartwood. Then *Coptotermes* come in through old roots or fire scars at ground level and eat their way up the heart. It takes years to progress up the trunk and out the main branches.

Coptotermes acinaciformis are effective destroyers but they leave no hollow pipe behind them. The workers bring up clay to mix with saliva and excreta, and they replace the eaten-out heart of the living tree with a brick-like material timbergetters disgustedly call 'mud guts'. It blunts saws. Only burrowing animals can make use of it.

When *Coptotermes frenchi* reach the end of the last branch and abandon the tree, they leave behind only spaces or fragile honeycomb. Then there is a good new nesting place for parrots, ducks and owls, or shelter for possums and gliders and so many other creatures.

In one genus of termites that swarm in huge colonies, the *Nasutitermes*, the soldiers have no offensive jaws. Their heads are extended in a long pointed snout through which the frontal gland opens. They make up for their lack of weapons by their numbers, thirty or forty per cent of hundreds of thousands. These termites build intricate mounds up to sixty centimetres high, usually with a rotten stump as a core. The top layers in which the soldiers congregate are about thirty centimetres deep and have small tunnels and chambers with strong woody walls. If these chambers are breached the soldiers pack the opening with their heads or run about outside pushing colourless blobs on the tips of their snouts. When the danger has passed workers are sent up from below to restore the damage.

The lower chambers are much bigger and the walls are made of a thin crisp material lighter in colour and easier to break into. This part of the mound is markedly warmer and is maintained at over ninety per cent humidity. This excellent incubating atmosphere is made use of for nesting by several species of parrots in other parts of Australia, and in the Pilliga forest by Sacred Kingfishers and Laughing Kookaburras.

These kingfishers prefer to nest above ground level. One species of snouted termites, *Nasutitermes walkeri*, builds high in a fault in a living tree. The kingfishers peck narrow tunnels through the hard outer layers of their muddy bulges then open out nesting chambers in the warm interior.

We watched a female Sacred Kingfisher feeding her December brood out near Ned Edwards Bridge on the Sixteen Foot Road in Pilliga East State Forest. She had built in a mound about nine metres up a Narrow-leaf Ironbark where a small dead branch forked off. In ten minutes she caught four small dragon lizards among the scrubby undergrowth and carried them into her noisy young.

Because of the huge insect population, there is a huge population of insect-eating lizards, and, because of these, many of the small snakes and bigger lizards that feed on insect-eating lizards. Some are brightly coloured and beautiful. All are interesting. The most interesting are the geckos, the night lizards, most of them termite-eaters though not exclusively.

When we moved from the river at Boggabri to the forest at Baradine we brought with us ten of the Native House Gecko, or Northern Dtella. We had grown to love these almost transparent lizards that fed each summer's night on little moths baffled by the gauze on verandahs and windows. There were none in the house at Baradine, so, as a last item of packing, Joan and our then young daughter, Kerry, went round the house on the last night and boxed up all the geckos they could find. They had to handle them gently lest they cast off their long cream tails. A gecko can grow a new tail but it is always inferior to the old.

In Baradine the previous owner's abandoned cats soon ate several geckos that moved too low on the gauze. So we shot the cats and the geckos have bred. There is now a constant population of about thirty. Each late spring a few young thirty millimetres long appear and a few of the older ones seem to be missing. But up to the summer of 1976 two or three of the originals brought as adults from Boggabri were still alive, then at least twelve years old. Towards the end of each summer the females show two round white eggs clearly through the skin on their bellies as they move heavily about the gauze.

Fingers and toes of this species broaden into pads on the end. The under surface of the pads is so remarkably laminated a gecko that has not grown too fat can run up vertical glass or walk upside down across a rough surface.

These delicate creatures were once feared as wood adders and thought to be poisonous. One old man, George Ruttley, told me that when he was a baby – he was born on 24 March 1896 – his mother was appalled one morning to find a dead wood adder tangled in his unusually long hair. She caught him up quickly and called to his father who harnessed the horse in the sulky and drove them fifty kilometres to the unqualified doctor in Boggabri. Dr Rogers, as ignorant of geckos as the parents, examined the baby carefully and said they were very lucky, he had not been bitten.

Although the Northern Dtella is as gentle as a moth – its only defence is to yield up as much of its tail as it has to to whatever has grabbed it – there is one species of gecko in the forest, the Soft-spined (*Diplodactylus williamsi*), that tries to make itself truly fearsome. This sluggish gecko can be found by day between the lifting bark and wood at the top of the metre-high stumps of thinned-out cypress pines. Geckos have been able to make use of the food supplied by man's interference because of the new homes supplied by man. They like narrow spaces to live in and the number of ideal cracks in logs or trees is very limited. After years of weathering the hundreds of thousands of stumps provided by thinning and milling make perfect homes. The wood shrinks from the bark leaving a safe space of four to ten millimetres.

If the bark is pulled away where a Soft-spined Gecko is resting, it usually does not move. They are drab geckos with four rows of a dozen or more short spines on their tails. If one advances a hand to pick it up, the gecko gapes its mouth, and one suddenly looks down a depthless purple cavern outlined in brilliant blue to accentuate its size. If a would-be predator does not recoil, the gecko chirps, throws up its tail, and squirts a brown liquid from the spines. Five or six fire at once. Aim is good. It can hit an enemy fifty centimetres away and leave it hung with sticky filaments.

The Thick-tailed Gecko, or Barking Gecko, lives under sandstone slabs in the decaying hills. Its body is cinnamon-coloured with dotted yellow stripes across it. The original tail is velvet black, broad at the base, then narrowing suddenly. Six white bands accentuate its blackness. If one reaches to pick it up it arches its back and props itself stiffly on straightened legs. Then it hisses harshly.

Geckos in the Pilliga forest were studied over an eight-year period by Dr Robert Bustard who marked out thirty-four hectares of suitable stumps with numbered stakes to give reference points for the movement of marked geckos. They were identified by toe-clipping. In order to make some of the geckos easier to find he set up about forty artificial stumps.

They were all made to the same pattern, cylinders of galvanised flat iron ninety centimetres high and forty-five centimetres in diameter. The ends were wooden discs with holes bored in the centre through which a length of pipe was driven into the ground to hold the cylinder firmly upright. The flat-iron was covered with termite-proofed linoleum with the rough underside facing out. About this was wrapped another sheet of linoleum with the rough side facing in. It was propped out six millimetres from the inside sheet by masonite spacers. An attractive ten millimetre crack was left where the ends of the outside sheet met to entice exploring geckos in. The top of the stump was roofed with sheet iron, an improvement missing on the stumps provided by timbergetters.

We inspected these stumps several years after Robert Bustard had finished his work. They had then been in place about twelve years. Flat, brown, hairy huntsman spiders that like the same conditions as geckos had taken over some of them in thousands. Others harboured one only of the solitary big grey and white huntsmen that often take up residence in houses. There were many pairs of Tree Dtellas, or Varigated Geckos, the species most studied by Bustard. They are of the same genus as our. house geckos and they, too, live to good ages. Two or three of those we found had had their toes clipped for identification. There were wary, fast-moving Tree Skinks in others and several pairs of the spectacular Ocellated Velvet Gecko. This is one of the largest and loveliest Australian geckos. It is speckled brown in a carpet pattern and feels as it looks, soft and velvety. Along its back there are big cream splotches outlined in purple.

The Tree Skink is a robust lizard, common in the forest. It shelters under the stacks of bark made by the sleeper cutters. It likes warmth so its cover must be substantial. About half-past four on the hottest summer day it stops foraging and seeks shelter lest the evening grow too cool. For a couple of years one came each afternoon into our kitchen to take scraps of bread and meat from the dish kept for the fowls. It came in through a hole in the brickwork at the back of the slow-combustion stove. For sixty centimetres of the passage it had to squeeze between the bricks and a steel plate at the back of the stove. This was often so hot it sizzled if a wet finger was placed against it. The lizard showed no discomfort though one's nose twitched expecting to smell burnt flesh.

The third year a young skink, born alive, began coming in occasionally, though not in company with its presumed parent. One afternoon the old one foraged in a different direction and tried to take the meat from a rat trap. The young one stopped visiting then, too, and no other of its kind has yet found the way in.

The several species of tiny swift inconspicuous skinks and the fascinating burrowing skinks that have almost worn their legs off were unidentifiable by amateurs until the publication of H. G. Cogger's great work, *Reptiles and Amphibians of Australia*. This book switched on lights in very dark rooms. Now one can find snake, lizard, turtle or frog and identify it.

The burrowing skinks are found after rain, rarely on the surface, usually beneath logs where they come up to eat termites. In the loose sandy soil of the Pilliga forest they can move an inch or two below ground where no burrows are prepared. Their scales are polished smooth and their limbs are ineffectual stubs with one, two or three digits. In some species the forelimbs are missing altogether.

There is another family of lizards, scaly-foots or flap-foots, that have dispensed with legs. A pair of short fin-like scales show where their hind legs were. They move above ground like snakes. Some of them are so snake-like one needs to check that their tongues are solid to be sure they are lizards. The beautiful Burton's Snake-Lizard, the largest of the family and the one most commonly found in the Pilliga forest, is often killed as a snake. It grows to sixty centimetres, but its pointed head distinguishes it and sometimes its bright colouring. Some are orange-yellow or rose pink, others light rusty-red with longitudinal stripes of dark red. Usually they are grey but not dull since the scales shine as though freshly polished and there is a black and white pattern about the head, and stripes of lighter and darker greys on the body.

Few snakes are so handsomely coloured and one that is, the Coral Snake, is a nocturnal burrower and seldom seen. One finds it occasionally by torch light moving across sandy roads. It is about thirty centimetres long and a bright salmon with a broad black band behind the head and narrow cream and brown rings all the way along the body.

There are usually a couple of Yellow-faced Whip Snakes in the garden, olive-green with yellow markings about the face, and ten centimetres of bright salmon behind the head. They are poisonous and big enough to be dangerous but they are inoffensive even when disturbed and glide away instead of striking. But they are not gentle in taking their prey. They move so fast they can catch skinks on the run.

Sometimes one comes into the house then gets worried when it finds itself sliding on unfamiliar surfaces. The easiest way to get it out is to roll up a *Sydney Morning Herald* diagonally and place it in its path. When the snake crawls into the cylinder the ends can be squeezed shut and the snake carried out.

The clowning Jacky Lizards, one of the dragons, are common in the forest. One has its territory outside the kitchen window. It comes out from beneath an old vine-covered room that was once the local school and climbs to the top of a fence post where it lies with its head hanging over the edge so that it can watch for insect movement on the lawn. Every now and then it hurtles down, snatches up something small, and climbs back up the post again. Sometimes it stops with its head poking over the top of the post, then raises its right foreleg and waves it in little circular motions as though trying to attract attention. All Jacky Lizards do this and nobody has suggested a reason.

Another member of the same genus without a common name, *Amphibolurus nobbi*, has a tail as pink as the sand where it is found and yellow stripes along the body. But if it is caught the colours fade in the hand and one holds just a drab little lizard. The colouring of many animals is fragile. The iridescent glow of tuna cannot be touched. As the fish is pulled from the water the colours slip away like oil.

Dragons lay eggs and dig little burrows when the soil is damp to lay them in. Our Jacky Lizard lays in the garden. She digs out an obvious burrow about thirty millimetres in diameter and slanting down twenty centimetres or so to an enlarged chamber. The soil is raked out into a mound behind the hole. As soon as her seven or eight eggs are laid she fills in the hole by scratching backward with all four legs and occasionally by turning round and bulldozing a pile of dirt along with outstretched front legs. She is meticulous about replacing all the dirt in the hole. The final tamping is done with her forehead. By scratching and sweeping her tail she smooths out the whole area. Then she selects litter from round about and places it naturally on the bare area. When she is finished it is impossible to see either where the hole was dug or where the soil was piled. I have never seen her begin a burrow and I would much like to know whether the rose petal she picks up and places down so carefully or the twig she seemingly arranges at an exact angle are the ones moved from those positions before she began work.

The great goannas have no need for subtlety. They thrash about the forest alarming all lesser creatures. In settled districts carrion eating exposes them to farmers' poisons and there are few goannas. In the forest they are safe from poison and they have thrived. There are enormous old goannas, some of them more coloured than is usual. One I saw out at the aloes on old Cumble was a good two metres long and predominantly bright yellow. There was a black cap on its head, bilious green about the mouth, and black bands across the yellow body no more than five centimetres wide and spaced ten to twenty-five centimetres apart. Generally those goannas, known as Lace Monitors, are speckled dark grey or blue with black and yellow bands on the tail. Like the Sacred Kingfisher they make use of termite mounds for breeding. The female digs deep down into the warm carton of a *Nasutitermes* mound on the ground and lays her eggs in the ideal atmosphere. Then she leaves them and, when the workers restore the damage, the eggs are well protected.

It is possible that the cries of the young call her back at hatching time to help them out through the woody upper sections. Female goannas have been found near termite mounds when there were newly-hatched goannas inside.

There are three species of goanna in the forest: the Lace Monitor, already described; Gould's Sand Goanna, a brightly speckled ground dwelling species; and a third which I have not seen. It might be *Varanus tristis*; it is possibly an unknown species. Bert Ruttley told me of it. 'Come three miles straight towards sundown from old Ayrlands' he told me, 'that's where you'll find them.' That area is on the southern boundary of the sometimes occupied Denobollie.

Bert knew the last of the tribal Kamilaroi Aborigines in this area. They had names for two species of goanna other than the sand goanna. One was called 'Goorie' the other 'Coorie'. Bert could not remember which of those names applied to the common Lace Monitor, a favourite food of the Aborigines. The other was regarded as inedible. It was smaller than the Lace Monitor, more wary, and spent most of its time in trees. Its body was the same colour as the dark Lace Monitor but its tail was banded with black and white instead of black and yellow.

The southern hemisphere is probably growing wetter. Certainly in this area there have been more years of exceptional summer rains in the last fifty years of record keeping than in the first fifty. It is after periods of extreme rains that insects are put on display.

In January 1971 a great band of tropical rain came down from the north of Queensland. In a couple of weeks more than one hundred millimetres soaked the whole of eastern Australia. Then there was a tremendous rain on the last night of January. It was warm rain, different rain. It was Cairns and Cooktown rain, not the Western Australian rain we usually get. I measured 207 millimetres in fifteen hours. And butterflies came with it, thousands of butterflies of species usually confined to the coast: Common Australian Crow, Common Eggfly, Blue Tiger. The air was striped with Blue Tigers unconcerned with the heaviest rain. Butterflies are not fragile sippers of nectar. Some can fly at fifty kilometres an hour for short bursts. Their appetites are lusty.

The rain continued through the first two weeks of February, another hundred millimetres or so. We had a heavy crop of grapes and they all fermented. The garden smelt like a brewery and the butterflies stayed about to feast on the rotten fruit.

Our own butterflies began to hatch in unusual numbers: the Meadow Argus, Chequered Swallowtail, and the big Orchard Butterflies that have learnt that citrus trees are good for their larvae and have spread wherever they are grown. Fourtail, the big handsome emperor, came from Kurrajong and acacia. It has a liking for alcohol and is attracted to country town hotels. And Lesser Wanderers came from the poisonous crotalarias known as Rattle Pods and Bird Flowers. These butterflies, as all of the danaids, are immune to attack by any bird or lizard that has ever eaten one. The larvae feed mainly on plants poisonous to vertebrates, even the imported oleander, and store poison

in their bodies which persists in the butterflies. The poison does not kill
but it is such a fast-acting emetic that any animal realises that the
vomiting was caused by what it ate. Till the end of that February we
had a butterfly garden, then hot weather and the shrivelling of the
grapes dispersed them.

Each time we have been to Baileys Peak it has been haloed with
Wood White Butterflies, males asserting their territory. They flap and
glide and swerve at right angles and chase one another for hours. The
larvae of this species feed on parasitic plants, mistletoes and the Native
Cherry. The larvae of the Icilius Blue Butterfly are legume feeders and
there are big areas of its chosen plants in the Pilliga forests, the Pilliga
Wattle and the Desert Cassia. But there are restrictions on its feeding
which keep it uncommon. Its larvae will eat only the tips of young
plants. Mature plants are ignored. And they are apparently very attractive to predators since they require the attendance of black ants to
protect them. The larvae exude honeydew from glands on the back
which attracts a bodyguard of ants to drink it. Few birds will pick up
meat covered with ants. The butterfly is a lovely thing, small with
shimmering blue wings.

In January 1974, three years after the visit of exotic butterflies, there
were over 200 millimetres of rain in a week. A shallow waterway
flooded forty centimetres deep through a paddock of dense lucerne
and put its insect population on show on the exposed tops of the plants.
Red-backed Spiders hung in quickly-made webs or bobbed in the
water like tiny buoys. Wolf Spiders from a distance looked fuzzy with
young clinging to backs and legs, or misshapen with blue-green egg
cases hanging to spinnerets. Those unencumbered were wary, and
plunged like turtles into the water as I approached. Green Tree Frogs
hung half in the water and half out and long yellow centipedes were
drowned or drowning or stretched alive on stiff stems. There was such
a multitude of beetles, bugs, grasshoppers, spiders, stick insects,
mantises, centipedes, frogs, skinks, finally only the odd, the beautiful
or the flamboyant could make impression.

Size was unimportant. Three-millimetre-long leafhoppers are remembered because they were no more than brown lucerne pods till one
looked closely. Then one saw that they were wedge-shaped and alive.
And the small cream Tree-Crickets are remembered with wings of
translucent parchment stretched tight over prominent struts. They
looked as though they had been built by a model-maker. Slim grasshoppers were twenty-five millimetres of pale green with prominent

pink eyes, colours that would look insipid on a bridesmaid but which looked superb on a grasshopper.

There were grotesque cricket-like animals with powerful jaws, long orange grasshoppers striped in black, and one Crested Grasshopper, pale green with brown Chinese-like characters apparently brushed on at intervals. Behind its head was a three-horned saddle supporting magnificently a semicircular green crest with a serrated edge outlined in black. Even more spectacular are the Mountain Grasshoppers found in the foothills of the Warrumbungles. At first sight they are unobtrusive. Indeed they are so well camouflaged they are difficult to find. They rest on the trunks of angophoras and their bodies are grey and grooved like the bark. The female is short, about twenty-five millimetres long, and heavy-bodied. She is almost as wide as she is long. She has no hind wings and her forewings are insufficient to lift her. She cannot fly. If one goes to pick her up she raises her stubby wings and exposes an astonishing flare of red and blue – there are raised blue saddles across her deep red abdomen. At the same time a salmon pink welt rises up from behind her head. One's hand withdraws as though from a hot coal.

Ants sought refuge from that lucerne paddock flood, too. Everywhere in the forest there are ants, probably several hundred species, and most of them are nameless. They have not even been picked up and tagged. There is a decidedly commercial outlook to scientific research in Australia. Knowledge is expected to earn profit, not understanding.

One very hot day I saw a twenty-metre line of ants racing along a road near the house. They were orange-brown in colour, about the length of the common meat ant but more lightly built, longer-legged and very swift, a species I had not seen before.

The leader turned off the road into grass and came to the heavy shadow of a pair of grain silos. The sunny ground was so hot it sizzled if one spat on it and the leader slowed immediately it came to the shadow. Those following slowed at the same point and ant began piling on ant where the shadow began. When the leader came out of the shadow it trebled its pace again.

Individuals near the leader broke off to investigate the nests of other species. Several had a cursory look at a single hole of little black ants. Others inspected the several entrances of a greenhead nest – those ants that sting so astonishingly hard – but they left quickly when dark green heads appeared at one of the holes. A few metres farther on the leader headed for a prominent mound eighty millimetres high. All those in the lead seemed to recognise the kind of mound from a couple of metres away, since they spread out as they approached it and raced over the top. A swarm of black ants almost as big as the raiders came out to defend. There was no battle. The black ants were too slow. Each of the raiders chose a victim and picked it up with ease. Sometimes black ants reared into defensive positions but the red ants simply swerved, ran around behind them and picked them up by the waist before they could turn. As each of the raiders caught its prey, it set off back the way it had come, carrying its struggling victim clear of the ground. There were now two lanes of red ants, those still approaching, and those returning.

By the time the last of the raiders were selecting their victims the few black ants left were trying to get eggs out of the hole and escape with them into the grass. Only fifty or sixty succeeded. The red ants realised what was happening and guarded the hole.

I never found out where the red ants lived. About one hundred and twenty metres from the black ants' nest the leading red ant came to a depression in the road. It looked like the deserted lair of an ant lion. The leading ant dropped its crumpled victim in the bottom, moved away a few centimetres and preened its legs. All those following did the same. Soon there was a pile of dead black ants. Then those that had rested began to run to the pile, pick up dead ants and distribute them on the ground near the hole. Other rested ants found them there and carried them back to the pile.

So it went on for an hour and a half till I had to leave – dead ants were taken out and the same ants put back. All the raiders had returned in the first half hour or so. Each behaved in the same way. What had seemed a well-planned raid ended up as a shemozzle.

Two big sand wasps I watched one afternoon expended enormous energy to no purpose. It had rained eleven millimetres the day before, enough to make them think of egg-laying. Sand wasps provide paralysed spiders for their young. The species I watched, red-brown with two black bands high on the abdomen, prey on the big Golden Orb-weaving Spiders that stretch yellow ropes of web between pine trees as guys for their orbs.

It is a dangerous manoeuvre for a twenty-millimetre wasp to take a spider whose body is as long as itself and almost twice the weight. The spider rests head down at the centre of her web. If something disturbs her she turns round and prepares to flee up the guy ropes. But when she sees the disturber is a wasp she freezes, stands out tensely from the web and raises her front legs in striking position. Her abdomen hangs like a cream and purple plum from the pedicel. The wasp comes in very fast beneath the spider. As the sting goes into her abdomen, the spider's eight long legs shoot out at an oblique angle and she falls. The wasp sideslips to avoid both the falling spider and the sticky web which is strong enough to hold a small bird.

The wasp comes to ground, seizes the paralysed spider by the pedicil and tows it backward. The spider's stiffened legs poke out one side, its abdomen the other. The wasp pulls at the apex of an acute angle and in grass moves the great load about one third of a metre a minute. Its legs strain and slip, its wings flutter. Sometimes it props its wings on the ground and levers itself backward. Every minute or so it rests.

The two wasps I watched had already towed two spiders forty metres through grass. The residents of webs at that distance were missing. Now they had left the spiders on a sandy track and each was scouting about on wing and on foot trying to find a suitable place to dig a hole in which to deposit spider and egg. It was difficult to find a place suitable for digging. The rain had been heavy and most had run off. They scratched here and there but found the ground too hard or so loose it would cave in.

After an unsuccessful search a wasp returned to her spider, pulled it about three metres farther along the road – she could negotiate that distance in a minute where there were no obstacles – rested for a while then scouted again. Six long searches were fruitless so each wasp dragged her spider off the road, propped it in a weed seventy or eighty millimetres off the ground and began flying greater distances. They zig-zagged low through the grass twenty to thirty metres away.

When it began to get late I made heel scrapes on the road to mark where the spiders were. This uncovered some damp ground. Immediately one of the wasps flew over to investigate. She ran up and down one of the scratches testing it here and there, then dragged her spider close. She began to dig hard, front legs scratching and jaws biting. In five minutes she had dug no more than three millimetres. Wheel tracks had hardened the surface. So she gave up and tested the scratch for somewhere softer. She seemed to decide it was all too hard.

She ran back to her spider, pulled it a few centimetres, then changed her mind and came back for another look at the scratch. Where I had begun the mark, just off the track, most of the dry sand had been moved. The wasp raked it about, decided it was too loose, ran toward the spider, stopped, turned back – one could almost hear her deciding

'The sand in that spot is not too deep' – and began scraping it away with all feet working together. Sand flew until there were six square centimetres of wet soil exposed. Then she began to burrow.

Two metres away the other wasp had found a patch of sand stabilised by twigs and leaves. She dug a few millimetres, then collected her spider from where it was propped in the weed about one and a half metres away and dragged it to the protection of a prickly piece of Khaki Weed near where she was digging. She dug in at an angle very quickly. It took no more than two minutes to dig twenty-five millimetres, just far enough to hide her whole length. Then she ran to the spider and stretched her front pair of legs from its spinnerets to its head – I am certain she measured it – then she ran back and dug again.

A third wasp of the same species flew overhead, saw the spider in the Khaki Weed, dropped down beside it and pulled it a metre away where she lifted it up into a weed. Then she ran another metre or so and began to dig very successfully in a place that both other wasps had several times tested and rejected. The owner of the spider had dug six centimetres and was satisfied. She went to collect her catch. And she ran over and under and around the plant of Khaki Weed for a couple of minutes before she would believe the spider had gone. Then she made a quick thorough search in nearby weeds and came to within forty centimetres of the spider. The wasp that had stolen it, perhaps by design but seemingly by lucky chance, came back at that moment and towed it to where she was digging. She was halfway there when its searching owner came to the weed where the spider had been propped. She knew it had been there. Every plant near it had been checked briefly but she searched that one as thoroughly as the Khaki Weed.

Then she continued the search in the wrong direction. When it was too dark to see any more she was still searching and the other two were still digging.

When I looked the next morning the three wasps were gone. Only the thief had been successful. Her hole was filled in. She was not nearly as particular as the Jacky Lizard. It was obvious where it had been dug. She had spread yellow sand from the bottom of the hole on the grey sand above. The wasp that had been digging in the boot scraping had got down no more than twenty millimetres and given up. The ground was too hard after all. The spider was abandoned where she had left it. Not more than two metres away was the empty hole completed by the wasp whose spider was stolen.

The Golden Orb-weaving Spiders are often attended by little spiders known as Dew-drop Spiders whose abdomens are glistening silver cones. They clean up the mosquito-sized insects too small to interest the great Orbweavers. The egg cases of the Dew-drop Spiders hang in groups like tiny flask-shaped gourds.

Another big red and black wasp seen here in numbers for the first time in the spring of 1979 builds a mud cell on a flat surface – a shaded cement path or a laundry tub are favourite places – stuffs it with caterpillars or even maggots, usually one species only to a cell, lays one egg, then seals the round opening. It builds five or six cells in the one complex then plasters them all over with a thick coating of mud. The wasp is big enough to carry a ball of mud six millimetres in diameter so it builds quickly. Then, astoundingly, it does not abandon its nest like the majority of mud-building wasps. On warm days it frequently soaks the top of the nest with water poured from its mouth. It carries enough each trip to wet about four square centimetres.

A very big grey wasp buries a wolf spider for its hatched grub to feed on. This wasp first digs a hole and then goes in search of prey, a sure method perhaps, but wolf spiders are dangerous game. They are big and powerful and stalk grasshoppers as patiently as cats after birds, or run down skinks like Dingoes after kangaroos. Often they lie in wait near the top of their dwelling holes with legs hooked over the rim so that they can heave themselves out and pounce if an insect crawls by. They themselves are preyed on by centipedes. I once saw a centipede fifteen centimetres long go down a hole after a wolf spider. There was an astonishing thumping and scuffling at the bottom of the hole and after several minutes a very big wolf spider backed out towing the dead centipede.

The grey wasps do not venture down the holes. They dive on the spiders in the open, and before carrying them away make them into neater parcels by cutting the legs off. It is still a great load to lift, an enormous load that defies the laws of aerodynamics. The spider is heavier than the wasp which flies slowly and very noisily to the prepared hole perhaps a hundred metres away. It is a fine piece of direction-finding to locate a hole twelve millimetres in diameter at that distance in a grass jungle.

The periodic exceptional rains fill swamps and lagoons in the forest and eggs of outlandish water creatures hatch that have lain in dust for years. For months the water seethes with life, water birds come to feed and breed, then the swamps dry up and, since the water has killed the dry season seeds and growth, they are barren places for a year or two.

No rains can bring the fish back to the sanded creeks. People used to drive in sulkies out of Narrabri to fish the Terradelba waterhole (pronounced Turradulbie) that persisted longer than most in Bohena Creek on old Thurradulba. Most of the waterholes dried up with the mud springs in the 1918 drought. 'George and me, we pulled the last hole there ever was in Coghill Creek,' Bert Ruttley told me. 'The hole was drying up fast so we got some wire netting and swept it. We got sixty-nine fish, one eighteen-pound cod. That was on old Coghill station. And there has never been water in that hole since.'

At the beginning of that drought the rail came through to Coonabarabran. The Castlereagh River was a series of waterholes and the railway gang dynamited every hole as they progressed from Binaway north. They lived well on Murray Cod. There have been no cod caught in that part of the river since.

There are fish still in the lovely, difficult-to-get-to holes in Borah Creek in the Pilliga Nature Reserve and in the creeks not yet much damaged by man's occupation coming out of the Warrumbungles. Bernie Emmott of Coonabarabran took us one night to Shawns Creek that runs into the Castlereagh River to show us what species the locals called Tailor, and we caught a good meal of River Blackfish. These little fish were once common in all the gravelly heads of creeks feeding the Murray-Darling system. They are now plentiful in localised areas only. Silt and imported trout are eradicating them. There are still plenty in the Warrumbungle waters which seem safe from silting. But the fishing club at Coonabarabran is releasing more and more trout fingerlings in these waters. The slow-breeding blackfish cannot compete where trout thrive. Apart from competition for food the big eggs of blackfish are relished by trout. Why replace a fish that is good to eat with trout that are poor eating? Some members of modern fishing clubs are as foolish as the acclimatisers that did so much harm in the 1860s.

Blackfish are slim. The biggest we caught weighed only eighty-five grams but was twenty-four centimetres long. They are scaleless and slippery. The locals fish for them with small hooks and floats on two-metre lengths of line tied to bamboo. The bait is bread or worms. When a cork goes under the little fish is poled to the bank like a tuna into a fishing boat. It croaks loudly when picked up.

They bite best on summer nights. It is good in the cool mountains testing pool after rocky pool. Sometimes a dozen can be taken out of a pool no bigger than a bath tub. If no lights are used they will come into seven centimetres of water forty centimetres wide. It is like fishing in a dish. The flesh is sweet and delicious. Provided one considers the anatomy, the bones can be slid away easily in five groups. A blackfish only eighteen centimetres long, the smallest we kept, can be eaten without getting a bone in the mouth.

Ted Morrissey carried six of these fish in a bucket northward over the mountains in the 1940s and released them in Yearinan Creek that runs through his fertile gardens. Those six have stocked that creek and a few smaller creeks that join it. In his youth Ted Morrissey caught these fish up to thirty centimetres long and 170 grams in weight.

In 1976 we pulled a prawn net through all the permanent holes along three kilometres of Borah Creek in the Pilliga Nature Reserve. I wanted to know what fish were in them; Ian Briggs of the Australian Museum wanted specimens. He was helping to map the distribution of freshwater fish in New South Wales. We worked carefully. Each hole was pulled once only. Two or three of each species were taken for the formalin bottle. The rest were returned quickly to the water by hands covered in wet surgical gloves.

Despite our care the Bony Bream dropped scales like confetti on the sand and many probably died later of bacterial infection where their protective slimy coating was broken. 'Forky-tails' the locals call these. They have trailing extensions on the top fin and move like flights of arrows through the water.

We found Freshwater Catfish and the common Spangled Perch with cinnamon-coloured crosses on them. These are often called Mud Gudgeons. Almost every little fish is termed Bobby Cod or Mud Gudgeon. We caught an Australian Little Grebe, a penguin-like diving bird, whose feathers were almost hair and whose legs were set so far back on its body it could barely waddle back into the water. We caught rare fish, the Mitchellian Freshwater Hardyhead, cream-coloured and dense-fleshed with a dark lateral line. The forest has saved those too. And we caught Rainbow Fish, bright as jewels. It hurt to take them. They dropped like opals into the formalin.

The flowers of the forest attract apiarists. They began to come in as the forest thickened and the forest began to thicken as good modern trucks came on the market to take them in. It was fortunate for the beekeepers who at that time were losing their permanent country to farmers. Modern tractors were allowing more country to be cleared and ploughed.

So the sedentary beekeepers became travellers, and more expert than ever in the flowering of eucalypt and acacia and plants they call by pet names: Honey Myrtle, Hangdown, Eggs-and-Bacon. They keep rainfall records for the whole of New South Wales, for beekeepers do not follow the flowering, they predict it. Their hives are in place when the country comes on. And they work from the coastal melaleuca to the far western Yapunyah, a little eucalypt on the low grey flats of the Paroo.

Most northern beekeepers some time come into the Pilliga forest, though sites are hard to get there now. The best are booked permanently with Forestry Commission or the National Parks and Wildlife Service, 260 hectare squares at twelve dollars a year. The honey flows in the Pilliga are infrequent. Mugga Ironbark comes on every few years at Cuttabri for those with sites there and in stormy humid summers the Blue-leaved Ironbark pours nectar all along the ridges. It produces a dense, light-coloured honey. From March to the middle of May White Bloodwood sometimes yields a second grade honey when little else is on anywhere, but it is an erratic producer.

Mostly the beekeepers come into the Pilliga forest for pollen. When the bees have dwindled on the massive nectar flows of Caley's Ironbark on the tablelands, and the few workers left are ragged-winged and tired, they are brought into the forest to feed on the pollens of oak, acacia, Hangdown (Common Fringe Myrtle), hopbush, until the colonies breed up again.

Merv Goodwin of Gunnedah went down Borah Creek from Rocky Glen in 1937 and was one of the first beekeepers to work the forest. Fred and Perc Norton of Tamworth went in with him, and the Varney brothers about the same time. All did well. By the time the forest came into full flower in the wet 1950s many had followed them. Kylie Tennant, then living at Coonabarabran, went out with Jack and Bill Koina from Inverell and wrote *The Honey Flow*, so real one can smell the forest.

At any time of the year on any road in the forest one now comes across hives set out in rows wherever there are clearings. Bees need to be within a kilometre of water. They evaporate water by wing-fanning to cool their hives. Sites near water are few. Most of the bees in the forest have to be watered. The beekeepers fill plastic-lined trenches with water and cover them with sleeper slabs to keep wild pigs and kangaroos out. The bees crawl through gaps left between the slabs. The Pilliga forest is one of the few big pollution-free areas available to apiarists and it is worth going to that trouble.

Bees placed on forest edges to feed on farmers' lucerne and sunflowers and that prolific weed, Paterson's Curse, as well as native flowers, are sometimes attacked by migratory Rainbow Birds. Bees and wasps are their favourite prey. There are hundreds of species of

Australian wasps and about three thousand native bees. Most of them sting. The Rainbow Bird is immune to stings. Nevertheless, after catching a bee, it flies to a branch and deftly wipes the sting off against it before swallowing.

They have learnt to relish the beekeeper's European bees. In some years they come in hundreds, green and brown and gold, and settle down on bare branches near the hives like long autumn leaves. They can take out most of the field force of a hundred hives so beekeepers string up wires for them to rest on and shoot them off the wires.

Most of the native bees are solitary. They hide little pots of honey in holes in trees or in the ground to feed their young instead of caterpillars or spiders like their relatives, the wasps. The majority confine their feeding to a few species of plants. Some specialise to an extreme extent. Generations build their lives about one tree. Other trees of the same species a few metres away are never visited.

European bees are promiscuous collectors. No one knows what effect they have on the food supplies of solitary bees or on those plants that require extraordinary contact with native insects for pollination.

One genus of native bees, the *Trigona*, live in colonies. Their nests turn up at sawmills in hollows in faulty pine, big wax pots of honey arranged hemispherically. A nest yields about a litre of honey, dark and very sweet. Aborigines traced a nest by catching a laden bee at water and sticking a downy feather to it with blood. Sometimes by looking through treetops towards the summer sun one sees a fuzz of these little bees about the entrance to a hollow limb. They do not work during the winter; entrances are waxed off.

Mosquito Bees, the colonists called them. They are black and about the size of Bush Flies. Men working in the summer were irritated by them. They are stingless but they settled on shirt or bare back in dozens to suck sweat. They have become markedly fewer. It is years since a swarm landed on my back. Escapees from hives of European bees have run wild as successfully as so many other imported animals and taken over too many hollows.

12

Animal Life
The Mammals

It will never be known how Australian plants and animals would have sorted themselves out in the new environment of our forests because their lives are disordered by coarse foreigners. European bees are one of a list. In all our unsettled lands there are stray cattle and wild horses. And there are cats, goats, pigs, rats, mice, hares, rabbits, foxes – universal mammals that tend to make everywhere the same. In National Parks they are all vermin because they frustrate the purpose of the park, to preserve Australian plants and animals. The worst of them are the wild pigs that spread through the heart of the Pilliga forest during the 1970s. Before that they lived in small numbers on the forest outskirts.

There are schoolboy legends of the Pilliga boar, massive and ageless, tusks like an elephant, hooves like a cow. The wild pigs are small, black and long-nosed. An occasional one is white enough to demonstrate its Large White grandfather or spotted brown if it has picked up a bit of Tamworth somewhere. They are prolific, intelligent and secretive.

The life of the sows is a cycle of suckling and pregnancy. They farrow twice a year. The boars are the scouts, the finders of food and water. They avoid obvious waters like farm ground tanks if possible and lead their mobs long distances to hidden soaks where they can wallow without exposing themselves to danger. The wallowing not only cools them, it fixes the big lice that plague them in a mud plaster that can be scraped off against trees.

Although small, the boars are formidable enough and, if cornered, charge without hesitation. They maintain no territory but there is always a dominant boar. Boars foraging alone announce their presence to sows by rubbing a scent gland beneath the chin against the trunks of trees. They scrape so vigorously their tusks make long scratches in the bark. One finds young pines almost ring-barked by boars. 'The boars have been sharpening their tusks' is the usual explanation. Tusks do not need sharpening.

On a mature boar the upper tusks grow out at right angles to the jaw for about five centimetres then curve downward. They are broad at the base and cone-shaped. Points are sharp as centre punches. The main tusks, the lower, have solid roots about ten centimetres long extending along the jawbone below the roots of the normal teeth. The exposed tusk projects upward out of the mouth at right angles to the root and meets the outer edge of the top tusk. The top tusks sharpen the bottom tusks to a chisel edge. They grow ten centimetres long and more and can rip like bayonets. The upper lips wrinkle over the upper tusks. Bottom tusks push the bottom lips outward. A boar's mouth looks uncomfortable. His lips have made no proper provision to accommodate his tusks.

Across his shoulders the wild boar grows a horny shield that is only slightly developed in domestic pigs. Keratin forms on keratin till the pad is forty millimetres deep. It turns the blade of a sticking knife and stops a high-powered .22 bullet in its own length.

The little sows come on heat a week or so after farrowing. The dominant boar mounts a sow first then permits the lesser boars a turn in order of rank until the sow refuses. She refuses definitely. A neighbour's domestic boar had his penis bitten off when he insisted on mounting a sow that did not want him.

Mating is protracted. The boar stays mounted for about twenty minutes and spurts out about a cupful of semen. His penis erects into a long corkscrew. The sow accentuates its strange shape by squealing as though the boar is indeed drilling a hole in her. But wild sows are too cautious to make as much noise as domestic sows.

Sometimes the lesser boars are too impatient to wait a turn with a sow. One mounts the busy dominant boar then boar mounts on boar behind until there is a line of thrusting boars masturbating against one another. It is unlikely they ever connect by the anus, though a young

domestic boar will often stand and let others of his age penetrate him.
There is a lot of homosexual behaviour among young mammals both
male and female. Ewes and cows on heat mount one another. Men who
fatten bulls in feedlots have found that one or two in the yard are willing to stand for the others. I once bought a couple of truckloads of
hemi-castrates that someone had used in a growth rate experiment.
They were fattened in the same paddock as a few steers. One of the
steers soon attached himself to the potent but infertile young males. He
stood willingly for full penetration. Later he began to seek their attentions and would walk across to where one was feeding and back up like
a cow on heat.

The pigs in the forest are a preserve of the forestry workers and
timbergetters. Pig catching is a general sport and wild pork a favourite
food. If pigs become too few in an area to supply the men working
there, someone goes up to the Barwon or up to the Moree watercourses
and brings back a utility load of sows in pig to release to breed up. If a
litter of young pigs is found, boars are castrated and released to grow
into long-legged barrows. There is a theory that boar meat stinks when
being cooked and tastes too strong to eat. Recent research has proved
this belief wrong, and in the late 1970s many domestic pig producers
stopped castrating boars. Boars grow faster to bacon weight than barrows and do not overfatten so readily. Centuries of castration wasted a
lot of time.

The wild pork is delicious, less fatty than domestic pork with the
slight tang all wild things possess. But it harbours a flesh worm,
Sparganosis, that makes it a dangerous food. The worms are carried in
the human bloodstream before burrowing out to make itchy lumps in
flesh. A single worm in the brain will kill. But there are few cases of
Sparganosis in humans since most of the meat is frozen before eating
and several days freezing kills the worms. We do not eat frozen foods.
Freezing destroys both taste and texture. So we do not eat wild pig.

Because of Sparganosis few abattoirs kill wild pigs. But there is a
ready sale for illegally slaughtered pigs. Men drive through north-west
New South Wales in refrigerated trucks looking for supplies. 'Hey
mate! Where can I get hold of a bit of long-nosed bacon?' A couple of
Baradine men had a fairly regular run to Sydney. 'Me mate and me,
we goes out with the dogs and catches twenty to thirty good pigs. Then
we dresses 'em and freezes 'em, loads 'em on the back of the ute and
covers 'em up with the tarp. Drives down be night. I pulls up next
morning outside one of them pubs in Redfern or down at the Quay.
Blows the horn a couple of times then I pokes me head in a door and I

yells, "Oo wants some pork?" Jesus! You should see them New Australians come out that pub. Like rabbits out a burrow at feed time. Thirty-five cents a pound and it's gone in no time. They uses it in their sausages. "When yer comin' back, mate?" is all I hear as I pull off. Don't do to hang around. Bloody coppers'll pick you up in no time.'

The pigs are caught by dogs. Half of any good pig dog is Bull Terrier, a breed with mighty jaws and no brains. They are too stupid to be taught to let go on order. Once the jaws clamp shut the only way to get them open is to choke the dog, not an easy thing to do even with a rope. Their necks are thick and solid. Luckily they are amiable with humans.

During a pig hunt on our own property a young dog with too much Bull Terrier caught a sucker. The little pig's ears were too small for a convenient hold so the dog grabbed it by the snout. The owner of the dog picked the pig up by the hind legs and tried to persuade his dog to let go. The jaws remained clamped. He kicked the dog in the ribs but it was impervious to everything but holding its jaws shut. The pig's snout crushed flat, its lower jaw broke up. The dog rolled back its lips and dribbled pig's teeth out of the corner of its mouth. Belting the dog on the nose with a stick had no effect so a noose was drawn tight around its neck. When its eyes glazed it let go.

So Bull Terriers are mated with more intelligent breeds to allow the jaws to be given some direction. Crosses with the Australian Cattle Dogs are often made. These are strong, intelligent dogs but too dangerous. Cattle dogs answer to one man only and are violently protective to all that he owns. Crosses with the gentle intelligent Labrador are good. The best pig dog of all is a cross with the old Staghound, not the extinct English breed but the big, intelligent Australian dog bred from the earliest days for kangaroo hunting by crossing English Greyhounds and Scottish Deerhounds. It has never been recognised as a breed.

Pig dogs prefer to work in pairs. One goes in each side of the pig and fastens to an ear. Then they press close against the pig so that no part of their bodies can be swung into the pig's champing jaws. When their master seizes the pig by the hind legs, the dogs should let go on the order 'Leave!' Very few are so well-trained. Usually the man tugs one end of the pig and the dogs the other. There is much squealing from the pig, barking from the dogs and bad-tempered shouting from the man before the dogs let go.

We went out with Penny Harris who lives at Harris Tank to see if a pig trap he had erected on a farm west of the Coonamble-Pilliga road had caught anything. Phil Ayoub, the charcoal-burner, came with us.

Pig traps are made of circular weldmesh wheat silos fitted with push-in entrance doors. The traps are baited with boiled grain, preferably a little sour so that it can be smelt a long way off. It was dark when we got there – Penny had underestimated the distance. By the lights of the Land-Rover we saw two pigs in the trap, a savage boar, bigger than usual, and a huge savage barrow, three times the weight of the usual wild pig. The silo had not been cut in half to make it easier to get the pigs out. The sides were 180 centimetres high.

'Bastards too cranky get in with 'em' said Penny in his clipped sentences. 'Got let one out. Hold dog.' So I held the quivering Digger, a cross between a Bull Terrier and a German Shepherd, while Penny held the door open with a stick. Phil walked round opposite the door to hunt one of the pigs out. The boar tried to attack Phil through the cage. The barrow charged at Penny, and rushed through the open door at about sixty kilometres an hour. I let Digger go. Penny dropped the door shut.

Pig dogs do not like working alone, they do not like working at night. Nevertheless Digger chased the barrow and we heard a squeal in the dark distance as he clamped on an ear. But one dog had no hope of holding a pig so big and so fast. Digger returned unhappily. 'Wrong bastard went' said Penny. He lifted the door of the cage, and Digger and Penny crawled in to catch the boar.

Digger grabbed an ear, Penny the hind legs. The boar squealed and struggled. His ear tore off. While Digger changed sides Penny lost his footing. Pig, dog and man rolled tangled together about the cage. The boar hooked at Penny with yellow tusks and each time Penny rolled clear with a centimetre or two to spare. Not many modern men risk death to secure their meat. The other ear began to tear. Phil Ayoub went in to help. Finally the frothing boar was dragged backward out of the pen. We pulled a bag over the head to mask the awful tusks and Penny and Phil sat on the boar in the back of the Land-Rover. We got back to Penny's camp about midnight. Reuben Harris, Penny's brother, helped us carry the boar to the pen where the pigs were kept until needed for meat. We had taken the bag off the boar's head and were just about to drop him in when Penny said 'Forgot. Boar. Got cut him. Get knife. Sharp.'

So Penny held the boar on its back while Reuben walked to the camp, found the knife and sharpened it. The camp was thirty metres away but we heard each draw of the knife against the steel. Reuben handed the knife to Penny and held the boar by its front legs. His own testicles were centimetres from the tusks that could rip them out with a flick of the boar's head. 'Hold torch' said Penny. He spread the boar's hind legs. I lit up the bulging scrotum and Penny made a quick definite slash above the left testicle. Then he pressed the edges of his palms beneath the testicle, squeezed it out the cut – it filled his hands – and threw it over his left shoulder. The throw broke ligaments and tubes and the heavy testicle thudded to the ground somewhere in the darkness. Penny was quick as a conjurer. The right testicle was in his hands as the left one landed. We dropped the pig in the pen. 'Good meat' said Penny. He had earned it.

During the 1974 Christmas fire in the Pilliga Nature Reserve seventy burnt Red-necked Wallabies hopped into a clearing near John Grosser's sawmill. Most would have died, a few might have lived. Wild pigs that somehow had escaped the fire gave none a chance. They ate the lot alive.

Wild pigs will travel ten kilometres by night to feed on a farmer's crop of sorghum and be well gone by daylight. An old boar moved ahead of me out of sight as I stalked him with a gun in a dense crop of wheat, and, after half an hour or so when he grew tired of being followed, he came in behind me and stalked me. A mob of sixty pigs scattered and froze and let twenty-four men with fifteen dogs move past them in a tangled crop of oats. Then they slipped away behind us and most escaped.

By 1977 many wild pigs lived in areas of the forest where they had no access to farmland or domestic stock. Foxes and feral cats lived there, too, and a few rabbits that had braved the dense growth they do not favour. There were no other imported animals; most plants were native. So the pigs lived on native animals and plants – there was nothing else to eat. They ate the dropped red fruit of Quandong and the sweet green fruit of Five Corners that Emus love. They rooted up two hundred square metre patches two-thirds of a metre deep in search of Bardie Grubs, the larvae of the Goat Moth. They rooted for the rhizomes of ferns, the tubers of orchids, worms, ant eggs, and lizards. They ate anything they came across. Their capacity for destruction is inordinate.

'The life went out of the scrub when the wild horses went,' Dick Burke of Kenebri told me. 'Up to 1962 there were a lot. You'd see mobs of ten to twenty crossing the road anywhere you drove. We were always out after them. We loved chasing them. When we were not actually yarding them, we'd just go out to see what was there, and give them a bit of a gallop.

'I yarded one mob with two stallions in it and when I got 'em on the truck the stallions started to fight. They were up on their hind legs squealing and biting and pawing at one another and plunging about all the way from Hunt's bore to Kenebri. I could hardly keep the truck on the road.

'Young Dan Casey yarded over 300 wild horses in 1956, some beautiful Clydesdales among them.'

And Wally Bateman yarded hundreds a few years after Dan Casey, and a lot of men before him and after him yarded lesser numbers. Old Jack Miller who travelled the district with his stripper and winnower used to run horses into his yards at Kiamber. He rode out in the 1880s to the Pilliga East Forest, ran a mob till his horse knocked up, rode home, changed horses, found the mob again, then ran them the rest of the way home. In the 1890s old Dan Jones who used to cart the tallow and cheese from the Euligal boiling-down works and Bill Sowden who selected the farm we now own used to pedal their pushbikes into the Pilliga West Forest, find a mob and drive them back to Kenebri on their bikes. The forest was so open they had no trouble keeping them in sight. Where did all the wild horses come from?

Many were abandoned when prices were low. Good mares escaped from T. G. G. Dangar's runs. The Gardners on Upper Cumble bred a lot of horses, confining them in the one fenced paddock until a dry time ran them out of feed, then they turned them out into the open forest. Gardner horses spread from Kenebri to Narrabri. Tom Heferen in this century had two good draught stallions at Kenebri and a trotting stallion he bought in Dubbo. Tom had only thirty-four hectares fenced. His horses ran in the forest most of the time. Tom's sons left home, he grew too old to muster thoroughly. Young unmarked colts escaped, took mares with them. Tom Heferen's crossbred draughts peopled the Pilliga West Forest. 'Heavy clumpers' the knackery dealers called them – sought-after horses. But Tom Heferen never ceased to proclaim ownership. He would ride fifty kilometres to inspect a yarded horse.

The wild horses were the preserve both of those who thought they had bred them and of those who found them and erected yards to catch them. There were others with no claim at all who wanted them anyway.

'I was out in the big scrub after a few I knew of,' Ron Cutts of Baradine told me. 'And there was this bastard followed me in, started annoying me, just following me round, frightening the horses. Then he cut me yards down while I was way out fencing off another water, so I back tracked the bastard, found out where he was camped, then came back at night and grabbed him in his bunk. Never did nothing to him that night, just tied him up real tight to a tree and left him wondering. In the morning I came back with me mate. I had a long length of barb wire and I hitched that round his neck, then let him loose and led him round a bit. He led real easy with that barb round his neck. You'd have swore he'd been taught to lead. Well after I got tired of doing that I thought I'd put a bit more of a scare in him so I threw one end of the barb over a leaning limb and I called to me mate "Here! Give us a hand to string this bastard up." Gawd! He looked real nervous then.

'But of course we never done nothing bad like that to him. We just tied him back up to the tree, gave him a bucket of water and a loaf of bread and left him till we caught our horses. We never had no trouble with him again after that. And never won't again. Did you read where that bloke was killed working under his car in Narrabri a few months ago? That was him. Had a jack under his car with the wheels off and the jack slipped. Wasn't no loss but. Real bad bastard he was.'

Running the wild horses – driving them at the gallop into winged yards – was a chancy and dangerous occupation. Only the hardest riders enjoyed it. A surer way of taking the horses was to build a trap yard on one water, then fence off other waters in the area during a hot dry spell. 'Perishing the horses' it was termed.

Trapped horses do not charge at the yards in an attempt to break out, so the yards do not have to be built massively strong. Light box or oak rails suffice. But the yards have to be high, almost three metres, because if a horse can lift its head above the top rail it will climb over. And the bottom rail has to be low with no spaces left anywhere where horses can force their heads beneath it. They go down on their knees inspecting every metre of that rail and, if one horse twists its head under it somewhere, it levers upward until the rail breaks, then the whole mob crawl out.

The entrances on the first yards built were all spear-point: V-shaped races of flexible green pine rails sharpened at the end. A gap of about one-third of a metre was left for the horses to push through. If a horse tried to walk back through it, the pointed rails prodded against him and closed tighter.

The horses knew that entrance was a trap. They padded around the other fenced-off waters night after night looking for ways over or under. They ignored the entrance to the trap yard and investigated the bottom rail on their knees. They resisted until they were staring-eyed and hollow-flanked, then they filed through the entrance.

Many of these yards were built in the 1940s. When a mob was

taken the yards were not pulled down and often they were not inspected regularly. Horses came into them and died of starvation. Bert
Ruttley found twenty horses dead in an old yard on Mallallee Creek
(he knew it as Basin Creek) that flows through Ayrlands into Yaminba
Creek. So foresters and timbergetters cut down or burnt yards as they
found them.

Young Dan Casey was not molested when he yarded the horses in
Pilliga West. He was a well-known local and the foresters at Baradine
knew what he was doing. When Wally Bateman, a big Queensland
horse dealer, came down to clean up Pilliga East, there was resistance
from jealous locals as well as Forestry Commission. He could not get a
permit to cut rails to build yards, a concession usually granted on request. When he put up illegal yards they were cut down. Bateman had
men with him as tough as he was. They persisted.

Big Dobbin Hamilton was with him, red-headed and dark. 'He'd be
a mate of Bateman's,' old Dan Casey, young Dan's father, told me.
'He had a bit of a camp put up out on Coghill Creek down near the
Wee Waa road. There was a family of them. They just used to knock
about. The big fellow – someone killed him about Narrabri later – used
to move about a bit. He went over to Coonamble and hung round there
for a spell. Got stuck into them all over there. Give all the principal
blokes a proper hiding. Then he pushed on somewhere else. He'd be
one of Bateman's mob.'

Lumley was with him off and on. 'Felt sorry horses sometimes,'
said Penny Harris. 'Pushed bike out one tank let mob go. Walked up
quiet to gate. Looked up. Lumley sitting behind tree. Cocking rifle.
Would shot me too. Tried once.'

And a man who became a good friend of ours, Dick Law, was with
him, thoroughly broke after a venture on his own running horses in
the channel country in the far south-west of Queensland. He had
difficulties with the freezing of the horse meat. It went unsalably black.
Then a lovely little mare he rode, black with white points, put her foot
in a hidden crack while he was racing on the wing of a wild mob.
She broke her neck and put Dick in hospital. Dick was no tough. He
was intelligent, interested and interesting and known to an astonishing
range of people over much of New South Wales and southern
Queensland.

Bateman himself could neither read nor write. 'I showed him how to
sign his name,' said Dick Law 'by pointing out the letters in comics.'
But he could work out instantly the dressed weight and the value of a
horse in his head and he could keep track of the hundreds of horses he

had moving on stock routes – the buying price and where he had bought them – without any written record that anyone could refer to. Young Dan Casey saw him in Queensland with a mob of eight hundred. 'Good horses, too. I'd never seen so many horses. You see that many cattle. But horses! Gorgeous to see all those horses together.'

Dick Law went down with Wally Bateman to Quirindi to see a solicitor and to pick up the mail that had been collecting at the post office for months. 'That bloody old mare in foal he should never have loaded – she died in the trucks and the RSPCA was charging him. Well after he had seen his solicitor – he got him out of it, he got him out of a lot, that solicitor – we went up and picked up a big bag of mail. And Bateman sat down in the gutter in the main street of Quirindi and started going through it. He couldn't read but he could pick bills from cheques by looking at the envelopes just as well as he could pick horses. "I'll keep that one" Wally would say. "That one's no good. And that. And that." The bills were thrown over his shoulder into the gutter. When he'd finished – look! He had a pile of bills that high and he got out his matches and burnt the lot.'

Forestry Commission and would-be horse catchers pestered Bateman for nearly ten years till he caught two foresters building a fire with one of his trap yards. They ended up in hospital. Then a couple of the huts forestry workers camped in during the week burnt down and signs appeared in charcoal on all the remaining huts, 'Burn my yards and I'll burn every hut in the forest'. Bateman got his permit to cut rails.

He put in traps at Dingo Bore (where Harry Kuhner who lost his shotgun and rifle to the Governors later camped for years), at Lucky Flat, Mollieroi – the list was given to me in the Imperial Hotel at Wee Waa – behind Jack Smith's, Black Creek, Middle Creek, Waterfall, Lane's mill. Every main water in the Pilliga East Forest was fenced in with a spear-point trap. Then lesser waters were fenced off, some small waterholes were pumped dry. The horses were loaded on to a motor truck, put on rail at Gwabegar, and consigned to Burns Animal Food Knackery at Rouse Hill. Australians do not eat horse meat. I have never tasted it and I do not intend to. But I realise that it is an absurd distaste. Horse flesh is a superior food. Like kangaroo meat most of the fat is polyunsaturated.

The few mobs taken in the last ten years were trapped at manned yards. A weighted canvas or hessian roll was fixed above a wide entrance. A rope lead to a man hidden on a little platform in a tree thirty to forty metres away. He always knew when the horses were coming because, although they come suspiciously, they do not come quietly. They trot around checking the yard for other ways in before they risk the obvious entrance.

A stallion reacts viciously when trapped. He turns on his mares, strikes, squeals and kicks in an attempt to force them to break out. Instead of crowding against the fence, the mares crowd into the water to escape him. Foals go down and are trampled into the mud hence the name Dead Filly Tank for one of the waters in the Pilliga West Forest. There are still the remnants of yards about that tank and about several others in that part of the forest. Rails from the dismantled yards decay in heaps. Wire hangs on the trees where the loading ramps were built. The sleeper offcuts that floored the ramps and the oak rails used as baulks behind the horses are scattered about.

Pappy Masman, a Baradine grazier, trapped a small mob in Pilliga West in 1972. There were a few good mares among them that Pappy wanted for breeding. They were wild so Pappy gave each a first lesson in restraint before loading them on to his float. They were lassoed in turn and tied to a tree in the yard. They jerked backward, choked themselves down and rose trembling. They knew it hurt to fight the rope. The stallion reacted so violently he choked himself too hard. 'He went down and stayed down and he looked like he was dead,' said a neighbour's son who was there. 'Pappy was jumping up and down on his belly trying to pump some air back into him. He came good and they ran him on to the truck but they couldn't do anything with him. Real mean he was, a nasty bugger. Kept coming at you with his ears lopped and his mouth open. Had to sell him for dog's meat.'

In 1977 there was a small mob of wild horses in the Pilliga West Forest. Their tracks could be found among domestic cattle tracks at Dead Filly Tank and Red Tank. The Harris brothers saw them sometimes. Out on Borah and Yaminba creeks in the Pilliga Nature Reserve numbers had built up substantially. Tracks showed along all creeks and roads. Dan Casey saw a mob of fifteen in 1965. None had been taken out in the twelve years since so they could have numbered well over a hundred.

They were shy and seldom seen. We saw a bay mare and her undersized foal in one drive down the creek. The foal was at least two years old and no bigger than a six-month foal on good country. Their black manes were long and tails dragged on the ground. They were swaybacked and long-headed, not attractive horses. Wary of the Land-Rover but curious, they kept galloping away, then circling and coming back to stare at us from a hundred metres away.

The most exciting wild cattle lived on those creeks, too: enormous roan and spotted bullocks of Jim Carr's that had been roped, branded and castrated as calves then had run too wild to muster. Only sixteen hectares of the first growth on Yaminba had been cleared. All of Carr's cattle ran where they would. Later when Jim Carr died and the best of the property was cleared and fenced the wildest of the cattle were abandoned.

The Caseys, old Dan and young Dan, had cattle in that area in 1932. Sometimes they mustered Carr's big bullocks and gave them a run. When they were moving freely the Caseys galloped to the lead and made them mill. There seemed to be hundreds. 'Gorgeous to see their horns,' young Dan remembered, 'you'd hear them rattling.' Then they let them go.

After World War II the Forestry Commission stopped the general practice of landholders near the forest using it for extra grazing. Yards were put up in east and west sections and all cattle mustered. Ben Harris, then District Forester, advised the brands of those yarded by radio to Baradine and landholders were given a fixed time to collect their cattle. Those unbranded or unclaimed were impounded and sold. Jim Carr's cattle by then had died out. 'They'd never have yarded them,' said old Dan Casey. 'In the end there were a lot of old bulls that had never been in a yard. Some of them would eat you.'

When cattle breeding became temporarily unprofitable after 1975, the forest began to fill up again with cattle. Most of them were there legally on the fenced-in twenty-five-year leases. Many were there illegally. In 1977 there were quiet branded cattle in the Pilliga Nature Reserve. Neither cattle nor horses have any place there; nor the plentiful feral goats.

South of Canyon Camp in the Warrumbungle National Park there are caves in the hills above Split Rock. Until well into the 1960s these caves housed a colony of Brush-tailed Rock Wallabies. Wild goats displaced them. Since they had nowhere else to live, they must have died. A few brush-tailed wallabies lived on in quieter caves to the west of the park. In 1977 they seemed to be extending their range. Occasionally one was seen at night hopping across the road to the park. Indeed, in 1978 John Johnston, a neighbour, drove for about two hundred metres beside a wallaby he did not know on Belar Road in the flat Merriwindi Forest many kilometres from rocks or hills. He described it as fast, agile, standing about sixty centimetres high with a pronounced black tuft on the end of a long tail. Only the Brush-tailed Rock Wallaby fits that description.

East of Borah Creek there is a hill with a complex of caves ideal for rock wallabies. Hundreds of wild goats have taken them over. They will maintain possession.

When Hans Brunner and Dr Brian Coman called in at the end of 1975, two brilliant Victorian scientists working at the Keith Turnbull Research Institute in Victoria, I took them to see the sandstone pools on Borah Creek. I told them confidently it was a lonely place a good fifteen kilometres from the nearest farmland and, although there were a few wild horses and a lot of pigs and goats, one could expect that the smaller mammals would be native.

The pigs, goats and two of the horses showed themselves as well as somebody's turned-out cattle. We found the droppings of cats, hares, rabbits and imported rats and mice. I did not know then of the interesting native fish in the pools. What fish we saw floating near the surface in little shoals were ancestral forms of the imported Goldfish. A few had retained their original colours to identify themselves. Along the road at the base of prominent low bushes, on top of soil mounded up by the grader, beside windblown sticks was the dung of foxes. Males had been marking out territories. The only sign of native mammals was the strange dung of Spiny Anteaters, sharply broken-off cylinders of sand with ant and beetle cases embedded in it, dropped on the lower tiers of sandstone shelves. Hans Brunner offered to examine fox scats to see if foxes were finding native mammals. He is the world authority on identification of mammals by hair.

Hans Brunner was born in Switzerland and came to Australia in 1953. He did not forsake his homeland, he became first yodeller with the Yodel Club Edelwyss in Melbourne. The Swiss have made fine music of that far-carrying mountain call and Hans was so good Swiss clubs begged him to stay when he returned on a visit. For several years he worked with the Vermin and Noxious Weeds Destruction Board spraying weeds and poisoning rabbits, jobs that did not engage his intelligence. Then he joined Brian Coman as technical assistant. Brian, a slight energetic doctor of science who had specialised in veterinary parasitology, was commissioned to find out if foxes spread Sheep Measles, parasitic worms with complicated life cycles that cause unsightly little nodules in meat. The disease worries exporters because it causes too much meat to be condemned. It was Hans's job to analyse the stomach contents of the foxes trapped and shot.

He began by using the broad methods available in the early 1970s. Plant remains were salvaged and sent to botanists for identification. Insects were identified when pieces were big enough to be recognisable.

Bones were sent to CSIRO. But little enough was then known about the skeletons of native mammals and most of the bone fragments were too small to be identified anyway. Teeth and claws were often absent. Hairs were often present, sometimes the fox's own hairs collected in grooming, often enough the hairs of some mammal it had eaten. These were sorted out obviously. Rabbit fur was recognisable, so was wool and some others if there were clumps in the stomach. Too many hairs were unclassifiable. So Hans Brunner sought information about the structure of hair. He began experiments of his own. His attention was wholly engaged and his work has been singularly brilliant.

A member of the forensic science team in the Victorian police force went to see him to discuss hair identification. He was particularly interested in sectioning equipment – the police force was considering buying an expensive machine. Cross-sections of hairs under the microscope are vital for identification. And a hair has to be cut at right angles. A round hair cut on the slant looks oval and confuses identification. 'I'll show you my machine,' said Hans. 'It is the best that can be got.'

He used a steel microscope slide bored with a row of several 0.8 mm holes. Through one of the holes he pushed a loop of fine nylon thread, then he centred a coil of several turns of cellulose acetate yarn in the loop and pulled it into the hole with the cord. The yarn sprang up in loops making a funnel down which a single hair or a small tuft could be dropped. When the cord was pulled again the hair was drawn down the hole with the yarn. It could then be cut off on the top and bottom of the slide with a razor blade leaving perfect cross-sections to be put under the microscope.

Hans worked very quickly and made the method look easy. But its success depends on exact judgment. If too much hair is drawn down with the yarn the hairs get squeezed out of shape and show a false cross-section. If there is insufficient yarn to hold the hair firmly it does not cut squarely. Perhaps a police officer doing the work occasionally would be better off with a machine costing several thousand dollars that did the job unthinkingly.

As well as cross-sections, the scale patterns on the hair surface have to be studied. Hans coated thin glass coverslips with polyvinyl acetate glue, embedded cleaned hairs in it, and when the solution had set, lifted the hairs carefully with tweezers. When the slide was turned over and looked at through a microscope the scale shapes were seen in a normal position.

Hair varies from the dumb-bell-shaped cross-section of rabbit's fur with the jagged overlaid scales that make it felt so well to the tiny dark oval section of the Lesser Long-eared Bat's hair built up of scales fitted together like a long line of wineglasses. The construction of the hair of all the small bats suggests the barbs of feathers. The long eye-shaped hair sections of Koalas with big rounded scales can be readily picked from the short round hairs of Yellow-footed Marsupial Mice with long narrow sharp diamond-shaped scales. But many hairs are difficult to distinguish especially if only one or two have been found. Hair patterns are not as exact an identification as finger-prints in humans.

Hans Brunner's work increased in accuracy as he built up his stock of pelts for reference. He had good photographic records of the hair of Victorian mammals but he did not often need to refer to them. The complicated features of dozens of hairs were carried in his head. Although the work was so new and was still developing when I first met him, he had already shown that the hairs in predator droppings – the dung of foxes, feral cats and dogs, and the casts of owls – revealed more species of mammals present in an area than any comparable method.

Before the Mitta Mitta River in north-east Victoria filled up a new dam site at Dartmouth, Hans Brunner and other workers at the Keith Turnbull Research Institute carried out a survey of the mammals present by scat analysis. The Victorian Fisheries and Wildlife Division made a separate survey using the conventional methods of trapping and searching at night with spotlights. Eight species were found by hair analysis that other methods did not find, and the hairs of Long-nosed Bandicoots, only five of which were seen or trapped, were found in 149 scats. The only mammals present not found in scats were the abundant small bats seen flying each evening. Astonishingly some scientists did not welcome this marvellous new aid in locating mammals and tried to discount the findings. Happily Hans Brunner's methods became widely accepted and by the end of the 1970s were used by research organisations throughout Australia.

The fluffy short-legged Broad-toothed Rat with wide molar teeth was thought to be nearly extinct in Victoria. Then its hairs showed up in fox scats collected at several places east and west of Melbourne. Later work using scat analysis to locate them and traps to catch them proved them fairly common at times over a wide area.

There was a grisly find in scats picked up in the Sherbrooke Forest, east of Melbourne. Human hair is often found in fox dung because foxes scavenge in garbage dumps if they have opportunity, but Hans found that one fox at Sherbrooke had eaten clumps of human hair with roots. The police were notified. A few days later bushwalkers found the part-eaten body of a suicide.

Hans Brunner examined 173 samples for me from the Pilliga forests. It was a considerable amount of work – one sample alone consisted of ten kilograms of pig dung. Each sample had to be soaked in water, washed in a fine sieve, then spread on a white tray so that hairs which are indigestible could be picked out by eye. Then each different hair had to be scale-printed, cross-sectioned and examined. Hans did enough work to find out that important discoveries could be made, then he ran out of time. Brian Coman and he began a three-year investigation of the effect of poisoning rabbits and Dingoes with 1080, a major job and an overdue one.

Wild pigs had eaten pigs, sheep, rabbits, grey kangaroos, a wallaby not definitely identified but probably the seldom-seen Swamp Wallaby that also showed up in two fox samples, and a Koala. There were big balls of Koala hair in dung collected on Dubbo Creek. The Koala might have been dead before the pigs ate it. But Koalas are clumsy on the ground and a wild pig could eat a live Koala as easily as a dead one.

Apart from the kangaroo family and one species of marsupial mouse, native mammals have not prospered in the new forest like insects, lizards and birds. But the new growth has saved some mammals that would not otherwise be here. The Koala is one that has been saved.

Koalas used to be common. They are solitary creatures and there were sufficient eucalypts in the old open forest to support perhaps one to twenty hectares as well as a good population of Brush-tailed Possums. Both possums and Koalas usually find enough water between rains by licking dew off leaves. In drought time when the trees protect themselves by dropping leaves and branches, possums and Koalas move on to creeks and rivers where the leaves are fresher.

Koalas began to disappear as foxes built up in this area. Foxes were first seen here about 1903 and by 1910 were plentiful. Then the men shooting Koalas for their skins frequently saw scraps of skin and bone on the ground especially along creeks. But the foxes might have eaten mostly sick Koalas. Eye diseases attacked them periodically and starving, blind Koalas sat crying at the foot of trees.

By the late 1970s Koalas had built up again in the forest after the 1951 fire and were seen where none had been seen for sixty years. We have a favourite creek where we can always find one or two to show visitors. They have no preference for trees to rest in and finding them is a matter of walking a long way and looking upward. They rest in oak, cypress pine, angophora, Blakelys Red Gum, River Red Gum – any tree that carries them high above ground. The gums are food trees, the others probably not, although Koalas do not feed exclusively on eucalypts. They have been seen to eat the flower buds of callistemon.

The Koalas in the forest are exceptionally big and beautifully furred. So many Koalas in sanctuaries have the look of well-worn toys. We often see females with young in the pouch, legs dangling unsupported out of the incongruous rear opening. The young are not even held securely by the pouch when the female climbs down from a tree. She climbs down backward, like a man not a possum. Older young ride on the mother's back and, even when they are almost two years old and too big to be carried, the mothers protect them as they sleep. The young one props its back against one branch of a narrow fork. The mother props her back on the other branch, then stretches her arms and legs around her young and grasps the branch behind it.

Koalas are at more risk from the wild pigs that have recently spread into their territory than they ever were from shooters for skins. They spend a lot of time on the ground. Apart from the clumsy ambling about inspecting trees, they periodically spend up to twenty minutes at a time licking soil or gravel perhaps in search of calcium. The forest roads are favourite places for soil-licking. Sleeper cutters see them in the early morning as they drive to work. The Koalas sit up blinking as the vehicle approaches.

A fox confirmed that there are pigmy possums in the forest by eating one out near Timmallallie Creek. These mouse-sized possums with prehensile tails are seen occasionally by men splitting hollow trees for firewood. The species are difficult to separate even when caught and it is not known which species is here. They are seen less often than the Pigmy or Feathertail Gliders, also mouse-sized in body, and delicately beautiful, with long feathery tails that trail behind them as they glide. Dr Kerr of Coonabarabran twice saw colonies of these creatures on the move on his property in the Warrumbungle foothills. It was in 1968 or 1969 shortly after he had bought a neglected grazing block. About dusk he saw what at first seemed to be long leaves drifting from the top of a gum towards the base of the next tree but when they reached it they scampered up it and drifted down again. Ten to twenty progressed like a wave through gums and angophoras. The much bigger Sugar Gliders are fairly common in the forest.

Another fox in a broom patch on Junction Road in Euligal State Forest ate a little kangaroo with hair like the Victorian potoroo. It is not impossible that potoroos (rat-kangaroos with long noses like bandicoots) live in the forest although they have never been reported. But until Liz Edmondson was appointed by National Parks and Wildlife in 1976 to work on mammals in this district, scarcely any scientific observation of mammals had ever been made. She found the skull of some species of bettong (rat-kangaroos with short, blunt noses) outside a cave near Binnaway fifty kilometres south of the Pilliga forest. General observers would have lost any bettongs or potoroos among the plentiful Rufous Rat-Kangaroos that Oxley first reported. That was probably what the fox on Junction Road ate. The forest seems to have saved a few of them. There are increasing reports from areas wide apart of small mammals that fit its description. They are bigger than the other species of rat-kangaroos. Hans Brunner had no hairs from this area for comparison and he found unexpected differences between Victorian and Pilliga forest samples of some known species. It was difficult work.

In 1910 when Ned Edwards of Baradine was fencing land newly cleared by Harry Joy north of Yarrie Lake, the guttural cries of squabbling rat-kangaroos kept him and his fencing mate awake at night. So they caught them with the old springer-and-noose traps baited with bread or potato or pumpkin, tied bells made of jam tins with stones inside to their necks, then let them go to frighten the others away. Often they ate them instead of releasing them – the flesh was white and good.

Rufous Rat-Kangaroos have nowhere been numerous since. That land was soon farmed and the colony disappeared. Earlier rat-kangaroos in other parts of the forest had been decimated by disease. They died in hundreds, little pink noses poking out of their grass nests. Farming and the rapid build-up of rabbits gave them no chance to recover.

All the kangaroo family are subject to periodic catastrophe, usually epidemics of coccidiosis. In 1944 Grey Kangaroos died throughout the forest. They lay dead in twos and threes under trees, in caves. Individuals crawled up hollow logs to die. In 1974 I saw many sick kangaroos. Enormous gaunt old bucks crawled about on four legs, too weak to hop.

Two lovely mammals disappeared about the same time as Rufous Rat-Kangaroos: the smoke-blue, long-haired Bilbies and the Bridle Nail-tailed Wallabies known affectionately as Flash Jack or Jacky Braces. The tail of both these mammals ends in a horny growth like a small finger nail. The Bilby was common in the late 1880s especially on the abandoned parts of the big runs south of Narrabri: Molly, Cooma,

Thurradulba (or Bohena), Tiberenah, Norfolk. They had burrowed
into every sandhill. The increasing local rabbits began to take over the
Bilby burrows in the 1890s. There might be a few Bilbies left near
Gilgandra in central-western New South Wales. My younger son saw a
long-eared mammal that was not a hare from a slow-moving train in
1974. In 1978 a property owner near Gilgandra told Liz Edmondson he
followed what might have been a Bilby for over an hour. If there are
any Bilbies left in the forest I feel sure they will be in the now wild Jacks
Creek State Forest that was old Norfolk.

Bridle Nail-tailed Wallabies are hare-sized and fast-moving. White
shoulder stripes something like the cheek straps of a bridle earned them
the more descriptive name of Jacky Braces. Phillip O'Malley who ran
the Mullali Wildlife Park between Coonabarabran and Gunnedah for
several years thinks he saw one about 1972. Perhaps they still exist in
very small numbers about some of the low hills.

The old men with good memories who gave me so much information
for this book all knew three wallabies by their Aboriginal names. The
Swamp Wallaby, once much more common than it is now, was called
wooroo. The Red-necked Wallaby, now common but very seldom seen
until recent years, was called *bullion*. And there was another common
little wallaby of the scrubby places called *woorion*, exceptionally good
eating I was told. Grey, with a black stripe on the tail, the male was
bigger than the female and both were intermediate in size between the
Rufous Rat-Kangaroo and the Red-necked Wallaby. What else could
they have been but pademelons, probably the Red-necked?

Whatever they were, some are still here. Several times in the dense
Wittenbra Forest where few timbergetters work a small wallaby has
flashed across the road in front of our Land-Rover. They crouch so low
and move so fast it is not obvious that they are hopping. In order to hop
through the dense undergrowth they carry their heads in the same position as a mammal running on four legs. One left clear tracks where the
narrow road was sandy, parallel marks ten centimetres apart every
thirty centimetres.

In 1978 Graeme Robertson, Dr Judy Caughley and Liz Edmondson,
all of the National Parks and Wildlife Service, made an exciting discovery of a colony of thirty-four Black-striped Wallabies in Brigalow
south of Wee Waa. Gould recorded them there in 1863 and no one else
had recognised them since.

Red Kangaroos moved into the forest with the Grey Kangaroos and
since the 1960s have been seen in increasing numbers. The division
which once existed between these species has been lost. Red Kangaroos

spread east into heavily timbered country they had never before entered though they feed out on farmers' crops and open grazing land whenever they can break through fences.

There are two species of Grey Kangaroos but they are not easily distinguished. The two species were confirmed by a study of blood samples in 1966. They might overlap in the Pilliga. One would expect to find the Forester or Eastern Grey Kangaroo (*Macropus giganteus*) but some of the hair samples studied by Hans Brunner were more typical of the Western Grey Kangaroo (*Macropus fuliginosus*). Many of the Grey Kangaroos lived in the forest where they had no access to open country. Their habits were changing in the 1970s. Bores and ground tanks supplied them with water in the northern and western sections of the forest, creek holes and permanent springs in the south. In many places they dug a metre or so to water in the sanded creeks and supplied wild pigs as well as themselves.

The bigger kangaroos are lavish with water. Through binoculars we watched a big buck Red-necked Wallaby on a sandy spit at one end of the Black Duck Waterholes on Borah Creek. For more than an hour he alternately bent down on four legs to drink and straightened up to groom himself with his tongue or soak his forearms and lower legs with saliva. Kangaroos sweat only at times of great exertion. Usually they depend on evaporation from special vascular structures to reduce body temperature. Even on mild spring days our pet Grey Kangaroo frequently soaked his forearms and lower legs where networks of small veins spread beneath the skin. He never dipped them in his water bucket, he always drank first then wet them with saliva. It streamed from his mouth as he licked, far more liquid than he could have held in his mouth after drinking. As soon as his arms and legs were dripping wet the massive saliva flow stopped. When he groomed the rest of his body his tongue just kept normally moist.

Hairy thick-set Wallaroos changed their habits, too, and spread from the mountains into flat country. I disturbed one asleep in the middle of a flat paddock of wheat twenty-five kilometres from the nearest hills, an extraordinary place for a mountain-dweller to be found. The plentiful Red-necked Wallabies began to build up in the mid 1950s as cover increased and most of the Dingoes had been taken. Doggers stopped work in the forest in 1954.

In the early 1900s Dingoes were so plentiful they ran in packs. Billy Mills of Baradine counted twenty-four one morning at daylight in 1910 as they ran away from a dead beast on Dandry Creek. Marc Lubb remembered them in packs of ten to fifteen howling about his tent at night and coming into the firelight to steal food scraps thrown away after the evening meal.

In such numbers Dingoes outstrip their preferred food supply of native mammals and kill sheep. A determined effort was made to get rid of them in the 1940s. Any gaps in landholders' high dog-proof fences were filled in right round the northern and eastern boundaries of the forest and professional doggers set to work with traps and poison. Sleeper cutters earned extra income shooting them for the scalp money placed on their heads. Many set trip guns across tracks to water. A rifle was lashed to a tree with the muzzle sighted at Dingo height. Then a wire tied to the trigger was stretched tightly across the track. Some men had up to six rifles set. It was dangerous to walk or ride along any but the main tracks.

A few Dingoes survived. In 1973 as we drove through old Gibbican in the Baradine State Forest a big red dog took off fast and straight from a Red-necked Wallaby run over by a truck on Mag's road. The dog had opened the Wallaby on the belly, not a place where a domestic dog would begin to feed. Mrs Jill Morphett of Uplands, Boggabri, on the eastern edge of the Pilliga Nature Reserve, watched through binoculars as a spotted yellow dog ran ahead of the Christmas Day fire in 1974. Tawny yellow, sometimes with spots, is one of the main colours of Dingoes. About a fortnight later Jack Taylor on Delwood, an adjoining property, found a ewe killed in the manner Dingoes kill. She was a strong shorn ewe. Her tracks and those of one dog led through the mud of a little creek to where she had been pulled down by the loin and her kidneys and kidney fat eaten. Another ewe nearby was still alive but so badly ripped about the loin her intestines dragged behind her as she walked.

We found two lots of droppings that were certainly dog and probably Dingo when collecting samples in 1974 for Hans Brunner to process. One had eaten a wild pig, the other a Brush-tailed Possum. Another dog, or possibly fox, had eaten part of a Spiny Anteater. The sharp spines of anteaters do not protect them as well as one would suppose. Among his collection Hans Brunner had the stomach of a Dingo that ate an anteater spines and all.

Pepper, our Beagle bitch, showed me how an anteater can be eaten. All food excited her but she was particularly excited by her own catches. When she nosed out an anteater she attacked cautiously at first. It was half-buried below a rotten pine branch. She felt its back with her paws then decided to dig under it. She dug quickly but the pine branch frustrated her so she bit hunks out of the rotten wood until it was nearly bitten through. Then she moved about thirty centimetres up the branch, seized it in her teeth, and propped one paw as a fulcrum in the hole she had chewed. She jerked backward with her head and pushed with her paw till the branch broke. She barked her pleasure, dragged it out of the way, then leapt back to dig under the anteater. By then it had wriggled itself almost out of sight. Pepper dug with all her energy but the anteater made little hunching movements and sank into the ground as fast as Pepper dug. She lay down panting and watched it for a while. Then she barked, cleared the dirt off its back, opened her mouth and struck downward with her top teeth. Three spines broke off. She leapt back, barked and came in again. Several more spines broke off. Blood ran from her mouth but she was too excited to feel pain. The third time she made it obvious she would soon break off enough spines to give her a clear bite. She was excited beyond obeying me so I picked her up and carried her away. Dingoes, bigger and stronger than Pepper, rake anteaters on to their backs and bite at the softer belly.

With a plentiful food supply anteaters are common in the forest. Signs are seen more often than the anteaters: dug-out ant holes, burrows in termite mounds, or piles of the peculiar sandy droppings of several ages under curved logs or in sandstone caves. Each wanders about in a home range of about forty hectares and returns to favourite night covers at irregular intervals. A range overlaps several others. At mating time the female drags her cloaca along the ground and soon collects a following of males attracted by the scent trail. Hollow logs have been found seemingly stuffed with Spiny Anteaters, a female and her coterie of males.

The hairs of Brush-tailed Possums were found in fox scats. Although their food supply has increased these possums are not as common as they were. In the 1930s thousands of possums were trapped for their skins with copper wire nooses on poles leant against trees. No possum could resist the easy way down the poles offered. Many more were poisoned with cyanide and flour. Yet the possums seemed to replace the numbers taken each year. Bushmen declare possums were devastated by myxomatosis in the 1950s along with rabbits. That did not happen but the observation that possums grew scarce then is undoubtedly sound. Almost certainly it was predation by foxes that reduced their numbers. Foxes had lived on rabbits ever since foxes were released in Australia. Then after eighty years their chief food supply had to be replaced suddenly.

Mrs Gwen Bower of Baradine was troubled by Brush-tailed Possums that lived between her roof and ceiling. They thrived on the fruit in her garden. When they grew too many and too noisy I lent her cage traps fitted with drop doors. The possums came readily to baits of pomegranate and honey and she caught them all in a few weeks. We released them among good food trees where there were no other possums.

The colony consisted of ten females of different ages, one young male, and one old male with a yellow belly. The young male was not mature or else the old male would not have tolerated him. Several times during the two years the possums were in residence Mrs Bower heard sharp fights in the ceiling. Each time a young male was found next morning crouched tightly in a corner where a verandah joined the house. Five times she heard prolonged fighting that continued for two or three nights and culminated in cries of pain that grew weaker and stopped abruptly. Each fight was followed a few days later by a bad smell above the ceiling, then the noise by night of something being dragged. The bad smells were transferred to a dense clump of bamboo at the bottom of the garden. Mrs Bower felt sure the old male killed any young males that did not willingly leave the colony and pulled them out of the house when they began to smell.

Out-of-town possums do not live in colonies. They lead solitary lives in defined territories with overlapping boundaries much like Spiny Anteaters.

Since there are few rabbits in dense parts of the forest far from settlement, fewer imported House Mice and, except near water, few imported rats, the foxes and feral cats that live in those places mostly eat native animals: insects in summer, small marsupials and native mice in winter. Food passes quickly through the stomachs of foxes and the hairs in their dung locate colonies of native mammals. Some of the marsupials eaten are rare enough but it is unlikely any species will be wiped out by this predation. What have suffered are the native cats that seek the same food as the foxes and feral cats. Some were still seen in the forest during the 1970s as a glimpse of something spotted in the headlights of a car. One was trapped in a Boggabri fowl-yard in 1972. The species is not known. They were probably the bigger Tiger Cats, creamy-brown with white spots that extend along the tail. The smaller native cats, now very rare, have no spots on the tail. They were creatures of the open eucalyptus forests and were once common. None of their original habitat is now available to them. If the forest has saved any it has saved them in a foreign atmosphere.

For more than forty years there have been reports of Panthers in the forest. Joe Rodgers who lived on Borah Creek twice saw a big black cat during the 1970s. He saw it once about thirty metres away just on dusk and again one night very clearly by spotlight. Several others who were with him saw it too. Joe is accustomed to estimating the weight of animals – his family breed pigs – and he judged it to weigh about fifty-five kilograms.

Big cats, black, tawny or striped, are persistently reported from many parts of Australia. Possibly seven different mammals are seen. The Pilliga cats might be Panthers. The creatures referred to as the Emmaville Panther are almost certainly Panthers. A circus trailer carrying two male Panthers and one female crashed off a New England road in 1959. The cage burst open and all three escaped.

Pumas are reported from the Grampians in Victoria. A few American airmen brought Pumas to Melbourne as cockpit pets during World War II and released them in the mountains when they learnt it was against the law to bring them into Australia. But the Grampian Pumas are confused with the big feral cats sometimes seen there, twice the size of the biggest domestic cat. And elsewhere there are big yellow foxes that look different to other foxes, and Dingoes and feral dogs of unusual colours.

Among these reports of several mammals there are some that seem to describe a big marsupial cat and others that describe the Thylacine, or Tasmanian Tiger. A photograph of a supposed mainland Thylacine published in the *Sunday Telegraph* 27 March 1977 was no proof of its existence. The head looks foxlike – the massive jaws of the Thylacine are missing – and the stripes might have been painted on the body. The heavy tail is cocked to one side in a position that looks unnatural. The Thylacine uses its tail for balance like a kangaroo. It does not swish its tail about like a milking cow.

Early one morning in the Willala hills I heard three inexplicable noises. They were loud deep coughs with a rolling growl at the end, the sort of noise one would expect to hear when approaching the big cat cages at the Zoo, not near an Australian hill. The animal was no more than thirty metres away but the growth was so dense it was impossible to leave the graded fire trail I was walking along to look for it.

Some of the small mammals in the forest are known from one specimen or one sighting. A farmer on the edge of Jacks Creek State Forest south of Narrabri sent an Ingrams Planigale caught by his cat to the National Parks and Wildlife Service. These tiny mice, about half the size of a House Mouse, are the smallest of the marsupials and few enough have been seen anywhere. Their skulls are extraordinarily flattened, no more than three millimetres thick, so that they can fit lizard-like into crevices in sandstone or cracks in timber, or squeeze under clumps of grass and leave no sign of their passing. David Fleay bred them in his Queensland sanctuary in the 1960s. His first female ate more than her weight in grasshoppers a day.

Keith Pickette who farmed a block of old Cumble described four rat-sized marsupials that must have been Brush-tailed Phascogales. He felled a dead tree for firewood and a hollow limb split open when it hit the ground. The four mammals tumbled out of a nest of leaves into the mouths of Keith's dogs. He could not prevent them being eaten but he did get a good look at them as they were being chewed. Phascogales are tree-dwellers, active and agile. One can race down a tree trunk with its tail fluffed out like a bottle-brush behind it, come to a sudden stop, hang motionless head down, then flip round and race up again.

On a sandy track near The Bulga, the hill north of Willala mountain, I found tracks in loose sand of some small hopping marsupial. The sand was too loose to record claw or pad marks but about every eighteen centimetres parallel indentations showed plainly thirty millimetres long and twenty-five millimetres apart. Mitchell's Hopping Mouse is the most likely to have made them. None have ever been reported from the Pilliga forests.

Droppings I found on Old No. 1 Break seem to confirm the presence of some species of hopping mouse. There were no tracks. The droppings had washed down the road after a storm on to a sand pile. I collected a big envelope full and sent them to Hans Brunner. The mammal seemed to be exclusively a herbivore. Hans found a few unidentifiable grooming hairs but no remains of insects. There are no mouse-sized herbivores other than hopping mice.

During the 1970s the New Holland Mouse, a delicately-built Australian rodent of the genus *Pseudomys*, was found in several places in New South Wales. Like the Broad-toothed Rat it was thought probably extinct until one was caught in 1967 near the garbage tip in Kuring-gai Chase National Park north of Sydney. Kent Keith of the Division of Wildlife Research, CSIRO, set traps systematically in coastal forest till he found that the mice were common in a small area south of Port Stephens, New South Wales. Since then they have been found in other places.

Several native mice thought at first to be New Holland Mice have been trapped in widely spaced parts of the Pilliga forest. My younger

son, Mitchell, caught one in an Elliott trap in January 1978 only a couple of hundred metres outside our boundary fence in the fairly open,
exploited Merriwindi Forest. We were delighted to find it but what we
were trying to catch was a Yellow-footed Marsupial Mouse so that
Kim, my elder son, could photograph its extraordinary feet.

The mouse Mitchell caught was a pregnant female. Pregnancy is
easy to recognise since the vulva, separate from the urethra, seals over
until birth is imminent. Barry Fox who was studying New Holland
Mice at Macquarie University kept her alive. She produced four
young. They all lived for three months, then one night a native rat, also
under study, chewed his way out of his cage, opened the mouse's cage
and ate the whole family.

Because the Pilliga mice are so isolated from other New Holland
Mice and because the several caught had all been measurably smaller
than New Holland Mice, Barry Fox suspected they might be a new
species. The rat left enough flesh for an electrophoretic study by Dr
David Briscoe and Sandra Ingleby. Using exquisitely selected dyes
they compared the movement in an electric current of the blood pro-
teins of the Pilliga mice with all known species of *Pseudomys*. They were
clearly distinct.

We caught another pregnant female. Barry Fox and David Briscoe
came to Baradine and caught a male and one more pregnant female.
Barry Fox bred enough to yield substantial measurements for comparison with the other species. As I made final revisions to this chapter
in August 1980 they had published their first paper in *Australian Mammalogy* convincingly cataloguing the mouse as a new species: *Pseudomys
pilligaensis*.

There are two genera of small marsupial mice with carnivorous
teeth: *Antechinus* with broad hind feet, of which the Yellow-footed Marsupial Mouse is a species, and *Sminthopsis* with narrow hind feet.

There are three species of *Sminthopsis* in the forest. It is not known
how plentiful they are since they are seldom caught in the neatly-built
Elliott folding traps. They are suspicious of even small strange objects
in their territory and a box of shining aluminium is a signal to keep
away. Hans Brunner found that foxes had eaten *Sminthopsis crassicaudata*, the species with a short fat tail that stores food for a brief winter
lay-up. *Sminthopsis murina*, more mouse like but prettily marked about
the head, with a long thin tail is present and also *Sminthopsis macroura*, a
species with a long fat tail. One sees these marsupials mostly when
tractor-driving at night though they prefer open grassland with fallen
timber on it to forest or farmland, a diminishing environment.

During the 1979 winter farming period these marsupials were more plentiful than usual. We were able to compare live *Sminthopsis macroura* and *S. crassicaudata*. A dead *Sminthopsis murina* fell out of a hollow tree pushed down by a bulldozer at Rocky Glen. Although the Australian Museum had no doubt of its identification, it was much bigger than two other members of the same species I have seen here.

The Yellow-footed Marsupial Mouse is common in the forest, especially in wet years. They trap readily and although nocturnal sometimes play about by day under cover of fallen pine tops or slabs of bark. The first I caught (and the first I had ever seen) was in 1970 when we were clearing a few rabbits off our newly bought property. A rabbit trap set at what looked like a breeding stop caught not a pregnant doe but a Yellow-footed Marsupial Mouse that was carrying a House Mouse. The jaws of the trap had closed across both their bodies and the jaws of the Yellow-footed Marsupial Mouse were still clenched on the body of the House Mouse.

They come to baits of meat or sultanas. Peanut butter is a favourite. They have bristly steel grey hair on the back with rusty yellow flanks and legs, and vary in size according to age and sex up to that of a half-grown rat. They, too, are extremely agile. A young male trapped near a big fallen Bimble Box on our own property raced out along one of the hollow limbs when released. They run unevenly but very fast and jump every few paces. It is a bouncing gait. Suddenly he dived over the side of the log and up into a small hole in its side. He knew exactly where the hole was because it could not be seen from the top of the log. The movement was so quick he gave the impression that he somersaulted in mid-air and sprang upward.

A female caught at the same place the next night showed how he had done it. She dived too quickly. Her forepaws caught the little bulge at the top of the knot hole (it was no more than thirty millimetres in diameter) but she could not bring her hindlegs up so she could dive into it. Her body swung out and over. She let go with one paw and twisted so that she faced the hole. She hung momentarily then dropped to the ground about thirty centimetres below. Then in a recoil movement with no hesitation she leapt straight upward into the hole.

Their feet are as marvellously made as the feet of the Native House Gecko but instead of laminations they have granulated pads that allow them to run upside down across the roofs of sandstone caves. Whenever we catch a small mammal we put it in a glass preserving jar. This allows us to get a good look at it without hurting it by handling it.

Yellow-footed Marsupial Mice can climb up the glass with ease but they cannot hold themselves still on it.

Most of them when taken out of the traps are wet with urine, bedraggled and frightened. One shivering female caught on Baileys Peak had eleven tiny naked young clinging to her teats. They have no real pouch. Skin folds that run the length of the belly gradually deepen and roll over the young as they grow. But they are never sufficient to enclose them. The young always poke out like parallel growths of proud flesh.

A night in a trap does not make them trap shy. I caught one old female on three successive nights and each time I had moved the trap about fifty metres. She was easily recognisable since I had plucked a tuft of hair out of one shoulder to send to Hans Brunner. I feel sure she was older than the maximum three years they are said to live. They usually have particularly sharp teeth. Molars are jagged and incisors needle-pointed. The teeth of this female were ground down to short smooth stubs of bone. Perhaps she trapped so enthusiastically because she was finding it difficult to capture food.

One species, *Antechinus stuartii*, the Brown Antechinus, has been well studied. They might live in the Pilliga forest but none had been found up to 1979. The males of this species die after a winter mating. The females bear their young and mate again with the new males the following winter. The year-old females also mate.

During 1974 R. W. Inns, a zoologist at the University of Adelaide, kept Yellow-footed Marsupial Mice in cages during a full breeding season. None of the males died. He concluded that 'the lack of die-off observed in captive males is probably due to the fact that they have an adequate supply of food and are not as heavily stressed as wild males'. I doubt that conclusion. Males of the Yellow-footed Marsupial Mouse do not die generally like the males of the Brown Antechinus. I have caught about ten males out of thirty-odd that were obviously older than the general breeding group. They were half as big again as year-old males and as tawny on the belly as an old possum. They looked healthy and they were in good breeding condition. Their testicles were big, firm, covered with hair and held close to the body. At the end of breeding they shrivel to little bald pendulous sacs.

Mating is a savage and lengthy process. Basil Marlow, curator of mammals at the Australian Museum, kept cages of Brown Antechinus under study for years during the 1960s. The females can ovulate only under shock. Gentle males are no use to them. So the male grabs the female by the scruff of the neck, drags her into position and mounts. He rides her for up to twelve hours without a break and shakes her about furiously if she tries to pull away.

There are small flying-fox camps in the forest though I know of no one who has found one. But when fruit is ripe in orchards round the forest perimeter Red Flying Foxes find it or the Grey-headed Flying Foxes. One hears their cries at night and sometimes sees their dark angled wings against the moonlight more like shadows than flesh.

And the little insect-eating bats have thrived with the insects, five species at least. Hans Brunner found hairs of the Chocolate Bat in two groups of fox scats. One wonders how foxes catch them. Perhaps they sometimes camp in hollow logs. A Little Bat hurtled into the dish I was washing up in one night when camped in the forest. Luckily the water was not too hot so we washed the soap off the squeaking little animal and put it up in a tree to dry. These small common bats trap themselves in odd places round farm homesteads. They drown in buckets of sump oil not emptied immediately or tangle themselves in fat from the killing pens hung out of reach of dogs until it is burnt.

Little Pied Bats get into houses sometimes, as do the marvellously ugly Long-eared Bats, the Greater and the Lesser. The ears of the last two species are joined together by a membrane and they spread in flight like secondary wings. One of the Greater species flew out of a coil of hessian stored for months in a shed as I unrolled it to clip it to the sides of a bulk storage bin in a paddock of ripe sunflowers. It fluttered about me bewildered by the sunlight then flew to the top of a tree fifty metres away. For half an hour the bat kept flying back to hang on the spread hessian as though it hoped it would roll up again and enclose it in comfortable darkness.

Apart from bats and Yellow-footed Marsupial Mice, all that can be said for small mammals in the forest is that some were still present during the 1970s. They are hard to find and harder to trap. They might not exist in sufficient numbers to be safe. They might be more plentiful than is thought.

13

Animal Life
The Birds

Birds above all have profited from the growth of the forest. In an area where explorers and, later, land surveyors commented on their scarcity there is now a miracle of birds. One sees not ten or twelve Magpie-Larks in a winter flock, but a hundred and fifty and many flocks; not twenty wood-swallows pressed together in a long feather bolster on a limb, but twenty thousand in noisy excitement feeding on Blue Lucerne Moths. Crested Pigeons and Common Bronzewings that once fed on the scant seeds of native grasses on the flats and acacia on the ridges now have the choice of thousands of hectares of acacias producing a succession of pods, and of farmers' crops and introduced weeds circling the whole forest and encroaching in long tongues into all parts. Both species of pigeons like to pick over worked ground, not the rough clods of first ploughing or even the deep furrows of the scarifier, but the smoother ground at sowing time when harrows are drawn behind the seed drill. The oval-bodied bronzewings come to ground with the trajectory of bullets and as they land they kick up little spurts of dust like bullets striking.

Birds that drink water such as honeyeaters, parrots and doves have the few springs and waterholes left in the sanded creeks, and the farm and forest troughs and ground tanks that more than replace the water that has been lost in the sand. The little insect-eaters that get their

water from their food and from dew on leaves, thornbills, wrens, pardalotes, instead of being restricted to narrow bands and patches of
scrub where the insects were, now have the whole new forest to feed in.

About forty members of a Gould League bird study group who
camped on Baradine showground at the end of August 1975 counted
144 species in seven days. They were expert observers and could
recognise birds from momentary glimpses. Dollar Birds and Rainbow
Birds, migratory species, had not yet arrived (Sacred Kingfishers arrived two days before the camp ended) and other species that are nomadic opportunists like Crimson Chats and Grass Whistle-Ducks did
not come at all. Crimson Chats came more often to the district when
hay was cut with a binder and the sheafs dried in stooks. The chats
buzzed about the stooks in little swarms like giant crimson bees. Some
of the rare birds – Grey Goshawks, Mallee Fowl, Brush Turkeys – did
not show themselves. There are over two hundred species in the forest
area.

Mallee Fowl and Brush Turkeys are two species that have not gained
by the change in conditions. They were once plentiful. Now they are so
rare very few people know of their existence in the forest. But without
the dense growth to protect them not even the present small numbers
would have survived.

The Mallee Fowl are the only members of their species so far east in
Australia; the Brush Turkeys are the only members of their species so
far west. It is remarkable that two birds requiring such different conditions were ever plentiful. Both are mound-builders. The males of
each species spend a big part of the year raking leaves and soil to maintain the mounds. An old mound might be six metres across and two
metres high. But whereas the Brush Turkey rakes damp litter into
the mound – the incubation warmth comes from fermentation – the
Mallee Fowl uses the warmth of the sun to hatch its eggs. The leaves
and litter raked in with the sand are merely to keep the mound in
workable condition. When the eggs are in the mound the male Mallee
Fowl is forever in attendance. He tests the temperature with his tongue
and opens the mound to the sun a little if it is too cool, closes it if it is
too warm. Sometimes on cloudy days he opens it deeply and almost exposes the eggs. Then, if the sun comes out hot or if rain threatens, he
fills it in frantically. Sudden changes in temperature cost him most of
his energy.

When the Brigalow scrub was thick south-west of Narrabri, one
Brush Turkey's mound could be seen from the other. Young Bert
Ruttley saw hundreds of mounds as he lifted the chain drawn between

Joy's steam traction engines. There was deep litter beneath the Brigalow and after good spring and summer rains the male Brush Turkeys sought out areas free of the tangle of black roots and raked furiously while the ground was wet. The long stiff dead leaves fermented slowly. Heat was maintained for weeks.

Brush Turkeys were shot in dozens in the 1930s along with kangaroos that were driven against the Dingo-proof fences. They can run fast and they prefer to run rather than fly. During the drives they were frightened by the cracking of whips and firing of guns, so they ran with the kangaroos. When they suddenly found themselves hard against the two-metre fences it was too late to lift over. They were shot as they beat helplessly against the netting.

Illegal shooters in coastal rainforests use little yapping terriers to force these birds off the ground into trees where they can be shot with ease. I could not bring myself to eat one of these birds. It seems such an unnecessary extravagance. There is flesh enough to satisfy any palate. A mother told me not many months ago that her son, walking with a party in the Mount Kaputar National Park, shot and ate a Brush Turkey. The birds are not as rare there as in the Pilliga forest but they are rare enough. I would not have been much more startled if she had told me they had eaten a piccaninny.

The birds were fairly common in the forest until the mid-1940s. Mrs R. Gunter who lived as a child on the now abandoned and overgrown Chromite Road remembered the flash of the cock's red head as he fanned his tail and strutted much like a domestic gobbler. The children walked or rode bicycles along the forest tracks and they came on the birds silently.

After 1946 none of these birds were seen in the forest for years. It might have been the shooting that eradicated them, it might have been foxes; or else the awful rabbit plague of the 1940s might have interfered with breeding. Rabbits destroy ground litter.

The few birds left were saved by the frantic growth of the 1950s. It gave them a chance to breed up again. Bloodwood country with dense undergrowth is their choice since the Brigalow was swept down. That country would never support the same population – it is drier – but several beekeepers and sleeper cutters each knew of a mound or two being worked in different parts of the forest until 1974. On one road in the far eastern section several birds used the banks of graded drainage cuts as mound bases.

Then came the Christmas day fire of 1974. No one knows how Brush Turkeys behave in a fire. Do they try to fly away from it or do they try to outrun it? I went in to inspect the mounds I knew of a month or two after the fire. They looked as though they had come out of a potter's oven: glazed and brick-hard. Even if the birds escaped there was no litter for rebuilding.

The Mallee Fowl is rarer now than the Brush Turkey but perhaps it is building up. Several were seen in the 1970s. One of those sightings was a quick flash of a bird in flight by a woman who grew up in mallee country. They fly distinctively. On 28 December 1977 Alan Morris, stationed at Coonabarabran as senior ranger of National Parks and Wildlife, caught a week-old chicken on the eastern edge of the Pilliga Nature Reserve. The chickens are unmistakable. Down covers their bodies but their wings are feathered in the adult pattern. They can fly as soon as they worm out of the mound.

Mallee Fowl were once common since the dry open forest suited them a great deal better than the modern tangle. On Taylor's old Dinby on the western side of the forest, they flew in and ate wheat with the fowls in the evening. Laura Purdy of Baradine who lived as a child at the old Rocky Creek sawmill remembers her mother rolling Mallee Fowl eggs in a flannel singlet and setting them to hatch beneath the oven of a bow-legged fuel stove. She does not remember what happened to the chickens but she is sure they hatched. Certainly they would have bolted out the kitchen door and taken to the bush. That is what they do after their long dark upward tunnelling through the sandy mound. The parent birds never see their young. Their whole attention is devoted to the mound.

Southern Stone-Curlews have also decreased. The forest would have pushed them out with the cattle and sheep because curlews like open country. They are companions of the Australian Spur-winged Plovers and the quiet trim Banded Plovers that always turn their backs to an observer. But the curlews are gone from plains adjacent to the forest where plovers are still common. Their call used to be as much a part of the night as the Southern Cross. Little parties of three or four, no more, gathered together on still clear moonlight nights. They made agitated little cries increasing in tempo and loudness until one broke out into the long wailing 'Kerloo'. Then another bird wailed and another. The cry is so desolate the Aborigines made legends to account for it. One tells of the souls of women lost somewhere after death and crying for lovers. I heard the cry at Baradine one night in 1969, and I have not heard it since. Some farmers still hear them a few kilometres to the west of our home.

The Southern Stone-Curlew was never a plentiful bird. They lived in pairs with a territory of perhaps 500 hectares. The calls carried a long way, two to three kilometres with ease, so they could be heard whenever they called.

Farming and over grazing probably reduced their numbers originally. The survivors are perilously exposed to foxes. They nest on bare ground and depend on camouflage for protection. Foxes do not eat many birds if there are rabbits and insects about. But they are omnivorous feeders. If the preferred food is not available they take whatever there is. There are few rabbits on the plains where the last curlews in the district live and in winter or in dry summers there are few insects. Birds then form a substantial part of the diet. Curlews cannot afford to supply any part of a fox's diet.

Out east in the lovely Willala hills among the well-grown Red Ash and the kangaroo-tails and pinnate-leaved hopbush, the angophora, ironbark, bloodwood and profusion of flowering shrubs and little plants, there are Spotted Pardalotes in hundreds. Wherever one stops within ten kilometres or so of the hills, their loud three note call beats out. We camped early one September right on top of the hills. Pardalotes were nesting under sandstone slabs, in burrows beneath roots and in the long mound of sand scraped out by a grader. We were setting Elliott traps for lizards and marsupials and it was difficult to find a hole that was not a pardalote's nest.

While we were camped a carload of young people drove in. Usually only Land-Rovers can travel the Scratch Road but they were taking advantage of recent grading. They came to us saying they had dug out a little hole – a bird had gone down it just like a mouse – and now there were four little birds, unfeathered, uncovered, and squeaking. What would they do? I took the shovel and we fitted a strong slab of bark over the top of them, then covered it with sand. We moulded a likely looking entrance from damp soil. The parent birds were suspicious for nearly an hour. The young ones kept squeaking and the female hopped about the nest inspecting the changes. Now and again she poked her head into the opening then hopped back in alarm as though she feared it might fall in if she ventured any farther. But she gained courage and went in. My younger son checked the next morning and the female was unconcernedly flying in and out with food.

There are Grey-breasted Silvereyes and Double-bar Finches in extraordinary numbers and communities of the lovely Purple-backed Wrens. Southern Yellow Robins quiet and curious have watched us make camp each time we have been there. They perch upright like treecreepers on the trunks of shrubs, then lean out sideways. If an insect moves on the ground they forget us and hop down to grab it.

There are thornbills and weebills, all seven species that can be there. And most of them are exasperatingly difficult to identify as they seek insects in the shrubs. They are never still. All one sees is a bit of chestnut rump as a bird dives away, or a bit of streaking on a breast or a bit of pale yellow as it flashes forward.

One usually has to wait for a thornbill to help identify itself by its actions. A thornbill that flies to the top of an ironbark and makes an inspection of leaf bunches by hovering like a warbler is probably, in that area, a Little Thornbill. And if a thornbill hops on the ground to feed and is buff about the tail it is a Buff-tailed Thornbill. Some species do not feed on the ground. The lovely Yellow-tailed Thornbill, mostly a ground feeder, is slower moving than the other species and the only one that presents itself for close inspection through binoculars. And binoculars are not needed to identify it – the bright yellow rump declares it without doubt.

Most thornbills and pardalotes and several other birds were as impossible as skinks for the amateur to identify until the publication of Peter Slater's two volumes comprising *A Field Guide to Australian Birds*. This great work makes what was impossible easy. One misses the artistry of Nevill Cayley's *What Bird is That?*. Cayley's birds are living birds but painted sometimes as if he saw them at a distance without binoculars. Slater's birds are flat shapes but he knows each feather and his colours are mixed and applied with mathematical accuracy.

Australian books on birds are of extreme standard. Klaus Immelmann in *Australian Finches* has identified the gaping naked young by mouth marks and followed their parents through every phase of their lives. H. J. Frith's *Waterfowl in Australia*, in its observation of the breeding and the feeding of ducks, reads like a journal of exploration. And David Fleay in *Nightwatchmen of Bush and Plain* reveals not only the habits of the secretive owls but the character of the birds. This has been seldom done at such depth for any animal.

The two great photographic works, *The Readers Digest Book of Birds* and *Every Australian Bird Illustrated*, are good to own but they are not books for identification. Strangely some of the photographed birds look less real than Cayley's paintings. They have been caught in unusual postures.

A number of the best photographs in both books were taken by Wilf

Taylor who lives on Bugaldi Creek where the early vegetable-growers had their farms. He, too, is a farmer and one of the best photographers of free birds in the world. He spends weeks waiting and watching to get the exact photograph he requires, and sometimes leaves his camera in place for days till a bird gets used to it. He once took a series of photographs of the hatching of Spur-winged Plover chickens. In the first the bird sits on her nest. In the next small round holes show in two of the eggs. In the last photograph taken about twelve hours later the feathered chicks are free of the eggs and ready to run. Many of his photographs are in the Australian Museum's *National Photographic Index of Australian Wildlife*. That collection was the idea of A. Donald Trounson, a British diplomat and photographer, who gave most of his time to photographing Australian birds after his retirement in 1967. In association with another photographer, Molly Clampett, he built a cage with transparent reflection-free sides that allowed a bird to be photographed against its natural surroundings from a distance of sixty centimetres. Special fast flashlights (an eighty millionth of a second) were set at calculated angles. They took this cage to the Simpson Desert and to Cape York and photographed birds caught in mist nets that had never before been photographed. The result was a perfection seldom attained.

Joseph Forshaw's magnificent expositions of parrots are fine for identification but their size and their value make them unfit to carry about on the rough front seat of a Land-Rover, especially in rainy weather beneath the little split in the roof of our old rover. *Parrots of the World* with William Cooper's paintings increases in value satisfyingly year by year. But ours will not be maintained in mint condition. It is well used.

We have seen a pair of the big black Yellow-tailed Cockatoos screeching from the top of a little angophora in the Willala hills. They are rare enough in the forest. The Glossy Cockatoo is the black cockatoo usually seen and heard flying over the forest. They feed wherever there is casuarina and they are noisy and tame in their feeding. One can approach within a few metres. They were thought to be rare until recent times because they were usually confused with Red-tailed Cockatoos.

Black cockatoos do not hang from low branches to drink like Galahs or bend down from part-submerged logs like Sulphur-crested Cockatoos. Those that feed in the eastern part of the forest water at Arthur Kensit's big ground tank on his Bulga property. In late afternoon little flocks of ten or twelve fly screaming out of the forest. They light on a high bare bank of the tank, then walk slowly down it and line up like sheep at the water's edge.

Mrs Win Kensit has seen three species of black cockatoos watering at that dam. Red-tailed Cockatoos, the females prettily spotted with yellow, come sometimes to the eastern part of the Pilliga forests not far from the Namoi River.

We crawled once through a kangaroo-torn hole in the old Dingo-proof fence to Neil Kemmis's Be-Bara and climbed the Willala Mountain, the highest point at the far eastern edge of the hills. The slopes are tumbled with big sandstone slabs and on the hill itself there are rock falls, caves and crevices, sheer faces and wide deep cracks. Trees and shrubs sprout wherever they can get a hold. One must circle halfway round to get to the top and as we climbed we saw a Peregrine Falcon circling below us over the valley of a little creek. Suddenly his mate began to scream to him from her nest in a crack on the top of the hill. The noise poured down the crack on top of us, indrawn screams as she took in breath, then rapid high notes as she poured it back out. They beat on the back of the neck like little stones.

There is a trig. station on the top as on the Bulga hill thirty kilometres to the north. They were put there in 1957. As we left the hill a Swamp Harrier, now becoming rare, watched us from a stunted ironbark. It moved down a couple of times as we moved, like a watchman descending stairs to see unwanted people off the premises.

Alan Morris, senior ranger, made a daily count of all birds seen as he drove about his huge district. A man with a deep knowledge of birds, he had not a great deal of faith in the tally of small species but he thought his list of birds of prey reliable. Here is that list for 1975:

Black-shouldered Kite	214	Spotted Harrier	10
Black Kite	54	Swamp Harrier	5
Whistling Kite	28	Black Falcon	8
Brown Goshawk	13	Peregrine Falcon	10
Collared Sparrowhawk	4	Little Falcon	7
Wedge-tailed Eagle	61	Brown Falcon	184
Little Eagle	20	Nankeen Kestrel	1056

Those birds were counted in a huge slab of the central west bounded north and south by Coonamble and Molong, east and west by Coolah and Nyngan. But all fourteen species are present in the forest or the circling plains. Seven or eight of them can usually be counted on a summer's day drive from Baradine to Coonamble. Telephone lines run one side of the road, electric light lines the other. Nankeen Kestrels and Brown Falcons use the poles as permanent look-outs for prey. Other species use them as temporary resting-places – even the huge Wedge-tailed Eagles.

Alan Morris saw Wedge-tails in satisfying numbers. It is not yet an endangered species. But it now has an uncertain food supply. Once it fed on rat-kangaroos and Bilbies. As rabbits replaced them it changed happily to a chief diet of rabbit. For sixty years it fed on rabbits from 1890 to the coming of myxomatosis in 1950. Thereafter it must have increased predation on birds – Galahs are a favourite meal, though hard to catch – and on carrion. What else was there? Young kangaroos are sometimes taken but by the time a joey leaves the pouch for long periods it is so heavy that it requires clever hunting by a pair of eagles to take it.

Although Wedge-tailed Eagles have lived successfully since 1950, their diet in many districts is precarious. They depend for a substantial percentage of their food on animals killed by fast cars on bitumen roads, never a safe feeding-place, and on dead sheep in paddocks. This last food exposes them to poison, to the rifles of graziers despite the birds' protection, and to changes in land use. More acres under plough in a district, or a switch from sheep to cattle, displaces eagles in search of food to the guarded territories of other eagles.

In *The Great Extermination*, edited by Dr A. J. Marshall shortly before his death, there is a photograph of an eagle with outstretched wings supposedly standing on a boy's arm. The caption states 'The wedgetail was taken from its nest as a baby and became the wild pet of Gary Ryder who lives near Coonabarabran'. The photograph worried me. Falconers have always used heavy gloves. Modern gloves are meshed with steel. No one, I thought, could allow owl or hawk to sit on a bare arm without risking talons being driven and locked into his flesh. So I asked a member of the Ryder family. The photograph was faked. An English visitor thought it would make a good photograph to string up a dead eagle and have Gary hold an arm beneath its legs. It is clear that the eagle is dead once one is told – the toes are curled unnaturally. The photograph was published in the English magazine *Field* with the imaginary caption and eventually came back to Australia.

The Wedge-tail has fed fairly safely on dead lambs and sheep since it likes meat fresh. The Whistling Kite is in danger because it is a carrion feeder. It arrives at a carcass after the ravens, after the eagles, after the silly graziers with an organo-phosphate poison to kill the harmless ravens. The summer's day call of the Whistling Kites as they circled, a long whistled glissando then a climb in seven or eight short notes up the scale again, was once as common as the curlew's wail at night. Now it is seldom heard.

The Little Falcon is not as rare as Alan Morris's count shows. These fast-flying birds do not haunt roads for carrion but follow tractors about paddocks taking grasshoppers, Little Quail, mice – anything that moves from the machinery – on the wing. Two or three often follow our tractor for an hour or so a day. They dive, snatch grasshoppers out of the air, then glide upward while they bend down to eat them, then turn quickly and dive for more. Sometimes one rockets down and snatches a grasshopper inches from the front wheel of the tractor. If a quail or a mouse is taken the bird usually flies off to a tree to eat it.

An old Spotted Harrier flies over sometimes, too, to see if the tractor has disturbed anything for it. That harrier was on the property when we bought it in 1968. The borders of its territory seem to be the boundary fences. It makes regular slow inspections of the paddocks flying up and down no more than a metre or two above the ground. When it makes a catch, always something bigger than a grasshopper, it comes to ground to eat it, or sits on top of a strainer post.

Since he made the list of hawks Alan Morris saw a pair of rare Grey Falcons on a property on the Baradine-Coonamble road. One of them had just caught a Brown Flycatcher. A casual observer might have mistaken them for the common Black-shouldered Kite.

I have seen two species of hawks not on the list, one only of each species. A Black-breasted Buzzard came to the farm at the end of April 1977 after the first draft of this chapter was written and stayed on for a couple of weeks. These are massively built hawks, unmistakable as they fly overhead because of a large oval white patch at the base of the flight feathers on each wing, much like the white circles on the Dollar Birds' wings. By its great size it was probably a female and she could usually be found somewhere each morning sitting quietly in Kurrajong, Whitewood or pine. Hawks are usually nervous of binoculars – probably they suggest guns – but she watched me as I watched her from the Land-Rover and she showed no fear, often breaking her gaze to groom herself. When Brolgas, Bustards and Emus nested on the grey Riverina plains, Black-breasted Buzzards were known to threaten the sitting birds. Groups of five or six dived on them or came to the ground and advanced on them with open beaks and outstretched wings. When the frightened bird abandoned the nest, the buzzards picked up stones or clods, dived at the eggs and dropped the missiles as they pulled out of the dive. Then all congregated to feast on the smashed eggs.

The other hawk was a lovely Grey Goshawk, rare in this district. There was a sudden racket one day among the Red-rumped Parrots that feed regularly in the wild garden. I went out expecting to find the enormous goanna that comes now and again to try to break into the Guinea Pig's cage. The goshawk was on the ground feeding on a parrot. It was a delicate arrangement of light greys with fine barring on the breast, thick yellow legs and red eyes. It stayed about for a couple of days terrorising the Red-rumped Parrots and upsetting all the regular inhabitants of the garden.

Strange small birds are usually allowed to fit in. A pair of White-winged Trillers, not often seen about the house, can come for a whole season without comment. Even a pair of silent Black-eared Cuckoos belonging to a generally hated family of birds, aroused resentment only among the Willie Wagtails when they stayed a week or two in July 1975. The cuckoos probed the wire holes in the garden fence for spiders, holes that the wagtails regularly inspect.

But any strange big birds, even harmless ones, are fiercely resented. A bedraggled Nankeen Night Heron flew late one afternoon into a big White Cedar outside the kitchen window. It was winter and the tree was bare, no resting place for night herons that like dense cover. Anyway it was almost dusk, feeding time for these birds. It was obviously sick or exhausted. It hopped down the bare branch and pressed itself against the trunk to make itself as inconspicuous as its white breast would allow.

Immediately there was an absurd outcry. Birds that had been settling down to roost came to attack from all parts of the garden: Magpies, Magpie-larks, Willie Wagtails, Restless Flycatchers (Scissors-grinders), a couple of visiting Ravens and a whole flock of Apostle Birds, astonishingly vicious. Three or four Sulphur-crested Cockatoos squawked in a tree a hundred metres away and a small flock of Galahs came screaming and tumbling about in the air above the heron. Red-rumped Parrots chattered nervously and kept on moving from tree to tree.

The heron was buffetted with wings and pecked all over. It stood the attack for a few minutes then laboured away across the paddock towards a timber belt. About twenty birds pursued it. As it grew dark they were still attacking, trying to drive it right off the property.

How many birds are in our garden? Always there are a hundred or more, sometimes several hundred. In the garden and small adjacent paddocks there are often several thousand.

The huge flock of wood-swallows mentioned at the beginning of this chapter were feeding on moths in lucerne that grew beside the house. The number stated was not a wild guess. It could be estimated accurately.

I woke one morning to a great volume of small chirps as though a summer's night call of crickets was many times amplified. When I walked out there was a haze of pale blue birds feeding: White-browed Wood-Swallows with a sprinkling of Masked. They kept plunging into the lucerne and up again so that the paddock seemed to be steaming.

Birds in flocks maintain safe distances apart. Each of these birds occupied about twenty-seven cubic metres. Three metres each way seems to be a usual distance for birds feeding on the wing. The flock was four birds high, a flat-topped cloud of birds ten metres deep that covered four hectares. I measured it. That makes twenty thousand birds. There might well have been more. The electric light wire was lined with resting birds and all the nearby Kurrajongs were full. As well, many were in the high lucerne itself, sitting on the flowering stems with heads turning constantly in search of movement of moth or caterpillar.

Galahs on the ground feed close together but they all move the same way so that the flock can take off in an instant without collisions. If it is windy, they feed into the wind. Birds flying in to join the flock from any direction always turn before landing and settle down in the same line. There are quarrels during feeding. Often a bird jumps round and squawks at the one behind it but it is always a quick move out of line. It soon swings round again. The birds at the back of the flock, feeding over ground that hundreds have already picked over, keep flying to the front. All birds have a turn at fresh ground.

As well as the regulars that took part in the attack on the Nankeen Night Heron, garden birds come and go according to season. Sometimes the bird population gets low and nervous. Then we know that wild cats are living under the shearing shed again. So we trap and shoot the cats, and gradually the birds build up. If a family of Superb Blue Wrens gets eaten or frightened away, it is often years before any come back. There are many always in the forest only one and a half kilometres to the north, but a wren does not take off like a pigeon or a currawong and fly across open paddocks. A wren must have a way furnished for it to hop and flit through with many stops: a high stiff crop of sunflowers, perhaps, or a fence line overgrown with weeds in a flush season.

Winter is the time for butcher-birds and Pied Currawongs. The currawongs do not roost in the garden. About sunrise they begin to straggle up out of the forest in twos and threes and fly the one and a half kilometres with full slow flaps of their pied wings. They water at low spots in the old house guttering, and set the whole garden ringing with their calls. They eat the berries of the big straggly Pepper Trees and regurgitate what is not wanted in long thick casts on paths, on posts, on roofs, in the stock troughs.

The pepper berries are eaten by many birds, honey-eaters, Olive-backed Orioles, Spotted Bower-birds, parrots. Only the currawongs eat so many and cast the leavings through their mouths. There is little enough nourishment in the berries, just a thin slimy coating of vilely pungent flesh between the red papery skin and the hard seed. The tiny red and black Mistletoe Birds eat this flesh, too, but they do not swallow the berries to get it. They hang from the fruit stems and probe through the split casing of ripe berries. They are so gentle and so dextrous they can quickly remove all the flesh and leave the stripped seed hanging in its skin. These beaks are used to weave their lovely nests: tear-shaped purses of cobwebs and pliable stems hung so that the slit-opening is to the side. The nests are decorated, perhaps camouflaged, with the brown wings of seeds and beetles, and shrivelled brown flowers.

The rich song of the Pied Butcher-birds carries above the cling-clang of the currawongs about the house. It is the most musical of all bird songs. The tunes can be written down – at least three that run through several bars of music. Grey Butcher-birds come sometimes to the house too. There are many in the forest. They make harmonious calls like the Black-backed Magpies, no tunes to be remembered. When the Grey Butcher-birds are about we sometimes find a dead bird or two hanging up in a larder. One morning the unpruned grape vine at the back door had two sparrows and a Jacky Winter (Brown Flycatcher) hanging from it. The bodies of the birds had been most cleverly dropped between two canes of the vine, then slipped along so that the necks of the birds fitted into the narrow fork where the canes joined. They dangled by their heads.

In spring the Pallid Cuckoos come, sounding glorious with the first few notes up the scale. But they keep up the same notes all spring to embarrassing inanity like an overexposed TV commercial. 'Brain-fever Bird' is an apt nickname.

In the first week in November when a Silky Oak sends ten-metre tongues of orange flame shooting way above the roof, the honeyeaters come. They sing or squawk harshly according to species and quarrel incessantly over feeding rights. Often seven species can be seen in the tree in half an hour and it is not often that there is more than one species in it at a time. Those waiting move restlessly in flocks about the White Cedars and swallow a few of the old berries. The Noisy Friar Birds, raucous and ugly but sometimes surprisingly musical, get the best of it since there are more of them. The Noisy Miners (Soldier Birds) do well because they are more savage. But the Spiny-cheeked Honeyeaters with the lovely bubbling song and the harsh-voiced Blue-faced Honeyeaters, the Striped Honeyeaters, the Little Friar Birds, even the small White-plumed Honeyeaters that live mostly on insects, take off in turn in small flocks, drive out the species feeding and themselves feed energetically for a few minutes.

There are twenty-one species of honeyeaters in the forest and War-rumbungle ranges including the Red Wattle-bird and the lovely Regent Honeyeater. All live substantially on fruit and insects sup-plemented by nectar and pollen. The ends of their tongues are split into fringes to facilitate the harvesting of flowers.

The tongues of lorikeets are even more specialised. Their tongues end in brush-like tufts of fleshy threads kept wet by a plentiful supply of thick saliva. 'On suspending a fresh-shot specimen by the toes' wrote John Gould, the great naturalist, of the Purple-crowned Lorikeet of Western Australia, 'a large teaspoon of liquid honey will flow from the mouth'. This liquid is mostly saliva.

Stephen Hopper and Andrew Burbidge of the Western Australian Wildlife Research Centre watched Purple-crowned Lorikeets feed-ing among low flowering mallee. The birds selected freshly-opened flowers, enclosed them gently in their beaks, and swept their tongues inside in a rolling motion that licked up the nectar and squeezed out the pollen in the one movement. They fed quickly, averaging about thirty flowers a minute.

There are flocks of Little Lorikeets on the Pilliga forest fringes and Musk Lorikeets along Borah Creek. They come to the Coonabarabran orchards when apricots are ripe. Scaly-breasted Lorikeets are rare visitors to the Warrumbungles, and perhaps the Rainbow Lorikeet. These lorikeets probably harvest pollen and nectar in the same way as the Purple-crowned Lorikeets but since they feed mostly in trees much taller than mallees, they are hard to observe.

This extensive pollen feeding helps explain the pollination of Australian plants. Anyone, scientist or layman, asked today 'What is the principal pollinator of native flowers?' would answer 'The honey

bee'. The honey bee was brought out with as much care as the first rabbits – Gregory Blaxland's hive travelled in his cabin – and spread with
settlement. In many districts it has been principal pollinator for no
more than a hundred years. One wonders whether more efficient
pollination allowed the heavy growth in modern forests. Could the
honeyeaters and lorikeets or the little *Trigona* bees have coped with
thousands of hectares of massed flowers or millions of extra solitary
bees found enough holes or dug enough burrows to store their individual honey pots? There is now a massive seeding in forests in good
years. Seed is cast on the ground as lavishly as spermatozoa into a
female animal.

Summer belongs to the Western Warblers, tiny grey birds with huge
musical voices and a song that sounds always a few notes short of being
complete.

When the grapes are ripe, Olive-backed Orioles and a pair of Spotted Bower-birds come to the feast. With these two expert mimics
about, a menagerie of animals not there call from the garden. One is
thankful that the bower-bird has not yet imitated the young orioles.
When as big as the parents they still demand to be fed with loud,
monotonous, insistent, strident cries over and over and over from
daybreak to dusk. The female oriole performs marvels for them, even
finding worms in dry summers by scratching down several centimetres
beneath the watered citrus trees.

After much experience in digging the big Coonamble and Wee Waa
worms for fish bait, I learnt the technique of pulling a long worm from
the ground without breaking it. It is remarkable to see that the currawongs know as much. After rain big sandy-coloured worms feed in
the leaf litter beneath the Kurrajongs in the garden. The currawongs
scratch there and, when a few centimetres of exposed worm is seen, a
currawong grabs it. Immediately the worm bulges out that part of it
still in the hole and holds firm. But in order to pull itself down into the
hole the worm has to relax. So the currawong keeps a firm grip and
bends forward to give the worm a few centimetres of slack. The worm
relaxes and begins to slide down. Then the currawong braces its legs
and draws back steadily. It gains several centimetres before the worm
bulges and resists again. So the currawong relaxes and worm and currawong repeat their moves. It often takes five minutes to pull a thirty-
centimetre worm up without breaking it.

Apostle Birds, those rather obtrusive birds that live in groups, also
tend to their young until they are as big as their parents. I went out one
afternoon to see what had grabbed a young Apostle Bird – it was

squawking alarm calls at top volume. Its parents had it on its back on the ground delousing it. The female had one foot firmly on the young one's breast while she raked through its neck feathers with her beak, frequently pecking and swallowing. The male bird stood on the struggling young one's legs and pecked lice from its vent. Galahs are sometimes seen sitting together like a pair of monkeys taking turns to comb one another for lice.

Ripe peaches and apricots bring the parrots: the big Mallee Ringnecks, Eastern Rosellas, Blue Bonnets, and the Red-winged Parrots – green and crimson marvels. What can one do with a dozen Red-wings eating peaches but gasp at their beauty and regret the peaches?

Both possible races of Blue Bonnet come to the house. The startling crimson circles on their yellow abdomens look as though they have bled from bullet holes. The race with the emerald patch on the shoulder is not common. Their wings flare like opal as they move, crimson, yellow, emerald and blue.

The big red and green Australian King-Parrots are in the Warrumbungles and the Willala hills and a few pairs of the delicate Superb Parrot. I watched a pair of these drinking at a cattle trough near the house. 'Green Leeks' they are called affectionately, and so they seemed, two superbly supple long green stalks bending down to the water.

Bird trappers come into the forest. They use mist nets for finches and snares for parrots, set them up for a few hours then move on before they are discovered. A trapper was seen in 1974 at the bore at Lucky Flat catching the Ringnecks that came to water. He had five or six as decoys in cages set on top of one and a half metre poles. Cross arms reached out a metre or so each side of the pole tops and on these arms were fixed nylon nooses to snare investigating parrots by the feet.

Occasionally Spine-tailed Swifts are found on the ground, forced down by hawk, or the stormy weather that excites them. They shrill their distress and claw their way along the ground with awkwardly long wings and feeble legs. Unless they can get to a tree or cliff and climb several metres up for a gliding take-off it is impossible for them to get off the ground. Most of their lives are spent in the air; perhaps they even mate in the air. They have never been seen to land willingly in Australia. Even when they nest in the broken tops of pines in northern hemisphere forests or on the coastal cliffs of Japan and Asia, the nesting materials – insect wings, seaweed, sticks and leaves – are taken on the wing. The birds cement them in place with gelatinous saliva while they prop themselves with their stiff tails and half flutter and half cling to cliff shelf or pine trunk.

I watched a flock of Spine-tails watering at a forest ground tank. The tank was in the middle of a dense pine forest in a patch of Fuzzy Boxes a good twenty-five metres high. Tank and clearing occupied less than a hectare. It must have looked small enough to the swifts circling very high above it. Four or five at a time spiralled down from the flock to within a couple of metres of the ground then each turned and swept low and fast over the water. Always the first time they went in too fast and were not brave enough to open their beaks. They rose over the banks of the tank, turned at the forest edge and came in again slower. Second time usually was still too fast. Most had to turn and come in again. The third or fourth time each opened its mouth and scooped up water in four or five quick dips – they looked like stones skipping – then rose over the trees and spiralled up to the flock while another dropped down to take its place.

I have always thought some species of small bats would get a nasty jerk when drinking if they misjudged their speed. We used to watch them at dusk on our river property at Boggabri. It was too dark to see what species they were. They flew slowly up and down the river with tails spread into scoops. Every fifty metres or so they dipped their tails into the water, lifted a few feet in the air, then bent their heads and drank.

The small flocks of Double-bar Finches that come to the house drink where a slow leak from a cemented rainwater tank leaks on to the path. There is no pool of water to drink from. These finches drink by sucking as pigeons do, and they can continue to live by the drying waterholes in the creeks long after other birds leave. The last patch of damp sand will yield them enough. But they drink often, about once an hour. One never has to wait long beside water to see if these finches are about.

The Double-bars, although most plentiful in the Willala mountains, associate with Plum-headed Finches along Baradine Creek. But the Plum-heads leave months before the Double-bars as the creek dries up. Plum-heads drink in single sips and are very fussy about their water. They like a clear trickle with a low twiggy branch or a strong reed to hang from as they sip.

We love the owls and nightjars that come to us at night: the laughing cackle of the Spotted Nightjar hawking for insects along the forest edge at dusk; and the cricket-like chirring of the Tawny Frogmouths that sit in the White Cedars; and the little Boobook Owl that sits on a corner of the roof and calls 'morepork, morepork' to other Boobooks that answer from every direction. One year a pair of Owlet Nightjars nested in a hollow in an old White Cedar. One wonders how such a gentle bird got there before the sparrows and the ringneck parrots that usually squabble over that site.

One late night as we drove back from fishing at Walgett by the Burren Junction road, Owlet Nightjars kept rising from the high grass at the side of the road and diving at the lights of the Land-Rover. No insects were rising to attract them. I had never known there were so many of these birds. Every forty or fifty metres one dived at the lights. There was no doubt of the species. Although I kept on braking, we arrived home with three bodies caught on the front of the Land-Rover.

The huge Powerful Owls are in the Warrumbungles – a long way west for a bird of rainforest and wet tableland. And a big female Masked Owl came out of a hollow tree near our boundary when I knocked on the trunk with a stick one afternoon. She sat in a small pine facing us from five or six metres. Little Thornbills set up an angry chatter and the uneasy owl turned her head constantly. She sat for a quarter of an hour or more while three of us watched her, then flew away. We brought her out twice more over the next few weeks to show children coming home from school and university, then she moved somewhere to a quieter tree.

A pair of Barking Owls nested in a timber strip on our eastern boundary. These owls move by day as much as by night and their mighty barked 'Hoo-hoos' distressed all the birds within a kilometre or so. They are big birds and it is startling to see one through the binoculars for the first time since the round yellow eyes suddenly glare as though they have been lit up. This is the owl that makes the terrified woman screams, usually at night. The nesting female made it about half-past four one afternoon when I was fencing, a single high agonised call for help. I knew the owls were there – I had been watching them. I knew immediately what the call was because I had been hoping to hear it. But still I dropped my pliers and my hair started on end. The call is a distillation of extreme terror and sounds absolutely human.

The pair hatched out two young but the mighty barks of the old ones attracted too much attention. We went away for a few days and someone came in and shot the young birds. The old birds were missing but I could not find their bodies. They have not nested there since.

Birds attach themselves to a homestead sometimes in a way that suggests intelligence. A Magpie Lark found the meat scraps on our open-air cutting block. Soon it learned that we had something to do with the meat being there because it followed and lit on the ground nearby as soon as anyone carried meat to the block. We cut small pieces off for it and it soon learnt that the sound of the chopper meant meat. If only a few lamb chops were being cut off a side, the bird heard. From somewhere in the garden there was a squawk and it came flying.

After three or four weeks it began perching on the meat block and squawking till we fed it. And when it found that meat could be called for it began hopping to the back door and calling. But it wanted no closer contact with us. It would take meat dropped at our feet, though nervously, but never out of our hands. It preferred to keep a metre length away. After a few weeks of being fed it moved off somewhere else.

A Magpie Lark that we all loved was picked up on a road with a bruised and torn wing. It looked stronger after three days in a cage so we let it out to peck around the garden. We fed it, too, and in a couple of weeks it began to fly, not strongly, but well enough. It stayed about for months and grew more and more friendly. If one of us walked away from the house, Peewit followed calling and circling overhead. It always came to greet us when we first walked out the door in the morning. 'Pee-o-wit' in the tones of a clarinet is a cheery 'good morning'. One early morning as I walked out to the woodheap, Peewit was chanting and flying in tight circles just above my head. Suddenly there was a rush of air, a thump and a squawk. A Brown Falcon, in an unusual attack on a bird in the air, had come in very fast and snatched Peewit. As I watched it glide over the garden fence, it was already bending down to eat the struggling body off its talons.

A Grey Shrike-thrush that spent a winter with us learnt somehow that if it sang it would be fed. About sunrise on frosty mornings it hopped to the gauzed verandah door and directed its several harmonies towards our open bedroom door. Thrushes seem to sing in chords. It always knew we were there since before flying down to sing, it would sit up in the grapevine looking in at us. If neither Joan nor I got up after the first series, the thrush repeated them but with a few harsh notes thrown in at the end of each phrase. If the songs ever had to be repeated a third time they grew very harsh indeed and usually ended with several piercing alarm calls.

Early in the spring a pair of strange thrushes came to the house. All one day the strange male chased our thrush about the garden and next day it was gone. The strange pair did not stay either. We hoped our thrush would come back the next winter but it did not. But whenever a thrush calls now from the garden we go out to see if it knows us.

What else is there? There is a bird list at the end of this book, but some wonders have been seen only once: a big Black-necked Stork (Jabiru) David Johnston, a near neighbour, saw beside a temporary lagoon; or the Rufous Whistler and the Golden Whistler he saw in the same tree; or the Cattle Egret, Plumed Egret and Little Egret all in breeding plumage Alan Morris saw in a dead tree beside a lagoon on Bettington's old Teridgerie. It was the first sighting (November 1976) of a Cattle Egret in the district. That dead tree, the only one near the lagoon, is the favourite perch of resting cormorants and darters and the lookout for herons and spoonbills. There are often over a hundred birds in it of fifteen species or more. Where will they perch when it falls down?

There are the three species of doves and two of pigeons all cooing at once, and the Rufous Songlarks that begin singing before any grey of dawn is detectable and have such a variety of calls they seem more than one bird. They run through all the calls several times, the only birds singing for a good half hour, until others begin to wake. There are the thirty Black-faced Cuckoo-shrikes that worked so energetically to keep Heliothis caterpillars out of forty hectares of linseed that we did not even have to consider spraying.

There are the pair of big Brown Quail that have lately taken up residence in the garden, and the Painted Quail running amongst forest shadows. And the Red-chested Quail that stunned herself against a kitchen window one night in 1979. These little Button-quail were thought to be rare till Alan Morris found them to be permanent residents near Mudgee and in fair numbers between Narrabri and Moree. Casual observers would not have distinguished them from the common Little Quail, another species of Button-quail.

Clim, Alan Morris's highly-trained German Short-haired Pointer, helped him in his quail studies. She let him know whether a Button-quail or a Stubble Quail was about to rise. Button-quail do not freeze like Stubble Quail. They squat briefly, then run forward a metre or so. Clim adjusted her classic points and pointed as she moved forward to keep the birds in sight.

Alan Morris found Little Quail and Red-chested Quail easy to distinguish in their short fast flight. Because of their different-coloured flanks, Little Quail present a creamy-white oval split by a brown streak that is the tail, Red-chested Quail an orange oval split by a brown streak.

There was a female Black Duck that came out of dense scrub and ran in front of the Land-Rover on Scratch Road, two kilometres from water, with fifteen tiny ducklings running in a cluster behind her. Both Wood Duck (Maned Duck) and Black Duck often nest far from water and then shepherd their young to the water they need to feed in.

Usually all walk. Modern scientists are emphatic that this is the only way the young get to water. But too many observant and honest men have seen young Wood Ducks carried.

Bert Ruttley watched ducklings being brought to a ground tank near Baradine. He had no binoculars and could not see how they were carried, but each time the mother landed in the water a duckling somersaulted in front of her. It righted itself quickly and floated like a bit of fluff. But it dived immediately if disturbed. Bert's older brother, George, was fencing one day near a hollow tree from which a Wood Duck was taking her young. Several times he saw the mother come out of a spout with a duckling in her bill.

There are Emus that run in front of vehicles on the long straight forest tracks. A male Emu frightened by a vehicle brings his eight or nine twelve-month-old chickens out on the road where they can run quickly. After pacing in front for eight kilometres or so at about fifty kilometres an hour, they begin to tire, so all dash off the road into the forest. The shrubs impede them, the noise of the vehicle comes closer, so they dash on to the road again where they can move freely. One often has to stop and wait for them to move off, otherwise they would drop exhausted.

It is the male that hatches the eggs and cares for the young, sometimes until they are eighteen months old and almost as big as their father. The female lays her clutch, up to twenty huge green eggs, then goes off on her own. Often she mates again and lays another clutch. In a good season a female Emu can have three males brooding for her.

A male Emu has been seen lifting his little striped chickens over a netting fence. He had blundered over it as Emus do by skating on his breast and flailing wildly with his legs. When the little ones did not follow and began the penetrating whistling they make when lost, the male came back to the fence and ran up and down it in agitation. Then he suddenly reached over the fence, picked up one chicken in his beak and dropped it on his side, then another and another. The last chicken was frightened and would not keep still long enough to be grabbed. It was Bert Ruttley who saw them when fencing on Goorianawa. He walked across and lifted the last chicken over.

And there was a Blue-winged Kookaburra that flew into a Kurrajong in the garden in March 1975. The regulars announced that there was an interloper with loud angry calls. They attacked him almost as fiercely as the Nankeen Night Heron. No notice is ever taken of the Laughing Kookaburras that come around often.

The Blue-wing was obviously lost and nervous. It did not stay long. I did no more than note down the date and wonder why the bird was so far from its territory. I knew of a colony of Blue-wings on Dubbo (or Etoo) Creek in old Cumble, twenty kilometres north-east of our house.

A few months later I told of that kookaburra in a talk to the Gould League bird-watchers. There was an ornithologist in the audience who came to me after the lecture and said 'You are quite wrong about that Blue-winged Kookaburra. They have never been reported in New South Wales'. When I said 'Well, I now report them' and explained that it was a male Blue-wing with a blue tail and his male rivals out on Etoo Creek also had blue tails and they all had wings that were mostly blue and paler bodies than the Laughing Kookaburras, and that they sat a little differently so that their beaks seemed to be set on at a different angle, and that they had never learned to laugh properly and finished off in a great howl when the laugh went wrong: when I had explained to him beyond doubt that they were Blue-winged Kookaburras he was as offended and unbelieving as if I had insisted on seeing a Dodo.

Wilf Taylor, the photographer, was in the audience. He has seen Blue-wings on Bugaldi Creek – these birds are never far from water. Between 1960 and 1964 there was a pair on a property four miles up the creek from his own. He saw them often. About 1966 he saw one bird only and he has seen none since. In 1964 he also saw one on his own place, a female, at close range.

I went the next day to find the colony on Etoo Creek. The holes where they watered had dried up and the birds had moved. Perhaps the male that came into the garden was one of them, split from the others as they tried to establish themselves in a new territory near permanent water.

Roni Parry Madeley, then of the University of New England, an energetic woman with enthusiastic and authoritative knowledge of kookaburras and magpies, sent me a tape of the calls of Blue-winged Kookaburras made in Queensland. We drive out to old Cumble, park the Land-Rover near the aloes that mark the site of the old homestead, and walk with the tape recorder along the wide sanded-up Etoo Creek. Every kilometre or so we stop to broadcast the calls. We also seek out permanent holes in other creeks and play the tape.

Bewildered Laughing Kookaburras search and challenge. But no Blue-winged Kookaburras have answered with high wild howls. They must be accidental visitors only, perhaps swirled down from Queensland like the Blue Tiger butterflies by north-east drifts of tropic rain.

14

Wood Chips and International Airports

A Businessmen's Game

What happened in the Pilliga forest happened on a lesser scale in most of Australia's forests. It was only by concentrating on one that I could bring the men and animals to life. Each district has its own life.

Many soils started no retaliatory growth. Some delayed them. A scrub of hopbush, eremophila and cassia spread wildly in westen New South Wales in the 1970s.

Because of the intensity of our modern forests they are more precious than remnants. They do not display the past as it was, they have concentrated it. And few of those who seek to save them and none of those who seek to destroy them understand that.

From 1973 to 1975 Coonabarabran Shire Council, greedy and irrational, promoted the Pilliga forest as a site for an international airport. The members once more saw the forest as waste land to be utilised. They slightingly referred to it as 'The Pilliga Scrub'. Orana Regional Council supported them. Narrabri later took up the proposal and pursued its own ends. In 1979 local councillors were still whispering 'The Pilliga Scrub' to politicians uneasily considering new airports.

The concept of establishing a huge airport where there is no population, unlimited room, clear air and flat surroundings is excellent. Passengers can be distributed to cities by smaller planes and by helicopter. But there is plenty of poor farming country already cleared

where such an airport could be established at little greater cost.
Nothing need be destroyed.

Those who value our forests and wish to preserve them declare, as in
this extract from *Save Colong Bulletin*, November 1976, 'More than half
the forest in eastern Australia – the dry sclerophyll and savannah
woodland – has disappeared since European settlement'. Hugh
Tyndale-Biscoe of the Society for Social Responsibility in Science
(ACT) irresponsibly exclaimed in the *Sydney Morning Herald* of 18
September 1978 'there is no equivalent in Britain to our great primeval
forests'. Over and over one finds similar statements in modern
writings. What forests? How many trees make a forest?

'Every where we have an open woodland', wrote Charles Darwin on
his 1836 visit. 'Nowhere are there any dense forests like those of North
America', explained *Chambers's Information for the People* in an article on
'Emigration to Australia' written in 1841. Such statements are made
over and over in early writings. De Beuzeville was aware of them. He
reasserted them in his *Australian Trees for Australian Planting*. 'Even along
the . . . gullies and the contiguous streams', he quoted, 'the country
resembled the "woodier parts of a deer park in England".' In the
seventy-two forests declared in New South Wales by 1879 the tree
count of those assessed varied from two and a half mature trees to the
hectare inland to eighty on the tablelands and coast. The Forestry
Commission in experimental plots in the Yerrinan section of the Pilliga
forest found that sixty-year-old White Cypress Pines thinned in 1940 to
two hundred to the hectare produced the best timber over the next thirty years, but, if thinned to six hundred to the hectare, they produced
the most timber. Nowhere, in a search lasting months, did I find
reference to former stands of timber as thick as those modern thinned
stands.

However, there were some stands of heavy timber. Arthur Dewhurst
in 1879 reported stringybark in the small Nundle Forest Reserve south-
east of Tamworth standing one hundred and fifty to the hectare and
'cutting on an average 600 feet surface'. Although they were well-
spaced, trees of that size would have formed a canopy. He wrote of
'ferns of great beauty and size' which do not grow in direct sunlight.
The Karri and Jarrah forests of south-west Western Australia, as mentioned in Chapter Two, were as thick or thicker and covered a much
bigger area than the Nundle forest. There was a belt of thick eucalypts
between Sydney and the Blue Mountains fifteen to twenty kilometres
wide that opened out into grass land broken by dense patches of mallee
and banksia scrub. A great mallee scrub in western Victoria extended

into South Australia. Both States cleared most of it. Mountain Ash closed in over mountain gullies in Victoria. Apart from these, Australia had patches only of dense eucalypts. About six hundred species of eucalypts grew mostly as individuals or in small clumps among grass.

The great eucalyptus growth on the Dividing Range and on every little hill in central-western New South Wales, the belts of Bimble Box in western New South Wales, of River Red Gum on the western rivers and Coolabah on flooded plains did not exist at the time of settlement. Between 1900 and 1930 gangs of up to a hundred Chinese ringbarked eucalypts in New South Wales and Queensland. The trees they killed were the new crop twenty to fifty years old.

Rainforest is a different story. There is less of the immoderately complex tropical rainforest in northern Queensland and much less of the more austere temperate rainforest in Victoria. Some of the Victorian forests drove out intruding men with new growth just as the Pilliga forest did, but the new growth was less beautiful than the old. Rainforests are fragile. And there is much less of the beautiful subtropical rainforest that grew in south-east Queensland and on the North Coast of New South Wales. The area of this forest was never great in New South Wales. It, too, extended for a time after first settlement, then the whole area was almost exterminated in a rush for land.

Rainforest was cleared for dairy farms, for canegrowing and banana growing. There are no eucalypts in rainforest and since the massive growth is tender it is comparatively easy to clear by fire. Moreover the soil was seemingly rich. Alas, much of the richness was cycled within the forest like coins passed around. There was no bank. When the forest was cleared and the cycle broken, planted crops spent it in a year or two, then the ground was poor.

Another forest that was almost wiped out was the cedar brush dominated by Red Cedar, *Toona australis*. It grew in brushes up to five kilometres wide along the Hunter, though certainly not in an unbroken line. It grew along the rivers and creeks of the central and northern coast of New South Wales and even on some of the western slopes of the Dividing Range. The timber was valuable. The soil where it grew was rich. Although the undergrowth was dense, settlers followed the cedargetters.

The cedar was grabbed in the same haste as the gold. Then there was nothing. It never grew thickly. One great tree to a hectare was a good stand. It is one of Australia's few deciduous trees and the only long-lived tree. Some of the giants that yielded seventy cubic metres of timber were two thousand years old and buttressed like Port Jackson

Figs. The cedargetters balanced on narrow planks up to five metres off
the ground and chopped them down above the buttresses. They
discarded the tops and branches. Often they roughly squared the log.
Perhaps half the timber was left to rot. Was that a thousand years of
growth squandered?

Despite the burning of rainforest and cedar brush and the years of
ringbarking, just as there are now more kangaroos in Australia than at
the time of settlement, there are more trees. That does not make our
forests less important. There are species of kangaroos at risk. Our
forests are vulnerable. Their concentration puts both plants and animals at risk. They are the packed containers of so much that has gone
from the rest of the country.

The forestry authorities of the different States are insufficient guard-
ians. All are sensitive to criticism since they handle so much public
money at such an enormous loss. But changes that should come from
increasing knowledge within too often have to await outside influence.
One suspects the Forestry Commission of New South Wales might still
be practising its awful monoculture if it had not been told it was wrong.
The science of forestry must be reinforced by all the sciences dealing
with plants, animals and soils, and by far-sighted accountants. Woodchippers working in the 1970s on the South Coast of New South Wales,
in the south-west of Western Australia, and in Tasmania were not
harvesting forests according to their sustained yields but disposing of
them by clear felling. And the several governments had sold the forests
secretly for absurdly insufficient money.

Arguments against woodchipping began in the late 1960s. Sometimes the arguments became violent. In 1976 one masked and armed
environmentalist held up a nightwatchman at a woodchip export plant
in Bunbury, Western Australia, while another distributed hundreds of
sticks of gelignite about the plant. They did not destroy its environment. Only one charge went off. Near Bega on the New South Wales
south coast stacks of logs were burnt and bulldozers put out of action
with sugar in the diesel tanks and sawdust in the hydraulic oil. The
energies directed against woodchipping would have been better spent
preparing for it. It is a sound and necessary industry.

But in ten years the industry has devastated too much of Australia's
too precious forests. And it is unnecessary destruction. Although ten
years had been lost by the end of the 1970s there was still time to plant
forests for woodchipping on ground already cleared. Farmers could
grow trees as a crop if a scheme was developed to compensate them for
the forty-year wait for income. Then the woodchippers would harvest

the trees with the remarkable machines now being developed that move into a forest like a header into ripe wheat, cut the trees off at ground level, strip off the bark and leaves, chip the wood, elevate it into a huge bin and throw the bark, leaves and twigs out the back. When a crop of eucalypts has been taken, it could be followed by tall-growing acacias, Yarran or Brigalow or Black Wattle (*A. decurrens*), to replace nitrogen and provide another crop of woodchips. The Forestry Commission of New South Wales, demonstrating a lack of knowledge of soils, replaced some of the harvested Radiata Pine plantations with another planting of Radiata Pine that is not doing well.

Eucalypts for woodchipping and for fuel are being grown on a huge scale overseas. By 1977 Brazil was planting 200,000 hectares of Australian trees a year. Australia, no longer with any sound reason, plants the imported Radiata Pine, which provides little food for Australian animals, yields no better timber, and which excludes most Australian shrubs from the understorey. Foreign trees from a wetter climate intercept too much rain and evaporate it from their leaves instead of funnelling it down their trunks to the ground. Radiata Pine plantations look deceptively beautiful from a distance. Within they are sterile areas which would be beautiful if planted with mixed eucalypts. When they have grown the eucalyptus forests of Brazil, unsuited to South American animals and understorey plants, will probably be as lifeless.

The management of the Pilliga State Forests by the Forestry Commission has been mostly sound. Until the astonishing new growth of the 1950s it milled the old pine with the expectation that the milling was controlled liquidation. Many foresters had never seen a White Cypress Pine seedling growing naturally. It was not possible to preserve the Old Greys nor the big ironbarks. If not cut they would soon have died. The new growth of the 1950s and the success of the thinning of the growth of the 1880s allowed full practice of sustained yield. Each area will be cut every thirty to forty years.

The few years of monoculture in the 1960s and early 1970s disrupted animal life in parts of the forest. A good growth of White Box and a couple of species of ironbark in the Vickery and Wandobah forests out of Gunnedah were popular with beekeepers. They yielded good flows almost every year. The pine was poor. The Forestry Commission ring-barked all except the pine. There might never be a yield of timber to pay expenses and most animal life has gone. As late as 1974 a gang of eight men were at work in the Kerringle Forest east of the Pilliga Nature Reserve cutting down oak. Bull Oak in quantity is worthless enough to men and animals. But they also ringbarked any eucalypts they came across.

Soon afterwards new ideas penetrated the public service armour. Work gangs cutting oak were told to leave big old eucalypts with hollow branches and any good clumps of younger eucalypts. Some scattered eucalypts were still ringbarked. They interfere markedly with the growth of pine about them.

No one knows how many eucalypts ought to be left to maintain the animal life of the forest and still permit the pine to grow. One hopes the District Forester has hit on the right number.

Certainly the District Forester does not allow for the effects of parasitic mistletoe. That plant illustrates the complexity of the management of forests. Since the sharp reduction in the number of possums in the 1950s, mistletoe, one of their favourite foods, grew unchecked. So the little red and black Mistletoe-birds that eat the fruit had an increased food supply and multiplied. They have an almost straight gut. The mistletoe seeds pass through them in less than an hour, sometimes within twenty-five minutes. They perch in line with branches instead of across them like other birds and soon deposit the sticky seeds all along the branches of any tree with mistletoe. Sufficient mistletoe kills slowly but certainly. A species has developed for each genus of trees.

Few attach any importance to the hollows in dead trees. They are as effective a shelter as hollows in live trees. Those with licences to cut firewood, those who think they have a right to firewood by long usage, cut down hollow trees without a thought. It takes over a hundred years to make a hollow tree and each year the number grows less.

The effect of fire in forests and nature reserves is so complicated no one can do anything with the certainty he is right. Modern scientists have done a great deal of work on fire, much of it brilliant. If they meet at a seminar each advances a disparate theory. Not even the elementary question 'If a fire starts do we put it out?' can be answered definitely. The effect of fire is different in different areas and one has to consider the purpose of the area. If a park is displaying acacias it will have to be burnt with a hot summer fire every ten years or so otherwise the acacias will die out. If a forest is growing White Cypress Pine logs for milling, hot fires are disastrous, any fire is damaging. If a reserve protects rare kangaroos like the Wertago Nature Reserve that in 1979 contained the last forty Yellow-footed Rock Wallabies in New South Wales, it should be burnt in sections and burnt often to maintain a short green pick of grass. Nothing matters but the welfare of the wallabies.

Generally, a return to the Aboriginal system of burning is not desirable. If frequent fires make country more open it will support less plants and animals that now have nowhere else to live. Fertilised farm land and grazing land is an unsuitable habitat for most Australian life. But mostly, in the present absence of mammals that eat tree seedlings, frequent fires will make dense growth denser. Frequent burning sharply reduces the numbers of small Australian mammals and the periods of recovery encourage the imported House Mouse and Black Rat.

Because fire in recent times burns growth thicker than Australian soil was accustomed to, it releases more phosphorus than most Australian plants can tolerate. The after-fire period favours imported weeds.

There is little experience of the rapid build-up of phosphorus. Prescribed burning began in the 1970s. The growth it was designed to control began in the 1950s. It was not only in the Pilliga forest that growth thickened when rabbits died. The terrifying top fires prescribed burning is meant to prevent are modern events. Aboriginal fires were grass fires. Eucalyptus vapour did not explode above forests till modern forests grew.

Every forest, every reserve must be assessed and an honest programme designed for it. If politicians have the final say it will be a politically expedient programme. Too many environmental impact studies are carried out by dubious scientists willing to substantiate whatever is desired of them.

The remarkable School of Natural Resources under Professor Burton of the University of New England produces the comprehensive scientists needed for this work. Permanent positions must be opened for them to advise in the management of all parks and forests. Foresters are not equipped for such work. The Department of Forestry at the Australian National University naturally concentrated on the growing and harvesting of timber. Students were taught to conduct tree farms. Plants and animals had to fit the programme. In some forests that was sound management. In the Central Highlands of Victoria, for example, it was unsound. The mature Mountain Ash forests house the only colony of the rediscovered Leadbeaters Possum. This active and beautiful creature was thought to be extinct. The programme decided for the forest in 1977 after a bad study would finally exterminate it. The Forests Commission of Victoria decided to clear fell 20-80 hectare blocks progressively – it calls them 'coupes' – slash them, burn them, reseed and replant them, then harvest them again in sixty years. The possum depends on a large number of mature trees. A young forest does not suit it. Timber is important. It would not be sound management to abandon eight thousand hectares of superb timber to a possum. But it is sound management to bring in the scientists who can show how a lesser quantity of timber can be harvested at no risk to the possum. By 1980 the Forests Commission had begun to appoint those scientists.

Whatever the decision for burning an area, there should be a sufficient break to contain fires, especially about areas to be burnt seldom or never. Lightning or lunatic will eventually start a fire. The longer fire is excluded the fiercer the fire. No park or forest has more than a token break about it. They threaten the surrounding land. And in those places where farmers burn stubble, the surrounding land threatens the forest.

Probably the plan of the Forestry Commission of New South Wales to use cattle to control the undergrowth that hampers timbergetting in the Pilliga forests is a good plan. It is a fortunate area. In the Pilliga East section the great Nature Reserve of about 65,000 hectares is enclosed on two sides by over 300,000 hectares of forest. Big areas of the forest are not exploited because there is no worthwhile timber. So foresters can happily give first thought to the pine and ironbark. Most animals and other plants have their separate establishment.

But even here foresters are not adequately trained to have full control. Scientists with more specialised knowledge of soils, plants and animals are needed to work with the Forestry Commission and monitor the area. For instance Koalas favour the forest to the nature reserve because there is less undergrowth to hamper their movements from tree to tree. And new fences run to confine cattle on 25-year leases could cut Koalas off from the creeks they seek in drought time. This probably has not yet happened. In the interests of economy lessees erect five barb fences that Koalas should be able to crawl under. But their movement is not considered in the specification for the fences. There is nothing to stop a lessee running a mesh fence tied to star-pattern iron posts that might confine Koalas as well as the cattle.

The broom plains in the Pilliga East State Forest have no like elsewhere. There is the one mass only of Fringed Heath Myrtle. These areas are surrounded by good timber and though an unfenced Broom Flora Reserve had been designated by 1979, there was no plan to protect other broom plains or any of the heath country. The Forestry Commission's policy of multiple land use – recreation, grazing, timbergetting, even wheat growing in a forest near Gunnedah – does not suit these areas. There are no cattle in them yet. If they are brought in they will destroy the delicate carpet of sundews and mosses among the broom. They will break down the spreading Fringed Heath Myrtle and the amazing tangle of heavy pollen-bearing plants the beekeepers flock to. Their hooves will destroy the mulch beneath the areas of dense heath plants and trample the fine roots. Heath plants are adapted to soils of very low fertility. Most of them are tap-rooted but a system of fine roots seeks the minute quantities of minerals in decaying leaves. Some of the genera of heath plants, *Banksia*, *Grevillea* and *Isopogon* for example, grow proteoid roots. They are fragile bundles of hairy rootlets that grow temporarily on normal surface roots and reach almost to the soil surface. No heath plant can tolerate disturbance of its roots. Indeed these sturdy-looking plants lead a delicate existence. They are susceptible also to phosphorus. European mammals excreting large amounts are intolerable to them. Some mammals secrete phosphorus in their faeces, some in their urine. The bush daisies (*Helichrysum* spp.), *Leucopogon* spp., and grass trees are particularly susceptible. The manure of one steer can poison three square metres of these plants each day. One man's urine can poison a square metre a day, a cat's one-third of a metre. A discarded orange peel, a banana skin is damaging. Two botanists, E. M. Heddle and R. L. Specht, who experimented on heath on the Ninety-Mile Plain in South Australia between 1950 and 1972, found that much of the phosphorus applied in 1950 was still being circulated among a changed vegetation in 1972. Heath plants are exceptionally beautiful, and home for birds, wallabies and Pigmy Possums. They are difficult to manage in forests and reserves. If the concept of 'parks for the people' means more tourist roads through heath plains, the plants will recede from the tourists year by year.

The management of national parks and nature reserves by the National Parks and Wildlife Service in New South Wales is insufficient. The Pilliga Nature Reserve and Warrumbungle National Park were fortunate in having Alan Morris as its first senior ranger. With his exceptional knowledge of birds he was enthusiastic about all studies of the area. Many parks were run by rangers of the old school who thought scientific investigation a waste of time, and whose chief interests were the maintenance of roads, attendance figures and kiosk sales.

Parks have to be big to conserve creatures such as the Greater Glider which needs about two thousand hectares to maintain a viable population of a thousand. But by the beginning of the 1980s the area of parks and reserves in New South Wales, still insufficient, had outstripped the men and the money needed to run them. It was beyond possibility to get much more than an obvious assessment of what plants and animals they conserved let alone maintain them. Neglected reserves tend to fill with vermin: pigs, goats, rabbits and foxes. Kangaroos breed in excessive numbers. But the question of how much a reserve should be managed is as difficult to answer as the question of fire.

'Parks for the people' would eventually mean more roads. Rabbits follow roads and the seeds of imported weeds are distributed by cars. Permanent roads in rainforests are especially damaging. Not only do they open a way for Lantana and Camphor Laurel but they give an advantage to the opportunist rai ʿorest plants with longlived seeds that wait any break in the canopy. The disruption of temporary logging tracks and snig furrows might not be damaging. The rainforests of New Guinea have survived the slash, burn, cultivate and move on technique of the natives for thousands of years.

Probably permanent roads in any nature reserve are undesirable. In forests they should be restricted to essential firebreaks. Nature reserves should not be regarded as drive-in botanical or zoological gardens. It is important that some effort be required to see them. The damage is less, the reward is greater. Walking trails as in the Warrumbungle National Park are ideal if supplemented by a boundary road on a wide firebreak and a substantial fence. The expensive fence, an essential, has never been considered.

Foxes, pigs and kangaroos in reserves depend for much of their food on adjacent farms. They feed in paddocks by night then cross back through insufficient fences to shelter in forest by day. The extra food allows them to increase their numbers. Landholders are responsible for their boundary fences against both forest and reserve. Those with the worst fences complain the most bitterly. Some complain foolishly. Kangaroos are gentle feeders and forty or fifty coming in to feed each night, even on crops, do very little damage. But by 1979 kangaroos over much of New South Wales had built up to numbers unacceptable to everyone. Licenced shooters began to harvest them, most of them shot for skins only. The flesh was wasted. Shooting is not a good method of getting rid of any unwanted animals. It splits up groups and makes the remainder wary. Both flesh and skin of kangaroos is so valuable a better method of taking them should be devised, possibly trapping on water in yards made of nylon netting. On dry country especially husbanded kangaroos might be more profitable and less damaging than sheep or cattle. The popular agitation against the marketing of kangaroos is mostly based on ignorance. Controlled harvesting keeps the breeding stock healthy and prevents the alternate build-ups and crashes of uncontrolled breeding. Worse, the publicity given to the protection of the bigger species of kangaroos takes attention from the animals that need protection: the Pretty-face Wallaby, for example, or the Straw-necked Ibis that is losing its principal breeding-grounds through irrigation works affecting the Macquarie Marshes.

Modern scientists are comparing the meat produced by conventional domestic animals with that produced by the native animals of different countries under the same conditions. Often the native animals are decidedly superior. Russell Kyle from the Bristol Veterinary School in England in his *Meat Production in Africa* reported the successful domestication of those imposing antelopes, the Eland and the Oryx. Where cattle, sheep and goats persistently overgrazed South African pasture, mixed wild ungulates produced four times the meat with no harmful effect. Since the greatest change in Australia was the damage to the structure of the soil caused by European mammals, meat and skin production based on kangaroos might eventually reverse the damage.

But meat production should play no part in the management of reserves. It might subtly change the outlook of the managers. If high netting fences backed up by electric wires were run where they could be maintained, Dingoes could be re-established to keep the population of kangaroos under control. Although they prefer native mammals, Dingoes might also keep down the wild pigs in forest and park. When collecting for Hans Brunner I found dog dung with many pig hairs in it in wild country where no domestic dog would have been. The introduction of Dingoes would add interest to forest and reserve. These fine dogs have been in Australia long enough to be regarded as native.

The National Parks and Wildlife Service, if it had more staff, could experiment with the re-establishment of several animals in New South Wales, the Bilby for instance, found now only in central Australia and in two isolated colonies on the coast of Western Australia, or the Australian Bustard and Brolga, once plentiful, now seen as rare travellers. Introductions should not be used to reinforce a small population. The newcomers might carry latent diseases that will wipe out the former occupants.

And it could experiment, on land already cleared, with the slow recreating of conditions as they were at settlement, of the open country favoured by Rufous Rat-Kangaroos and Eastern Native Cats. The only country many of our animals knew is now nowhere available to them. There would be scattered big eucalypts developing hollows, and here and there a seedling started by a fire. There would be fallen branches and hollow logs littered about. Imported plants would have to be eradicated with hoes and mowers, perhaps even sprayed in the first few years before tyres and boots and shoes and all that pressed the soil were banned. And eventually perhaps the soil in the park would loosen again and among the predominate grasses would grow the scattered shrubs and smaller plants that made early New South Wales 'a perpetual flower garden'.

The Forestry Commission does nothing towards getting rid of noxious weeds or animals. National Parks and Wildlife Service does what it can with limited funds. Its methods are not always the best. The shooting of goats in Warrumbungle National Park by one or two men on foot can do little more than keep the present numbers in check. The goats move in small flocks. Only one or two can be shot before the rest disappear over a hill. Men on horseback with trained sheep dogs can hold flocks together until all are shot. It would not be possible in that country to drive them to yards for marketing. The same method could be used in the Pilliga Nature Reserve where no attempt had been made by 1979 to rid it of the hundreds of goats.

Although our forests are valuable for what they have conserved, Australia would be a poorer country without the timber they produce. Used without imagination, often unregarded, our timbers are magnificent. In the 1970s the Standard Sawmill Company of Murwillumbah began to treat them with respect. The four Withey brothers who owned the mill experimented with the seasoning of timber. They met Peter Marshall of the great Wood Technology and Forest Research Division of the Forestry Commission of New South Wales and induced him to work with them. He spent two years designing the first big seasoning plant in Australia. Logs of many species of coastal softwoods and hardwoods dried in the bark in log dumps in the yard for four or five months. Then they were sawn into slabs and treated in a pressure chamber to make them termite-proof. From there the slabs went into huge hot-air kilns that reduced them to 8 per cent moisture in three or four weeks. But it was not possible to get even drying. Wet patches remained in the timber that would cause it to warp and crack if suddenly exposed to the air. So the slabs were wheeled from the drying room to a steam bath which stabilised them at 12 per cent moisture. From there they were moved to covered storage sheds.

Two brothers, Jeremy and Gervase Griffiths, erected a huge pole shed in a beautiful valley in Murwillumbah and made superb furniture from the last of the rare, fragrant Rosewood seasoned by this method.

Their numbered, polished, solid tables kept the natural edge of the timber. Sometimes grooves showed on an edge where a chain binding it to a trailer had scored it.

Timber from the Pilliga forest has never been seasoned. Apart from the use of polished White Cypress Pine as flooring it has seldom been used well. It is the custom to saw it and use it as it comes dripping with sap from the forest. In other countries logs of fine timbers were stood on end with iron bands about them. As the logs dried over three or four years the bands were tightened to prevent cracking.

Houses built of pine are condescendingly referred to as 'weatherboard' and have less value than brick houses. They are designed to be of less value. White Cypress Pine weatherboards are put on as cheap sheeting and painted. The unseasoned knots do not hold paint well. It bubbles off within a year or two. Pine is beautiful used unplaned, fitted upright with battens covering the joins, then oiled at least twice. The oils so far developed do not give lasting protection. The surface of the pine crazes but the very fine cracks merely roughen the finish a little more. They do not affect its long life.

Because of its great strength and weight ironbark has been relegated to work-horse jobs, fence posts, sleepers, telegraph poles, bridge bearers. If seasoned it planes well and finishes in different shades of red. As flooring it is the equal of Jarrah and as beautiful as pine. Its weight is a disadvantage for use on exterior walls but it is worth the trouble to fix it. It does not crack or warp and weathers slowly to the colour of old silver. A light sanding brings up the red again. Used rough as thick wide door jambs and window framing it makes a house look solid. A timber table, a timber house is not something made easily. They grow during more than one man's lifetime.

So that is how it was, so that is how it is, between Narrabri and Coonabarabran, between Baan Baa and Baradine. Once we lived on the eastern fringe of the forest. Then we lived hard against the western border. And both were good places to live.

Bird List

This bird list for the Pilliga forests, Pilliga Nature Reserve and the Warrumbungle National Park has been compiled from Alan Morris's lists, from the sightings of A. R. McGill and a Gould League bird study group camped at Baradine Showground in 1975, and from my own sightings. The first column gives the familiar names as used in the text from Peter Slater's *A Field Guide to Australian Birds*. The second column gives the names recommended in 1977 by the Royal Australasian Ornithologists Union (the *Emu*, vol. 77, Supplement May 1978). I find some of these names unacceptable, especially Bush Thick-knee for the Southern Stone-Curlew. Etymologists are uncertain whether the onomatopoeia of curlew is imposed or contained but in disposing of the marvellous cry the RAOU has almost disposed of the bird. And the changing of Nankeen Night Heron to Rufous Night Heron because nankeen as a colour has become obsolete is pedantic. Let the bird preserve the old word.

Name according to Slater	Name recommended by RAOU (noted only if different)
Apostle Bird	Apostlebird
Babbler, Grey-crowned	

White-browed	
Bell-bird, Crested	Crested Bellbird
Bittern, Brown	Australasian Bittern
Blue-bonnet (Both *Northiella haematogaster*	Blue Bonnet
haematogaster and *N. haematogaster*	
haematorrhous)	
Bower-bird, Spotted	Spotted Bowerbird
Brolga	
Bronzewing, Common	
Brush Turkey	Australian Brush-turkey
Budgerigar	
Bushlark, Singing	
Butcher-bird, Grey	
Pied	
Buzzard, Black-breasted (Recorded	
30 April 1977 on author's farm	
16 km north-west of Baradine)	
Chat, Crimson	
Chough, White-winged	
Cicada-bird	Cicadabird
Cockatiel	
Cockatoo, Glossy	Glossy Black-Cockatoo
Major Mitchell's (No recent	Pink Cockatoo
sightings. Last seen by author	
near Rocky Glen *c.* 1966)	
Red-tailed	Red-tailed Black-
	Cockatoo
Sulphur-crested	
Yellow-tailed	Yellow-tailed Black-
	Cockatoo
Coot	Eurasian Coot
Corella, Little	
Cormorant, Black	Great Cormorant
Little Black	
Little Pied	
Crake, Marsh	Baillon's Crake
Crow, Little	
Cuckoo, Black-eared	
Brush	
Channel-billed	
Fan-tailed	

Golden Bronze   Shining Bronze-Cuckoo
Horsfield Bronze   Horsfield's Bronze-
                     Cuckoo

Pallid
Cuckoo-shrike, Black-faced
    Ground
    Little   White-bellied Cuckoo-
                     shrike

Currawong, Pied
Darter
Dollar Bird   Dollarbird
Dotterel, Black-fronted   Black-fronted Plover
    Red-kneed
Dove, Bar-shouldered
    Diamond
    Peaceful
Duck, Black   Pacific Black Duck
    Grass Whistle-   Plumed Whistling-Duck
    Musk
    Pink-eared
    White-eyed
    Wood
Eagle, Little
    Wedge-tailed
Egret, Cattle (Recorded by Alan Morris
    Nov. 1976)
    Little
    Plumed   Intermediate Egret
    White   Great Egret
Emu
Falcon, Black
    Brown
    Grey (Pair seen by Alan Morris
    20 km west of Baradine)
    Little   Australian Hobby
    Peregrine
Fantail, Grey
Finch, Double-bar   Double-barred Finch
    Plum-headed
    Red-browed   Red-browed Firetail
    Zebra

Firetail, Diamond
Flycatcher, Brown   Jacky Winter
     Leaden
     Restless
Fowl, Mallee   Malleefowl
Friar-bird, Little   Little Friarbird
     Noisy   Noisy Friarbird
Frogmouth, Tawny
Galah
Goshawk, Brown
     Grey
Grassbird, Little
Grebe, Australian Little   Australasian Grebe
     Hoary-headed
Gull, Silver
Harrier, Spotted
     Swamp   Marsh Harrier
Heath-Wren, Chestnut-tailed   Chestnut-rumped
                            Hylacola
Heron, Nankeen Night   Rufous Night Heron
     White-faced
     White-necked   Pacific Heron
Honeyeater, Black-chinned
     Blue-faced
     Brown
     Brown-headed
     Fuscous
     Regent
     Singing
     Spiny-cheeked
     Striped
     White-eared
     White-naped
     White-plumed
     Yellow-faced
     Yellow-tufted
Ibis, Straw-necked
     White   Sacred Ibis
Jabiru   Black-necked Stork
Kestrel, Nankeen   Australian Kestrel
Kingfisher, Azure

Red-backed
Sacred
Kite, Black
Black-shouldered
Whistling
Kookaburra, Blue-winged (A pair seen
often by Wilf Taylor near Bugaldi
Creek 1960 to 1964, a female seen
1964 on his own property, another
seen 1966. Author saw a distressed
male in his homestead garden
March 1975)
Laughing
Lorikeet, Little
Musk
Scaly-breasted
Magpie, Black-backed　　　　　　　　Australian Magpie
Magpie-lark　　　　　　　　　　　　　Australian Magpie-lark
Martin, Fairy
Tree
Miner, Noisy
Yellow-throated
Mistletoe-bird　　　　　　　　　　　　Mistletoebird
Moorhen, Dusky
Native Hen, Black-tailed
Nightjar, Spotted
White-throated
Oriole, Olive-backed
Owl, Barking
Barn
Boobook
Masked (One brought out of a
hollow tree by author on three
separate occasions in 1975)
Powerful
Owlet-nightjar　　　　　　　　　　　Australian Owlet-nightjar
Pardalote, Spotted
Striated
Parrot, King　　　　　　　　　　　　Australian King Parrot
Mallee Ringneck　　　　　　　　　Mallee Ringneck
Red-rumped

Red-winged
Superb
Swift
Turquoise
Pelican, Australian
Pigeon, Crested
   Domestic   Feral Pigeon
Pipit, Australian   Richard's Pipit
Plover, Australian Spur-winged   Masked Lapwing
   Banded   Banded Lapwing
Quail, Brown
   King (Shot by Merv Goodwin of
   Gunnedah *c.* 1976)
   Little   Little Button-quail
   Painted   Painted Button-quail
   Red-chested   Red-chested Button-quail
   Stubble
Quail-thrush, Spotted
Rainbow Bird   Rainbow Bee-eater
Raven, Australian
   Little
Reed-warbler   Clamorous Reed-Warbler
Robin, Hooded
   Red-capped
   Rose
   Scarlet
   Southern Yellow   Eastern Yellow Robin
Rosella, Eastern
   Crimson
Scrub-Wren, White-browed   Whitebrowed Scrubwren
Shrike-thrush, Grey
Shrike-tit, Eastern   Crested Shrike-tit
Silver-eye, Grey-breasted   Silvereye
Sittella, Orange-winged   Varied Sittella
Snipe, Japanese   Latham's Snipe
Songlark, Brown
   Rufous
Sparrow, House
Sparrowhawk, Collared
Spinebill, Eastern
Spoonbill, Royal

Yellow-billed
Starling, English
Stilt, Black-winged
Stone-Curlew, Southern (Now rare   Bush Thick-knee
    and endangered but heard on two
    properties during 1980 by Mrs
    A. Rich and David Hadfield. Both
    properties are about 20 km west
    of Baradine)
Swallow, Welcome
    White-backed
Swamphen   Purple Swamphen
Swan, Black
Swift, Fork-tailed (Rare — seen above
    author's house 15 Dec. 1977)
    Spine-tailed   White-throated Needletail
Teal, Grey
Tern, Gull-billed (Seen by author 29 Oct.
    1977. Caught several insects
    disturbed by scarifier)
    Marsh   Whiskered Tern
Thornbill, Broad-tailed   Inland Thornbill
    Buff-tailed   Buff-rumped Thornbill
    Chestnut-tailed   Chestnut-rumped
                                                        Thornbill

    Little   Yellow Thornbill
    Striated
    Yellow-tailed   Yellow-rumped Thornbill
Tree-creeper, Brown   Brown Treecreeper
    White-throated   White-throated
                                                        Treecreeper

Triller, White-winged
Tropicbird, Red-tailed (Found exhausted
    on the ground 20 km north-west of
    Baradine by David Hadfield on
    20 March 1978 after cyclonic
    rains from the east. Indentified by
    Alan Morris. Another found at
    Coonabarabran 21 March 1980)
    White-tailed (Also found 20 March

1978. Exhausted bird was brought to
Warrumbungle National Park)

Warbler, Speckled	
White-tailed	
White-throated	
Wattle-bird, Red	Red Wattlebird
Weebill	
Whistler, Golden	
Rufous	
Whiteface, Southern	
Willie Wagtail	
Wood-Swallow, Black-faced	Black-faced Woodswallow
Dusky	Dusky Woodswallow
Little	Little Woodswallow
Masked	Masked Woodswallow
White-breasted	White-breasted Woodswallow
White-browed	White-browed Woodswallow
Wren, Purple-backed	Variegated Fairy-wren
Superb Blue	Superb Fairy-wren
White-winged	White-winged Fairy-wren

Plant List

A full list of the plants in the Warrumbungle National Park and the Pilliga Nature Reserve and State forests would take up substantial space – about a thousand species have been recorded. Ms Gwen Harden of the University of New England has compiled an excellent list of over five hundred species for the Warrumbungle National Park. It is available from the National Parks and Wildlife Service. A preliminary list for the Pilliga Nature Reserve is also available.

The following list is selected to show some of the rarer plants and also the extraordinary numbers of the orchid family and of species within some genera confined in an area of 14,000 square kilometres. It is extracted from Gwen Harden's list, from Barry Fox's collection made during his study of the Pilliga Mouse, from George Althofer's study of the genus *Prostanthera*, and from my own collection.

DROSERACEAE

Drosera auriculata　　　　　　　　　Tall Sundew
　　　burmannii
　　　indica

LAMIACEAE

Prostanthera cruciflora　　　　　　Cross-flowered Mint Bush
　　　denticulata sp. aff. *P. denticulata*

granitica
sp. aff. *P. granitica*
howelliae
leichhardtii
sp. aff. *P. leichhardtii*
nivea var. *nivea* — Snowy Mint Bush
nivea var. *induta* — Snowy Mint Bush
rotundifolia — Round Leaf Mint Bush
saxicola var. *bracteolata* — Slender Mint Bush
stricta — Hairy Mint Bush (Found in one gully only in the Warrumbungles; equally restricted elsewhere.)

MIMOSACEAE

Acacia amblygona — Prickle-bush
burrowii — Burrow's Wattle
buxifolia — Box-leafed Wattle
caesiella — Blue Bush
caroleae (Formerly *A. doratoxylon* var. *angustifolia*)
cheelii — Motherumbah
conferta — Crowded-leafed Wattle
concurrens — Curracabah
cultriformis — Knife-leafed Wattle
deanei ssp. *deanei* — Deane's Wattle or Western Green Wattle (I found one form with sensitive leaves.)
decora — Western Golden or Silver Wattle
doratoxylon — Currawong or Spearwood
flexifolia — Bent-leaf Wattle
forsythii — Forsyth's Wattle
gladiiformis — Sword Wattle
hakeoides — Western Black Wattle
harpophylla — Brigalow
implexa — Hickory
ixiophylla
ixodes (Formerly *A. gnidium* var. *latifolia*) — Gin Gin
lanigera — Woolly Wattle

leucoclada ssp. *leucoclada*
lineata
mearnsii   Black Wattle
neriifolia   Silver Wattle
oswaldii   Umbrella Bush
paradoxa (formerly *A. armata*)   Kangaroo Thorn
pendula   Myall
penninervis   Mountain Hickory
pilligaensis   Pilliga Wattle
polybotrya   Coonabarabran Wattle
rigens   Needlewood
salicina   Cooba or Native Willow
spp. undescribed (*A. homalo-*   Wrongly called Yarran locally
    phylla-A. Pendula
group)
spectabilis   Mudgee Wattle
stenophylla   River Cooba
subulata   Awl Wattle
tindaleae
triptera   Spurwing Wattle, once known
                                        as Hookbill
ulicifolia   Prickly Moses
uncinata   Wavy-leafed Wattle
victoriae   Prickly Wattle
viscidula   Sticky Wattle

MYRTACEAE

Eucalyptus albens   White Box
    blakelyi   Blakely's Red Gum
    bridgesiana   Apple Box
    camaldulensis   River Red Gum
    conica   Fuzzy Box
    crebra   Narrow-leaved Ironbark
    dealbata   Hill Red Gum
    dealbata var. *chloroclada*   Sand Red Gum (a new name
                                        suggested by Dr Johnson for
                                        this attractive small tree)
    dwyeri   Dwyer's Hill Red Gum
    fibrosa   Blue-leaved Ironbark
    goniocalyx   Bundy or Long-leaved Box

macrorhyncha	Red Stringybark
melanophloia	Silver-leaved Ironbark
melliodora	Yellow Box
pauciflora	Snow Gum (On Mount Wambelong)
pilligaensis	Pilliga Box
populnea	Bimble Box or Poplar Box
rossii	White Gum
sideroxylon	Mugga or Red Ironbark
spp. (common intergrade between *E. microcarpa* and *E. pilligaensis*)	
spp. (probable cross between *E. crebra* and *E. melliodora*)	Gunnedah Ironbark
tessellaris	Carbeen
trachyphloia	White Bloodwood
viminalis	Ribbon or Manna Gum
viridis	Green Mallee

ORCHIDACEAE

Acianthus fornicatus	Pixie Caps (the botanical name refers to the stem jutting up from the vulva-shaped leaf)
Caladenia caerulea	Blue Fingers
catenata (Formerly *C. carnea*)	Pink Fingers
cucullata	Hooked Caladenia
dilatata	Green or Fringed Spider Orchid
filamentosa	Common Spider Orchid
reticulata	Plain-lip Spider Orchid
testacea	Honey Caladenia
Calochilus robertsonii	Purplish-beard Orchid
Chiloglottis formicifera	Ant Orchid
Cymbidium canaliculatum	Banana Orchid
Dendrobium speciosum	Rock Orchid
Dipodium hamiltonianum	Green Hyacinth Orchid
punctatum	Hyacinth Orchid
Diuris abbreviata	Donkey Orchid
platichila	Donkey Orchid
punctata	Purple Diuris

sulphurea	Tiger Orchid
Eriochilus cucullatus	Parson's Band
Glossodia major	Wax-lip Orchid
Lyperanthus suaveolens	Blady Leaf
Microtis parviflora	Slender Onion Orchid
unifolia	Common Onion Orchid
Prasophyllum rufum	Red Leek Orchid
Pterostylis boormanii	
biseta	Rusty Hood
coccinea	Red Hood
curta	Blunt Greenhood
hamata	Scaly Greenhood
longicurva	Greenhood
longifolia	Tall Greenhood
mutica	Midget Greenhood
nutans	Parrot's Beak Orchid
parviflora	Baby Greenhood
revoluta	Autumn Greenhood
rufa ssp. *aciculiformis*	Rusty Greenhood
Thelmitra aristata var. *megcalyptra*	Scented Sun Orchid
pauciflora	Slender Sun Orchid

PAPILIONACEAE

Daviesia acicularis	Prickly Bitter Pea
genistifolia	Broom Bitter Pea
latifolia	Hop Bitter Pea or Native Hops
pubigera	Bitter Pea
squarrosa	Prickly Pea
ulicifolia	Native Gorse
umbellulata	
virgata	
Pultenaea boormanii	
cunninghamii	Grey Bush-Pea
foliolosa	Small-leaved Bush-Pea
microphylla var. *microphylla*	Bush Pea
microphylla var. *cinerascens*	

RHAMNACEAE

Alphitonia excelsa	Red Ash

RUTACEAE

Philotheca salsolifolia

SAPINDACEAE

Dodonaea attenuata	Slender Hopbush
boroniifolia	Hairy Hopbush
cuneata	Wedge-leaved Hopbush
filifolia	
peduncularis	Stalked Hopbush
tenuifolia	
truncatiales	Sticky Hopbush
viscosa var. *angustifolia*	
viscosa var. *spathulata*	

Bibliography

Many sources were used in more than one chapter. The first use only has been recorded. Where some obvious sources were found too inaccurate for use that has been noted. All manuscripts and documents, unless otherwise stated, were consulted at the Mitchell Library or the Archives Office of New South Wales.

1: Explorers and Livestock

BOOKS

A Journal of a Voyage Round the World. London, 1771.

'Afrikander Cattle'. *Standard Encyclopaedia of Southern Africa*. n.d.

An Illustrated World History of the Sheep and Wool Industry. South African Wool Board, Pretoria, 1970.

An Authentic and Interesting Narrative of the Late Expedition to Botany Bay . . . by 'an officer'. 1st edn., London, 1789. Library of Australian History, Facsimile Series no. 12, Sydney, 1978.

Barrallier, Francis. *Journal of the Expedition into the Interior of New South Wales 1802*. Marsh Walsh Publishing, Melbourne, 1975.

Beaglehole, J. C. (ed.). *The Endeavour Journal of Joseph Banks*. Angus and Robertson, Sydney, 1962.

Bosman, A. M. *Cattle Farming in South Africa*. Central News Agency Ltd, 1931.

Bosman, S. W. and Nel, J. W. 'The Fat-tailed Types' in *The Smallstock Industry in South Africa*.

Briggs, Hilton M. *Modern Breeds of Livestock*. Macmillan Co., New York, 1958.

Captain Cook's Original Voyages Round the World. London, 1815.

Cobley, John. *The Convicts 1788–1792*. Wentworth Press, Sydney, 1965.

Dallas, K. M. *Trading Posts or Penal Colonies*. Fullers Bookshop, Hobart, 1969.

426

Eastoe, R. D. 'Breeds of Sheep' in *Sheep Production Guide*. Graziers' Association of New South Wales, Sydney, 1976.

Fison, E. Herbert. *Flocks and Fleeces*. Wyman and Sons Ltd, London, 1894.

Guthrie, J. F. *A World History of Sheep and Wool*. McCarron Bird Pty Ltd, Melbourne, 1957.

Historical Records of Australia (ed. F. Watson). Government Printer, Sydney, 1914–25.

Historical Records of New South Wales (ed. F. M. Bladen). vols I–VII, 1762–1811. Government Printer, Sydney, 1893–1901.

Kelley, R. B. *Principles and Methods of Animal Breeding*. Angus and Robertson, Sydney, 1946.

——. *Native and Adapted Cattle*. Angus and Robertson, Sydney, 1959.

Laseron, Charles F. *Ancient Australia*. Angus and Robertson, Sydney, 1955.

Lydekker, R. *The Sheep and its Cousins*. George Allen and Co., London, 1912.

McIvor, Clarence. *History and Development of Sheep Farming from Antiquity to Modern Times*, Part 1. Tilghman and Barnett, Sydney, 1893.

Morton, P. H. *The Cattle of NSW from 1788, more especially the Cattle of Illawarra from 1804 to 1930*. Waite and Bull, Sydney, 1930.

Opperman, H. B. K. *Africander Cattle of South Africa*. Africander Cattle Breeders' Society of SA, Bloemfontein, 1952.

Oxley, John. *Journals of Two Expeditions into the Interior of New South Wales, undertaken by order of the British Government in the years 1817–18*. John Murray, London, 1820.

Richards, Joanna Armour (ed.). *Blaxland – Lawson – Wentworth 1813*. Blubber Head Press, Hobart, 1979.

Rouse, J. E. *World Cattle*, vol. II. University of Oklahoma Press, 1970.

Tench, W. *A Complete Account of the Settlement at Port Jackson, in New South Wales* . . . London, 1793.

The Voyages of Captain James Cook . . . 7 vols, London, 1813.

The Voyages of Captain James Cook. London, 1846.

Wharton, Captain W. J. L. (ed.). *Captain Cook's Journal*. London, 1893.

Whitehead, J. R. *John Oxley's Journey to the Warrumbungle Mountains and through the Coonabarabran District 1818*. Warrumbungle Historical Society, n.d.

The World's Sheep Farming for Fifty Years 1843–1893. William Cooper and Nephews, Berkhamsted, 1893.

Wright, Phillip A. *Memories of a Bushwacker*. University of New England, Armidale, c. 1971.

Young, Rev. George. *Life and Voyages of Captain Cook*. London, 1836.

PERIODICALS, BOOKLETS

Atkinson, Alan. 'Whips and Tories and Botany Bay'. *Journal of the Royal Australian Historical Society*, vol. 61, part 5, 1976.

Bonsma, Jan C. 'The Africander Breed'. *Farming in SA*, March, 1952.

Bosman, S. W. and Mostert, L. 'Mutton Production in the North-Western Cape Province'. *Handbook for Farmers in South Africa*, vol. III, 1957.

Brooker, M. G. and Dolling, C. H. S. 'Pigmentation of Sheep'. *Australian Journal of Agricultural Research*, vol. 16, 1965.

'Excursion into History'. Blue Mountains Historical Society, 1968.

Fletcher, Brian H. 'Government Farming and Grazing in New South Wales, 1788–1810'. *Journal of the Royal Australian Historical Society*, vol. 59, part 3, 1973.

Gandevia, Bryan. 'Socio-Medical Factors in the Evolution of the First Settlement at

Sydney Cove 1788–1803'. *Journal of the Royal Australian Historical Society*, vol. 61, part 1, 1975.

Garran, J. C. 'Indian Sheep in Early New South Wales'. Royal Australian Historical Society, *Newsletter*, no. 135, 1974.

Harris, John. 'Shane's Park, South Creek'. Royal Australian Historical Society, *Newsletter*, no. 168, 1977.

'Historical History of the Blue Mountains'. Council of City of Blue Mountains, 1968.

Johnson, K. A. 'Marriage Licences 1813–1827'. *Descent*, vol. 8, part 2, 1977.

Joubert, D. M. 'Indigenous South African Sheep and Goats: Their Origin and Development'. *Tropical Science*, vol. XI, no. 3.

Martin, Ged. '"A Striking Instance of the Want of Enterprise": the Discovery of the Cowpastures in 1795'. Royal Australian Historical Society, *Newsletter*, no. 169, 1977.

Moore, Kevin. 'The Finding of the Seven Hills Farm'. Royal Australian Historical Society, *Newsletter*, no. 188, 1980.

Nel, J. W. 'South African Bantu Sheep'. *Farming in SA*, June, 1963.

Parsons, T. G. 'Courts Martial, the Savoy Military Prison and the New South Wales Corps'. *Journal of the Royal Australian Historical Society*, vol. 63, part 4, 1978.

Starke, Dr J. S. 'Development of the Non-woolled Sheep'. *Farming in SA*, March, 1952.

'The Drakensberger 1659–1947'. Unidentified photostat copy from South African Embassy.

Wilton, Rev. P. N. (ed.). 'The Late Tour of A. Cunningham'. *Australian Quarterly Journal*, vol. 1, no. 1, 1828.

NEWSPAPERS

Green, L. L. 'The Northern Journeyings of Explorer Oxley'. *Northern Daily Leader*, 29 September 1959.

'History and the sheep will keep Camden Park'. *Sydney Morning Herald*, 22 May 1976.

Narrabri Herald, 21 August 1886, quoting the *Bligh Watchman*.

'Sydney Built in Wrong Place — CSIRO Man'. *Sydney Morning Herald*, 16 June 1976.

MANUSCRIPTS AND UNPUBLISHED TYPESCRIPTS

Collins, E. C. Recollections of the Clarke Family of Bulga via Singleton, c. 1916. Library of Royal Australian Historical Society.

Archives of New South Wales. Colonial Secretary In-Letters 1815. Edict by Lachlan Macquarie, 9 Dec. 1815 (re impounding of trespassing stock and arrest of trespassers).

Cook, Captain James. Official Log May 1768–July 1771. Mitchell Library photocopy from British Museum.

Gardner, William. Productions and resources of the Northern and Western districts of New South Wales, 1854.

2: The First Moves

BOOKS

Australian Dictionary of Biography, vols 1–6. Edited by Douglas Pike, Melbourne University Press, Melbourne, 1966–76.

Australian Encyclopaedia, The. Angus and Robertson, Sydney, 1958.

Barton, G. B. *The True Story of Margaret Catchpole*. Cornstalk Publishing Company, Sydney, 1924.

Clark, C. M. H. *A History of Australia* (vol. II) *New South Wales and Van Dieman's Land 1822–1838*. Melbourne University Press, Melbourne, 1968.

Collins, David. *An Account of the English Colony in N.S.W.* Whitcombe and Tombs Ltd, Melbourne and London, n.d.

Ellis, M. H. *John Macarthur*, Angus and Robertson, Sydney, 1967.

Fletcher, Brian H. *Landed Enterprise and Penal Society*. Sydney University Press, Sydney, 1976.

Harris, Godfrey. *Mudgee Past and Present*. Commonwealth Jubilee Committee, Mudgee, 1951.

Mudgee Centenary Souvenir 1821–1921. Compilers and publisher not stated, c. 1921.

Spriggs, P. W. *Our Blue Mountains' Yesterdays*. Published by author, Leura, ?c. 1962.

PERIODICALS, BOOKLETS

The Discovery of Saint Patrick's Plains. Singleton Argus Print, author unknown, n.d.

Gundungura: a Guide to the Greater Southern Blue Mountains. Sydney University Rover Crew, Sydney, 1970.

Whitton, Evan. 'The Convict in Us All'. *National Times Magazine*, 7–12 November 1977.

MANUSCRIPTS AND UNPUBLISHED TYPESCRIPTS

Bonwick Transcripts 17, Bigge, Blaxland's Prospectus of Co.

Bonwick Transcripts 20, Bigge, (Gregory Blaxland, November, 1819).

Colonial Secretary. Copies of letters sent within the Colony: all permits for movement of stock in AO series 4/3506 to 4/3516, 1822 to 1825; also 'approval for temporary occupation' from same series.

Colonial Secretary. In-Letters 1815–23.

Colonial Secretary. In-Letters Bathurst 1824–6.

Colonial Secretary. Letters re Land (Searched 2/7791 to 2/8013 for all relevant names. It is a singularly valuable series of letters, memorials, applications, statements, Land Board reports, Surveyor-General's reports, memoranda, petitions, schedules of capital, newspaper cuttings, official jottings on folded-down corners, dated mostly from 1823 to 1835, contained in about two hundred boxes that often reveal not only the possessions of the landholders but their lives and their characters.)

Colonial Secretary. Letters sent within the Colony, 1 January 1814 to 28 March 1815.

Colonial Secretary. Letters sent within the Colony, 30 December 1819 to 19 April 1820.

Lawson, W. Expedition across the Blue Mountains. Photostat of original held in Mitchell Library safe.

Maxwell, John. Superintendent of Government Stock at Bathurst 1823–1826. Register of Female Herds of Government Cattle.

———. Letters 1824, 1825 (Bathurst Historical Museum).

Mitchell, T. L. Report on the New Line of Road Towards Bathurst 29 November 1827. Papers transferred from the Lands Department.

Papers relating to Margaret Catchpole, collected by James Bonwick, 'From Mr E. Brooke's Collection'.

Selkirk, Henry. Discovery of Mudgee. 1920.

Singleton, Benjamin. Journal of a party to the Northward an Westward. Colonial Secretary In-letters 1818 pp. 209–14.

Wentworth, William Charles. Journal. Photocopy of original held in Mitchell Library.

Wentworth Papers, letter from D'Arcy Wentworth re crossing of Blue Mountains dated 15 October 1814.
Wentworth Papers, W. C. Wentworth to Bathurst applying for new position of tender master, undated (?1817 in pencil).

3: The Squatters

BOOKS

Boyce, Dean. *Clarke of the Kindur.* Melbourne University Press, Melbourne, 1970.
Carter, H. R. *The Upper Mooki.* Quirindi and District Historical Society, Quirindi, 1974.
Dangar, H. *Index and Directory to Map of the Country Bordering upon the River Hunter . . . a complete emigrant's guide.* Joseph Cross, London, 1828.
Dawson, Robert. *Statement of the Services of Mr Dawson as Chief Agent of the Australian Agricultural Company.* Smith, Elder and Co. for the author, London, 1829.
Field, Barron. *Geographical Memoirs on New South Wales by various hands.* 'Journal of a Route from Bathurst to Liverpool Plains explored by Allan Cunningham'. together with map; and 'Journal of an Excursion across the Blue Mountains', author unknown. John Murray, London, 1825.
Fletcher, C. Brundson. *Coolah Valley and the Warrumbungle Range.* Cornstalk Publishing Co., Sydney, 1927.
[?Harris, Alexander]. *Settlers and Convicts By an Emigrant Mechanic.* C. Cox, London, 1847.
Kelley, R. B. *Sheep Dogs.* Angus and Robertson, Sydney, 1947.
Lea, David A. M., Pigram, John J. J. and Greenwood, Lesley M. (eds). *An Atlas of New England Vol. 2 — The Commentaries* (J. F. Atchison). University of New England, Armidale, 1977.
McMinn, W. G. *Allan Cunningham.* Melbourne University Press, Melbourne, 1970.
Memoirs of William Cox, J. P. (Authors probably daughters of George Henry Cox, grandson of William Cox.) William Brooks and Co. Printers, Sydney and Brisbane, 1901.
Mitchell, Sir T. L. *Journal of an Expedition into the Interior of Tropical Australia . . .* Longman, Brown, Green and Longmans, London, 1848.
Mitchell, Major T. L. *Three Expeditions into the Interior of Eastern Australia; with Descriptions of the Recently Explored Region of Australia Felix, and of the Present Colony of New South Wales.* 2 vols, 2nd edn. T. and W. Boone, London, 1839. (Author's copy, bought by an unknown landseeker in 1841, has long comments on margins and end-papers about the best country to take up.)
Mowle, P. C. *A Genealogical History of Pioneer Families of Australia.* 4th edn., J. Sands Pty Ltd, Sydney, 1948.
Perry, T. M. *Australia's First Frontier.* Cambridge University Press, London and New York, 1963.
Walker, John. *Two Hundred Years in Retrospect.* Bi-centenary Publication Syndicate of Cronulla, Cronulla, 1970.
Wood, W. Allan. *Dawn in the Valley.* Wentworth Books, Sydney, 1972.

PERIODICALS, BOOKLETS AND MONOGRAPHS

Bertie, Charles H. 'Pioneer Families of Australia No. 25 — The Chisholms'. *The Home,* 1 February 1932.

Blair, Sandra J. 'The Revolt at Castle Forbes: A Catalyst to Emancipist Emigrant Confrontation'. *Journal of the Royal Australian Historical Society*, vol. 64, part 2, 1978.

Froggatt, Walter W. 'The Curators and Botanists of the Botanic Gardens, Sydney'. *Journal of the Royal Australian Historical Society*, vol. 18, 1932.

'Paper to be Read'. Royal Australian Historical Society, *Newsletter*, no. 160, September 1976.

'Sir Thomas Mitchell's Map'. Royal Australian Historical Society, *Newsletter*, no. 165, 1977.

Tilley, G. A. 'Brave Men and Fit Governors: The Recall of Governor Darling from N.S.W.' *Journal of the Royal Australian Historical Society*, vol. 61, part 4, 1975.

Torr, Harry. *The Singletons*. Singleton Historical Society, Singleton, n.d.

Whitelaw, Ella. *A History of Singleton*. Singleton Historical Society, n.d.

NEWSPAPERS

'AA Company adjourns first meeting'. *Northern Daily Leader*, 9 July 1976.

Allison, Colin. 'A sad and sorry rest for our pioneers'. *Sydney Morning Herald*, 1 February 1978.

Atchison, John. 'Played like a trout by a set of rascals'. Letter to *National Times*, 21–6 November 1977.

Australian, 9 May 1827 (ten thousand head of cattle on Liverpool Plains).

Australian, 3 May 1833 (five murdered at The Barber's stockyard).

Gill, Alan. 'The Barossa Valley's vintage settlers'. *Sydney Morning Herald*, 3 June 1978.

Green, L. L. 'Mitchell's Movements in Tamworth District'. *Northern Daily Leader*, 6 October 1959.

'It'll be dinkum Aussie AA Co. from January'. *Northern Daily Leader*, 24 November 1975.

Maitland Mercury, 28 January 1843 (letter to C. M. Doyle from his son).

McLeay, Alexander. 'Government Notice. 29 September 1826' (re prisoners assigned to wives attending Church muster). Undated newspaper cutting among William Lawson's papers.

Nowland, William. 'A squatter'. Letter to *Sydney Morning Herald*, 23 January 1861.

Sydney Gazette, 30 April 1828 (suspension of Dawson from A.A. Co.)

Sydney Gazette, 2 June 1832 (re males outnumbering females 10 to 1).

Sydney Monitor, 12 January 1831 (trial of Edwin Baldwin).

'. . . the undermentioned prisoners having absconded . . .' *Sydney Gazette*, 8 February 1831.

'"The Upper Mooki" Tells story of opening of gate to plains'. *North West Magazine*, 23 September 1974, in *Coonabarabran Times*.

MANUSCRIPTS AND TYPESCRIPTS

A Journal kept by Mr George Cox on his late Tour to the Northward and Westward of Bathurst (30 November 1821–4 December 1821).

Colonial Secretary. In-Letters Newcastle 1825.

Colonial Secretary. In-Letters Naval and Military 1833 (ref. mounted police and settlement at Gourada).

Cunningham, Allan. Journal 11 April 1825 to 13 May 1825. (Fair photographic copy of original. Diary ends 31 May not 13 May – pages are out of order.)

Cunningham's report 1827 Liverpool Plains to Moreton Bay.

Executive Council. Appendix No. 4. Judge's Minutes.

Governor's despatches vol. 2, p. 677.

Hoddle, R. Letters 1824–33.

Supreme Court Criminal Jurisdiction Informations 1831 3 term, 4 term; 1832 1 term, 2 term.

MAPS

Cunningham, Allan. A Sketch of Portion of the Interior of New South Wales.

Dangar, Henry. 'Map of the River Hunter and its Branches'. J. Cross, London, 1828.

'Liverpool Plains District South West Portion Sheet No. 2'. Occupation of Lands Office, Sydney, 1881.

'Pilliga Project Map'. Forestry Commission of New South Wales, 1969.

4: Licences to Depasture Beyond the Limits;   5: Runholders and Selectors

BOOKS

Australian Dictionary of Dates and Men of the Time. J. H. Heaton, London, 1879.

Australian Men of Mark, vols I, II. 'John Eales, Senior, Esquire' and 'The Hon, John Eales, Esquire, MLC', Charles F. Maxwell, Sydney, 1889. (Inaccurate and obsequious.)

Bayley, William A. *Golden Granary*. Grenfell, 1954.

Bennett, George. *Wanderings in New South Wales* . . . Richard Bentley, London, 1834.

Black, Lindsay. *Stone Arrangements*. The author, Perth, 1950.

Blainey, Geoffrey. *The Rush that Never Ended*. Melbourne University Press, Melbourne, 1964.

Burke, James Lester (ed.). *The Life and Adventures of Martin Cash*. 'Mercury' Steam Press Office, Hobart Town, 1870.

Cameron, James. *Centenary History of the Presbyterian Church in New South Wales*. Angus and Robertson, Sydney, 1905 (Archives of Presbyterian Church, Margaret Street, Sydney).

Campbell, J. F. *'Squatting' on Crown Lands in New South Wales*. Royal Australian Historical Society in association with Angus and Robertson, Sydney, 1968.

Cannon, Michael. *Life in the Country*. Nelson, Melbourne, 1974.

?Clements, the Rev. Stuart. *The Parish of Bowenfels to the year 1865*. Lithgow, n.d. (Inaccurate.)

Dargin, Peter, *Aboriginal Fisheries of the Darling-Barwon Rivers*, Brewarrina Historical Society, 1976.

Darwin, Charles. *Journal of researches into the geology and natural history of the various countries visited by H. M. S. Beagle*. Henry Colburn, London, 1839.

Dawson, Robert. *The Present State of Australia*. Smith Elder and Co., London, 1830.

Fetherstonhaugh, Cuthbert. *After Many Days*. John Andrew and Co. Printers, Sydney, 1918 (published by the author).

First Annual Report upon the Occupation of Crown Lands . . . Department of Mines N.S.W. for the year 1879. Government Printer, Sydney, 1880. (And all subsequent annual reports of the variously named departments of lands to 1930, at Department of Lands.)

Fraser, Allan and Stamp, John T. *Sheep Husbandry and Diseases*. Crosby Lockwood and Son, London, 1968.

Greaves, Bernard (ed.). *The Story of Bathurst*. Angus and Robertson, Sydney, 1976.

Hanson, William. *Pastoral Possessions of N.S.W.* Gibbs, Shallard and Co., Sydney, 1889.

Haydon, A. L. *The Trooper Police of Australia.* Andrew Melrose, London, 1911.

Idriess, Ion L. *The Red Chief.* Angus and Robertson, Sydney, 1965.

Ingleton, Geoffrey C. *True Patriots All . . .* Angus and Robertson, Sydney, 1952.

Kiddle, Margaret. *Men of Yesterday.* Melbourne University Press, Melbourne, 1963.

Lamond, Henry G. *From Tariaro to Ross Roy: Wm Ross Munro 20-2-50—20-2-43.* Jackson and O'Sullivan Pty Ltd, Brisbane, ?1943.

Leslie, John. *Stockyards to Streets.* Pub. by author (L. J. Gibson), ?1955.

Levi, J. S. and Bergman, G. F. J. *Australian Genesis.* Rigby, Adelaide, 1974.

Marriott (Lee), Ida. *Early Explorers in Australia.* Methuen and Co. Ltd, London, 1925.

Maxwell, Eileen. *Written in Gold. The Story of Gulgong.* The author, Dubbo, 1975.

New South Wales Government Gazette. July—December 1848. 'Claims to Leases of Crown Lands Beyond the Settled Districts', also 'The undermentioned prisoners having absconded . . .'

Parliamentary Papers. *Legislative Assembly New South Wales 1865—66.* 'Crown lands held under Pastoral Occupation'.

Reed, A. W. *Place Names of Australia.* A. H. and A. W. Reed, Sydney, 1973.

Ridley, Rev. William. *Kamilaroi and other Australian Languages.* Government Printer, Sydney, 1875.

Ridley, William. *Gurre Kamilaroi.* Sydney, 1856.

Roberts, Stephen H. *The Squatting Age in Australia 1835—1847.* Melbourne University Press, Melbourne, 1975.

Smith, Bertha Mac. *Quench Not the Spirit.* Hawthorne Press, Melbourne, 1972.

Sommerlad, Ernest C. *The Land of the Beardies.* Facsimile reproduction in *The Beardies Heritage.* Glen Innes Municipal Council, 1972.

Steele, Jas. *Early Days of Windsor.* Facsimile reprint by Library of Australian History, Sydney, 1977.

Therry, R. *Reminiscences of Thirty Years Residence in New South Wales.* Sampson Low, Son and Co., London, 1863.

Turner, F. *Australian Grasses.* Government Printer, Sydney, 1895.

Webb, R. J. *'The Rising Sun' A History of Moree and District. Moree Champion,* Moree, 1972.

Yarwood, A. T. *Samuel Marsden The Great Survivor.* Melbourne University Press, Melbourne, 1977.

PERIODICALS, BOOKLETS AND MONOGRAPHS

'A History of Coonamble District Properties compiled from the notes of Alan Mears Ibbott'. Coonamble Historical Society, 1974. (Inaccurate.)

'An Agriculturist's Tour to the West'. *Town and Country Journal,* 2 May 1874.

Atchison, J. F. 'The P.G.K. Post'. Royal Australian Historical Society, *Newsletter,* no. 175, 1978.

Atchison, John and Gray, Nancy. *Henry Dangar Surveyor and Explorer.* Scone and Upper Hunter Historical Society, Scone, 1974.

Back to Coonabarabran Week — 26 February—3 March 1934.

Back to Gilgandra Week Celebrations. Chamber of Commerce 'Back to Gilgandra' Week Committee, 1976.

Coonabarabran Centenary Celebrations 1860—1960.

Dalton, W. 'With the Pioneers. The Cormie Family of Early Scone'. Scone Historical Society, *Journal,* vol. 2, 1961. (Inaccurate.)

Dickey, Brian. 'Responsible Government in N.S.W.: the Transfer of Power in a

Colony of Settlement'. *Journal of the Royal Australian Historical Society*, vol. 60, part 4, 1974.

Doyle, Alec B. *Interim Notes on the Doyle Families in Ireland and Andrew Doyle of Ulitedinburra Lodge, Lower Portland, in the Hawkesbury District of New South Wales and his Descendants.* Privately bound and printed, 1960. (Inaccurate.)

Dwight, A. 'The Use of Indian Labourers in New South Wales'. *Journal of the Royal Australian Historical Society*, vol. 62, part 2, 1976.

Eipper, F. R. 'Hunting Wild Cattle by Moonlight'. Scone and Upper Hunter Historical Society, *Journal*, vol. 2, 1961.

Fletcher, Brian. 'Sir John Jamison in New South Wales 1814–1844'. *Journal of the Royal Australian Historical Society*, vol. 65, part 1, 1979.

Forster, Harley W. (ed.). *The Dillingham Convict Letters.* Cypress Books, Melbourne, 1970.

Geeves, Philip. 'Whatever Became of Thos. Hamblett?' Royal Australian Historical Society, *Newsletter*, no. 156, 1976.

Historical Narrabri. Narrabri and District Historical Society, 1967.

Jervis, James. 'Exploration and Settlement of the North-Western Plains'. *Journal and Proceedings of the Royal Australian Historical Society*, vol. 48, 5, 1962 and 6, 1963. (Inaccurate.)

Karr, Clarence. 'Origins of the New South Wales Farmers' Union Movement'. *Journal of the Royal Australian Historical Society*, vol. 61, part 3, 1975.

King, C. J. 'An Outline of Closer Settlement in New South Wales Part 1 the Sequence of the Land Laws 1788–1956', *Review of Marketing and Agricultural Economics*, vol. 25, nos. 3, 4, 1957.

King, G. B. Gidley. 'Aspects of the First Decade of the Australian Agricultural Company'. *Descent*, vol. 4, part 1, 1968.

King, Hazel. 'Pulling Strings at the Colonial Office'. *Journal of the Royal Australian Historical Society*, vol. 61, part 3, 1975.

Lea-Scarlett, E. J. (ed.). 'Recollections of a Pioneer George Whiting Crommelin (Part II)'. *Descent*, vol. 3, part 2, 1967.

Lea-Scarlett, Errol. 'An Outline History of the Eather Family in Australia'. *Descent*, vol. 6, part 3, 1973.

Lenehan, Marjorie. 'Richard Rouse of Rouse Hill'. *Descent*, vol. 3, part 2, 1967.

Lithgow and District Festival of the Valley 1973.

Littlejohn, R. A. 'The Shepherd'. Royal Australian Historical Society, *Newsletter*, no. 164, 1977.

'100 Years of Education', 1969. (Dealing with schools – Lithgow area.)

Smith, Bertha Mac. 'John Maxwell of Bathurst and Hartley'. *Descent*, vol. 4, part 1, 1968.

Stewart, Gordon Neil. Quote from talk re convicts at Bathurst. *The Australian Author*, vol. 8, no. 1, 1976.

Winchester, F. *James Walker of Wallerowang*, Lithgow Historical Society, 1972.

NEWSPAPERS

'Apprehension of a Supposed Cattle Stealer'. *Sydney Morning Herald*, 24 March 1864.

A Squatter. 'Law at Mudgee'. Letter to *Sydney Morning Herald*, 8 July 1864.

'Aust. Shorthorns not well muscled' and 'Steers too small say Canadian Visitors'. *Country Life*, 6 April 1977.

'Blue Gum'. 'How Settlement dawned around Pilliga'. Undated newspaper cutting from the *Land* (in possession Mrs A. Kensit).

'Capture of Portion of a Gang of Wholesale Cattle Lifters'. *Sydney Morning Herald*, 2 March 1864.

Cormie, W. C. (Bill). 'Wee Waa is the Oldest Town on the Namoi', 'Wee Waa Was Once a Huge Cattle Station', 'The Pilliga School Bell', 'Memories of the 1880s at Pilliga', *Western Stock and Station Journal*, 14 December 1956, 21 December 1956, 2 April 1957, 5 April 1957, 25 July 1957. (Inaccurate.)

'Crossing Strains to Improve Quality'. *Country Life*, 23 November 1977.

Cunningham, James. 'The House That Tradition Built'. *Sydney Morning Herald*, 15 June 1978.

Frizell, Helen. 'How they switched on the city of light'. *Sydney Morning Herald*, 16 March 1976.

'Historic Windsor House – the Loder Mansion'. *Windsor and Richmond Gazette*, 25 November 1921 (photocopy in library of the Society of Australian Genealogists, Sydney).

Hobden, Jim. 'Tamworth's First Stores'. *Northern Daily Leader*, 12 July 1978.

MacKenzie, Harold M. 'Among the Pastoralists and Producers'. Book of newspaper clippings from *Maitland Weekly Mercury*, 1896 and 1897.

Maitland Mercury. June, July 1844, 1846, 1847, 1848, 1851, 1854, 1855, 1859 (many refs).

Morse, Clive W. 'The Good Shepherds of Down Under'. *Land*, 18 April 1957.

'Mudgee Quarter Sessions'. *Sydney Morning Herald*, 8 July 1864 (re Joe Launt).

Mullholland, W. J. (ed.). *Narrabri Jubilee Celebrations Back to Narrabri Week*. 4–10 September 1933.

Narrabri Herald and Northern Districts Advocate, 1883–1889, 1899 (many refs).

'Rail Line Junction Gave Birth to "Creek"', *North West Magazine*, 29 August 1977, in *Coonabarabran Times*.

'Rust in Wheat'. *Sydney Morning Herald*, 13 May 1864.

Sydney Gazette. 23 October 1823. Re Joseph Capp brought before Bench (photocopy in library of the Society of Australian Genealogists).

Sydney Morning Herald. 27 October 1824 (Aborigines on the Gwydir).

———. 14 June 1850 (Brown's Mill at Cooerwull to be converted to steam).

———. 24 October 1863 (Patrick Quinn stuck up by bushrangers, also advertising sales of Pilliga and Milchomi and Walker properties).

———. February–May 1864 (flood in Namoi).

———. 11 January 1899 (obituary – Frederick York Wolseley).

Tamworth Historical Society. 'The Flood of 1864 Possibly the Worst'. *Northern Daily Leader*, 13 November 1974.

———. 'Postal Service Began in 1840'. *Northern Daily Leader*, 22 January 1975.

———. 'Sheep Washing Was Always a Regular Event Before Shearing'. *Northern Daily Leader*, 6 August 1975.

———. 'No Shortage of Industries in City's Early Days'. *Northern Daily Leader*, 10 November 1976.

'The Death of Arthur W. Eales . . .' *Bulletin*, 24 September 1925. (Photocopy in library of the Society of Australian Genealogists, Sydney.)

Town and Country Journal quoting the *Narrabri Herald*, 20 May 1876 (re Patrick Quinn).

'Villages Disappear in Path of Progress', *North West Magazine*, 11 July 1977, in *Coonabarabran Times*.

MANUSCRIPTS, TYPESCRIPTS AND DOCUMENTS

Archer Family Correspondence. Letters from James Walker 1836–50.

Archer Papers. Letters from Edward Walker 1838–53. Personal and Business Papers 1833–1929.

Archer, Thomas. 'Recollections of a Rambling Life'.

Barton Estate. Perpetual Trustee Co. Ltd.

Bigge's Appendix. Returns, births, deaths and marriages New South Wales, 1816–19.

Brown, A. Journal 1838–93.

Capp, Joseph. 'Certificate of Freedom, 24 April 1823'. (Society of Australian Genealogists.)

Central Division Occupation Licences (all relevant holdings).

Colonial Secretary's Papers: Commissioners of Crown Lands
　Case of Ed Mayne
　Half-yearly return of population and livestock (Liverpool Plains) first Day of July 1845.
　Itineraries.
　Letters sent from Liverpool Plains, 1846–69.
　Liverpool Plains – Copies of letters sent to the Colonial Secretary and Chief Commissioner 1848–58.
　Liverpool Plains – Return of Licensed Occupiers of Crown Lands 1847–51 (but includes 1845–46).
　Reports 1837–47.
　Reports re Border Police.
　Yearly return (Liverpool Plains) 1846–51.
　Yearly return of the Licensed Occupants of the Crown in the District of Liverpool Plains for the year ending 30th June 1851.
　Yearly Return of Sheep and Lambs in the District of Liverpool Plains in the Colony of New South Wales on the 1st January 1855 (also 1857. These manuscript records were not kept consistently nor have all been preserved.)

Correspondence and Papers relating to Australia 1844–6. Extract from a Despatch from the Commissioner of the Australian Agricultural Company dated Port Stephens May 24th 1844; Despatch, Governor Sir George Gipps to Lord Stanley, 3 April 1844 and Letter from 'A Young Colonist' to the Right Hon. Lord Stanley, 1 January 1845.

Court of Claims Papers 1841–73 (among other valuable papers contains what are probably the only extant pay chits).

Court of Criminal Jurisdiction – Miscellaneous Criminal Papers 1788–1816.

Crew, Bernard Henry. The History of the Walker and Archer Familes in Australia 1813–1868. MA Thesis, Australian National University, Canberra.

Currey, C. H. The Hon. T. D. Mutch: in memoriam.

Gardner, William. Discription of a Map of the Five Northern Districts Beyond the Boundary of Location in New South Wales. 1844–5 and 1846.

Garnsey, E. J. History of Dubbo.

Gipps's despatches 1839 (including letter from Alexr Patterson 6 December 1837, depositions ref. Major Nunn's shooting of Aborigines, *Government Gazette* notice 21 May 1839 ref. chaining of Aboriginal women in huts).

Goodin, V. W. E. The Hon. T. D. Mutch and his work.

Lloyd Papers.

Lloyd Papers – Reminiscences.

Lloyd, C. W. Notes and Reminiscences.

Norton Smith papers. Lawson Estate – papers concerning land.

NSW Governor's Despatches. Geo. Gipps to Lord Stanley, Government House, Sydney, 17 May 1844.

Parry, Sir Edward. Journal 23 December 1829–19 November 1834.

Pastoral Holdings Central Division (all relevant holdings).

Pilliga Scrub Lands. Nine blocks available for special leases (undated Government advertisement).

Return Applications Depasture Stock 1836–7.

Sir Thomas Brisbane. Letterbook pp. 85–93 (re Jamison).

Telfer, William. Reminiscences.

Transcripts of missing Despatchs from Governor of New South Wales 1823–32, p. 110 (Brisbane re Jamison).

'Transfers of runs in Liverpool Plains Distric' 1849–66. Extracts from New South Wales *Government Gazette* prepared at Department of Lands.

White, G. B. Surveyors' Field Books 1848, 1849.

MAPS

New South Wales Showing Pastoral Holdings, 1886.

Rowley, G. B. Map of the Colony of New South Wales, 1886.

Squatting Map. F. H. Reuss and J. L. Browne, surveyors and architects ?1860.

6: The Forest Takes Over

BOOKS

Ferry, John. *Walgett Before the Motor Car*. Walgett and District Historical Society, 1978.

Hardy, Bobby. *West of the Darling*. Jacaranda Press, Brisbane, 1969.

Idriess, Ion L. *The Cattle King*. Angus and Robertson, Sydney, 1942.

_____. *The Silver City*. Angus and Robertson, Sydney, 1976.

Jose, Arthur W. *History of Australasia*. Angus and Robertson, Sydney, 1911.

Mudie, Ian. *River Boats*. Rigby, Adelaide, 1972.

Roberts, S. H. *History of Australian Land Settlement (1788–1920)*. Melbourne, 1924.

Wheelhouse, Frances. *Digging Stick to Rotary Hoe*. Rigby, Adelaide, 1972.

White, Rev. C. A. *The Challenge of the Years (A History of the Presbyterian Church of Australia)*. Angus and Robertson, Sydney, 1951.

PERIODICALS

Agricultural Gazette of N.S.W. October 1909. (Long article on wheatgrowing.)

Dougan, Rev. Alan. 'The Kirk and Social Problems of the Eighteen Thirties in New South Wales'. *Journal and Proceedings, of the Royal Australian Historical Society*, vol. 48, part 6, 1963.

Fitzsimmons, R. W. 'Fifty Years of Changes in Wheat Varieties'. *Agricultural Gazette of New South Wales*, December 1978.

Frost, W. S. 'More About Coaching'. Royal Australian Historical Society, *Newsletter*, no. 149, July 1975.

Jacob, E. H., Wrigley, C. W., and Blakeney, A. B. 'Quality Wheat for Australia'. *Agricultural Gazette of New South Wales*, October 1975.

Karr, Clarence. 'Mythology vs Reality: The Success of Free Selection in N.S.W.'. *Journal of the Royal Australian Historical Society*, vol. 60, part 3, 1974.

Ridley, Rev. W. 'The Namoi and the Barwon'. *The Presbyterian*, 1, 6, September 1871. (Presbyterian Church Archives.)
Rogers, Dick. 'Coaching Days'. Royal Australian Historical Society, *Newsletter*, no. 148, June 1975.

NEWSPAPERS

'Bob Hits the Century'. *North West Magazine*, 5 December 1977 in *Coonabarabran Times*.
'Boggabri Man Dies Aged 100'. *Northern Daily Leader*, 13 May 1978.
Buchanan, John. 'Burburgate Break-up Heralded North West Closer Settlement'. *North West Magazine*, 24 January 1977, in *Coonabarabran Times*.
Buchanan, John. 'Settlement Schemes Produced Emerald Hill Farms'. *North West Magazine*, 7 February 1977, in *Coonabarabran Times*.
Grosser, Alec. 'Grosser family founder migrated to Australia in 1841'. *North West Magazine*, 20 January 1976, in *Coonabarabran Times*.
——. 'Pioneering of new farm big task in 1909'. *North West Magazine*, 2 February 1976, in *Coonabarabran Times*.
——. 'Veteran farmer tells of depression year farming at Milroy'. *North West Magazine*, 9 February 1976, in *Coonabarabran Times*.
Holliday, Ron. 'Sheds of Our Forefathers'. *Land*, 3 February 1977.
'Openings of Railway Extension from Binnaway to Coonabarabran'. *Coonabarabran Times*, 16 September 1976.
Scott, E. R. 'Bogamildi — and 50 Years in the North-west'. *North West Magazine*, 11 February 1974 in *Coonabarabran Times*.
'Secret Pact with a Dying Judge'. *Sydney Morning Herald*, 2 November 1977.

MANUSCRIPTS, TYPESCRIPTS AND DOCUMENTS

Bureau of Meteorology. Rainfall records for north-west towns.
Bowenfels, Presbyterian Church. Minute Book for meetings of Congregation and Finance Committee 1864–1907.
——. Session Book — Bowenfels — 1858–1932.
——. Visitors' Book, Public School, Bowenfels South 1880–1932.
O'Reilly, Jim. Soils in the North-west, extract from his memoirs (in possession of Jim O'Reilly).
Ruttley, George. Diary 1895 (in possession of his granddaughter, Mary Hitchen).
Sheet No. 1. Pilliga Lands 58 Crown Leases Baradine . . . available on and after 3rd March 1924 (23 blocks for returned soldiers, 35 for general application).
Sheet No. 2. Pilliga Lands 22 Crown Leases County of Baradine . . . (7 blocks for returned soldiers, 15 for general application, c. 1924).
Wolseley, Frederick York and Creagh, Erle Wolseley. Extracts from *Burke's Irish Family Records, Peerage, Baronetage and Knightage*, and family wills, probate engrossments, and inland revenue affidavits in England and Ireland compiled by Ms Hilary Marshall, genealogical researcher, London.

7:   The Breelong Blacks

BOOKS

Hornadge, Bill. *Old Dubbo Gaol*. Dubbo Museum and Historical Society, Dubbo, 1974.
Keane, Eve. *Valley of the Winds*. Sponsored by Coolah Shire Council, Sydney, c. 1953.

Prior, Tom, Wannan, Bill and Nunn, H. *Plundering Sons*, Lansdowne Press, Melbourne, 1966.

NEWSPAPERS

Donald, Jim. 'Yesterday' (the Breelong Blacks). *Daily Mirror*, May, June, 1948.

Mudgee Guardian, 23 July 1900, 13 August 1900.

Robertson, Anne. 'The Little Explorer'. *Sydney Morning Herald*, 14 May 1976.

Singleton Argus November 1900 (many refs).

Sydney Morning Herald. 23 July 1900, 24 July 1900, 25 July 1900, 26 July 1900, 9 August 1900, 13 August 1900.

'The Black Outlaws'. *Evening News*, 1 September 1900.

MANUSCRIPTS AND VARIOUS DOCUMENTS

Carr, George. Letter. Typewritten copy in Gulgong Pioneer Museum.

Driscoll, Frank. 'The Black Bushranger', undated newspaper cutting in Gulgong Pioneer Museum.

Jimmy Governor. Papers 1900 (boxes of telegrams; newspaper cuttings; letters; reports; statements; detailed: Synopsis of Offences committed by the Outlaws Jimmy and Joe Governor; police descriptions of Breelong murderers; maps and claims for expenses).

Marriage certificate James Governor and Ethel Mary Jane Page: copy in Gulgong Pioneer Museum.

Noonan, Arthur. 'The Breelong Blacks'. Typescript of a poem published originally in pamphlet form in the early 1900s. Copies still in circulation.

Police papers re Jimmy Governor 1900–13.

Police Special Bundles. Warrant of Apprehension . . . Joe Governor and Jimmy Governor, 25 July 1900.

8: Timber and Scrub

BOOKS

Althofer, George W. *Cradle of Incense*. The Society for Growing Australian Plants, Sydney, 1978.

Anderson, R. H. *The Trees of New South Wales*. New South Wales Dept of Agriculture, Sydney, 1956.

Armitage, Inez. *Acacias of New South Wales*. The Society for Growing Australian Plants, Sydney, 1977.

Blainey, Geoffrey. *Triumph of the Nomads*. Macmillan, Melbourne, 1975.

Cribb, A. B. and J. W. *Wild Food in Australia*. Collins, Sydney, 1975.

de Beuzeville, W. A. W. *Australian Trees for Australian Planting*. Forestry Commission of New South Wales, 1947.

Dockrill, A. W. *Australian Indigenous Orchids*. The Society for Growing Australian Plants, Sydney, *1969*.

Fitzpatrick, Kathleen. Australian Explorers. Oxford University Press, London, 1959.

Hallam, Sylvia J. *Fire and Hearth*. Australian Institute of Aboriginal Studies, Canberra, 1975.

Harris, Thistle Y. *Wild Flowers of Australia*. Angus and Robertson, Sydney, 1943.

Hodgson, Margaret and Paine, Roland. *A Field Guide to Australian Wildflowers*. 2 vols. Rigby, Adelaide, 1976, 1977.

Howitt, A. W. *The Native Tribes of South-east Australia*. Macmillan and Co. Ltd, London, 1904.

Macdonald, Ross and Westerman, John. *A Field Guide to Fungi of South-eastern Australia*. Nelson, Melbourne, 1979.

Nicholls, W. H. *Orchids of Australia*. Nelson, Melbourne, 1969.

Whittet, J. N. *Weeds*. New South Wales Department of Agriculture, Sydney, 1958.

Worgan, George B. *Journal of a First Fleet Surgeon*. Library of Australian History, Sydney, 1978.

Wrigley, John W. and Flagg, Murray. *Australian Native Plants*. Collins, Sydney, 1979.

PERIODICALS

Andrews, G. J. 'Fungus'. *Wildlife in Australia*, vol. 15, no. 2, 1978.

Ashton, D. H. 'The Seasonal Growth of *Eucalyptus regnans*'. *Australian Journal of Botany*, vol. 23, no. 2, 1975.

Burrendong Arboretum. *Brigge*. January 1979, April 1979.

Carlquist, Sherwin. '*Alexgeorgea*, a Bizarre New Genus of Restionaceae from Western Australia', *Australian Journal of Botany*, vol. 24, no. 2, 1976.

Coleman, Edith. Royal Entomological Society, London. *Proceedings* (a) 5:15, 114 (1930), 6:22 (1931), 13:82 (1938).

Coleman, Edith. *Victorian Naturalist*, 44:20, 333 (1927), 46:62, 236 (1929), 50:41 (1933).

'Firing Our Grass Trees'. *Ecos*, no. 12, 1977.

'Fuels and Future Fires'. Bush Fire Council of New South Wales. *bush fire bulletin*, Winter, 1974.

Gill, A. M. 'Fire and the Opening of *Banksia ornata* Follicles'. *Australian Journal of Botany*, vol. 24, no. 3, 1976.

Griffiths, Jeremy. 'Crafts as a Successful Livelihood'. *Craft Australia*, no. 1, 1978.

Hadlington, Phillip W. *Common Insect Pests of Trees*. Forestry Commission of NSW, 1972.

'Lightning More Suspect'. Bush Fire Council of New South Wales. *bush fire bulletin*, Spring, 1974.

National Herbarium of New South Wales. *Flora of New South Wales* and *Flora Series*. All published volumes.

'On Food and the Future'. *Ecos*, no. 12, 1977.

The Society for Growing Australian Plants. *Australian Plants* vols 2–10. Many references to relevant plants especially:

Clemesha, Stephen. 'Sundews' vol. 5, no. 37.

Conrick, P. 'Common Fringe-Myrtle'. vol. 5, no. 43.

Conrick, P. E. 'Desert Lime'. vol. 8, no. 66.

Curtis, B. V. 'Plants for Inland Planting'. vol. 7, no. 59.

Curtis, B. V. 'Spare a Spot for the Santalum'. vol. 7, no. 59.

Erikson, Rica. 'Australian Carnivorous Plants'. vol. 3, no. 27.

———. 'Tiny Plants that Prey on Living Creatures'. vol. 4, no. 29.

Grant, W. J. R. and Buttrose, M. S. 'Santalum Fruit'. vol. 9, no. 75.

Hawkeswood, T. J. 'The Genus *Melichrus*'. vol. 10, no. 77.

Hockings, F. D. 'Banksias'. vol. 9, no. 71.

Jones, David L. 'Cultivation of the Genus *Diuris*'. vol. 7, no. 54.

Lamont, Dr Byron. 'Some Current Research on Australian Plants'. vol. 8, no. 64.

Lothian, T. R. 'Lilies? Iris?'. vol. 5, no. 38.

Mass, Nuri. 'Trees with a Hundred Thousand Lives'. vol. 8, no. 61.

McIntyre, D. K. 'Raising Natives from Seed'. vol. 6, no. 50.

Powell, R. 'Native Grasses'. vol. 8, no. 61.

Stone, Frank H. 'Growing Waratahs'. vol. 4, no. 29.

Verdon, D. 'Melaleuca'. vol. 7, no. 54.

The Society for Growing Australian Plants. *Native Plants for N.S.W.* vols 5–13. Many references to relevant plants especially:

Cooper, Arthur. 'Nomenclature for the ordinary people'. vol. 12, no. 1.

Ganger, Jeath. 'Banksias of New South Wales'. vol. 5, no. 7.

_____. 'Grass'. vol. 7, no. 2.

Hawkins, Lester. 'Landscape uses of Australian plants in California'. vol. 11, no. 5.

Lassak, Dr E. 'The Chemistry of Australian Plants'. vol. 8, no. 1.

Stanley, Patrick. 'News from Kuring-Gai Wildflower Garden'. vol. 5, no. 4.

NEWSPAPERS

'"Bush" Grasses Go to Town'. *Northern Daily Leader*, 26 May 1977.

'CSIRO Tries to Tame Quandong'. *Northern Daily Leader*, 3 November 1976.

Morris, Alan. 'Wildlife Notes'. *Coonabarabran Times*, 23 September 1976.

Prineas, Peter. 'Not Just Singed Tails'. Letter to *Sydney Morning Herald*, 29 May 1975.

'Scientists from overseas in search of native Australian citrus trees'. *Western Magazine*, 26 March 1976, in *Coonamble Times*.

MANUSCRIPTS AND DOCUMENTS

The following were in a box of miscellaneous Forestry Commission papers donated to New South Wales State Archives by W. P. de Beuzeville.

de Beuzeville, W. A. W. The Forest Resources of the Pilliga. Ms dated 7–10–15.

'Rate of Growth of Indigenous Commercial Trees'. *Bulletin*, Forest Department, 1914.

'Report on the Forest Department', 1914.

9: Timbergetters and Scrub Dwellers

BOOKS

Braden, L. *Bullockies*. Rigby, Adelaide, 1974.

Brock, Daniel George. *To the Desert with Sturt*. Royal Geographical Society of Australasia, South Australian Branch, Adelaide, 1975.

Dallas, K. M. *Horse Power*. Fullers' Bookshop, Hobart, 1968.

Freeland, J. M. *Architect Extraordinary The Life and Work of John Horbury Hunt: 1838–1904*. Cassell, Melbourne, 1970.

Harris, Douglas. *The Teams of the Blacksoil Plains*. Rohan Rivett, Melbourne, 1977.

Hassall, Rev. James Samuel. *In Old Australia*. Library of Australian History, Facsimile Series number 7, Sydney, 1977 (originally pub. 1902).

Legislative Council of New South Wales, *Journal Session 1890*. 'Forest Conservancy Branch (Report on, for 1889)'.

Stringer, Michael. *Australian Horse Drawn Vehicles*. Rigby, Adelaide, 1980.

Walker, R. B. *Old New England*. Sydney University Press, Sydney, 1966.

JOURNALS, MAGAZINES, BOOKLETS AND MONOGRAPHS

Adams, Bruce. 'Last of the Bullock Teams'. *Walkabout*, October 1966.

Baradine Centenary 1865–1965. Souvenir Booklet and Programme, Baradine Centenary Committee, 1965.

Black, E. Leighton. 'The Australian Verandah'. Royal Australian Historical Society, *Newsletter*, no. 151, September 1975.

——. 'The Australian Verandah (Concluded)'. Royal Australian Historical Society, *Newsletter*, no. 154, January–February 1976.

Boggabri The Story of Our Town. Compiled by members of the Boggabri Adult Education Committee, Golden Grain Festival, September 1957.

Burrell, John. 'Which Australian Cattle Dog?' Letter to editor R. A. S. Kennel Control, *Journal*, July 1976.

Carter, H. R. 'History of Blackville, Yarraman, Coomoo Coomoo Areas', Quirindi and District Historical Society, *Journal*, vol. 11, no. 2, 1971.

Carter, Jeff and Mare. 'Bullock Drivers Don't Swear'. *Walkabout*, June 1961.

Cotter, W. M. 'Recollections of an Unmelodious Bullocky'. Royal Australian Historical Society, *Newsletter*, 156, 1976.

Courier Centenary of Publishing 1873–1973, The. The *Courier*, Narrabri, November 1973.

de Beuzeville, W. A. W. 'The Climatological Basis of Forestry'. NSW Forestry Commission, *Bulletin*, 1943.

Eipper, F. R. 'Hunting Wild Cattle by Moonlight'. Scone and Upper Hunter Historical Society, *Journal*, vol. 2, 1961.

Foley, J. 'The Australian Cattle Dog' R. A. S. Kennel Control, *Journal*, October 1978.

'Forest Tour – Radiata Pines'. *Blue Lake Holiday Guide*, Mount Gambier, Spring, 1969.

Geeves, Philip. 'Darwin in New South Wales'. Royal Australian Historical Society, *Newsletter*, no. 147, 1975.

——. 'The Switched-on Generation'. Royal Australian Historical Society, *Newsletter*, no. 139, 1974.

Grainger, Rodney. 'The Inspector of Forests Was Also a Poet'. Forestry Commission of New South Wales, *Forest and Timber*, extract only, c. 1967.

Gray, Nancy. 'The Promised Land'. *Scone Historical Monograph*, no. 3, Scone and Upper Hunter Historical Society, 1975.

Hemmings, Leigh and Barbara. 'Shingle Splitting: A Country Craft'. *Craft Australia*, 3, 1978.

Irving, Robert. 'Early "Galvanized Iron" in Australia'. Royal Australian Historical Society, *Newsletter*, no. 172, April 1978.

'Largest Tree in New South Wales, The' Forestry Commission of New South Wales, *Forest and Timber* (extract only, c. 1967).

Littlejohn, R. A. 'The Universal Fluid'. Royal Australian Historical Society, *Newsletter*, no. 140, September 1974.

'More About the Australian Verandah'. Royal Australian Historical Society, *Newsletter*, no. 152, October 1975.

Museum of Applied Arts and Sciences, N.S.W. 'The Bloodwoods'. *Australian Plants*, vol. 2, no. 14, 1963 (Kino and Tanning).

'Peep in the Past'. *Forest and Timber*, Forestry Commission of New South Wales, May 1965.

Ryan, M. 'The Verandah'. Royal Australian Historical Society, *Newsletter*, no. 150, 1975.

Scott, Bill. 'He's Got a Head Like a Diseased Paw Paw'. *The Australian Author*, vol. 7, no. 2, 1975.

Shoalhaven Historical Society. 'The Possum Rug'. Royal Australian Historical Society, *Newsletter*, no. 140, September 1974.

Snowie, Jenny. '"Pale Washy" Colours'. Letter to editor, R. A. S. Kennel Control, *Journal*, 18, 8, 1975.

Starr, Joan. 'To the Tone of a Texas Bell'. *Hoofs and Horns*, September 1972.

Swan, Keith. 'Bullock Bells'. Royal Australian Historical Society, *Newsletter*, 132, January 1974.

Welch, R. 'Chain Saws and Vibration'. *The Agricultural Gazette of New South Wales*, October 1971.

Woolley, Percy. 'Cedar and the Pitsaw'. Royal Australian Historical Society, *Newsletter*, November 1974.

NEWSPAPERS

Brien, Steve. 'There's no concrete answer'. *Sun*, 11 February 1977 (concrete sleepers).

Buhrich, Eva. 'You can't see the wood experts for the trees'. *Sydney Morning Herald*, 1 August 1973.

Cochrane, Peter. 'Jack Schikowski: Condamine character comes south with bells and boomerangs'. *Northern Magazine*, 29 January 1978, in *Northern Daily Leader*.

'Combining the old and new'. *North West Magazine*, 20 May 1974, in *Coonabarabran Times* (tanning).

'Cypress Pine: Our great inland timber nearly perished?'. *North West Magazine*, 27 October 1975, in *Coonabarabran Times*.

'Giving new life to old vehicles'. *North West Magazine*, 11 July 1977, in *Coonabarabran Times*.

Russell, Glenn. 'The draughthorse is being put in his place'. *Country* Life, 27 April 1977.

Scott, E. R. 'Bogamildi — and 50 Years in North-West'. *North West Magazine*, 29 April 1974, in *Coonabarabran Times*.

'Survey of Pilliga Scrub'. *Land*, 9 July 1948.

'Town will die if forestry is moved'. *Coonabarabran Times*, 27 February 1975.

MANUSCRIPTS AND DOCUMENTS

Gipps despatches: Correspondence relative to Crown Lands and Emigration in New South Wales. 'Licences for Cutting Cedar or Other Timber', 1839.

Ruttley, Arthur. Letters from Forestry School, Canberra, to Bert Ruttley, 21 March 1933 and 11 October 1933 (in possession of Mary Hitchen).

10: Mud Springs and Soda Plains

BOOKS

Black, Lindsay. *Aboriginal Art Galleries of Western New South Wales*. The author, 1943.
_____. *Cylcons The Mystery Stones of the Darling River Valley*. The author, 1942.
_____. *The Bora Ground*. The author, 1944.

Fairley, Alan. *A Complete Guide to Warrumbungle National Park*. Murray Child, Sydney, 1977.

JOURNALS, MAGAZINES, BOOKLETS

Fox, Allan M. *Warrumbungle National Park*. 2nd edn. National Parks and Wildlife Service, Sydney, 1972.

Fry, W. R. 'The Pilliga Scrub'. *Agricultural Gazette of NSW*, July 1909.

Jensen, H. I. 'The Agricultural Prospects and Soils of the Pilliga Scrub'. Department of Agriculture New South Wales, *Farmers' Bulletin*, no. 54, 1912.

The Pilliga National Forest. Various contributors. Forestry Commission of NSW, c. 1933.

Richardson, Michael. 'The Mountains of Madness'. *Overlander*, vol. 2, no. 4, 1977/8.

NEWSPAPERS

'Discovery made by observatory at Siding Spring'. *Northern Daily Leader*, 16 October 1975.

'Faintest star seen is Photographed'. *Sydney Morning Herald*, 28 February 1977.

Keay, Professor Colin. 'Telescope "one of the finest"'. *Newcastle Morning Herald*, 5 February 1979.

'Schmidt Telescope Most Powerful Camera in World'. *Coonabarabran Times*, 14 July 1978.

'Space Discovery by Scientists at Siding Spring'. *Coonabarabran Times*, 8 March 1979.

MANUSCRIPTS AND DOCUMENTS

Flack, D. S. and Suppell, D. W. Chromium, in The Mineral Industry of New South Wales. Geological Survey of New South Wales, Department of Mines, 1968.

Department of Mines. Various extracts re minerals in Pilliga Forest—Coonabarabran area.

Salvation Army Almanac 1915. 'A Little Australian Hero'. Supplement to *War Cry*, 19 December 1914 (in possession of J. E. Taylor).

11: Animal Life — Insects, Reptiles and Others

BOOKS

Barrett, Charles and Burns, A. N. *Butterflies of Australia and New Guinea*. N. H. Seward Pty Ltd, Melbourne, 1951.

Bustard, Robert. *Australian Lizards*. Collins, Sydney, 1970.

Child, John. *Australian Insects*. Periwinkle Press, Sydney, 1961.

Cogger, H. G. *Reptiles and Amphibians of Australia*. A. H. and A. W. Reed, Sydney, 1975.

CSIRO, Division of Entomology. *The Insects of Australia*. Melbourne University Press, Melbourne, 1970.

———. *The Insects of Australia Supplement 1974*. Melbourne University Press, Melbourne, 1974.

Hill, Gerald F. *Termites (Isoptera) from the Australian Region*. Council for Scientific and Industrial Research, Melbourne, 1942.

Kinghorn, J. R. *The Snakes of Australia*. Angus and Robertson, Sydney, 1956.

Lake, John S. *Freshwater Fishes and Rivers of Australia*. Nelson, Melbourne, 1970.

———. *Freshwater Fish of the Murray-Darling River System*. State Fisheries Research Bulletin Number Seven, Government Printer, Sydney.

Lee, K. E. and Wood, T. G. *Termites and Soils*. Academic Press, London and New York, 1971.

McCubbin, Charles. *Australian Butterflies*. Nelson, Melbourne, 1971.

McKeown, Keith C. *Australian Spiders*. Angus and Robertson, Sydney, 1952.

Main, Barbara York. *Spiders*. Collins, Sydney, 1976.

Mascord, Ramon. *Australian Spiders in Colour*. A. H. and A. W. Reed, Sydney, 1970.
Ratcliffe, F. N., Gay, F. J. and Greaves, T. *Australian Termites*. CSIRO, Melbourne, 1952.
Roughley, T. C. *Fish and Fisheries of Australia*. Angus and Robertson, Sydney, 1953.
Swanson, Stephen. *Lizards of Australia*. Angus and Robertson, Sydney, 1976.
Williams, W. D. *Australian Freshwater Life*. Sun Books, Melbourne, 1968.
Worrell, Eric. *Reptiles of Australia*. Angus and Robertson, Sydney, 1966.

PERIODICALS

Doull, Keith. 'Bees and their role in pollination' *Australian Plants*, vol. 7, no. 57, 1973.
Edgar, J. A. and Culvener, C. C. J. 'Coevolution of Danaid butterflies with their host plants'. *Nature*, vol. 250, 23 August 1974.
Houston, Terry F. 'A Revision of the Australian Hylaeine Bees (Hymenoptera; Colletidae)'. *Australian Journal of Zoology*, Supplementary Series, no. 36, 1975.
'Termites turn the nutrient cycle'. *Ecos*, no. 10, November 1976.

NEWSPAPERS

'Generations of hard work gave them a "sweet life"'. *North West Magazine*, 20 May 1974, in *Coonabarabran Times*.
Gulliford, Bob. 'Studying bees — a pastime and scientific pursuit'. *Northern Magazine*, 8 December 1974, in *Northern Daily Leader*.
Gulliford, Bob. 'The sweet north is rich in honey'. *Northern Magazine*, 15 December 1974, in *Northern Daily Leader*.
Mant, Gilbert. 'Hot on the tracks of the elusive Icilius Blue'. *Land*, 24 March 1977.
Morris, Alan. 'Wildlife Notes. Butterfly Migration'. *Coonabarabran Times*, 15 January 1976.
Morris, Alan. 'Bee Farming and the Pilliga Nature Reserve'. *Coonabarabran Times*, 10 March 1977.

12: Animal Life — The Mammals

BOOKS

Brunner, Hans and Coman, Brian. *The Identification of Mammalian Hair*. Inkata Press, Melbourne, 1974.
Davey, Keith. *Australian Marsupials*. Periwinkle Books, Melbourne, 1970.
Ride, W. D. L. *A Guide to the Native Mammals of Australia*. Oxford University Press, Melbourne, 1970.
Troughton, Ellis. *Furred Animals of Australia*. Angus and Robertson, Sydney, 1957.

PERIODICALS, PAMPHLETS

Archer, Michael. 'The Dasyurid Dentition and its Relationships to that of Didelphids, Thylacinids, Borhyaenids (Marsupicarnivora) and Peramelids (Peramelina: Marsupialia)'. *Australian Journal of Zoology*, Supplementary serial no. 39, 15 April 1976.
Augee, M. L., Ealey, E. H. M. and Price, I. P. 'Movements of Echidnas, *Tachyglossus aculeatus*, Determined by Marking—Recapture and Radio-Tracking'. *Australian Wildlife Research*, vol. 2, no. 2, 1975.
'Australian Native Dog Training Society of N.S.W. Limited'. R. A. S. Kennel Control, *Journal*, vol. 20, no. 6, 1976.
Brunner, H., Amor, R. L. and Stevens, P. L. 'The Use of Predator Scat Analysis in a

Mammal Survey at Dartmouth in North-eastern Victoria'. *Australian Wildlife Research*, vol. 3, no. 1, 1976.

Brunner, Hans and Bertuch, I. D. 'The Broad-Toothed Rat Still in Sherbrooke Forest. A Successful Search for *Mastacomys fuscus* Thomas'. Victorian Naturalist, vol. 93, 1976.

Brunner, Hans, Lloyd, John W. and Coman, Brian J. 'Fox Scat Analysis in a Forest Park in South-eastern Australia'. *Australian Wildlife Research*, vol. 2, no. 2, 1975.

Brunner, H., Wallis, R. L. and Voutier, P. F. 'Locating and Trapping the Broad-Toothed Rat (*Mastacomys fuscus* Thomas) at Powelltown'. *Victorian Naturalist*, vol. 94, 1977.

Cheal, Peter D., Lee, Anthony K. and Barnett, John L. 'Change in the Haematology of *Antechinus stuartii* (Marsupialia) and their Association with Male Mortality'. *Australian Journal of Zoology*, vol. 24, no. 3, 1976.

Coman, B. J. and Brunner, Hans. 'Predators on Trial'. Keith Turnbull Research Station, Pamphlet no. 46, December 1973.

Coman, B. J. and Stevens, P. L. 'The Fox in Victoria'. Vermin and Noxious Weeds Destruction Board, Pamphlet no. 37, 1972.

'Domestic animals gone bush'. *Ecos*, 13 August 1977.

Fox, B. J. and Briscoe, D. A. '*Pseudomys pilligaensis*, a new species of murid rodent from the Pilliga Scrub, northern New South Wales'. Extract from *Australian Mammalogy*, vol. 3, 1980.

Harrop, C. J. F. and Degabriele, Robert. 'Digestion and Nitrogen Metabolism in the Koala, *Phascolarctos cinereus*'. *Australian Journal of Zoology*, vol. 24, no. 2, 1976.

Hudson, J. W. and Dawson, T. J. 'Role of Sweating from the Tail in the Thermal Balance of the Rat-kangaroo *Potorous tridactylus*'. *Australian Journal of Zoology*, vol. 23, no. 4, 1975.

Inns, R. W. 'Some Seasonal Changes in *Antechinus flavipes* (Marsupialia: Dasyuridae)'. *Australian Journal of Zoology*, vol. 24, no. 4, 1976.

James, Bill. 'On the track of the thylacine'. *Australian Outdoors*, June 1965.

Johnson, C. V. 'Dingo'. R. A. S. Kennel Control, *Journal*, October 1975.

Kemper, C. M. 'Reproduction of *Pseudomys novaehollandiae* (Muridae) in the Laboratory'. *Australian Journal of Zoology*, vol. 24, no. 2, 1976.

Nolan, Jack. 'Eucalypts Not Koalas' Only Food'. *Wildlife in Australia*, 6, 3, 1969.

'The Notorious Dingo'. Wildlife Preservation Society of Australia, *Newsletter*, September 1976.

Smith, Malcolm. 'The Koalas of Lone Pine'. *Wildlife in Australia*, 13, 2, 1976.

NEWSPAPERS

'Couple discover success in a wildlife sanctuary'. *Sydney Morning Herald*, 9 January 1973.

Edmondson, Liz. 'Wildlife Notes Wallabies'. *Coonabarabran Times*, 14 September 1978.

'Feral Cat the "Puma"?' *Stawell Times-News*, 16 August 1977.

'Forests and Settlement'. *Country Life and Stock and Station Journal*, 2 October 1936.

'Headless body is found in bush'. *Sun* (Melbourne), 3 December 1973.

Morris, Alan. 'Wildlife Notes The New Holland Mouse'. *Coonabarabran Times*, 2 September 1976.

'3.5 m Kangaroos'. *Sydney Morning Herald*, 11 September 1976.

'"Tiger" now in baby mystery'. *Sunday Telegraph*, 27 March 1977.

'W.A. feral cats shot'. *Sydney Morning Herald*, 31 May 1978.

13: Animal Life — The Birds

BOOKS

Cayley, Neville W. *What Bird Is That?* Angus and Robertson, Sydney, 1958.
Complete Book of Australian Birds. Readers' Digest, Sydney, 1976.
Every Australian Bird Illustrated. Rigby, Adelaide, 1975.
Fleay, David. *Nightwatchmen of Bush and Plain.* Jacaranda Press, Brisbane, 1968.
Forshaw, Joseph M. and Cooper, William T. *Parrots of the World.* Lansdowne Press, Melbourne, 1973.
Frith, H. J. *Waterfowl in Australia.* Angus and Robertson, Sydney, 1968.
Immelmann, Klaus. *Australian Finches.* Angus and Robertson, Sydney, 1974.
Slater, Peter. *A Field Guide to Australian Birds. Non-Passerines.* Rigby, Adelaide, 1970.
_____. *A Field Guide to Australian Birds. Passerines.* Rigby, Adelaide, 1974.

PERIODICALS

'Australian birds — migrants or nomads?' *Ecos*, no. 4, 1975.
'The Brush-Tongued Lorikeets'. *Wildlife in Australia*, vol. 9, no. 3, 1972.
'Emus Outback'. *Wildlife in Australia*, vol. 13, no. 3.
Frith, H. J., Brown, B. K. and Barker, R. D. 'Food of the Crested and Common Bronzewing Pigeons in Inland New South Wales'. *Australian Wildlife Research*, vol. 1, no. 2, 1974.
Hopper, Stephen D. and Burbidge, Andrew A. 'Feeding Behaviour of a Purple-crowned Lorikeet on Flowers of *Eucalyptus buprestium*'. *Emu*, 79, 1979.
Llewellyn L. C. 'New Records of Red-Tailed Black Cockatoos in South-Eastern Australia with a Discussion of their Plumages'. *Emu*, 74, 1974.
Morris, Alan K. 'Some Doubtful Records for the Pilliga Scrub'. *Australian Birds*, vol. 10, no. 3, 1976.
Morris, A. K. 'The Red-chested Quail in New South Wales'. *Emu*, 71, 1971.
Morris, A. K. and Kurtz, N. 'Red-chested and Little Button-quail in the Mudgee District of New South Wales'. *Corella*, vol. 1, no. 4, 1977.
Rowley, Ian. 'The Comparative Ecology of Australian Corvids'. *CSIRO Wildlife Research*, vol. 18, no. 1, 1973.
Trounson, Donald. 'The Elusive Desert Sprite'. *Wildlife in Australia*, vol. 15, no. 3, 1978.

NEWSPAPERS

Morris, Alan K. 'Wildlife Notes' *Coonabarabran Times*:
  'Apostlebirds Early Morning Nest Builders', 27 April 1978.
  'Australian Bird Atlas', 15 September 1977.
  'The Cattle Egret', 11 November 1976.
  'Mallee Fowl in Pilliga Scrub', 26 January 1978.
  'The Pied Currawong', 5 May 1977.
  'Return of the Migrants', 10 February 1977.
  'The Use of Tools by White-winged Choughs', 8 June 1978.
  'Tropical Seabirds in Coona District', 22 March 1978.
  'Wedge-Tailed Eagles in Central Western N.S.W.', 3 June 1976.
  'Where Do Kingfishers Go in Winter?', 6 November 1973.

14: Wood Chips and International Airports

BOOKS

Frith, H. J. *Wildlife Conservation.* Angus and Robertson, Sydney, 1973.

Goldstein, Wendy (ed.). *Rain Forests.* National Parks and Wildlife Service, Sydney, 1977.

Kyle, Russell. *Meat Production in Africa – the case for new domestic species.* University of Bristol, 1972.

Legislative Assembly New South Wales 1878–9. *Namoi-Narrabri Timber Reserve (Surveyors' reports and plans).* Printed by order Legislative Assembly, 7 May 1879.

Maiden, J. H. *The Useful Native Plants of Australia.* Compendium, Melbourne, 1975. (Facsimile reproduction of 1889 edition.)

Marshall, A. J. (ed.). *The Great Extermination.* Heinemann, Melbourne, 1966.

Routley, R. and V. *The Fight for the Forests.* Australian National University, Canberra, *Victorian Yearbook 1973.* 'The Land'. [1975.

PERIODICALS, BOOKLETS, DOCUMENTS AND PAMPHLETS

'Burning question in the Snowy', *Ecos*, no. 11, 1977.

Colley, Alex. 'Rainforests and New South Wales', extract from 'The Last Rainforest'. Wildlife Preservation Society of Australia, *Newsletter*, March 1976.

'Current Woodchip Activities'. *Wildlife in Australia*, 11, 2, 1974.

Edwards, Peter H. 'Aerial Ignition Burns in the Blue Mountains'. *Wildlife in Australia*, 11, 3, 1974.

'Emigration to Australia'. *Chambers's Information for the People*, no. 19, c. 1841.

'Eucalypt Forests: A Resource or a Refuge?' Wildlife Preservation Society of Australia, *Newsletter*, December 1976.

Faculty Handbook 1975. The Australian National University, Canberra, 1974.

Fitzgerald, Adrian. 'I.N.S.P.E.C.T. Report on the Woodchip Industry'. Wildlife Preservation Society of Australia, *Newsletter*, September 1973.

'Forestry as a Career'. Forestry Commission of New South Wales, 1972.

Groves, R. H. and Keraitis, K. 'Survival and Growth of Seedlings of Three Sclerophyll Species at High Levels of Phosphorus and Nitrogen'. *Australian Journal of Botany*, vol. 24, no. 6, 1976.

Harrold, Arthur. 'The Ecosystems of the Wallum'. *Wildlife in Australia* 13, 1, 1976.

Heddle, E. M. and Specht, R. L. 'Dark Island Heath (Ninety-Mile Plain, South Australia). VIII The Effect of Fertilizers on Composition and Growth, 1950–1972'. *Australian Journal of Botany*, vol. 23, no. 1, 1975.

Information Handbook. Department of Forestry, Australian National University, 1975

'Inside our rain-forests', *Ecos*, 6 November 1975. [and 1977.

'In the timeless region they call "The Pilliga"'. *Forest and Timber*, Spring, 1972.

Lamont, Byron. 'Proteoid Roots'. *Australian Plants*, vol. 9, no. 72, 1977.

'New Policy for National Parks'. Wildlife Preservation Society of Australia, *Newsletter*, March 1977, quoting *Sydney Morning Herald*, 29 March 1977.

Ramsland, John. 'The cedarcutters of northern New South Wales'. *Forest and Timber*, vol. 13, no. 1, 1977.

Rawlinson, P. A. and Brown, P. R. 'The Fairy Possum'. *Wildlife in Australia*, vol. 14, no. 3, 1977.

Roberts, Greg. 'The Cape York Peninsular Wilderness'. *Wildlife in Australia*, vol. 15, no. 4, 1978.

Ryan, David. 'Cypress Pine: A New Lease of Life'. *Forest and Timber*, undated extract c. 1969.
'Secret threat to our forests'. *Bulletin*, 3 March 1973.
Serventy, Vincent. 'Along the Nature Trail Mistletoe-birds'. *Wildlife in Australia*, vol. 3, no. 5, 1966.
Specht, R. L. 'Phosphorus Nutrition of Heath Plants'. *Australian Plants*, vol. 3, no. 27, 1966.
Thorpe, Geo. W. 'The Rainforest'. *Australian Plants*, vol. 9, no. 76, 1978.
'Understanding fire in the forest'. *Ecos*, no. 7, 1976.
Vickery, J. R. 'Fertilizer requirements of Australian plants'. Society for Growing Australian Plants, *Newsletter*, vol. 7, no. 6, 1973.
'What happens to animals in a bushfire?' *Ecos*, no. 8, 1976.
Wilderness Conservation. Australian Conservation Foundation, Nunawading, n.d.
Withers, Jennifer R. 'Studies on the Status of Unburnt *Eucalyptus* Woodland at Ocean Grove, Victoria'. *Australian Plants*, vol. 10, no. 82, 1980.
'Your Forests', Forestry Commission of New South Wales, undated pamphlet, c. 1972.

NEWSPAPERS

'All world wants our gum trees'. *Northern Daily Leader*, 5 April 1977.
'By health research science may solve domestic meat problem'. *Northern Magazine*, 11 October 1974, in *Northern Daily Leader*.
'Council to press for airport in Pilliga Scrub'. *Coonabarabran Times*, 27 September 1973.
Glascott, Joseph. 'A valuable ally votes for Border Ranges'. *Sydney Morning Herald*, 3 March 1978.
_____. 'State forests likely to stay in red'. *Sydney Morning Herald*, 1 January 1979.
Graham, Vernon. 'Scrub takes mounting toll in western NSW'. *Land*, 10 May 1979.
'International airport proposal'. *Coonabarabran Times*, 10 May 1975.
Moriarty, Oliver. 'Only the careful rural people can conserve Australia's bushland'. *Northern Magazine*, 3 October 1976, in *Northern Daily Leader* (sound history leading to a wrong conclusion).
Morris, Alan K. 'Wildlife notes: Rock Wallabies'. *Coonabarabran Times*, 23 February 1978.
_____. 'Wildlife notes: Prescribed burning programme'. *Orana Shopper*, 16 May 1979.
Stannard, Bruce. 'Violence explodes in W.A.'s lucrative woodchip industry'. *National Times*, 26–31 July 1976.
Tyndale–Biscoe, Hugh. 'The concept of "countryside" rather than "national" parks'. Letter to editor, *Sydney Morning Herald*, 18 September 1978.
Wright, Peter A. 'Native forest destruction is questioned'. Letter to editor, *Northern Daily Leader*, 12 July 1973.

PAPERS

Cameron–Smith, Barbara and Good, Roger. Fire Seminar Review of Papers. Stapled printed sheets. National Parks and Wildlife Service, c. 1977.
Curtin, R. A. 'Experiment 021216 – Pulpwood Plots – Yerrinan S. F.' Printed paper, Forestry Commission of NSW, 1974.
Humphreys, F. R. 'Wood Technology a sketched outline history with some reference to personalities'. Forestry Commission of NSW. Stapled printed sheets c. 1978.

Index